USA
The Unfolding Story of America

Philip L. Groisser, Ph.D.
Former Superintendent of Brooklyn
High Schools, New York City

Sol Levine
Principal, Beverly Hills High School
Beverly Hills, California

Dedicated to serving

AMSCO

our nation's youth

When ordering this book, please specify:
either **R 431 H** or **USA**

AMSCO SCHOOL PUBLICATIONS, INC.
315 Hudson Street / New York, N.Y. 10013

Grateful acknowledgment is made to the following sources for permission to use copyrighted materials.

From SMOKE AND STEEL by Carl Sandburg, copyright 1920 by Harcourt Brace Jovanovich, Inc.; renewed 1948 by Carl Sandburg. Reprinted by permission of the publisher.

From THE PROMISED LAND by Mary Antin, copyright 1912 by Houghton Mifflin Company; copyright renewed 1940 by Mary Antin. Reprinted by permission of Houghton Mifflin Company.

From READERS' GUIDE TO PERIODICAL LITERATURE, copyright © 1984 by The H. W. Wilson Company. Material reproduced by permission of the publisher.

From THE WORLD ALMANAC & BOOK OF FACTS, 1985 edition, copyright © Newspaper Enterprise Association, Inc. 1984, New York, New York 10166.

From THE WORLD BOOK ENCYCLOPEDIA, © 1985 World Book, Inc. By permission of World Book, Inc.

ISBN 0-87720-643-0

Printed in the United States of America

PREFACE

American history did not begin when Thomas Jefferson penned the Declaration of Independence. It did not end when U.S. spaceships began exploring distant planets. American history is ongoing. You are a part of this exciting process, and *USA: The Unfolding Story of America* provides the background you need to understand the past and prepare for the future.

The book has been written with you, the reader, in mind. Lessons, or chapters, are brief and to the point. We have organized them in a logical manner, with many headings and subheadings to introduce important topics. Before you begin each lesson, we suggest that you skim through and read the headings and subheadings. They will give you a preview of what the chapter contains. Later, when you are reviewing the material, the headings (along with the "Summing Up" section) will provide a convenient framework to help you organize what you have learned.

You will find interesting highlights of history enclosed in boxes that appear throughout the book. Other special features include numerous maps for easy reference, and graphs and charts to supplement information provided in the narrative. At the back of the book, you will find the full texts of two of American history's key documents—the Declaration of Independence and the U.S. Constitution. You will also find a glossary, giving definitions of the more difficult words used in the book. Finally, you will find an index to help you locate material on specific topics and people.

The 87 lessons are grouped into nine major units. Most of the units follow a chronological order, but some units are organized around important themes. Unit Two, for example, describes the United States government not only through its historical development but also as it exists today. The last four units treat specific aspects of 20th-century American life, combining chronological order with the treatment of significant topics. An example of a lesson in these units is "Environmental Protection Today."

We hope that by using this text, you will gain a much deeper understanding of the unfolding story of America and a new appreciation of the people and events that have made our nation what it is today.

Philip L. Groisser / Sol Levine

CONTENTS

UNIT ONE: A New Nation

UNIT TWO: The United States Government

UNIT THREE: A Growing Nation

UNIT FOUR: A Nation at War With Itself

UNIT FIVE: America Looks to the 20th Century

UNIT SIX: American Politics in the 20th Century

UNIT SEVEN: The American Economy in the 20th Century

UNIT EIGHT: Americans in the 20th Century

UNIT NINE: America's Foreign Relations
in the 20th Century

Reference and Resource Unit

SKILLS DEVELOPMENT

The text's sequential and spiraling skills development program is outlined below. You are challenged to learn and use many basic skills, including reading and interpreting passages; analyzing charts, graphs, and maps; and understanding political cartoons.

x   *Skills Development*

MAPS

GRAPHS, TABLES, CHARTS, AND DIAGRAMS

PAGE

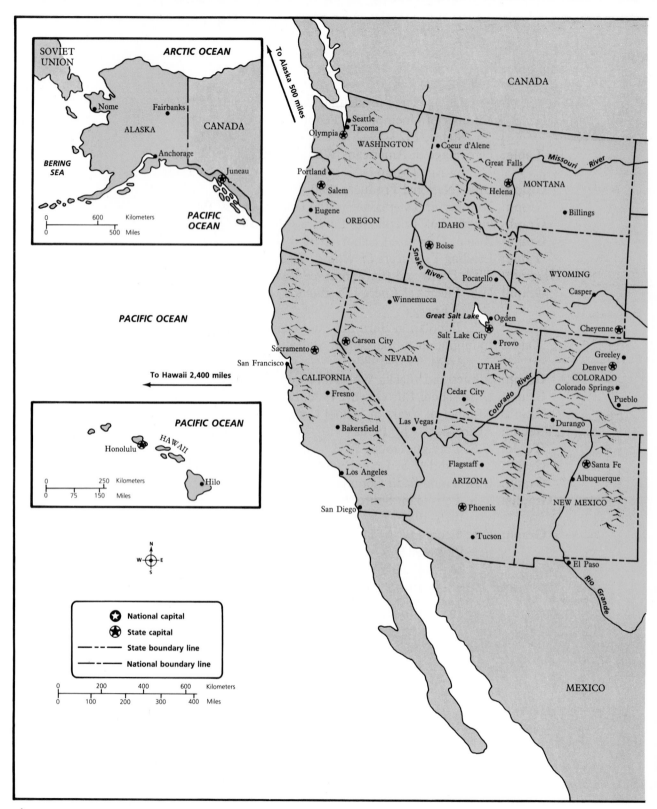

SOVIET
UNION

ARCTIC OCEAN

To Alaska 500 miles

Nome

Fairbanks

ALASKA

CANADA

BERING
SEA

Anchorage

Juneau

PACIFIC
OCEAN

0   600
Kilometers
0   500   Miles

PACIFIC OCEAN

To Hawaii 2,400 miles

PACIFIC OCEAN

Honolulu

HAWAII

Hilo

0   250   Kilometers
0   75   150   Miles

N
W   E
S

National capital
State capital
State boundary line
National boundary line

0   200   400   600   Kilometers
0   100   200   300   400   Miles

xiv

CANADA

Seattle
Tacoma
Olympia
WASHINGTON

Coeur d'Alene

Great Falls

Missouri River

MONTANA

Helena

Billings

Portland

Salem

Eugene

OREGON

IDAHO

Boise

Snake River

Pocatello

WYOMING

Casper

Winnemucca

Great Salt Lake

Ogden

Cheyenne

Salt Lake City

Provo

Greeley

Carson City

Denver

Sacramento

NEVADA

UTAH

Colorado River

COLORADO

San Francisco

Colorado Springs

CALIFORNIA

Fresno

Cedar City

Pueblo

Las Vegas

Durango

Bakersfield

Flagstaff

Santa Fe

Los Angeles

ARIZONA

Albuquerque

Phoenix

NEW MEXICO

San Diego

Tucson

El Paso

Rio Grande

MEXICO

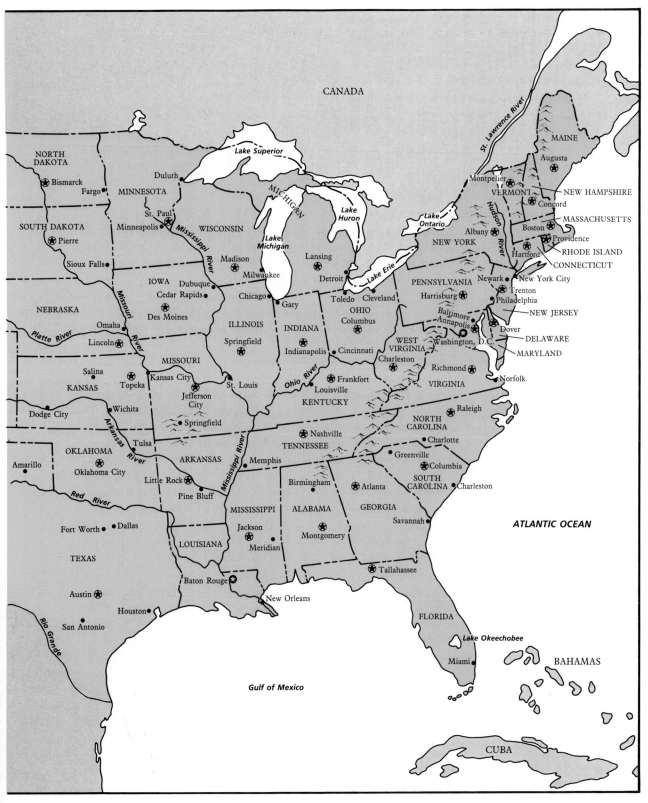

CANADA

NORTH DAKOTA
● Bismarck
Fargo ●

MINNESOTA
Duluth ●

Lake Superior

MICHIGAN

Lake Huron

St. Lawrence River

MAINE
● Augusta

Montpelier ●
VERMONT
NEW HAMPSHIRE
● Concord

SOUTH DAKOTA
● Pierre

St. Paul ●
Minneapolis ●

WISCONSIN
Mississippi River

Madison ●
Milwaukee ●

Lansing ●

Lake Michigan

Lake Ontario

NEW YORK
Albany ●

Hudson River

MASSACHUSETTS
Boston ●
● Providence
RHODE ISLAND
Hartford ●
CONNECTICUT

Lake Erie

Detroit ●

Sioux Falls ●

IOWA
Dubuque ●
Cedar Rapids ●

Chicago ●
Gary ●

Toledo ● Cleveland ●

OHIO
Columbus ●

PENNSYLVANIA
Harrisburg ●

Newark ●
● New York City
● Trenton
Philadelphia ●
NEW JERSEY

NEBRASKA

Des Moines ●

ILLINOIS

INDIANA

Omaha ●
Lincoln ●

Missouri River
Platte River

Springfield ●

Indianapolis ●

Cincinnati ●

Ohio River

WEST VIRGINIA
Charleston ●

Baltimore ●
Annapolis ●
Washington, D.C. ●

Dover ●
DELAWARE

MARYLAND

Salina ●
KANSAS
Topeka ●

Kansas City ●
St. Louis ●

MISSOURI
Jefferson City ●

Frankfort ●
Louisville ●

Richmond ●

VIRGINIA

● Norfolk

Dodge City ●

Wichita ●

Springfield ●

KENTUCKY

Raleigh ●

NORTH CAROLINA

OKLAHOMA

Arkansas River

Tulsa ●

Nashville ●
TENNESSEE

● Charlotte

Greenville ●

Amarillo ●

Oklahoma City ●

ARKANSAS

Memphis ●

Columbia ●

SOUTH CAROLINA
● Charleston

Little Rock ●
Pine Bluff ●

Red River

Mississippi River

Birmingham ●

Atlanta ●

GEORGIA

Fort Worth ● ● Dallas

MISSISSIPPI
Jackson ●
Meridian ●

ALABAMA

Montgomery ●

Savannah ●

ATLANTIC OCEAN

TEXAS

LOUISIANA

Tallahassee ●

Austin ●

Rio Grande

Houston ●
San Antonio ●

Baton Rouge ●
New Orleans ●

FLORIDA

Lake Okeechobee

BAHAMAS

Gulf of Mexico

Miami ●

CUBA

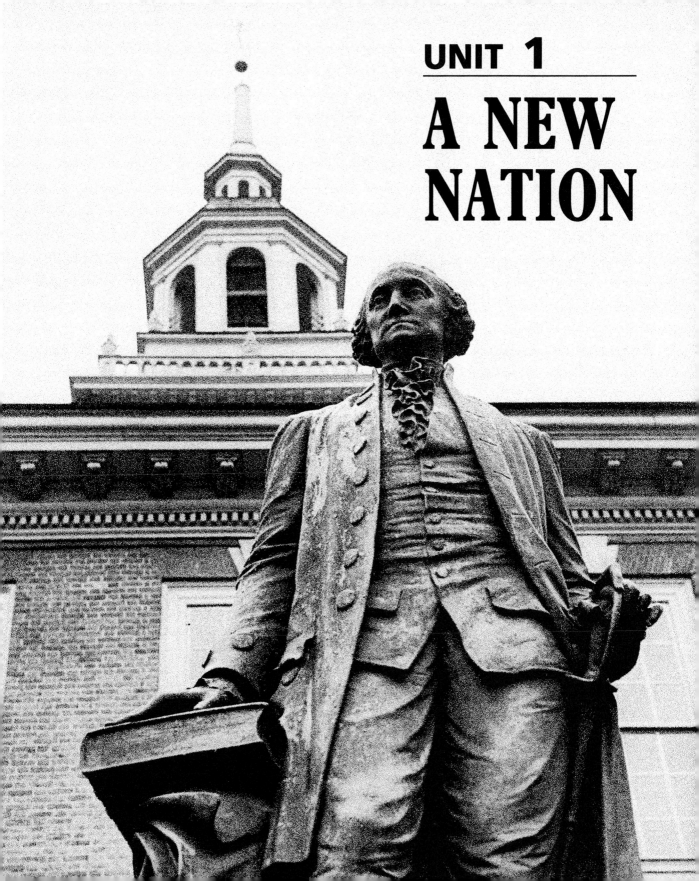

UNIT 1

A NEW NATION

Indians in America Before the Europeans

Thousands of years before Europeans came to America, other people already lived here. Many different Indian nations inhabited what the Europeans later called the "New World." Over the centuries, each Indian nation had developed its own ideas, inventions, and habits. In other words, each had created its own way of life.

The explorer Christopher Columbus first called the people of the New World "los indios"—the Spanish term for Indians. He used that name because he thought he had landed in the East Indies, off the southeastern coast of Asia. Though Columbus was in error, the name "Indians" has stuck. Today, many Indians prefer to be called "Native Americans."

The First Migration to the New World

Although now there is no way to walk from Asia to North America, a land bridge once connected the two continents. (See the map on page 3.) The ancestors of the American Indians *migrated* (moved) from northern Asia about 25,000 to 30,000 years ago. Such a journey was possible then because the world's oceans were at a lower level. There was less water in the oceans because so much was held by gigantic *glaciers* (thick ice). Because these glaciers cov-

ered large areas of North America, Asia, and Europe, we call this time the "Ice Age." At a later time, most of the glaciers melted and the oceans rose to their present levels.

The earliest Americans settled in various parts of North America. Later generations went on to Central and South America. Because the lands were vast and most groups lived far apart from one another, American Indians developed separate cultures.

A *culture* is the distinct way in which a group of people lives. How they work, play, obtain food, communicate, practice a religion, and organize themselves all contribute to making a culture. Like most cultures, those of the Indians developed slowly. Their cultures changed over the years and are still changing.

Major Cultures South of the Rio Grande

Some of the most advanced of all Indian cultures developed thousands of years ago south of the Rio Grande. The Rio Grande is a river that forms part of the southern boundary of the

2

MIGRATION FROM ASIA TO THE AMERICAS

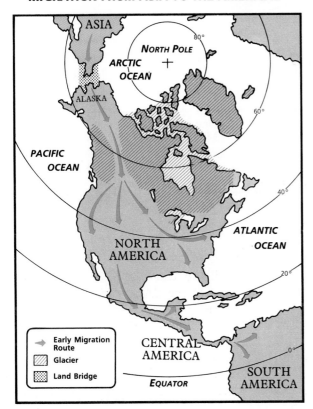

ASIA

NORTH POLE
ARCTIC OCEAN

ALASKA

PACIFIC OCEAN

NORTH AMERICA

ATLANTIC OCEAN

CENTRAL AMERICA

SOUTH AMERICA

EQUATOR

→ Early Migration Route
Glacier
Land Bridge

United States. Three of the most noteworthy cultures were those of the Mayas, Aztecs, and Incas.

Mayas The remarkable Mayan culture took shape in a number of cities in Central America beginning about the year 300 A.D. Each city was like a separate state, controlling the area around it. The Mayas were mainly farmers. They grew *maize* (corn) and other crops. The Mayas made important advances in the arts and sciences. These people developed accurate calendars, a numbering system, and a form of writing that used symbols.

Aztecs Hundreds of years before Spanish soldiers under Hernando Cortés arrived in 1519, powerful Aztec emperors ruled a large region of what is now Mexico. Their capital, Tenoch-

titlán, was built on an island in a lake. Tenochtitlán had more people than most cities in Europe at the time. Now we know Tenochtitlán as Mexico City.

Most Aztecs worked as farmers. Others entered government or military service or became traders. Boys went to schools for training to become priests, soldiers, or government workers. The education of girls was less common, although some became priests. Aztec education was aided by a system of writing that used pictures to represent objects, people, and ideas.

Incas High in the Andes Mountains of Peru, a large Incan empire emerged about the year 1000. It stretched north and south along the Pacific coast of South America. The Indian people who built this empire called their emperor the "Inca." Today, we use that title to refer to the people themselves—the Incas.

The Incas produced skillful works of art in clay, metal, and textiles. Moreover, they are well-known for the work they did in stone. Slaves and other laborers carried giant-sized stones from quarries to building sites. Then masons carved the stones into blocks, each to fit almost perfectly with adjoining blocks.

Francisco Pizarro and other Spaniards defeated Inca forces in 1532. Soon the Incan empire collapsed.

Major Indian Cultural Areas of the North

By the time Columbus reached America, over 1 million Indians lived in what are now Canada and the United States. Where and how did they live? People who study Indian cultures often combine them into groups. Each cultural group lived in a specific area. The map on page 5 shows six major cultural areas in North America.

The Far North Because of its harsh climate, this area was never heavily populated. It was

One Eastern Woodlands tribe, the Manhattans, lived in villages made up of many longhouses. Among other places, they inhabited the island of Manhattan, which they sold to the Dutch in 1626.

occupied by Algonquins, Chippewas, Crees, and other tribes that shared a common culture. During the long winters, these people wore heavy clothes made of moose or caribou hides. They traveled through the snow on snowshoes or by toboggan. In the summer, they used birchbark canoes to cross lakes and paddle along rivers.

For food, the Indians of the Far North fished, gathered berries, and hunted moose, caribou, and other animals. They built homes in varied shapes, but usually the homes had wooden frames covered with skins, brush, or bark.

At some time between 10,000 and 11,000 years ago, Eskimos moved into areas of the Far North. Most of them settled near the sea, where they hunted whales and seals and caught fish. We often link Eskimos with snowhouses that we call *igloos.* Actually, Eskimo sod houses and tents were much more common. For the most part, Eskimos built snowhouses only when traveling during the winter.

Like the ancestors of Indians, Eskimos first came to America from Asia. Nevertheless, they arrived much later than the first Indians, and, thus, are not considered part of any Indian group.

The Eastern Woodlands   This area included the lands east of the Mississippi River. It was the home of the Fox, Iroquois, Cherokees, Creeks, Seminoles, and other Indian nations. All these people hunted, fished, and gathered nuts and berries. During the warm summer months, some tribes also grew corn, beans, and squash. Women did most of the farming and gathering, while the men fished and hunted.

Their homes varied according to location. In the sometimes chilly Northeast, many Indians lived in round, bark-covered *wigwams.* In the South, Seminoles built thatched huts with sides that were open to allow breezes to pass through. Each wigwam or hut gave shelter to a single family. The Iroquois longhouse, however, was large enough to hold several families at once.

In the Mississippi and Ohio River valleys, some Indians developed an advanced culture as early as the year 1000. These people are now known as the "Mound Builders" because they built large mounds of earth. Some of the earthworks were burial sites. Others had temples on top of them and were used for religious purposes.

In 1570, five Indian nations in the Northeast joined together in a *political union.* The League of the Iroquois, as it was called, became a strong military force. At a later period, in the Southeast, five other tribes formed a similar union—the Creek Confederacy.

The Plains The Blackfeet, Crows, Sioux, Arapahos, Comanches, and other nations lived in scattered settlements on the Great Plains. They built most of their villages on strips of land along rivers and streams. The villages were made up of large, earth-covered lodges. Farmland was located nearby.

On the Plains, the Indians hunted buffalo and other animals. When these people traveled, they set up *tepees*—cone-shaped tents made of buffalo hides. Hunting buffalo was quite difficult because the Indians did not have horses. Horses, brought to the New World by the Spaniards, were first used by the Indians in the 1600s.

The Northwest Coast In a narrow strip of dense forest along the Pacific Ocean lived the Chi-nooks, Tlingits, and other tribes. Although their climate was mild and misty, these Indians did not farm the land. They found plenty to eat by fishing in the ocean and rivers and hunting and gathering in the forests.

These people were almost always surrounded by giant trees. Not surprisingly then, they learned to build impressive houses and totem poles of wood. They also made oceangoing canoes large enough to hold 60 people. Unlike most other Indians, the Indians of the Northwest Coast valued wealth. They accumulated blankets, canoes, copper shields, and other possessions. The wealthiest families held great power over other villagers.

California and the Great Basin California had one of the largest Indian populations of any area

INDIAN CULTURAL AREAS OF NORTH AMERICA

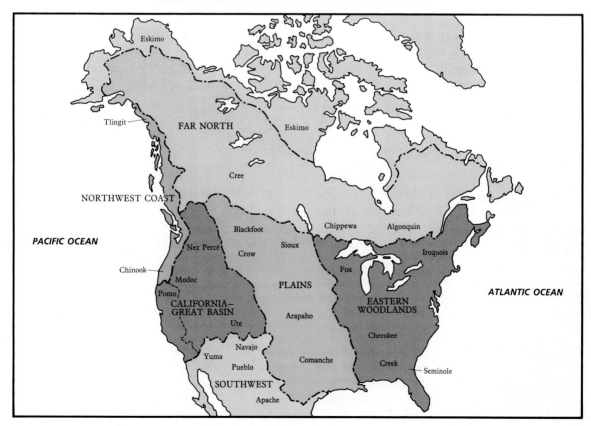

in North America. The Great Basin—the area between the Rocky Mountains in the east and the Sierra Nevada and Cascade ranges in the west—had one of the smallest populations. The reason for the difference was geography. California had a mild climate and offered food for the taking, including deer, elk, rabbits, coyotes, berries, nuts, roots, and fruits. The Great Basin was too dry for farming and did not support much game for hunting.

Indians of the two regions included the Modocs, Nez Percés, Pomos, and Utes. They obtained food by gathering seeds, nuts, and wild plants. To this diet, they added the meat of small game and fish. These Indians turned out art objects of a useful nature. For instance, the baskets that they wove were used in gathering food, carrying supplies, and cooking.

The Southwest   In the hot, dry lands north of Mexico lived the Apaches, Navajos, Pueblos, Yumas, and other tribes. There was quite a wide variety of cultures among these Indian nations.

The Pueblos lived in buildings made of *adobe* (clay bricks). Many of these buildings held more than one family and were several stories high. A few of them were built on the sides of cliffs.

The Pueblos were farmers. Because the Southwest was dry, they dug *irrigation ditches* to carry water from the streams to their fields. The Pueblos depended on the food they could coax from the stubborn soil. For that reason, they performed rain dances to insure the survival of their corn and other crops.

The Apaches and Navajos also grew some crops. Nonetheless, they spent more time hunting animals and gathering cactus fruit and other foods. Like the Pueblos, the Navajos built permanent homes. Their *hogans* were log structures covered with mud. The Apaches, on the other hand, were constantly moving about. They lived either in tepees or in huts made of sticks.

The Pueblos were known for multi-storied structures such as these in Canyon de Chelly, Arizona.

The Indians of the Southwest still practice their ancient crafts today. They make pottery vessels, cotton cloth, baskets, and buckskin moccasins similar to those made more than 500 years ago.

SUMMING UP　　We have seen that America's first immigrants came from Asia many thousands of years ago. Slowly these people settled the land and developed distinct cultures. Today, scholars who study Indians of the United States and Canada often divide them into six culture areas. These Indian people made some important advances in farming, crafts, and government organization.

Understanding the Text

On a separate sheet of paper, write the letter of the word or phrase that best completes each of the following statements.

1. The first people to settle in America came about (*a*) 250 years ago (*b*) 500 years ago (*c*) 25,000 years ago (*d*) 5 million years ago.

2. A culture consists of ways in which a group of people (*a*) works (*b*) communicates (*c*) practices a religion (*d*) does all of these things.

3. All of the following Indian nations built large structures, *except* the (*a*) Apaches (*b*) Incas (*c*) Pueblos (*d*) Mound Builders.

4. Tenochtitlán was the capital city of the (*a*) Aztecs (*b*) Algonquins (*c*) Pueblos (*d*) Incas.

5. All of the following Indians grew crops, *except* the (*a*) Pueblos (*b*) Indians of the Far North (*c*) Mayas (*d*) Indians of the Plains.

6. The Indians who put great stress on accumulating wealth were those of the (*a*) Plains (*b*) Northwest Coast (*c*) Far North (*d*) Eastern Woodlands.

7. Of the following peoples, those usually *not* considered Indians are the (*a*) Cherokees (*b*) Eskimos (*c*) Mayas (*d*) Utes.

8. The Indians who built large adobe houses of several stories were the (*a*) Sioux (*b*) Crees (*c*) Nez Percés (*d*) Pueblos.

9. A culture area where the hunting of buffalo was important was (*a*) the Eastern Woodlands (*b*) the Plains (*c*) the Northwest Coast (*d*) California and the Great Basin.

10. One of the main points of this lesson is that the Indians of North America (*a*) made up a single cultural group (*b*) made up two different cultural groups (*c*) consisted of three different cultural groups (*d*) developed many different cultures.

Developing Map Skills

Study the map on page 5. Then choose the letter of the word or phrase that best completes each sentence. On a separate sheet of paper, match the sentence number with the correct letter.

1. The main land area shown on the map is (*a*) South America (*b*) North America (*c*) Antarctica (*d*) Australia.

2. The map identifies main culture areas of the (*a*) Europeans (*b*) Peruvian Incas (*c*) North American Indians (*d*) New Zealand Maoris.

3. According to the map, the Pueblo Indians lived in the region labeled *(a)* Southwest *(b)* Far North *(c)* Plains *(d)* Northwest Coast.

4. One group of Eastern Woodland Indians was the *(a)* Modocs *(b)* Tlingits *(c)* Crows *(d)* Iroquois.

5. Another title for this map might be *(a)* How Some Early Travelers Arrived in America *(b)* Prehistoric Cities of the Western Plains *(c)* Indian People of the Antarctic *(d)* Where Some Indian People Lived in North America.

Thinking About the Lesson

1. What reasons can you give for the development of more than one culture among the Indians of America?

2. Why did some Indians of the Eastern Woodlands become farmers, while the Indians of the Great Basin did not?

3. What, in your opinion, was the value of a political union such as the League of the Iroquois? What benefits do you suppose members of the League drew from their union?

4. Name two characteristics of Indian cultures of the Northwest Coast not shared by Indians of the Eastern Woodlands. Explain one of these differences.

The European Age of Exploration

Until about 1,000 years ago, the Indians had America almost entirely to themselves. Their isolation, however, was not to last. In time, Europeans learned of what they called the New World. Once they did, they too helped to settle America.

> The Vikings are usually given credit for having been the first Europeans to reach America. In the late 900s, these Scandinavian sailors established small colonies in Greenland. From Greenland, in about the year 1000, Leif Ericson sailed along the North American coast.
>
> Some Vikings probably settled in America for a few years. Nevertheless, they made no lasting impact on American history. By the 1400s, Viking voyages to the New World were all but forgotten.

Trade Routes to the East

During the 11th, 12th, and 13th centuries, Europeans waged several religious wars known as *Crusades*. These wars took place along the eastern shore of the Mediterranean Sea in an area known as the Holy Land. The Holy Land had been the birthplace of three great religions—Judaism, Christianity, and Islam. In the Crusades, Christians attempted to drive *Moslems*, followers of Islam, out of the Holy Land.

When Europeans traveled to the Holy Land, they became familiar with many new things—spices, silks, and valuable stones. Most of these items came from India and China. As these goods arrived in Europe, they created a demand for trade. Italian *merchants* (traders) bought Eastern goods in the Holy Land. They shipped the goods across the Mediterranean and resold them in Europe at much higher prices. Since the Italians controlled the Mediterranean, they also controlled the supply of Eastern goods to Europe.

Other Europeans resented the Italian trade. They wanted to avoid the high costs of doing business in Italian ports. They also wished to avoid the long, dangerous land travel to and from the eastern Mediterranean. Chief among these Europeans were the Portuguese. By the mid-1400s, they were making risky voyages into the unknown Atlantic Ocean, partly to set up trade with Africa. In 1488, a Portuguese sailor, Bartholomeu Dias, journeyed around the southern tip of Africa. He showed future explorers that they could reach Asia by an all-water route.

9

Educated Europeans at this time believed that the world is round. They thought that one could reach the East by sailing west. This belief led the Italian Christopher Columbus to take a daring route across the Atlantic in 1492. (See the map on page 11.) Sailing under the Spanish flag, Columbus landed on one of the Bahama Islands, in the West Indies. He believed the islands to be in the East Indies, in Asia.

> Historians refer to 100-year periods of time as *centuries*. The first century was all the years from one to 100. Following are some of the centuries mentioned in this lesson:
>
> 14th century: 1301–1400
> 15th century: 1401–1500
> 16th century: 1501–1600

New Knowledge Brings Exciting Changes

The desire for new trade routes was not the only factor explaining European exploration of the 15th and 16th centuries. Another was a renewed interest in learning, science, and the arts. Early in the 1300s, Europe entered a period known as the *Renaissance*. (The word "Renaissance" comes from a French word meaning "rebirth.") The period lasted until about 1600.

Renaissance knowledge made voyages far beyond Europe possible.

New inventions and developments of the period included the:

• *Magnetic compass.* With a needle that always pointed north, this compass made it easier to steer a ship in the right direction.

• *Astrolabe.* Sailors used the astrolabe to measure the angle between the horizon and certain stars. With this information, they could figure out how far north or south they were from certain places.

• *Printing press.* In the 1400s, Europeans began to print books instead of having to copy each book by hand. More books became available to more readers, helping to spread Renaissance knowledge.

• *Caravel.* This type of Portuguese ship was more efficient and safer than earlier types. Explorers could travel more quickly on these ships. And they were more likely to survive dangerous storms.

In addition, Europeans were improving their skills at making maps. In the 1300s and 1400s, sailors began drawing more accurate outlines of the Mediterranean coast. Their charts also indicated the location of shipping ports. Such work added greatly to knowledge of the Mediterranean, and in time, of other parts of the world.

Christopher Columbus (kneeling) obtained financing for his 1492 voyage across the Atlantic from King Ferdinand and Queen Isabella of Spain. The Queen shared Columbus's vision of a westward route to India.

MAJOR EUROPEAN VOYAGES OF EXPLORATION

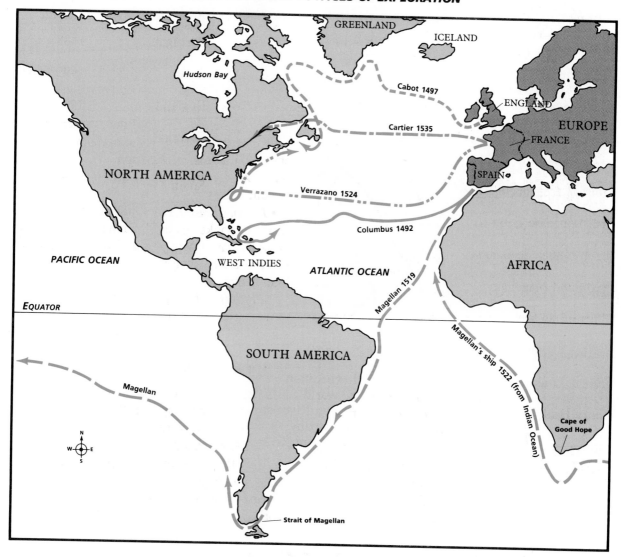

Other Reasons for Exploration

Sailors could not have begun their long voyages without the support of European rulers. Why, though, did these rulers want to *finance* (pay for) such projects? The rulers were curious to learn more about distant countries. They also hoped to open up new trade routes. In the main, however, the reasons for their interest can be summed up as: gold, glory, and gospel.

Gold Rulers, explorers, and merchants were all hungry for riches. Rulers and explorers hoped to find gold and silver in the New World. Merchants wanted new products for trade and profits.

Glory Rulers hoped to gain glory for their nations. They could do this by gaining control of lands and people in the New World. In setting up *colonies* (groups of people in new

MAJOR EUROPEAN EXPLORERS, 1488–1673

Explorer	Achievement	Country	Date
Bartholomeu Dias	Sailed around Cape of Good Hope	Portugal	1488
Christopher Columbus	Explored West Indies	Spain	1492
John Cabot	Explored coast of New-foundland	England	1497
Vasco da Gama	Reached India after sailing around Cape of Good Hope	Portugal	1498
Amerigo Vespucci	Explored eastern coast of South America	Spain	1499
Juan Ponce de León	Explored Florida	Spain	1513
Vasco Núñez de Balboa	Crossed Panama and saw Pacific Ocean	Spain	1513
Ferdinand Magellan	Led first expedition to sail around world	Spain	1519–1522
Giovanni da Verrazano	Explored eastern coast of North America	France	1524
Jacques Cartier	Explored St. Lawrence River	France	1534–1535
Francis Drake	Led second expedition around the world	England	1577–1580
Henry Hudson	Explored Hudson River as far north as Albany	Netherlands	1609
Père Jacques Marquette and Louis Joliet	Explored Mississippi River Valley	France	1673

lands with ties to a parent country), each nation tried to outdo the others. Sometimes the rivalries among nations led to war.

Gospel   Many Europeans had religious reasons for colonizing the New World. They wanted to spread the *gospel* (set of beliefs) of Christianity among the native peoples of two continents.

Some Major Achievements of the Explorers

Who were these European explorers? Christopher Columbus was the first in America during this era and the man whose voyage changed world history. A number of other explorers followed, sailing under the flags of several countries. Four of the most important were:

• John Cabot, an Italian seaman who sailed under the English flag. In 1497, Cabot crossed the Atlantic and explored the east coast of Canada. During the next year, he may have explored as far south as Virginia. The English believed that his voyages gave them a claim to settle North America.

• Ferdinand Magellan, a Portuguese who sailed under the Spanish flag. In 1519, Magellan began a voyage that would take one of his ships completely around the world. He and his crew crossed the Atlantic and then journeyed southward along the east coast of South America. They passed through the Strait of Magellan at the southern tip of South America and set out across the Pacific. Magellan explored the Philippine Islands in Southeast Asia, where he was killed by natives. One of his ships finished the voyage around the southern tip of Africa and back to Spain in 1522. This journey showed beyond all question that the world is round.

• Giovanni da Verrazano, an Italian who sailed under the French flag. In 1524, Verrazano explored the east coast of North America from North Carolina to Nova Scotia. He is thought to have been the first European to enter New York Harbor and Narragansett Bay in Rhode Island.

• Jacques Cartier, a Frenchman who sailed to America for the French king. On his second voyage, in 1535, Cartier became the first European to explore the St. Lawrence River.

Jacques Cartier claimed for France important areas of Canada, including lands along both sides of the St. Lawrence River.

European Empires in the New World

The Age of Exploration paved the way for European nations to establish *empires* (several territories under one ruler) in the New World.

Spain built the largest of these empires. Spaniards set up colonies in North America, Central America, the West Indies, and South America. In North America, their colonies were located in Mexico and the extreme southern and southwestern part of what is now the United States.

France built a great empire, too, mainly in Canada and the Ohio River Valley. The French settled also in the West Indies.

Portugal settled the eastern half of South America—an area that today is the country of Brazil.

Sweden and the Netherlands settled much smaller parts of the New World. Swedes set up a colony on the Delaware River centered around Fort Christina (now Wilmington, Delaware). This colony, New Sweden, fell to the Dutch in 1655 and was later taken by the English. The Dutch turned the Hudson River Valley into the colony of New Netherland. In 1664, the Dutch surrendered New Netherland to the English, who renamed it New York.

England started its empire building much later than Spain or Portugal. By 1750, however, the English had 13 colonies stretching along the Atlantic coast of North America. In Canada, the English controlled the Hudson Bay region and Nova Scotia. In addition, the English established colonies in the Bahamas and other parts of the West Indies. As time went on, in fact, it became clear that England had built the most powerful empire of all.

SUMMING UP   We have seen that the Age of Exploration began in the late 15th century because of many factors. Desire for new trade routes, new inventions, and the quest for gold and glory and the urge to spread the gospel were all important. During this period, several major powers of Europe set up colonies in the New World.

Understanding the Text

On a separate sheet of paper, write the letter of the word or phrase that best completes each of the following statements.

1. Before the discovery of the New World, most European trade in goods from the East was carried on by the *(a)* Spaniards *(b)* French *(c)* English *(d)* Italians.

2. Christopher Columbus reached America in the *(a)* first half of the 14th century *(b)* last years of the 14th century *(c)* last years of the 15th century *(d)* middle of the 16th century.

3. Bartholomeu Dias made sailing history by *(a)* discovering the Canary Islands *(b)* accompanying Columbus to America *(c)* attempting to circle the globe by sea *(d)* rounding the southern tip of Africa.

4. The phrase "gold, glory, gospel" explains *(a)* why Europeans desired to control the New World *(b)* advances in learning, science, and the arts *(c)* causes of the Renaissance *(d)* effects of missionary work.

5. The astrolabe helped European explorers to *(a)* forecast the weather *(b)* reach agreements with American Indians *(c)* show the position of a ship at sea *(d)* teach Christian beliefs.

6. The Renaissance is a term applied to a *(a)* series of voyages of discovery and exploration *(b)* period of renewed interest in learning, science, and the arts *(c)* set of religious beliefs *(d)* book about strange places in Asia.

7. Ferdinand Magellan made sailing history by *(a)* discovering the Canary Islands *(b)* accompanying Columbus to America *(c)* attempting to circle the globe by sea *(d)* reaching the southern tip of Africa.

8. The European nation whose colonies covered the greatest area in North, Central, and South America was *(a)* Spain *(b)* England *(c)* the Netherlands *(d)* Portugal.

9. Which of the following true statements is found in the lesson? *(a)* There was great wealth to be uncovered in Mexico. *(b)* Educated people at the time of Columbus knew that the world is round. *(c)* Spanish colonization changed the language and culture of Central and South America. *(d)* Many great painters lived during the Renaissance.

10. Which of the following statements is supported by information in this lesson? *(a)* Military strength may be of greater importance to a nation than scientific knowledge. *(b)* It has always been known that the world is round. *(c)* There are periods in history when great changes take place and much progress is made. *(d)* When nations set up colonies, they bring great benefits to the people living in those areas.

THE ORIGINAL THIRTEEN COLONIES

Colony	Date first settled	By whom first settled	First permanent settlement
Virginia	1607	England	Jamestown
Massachusetts	1620	England	Plymouth
New Hampshire	1622	England	Dover
New York* (New Netherland)	1624	Netherlands	Fort Orange (Albany)
New Jersey* (New Sweden/New Netherland)	1624	Sweden/Netherlands	Fort Nassau (now Camden area)
Delaware* (New Sweden/New Netherland)	1631	Sweden/Netherlands	Zwaanendael (now Lewes)
Maryland	1634	England	St. Marys
Pennsylvania	1634	Sweden	Tinicum Island (near Philadelphia)
Connecticut	1635	England	Windsor
Rhode Island	1636	England	Providence
North Carolina	1653	England	(uncertain)
South Carolina	1670	England	Charleston
Georgia	1732	England	Savannah

*In 1664, England took control of the lands that had been New Netherland.

Growth of the Colonies

By 1750, about 1.2 million people were living in the British colonies of North America. Many of these people had been born in America.

A *population* (number of people) of 1.2 million seemed much larger in the 18th century than it does today. The population of Great Britain itself at that time was only about 6.5 million.

Reasons for Moving to the New World

Why did so many British people decide to risk the dangers and hardships of moving to the New World? We can name three different reasons: economic, political, and religious.

Economic Reasons Most people came mainly because of poor economic conditions in England. More and more people there had a difficult time making a living. Many farm families lost their land. Prices rose rapidly—a problem called *inflation*. This problem made it even harder for poor people to live decently.

The colonies offered all sorts of economic opportunities. Farmers could buy good land at low cost. The forests could provide valuable lumber and ship masts. There was good fishing in coastal waters and in rivers and lakes. The growing trade with Britain created a brisk business for shopkeepers and merchants. Many kinds of skilled workers, such as carpenters and blacksmiths, also were needed.

> In your study of American history, you will often meet the following words:
> *economic*—having to do with earning and spending of money; relating to the making and using of goods and services.
> *political*—having to do with government and the exercise of power.

Developing Chronology Skills

IMPORTANT EVENTS IN EUROPEAN EXPLORATION

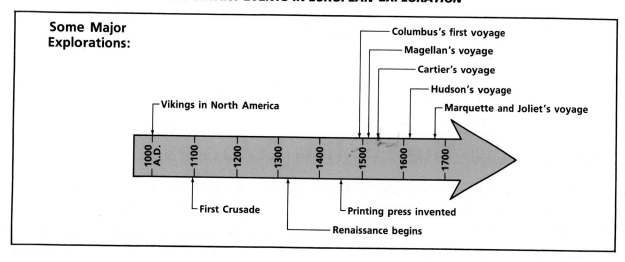

Study the timeline above. Then choose the letter of the word or phrase that best completes each sentence. On a separate sheet of paper, match the sentence number with the correct letter.

1. The event on the timeline that took place *last* was (a) the first voyage of Columbus (b) the Vikings' voyage to North America (c) Cartier's voyage (d) Magellan's voyage.

2. An event that took place in the *same* century as Columbus's first voyage to America was (a) the beginning of the Renaissance (b) the Vikings' voyage to North America (c) Cartier's voyage (d) the invention of the printing press.

3. The date of the First Crusade is (a) 950 (b) 1096 (c) 1150 (d) 1492.

4. No event is listed on the timeline for the (a) 11th century (b) 12th century (c) 14th century (d) 15th century.

5. Which of the following could *not* be considered a reason why Columbus made a successful journey to America in 1492? (a) the Crusades (b) the invention of the printing press (c) Magellan's voyage (d) the Renaissance.

Thinking About the Lesson

1. How did new inventions help make possible Europe's Age of Exploration?

2. Why do you think that some European rulers wanted to finance voyages of exploration in the 1400s and 1500s?

3. In your opinion, which single reason—gold, glory, or gospel—was most important as a basis for the rapid growth of European colonies in the New World? Explain your answer.

The English Colonies

More than 100 years after Columbus had come to the New World, England began to set up colonies there. In time, the 13 English colonies along the Atlantic coast of North America formed the United States.

England's Need for Colonies

England founded its colonies in America for several reasons:

• English rulers wanted greater power and prestige among European nations. Extending English rule to the New World was one way to obtain these goals.

• English merchants expected to make profits from trade with the colonies.

• The English ruling class hoped that people dissatisfied with life in England would move to the colonies.

Founding the Colonies

On April 26, 1607, three small English ships reached the southeastern coast of North America. The ships belonged to the London Company, which had a *charter* (legal document) from King James I. This charter allowed people to settle a huge section of North America, which

16

the English called "Virginia." The ships carried 120 people who wanted to settle in the new colony.

The ships sailed up a river, which the sailors named the "James" after the English king. In a lowland area near the mouth of the river, the settlers chose a site for a fort. They called this site "Jamestown." It was to be the first successful English settlement in America.

In the beginning, the settlers had a difficult time. They did not have enough food or adequate clothing. Yet many of them spent time looking for gold instead of building shelters or planting crops. Some fell ill with the disease *malaria*, probably from mosquitoes that lived in nearby marshes. Only 53 out of the original 120 settlers survived the first year.

During the second year, under the leadership of Captain John Smith, conditions at Jamestown improved. The settlers worked harder, and fresh supplies arrived from England. The Virginians learned how to grow and *cure* (dry) tobacco. Soon they were shipping this crop back to England and selling it at a profit. Slowly the colony expanded to nearby rivers, such as the Rappahannock and the York.

Over the course of several decades, the same pattern would be repeated again and again. First, a small band of settlers would put down

In 1587, John White and 120 others from England landed in Roanoke Island, North Carolina, to establish colony. After a month, White returned to England for supplies. When he returned to Roanoke in 1590, colonists had disappeared. The only trace ever found of the "lost colony" was the word "Croatoan"—t name of a nearby island inhabited by friendly Indians.

roots along a coastline or riverbank. Then the number of settlements would slowly grow. In this way, 12 other colonies were established on the eastern coast of North America between 1620 and 1732.

Types of English Colonies

There were three different kinds of colonies: charter, proprietary, and royal.

Charter Colonies As we learned on page 16, English rulers sometimes issued charters to trading companies. A charter gave a company land and certain rights to govern in the New World. Virginia, for example, was founded as a *charter colony.*

Proprietary Colonies English rulers gave gifts of land to close friends and people of high birth. Those who received such royal grants were called

proprietors. Proprietors in the New World allowed to set up colonies on their lands. Maryland and Pennsylvania began as *propr colonies.*

Royal Colonies The English rulers put colonies under their direct control. These were called *royal colonies* or crown colonie such colonies, laws made by the people there had to have royal approval. Contr the crown was maintained by royal gover appointed by the king.

A number of charter colonies, including ginia, were later taken over by the English Thus, they became royal colonies. By 17 of the 13 colonies were crown or royal col The British kings, far away in England, busy with matters closer to home. As a r royal colonies enjoyed a large amount o *government,* an arrangement whereby peopl themselves.

Political Reasons Many English people disagreed with the actions of their government. They wanted more political freedom, but there was little that they could do to bring about changes in Britain. Therefore, they came to America, where the power of the British government was not so strong.

Others left England to get away from a *civil war* (a war among groups within a country). During the English Civil War (1642–1660), there was much fighting between the army of the King and an army loyal to Parliament, England's lawmaking body.

Religious Reasons In the 17th century, religious differences caused great conflict. For most of the time, the Anglican Church was the *established church* (official religion) in England. Many fellow Protestants, though, refused to worship as directed by the established church. These people, known as *dissenters*, included the following groups:

• Puritans, who wanted to simplify the practices of the Anglican Church.
• Separatists, who wanted to break away from the Anglican Church. The Pilgrims were one group of Separatists.
• Quakers and others seeking freedom to worship in their own ways.

Additional groups also sought freedom of worship. Of special importance were Roman Catholics, who belonged to the Church headed by the Pope in Rome. Roman Catholics were entirely outside the Anglican Church. So were England's Jews.

In England, authorities *persecuted* (made suffer because of beliefs) religious dissenters, depriving them of their rights. In the colonies, on the other hand, dissenters were usually welcomed and well-treated.

In the mid-1600s, Puritans briefly took political control of England. They made their religion the established church and persecuted members of other religions. As a result of this religious persecution, many Anglicans fled to the colonies to obtain religious freedom.

Not all the people in the British colonies were from Great Britain. By 1750, one third of the colonists had come from other countries or descended from these people. Ireland, France, Germany, and Holland were major sources of *immigrants* (people who come from another country to settle). Non-British immigrants sought the same freedoms in America as did immigrants from Great Britain.

In addition to European immigrants, many Indians and black Africans lived in the colonies. Most blacks had been brought to America as slaves.

THE ORIGINAL THIRTEEN COLONIES, 1750

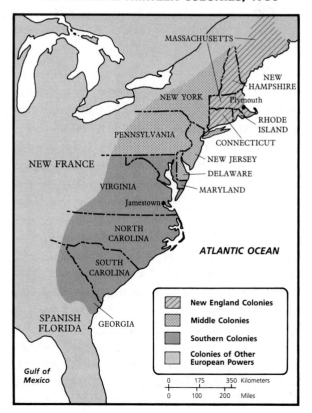

New England Colonies	
Middle Colonies	
Southern Colonies	
Colonies of Other European Powers	

SUMMING UP   We have seen that the British colonies were set up to meet some important needs of Britain. America also met the needs of other European immigrants. People came to America for a variety of economic, political, and religious reasons.

Understanding the Text

On a separate sheet of paper, write the letter of the word or phrase that best completes each of the following statements.

1. The 13 colonies in North America were founded over a period of about *(a)* 10 years *(b)* 125 years *(c)* 1,000 years *(d)* 1 year.

2. The English rulers were eager to set up colonies in America in order to do all of the following, *except* *(a)* increase national power *(b)* bring wealth to England *(c)* get rid of dissatisfied people *(d)* provide more political freedom for people.

3. By 1760, more than half of the 13 British colonies were *(a)* under direct royal control *(b)* governed by proprietors *(c)* independent of Britain *(d)* partly controlled by the king of France.

4. Most English people came to America to *(a)* create new religions *(b)* fight in the Civil War *(c)* help the Indians *(d)* make a better living.

5. All of the following terms belong together, *except* *(a)* inflation *(b)* economics *(c)* money *(d)* religious freedom.

6. In the early 1600s, the established religion in England was *(a)* Roman Catholic *(b)* Anglican *(c)* Separatist *(d)* Puritan.

7. The American colonies were important to British merchants mainly because merchants could *(a)* make profits from overseas trade *(b)* carry on trade with the Indians *(c)* set up factories *(d)* make land grants to friends.

8. An important factor in the eventual success of the Jamestown colony was the *(a)* Civil War in England *(b)* importation of debtors *(c)* cultivation of tobacco *(d)* discovery of gold.

9. In 1750, the people living in the 13 colonies had *(a)* come only from Great Britain *(b)* come mainly from Britain *(c)* come mainly from countries other than Britain *(d)* all been born in America.

10. One main point of this chapter is that *(a)* the first English settlement in North America was at Plymouth, Massachusetts *(b)* New Hampshire was first settled by the Dutch *(c)* English rulers were interested in settling North America partly because they wanted greater national power and prestige *(d)* charter colonies were governed directly by the English king.

Developing Table-Reading Skills

ESTIMATED BLACK POPULATION OF THE AMERICAN COLONIES, 1680–1740

	1680	1700	1720	1740
New Hampshire	75	130	170	500
Massachusetts	170	800	2,150	3,035
Rhode Island	175	300	543	2,408
Connecticut	50	450	1,093	2,598
New York	1,200	2,256	5,740	8,996
New Jersey	200	840	2,385	4,366
Pennsylvania	25	430	2,000	2,055
Delaware	55	135	700	1,035
Maryland	1,611	3,227	12,499	24,031
Virginia	3,000	16,390	26,559	60,000
North Carolina	210	415	3,000	11,000
South Carolina	200	2,444	12,000	30,000

Note: Georgia, founded in 1732, did not have a black population before 1740.

Study the table above. Then choose the letter of the word or phrase that best completes each sentence. On a separate sheet of paper, match the sentence number with the correct letter.

1. The table clearly shows that between 1680 and 1740 (a) most Americans were slaves (b) most Americans came from Europe (c) the number of blacks increased many times (d) blacks' political power increased greatly.

2. The year in which the black population was larger in North Carolina than in South Carolina was (a) 1680 (b) 1700 (c) 1720 (d) none of the above.

3. In 1680, the colony that had the smallest black population was (a) New Hampshire (b) Connecticut (c) Pennsylvania (d) Maryland.

4. In 1720, the colony that had the third largest black population was (a) Maryland (b) South Carolina (c) Virginia (d) New York.

5. In 1700, the total black population of the American colonies was about (a) 2,900 (b) 16,400 (c) 28,000 (d) 210,000.

Thinking About the Lesson

1. Were the problems that the first Jamestown settlers had typical of the problems of most early settlers in the English colonies? Why or why not?

2. Europeans moved to the English colonies for economic, political, and religious reasons. Which of these three reasons was the most powerful one? Explain your answer.

3. Imagine that you were king of England in the 1600s. Give two reasons why you would favor spending large sums of money to set up colonies in the New World.

LESSON 4

Self-Government in the English Colonies

Today our nation follows many democratic traditions. Some of them took root during the Colonial era. This period of time began in 1607, with the founding of Jamestown, and lasted almost 170 years.

> As you read this lesson, think about these two meanings of the word *democracy:*
>
> • A government in which people rule themselves, usually by means of elected representatives.
> • A way of life that provides personal freedom and equal rights and opportunities.

Beginnings of Representative Government

In 1619, colonists in Jamestown, Virginia, created a *legislature*, or lawmaking body—the House of Burgesses. The *burgesses*, or delegates, were chosen by Virginia's landowners. Thus, the House of Burgesses represented the colony's people of property. This legislature became the first example of *representative government* in the colonies.

In time, most American colonies created such legislatures made up of elected representatives. The right to vote and hold office, however, was limited to free males with a certain amount of property.

The colonial legislature usually made a colony's laws. In most colonies, though, the governor could *veto* (refuse to approve) a law. Unlike legislators, governors were not elected. Instead, they were chosen by the English king.

Colonial legislatures usually paid the governors' salaries. So to help "persuade" a governor not to veto a law, a legislature sometimes held back on paying the salary. Payments would resume when the governor accepted the wishes of the lawmaking body.

Self-Government in Massachusetts

Colonial self-government was strongly favored by the Pilgrims in Massachusetts. The first group of these English dissenters sailed for America on the ship *Mayflower*. In 1620, they entered the harbor of what is now Provincetown, Massachusetts. Even before landing, the new settlers signed an agreement, the *Mayflower Compact*. They agreed to form a government and obey its laws. Soon afterward, they came ashore, settling in Plymouth, Massachusetts.

Ten years later, neighboring Massachusetts Bay Colony developed a representative government. Its lawmaking body was the General Court. At first, membership in this body was

22

Forty-one male Pilgrims signed the *Mayflower Compact* while still on board their ship. The document provided for self-government of the Plymouth colony, but not for participation by females.

limited to the few men who held part ownership in Massachusetts Bay Company. Then, in 1634, a decision was reached to allow each town in the colony to elect representatives to the General Court. Even so, only males who were members of the Puritan religion could vote.

Town Meetings On the local level, residents of Massachusetts created their own form of self-government. They held town meetings, made up of all free men who belonged to the established church. Those present at the meetings discussed and voted on important matters and elected local officials. Today, people in different parts of New England still come together regularly in town meetings.

Early Personal Freedoms

To protect their rights, people in several colonies drew up written *constitutions* (sets of basic principles and laws of a group). The first constitution was the *Fundamental Orders of Connecticut* in 1639. This document explained how the colonial government in Connecticut was to work. It also listed the rights or personal freedoms of the colonists.

Two personal freedoms were especially important to the colonists. These were freedom of religion and freedom of the press.

Religious Freedom Many early settlers came to America to seek *freedom of religion* (the right to practice the religion of one's choice). Not all of the settlers, however, found the liberty that they sought. Some immigrants settled in colonies where the right to practice a religion was limited to people of only one faith.

Three colonies, though, protected religious freedom to some extent. Rhode Island, founded by Roger Williams, welcomed people of all faiths. Williams, a minister, believed that a government should not interfere with an individual's religion. He also believed that churches should stay out of affairs of government.

Maryland was founded by Roman Catholics who had been persecuted in England. They established their colony as a place where they could worship in their own way, without being bothered. In 1649, the Toleration Act extended religious freedom to all Christians in Maryland.

In the late 1600s, William Penn, the proprietor of Pennsylvania, set up his colony for Quakers. They, too, had faced religious persecution in England. Penn welcomed to his colony all people who believed in God.

Freedom of the Press   The principle of *freedom of the press* (the right of newspapers to publish what they want) was strengthened in 1735. In that year, John Peter Zenger, a newspaper publisher in New York City, went on trial. Zenger had criticized the royal governor of New York. Zenger's enemies accused him of misusing the power of the press to damage the governor's reputation. Zenger's lawyer argued that open discussion of public questions was necessary among free people.

A jury composed of men of the community heard Zenger's case. Women did not serve on juries at this time. The jury decided that Zenger had not misused his newspaper because he had printed the truth.

Other Rights and Freedoms

English colonists brought to America certain rights they had enjoyed in England:

• *Trial by jury* (a court trial with a group of citizens deciding the guilt or innocence of the accused).

• Protection of life, freedom, and property.

• *Habeas corpus.* This term refers to people's right to know about any criminal charges made against them. By knowing these charges, people can defend themselves. The term also refers to people's right not to be held in jail except as the law provides.

• Protection from having one's house searched without legal permission in the form of a written *search warrant.*

• *Freedom of speech* and *freedom of assembly* (the right to speak and meet in public without being bothered).

The Frontier   The area to the west of most settlements, called the *frontier*, encouraged a democratic spirit. On the frontier, life was hard. Settlers had to manage by themselves, with little

Anne Hutchinson was tried by the General Court of Massachusetts Bay Colony for challenging the authority of the Puritan clergy. After being banished from Massachusetts, she helped found Rhode Island. (*Granger Collection*)

government or community help. People in unsettled areas tended to judge others by what they could do, rather than by social standing or wealth. As a result, there was more equality on the frontier than in settled areas.

Undemocratic Aspects of Colonial Life

Colonial Americans had a number of basic rights and freedoms. Nevertheless, they did not enjoy the degree of self-government we have today. Nor did most of them have as much freedom. Slavery of black people was legal. In most colonies, women could not vote or own property.

Even free males had to meet certain requirements before being allowed to vote. *Property qualifications* (having to own a certain amount of property) usually limited voting to men who owned a certain amount of land or other wealth. And in some areas—although not everywhere— voters had to be members of an approved church.

SUMMING UP   We have seen how colonists in Virginia, Massachusetts, and elsewhere developed representative governments. Colonists enjoyed certain rights and freedoms, many of which had come from England. Democracy was growing, but one could not say that the English colonies were fully democratic.

Understanding the Text

On a separate sheet of paper, write the letter of the word or phrase that best completes each of the following statements.

1. The colonial period began with (*a*) the landing of the Pilgrims at Plymouth, Massachusetts (*b*) the settling of the frontier (*c*) Connecticut's written constitution (*d*) the settlement of Jamestown, Virginia.

2. The way the United States elects members of Congress shows that this nation has a form of (*a*) representative government (*b*) proprietary government (*c*) *habeas corpus* (*d*) royal government.

3. The *Mayflower Compact* (*a*) was drawn up by the English king (*b*) gave power to colonial governors (*c*) was drawn up by the House of Burgesses (*d*) strengthened the principle of self-government.

4. A colonial governor could (*a*) jail people without a trial (*b*) veto laws passed by a colonial legislature (*c*) grant a royal charter (*d*) choose all members of a colonial legislature.

5. An example of representative government in Virginia was (*a*) the General Court (*b*) the House of Burgesses (*c*) Peter Zenger's trial (*d*) the Fundamental Orders.

6. Roger Williams did much to (*a*) free black slaves (*b*) strengthen religious freedom (*c*) spread freedom of the press (*d*) give women the vote.

7. A colony initially settled by Quakers was (*a*) Maryland (*b*) Massachusetts (*c*) Pennsylvania (*d*) Connecticut.

8. The colonists with the most rights were (*a*) black slaves (*b*) male property owners (*c*) women (*d*) laborers.

9. After 1649, all of the following could worship freely in Maryland, *except* (*a*) Roman Catholics (*b*) Jews (*c*) Puritans (*d*) Anglicans.

10. From reading this lesson, it is clear that (*a*) the colonies had few forms of self-government (*b*) some colonists enjoyed democratic rights and freedoms (*c*) all colonists enjoyed the right to vote (*d*) all colonies except Rhode Island and Connecticut governed themselves.

Developing Reading Comprehension Skills

Read carefully the following paragraphs on Roger Williams. You will be asked questions about this reading.

ROGER WILLIAMS

He had "strange opinions" and was "to be pitied and prayed for." This is how Roger Williams, fighting for religious freedom, was described by Governor William Bradford of Massachusetts.

As a Christian minister in Salem, Massachusetts, Williams preached his "strange opinions":

Separation of church and state (no government control of religion or religious control of government.)

Freedom for Protestants, Catholics, and Jews to worship as they believed.

Williams was also worried about what was happening to the American Indians. These Native Americans, he argued, were the rightful owners of the land in the New World. Therefore, the English ruler had a duty to pay them for their land before granting charters to Europeans who wanted to settle it. Williams even made the daring suggestion that the religions of the Indians were just as acceptable to God as Christianity was.

In 1635, Williams was put on trial for expressing these ideas. He refused to give up his opinions and was found guilty. He escaped from Massachusetts with the help of Indians, who had come to love him.

In 1636, Williams founded the settlement of Providence, Rhode Island. In 1644, he obtained a charter for the Rhode Island colony. For the first time, true freedom of religion for Christians and others became a fact of colonial life.

On a separate sheet of paper, write *True* if the sentence is correct. If the sentence is not correct, change the word or phrase in italics to make it correct.

1. Roger Williams *hid* his "strange opinions."

2. To Roger Williams, it seemed *wrong* for church leaders to control the government.

3. Williams said that the English ruler did not respect the *land rights* of Indians.

4. The trial of Roger Williams took place in *Rhode Island*.

5. Another term for American Indians is *Native Americans*.

Thinking About the Lesson

1. To what extent did the colonists obtain their democratic rights and traditions from England?

2. Why was life on the frontier more democratic than life in settled areas of the colonies?

3. Would you characterize the 13 colonies as democratic, slightly democratic, or undemocratic? Explain your answer.

Life in the British Colonies

Most people who settled in the 13 colonies were European. They brought to America their European *customs*—their ways of doing things in everyday life. In time, however, colonists changed many customs, fitting them to their new surroundings and living conditions.

Population

At the end of the colonial period, in 1775, the 13 colonies had nearly 3 million people. Most of them were settled on farms not too far from the Atlantic Ocean. Some colonists lived in small towns. Others preferred the cities such as Boston, New York, Philadelphia, and Charleston.

As the population grew, many colonists moved west. First they settled in the foothills of the Appalachian Mountains. Then frontier travelers, such as Daniel Boone, crossed the mountains into Kentucky and Tennessee. Settlers soon followed the routes of these pioneers.

Daily Life

Most colonial Americans lived simply. They dressed in warm, dark clothes and ate homegrown foods. Using handmade tools, they built simple wooden houses and furniture. A few who were well-to-do wore fine clothes and filled their houses with expensive furniture. Such *luxuries* (goods that provide pleasure and comfort but are not necessary) had to be brought from Europe.

Religion Generally, colonists were deeply religious Christians. Their religious beliefs differed, however, and they were divided into various *sects* (religious groups). Even so, in most of the colonies there was a single established church, supported by local taxes. The established church was not the same for every colony.

The Puritans of New England were one of the important sects. They insisted on regular church attendance. In addition, they forbade dancing, playing cards, and going to the theater.

Education Most colonial children were educated at home. Some attended *parish schools* (schools run by the churches). Commonly, children learned about the *Bible* and the "three R's": reading, writing, and arithmetic.

Some New England towns were required by law to set up public grade schools, called *grammar schools*. In addition, a number of private *academies* were established. The academies offered training at a level similar to that of present-day high schools.

Academies, however, did not necessarily represent the final step in education. Some young

The tradition of free public education began in New England. A Massachusetts law of 1647 called on every town of at least 50 households to hire someone to teach reading and writing.

men went to Europe for a college education. (Women did not attend college in colonial times.) After a while, students did not need to go such distances. By 1775, America had some colleges of its own—Harvard, Yale, and seven others.

Culture Gradually, Americans grew more independent of European culture. They published their own books and newspapers. They ventured into the arts. John Singleton Copley and Benjamin West became well-known American painters. Copley painted many fine portraits in New England during the 1760s and 1770s. One of West's famous paintings, *The Death of Wolfe*, is reproduced on page 34.

American scientists won fame at home and in Europe. Benjamin Franklin, the inventor of the lightning rod, proved that lightning is electricity. He showed this by flying a kite during an electrical storm. A bolt of lightning traveled down the kite string and caused a spark where a key had been tied.

Daily Work

The main task of most colonists was to make a living. Colonial families, whether in towns or on farms, worked very hard.

Farming Nine out of every ten workers were farmers. There was plenty of work for everyone in a farm family. Women worked just as hard as the men did. Even children performed some important tasks.

New England's long winters and rocky soil made farming very hard. Families lived mainly by *subsistence farming*. In this type of agriculture, families used whatever they produced. Little or nothing was left for outside sale. Many subsistence farmers also held part-time jobs to help support their families.

In the Middle Colonies, winters were shorter and the soil was richer. Farmers raised many animals and produced large yields of wheat and other grains. What the farmers did not need for their own use, they sold to people within the colonies or overseas. As a result of the sale of these *surpluses*, the Middle Colonies became known as the *bread colonies*.

In the South, winters were even milder, allowing a longer growing season. Along the Atlantic coast, much of the land was turned into *plantations*. These large farms often grew great amounts of just one crop, such as rice or tobacco. The crops were known as *cash crops* because most were grown to be sold. Large quantities of the South's tobacco, for example, were sold in Europe.

Non-Farming Occupations Throughout the colonies, people started small businesses. Some became shopkeepers or workers skilled in making objects of metal, stone, or wood. Traders went everywhere in the colonies. Fur trading, in particular, became a major occupation. Other colonists became doctors, lawyers, teachers, or religious officials.

A large number of New England colonists earned their living from the sea. They fished, hunted whales, and made commercial voyages, carrying goods and people to and from various ports by ship. Shipbuilding served as an important occupation for carpenters and other skilled workers.

Since America was a land of great forests, lumbering was important. Colonists constructed not only ships, but houses and other buildings out of wood. Wood was valuable also in making furniture, tools, and household utensils. In most parts of the colonies, wood served as the main fuel.

Indentured Servants and Slaves

Many colonists had the help of *indentured servants*. These workers were mostly Europeans who had not been able to pay their passage to America. To make the voyage, they agreed to work for up to seven years without pay. After serving out the period of indenture, these people became as free as anyone else.

Quite a few of the indentured servants were single women. After serving their time, they did not usually remain single for long, since many male colonists were looking for wives.

Candlemaking was just one of the many small industries that developed in colonial America. Young Benjamin Franklin (center) was employed in the candlemaking shop owned by his father.

Black slaves from Africa were brought to the New World on ships such as this one. (*Granger Collection*)
The Africans were chained and made to lie down (as shown in the cross section of a slave ship). Because of unsanitary conditions, many slaves died before reaching America.

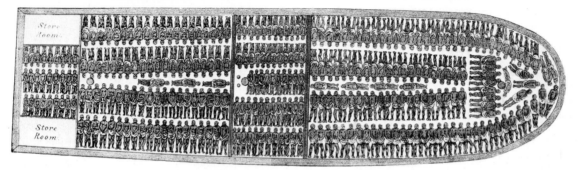

Criminals and *debtors* (people who could not pay their debts) also came to the New World as indentured servants.

So, at first, did black people. Some of them gained their freedom and purchased land in America. By the late 1600s, however, most blacks brought from Africa were slaves.

Slaves did many different kinds of work and were found in all of the colonies. Most of them, though, lived on plantations in the South. Unlike indentured servants, slaves remained in bondage throughout their lives. Their owners regarded them as human property. Slaves were bought and sold like other possessions—sometimes resulting in the splitting up of families. A husband could be sold to one owner and his wife to another. Children of slaves were considered slaves from birth.

Slavery lasted for hundreds of years, while the system of indentured servants died out much earlier. By 1789, there were few indentured servants in America.

Women in Colonial America

Colonial women did not have the same rights as men. Women could not obtain much formal schooling. Outside of New Jersey, they could not vote. Husbands controlled any property or wages that their wives might receive.

Most colonists were farmers, and in farm families men and women performed different tasks. Women fed and clothed the family and raised the children. They also tended dairy animals and poultry and made household products such as soap and candles. Women often did not live as long as men. Because of poor health care, many women died during childbirth. Men commonly outlived two or three wives.

In the towns and cities, a woman's life proved somewhat easier. There women ran shops, inns, or boarding houses. Some even became teachers, tailors, or printers, or entered other occupations.

SUMMING UP   We have seen how some 3 million people lived and worked in colonial America before 1775. Life was difficult for most colonists then, but even more difficult for indentured servants and slaves. Nevertheless, colonists were able successfully to adapt European ways of life to American conditions.

Understanding the Text

On a separate sheet of paper, write the letter of the word or phrase that best completes each of the following statements.

1. Most people in the 13 colonies lived (a) on farms (b) in cities (c) on the frontier (d) in the forests.

2. The luxury items that wealthy colonial Americans owned were (a) made in the colonial cities (b) made in the foothills of the Appalachian Mountains (c) brought from Europe (d) brought from Africa.

3. In the colonies, (a) the established church was the same in every colony (b) there was complete separation of church and state (c) some churches ran parish schools (d) all of the churches favored complete religious freedom.

4. Benjamin West was known for (a) killing wolves (b) painting historical scenes (c) leading settlers into Kentucky (d) performing scientific experiments.

5. In colonial America, private academies offered courses similar in level to those offered now by (a) elementary schools (b) middle schools (c) high schools (d) graduate schools.

6. A colonial scientist who won fame in Europe was (a) Daniel Boone (b) Benjamin West (c) John Singleton Copley (d) Benjamin Franklin.

7. Most indentured colonial servants came from (a) Africa (b) Asia (c) Europe (d) South America.

8. Of the following kinds of workers in colonial America, one *not* common was the (a) subsistence farmer (b) indentured servant (c) slave (d) factory worker.

9. Many women in colonial America (a) died while giving birth (b) went to college (c) held property jointly with their husbands (d) could vote in elections.

10. Which general theme of colonial history does this lesson emphasize? (a) government (b) everyday life (c) exploration (d) Britain's foreign policy.

Developing Chart-Reading Skills

PATTERNS OF TRIANGULAR TRADE

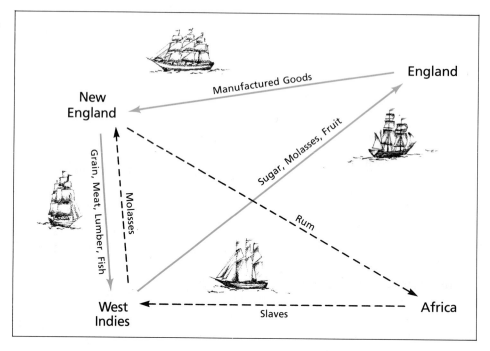

Study the chart above. Then choose the letter of the word or phrase that best completes each sentence. On a separate sheet of paper, match the sentence number with the correct letter.

1. All of the following geographical areas are indicated on the chart, *except* (*a*) Africa (*b*) South America (*c*) England (*d*) West Indies.

2. England was the source of (*a*) slaves (*b*) manufactured goods (*c*) fruits and wine (*d*) grain and lumber.

3. New England was the source of (*a*) manufactured goods (*b*) slaves (*c*) molasses (*d*) lumber.

4. The chart shows that (*a*) New England had cold winters (*b*) New England sold raw materials to other areas of the world (*c*) Africa bought slaves from other areas of the world (*d*) England controlled the slave trade.

5. An English ship left England with manufactured cloth. It went to New England, where it unloaded the cloth and obtained a cargo of grain. It took the grain to the West Indies. According to the chart, on its return home, the ship carried (*a*) slaves (*b*) fish (*c*) sugar (*d*) rum.

Thinking About the Lesson

1. How were educational opportunities in colonial America different from those enjoyed today?

2. Would you have enjoyed living in colonial New England? Why or why not?

3. In what ways was farming more profitable in the South than in New England?

4. How is the role of women in the United States today different from their role in colonial times?

Britain's New Colonial Policy

The government of Great Britain made many rules and regulations in order to control its New World colonies. At first, these laws were not strictly enforced. In the 1760s, however, the British Parliament decided to make the colonists obey its rules. It adopted some tough, new laws. The colonists viewed this stricter way of doing things as a new colonial policy.

Mercantilism

European leaders in the 18th century believed in a theory known as *mercantilism.* According to this set of ideas, the best way for a country to become powerful was to store up large amounts of gold and silver. Some colonies, such as those of Spain, had rich deposits of these two metals. They sent the gold and silver back to the home country.

Britain's 13 American colonies did not have deposits of these precious metals. Nevertheless, British leaders still used the colonies to help their country gain gold and silver.

The colonies *exported* (sent out of the country) to Britain *raw materials,* such as lumber, furs, and iron ore. In return, the colonies *imported* (brought into the country) *manufactured goods* (goods that people have made). Since these manufactured goods cost more than raw mate-

rials, the colonies had to pay the difference in gold and silver obtained in trade from elsewhere.

Early Control of Colonial Trade

During the colonial period, Britain tried to profit from the growing trade with its colonies in several ways.

Control of Manufactures Britain did not allow colonists to *manufacture* (make) certain items that English factories made for export. For instance, iron products could not be made in the colonies.

Control of Exports The colonies could not export certain products that would compete with similar British goods. Woolens were among the products that could not be exported from America.

Control of Shipping Between 1650 and 1767, Parliament passed a series of Navigation Acts. One of these acts required the colonies to use only British ships in trading with *any* European country.

Taxes The colonists had to pay extra *duties* (taxes on imports) on goods bought from non-British colonies and countries. Molasses, for example, was bought mostly in the Dutch and

French West Indies. Under the terms of the Molasses Act of 1733, the British taxed the product heavily when colonists imported it.

All of these laws were annoying to the colonists, but the regulations did not immediately lead to trouble. For one thing, Britain did not make much effort to enforce the laws at first. For another thing, the colonists became experts at *smuggling* (importing or exporting goods illegally, usually to avoid duties). They regularly smuggled goods in and out of America. Then a war between Great Britain and France changed this free and easy situation.

The French and Indian War

Ever since the European Age of Exploration, Britain and France had been rivals. In America, they both wanted: (1) profits from the fur trade, fishing, and other sources; (2) control of the Ohio and Mississippi river valleys, as well as Canada.

In 1754, this rivalry finally led to the French and Indian War. In this war, some powerful Indian nations sided with the French. Others, equally strong, came to the aid of the British.

Although the British suffered a number of defeats at the hands of the French, they finally won the war. An important British victory took place in 1759 at the city of Quebec. The French had long held this city, situated on a cliff above the St. Lawrence River. The British sent troops to scale the cliff and stage an attack on the French. The attack surprised the French, causing their defeat. Both the British and French commanders (General James Wolfe and the Marquis de Montcalm) died in the fierce battle.

American artist Benjamin West painted this scene from the French and Indian War. Here British General James Wolfe lies dying during the 1759 battle that led to the capture of the city of Quebec from the French.

Treaty of Paris   Britain was the victor in the war. In the Treaty of Paris of 1763, France lost its power base in North America. France had to *cede* (give up) both Canada and the Ohio and Mississippi river valleys to Britain. Spain had been on the losing side as France's ally. As a result, Spain had to give up Florida to England. To make up for this loss, France ceded Louisiana, including the city of New Orleans, to Spain. (See the map to the right.)

These vast territories were shifted from one country to another as though they were small pieces of real estate. Probably the European rulers had no idea of the great value of these possessions.

Stricter Control of the Colonies

In the years following the war, Britain enacted many policies that made growing numbers of colonists angry.

The Proclamation of 1763   Britain forbade colonists from traveling or settling west of the Appalachian Mountains. This area was to be reserved for Indian nations. By enacting this measure, the British wanted to avoid future troubles with the Indians. (The Proclamation Line, over which colonists were not supposed to cross, is shown on the map.)

The Proclamation was unpopular with colonists who wanted to live in the Ohio River Valley and other Western lands. *Land speculators* (people who bought and sold land for profit) were also upset by the new British policy. The Proclamation deprived them of sources of income.

New Taxes   A war between British forces and Indians under Chief Pontiac continued on the frontier. Fighting the Indians and administering the colonies were very costly to the British. Parliament felt that the colonists should pay higher taxes to help pay for these rising expenses.

NORTH AMERICA AFTER THE TREATY OF PARIS, 1763

Some of the new taxes included:

• The Sugar Act of 1764. This act raised existing duties on refined sugar.
• The Stamp Act of 1765. This law required special stamps to be attached to newspapers, pamphlets, playing cards, and documents of various types. Since the stamps were expensive, they naturally increased the cost of such items.
• The Townshend Acts of 1767. These laws put duties on tea, paper, glass, and paint.

Currency Act.   Some of the colonies had manufactured their own *currency* (coins and paper money). The Currency Act of 1764 forbade the practice. The new law made money scarce, resulting in higher prices for many goods.

Quartering Act   Because of the Indian wars, British soldiers were sent to the colonies in larger numbers than ever before. The Quartering Act of 1765 required the colonists to provide troops with supplies and *living quarters* (places to eat and sleep). Many soldiers were lodged in private homes.

Enforcement of Older Laws In addition to enacting all of the above-mentioned new laws, Great Britain began to enforce its existing laws more strictly. For instance, British officials made increasing use of *writs of assistance*. These writs were search warrants—documents that allowed officials to search buildings and ships for smuggled goods.

All of these measures were enacted early in the reign of George III, who became King of England in 1760. The young King followed the advice of powerful leaders in Parliament. His policies were to cause much trouble in the years to follow.

Much to the surprise of the British Parliament, its Stamp Act was strongly protested in the colonies. An angry crowd in Boston expressed its disapproval by burning paper sent from England to make stamps.

SUMMING UP We have seen that in the mid-1700s the British had a complex set of laws relating to its American colonies. Some of the laws reflected the government's policy of mercantilism. After the French and Indian War, British control over the colonies increased even more.

Understanding the Text

On a separate sheet of paper, write the letter of the word or phrase that best completes each of the following statements.

1. In the 18th century, a country that regulated its colonial trade so as to build up its holdings of gold and silver was said to be following a policy of (*a*) quartering (*b*) exploration (*c*) writs of assistance (*d*) mercantilism.

2. Americans in the British colonies were prevented from moving west of the Appalachian Mountains by the (*a*) Stamp Act (*b*) Navigation Acts (*c*) Currency Act (*d*) Proclamation of 1763.

3. The Dutch and French West Indies supplied the colonists with most of their (*a*) molasses (*b*) woolens (*c*) playing cards (*d*) iron products.

4. The Navigation Acts *(a)* shortened the sailing time from London to New York *(b)* required the colonists to use only British ships in overseas trade *(c)* helped the colonists to produce more manufactured goods *(d)* required colonists to provide living quarters for troops.

5. France's main enemies in the French and Indian War were the *(a)* American colonists *(b)* British *(c)* Indian nations *(d)* Spanish.

6. One territorial change that did *not* result from the Treaty of Paris in 1763 was *(a)* France's loss of Canada *(b)* Spain's loss of Florida *(c)* Britain's loss of the 13 American colonies *(d)* France's loss of the Mississippi Valley.

7. As a result of the French and Indian War, *(a)* Britain began to control its American colonies more strictly *(b)* France built forts along the Ohio River *(c)* Spain took over Florida

(d) Britain rewarded the colonists for their support by reducing taxes.

8. Britain passed all of the following laws after the French and Indian War, *except* the *(a)* Currency Act *(b)* Stamp Act *(c)* Quartering Act *(d)* Molasses Act.

9. The Townshend Acts *(a)* taxed tea *(b)* taxed sugar *(c)* required colonists to provide quarters for British troops *(d)* forbade the colonists from printing their own money.

10. Which of the following statements best describes the results of Britain's colonial policy in America after the French and Indian War? *(a)* It was welcomed by the colonists. *(b)* It caused much dissatisfaction among the colonists. *(c)* Since it was not enforced, it made little difference. *(d)* It caused an immediate revolt against the British government.

Developing Graph-Reading Skills

COLONIAL TRADE WITH ENGLAND, 1761

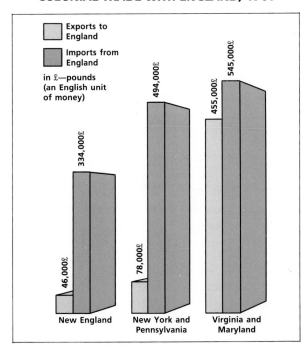

Study the graph on the left. Then choose the letter of the word or phrase that best completes each sentence. On a separate sheet of paper, match the sentence number with the correct letter.

1. The darker bars represent *(a)* the population of each region or group of states *(b)* duties on trade between England and the colonies *(c)* exports to England *(d)* imports from England.

2. The lighter bars represent *(a)* the population of each region or group of states *(b)* duties on trade between England and the colonies *(c)* exports to England *(d)* imports from England.

3. The region or group of states with the greatest amount of exports to England was *(a)* New England *(b)* New York and Pennsylvania *(c)* Virginia and Maryland *(d)* the West Indies.

4. The region or group of states where imports and exports were closest to being equal was *(a)* New England *(b)* New York and Pennsylvania *(c)* Virginia and Maryland *(d)* the West Indies.

5. From reading this graph, one can assume that *(a)* the colonies' imports from England were much greater than their exports *(b)* the colonies' exports to England were much greater than their imports *(c)* the colonies' exports and imports were roughly equal *(d)* the colonies' trade with one another was greater than their trade with England.

Thinking About the Lesson

1. Why did the British Parliament pass laws that strictly controlled manufacturing, trading, and shipping in the colonies?

2. Imagine that you had been living in the colonies in the 1760s. What would you have thought of Britain's Stamp Act?

3. Why did more British soldiers come to the 13 colonies after the French and Indian War? Why did some colonists object to their coming?

Resistance to the New Colonial Policy

As time went on, the bitter feelings stirred up by Britain's new colonial policy grew worse. Colonists strongly resisted Parliament's attempts to control colonial trade and government.

Peaceful Resistance to British Policies

At first, colonists were not ready for armed rebellion. They showed their opposition to British policies in non-violent ways. Some colonists refused to cooperate with the British or to obey hated British laws. They continued to smuggle goods into America. In spite of British prohibitions, they continued moving west. This *non-violent resistance* spread throughout the colonies.

Colonists sent written protests to Parliament. In their letters, they argued that Parliament was taking away their rights as English people. Although British property owners elected some members of Parliament, colonists elected none. As the colonists saw it, their major problem was being taxed without having a representative in Parliament. Thus, colonists voiced the slogan, "No taxation without representation!"

Stamp Act Congress The colonies began to work together more closely. In 1765, nine of them sent representatives to a Stamp Act Congress. The group, meeting in New York City, wrote a formal statement protesting the stamp tax. Their statement was called the "Declaration of Rights and Grievances."

Some colonial leaders urged their neighbors to *boycott* (agree not to buy) British goods. Since many colonial merchants and their customers cooperated, the boycott worked well. Parliament soon *repealed* (declared no longer legal) the Stamp Act.

Several years later, Parliament repealed other taxes, but it kept the hated tax on tea.

Violent Resistance Begins

After a time, colonial resistance occasionally became violent. In protesting against the British, property was destroyed and people were injured. A group called the "Sons of Liberty" led riots against the Stamp Act. On a number of occasions, they attacked and burned homes of British officials. During the boycott, merchants who continued to trade with Britain also became targets of this group's actions.

Boston Massacre In 1770, an angry crowd insulted British soldiers who were guarding a government building in Boston. The soldiers became enraged and fired into the crowd. Five Americans died. The "Boston Massacre," as the

Tension in the colonies led to this confrontation between colonists and British troops in Boston, on March 5, 1770. Angered by a mob, soldiers fired into the crowd and killed five Americans, including a black man—Crispus Attucks.

incident was called, was the first major act of violence between Americans and British soldiers.

Colonial Leaders With Fighting Spirit

Until the early 1770s, most colonists were *moderates*. A moderate is someone who holds views that are not extreme or "far-out." Although angry at the British government, moderates were willing to "forgive and forget." In return, they wanted Britain to go back to more easy-going policies of the past. Benjamin Franklin was one of the best-known moderates of the time.

More and more colonists were becoming *radicals*. A radical is someone who holds extreme views. Radicals among the colonists wanted to defend colonial rights—by the use of force, if necessary. Patrick Henry was a radical member of the Virginia House of Burgesses. In a speech before that body in 1765, Henry accused England of tyranny.

Another radical was Samuel Adams of Massachusetts. He had played a major role in setting up the Sons of Liberty. Adams helped create Committees of Correspondence as well. These letter-writing committees kept leaders of the various colonies in touch with one another.

The Boston Tea Party

In 1773, Parliament granted a British firm, the East India Company, a favored place in the American tea market. Colonists now were forced to buy all their tea from this one source. Even though duties on tea were low, colonists objected to being taxed without first being consulted. In New York City, angry colonists prevented ships carrying tea from entering the harbor.

In December, 1773, some Bostonians went even further. Under the influence of Samuel Adams, they decided to show their contempt for East India tea. Dressed as Mohawk Indians, they boarded ships of the East India Company and dumped the tea into the Boston Harbor. This event was soon called the "Boston Tea Party."

British Punishment of the Colonies

Parliament looked upon the Boston Tea Party as the final insult. British lawmakers acted quickly to show the colonists that the government meant business.

Intolerable Acts In 1774, Parliament decided to punish not only Boston but all of the people of Massachusetts. This action was supposed to be an example for the other colonies to note. By the laws that the colonists called the Intolerable Acts, Parliament imposed the following punishments:

• The port of Boston was closed to shipping. The harbor would be reopened only when Massachusetts paid for the tea that had been dumped into the harbor.

• Self-government in Massachusetts was severely limited in several ways. For instance, local leaders could now call town meetings only with the consent of the governor.

• Under a new Quartering Act, colonists in Massachusetts had to provide housing for soldiers within 24 hours after being notified by military officials.

• British officials and soldiers who were charged with crimes in Massachusetts could be tried in Great Britain.

First Continental Congress

The Intolerable Acts convinced even moderates that Britain had gone too far. In September, 1774, representatives from 12 colonies met in Philadelphia to protest these laws. Members of this First Continental Congress spoke out strongly against British actions. Congress advised each colony to draft and train a *militia*—a group of armed and trained civilians. In this way, each colony would have a force ready to fight the British, if needed.

The Congress also planned a boycott of all trade with Britain. This boycott would go into effect if Parliament did not repeal the Intolerable Acts.

This scene is what Bostonians might have observed if they had been out walking on the evening of December 16, 1773. Disguised as Indians, angry colonists threw some 342 chests of tea into the water.

SUMMING UP   We have seen that bitter feelings between Britain and its 13 American colonies increased after the passage of the Stamp Act. Some colonists resorted to protests and even violent acts against the British. Parliament repealed some taxes, but it kept others and enacted new laws to control the colonies.

Understanding the Text

On a separate sheet of paper, write the letter of the word or phrase that best completes each of the following statements.

1. The anger caused by Britain's colonial policy after 1764 (a) was limited to New England (b) was limited to merchants and other wealthy people (c) became deeper and more widespread (d) faded away within a short time.

2. The first major outbreak of violence between colonists and British soldiers was the (a) Boston Tea Party (b) Boston Massacre (c) Proclamation of 1763 (d) Stamp Act Congress.

3. The term "radical," as applied to colonists of this period, refers to people who (a) wanted to defend colonial rights by force, if necessary (b) were willing to "forgive and forget" (c) were loyal to the king (d) believed in communism.

4. The event among the following that occurred *last* was the (a) meeting of the First Continental Congress (b) Boston Tea Party (c) passage of the Intolerable Acts (d) Boston Massacre.

5. To oppose British taxes, colonists did all of the following, *except* (a) organize boycotts (b) riot against the Stamp Act (c) ask for a stricter Quartering Act (d) disobey laws.

6. The colony most affected by the Intolerable Acts was (a) Massachusetts (b) New York (c) Virginia (d) Pennsylvania.

7. To work together against the Intolerable Acts, representatives from 12 colonies met in the (a) British Parliament (b) First Continental Congress (c) Committees of Correspondence (d) Boston Massacre.

8. "Taxation without representation," meant that colonists (a) were not allowed to print paper money (b) did not have their own representatives in the British Parliament (c) could not vote for members of a colonial legislature (d) could not hold town meetings.

9. The Boston Tea Party (a) was held in the halls of Parliament (b) involved cargo belonging to the East India Company (c) was carried out by Mohawk Indians (d) ended in a massacre.

10. A statement supported by the events described in this lesson says that (a) people would rather fight than settle their disagreements peacefully (b) no serious disagreement can ever be settled except by force (c) when people fail to settle a disagreement peacefully, the use of force may result (d) force is better than peaceful methods for settling disagreements.

Developing Cartoon-Reading Skills

**THE GOOSE THAT LAID
THE GOLDEN EGG**

This cartoon is based on one that appeared in a London publication in 1776. Already political cartoonists were using their craft to criticize government policies.

Study the political cartoon above. Then choose the letter of the word or phrase that best answers each question. On a separate sheet of paper, match the question number with the correct letter.

1. Who or what does the man with the sword represent? *(a)* the British Parliament *(b)* Samuel Adams *(c)* Benjamin Franklin *(d)* the First Continental Congress.

2. Who or what does the goose represent? *(a)* the British Parliament *(b)* the king of England *(c)* the 13 American colonies *(d)* England's poultry industry.

3. What do the eggs in the basket represent? *(a)* British dairy products *(b)* colonial protests *(c)* the next generation of Americans *(d)* profits from the American colonies.

4. What relationship between the sword and the eggs does the cartoonist suggest? *(a)* The sword will smash the eggs. *(b)* The sword will kill the goose so that no more eggs can be laid. *(c)* The sword will push the goose away to reveal more eggs. *(d)* The sword will frighten the goose into laying more eggs.

5. Which of the following views does the cartoonist express in the cartoon? *(a)* The colonists should not resort to violence. *(b)* The British should not punish the colonies so harshly. *(c)* The colonies deserve any punishment that they can get. *(d)* Meat-eaters are cruel.

Thinking About the Lesson

1. Do you think that colonial groups such as the Sons of Liberty should have used violence in resisting the British? Why or why not?

2. Do you think that the British were right in punishing the whole Massachusetts colony for the Boston Tea Party? Explain your answer.

3. Compare the actions of the Stamp Act Congress and the First Continental Congress.

The Colonial Movement Toward Independence

By early 1775, colonists were getting ready for a serious conflict. Radicals enforced the boycott more strictly than before. Local groups began storing arms and learning how to use them. At first, few people realized that a *revolution* (attempt to overthrow a government) was brewing. In effect, though, colonists were moving toward independence from Great Britain.

Battle of Lexington and Concord

In April, 1775, the British made plans to seize colonial military supplies stored at Concord, Massachusetts. They also wanted to find and arrest two radical leaders, Samuel Adams and John Hancock, in nearby Lexington. Their attempt to carry out these plans led to the first battle of the American Revolution—the Battle of Lexington and Concord. (See the map on page 45.)

On the night of April 18, 700 *redcoats* set out from Boston. They had been ordered to march to Lexington by General Thomas Gage, the British military governor of Massachusetts. The same night, two colonists, Paul Revere and William Dawes, rode ahead to warn members of the militia, called *Minutemen*. When the British arrived at Lexington the next morning, the Minutemen were waiting for them. In the fighting that followed, several Americans were killed. Hancock and Adams were not caught, since they had already left town.

> "Minutemen" were so named because they were supposed to be ready at a minute's notice. The term "redcoats" refers to British soldiers. Colonists thought up this name, as well as "bloody backs" and "lobsters," because of the British soldiers' red jackets.

The fighting continued at Concord, where the redcoats burned whatever military supplies they found. Then the British troops began to march back to Boston. Along the way, colonists attacked them from behind buildings and trees. The British suffered heavy losses before completing their retreat.

Now the colonists began a year-long *siege* (military blockade) of Boston. They surrounded the city and shut in the British troops there.

BATTLE OF LEXINGTON AND CONCORD, 1775

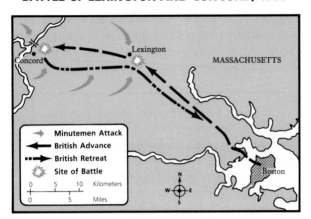

Meanwhile, more troops arrived in America from Britain. Among them were German *mercenaries* (soldiers who fought only for pay), whom the British had hired to defend the colonies. (These soldiers were also called "Hessians" because many of them came from the German state of Hesse.) The British sought help from some of the many Indian nations in America. They encouraged Indians to raid colonial frontier settlements.

The Desire for Independence Grows

Before 1775, most Americans simply wanted the British Parliament to stop treating them unfairly. Then as the fighting spread, so did bitter feelings. Many colonists began to hope for *independence* (complete self-government) from Great Britain.

On May 10, 1775, the Second Continental Congress met in Philadelphia and soon took four important steps:

• It asked King George III to end Parliament's punishment of the colonies.

• It declared that if the punishment continued, the colonists would fight to the death.

• It named the colonial troops surrounding Boston as the official "Continental Army."

On April 19, 1775, in Lexington, some 70 Minutemen led by Captain John Parker stood face to face with the British. Then the Captain gave a soon-to-be famous command to his men: "Stand your ground. Don't fire unless fired upon. But if they mean to have a war, let it begin here." Soon someone fired a shot. When the smoke cleared, eight colonists were dead and ten wounded. (Granger Collection)

• It appointed George Washington of Virginia to be Commander in Chief of the Continental Army.

In May of 1775, the Second Continental Congress was not yet ready to declare independence for the colonies. Over the next few months, however, the move for independence grew rapidly. Historians see a number of reasons for the change:

• King George and Parliament refused to grant the colonists' requests.
• The British closed all American ports.
• The undeclared war continued. In May, 1775, two colonial forces seized Fort Ticonderoga, on Lake Champlain. One force, under Ethan Allen, was from the Green Mountains, while the other force, from Massachusetts, was led by Benedict Arnold.
• In June, 1775, redcoats drove the colonists from their positions overlooking Boston. Yet Americans fought bravely and killed many of the attackers. The actual site of the main battle was Breed's Hill, near Bunker Hill. But the conflict is remembered as the Battle of Bunker Hill.

• In the fall of 1775, American forces invaded Quebec, in eastern Canada. There the British were organizing a force to march against New York. After early victories, the Americans were forced to retreat to New York in 1776.

In early 1776, Thomas Paine published a booklet, *Common Sense.* In it, Paine, a recent arrival from England, called for a revolt against Great Britain. Paine wrote that it made no sense for an island (Britain) to govern a *continent* (North America). *Common Sense* soon became very popular because it made the idea of revolution seem sensible to the colonists.

The Vote for Independence

On July 4, 1776, the Second Continental Congress adopted one of the most important documents in American history, the Declaration of Independence. (See pages 599–601.)

Thomas Jefferson wrote the original version of the document. Other members of Congress

On July 4, 1776, delegates to the Second Continental Congress gathered around to adopt the Declaration of Independence. This engraving was taken from a painting by John Trumbull, an American artist who studied under Benjamin West.

made some changes. The Declaration's opening sentences state *principles* (basic truths) about democracy and human rights, as follows:

• *Equality.* All people are born with the same or equal rights.

• *Unalienable rights.* Governments have no authority to take away certain rights from people. These rights include "life, liberty, and the pursuit of happiness."

• Purpose of government. Governments exist to protect the rights of the governed—that is, the people.

• *Consent of the governed.* A good government serves its people. People willingly give their government the powers it needs to do its job.

• Right of revolution. When a government becomes unfair, people have the right to overthrow it and to set up another one.

The second section of the Declaration contains a long list of complaints against actions of the king and Parliament. Included were taxation without representation, the closing of colonial legislatures, and the quartering of troops in private homes.

Finally, the Declaration states that all colonial efforts to keep the peace with Britain have failed. It concludes by saying that the colonies have the right to be "free and independent states."

Immediate Effects of the Declaration

American colonists felt the force of the Declaration almost at once. The Declaration gave their fighting a clear and important aim—independence. At the same time, colonists with doubts about independence had to take sides. Now they would have to be either Patriots or Loyalists. *Patriots* were those colonists who favored independence. *Loyalists* were those who supported British rule over the colonies.

Colonial leaders knew that they would need help against the British. Now that they were free to form *treaties* (formal agreements with other nations), they began to look for *allies*. (Allies are nations united by treaty to act together in time of war.) France, a longtime enemy of Britain, was an obvious choice to be an ally of the colonists.

The Declaration of Independence inspired fighters for freedom around the world. In 1789, leaders of the French Revolution used the document as a model for their own Declaration of the Rights of Man. In the 19th century, Jefferson's Declaration guided South Americans in their fight for independence from Spain. In this century, the Declaration of Independence has influenced many leaders of developing nations in Asia and Africa. It still serves as a "living document," guiding and inspiring the people of the United States and other countries.

SUMMING UP   We have seen that fighting between Britain and the colonists began in April of 1775. Yet more than a year passed before the colonists declared their independence. Many Americans were reluctant to conclude that independence was the right step. Even so, the quest for freedom gained strength, aided by the Declaration of Independence. Through the years, people around the world have found new hope in this document's forthright statement of principles.

Understanding the Text

On a separate sheet of paper, write the letter of the word or phrase that best completes each of the following statements.

1. Samuel Adams and John Hancock were both (a) mercenaries (b) radical Patriot leaders (c) Loyalists (d) British officials.

2. Lexington and Concord were (a) important ports in Connecticut (b) frontier settlements in Virginia (c) Spanish colonies in America (d) the location of the first battle in the American Revolution.

3. Thomas Paine believed that American Patriots (a) were traitors (b) had cause for complaint but should not fight British troops (c) could peacefully settle their differences with the British (d) were justified in rebelling against the British.

4. Of the following events, the one that occurred first was the (a) Battle of Bunker Hill (b) signing of the Declaration of Independence (c) fighting at Lexington and Concord (d) American invasion of Quebec, Canada.

5. July 4 is considered the birthday of the United States because on this date in 1776 (a) the Second Continental Congress adopted the Declaration of Independence (b) the United States Constitution was approved (c) the British Army in America was defeated (d) the Battle of Bunker Hill was fought.

6. The Declaration of Independence includes all of the following ideas, *except* that (a) all people are born with equal rights (b) a government's powers are given by the people who are governed (c) it is wrong for some people to be richer than others (d) people have the right to overthrow an unfair government.

7. An event that could *not* have influenced the Second Continental Congress to adopt the Declaration of Independence was the (a) French Revolution (b) closing of colonial ports by the British (c) Battle of Bunker Hill (d) publication of Thomas Paine's *Common Sense*.

8. The famous rides of Paul Revere and William Dawes in 1775 were made to (a) put George Washington in command of the Continental Army (b) gather together the members of the Continental Congress (c) warn the Patriots that British forces were on the march (d) raise funds for a colonial army.

9. Of the following people, ones usually considered mercenaries were the (a) Loyalists (b) Minutemen (c) Hessians (d) Continental Army soldiers.

10. The Declaration of Independence is considered a "living document" mainly because (a) its principles still inspire a love of freedom around the world (b) the document is still mentioned in history books (c) the original document still exists (d) the document was written by Thomas Jefferson.

Developing Reading Comprehension Skills

Study the Declaration of Independence, printed on pages 599–601. Then choose the letter of the word or phrase that best answers each question. On a separate sheet of paper, match the question number with the correct letter.

1. Read the Preamble (introduction) to the Declaration. What is meant by the phrase ". . . to dissolve the political bands which have connected them with another . . . "? (a) to declare independence (b) to unite two countries (c) to govern more effectively (d) to improve relations between two countries.

2. Read the second paragraph of the Declaration. What is another way of saying, "We hold these truths to be self-evident: that . . . "? *(a)* We know all about that . . . *(b)* Did you not know that . . . *(c)* It is obviously true that . . . *(d)* Truth cannot be known in that . . . .

3. In the second paragraph, the authors of the Declaration talk about rights that cannot be taken away from people. Such rights include *(a)* liberty *(b)* life *(c)* the pursuit of happiness *(d)* all of the above.

4. Read the third section of the Declaration, "Why We Want to Separate." In this section, many sentences begin with the word "he." To whom does the word "he" refer? *(a)* John Hancock *(b)* King George III *(c)* the King of Spain *(d)* God.

5. Read the last paragraph of the Declaration, the Conclusion. Who gave Congress the right to issue this document? *(a)* the people of the colonies *(b)* the British crown *(c)* the Supreme Court *(d)* God.

Thinking About the Lesson

1. In your opinion, who won the Battle of Lexington and Concord? Explain your answer.

2. Over a year passed between the first battle of the Revolution and the Declaration of Independence. Why did the Second Continental Congress take so long to issue that document?

3. In what sense is the Declaration of Independence a "revolutionary" document?

The American Revolution

Declaring independence was only the first step in creating the new nation. Before the United States could come into being, the colonists had to fight a long, hard war. The Revolutionary War lasted about six years. Furthermore, the British and Americans did not sign a peace treaty until 1783.

The Home Front

During the Revolution, most American civilians did not actually fight. Nevertheless, nearly all Americans were affected by the conflict.

Divisions Among the Colonists In the last lesson, we discussed the Patriots. Another group of colonists was made up of those who "sat on the fence." They supported neither the Revolutionary cause nor the British throne.

Still another group—about one third of the population of the colonies—opposed the Revolution. These people liked to call themselves "Loyalists" because they remained loyal to Britain and the crown. They were also called *Tories*, after members of the British political group—the Tory party.

Tories who aided the British were considered *traitors* (disloyal people) by the Patriots. A number of Tories were arrested. Many fled to Britain or Canada. The Revolutionary governments of the colonies *confiscated* (seized) the lands and

other possessions of the fleeing Tories. Most Tories, however, never left their homes. For the most part, they did not actively help the British.

Financing the Revolution Wars cost a lot of money. The colonies obtained their war funds by collecting taxes and by borrowing from foreign nations and rich patriots. Robert Morris and Haym Salomon were two wealthy Americans who contributed money to the Revolutionary cause.

In addition, the Revolutionary government issued its own money. This Continental currency was paper money not backed by gold or silver. At first, this currency was used successfully. By 1781, it could not buy anything. People who had something to sell would not accept it. The saying "not worth a Continental" was long used to describe something without value.

Difficulties Faced by the British

Great Britain sent about 50,000 troops to fight in America. They were commanded by experienced officers, such as Generals William Howe and Charles Cornwallis.

During most of the war, Britain controlled the seas. Yet the sea itself presented an obstacle since Britain was 3,000 miles from America. Sailing ships took many weeks to bring soldiers

50

and supplies across the Atlantic Ocean. The British government had trouble keeping fully up-to-date about the needs of its forces in America. As a result, British generals often could not get the supplies and additional troops they needed.

As the war went on, France entered it on the side of the Americans. Then Spain also waged war on Britain, and Holland followed Spain's example. These developments added greatly to the worries of the British government. Divided by its enemies, it could not give complete attention to the fighting in North America.

The vast size of the American territory also worked against the British. They could control only a few areas and key cities at any one time.

Before the Revolution, colonists had looked upon Great Britain as the "home country." After 1776, however, their viewpoint changed. They began thinking of Britain as a foreign power. They now referred to themselves as "Americans."

British Victories

Most of the important British victories took place early in the war. We have already mentioned the Battle of Bunker Hill and the British removal of American forces near Boston. The British also repulsed an American invasion of Quebec, Canada, in 1775. By mid-1776, those American forces were retreating home.

Another important British victory occurred on Long Island, New York, in August, 1776. The British advanced against Washington's main force in what is now Brooklyn. The Americans suffered heavy losses, but they escaped a trap by moving north to White Plains. (See the map on page 52.) The British were then able to win control of New York City, with its important port.

The American Strategy

In contrast to the large British force, the Continental Army rarely numbered more than 20,000 soldiers. From time to time, its ranks were

Sometimes Patriots and Tories living near each other came into conflict. Here a Tory is being expelled from town by an angry mob of Patriots.

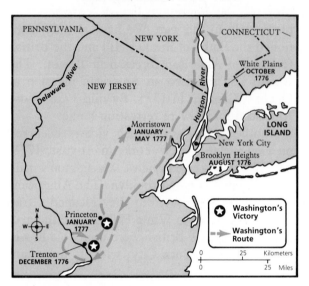

WASHINGTON'S RETREATS AND VICTORIES, 1776–1777

enlarged by state militias that became available for short periods of time.

Washington's able leadership and concern for duty helped make up for small numbers. Then, too, the rifle used by some of the American troops was superior to the standard *musket* (type of gun) used by the British. Above all, American soldiers were defending their own land. They fought with a determined spirit that the enemy often lacked.

General Washington's main *strategy* (overall plan) was to retreat just out of reach of the British. This plan not only tired the enemy, but also kept Americans together as a single force. At first, Washington knew that he did not have the soldiers needed to defeat the British in a major land battle. He rightly believed, though, that the war would not be lost as long as his army remained undefeated. Washington planned to build up the Continental Army so that it would be ready to attack at the right moment.

Washington's strategy led to the following moves:

• In one brilliant stroke, the Americans forced the British from Boston in March, 1776. Amer-icans had hauled heavy cannons from Fort Ticonderoga, New York, some 300 miles to Boston. Placing the cannons on Dorchester Heights, to the south of the city, the Americans threatened all of the British artillery. The British withdrew from Boston rather than fight it out.

• Later in 1776, Washington left White Plains and retreated to Pennsylvania.

• On December 26, 1776, Washington launched a surprise attack on enemy troops at Trenton, New Jersey.

• A week later, he earned another victory, this time at Princeton, New Jersey.

• Then General Washington took his troops to Morristown, New Jersey, where he spent the rest of the winter.

Valley Forge   In 1777, Washington suffered a number of defeats. The lowest point for his army came at Valley Forge, Pennsylvania. During the bitter winter of 1777–1778, his soldiers suffered greatly. Clothing supplies ran very low. Food was also scarce. Despite these conditions, soldiers who stayed with Washington revealed courage and the determination to win.

American Victories

While Washington was busy in New Jersey and Pennsylvania, American forces elsewhere were beginning to turn the tide of the war:

• Battle of Moore's Creek Bridge, 1776. In North Carolina, Patriot forces defeated a group of Loyalists on February 27, 1776.

• Battle of Charleston, June, 1776. Residents of Charleston, South Carolina, stood up to a British bombardment and forced the British fleet to withdraw. Years later, though, in May, 1780, the British returned and easily took the city.

• Saratoga, New York, 1777. At Saratoga, Americans under General Horatio Gates defeated British forces under General John Burgoyne. With this victory, the Americans upset

While Gen. Washington's men suffered through the winter of 1777–1778 at Valley Forge (above), British soldiers were well-fed and well-housed in nearby Philadelphia.

the British plan to split New England from the rest of the colonies. For once, the Americans outnumbered the enemy and captured an entire force of more than 5,000 soldiers. The Battle of Saratoga proved to be a turning point in the war. It encouraged France to ally itself openly with the Americans in 1778. Soon, the French sent land and sea forces, along with money and supplies, to the aid of the Patriots.

• Northwest Campaign, 1778–1779. George Rogers Clark led American forces in taking the British forts of Kaskaskia and Vincennes. These victories halted Indian raids and British control in the Northwest for a while. By 1780, however, the British had regained control of this region.

Both female and male *civilians* (those not members of armed forces) helped the Continental Army fight. Molly Pitcher (right) took over a cannon after her husband was overcome by heat in the Battle of Monmouth Court House, New Jersey, June 28, 1778.

• The War at Sea. The powerful British fleet controlled the Atlantic Ocean. Nonetheless, the Americans organized a small navy that fought well. After 1778, French naval forces made it harder for the British to move men and supplies by sea. Then in 1779, John Paul Jones, considered America's first great naval hero, won an important victory off the coast of England. Commanding the *Bonhomme Richard*, Jones forced the more heavily armed British warship *Serapis* to surrender.

• Battle of King's Mountain, 1780. Between 1778 and 1780, the British had occupied key cities in South Carolina and Georgia. But in October, 1780, Patriots delayed a planned British invasion of North Carolina. The Americans did this by defeating a Loyalist brigade at King's Mountain, South Carolina. Soon afterwards, in January, 1781, Patriots under General Nathanael Greene defeated Loyalists at Cowpens, South Carolina. That March, however, Greene was defeated by British General Charles Cornwallis at Guilford Courthouse, North Carolina. Cornwallis then proceeded north into Virginia.

The outcome of the Revolution was decided at Yorktown, Virginia, in 1781. There American and French troops and French naval forces caught the British in a trap. General Cornwallis and his army of 7,000 surrendered to General Washington. Although minor fighting continued for about a year, this battle was the last major one of the American Revolution.

Outcome of the American Revolution

The Treaty of Paris of 1783, which officially ended the war, included the following terms:

• Great Britain accepted the independence of the 13 colonies.

• The new nation's boundaries were greatly expanded. The United States now extended to the Great Lakes in the north, the Mississippi River in the west, and the northern border of Florida in the south. (See the map on page 56.)

• Congress promised to urge the states to return land and other possessions taken from Loyalists during the Revolution. Yet only a few states did what Congress requested. In time, many Loyalists who had fled came back to become loyal citizens of the United States.

• Britain had to give Florida to Spain, which had held it earlier. Nevertheless, the loss of Florida did not put an end to the British empire in the New World.

The British are shown surrendering at Yorktown in October, 1781, to officers of the combined American and French forces. British General Cornwallis refused to appear to present his sword to the victors, as was customary. Instead, he sent another officer to perform this duty.

SUMMING UP   We have seen how the colonies won their independence from Great Britain by force of arms. The British defeat was caused by many factors, the most important being the great distance separating Britain from the American colonies. In the end, the United States not only won its independence, but gained large territories as well.

Understanding the Text

On a separate sheet of paper, write the letter of the word or phrase that best completes each of the following statements.

1. In their fight to win the American Revolution, the colonists were *not* helped by *(a)* aid from France *(b)* the fighting spirit of American soldiers *(c)* the actions of the Loyalists *(d)* the leadership of George Washington.

2. Loyalists during the American Revolution were loyal to *(a)* the king and government of Britain *(b)* the cause of independence *(c)* the governments of the various colonies *(d)* France.

3. Americans are most likely to remember Haym Salomon for *(a)* providing financial aid *(b)* providing military leadership *(c)* forming the French alliance *(d)* providing medical services to the Continental Army.

4. One of the colonists' greatest problems during the Revolution was *(a)* finding an able Commander in Chief *(b)* keeping in touch with Parliament *(c)* paying the costs of the war *(d)* protecting Tory property.

5. A battle fought outside the borders of the 13 colonies took place at *(a)* Trenton *(b)* Long Island *(c)* Bunker Hill *(d)* Quebec.

6. In their efforts to defeat the Americans, the British were handicapped by *(a)* a lack of sea power *(b)* a shortage of money *(c)* poorly trained troops *(d)* the great distance between Britain and America.

7. The Battle of Saratoga is considered a turning point of the Revolution because it *(a)* caused the British government to ask for peace *(b)* led France to join the American side *(c)* gave the Americans control of the sea *(d)* brought all of the Indians over to the American cause.

8. The defeat of the British at Yorktown *(a)* decided the outcome of the Revolution *(b)* brought all fighting to an immediate end *(c)* encouraged France to enter the war *(d)* ended the British empire in North America.

9. The Treaty of Paris of 1783 provided for all of the following, *except* *(a)* American independence *(b)* the boundaries of the new nation *(c)* the payment of damages by Great Britain *(d)* the promise to protect property of Loyalists.

10. The American Revolution is a major event in world history because it led to the *(a)* downfall of the British empire *(b)* formation of a great nation based on principles of self-government *(c)* triumph of democracy in Europe *(d)* end of slavery in America.

Developing Map Skills

NORTH AMERICA, 1783

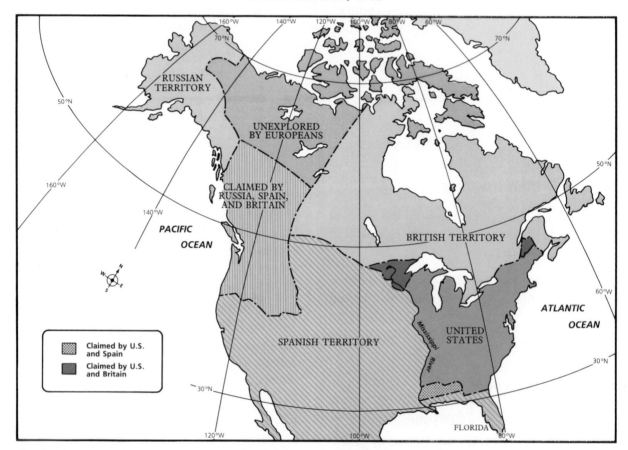

Study the map above. On a separate sheet of paper, number one through five. Then write *T* if the sentence is true, *F* if it is false, and *I* if there is *insufficient* (not enough) information to answer the question.

1. In 1783, the United States planned to gain control of Florida from the Spanish.

2. After the signing of the Treaty of Paris of 1783, part of the western boundary of the United States was the Mississippi River.

3. As a result of the Treaty of Paris of 1783, Britain no longer owned any territory in North America.

4. All of the United States in 1783 lay to the north of latitude 30°N.

5. Most of the United States in 1783 lay to the west of longitude 100°W.

Thinking About the Lesson

1. During the Revolution, why did not all American colonists become Patriots?

2. Why did France side with the American revolutionaries in the conflict?

3. Was General Washington's early strategy of retreating from the British main force a good one? Why or why not?

Forming a New Nation

America's economic, social, and political life had already begun to change during the Revolution. After the military victory at Yorktown, in 1781, this process continued. Above all, Americans saw a need to set up a new government to hold their nation together.

Economic Changes

During the war, trade had been disrupted. Prices had soared, and money had lost value. After the Revolution, however, the American economy was free from British controls. It began to grow in several ways.

Trade   American ports became busy centers of *free trade* (trade free of government restrictions). Foreign ships brought in needed manufactured goods and left with American meat, rice, and wheat. As trade grew, so did the number of American ships. Some of these ships sailed to far corners of the world.

Industry   The wartime need for weapons had given a boost to American iron manufacturing. After the war, this industry continued to grow. Cloth making—once restricted to Great Britain—now became a big business in the former colonies too. As new businesses such as these developed, new banks opened to serve them.

Farming   Ways of farming did not change much from the way they had been before the war. Nevertheless, as the country's population and size grew, more land was farmed. As a result, there was an increase in *farm production* (the growing of crops and raising of livestock).

Social Changes

The Revolution caused a number of social changes in American life.

Property Ownership   The number of small property owners grew. As Loyalists and British officials fled, local governments divided their lands into smaller pieces and sold them.

Western Movement   Many families moved west and settled on lands that Britain had closed off with the Proclamation of 1763. Since the lands were inhabited by Indian nations, there were frequent conflicts between the Indians and the new settlers.

Religious Freedom   In all but three of the new states, ties between religions and governments were broken. This change meant that the people of most states were no longer required to support any church with their tax money. Moreover, some religious requirements for holders of public office were dropped.

57

Slavery   About 5,000 blacks had fought in the Revolution in both the state militias and the Continental Army and Navy. As one result, some black war veterans obtained their freedom. As another result, several Northern states ended slavery. Still, efforts by a few government leaders to get Congress to abolish slavery throughout the United States failed. Slavery continued to be legal in most states.

Political Changes

At the end of the war, one of the most urgent tasks facing the new nation was to set up new governments.

State Governments   The former colonies were now independent states. Most of them adopted written constitutions containing features that were democratic for the times:

• Both state legislators and state governors were elected by the people. The legislatures were given important lawmaking powers and made independent of the state governors.

• In most states, individual legislators did not serve the whole state. Instead, they represented the *districts* (parts of a state) that elected them. Many legislators came from *rural* (country) districts that had not been represented in the past.

• State constitutions were approved by *assemblies* (legislatures), by *conventions* (meetings of delegates called for one purpose), or directly by voters. In stressing the need for voter approval, Americans supported the idea that powers of government come from the people.

• Many people worried that their individual rights might be ignored by the states. As a result, seven states included as part of their constitutions a *bill of rights* (list of rights guaranteed by a government).

Daniel Boone was responsible more than any other individual for settling Kentucky. In this picture, Boone (center) rests before leading settlers west across the Appalachian Mountains.

National Government The 13 states joined together as the United States of America. Before the end of the Revolution, they outlined the national government in a written constitution. They called this document the Articles of Confederation.

The Articles of Confederation

The Articles went into effect in 1781. In drawing up this document, U.S. leaders remembered their power struggle with Great Britain and its strong central government. Therefore, they wanted to make the states more powerful than the central government. They also wanted to prevent any one person or group from gaining too much power. These two desires became apparent in the sort of government that the Articles described.

Powers of Congress The new national government did not have an executive branch. Nor did it have a judicial branch. The Articles of Confederation set up only one branch of government—a legislature. Moreover, the powers of this legislature were sharply limited to the following activities:

• Dealing with foreign nations on all necessary matters, including war and peace.
• Organizing and maintaining an army and navy.
• Issuing and borrowing money.
• Creating and running a *postal system* (a system of delivering mail).
• Dealing with Indian groups.

Powers of the States The Articles left no room for doubt about the powers of the states. States were to keep all powers not specifically given to the national government. Therefore, the states, not Congress, could set taxes and control trade. When the national government found itself without funds, as it often did, it had to ask the states for money.

Nine of the thirteen states had to agree before Congress could pass a law. The law then had to be enforced by the states themselves. The states, however, often disagreed about what certain laws meant and what methods should be used to carry them out.

An *amendment* to (change in) the Articles could be passed only if all the states agreed to the change. Yet state rivalries made such *unanimous consent* all but impossible.

Each state had only one vote in Congress. As a result, states with small populations had as much influence as the more populous ones.

Achievements Under the Articles of Confederation

The Articles of Confederation held the country together for eight years. During that time, Congress passed two important acts, both involving the West.

The Land Ordinance of 1785 During the war, the states had agreed to give up their claims to Western lands. The Land Ordinance of 1785 outlined an orderly way to settle the lands. It also provided the national government with badly needed income. The ordinance directed that public lands be split into *townships* of 36 square miles. Within townships, *sections* of one square mile or parts of a section were put up for sale. The income from the sale of one section in each township was to be used to support the township's system of public education. (See the chart on page 61.)

The Northwest Ordinance, 1787 This law was passed to provide for the administration of the Northwest Territory—the lands north of the Ohio River and east of the Mississippi. (See the map on page 60.) At first, settlers in the territory would be ruled by a governor, appointed by Congress. They could also elect a legislature.

The Northwest Ordinance guaranteed settlers many personal freedoms, such as freedom of religion and the right of a trial by a jury. Moreover, the law prohibited slavery in the territory. Of great importance, the ordinance set up rules for governing all new territories and admitting them into the Union as states. To become a state, an area had to attract at least 60,000 free settlers. Then, settlers would need to draw up a constitution and have it approved by Congress.

In time, five states were formed from the Northwest Territory. They were Ohio (1803), Indiana (1816), Illinois (1818), Michigan (1837), and Wisconsin (1848). The Northwest Territory also included a portion of Minnesota, which became a state in 1858.

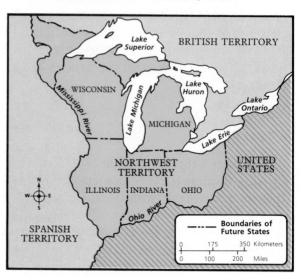

NORTHWEST TERRITORY, 1787

SUMMING UP   We have seen that the Revolution brought about some important economic, social, and political changes in America. With independence came the need for new state governments and a new national government. The national government achieved some important results in spite of the fact that it had few real powers.

Understanding the Text

On a separate sheet of paper, write the letter of the word or phrase that best completes each of the following statements.

1. Economic changes during and after the Revolution had the *least* effect on American (*a*) merchants (*b*) shipbuilders (*c*) farmers (*d*) bankers.

2. Black Americans during and after the Revolution (*a*) experienced no important changes in personal freedom (*b*) were freed in every state (*c*) were freed in some states (*d*) were called "Loyalists."

3. Most of the new state constitutions provided for all of the following, *except* a (*a*) strong, appointed governor (*b*) strong, elected legislature (*c*) representative government (*d*) bill of rights.

4. The Articles of Confederation were (*a*) local laws (*b*) treaties (*c*) a state constitution (*d*) a national constitution.

5. The national government under the Articles was weak because it lacked (*a*) an army and a navy (*b*) a president and a legislature (*c*) courts and a legislature (*d*) courts and a president.

6. Under the Articles of Confederation, most real power was held by (*a*) the states (*b*) Parliament (*c*) Congress (*d*) the army and the navy.

7. The Articles gave Congress the right to do all of the following, *except* (*a*) declare war (*b*) make peace (*c*) set and collect taxes (*d*) deal with Indians.

8. The Articles could be changed only with the consent of (*a*) nine states (*b*) Congress (*c*) all of the states (*d*) the president.

9. The Northwest Ordinance was important because it (*a*) set up a plan for creating future states (*b*) gave several New England states control of the Northwest (*c*) ended the Revolution (*d*) provided for a new and stronger national constitution.

10. Which of the following best describes the national government under the Articles of Confederation? (*a*) It was so weak that it accomplished nothing. (*b*) It was strong and successful. (*c*) It had a number of achievements, but it was too weak to meet the needs of the new nation. (*d*) It was given so much power that it controlled the states and denied the rights of the people.

Developing Chart-Reading Skills

A TYPICAL TOWNSHIP, LAND ORDINANCE OF 1785

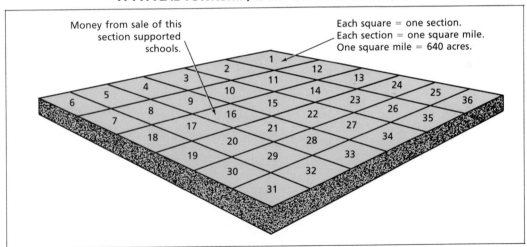

Money from sale of this section supported schools.

Each square = one section.
Each section = one square mile.
One square mile = 640 acres.

Study the chart above. Then choose the letter of the word or phrase that best completes each of the following sentences. On a separate sheet of paper, match the sentence number with the correct letter.

1. Each small box in the chart represents a (*a*) Western state (*b*) township (*c*) section (*d*) land ordinance.

2. In each township, schools are supported from the sale of (*a*) section 16 (*b*) any section (*c*) all sections (*d*) school bonds.

3. If one walked from anywhere on the northern boundary of a township straight south to the southern boundary, the number of miles one would have walked is (*a*) 1 (*b*) 6 (*c*) 16 (*d*) 36.

4. The number of acres in a section is *(a)* 1 *(b)* 36 *(c)* 360 *(d)* 640.

5. To purchase one section cost *(a)* $1.00 *(b)* $36 *(c)* $640 *(d)* none of the above.

Thinking About the Lesson

1. Do you think that the Revolution helped the American economy to develop? Why or why not?

2. Name some social groups that benefited from the Revolution. How did each benefit?

3. In what ways were the new state constitutions democratic?

4. Would you label the government under the Articles of Confederation as either "strong" or "weak"? Explain your answer.

5. How might the West have been settled differently if Congress had not passed the Land Ordinance of 1785 or the Northwest Ordinance?

The Critical Period

The goal of winning the Revolution had brought Americans together. After the war, however, the government of the Articles of Confederation failed to keep the nation united. Americans thought of themselves as belonging to their states first and the nation second. Many Americans wondered whether their new nation would ever manage to overcome its problems. As a result, the years from 1781 to 1789 are often called the "Critical Period."

Foreign Problems During the Critical Period

Several foreign countries took advantage of the weaknesses of the United States. These unfriendly countries limited U.S. trade and added to the economic problems of the young nation.

Great Britain British troops and traders remained in the Northwest Territory in violation of the terms of the Treaty of Paris. Britain refused to leave key forts there until the United States met the following demands:

• Congress was to make the states repay money U.S. citizens owed to British merchants.
• The United States was to pay for land and other property that Patriots had seized from Loyalists.

Most members of Congress were unwilling to give in to these demands. But under the Articles, the national government had no authority to take action either way.

The British provided the new nation with another problem as well. They prevented the United States from trading in the British West Indies. In doing so, they revived some parts of the Navigation Acts, which had been in effect before the Revolution. As a result, those American farmers who had been selling their products in the West Indies now suffered.

Spain Spain controlled the mouth of the Mississippi River, including the port of New Orleans. The Spanish now closed this part of the river to free trade by Western settlers. Settlers were also denied the *right of deposit*. That is, they could no longer take goods to New Orleans for loading onto oceangoing ships. This situation made life difficult for the settlers. There was no other easy way for them to bring goods and supplies into and out of the Western territories.

Barbary States The young nation had even worse troubles with the Barbary states of North Africa (present-day Morocco, Algeria, Tunisia, and Libya). For years, Barbary *pirates* (seagoing robbers) had attacked and robbed trading ships sailing the Mediterranean Sea.

Americans are shown beating back a Barbary pirate attack. Pirates preyed on U.S. ships in hopes of demanding money from the U.S. government for return of ships and crews.

Before the Revolution, the British fleet had protected American ships. In the 1780s, however, the pirates began to seize American ships and make slaves of the crews. The United States was too weak to stop the pirates and too poor to buy back its enslaved sailors. American trade in the Mediterranean nearly stopped.

Domestic Problems During the Critical Period

Foreign policy was not the only area of trouble. Congress's lack of power also created domestic problems.

Depression From the start, the states were slow to support Congress financially. Soon they became almost completely unable to do so because of a post-war *depression* (a period of time with a low level of economic activity and high level of unemployment). Business activity of all kinds fell off sharply. Farmers and merchants had to lower their prices. Even after the prices were lowered, sellers found that there were few buyers.

Lack of Money Since Congress lacked enough funds to meet its needs, it created its own currency. This paper money was not backed by gold or silver. As more paper money was printed, its value dropped.

Debtors liked to see the value of money drop. They found it easier to pay back their debts with money that was less valuable than it was when they borrowed it. Thus, debtors favored having Congress issue more paper money. *Creditors* (those who had lent money), on the other hand, opposed printing more paper money. They wanted the value of money to remain high.

Congress had money troubles of its own. It had to pay government employees, support the small army and navy, and make payments on its loans. Congress had still another worry. It had not yet paid all the salaries of soldiers who had served in the Revolution.

Rivalries Among States Under the Articles, Congress could not control *commerce* (trade) among the states. As a result, certain states taxed goods brought in from other states. This policy led to quarrels and weakened national unity.

States also had disagreements among themselves over boundaries, control of rivers, and other matters.

Shays's Rebellion

Many farmers in the 1780s owed money to banks and other creditors. A bank that lent money to a farmer usually held a *mortgage* on

In 1786, Shays's forces temporarily occupied the State Supreme Courthouse in Springfield, Massachusetts.

the farm. (A mortgage is a document showing that a loan has been made and will be repaid according to agreed-upon terms.) If the farmer had not made regular payments on the loan, the bank could have gone to court. The court might have taken the farm away from its owner and sold it so that the bank would be repaid.

Some states, such as Rhode Island, agreed to print more paper money or to delay payments on mortgages and other debts. Massachusetts, however, did nothing, and many people there lost their mortgaged farms.

Hundreds of angry farmers held meetings and wrote to the Massachusetts legislature, demanding more paper money, lower taxes, and a delay of debt payments. The legislature, which was controlled by rich creditors, still did nothing.

The farmers and debtors found a leader in Daniel Shays. Shays himself was a poor farmer. He had been a captain in the Continental Army and had fought in the Battle of Bunker Hill. In September, 1786, he led about 600 people in a march on the courthouse at Springfield, Massachusetts. (In the months ahead, the rebel force more than doubled.) The rebels' aim was to stop the jailing of debtors and to seize weapons stored at Springfield. They were almost successful, but Governor James Bowdoin of Massachusetts sent an armed militia to deal with the rebels. Shays's poorly armed rebels were defeated, and many of them were taken prisoner.

Little blood was shed in this *rebellion* (open resistance to authority). The captured leaders were tried and sentenced to death but eventually *pardoned* (forgiven). Shays fled to Vermont, but he, too, received a pardon, in 1788.

Shays's Rebellion shocked many Americans. Well-to-do people saw this as a "mob action"—clear proof that the Articles of Confederation had to be changed. Others, such as Thomas Jefferson, did not seem too upset. He wrote from Paris, "A little rebellion now and then is a good thing . . . . It is a medicine necessary for the sound health of government."

SUMMING UP We have seen that the Critical Period was marked by problems both at home and abroad. The new nation was not able to assert itself with many foreign powers. Nor could the United States solve its economic problems. Shays's Rebellion occurred at a time when some of the nation's leaders were worried about the weakness of their government.

Understanding the Text

On a separate sheet of paper, write the letter of the word or phrase that best completes each of the following statements.

1. After the Revolution, there was bad feeling between the United States and Great Britain because of (*a*) the Articles of Confederation (*b*) settlers who used the Mississippi River to transport goods (*c*) the presence of British troops and traders in the Northwest Territory (*d*) the seizure of state lands by Tories.

2. After the Revolution, Spain limited American trade (*a*) on the Mississippi (*b*) in the Mediterranean (*c*) in the Pacific Ocean (*d*) between New England and the South.

3. In the 1780s, the Barbary states of North Africa had a well-deserved reputation for (*a*) friendliness toward Americans (*b*) piracy (*c*) shrewd trading (*d*) international banking.

4. The United States after the Revolution may be described best as being in a period of (*a*) economic depression (*b*) rapid growth (*c*) widespread prosperity (*d*) drought.

5. Under the Articles of Confederation, the national government (*a*) had no lawmaking body (*b*) controlled the states (*c*) violated the civil rights of the people (*d*) could not pay all of its debts.

6. During the Critical Period, Congress did not stop the states from taxing goods brought in from other states. The failure to do so showed that (*a*) Congress had no control over interstate commerce (*b*) no one objected to such taxes (*c*) the states were not represented in Congress (*d*) taxes on these goods were paid to the national government.

7. Shays's Rebellion was put down by (*a*) the national army led by Gen. Washington (*b*) the Massachusetts militia (*c*) the Boston police (*d*) an alliance of foreign nations.

8. Shays's Rebellion led to a demand for (*a*) stricter courts of justice (*b*) free trade in the West Indies (*c*) United States control of the Mississippi River (*d*) a stronger central government.

9. If a bank holds a mortgage, the bank acts as a/an (*a*) creditor (*b*) debtor (*c*) borrower (*d*) issuer of paper money.

10. In general, the Critical Period was a time of (*a*) rapid economic growth (*b*) law and order (*c*) national power and prestige (*d*) political weaknesses and economic troubles.

Developing Graph-Reading Skills

PERCENT DISTRIBUTION OF U.S. WHITE POPULATION, BY NATIONALITY, 1790

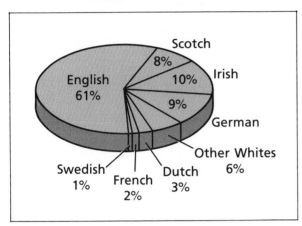

The pie or circle graph above shows the percent distribution of the U.S. white population by nationality groups in 1790. In that year, the federal government conducted its first *census* (national head count). Study the graph. Then choose the letter of the word or phrase that best completes each sentence. On a separate sheet of paper, match the sentence number with the correct letter.

1. The graph clearly shows that for the year 1790 (a) most Americans had come from Germany or were of German descent (b) the Germans were the dominant group in New England (c) the United States was a mixture of people from many countries (d) all residents of the United States were of European descent.

2. The second largest group of white Americans in the United States in 1790 was the (a) English (b) Germans (c) Scottish (d) Irish.

3. According to the graph, it was *not* true that (a) there were more German-Americans than French-Americans (b) the English and Dutch populations made up about 40 percent of the total (c) there were more Americans from England than from all other places combined

(d) "Other Whites" made up about 6 percent of the total white population.

4. A pie graph is characterized by (a) its round shape with wedge-shaped sections representing percentages (b) bars that represent quantities (c) lines connecting dots that represent quantities (d) all of the above.

5. Another good title for this graph might be (a) "Population of the Thirteen Colonies Just Before the Revolution" (b) "The United States—One Hundred Years of Growth" (c) "Europeans in America" (d) "Population Distribution, by States."

Thinking About the Lesson

1. Why did American settlers in the West want the right of free trade on the lower Mississippi River?

2. Why did debtors want more paper money not backed by gold or silver?

3. Some foreigners saw Shays's Rebellion as an indication that the United States could not govern its people. Do you agree with this point of view? Why or why not?

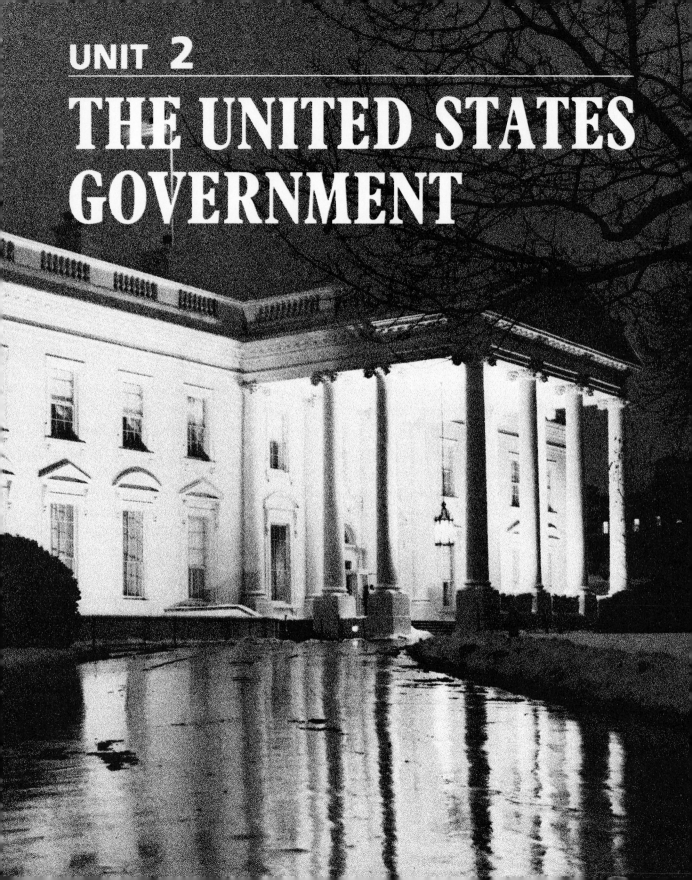

UNIT 2

THE UNITED STATES GOVERNMENT

 **LESSON 12**

Writing and Adopting the Constitution

During the late 1780s, the troubles of the Critical Period, discussed in Lesson 11, grew worse. Most influential Americans agreed that the government under the Articles of Confederation was not working well. Many wanted something done to make the national government stronger.

The Constitutional Convention

In the summer of 1787, 55 *delegates* (people who represent others) met in Philadelphia to deal with the country's problems. These men came from all of the states except Rhode Island. The stated goal of the delegates who gathered in the Pennsylvania State House was to *amend* (change) the Articles of Confederation.

The delegates met in secret. They wanted to be able to speak freely without fear of stirring up a public fuss. The delegates also wanted to be able to change their minds about issues without being embarrassed.

The Convention Leaders A number of prominent individuals had important roles in the Convention:

• James Madison, who played an active part in the debates, took careful notes during the discussions. Largely because of these notes, historians know what the delegates said.

• George Washington took charge as the *presiding officer* (person who runs a meeting). He rarely spoke out during Convention debates, but privately he called for a stronger government.

• Benjamin Franklin, Alexander Hamilton, and Gouverneur Morris also made lasting contributions to the Convention. When disagreements arose, Franklin's advice helped greatly to keep the Convention together. Hamilton became a leading spokesperson for a strong central government. The wording of the proposed constitution was in large part the work of Gouverneur Morris.

An Important Decision The Convention delegates quickly realized that they could not save the Articles of Confederation. They thought that a fresh start was needed. Therefore, they agreed to draw up a new constitution. For this reason, the meeting became known as the Constitutional Convention.

70

American artist Junius Brutus Stearns made this oil painting in 1856. It is titled "Washington Addressing the Constitutional Convention."

The delegates to the Constitutional Convention believed that they were working in the best interests of all Americans. Who were the delegates? All of them were males, and their average age was 43. In general, they were well-known, well-educated, and well-to-do. About half of the delegates were lawyers. Most were native-born Americans of British ancestry. Of greatest importance, many had outstanding abilities and a great sense of public duty.

Compromises in Writing the Constitution

Most delegates to the Constitutional Convention wanted a more powerful national government—one with a strong Congress. This Congress would have the authority to set and collect taxes in all of the states. It would also be able to issue money, raise an army, and regulate commerce.

The delegates disagreed, however, on other matters. To get around these differences, they worked out some important *compromises*. In compromising, each side gave up something it wanted in order to satisfy the other side.

The Great Compromise The large states wanted to have more representatives in Congress than the small states. Small states wanted *equal representation*. With equal representation, each state would have the same number of representatives. The so-called "Great Compromise" satisfied both sides by setting up a two-house Congress. To the upper house, the Senate, each state would send two senators. Here there would be equal representation. In the lower house, the House of Representatives, however, different states would have different numbers of representatives. The size of a state's population would determine how many representatives could be elected.

The Three-Fifths Compromise How was a state to count its slaves when deciding on the number

Delegates to the Constitutional Convention met in the Pennsylvania State House. Visitors to Philadelphia today can tour this building, since renamed Independence Hall.

of representatives to send to the House? How was a state to count these people when deciding on the amount of taxes to pay to the central government? Delegates disagreed on these two matters.

Delegates from Southern states wanted to count all slaves for representation and none for taxation. Delegates from Northern states wanted the opposite. They wanted to count no slaves for representation and all slaves for taxation.

Under the Three-Fifths Compromise, the delegates agreed to count five slaves as equal to three free persons. This figure would be used for both representation in Congress and payments of direct taxes.

The Compromise on the Slave Trade Slaves were still being imported from Africa and the West Indies. Many Northern delegates wanted to stop this *slave trade*. Most Southern delegates, however, wanted the trade to go on.

Again the delegates compromised. For 20 years (until 1808), Congress would have no power to stop the importation of slaves. After that time, Congress could take any action that it wanted on the matter. (In 1808, Congress did

declare illegal the importation of slaves into the United States.)

Basic Features of the Constitution

Within four months, the delegates had finished writing a Constitution. This basic law called for a three-part national government. The three parts or branches are:

• An *executive branch*, headed by a President.
• A *judicial branch*, headed by a Supreme Court.
• A *legislative branch*, headed by a Congress. As mentioned above, Congress consisted of a Senate and House of Representatives.

The document also provided for ways to make changes, or amendments, in the Constitution.

Debating the Constitution

The delegates finally signed the Constitution on September 17, 1787. The Constitutional Convention was over. *Ratification* (official approval) by nine states was needed, however, before the document became law. Parts of the new document were still quite controversial. For the next year, two opposing groups of Americans debated the ideas put forth by the Convention.

The Federalists Those in favor of the Constitution as written were called *Federalists*. They believed that a strong central government was needed. Under such a government, they thought, the new nation would grow wealthier, more stable, and more respected.

Many of the Federalists were well-to-do business leaders, landowners, and professionals. Three of their leaders—Alexander Hamilton, James Madison, and John Jay—wrote a number of newspaper articles. In these articles, later published together as *The Federalist*, the authors urged that the Constitution be ratified.

The Anti-Federalists Opponents of the Constitution were called *Anti-Federalists*. They feared a strong central government. Instead, they preferred to leave most powers in the hands of the states. If there were going to be a new constitution, they said, then it should state clearly that personal freedoms were to be protected.

Anti-Federalists won the support of many poorer Americans, including farmers, laborers, and debtors. Some people of wealth and high social position also were Anti-Federalists. Among the Anti-Federalist leaders, Patrick Henry, John Hancock, and Samuel Adams stood out. These men were articulate and forceful in criticizing the Constitution.

Ratification of the Constitution

By June 21, 1788, nine states had ratified the Constitution. Nine was the number needed to make the document legal. Approval by Virginia and New York followed that summer. Within the next two years, the last two states (North Carolina and Rhode Island) also approved.

The Bill of Rights The ratifying conventions of five states asked for changes in the Constitution. They wanted amendments that would guarantee important personal freedoms. Congress met this request in 1789, sending 12 amendments to the states for ratification. By 1791, ten of these amendments had been ratified. The first ten amendments became known as the *Bill of Rights*.

The new government held its first election in February of 1789. The newly elected Congress met in New York in March. At the time, New York City was the capital of the new government. Thus, George Washington was *inaugurated* (officially installed) as President in New York, but not until April 30.

SUMMING UP   We have seen that the Constitution was drawn up by a talented group of men. They believed that the existing government was not strong enough. By compromising, they were able to write a document that has met the test of time. The addition of the Bill of Rights helped to strengthen the Constitution.

Understanding the Text

On a separate sheet of paper, write the letter of the word or phrase that best completes each of the following statements.

1. The delegates to the Constitutional Convention were chosen for the task of (*a*) writing a completely new Constitution (*b*) revising the Articles of Confederation (*c*) carrying on the war against Great Britain (*d*) choosing Washington to be President.

2. Which of the following phrases best describes the delegates to the Convention? (*a*) ordinary citizens (*b*) men of property, public spirit, and outstanding abilities (*c*) enemies of a strong central government (*d*) able men interested only in protecting their own interests.

3. Although the Convention met in secret, we know much of what happened because of notes taken by (*a*) James Madison (*b*) Thomas Jefferson (*c*) Benjamin Franklin (*d*) George Washington.

4. The decision to create a two-house Congress was the result of a compromise on (*a*) slavery (*b*) taxation (*c*) division of power between the national government and the states (*d*) division of power between large and small states.

5. Of the following people, those most opposed to the Constitution were (*a*) poorer Americans (*b*) creditors (*c*) merchants and landowners (*d*) Federalists.

6. *The Federalist* was written by men who (*a*) opposed the new Constitution (*b*) favored the new Constitution (*c*) were looking for government jobs (*d*) favored a new Constitution, but not the one approved by the Convention.

7. Which of the following statements about the compromises made at the Convention is correct? (*a*) They were not necessary because the delegates were in close agreement on what kind of government was needed. (*b*) They were necessary to make the Constitution acceptable to different states and different groups of Americans. (*c*) They were necessary to make the Constitution acceptable, but they prevented the new government from working efficiently. (*d*) They had little effect on the makeup and workings of the new government.

8. Of the original 13 states, the last to ratify the Constitution were (*a*) Delaware and Virginia (*b*) New Hampshire and Virginia (*c*) Rhode Island and North Carolina (*d*) Rhode Island and Virginia.

9. Of the following events, the one that occurred last was (*a*) the ratification of the Bill of Rights (*b*) George Washington's inauguration (*c*) the ratification of the Constitution by nine states (*d*) the last meeting of the Constitutional Convention.

10. The Bill of Rights was (*a*) approved by the Constitutional Convention (*b*) approved by Congress and the states (*c*) approved by Congress, but opposed by most states (*d*) never approved by the Convention, Congress, or the states.

Developing Map Skills

Study the map on page 75. Then choose the letter of the word or phrase that best completes each sentence. On a separate sheet of paper, match the sentence number with the correct letter.

1. The state that first ratified the U.S. Constitution was (*a*) Pennsylvania (*b*) New Jersey (*c*) Delaware (*d*) North Carolina.

2. The last state to ratify the Constitution was (*a*) New Hampshire (*b*) Rhode Island (*c*) North Carolina (*d*) Georgia.

3. On April 28, 1788, the vote for ratification in Maryland was (*a*) 30–0 (*b*) 89–79 (*c*) 63–11 (*d*) 34–32.

4. The state with the largest number of votes against ratification was (*a*) Massachusetts (*b*) Virginia (*c*) Connecticut (*d*) none of the above.

5. A state where ratification was approved by unanimous consent was (*a*) South Carolina (*b*) Rhode Island (*c*) New Hampshire (*d*) Georgia.

Thinking About the Lesson

1. Why did the Convention delegates decide to write a new Constitution instead of just amending the Articles of Confederation?

2. How important to the success of the Convention was the delegates' willingness to compromise? Explain your answer and provide an example of a compromise.

3. What reasons did the small states have for wanting equal representation in Congress? Why did the large states oppose this idea?

THE STATES RATIFY THE CONSTITUTION

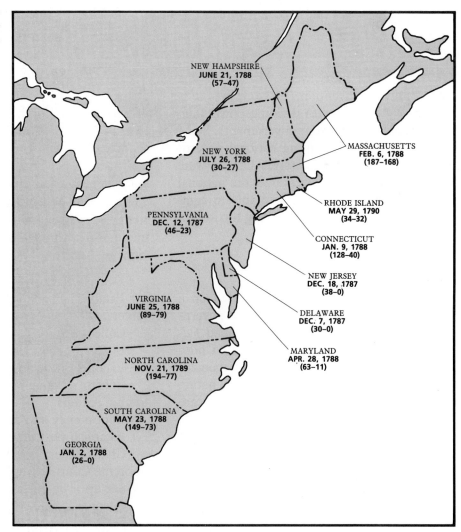

NEW HAMPSHIRE
JUNE 21, 1788
(57–47)

MASSACHUSETTS
FEB. 6, 1788
(187–168)

NEW YORK
JULY 26, 1788
(30–27)

RHODE ISLAND
MAY 29, 1790
(34–32)

PENNSYLVANIA
DEC. 12, 1787
(46–23)

CONNECTICUT
JAN. 9, 1788
(128–40)

NEW JERSEY
DEC. 18, 1787
(38–0)

VIRGINIA
JUNE 25, 1788
(89–79)

DELAWARE
DEC. 7, 1787
(30–0)

MARYLAND
APR. 28, 1788
(63–11)

NORTH CAROLINA
NOV. 21, 1789
(194–77)

SOUTH CAROLINA
MAY 23, 1788
(149–73)

GEORGIA
JAN. 2, 1788
(26–0)

The Federal System

Many important ideas were debated at the Constitutional Convention. One of the most important had to do with dividing powers between the national and state governments. Some delegates feared that a strong national government might become oppressive. Others were more fearful of states' powers over the national government. The delegates were able to compromise on this issue by introducing the idea of the federal system.

Federalism

The United States government is based on a division of powers between the national government and the states. This division, called *federalism*, is outlined in the Constitution. Under federalism, the *federal* (national) government has power to deal with problems of the nation as a whole. States, cities, and counties take care of local matters. The U.S. Constitution and acts of Congress rank above state constitutions and laws. If disagreements arise between states and the federal government, the federal government generally dominates. Moreover the federal government can intervene if two or more states cannot settle their differences.

For the most part, the Constitution is clear about how power is to be divided among levels of government. Four different kinds of powers exist—delegated, implied, concurrent, and reserved.

Delegated Powers Article I, Section 8, of the Constitution *delegates* (sets aside) certain powers to the federal government. (See page 605.) Some of the *delegated powers* of Congress include the right to:

• Declare war.
• Establish an army, a navy, and other armed forces.
• Collect taxes.
• Borrow money.
• Establish laws for patents and copyrights.
• Control commerce among states and with foreign nations.
• Coin money and control its value.
• Establish post offices.
• Create federal courts that rank below the Supreme Court.
• Set up laws on how foreign-born residents can become U.S. citizens.
• Govern the national capital.

76

One of the delegated powers of Congress is to govern the national capital. Although New York City served as the country's temporary capital in 1789 and 1790, national leaders wanted a permanent site. Therefore, Congress set aside ten square miles of swampy land on the Potomac River—the District of Columbia. President Washington hired a French engineer, Pierre Charles L'Enfant, to draw the plans for the new city. Meanwhile, Philadelphia served as the second temporary capital, from 1790 to 1800. By the latter date, construction was far enough along for the national government to move to Washington, D.C. The initials "D.C." refer to "District of Columbia."

Implied Powers According to the Constitution, Congress may pass other laws that will help it carry out its delegated powers. The Constitution, though, does not say exactly what these other laws might be. Thus, Congress's right to pass such laws is *implied* (indirectly indicated). The section of the Constitution that gives Congress the right to exercise its implied powers is called the *elastic clause*. (See page 606.) Using the elastic clause, Congress has expanded its lawmaking powers into many matters not dreamed of in 1787. Here are some examples of Congress's implied powers:

• Congress has the delegated power to borrow money. Implied from this is the power to sell *bonds*. Selling bonds is a way for the government to borrow money from those who buy bonds. People buy bonds with the idea that at a future date they can get back their money, plus interest.

• A *national bank* is not mentioned in the Constitution. But during the administration of

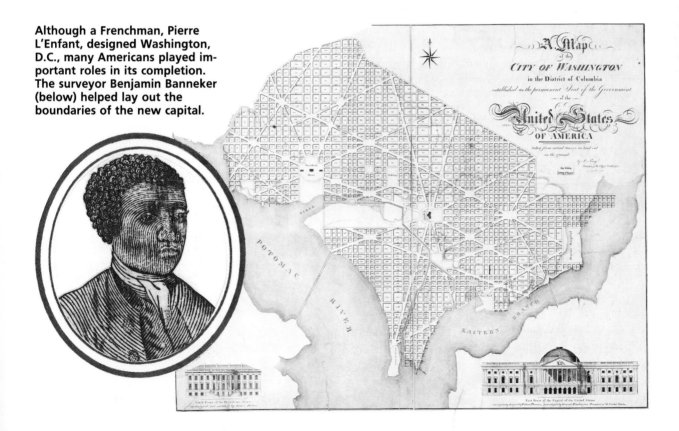

Although a Frenchman, Pierre L'Enfant, designed Washington, D.C., many Americans played important roles in its completion. The surveyor Benjamin Banneker (below) helped lay out the boundaries of the new capital.

The power to control what is studied in public school classrooms, such as this one, is reserved to the states.

Washington, such a bank was set up. Congress has the implied power to establish a bank from its delegated powers to collect taxes and borrow money.

• Many congressional actions result from the delegated power of Congress to control commerce. For instance, Congress has passed many laws affecting land, sea, and air travel. Under the same power, Congress regulates telephone, radio, and television communications.

Concurrent Powers The Constitution clearly denies to the states some of the powers delegated to Congress. These powers include the right to enter into treaties with foreign governments, coin money, control interstate commerce, and declare war. There are, however, *concurrent powers*—ones shared by the federal and state governments. Among the concurrent powers are the following:

• Collecting taxes.
• Borrowing money.

• Holding elections.
• Building roads.

Reserved Powers The Tenth Amendment to the Constitution says that all powers not given to the United States belong to the states. These *reserved powers* affect the daily lives of all Americans. Among the many powers reserved to the states are the following:

• Controlling marriages and divorces.
• Controlling public education.
• Providing health services.
• Regulating businesses.
• Licensing doctors, dentists, and other health professionals.
• Setting up voting requirements.

Federal-State Cooperation

Today, the federal government and the governments of the 50 states have many problems in common. These problems are often solved by close cooperation between the two levels of government. Thus, Congress gives money to the states for purposes of providing low-cost housing and improved health care. Education, public transportation, and welfare are other areas for which states obtain federal aid.

Experience has shown, however, that federal-state cooperation may cause problems. By helping states, the federal government has come to play a more important part in state affairs. To get federal aid, state governments must follow certain rules established by the federal government. For instance, federal educational aid is given on condition that the states set up certain educational programs.

Some Americans object to such conditions for federal aid. They would rather have states not accept federal aid that involves restrictions. Other Americans believe that the role of the federal government should be expanded. They believe that federal funds and rules are needed in helping states and cities solve their problems.

SUMMING UP We have seen that the authors of the Constitution wanted the new national government to be strong and helpful. But they did not want it to be too strong. They compromised by setting up a federal system whereby the states share power with the federal government. In this system, the central government is the *dominant* (stronger) partner.

Understanding the Text

On a separate sheet of paper, write the letter of the word or phrase that best completes each of the following statements.

1. In a federal system of government, powers are divided between states and the (a) people (b) President (c) courts (d) national government.

2. According to the Constitution, only the federal government can (a) control interstate commerce (b) hold elections (c) control marriages and divorces (d) license doctors.

3. Although television did not exist when the Constitution was being written, Congress is now able to regulate this type of communication because of (a) the Bill of Rights (b) implied powers (c) states' rights (d) the congressional power to establish post offices.

4. The implied powers section of the Constitution tends to increase the powers of (a) local governments (b) the courts (c) private businesses (d) Congress.

5. One right shared by the federal government and state governments is the power to (a) tax (b) declare war (c) issue coins and paper money (d) deal with foreign nations.

6. The Constitution gives states the sole right to (a) borrow money (b) establish post offices (c) control public education (d) govern the national capital.

7. When Congress made Washington, D.C., the nation's capital, it used its (a) delegated powers (b) implied powers (c) shared powers (d) principle of national supremacy.

8. The power to control marriages and divorces is said to be *(a)* concurrent *(b)* reserved *(c)* delegated *(d)* implied.

9. Increased federal aid to the states is *(a)* desired by all Americans *(b)* opposed by all Americans *(c)* contrary to the Constitution *(d)* sometimes accompanied by increased federal regulations.

10. The main idea of this lesson is that the Constitution *(a)* insures representative democracy *(b)* limits the powers of the courts *(c)* divides powers between the federal and state governments *(d)* solves all problems that may arise in American society.

Developing Dictionary Skills

Read the following entry from *Webster's Ninth New Collegiate Dictionary*.

fed·er·al·ism/'fed(-ə)-rə- ˌliz-əm/*n* (1789) **1 a** *often cap* : the distribution of power in an organization (as a government) between a central authority and the constituent units—compare CENTRALISM **b** : support or advocacy of this principle **2** *cap* : the principles of the Federalists

By permission. From *Webster's Ninth New Collegiate Dictionary* © 1984 by Merriam-Webster Inc., publisher of the Merriam-Webster® Dictionaries.

Choose the letter of the word or phrase that best answers each question. On a separate sheet of paper, match the sentence number with the correct letter.

1. In pronouncing the word "federalism," the main stress is on which syllable? *(a)* first *(b)* second *(c)* third *(d)* fourth.

2. Which part of speech is the word "federalism"? *(a)* an adverb *(b)* an adjective *(c)* a noun *(d)* a verb.

3. When was the word "federalism" first used? *(a)* in the 17th century *(b)* in the 18th century *(c)* in the 19th century *(d)* in the 20th century.

4. Which of the following statements about the word "federalism" is true? *(a)* It has only one definition. *(b)* It has more than one definition. *(c)* It cannot be defined. *(d)* It can be defined only by looking up the word "centralism" in a dictionary.

5. Which of the following statements about using the word "federalism" in the middle of a sentence is true? *(a)* It is always capitalized. *(b)* It is never capitalized. *(c)* It is always capitalized when it means, "the principles of the Federalists." *(d)* It is always capitalized when it means, "the distribution of power in an organization . . . between a central authority and the constituent units."

Thinking About the Lesson

1. Do you think that the federal system, under which the federal government has more powers than the states, is a good idea? Why or why not?

2. How does the federal system differ from the system of government under the Articles of Confederation?

3. Do you think that states should have any of the following powers—to make treaties with foreign governments? to coin money? to control interstate commerce? to make war? Explain your answers.

4. Why do the federal and state governments share certain powers, such as imposing and collecting taxes and holding elections?

5. Do you think that more federal involvement in educational matters is a healthy trend? Why or why not?

Checks and Balances in the Federal Government

Federalism is only one way that the Constitution works to prevent an unjust government. *Separation of powers* serves as another method. Under separation of powers, each of three main branches of the federal government plays an important role. No single branch can become too powerful because the branches check and balance one another.

Three Branches of the Federal Government

The three main branches of the federal government are the legislative, executive, and judicial.

The Legislative Branch The U.S. Senate and House of Representatives together make the laws. These two legislative bodies of Congress have many powers in common, but each exercises some additional, separate powers. For instance, tax bills must begin in the House of Representatives. On the other hand, only the Senate approves treaties with foreign nations.

The Senate and the House have set up special bodies to help them carry out their functions. These special organizations, such as the General Accounting Office and the Library of Congress, also are part of the legislative branch.

> The following terms are used in discussing Congress:
> • The *Senate* refers to the upper house, acting alone.
> • The *House* (or House of Representatives) refers to the lower house, acting alone.
> • *Congress* refers to both houses, acting together.

The Executive Branch The President enforces or carries out the laws. The Chief Executive also deals with foreign nations and *appoints* (chooses) important government officials. As head of the executive branch of government, a President is assisted by several million government employees. They work in the various executive departments and agencies of the government—all part of the executive branch.

> The *White House* is the mansion assigned to the use of the President of the United States. The President both lives and works in this building. Sometimes the term "White House" is used to mean "the President" or, more broadly, those who work directly for the President.

81

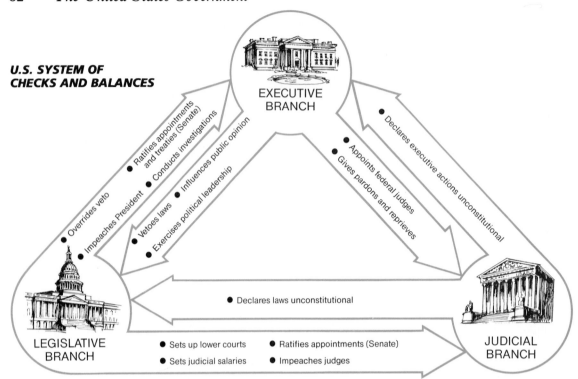

**U.S. SYSTEM OF
CHECKS AND BALANCES**

EXECUTIVE
BRANCH

Ratifies appointments
and treaties (Senate)

Conducts investigations

Influences public opinion

Overrides veto

Impeaches President

Vetoes laws

Exercises political leadership

Appoints federal judges

Gives pardons and reprieves

Declares executive actions unconstitutional

Declares laws unconstitutional

LEGISLATIVE
BRANCH

• Sets up lower courts
• Sets judicial salaries

• Ratifies appointments (Senate)
• Impeaches judges

JUDICIAL
BRANCH

The Judicial Branch Employees of the United States Supreme Court and the lower federal courts make up the judicial branch. The most important of these employees are the federal judges, who preside over cases brought before them. In making decisions, federal judges often *interpret* (explain the meaning of) laws passed by Congress.

Some students of government say that there exists a fourth branch of government. They refer to the many independent *regulatory agencies,* such as the Interstate Commerce Commission and the Federal Communications Commission. Not mentioned in the Constitution, the regulatory agencies were formed by acts of Congress. They are said to be independent because they do not come under the direct control of any of the three main branches of government.

Checks and Balances

The Constitution gives each of the three main branches of the federal government certain powers. Each branch can limit, to some degree, the powers of the other two. This arrangement is called the system of *checks and balances.*

Checks on the President Both the legislative and judicial branches of government can balance the power of the executive branch.

Congress may check the President's powers in the following ways:

• Congress sets the amount of money that may be spent by executive departments and agencies. Congress can also decide how much money should be spent on individual programs within these departments and agencies.

• Congress can refuse to pass a law that the President wants.

• Congress can pass a law even though the President has vetoed it. To take this action, however, Congress needs the approval of two thirds of both houses.

• Although the executive branch arranges all foreign treaties, the Senate must approve them by a two-thirds vote.

• The Senate must also approve whomever the President names to a number of important federal jobs. Justices of the Supreme Court fall into this category.

• The House can charge the President with misconduct in office. Such a charge is called *impeachment*. The Senate then has the power to try a President on these charges. A President who is found guilty by the Senate will be removed from office.

Judicial checks on the President are more general. In many court cases, federal judges review actions of the President and other officials

In 1868, the House impeached President Andrew Johnson and the Senate tried him. Here the President receives an impeachment summons from the Senate Sergeant at Arms. Opponents of Andrew Johnson were unable to get enough senators to vote to convict the President.

in the executive branch. If the judges decide that an action does not obey the Constitution, they declare it *unconstitutional* (illegal according to the Constitution). If that happens, then the executive branch must stop its illegal action.

The Constitution does not specifically mention the power of the *judiciary* (judicial branch) to review actions of the executive branch. The Supreme Court assumed this power early in the 19th century. This power and the power to review acts of Congress are known collectively as the power of *judicial review*.

Checks on Congress Checks by the executive branch on Congress are numerous and powerful.

• The President can veto any bill passed by Congress, in which case the bill does not become a law. As already mentioned, Congress has the power to pass a bill again over a President's veto. However, a two-thirds vote in both houses is difficult to obtain.

• The President can refuse to spend money approved by Congress for a specific purpose. This power is called *impoundment*.

• The President can speak for or against the re-election of senators and representatives. Many voters are likely to be influenced by what the President says.

• The President has the power to call Congress to meet in special *sessions* (series of meetings). Presidents do not use this power very often. They call a special session only when there is some good reason to do so.

• The President can ask Americans for their support when Congress does not cooperate with the executive branch. In this way, public opinion may be influenced to favor or oppose certain measures. Members of Congress are usually very sensitive to public opinion.

Federal judges can check Congress when they review federal laws in cases that come before them. In deciding these cases, the federal judges sometimes declare the laws unconstitutional.

Checks on the Federal Courts Both the executive and legislative branches have some control over the judicial branch.

The President's main check on the judicial branch is the power to appoint federal judges. Presidents usually name judges who they believe have views similar to theirs on important legal matters. Nevertheless, there is no way for a President to guarantee that judges will decide cases the way the President wants.

Congress has broad checks over the judicial branch:

• Congress controls the size of the U.S. Supreme Court, which, at present, has nine members.

• Congress can establish or do away with lower federal courts. The Supreme Court, however, was set up by the Constitution and cannot be abolished by an act of Congress.

• Congress sets the salaries of all federal judges.

• The Senate must approve all judges who are appointed by the President.

• The House and Senate can remove federal judges from office. They can accomplish this removal by the same impeachment process that they can use against the President.

> Federal judges are less influenced by public opinion than are Presidents and members of Congress. If judges do not commit crimes, they can keep their jobs for life. On the other hand, Presidents and members of Congress must face re-election. Senators are elected for six-year terms; representatives, for two-year terms. Presidents serve terms of four years, but they can seek office only twice.

Pros and Cons of Checks and Balances

Checks and balances help to keep the nation democratic and encourage all three branches of government to work together. No one branch can become too powerful. If any branch does

President Jimmy Carter, like most modern U.S. Presidents, gave many press conferences. By speaking directly to the American public, he was able to influence the passage of certain laws.

something that is improper or unwise, the other branches have a chance to stop this action.

Unfortunately, disagreements among the branches sometimes get in the way of government business. When disagreements prevent action, *deadlocks* (standstills) occur. Deadlocks are more likely to arise when the Presidency and Congress are controlled by different political parties.

Another problem with checks and balances has to do with the way federal courts work. Courts are not able immediately to check the other two branches. Courts have to wait for a relevant case to come before them. Then sometimes court cases take years before they are finally decided. Thus, for instance, federal judges may declare a law unconstitutional years after it has been passed.

SUMMING UP   We have seen that the federal government is divided into three main branches. Each branch has its own powers. In addition, each branch has special means of checking the powers of the other two. The different ways of balancing powers prevent any part of the federal government from becoming too strong.

Understanding the Text

On a separate sheet of paper, write the letter of the word or phrase that best completes each of the following statements.

1. The Constitution provides for all of the following safeguards in government, *except* (a) impeachment of the President (b) separation of powers (c) election of federal judges (d) checks and balances.

2. The President's powers do *not* include the right to (a) pass laws (b) enforce laws (c) make treaties (d) appoint important officials.

3. Of the following words, the one that does *not* belong with the other three is (a) judicial (b) executive (c) legislative (d) unconstitutional.

4. A good example of cooperation between the legislative and executive branches is (a) the President's appointment of a Supreme Court justice (b) a deadlock in Congress (c) a presidential veto (d) a bill passed by Congress and signed by the President.

5. Congress has no power over the President's (a) speeches (b) spending of money (c) appointments (d) ability to veto laws.

6. Removal of the President from office by impeachment proceedings is an example of a check of (a) the legislative branch over the judicial (b) the judicial branch over the executive (c) the legislative branch over the executive (d) the executive branch over the other two main branches.

7. A new federal judge must be approved by (a) the House of Representatives (b) both houses of Congress (c) the Supreme Court (d) the Senate.

8. Federal judges keep their jobs (*a*) for eight years (*b*) until the President removes them (*c*) until the next election (*d*) for life or until resigning.

9. A law that the Supreme Court finds unconstitutional is (*a*) sent back to Congress for changes (*b*) no longer a law (*c*) subject to the President's veto (*d*) subject to review by lower courts.

10. A central idea of this lesson is that checks and balances (*a*) speed up the work of government (*b*) prevent any one branch of government from becoming too strong (*c*) prevent people in government from making mistakes (*d*) are no longer as important as they once were.

Developing Diagram-Reading Skills

Study the diagram on page 82. Then choose the letter of the word or phrase that best answers each of the following questions concerning the diagram. On a separate sheet of paper, match the sentence number with the correct letter.

1. What building is depicted at the top, center part of the diagram? (*a*) White House (*b*) U.S. Supreme Court (*c*) House of Representatives (*d*) U.S. Senate.

2. The arrow leading from the "Legislative Branch" to the "Judicial Branch" represents (*a*) checks on the legislative branch (*b*) checks on the executive branch (*c*) checks on the judicial branch (*d*) checks on the states.

3. Which of the following is an example of a check by the judicial branch on the legislative branch? (*a*) It can appoint Supreme Court justices and other federal judges. (*b*) It can declare laws unconstitutional. (*c*) It can impeach the President. (*d*) It can establish lower federal courts.

4. What power does the U.S. Senate, but not the House of Representatives, have over the executive branch? (*a*) power to veto legislation (*b*) power to override vetoes (*c*) power to set up lower federal courts (*d*) power to approve or refuse to approve treaties.

5. Which of the three major branches of government has the *least number* of powers over the other two? (*a*) legislative branch (*b*) executive branch (*c*) judicial branch (*d*) independent regulatory agencies.

Thinking About the Lesson

1. List and explain some recent examples of how one branch of the federal government checks another.

2. Do you think that it is a good idea for the legislative branch to have the power of impeachment? Why or why not?

3. Do you think that the President should have the right to veto bills passed by Congress? Explain your answer.

4. Why are federal judges appointed for life terms? Do you think that the President and members of Congress should also serve for their lifetimes? Why or why not?

5. In your view, which of the three major branches of the federal government is the most powerful? Least powerful? Defend your answers.

How Laws Are Passed

Congress is the head of the legislative branch of the federal government. As such, Congress's most important duty is to consider proposed laws and to act on these proposals. There are several steps in this *legislative process*.

How Laws Begin

All laws start out as *bills* (written drafts of laws) which are introduced in either the House of Representatives or the Senate. To be introduced, each bill must have the backing of one or more members of Congress. Members of Congress, though, are not the only people who think up ideas for bills. Private citizens and interest groups often submit proposed laws to senators and representatives. The White House is another major source of legislative ideas.

Special-Interest Legislation While some bills will benefit the entire nation, others have to do with only local problems. Members of Congress want to help people in the states or districts that they represent. For this reason, senators and representatives often introduce bills that will bring money, jobs, or other benefits to their state or district. Many bills, for instance, call for construction of federally funded roads, post offices, hospitals, and similar projects.

A number of these projects are useful, but others are a waste of money. Whether useful or not, laws that benefit only one state or district are often called *pork-barrel legislation*.

The Committees

At the heart of the lawmaking process are *committees*, made up of groups of senators or representatives. All new bills are referred to a committee. In the House, the Speaker of the House makes these referrals. The Vice President of the United States, as presiding officer of the Senate, has that power in the upper house.

Chairpersons At the head of each congressional committee sits a *chairperson*. This leader exercises a great deal of control over the work of a committee. To be selected for the job, he or she usually must:

• be a member of the *majority party* (the party that controls the House or the Senate). Because of this qualification, one party usually holds all of the leading committee positions in the Senate or the House.

• have served on that committee longer than any other member of the majority party. This qualification is referred to as *seniority*.

87

The Capitol Building is usually lit up at night. Both the Senate and the House of Representatives meet here.

Committee Work   Committee members discuss and debate bills. During the course of this discussion, members often make amendments to the proposed laws.

If a committee needs to know more about a particular subject, it may hold public meetings, called *hearings*. People who want to express their views on bills are welcome to attend these meetings. Also, members of Congress will invite experts on a subject to speak at hearings.

Lobbyists   Hearings provide opportunities for *lobbyists* to speak. Lobbyists are hired by pressure groups to try to persuade members of Congress on how they should vote. *Lobbying* is a legal way to influence the vote on a bill before Congress. Lobbyists present many facts and figures to support their views. For this reason, lawmakers often find lobbyists' presentations useful when writing laws or deciding which way to vote.

Although lobbying is useful, it tends to help mostly the more powerful groups. Poorly organized groups and individual citizens usually have less influence with members of Congress.

> Lobbyists do more than talk to senators, representatives, and their staffs. They also visit the many executive departments and agencies. Sometimes lobbyists appeal directly to the American public by means of newspaper ads and television commercials.

Committee Approval or Disapproval   Most bills never receive the approval of a committee. They are simply *pigeonholed*—that is, set aside. If a committee "kills" a bill in this way, it is not likely ever to reach the floor of the House or Senate.

Only a few bills are approved by a committee. If approved, a proposed law is listed on the *calendar* (chart of dates and events) of the House or the Senate. In the Senate, bills usually come up for consideration in the order in which they come from committee. The House, however, has a Rules Committee that determines when a bill can reach the floor for debate.

Action on the Floor

Bills that reach the floor of the Senate or House are subject to debate and amendments.

Debate   While some bills are hardly discussed, more controversial ones are debated for long periods. Records of every day's debates, printed in the *Congressional Record*, show how much consideration is given to each bill.

House and Senate rules on debates differ. In the House of Representatives, members are limited as to how long they can speak on any piece of legislation. In the Senate, however, members are usually allowed to talk as long as they wish.

HOW ONE BILL BECOMES A LAW

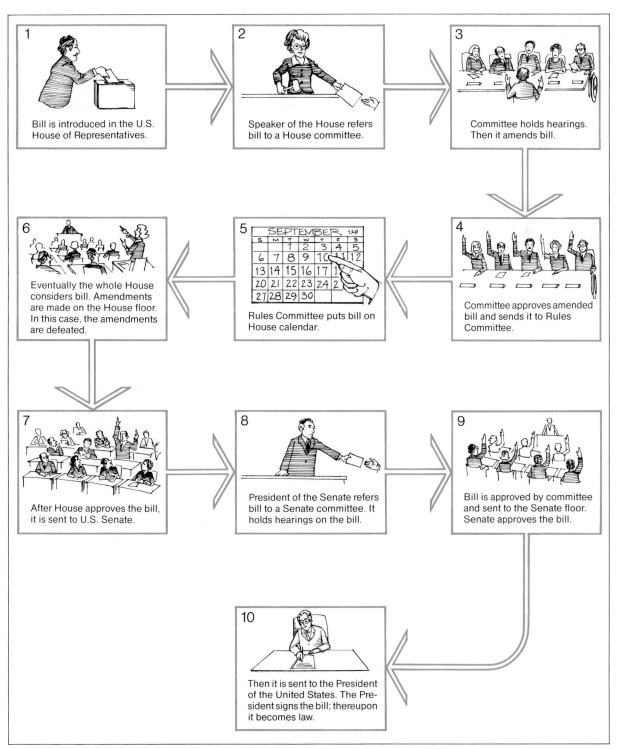

1. Bill is introduced in the U.S. House of Representatives.

2. Speaker of the House refers bill to a House committee.

3. Committee holds hearings. Then it amends bill.

4. Committee approves amended bill and sends it to Rules Committee.

5. Rules Committee puts bill on House calendar.

6. Eventually the whole House considers bill. Amendments are made on the House floor. In this case, the amendments are defeated.

7. After House approves the bill, it is sent to U.S. Senate.

8. President of the Senate refers bill to a Senate committee. It holds hearings on the bill.

9. Bill is approved by committee and sent to the Senate floor. Senate approves the bill.

10. Then it is sent to the President of the United States. The President signs the bill; thereupon it becomes law.

Filibuster   Sometimes senators use their right to debate in order to kill a bill. When several senators talk on and on for this purpose, they are engaging in a *filibuster*. By holding the floor for several days, the senators may prevent a vote on a bill. Eventually the Senate will want to move on to new business. Therefore, supporters of the bill may agree to drop their support if the bill's opponents stop filibustering.

A filibuster can be stopped in another way. Three fifths of the Senate can vote to limit debate to one hour per member. But such a vote, called *cloture*, is hard to obtain since most senators take pride in their right to talk.

Amendment   During a debate, senators and representatives have many more chances to amend a bill. Sometimes amendments are made to other amendments.

Some amendments have nothing to do with the contents of the original bill. Unpopular amendments may be added as a way of defeating legislation. If amendments make great changes in a bill, even its original supporters may not want to vote for it.

Voting on a Bill

A bill is passed by the House or Senate when a majority of the members present vote in favor of the bill. A *majority* is any number over half of the total. For example, if there are 405 representatives voting, 203 of them must vote *aye* (yes) for the bill to pass.

Logrolling   Some laws get passed through *logrolling*. With this practice, members of Congress do favors for each other. For example, Senator *A* might agree to vote in favor of a bill being pushed by Senator *B*. In return, Senator *B* will vote for a bill favored by Senator *A*.

Action by the Other House   Once a bill is passed by one house of Congress, it must go on

to the other. There it will go through many of the same procedures all over again. If the bill's sponsors are lucky, both houses will enact the bill during the same session of Congress. Sometimes only one house will pass a bill.

Conference Committee   Very often, the two houses of Congress will pass similar bills in somewhat different forms. When this situation develops, Congress must set up a *conference committee,* made up of both representatives and senators. This group works to iron out differences between two forms of a bill. After completing its work, the conference committee sends back a single bill to both houses for a vote.

Presidential Action

When a bill has been passed in identical form by both houses of Congress, it is sent to the President. In favoring the legislation, the President has a number of choices on what to do. The President can sign the bill, thereby making it a law. Or a bill can become a law when the Chief Executive takes no action at all on the measure. If a President does nothing (and Congress is still in session), a bill automatically becomes a law after ten working days.

There are two ways for a President to veto or disapprove a bill:

• A President can send a bill back to Congress, refusing to sign it. Usually, a President who does this gives reasons for the veto. A two-thirds vote of both houses is needed to *override* a presidential veto. If the bill is overridden, it becomes law without the President's signature.

• A President can also use the *pocket veto.* This type of veto can occur only when Congress *adjourns* (ends its session) within ten days after passing a bill. Then, for the pocket veto to take effect, a President just "pockets" the bill (takes no action on it), and it is considered killed.

U.S. SENATE AND HOUSE OF REPRESENTATIVES

SENATE	HOUSE OF REPRESENTATIVES
100 MEMBERS	435 MEMBERS
FLORIDA ELECTED BY ENTIRE STATE	FLORIDA — 15th Congressional District — Fort Lauderdale ELECTED BY CONGRESSIONAL DISTRICT
2 ALASKA 2 CALIFORNIA TWO SENATORS FOR EACH STATE	1 ALASKA 45 CALIFORNIA REPRESENTATION BASED ON POPULATION
ELECTED FOR 6-YEAR TERMS	ELECTED FOR 2-YEAR TERMS

SUMMING UP We have seen that a bill does not become law quickly or easily. In fact, most bills never achieve legal status. To become law, a bill must first be introduced and sent to a committee. After hearings and debate, the bill might be put on a floor calendar. On the floor of the House or Senate, a bill may be amended. Senators or representatives debate the bill further. If the bill is approved in identical form by both houses of Congress, it goes on to the White House for approval or veto.

Understanding the Text

On a separate sheet of paper, write the letter of the word or phrase that best completes each of the following statements.

1. A part of the government that does *not* play a direct role in the lawmaking process is the (*a*) President (*b*) House (*c*) Senate (*d*) Supreme Court.

2. Congress is able to deal with many bills at the same time because of (*a*) the House calendar (*b*) its long workday (*c*) the committee system (*d*) help from the executive branch.

3. A representative makes a speech on the floor of the House in favor of a certain bill. This speech is certain to be (*a*) vetoed (*b*) printed in the *Congressional Record* (*c*) sent to the President (*d*) filibustered.

4. A bill is killed in committee if (*a*) it is not sent back to the House or Senate floor (*b*) many changes are made in it (*c*) a senator begins a filibuster (*d*) the President makes a speech against it.

5. The work of a congressional committee includes all of the following, *except* (*a*) cloture (*b*) debates (*c*) hearings (*d*) making changes in a bill.

6. A two-thirds vote of both houses is needed to (*a*) pass a bill (*b*) override a presidential veto (*c*) stop a filibuster (*d*) all of the above.

7. The purpose of a conference committee is to (*a*) get information from lobbyists (*b*) introduce money bills (*c*) change the boundaries of election districts (*d*) make a bill acceptable to both houses of Congress.

8. One serious criticism of lobbying is that it (*a*) keeps information from lawmakers (*b*) feeds false information to the public (*c*) is used to bring about enactment of laws that favor powerful groups (*d*) is illegal.

9. An example of pork-barrel legislation is a bill to (*a*) regulate the meat-packing industry (*b*) provide more educational benefits for all veterans (*c*) build unneeded government offices in a few states (*d*) provide tax refunds for all U.S. citizens over age 65.

10. A pocket veto is possible only when (*a*) Congress is in session (*b*) the President is on vacation when Congress passes a bill (*c*) the Supreme Court asserts its rights to pocket a bill (*d*) Congress adjourns within ten days after it passes a bill.

Developing Reading Comprehension Skills

Read the first two pages of the U.S. Constitution, printed at the back of this book beginning on page 602. Then choose the letter of the word or phrase that best completes each sentence. On a separate sheet of paper, match the sentence number with the correct letter.

1. The first paragraph of the Constitution, the *Preamble* (introduction) to the document, lists (*a*) the powers of the Presidency (*b*) the powers of Congress (*c*) reasons why the United States declared its independence from Great Britain (*d*) none of the above.

2. Article I, which runs from page 602 to page 607, discusses (*a*) Congress (*b*) the Presidency (*c*) the judicial branch (*d*) none of the above.

3. According to Article I, Section 2, a requirement for one's election to the U.S. House of Representatives is (*a*) to be at least 25 years old (*b*) to have been a U.S. citizen for at least seven years (*c*) to be a resident of the state that one wants to represent (*d*) all of the above.

4. The *minimum* (fewest) number of representatives that any state will have in the House of

Representatives is *(a)* one   *(b)* two   *(c)* ten
(d) not mentioned in Article I, Section 2.

5. According to Article I, Section 3, the president of the U.S. Senate is normally the
(a) Speaker of the House   *(b)* President *pro
tempore* *(c)* Vice President of the United States
(d) President of the United States.

Thinking About the Lesson

1. Whose interests should members of Congress
be more concerned about serving—those of the
people whom they represent or those of the
nation as a whole? Explain your answer.

2. Why do only a small percentage of bills
introduced in Congress ever become laws?

3. Do you think that lobbyists should be allowed
to attend congressional committee hearings?
Why or why not?

4. In what ways can political parties influence
the outcome of national legislation?

5. In what ways can a President affect legislation? Do you think that presidential power over
legislation is too strong, too weak, or just about
right? Explain.

 **LESSON 16**

Powers and Duties of the President

The President is the most powerful person in the United States government. As head of the executive branch, the President enforces laws, conducts foreign policy, and runs the military. In addition, the President has some important legislative and judicial powers.

Executive Powers of the President

The President is responsible for seeing that laws passed by Congress are carried out correctly. Of course, a President cannot do this alone. Hundreds of advisers and personal assistants help the President do this job. In addition, executive departments, agencies, and commissions employ millions more in this work.

Foreign Affairs The Constitution puts the President in charge of running the foreign affairs of the country:

• With Senate approval, the President appoints *ambassadors*, people who represent the United States in foreign nations.

• The President receives *foreign diplomats* (representatives of foreign governments). As head of the U.S. government, the President enjoys the respect of world leaders.

• With Senate approval, the President makes treaties with other nations. The President can also make executive agreements with foreign leaders, without Senate approval.

• The President, both personally and through assistants, keeps in constant touch with leaders of foreign nations.

Military Affairs Although a civilian, the President is Commander in Chief of the Armed Forces. The President has the power to accept or turn down decisions of Army, Navy, or Air Force leaders. These top military officers are appointed to their posts by the President. The President can also remove them from office.

> Presidents have used their powers as Commander in Chief to send troops to other countries. In some cases, these troops have become involved in fighting a war. Because the Constitution gives only Congress the power to declare war, these presidential actions are controversial. In 1973, Congress passed a law limiting presidential actions in this area. It required the President to get congressional approval within 60 days after sending troops overseas.

94

Legislative Powers of the President

As noted previously, the President has the power to approve or veto bills passed by Congress. The President can also ask Congress to consider all kinds of legislation. The Chief Executive has other legislative powers as well.

State of the Union Message According to the Constitution, from time to time Presidents must give Congress their views on the "state of the union." In their annual State of the Union Message, Presidents tell Congress how they think the country is doing. They also suggest new legislation to solve some of the country's problems. These messages and other presidential speeches can strongly influence what laws Congress passes.

Special Session of Congress Presidents have the power to call a special session of Congress. Such a meeting might be needed, for instance, if there is a national emergency and Congress is not in session. Presidents can also call Congress into special session when Congress adjourns and leaves some important business unfinished.

In 1939, the United States was not yet involved in the fighting going on in Europe and East Asia. The country's policy was to be *neutral*—not to take sides. Then in September, Germany attacked Poland, causing World War II to break out in Europe. President Franklin D. Roosevelt immediately called a special session of Congress. He wanted Congress to help decide what, if anything, the United States should do. After considerable debate, Congress decided that the United States should remain neutral, but sell arms to any country that was fighting. In practice, this policy helped Great Britain and France the most.

President Franklin D. Roosevelt (center) met with Allied leaders Sir Winston Churchill (left) and Joseph Stalin at Yalta, USSR, toward the end of World War II. What power or powers was the President exercising at this meeting?

After the Battle of Antietam in 1862, Abraham Lincoln visited General George McClellan at the latter's headquarters near Harpers Ferry, Virginia. What power or powers was the President exercising?

Judicial Powers of the President

With Senate approval, the President appoints federal judges, including Supreme Court justices. Those appointed can serve for their lifetimes. A President cannot fire them for making decisions that the President does not like.

Another judicial power of the President is the right to issue pardons and reprieves. A *pardon* is a release from punishment for a person found guilty of a federal crime. The President cannot pardon a federal official who has been impeached and convicted. A *reprieve* delays a punishment that has been ordered by a court.

A third power of the President in the judicial area has to do with the power to approve or veto bills. This power is a judicial one when the President considers bills on the judiciary. The President might veto a law, for example, that would increase the number of justices sitting on the Supreme Court.

Leader of a Political Party

Although not mentioned in the Constitution, one of the duties of a President is to serve as leader of a political party. Presidents are often called upon to campaign for those members of their party who are running for a seat in Congress. Presidents can help their party in another way—through *patronage*. They can reward party workers for years of service to the party by appointing them to federal posts.

Assistants and Advisers to the President

Presidents need plenty of help. They are assisted indirectly by the millions of workers in the federal departments and agencies. Most of these employees obtain their jobs on the basis of examinations. Those who work closest to the

President, however, are usually appointed to their jobs by the Chief Executive.

Executive Office of the President Some of the federal employees most directly responsible to the President serve in the Executive Office of the President. They give the President information and help make policies. These workers are appointed by the President, some with Senate approval and some without. Units of the Executive Office include:

• The White House Staff, a group of some 500 people that serves as the President's personal team. It includes many experts on domestic and foreign issues, as well as speechwriters, photographers, secretaries, and others. The White House staff serves at the pleasure of the President and does not need the approval of the Senate.

• The National Security Council, which deals with the problems of safeguarding the nation against a foreign attack.

• The Council of Economic Advisers, which is concerned with economic issues.

• The Office of Management and Budget, which closely watches federal income and expenses. The OMB plans the annual budget of the United States government. The *budget* provides a detailed estimate of the money that the government will spend and bring in.

Cabinet The *Cabinet* is the oldest and highest-ranking group of presidential advisers. Most Cabinet members also serve as heads of the executive departments—that is, the departments of:

State	Agriculture	Housing and
Treasury	Commerce	Urban De-
Defense	Labor	velopment
Justice	Health and	Transportation
Interior	Human	Energy
Education	Services	

Heads of executive departments are named by the President and must be confirmed by the Senate. The Secretary of State and Secretary of Defense are considered to be the most important Cabinet members.

Like other Presidents, Ronald Reagan meets regularly with members of his Cabinet.

The heads of all executive departments (except the Attorney General, who heads the Justice Department) are called "Secretaries." This use of the word is a special one. Generally, we use the word "secretary" to refer to an employee who handles correspondence, typing, and other office work.

Increase in Presidential Powers

Over the years, the United States has been led by some strong and some weak Presidents. The stronger ones have increased their powers by assuming duties or privileges not specifically mentioned in the Constitution. They have done this in the course of carrying out their regular responsibilities. In time, many of these expanded presidential powers have become accepted as necessary by most Americans.

Executive Privilege   One example of expanded powers involved President George Washington. In 1796, the House of Representatives demanded from him some papers relating to a foreign treaty. Washington, however, refused. He said that the President and the Senate had treaty-making powers, not the House. Since then, other U.S. Presidents have refused demands by Congress for information. Citing Washington's example, these Presidents have said that they have an *executive privilege* in such matters.

SUMMING UP   We have seen that the Constitution gives U.S. Presidents several key powers. The President is concerned not only with executive functions, but has legislative and judicial powers as well. To aid the President, millions of people are employed by the executive branch of government. Over the years, some Presidents have gone beyond what the Constitution says about the Presidency and have expanded their powers.

Understanding the Text

On a separate sheet of paper, write the letter of the word or phrase that best completes each of the following statements.

1. The President's title of "Chief Executive" refers to this person's primary responsibility for (*a*) making laws (*b*) seeing that laws are enforced (*c*) declaring wars (*d*) deciding how money is to be spent.

2. All treaties and many important appointments made by the President must be approved by (*a*) the Supreme Court (*b*) both houses of Congress (*c*) the Senate (*d*) voters.

3. The President is able to recommend new laws (*a*) through the Office of Management and Budget (*b*) by executive order (*c*) in a State of the Union Message (*d*) by vetoing bills.

4. A President often can influence voting in Congress because a President is usually (*a*) unpopular (*b*) the head of a political party

(c) a member of the Senate (d) free from criticism.

5. The President's judicial powers include all of the following, *except* (a) naming federal judges (b) granting pardons (c) approving new laws on the judiciary (d) doing away with the Supreme Court.

6. All of the people on the White House Staff are (a) personal assistants to the President (b) approved by Congress (c) members of the Armed Forces (d) elected by American voters.

7. The President's Cabinet includes the heads of all of the executive departments. Of the following, which one is *not* such a department?

(a) State (b) Environmental Protection (c) Treasury (d) Defense.

8. An executive department *not* headed by someone with the title of "Secretary" is (a) Justice (b) Interior (c) Labor (d) HUD.

9. Since the time of George Washington, powers of the President have (a) decreased (b) increased (c) remained roughly the same (d) become the only important force in the federal government.

10. A power of the President *not* mentioned in the Constitution is the right to (a) appoint federal judges (b) claim executive privilege (c) veto bills (d) address Congress.

Developing Cartoon-Reading Skills

"YOU HOLD IT WHILE I SIT IN THAT CHAIR"

Don Hesse, © 1976, *St. Louis Globe-Democrat.* Reprinted with permission, Los Angeles Times Syndicate.

Study the political cartoon on the left. Then choose the letter of the word or phrase that best completes each sentence. On a separate sheet of paper, match the sentence number with the correct letter.

1. The man wearing glasses in the cartoon represents the (a) Congress (b) President (c) Supreme Court (d) American public.

2. The other character in the cartoon probably represents (a) Congress (b) the Soviet Union (c) the U.S. government (d) Great Britain.

3. In this cartoon, Congress seems to want to (a) support the President (b) refuel the economy (c) balance the budget (d) run the country's foreign policy.

4. The cartoonist seems to be most critical of actions of the (a) Congress (b) President (c) country's economic policy (d) oil producers.

5. An appropriate title for this cartoon would be (a) "Balancing the Budget" (b) "Do We

Want a Three-Term President?" *(c)* "What's Wrong With U.S. Foreign Policy?" *(d)* "The Federal System."

Thinking About the Lesson

1. Should the framers of the Constitution have put Congress in charge of foreign affairs instead of the President? Explain your answer.

2. Why do you suppose the framers of the Constitution wanted the President to have more authority than any other officer of the U.S. Armed Forces?

3. Why is it important for Presidents to address Congress from time to time and be able to call it into special session?

4. Why does the President have so many advisers and assistants?

How the President Is Elected

Every four years, Americans are asked to participate in a presidential election. These elections are especially important because they are the only nationwide ones. In a sense, the whole nation speaks on Election Day in November.

Qualifications for Candidates

The Constitution sets only three qualifications for a presidential candidate. The candidate must be:

• At least 35 years of age.
• A *natural-born citizen* (someone born in the United States).
• A resident of the United States for at least 14 years.

Exactly the same qualifications apply to a candidate for the office of Vice President. The qualifications are the same because the Vice President may become President if the President dies or has to leave office.

In the past, all successful presidential candidates have been men. Many of them (though not all) have had other things in common, such as:
• Training as a lawyer or military leader.
• Political success, usually as a state governor or U.S. senator.
• Moderate political views—somewhere in the center, rather than at an extreme or "far out."
• Residence in a large state, often having grown up in a small town.
• Age of more than 50 years.
• Being married and never having been divorced.
• Protestant religion and British ancestors.

The Election Process

The process of running for President begins long before the election date. In many states,

101

In February, 1980, Ronald Reagan greeted voters in New Hampshire in his bid for the Republican nomination for President. Reagan won this Republican primary—the first one of the election campaign.

candidates enter *primary elections* to test their popularity with the voters of their party. Winners of the spring primaries gain delegates to their party's national convention.

Nomination During the summer before a presidential election, both major parties hold large national conventions. The main business of a party convention is to *nominate* (name) a candidate for President. Once delegates have made this selection, they then choose a *running mate*—someone to run for the office of Vice President. Delegates almost always follow the wishes of the presidential candidate in making the vice-presidential nomination.

Meanwhile, the convention has drawn up a party *platform*. A platform states the party's views on key issues. Each of the main items of the platform, called *planks*, is debated at the convention.

Campaign Candidates use the time between the convention and Election Day in November to campaign. An *election campaign* is a large-scale effort to win the support of voters.

During the campaign, candidates explain why they think they deserve to be President. They travel widely, speaking to as many important groups as possible. They use the *media*—radio, television, newspapers—to reach voters whom they cannot see in person. More and more, television is becoming the most effective way for candidates to influence voters.

Election On Election Day, citizens go to the polls to vote. Once there, though, they do not vote directly for a candidate. Instead, they vote for a group of *electors* who have promised, in turn, to vote for a particular candidate. Usually the results of a presidential election are known soon after the polls close on Election Day.

The Electoral College

As we just mentioned, Americans vote for electors instead of voting directly for presidential candidates. The *Electoral College* is the name we give to all of these electors. Nevertheless, this body is not at all like a college attended by students, nor do electors meet together as one body.

In every state, each political party has its own electors. If a party carries a state, all of its electors in that state assemble. They meet in their own state capitals in the middle of the December that follows a presidential election. Electors are not bound by law to vote for their party's winning candidate, but most electors do this anyway.

Each state is allowed the same number of electors as it has members of Congress—that is, the total number of senators and representatives. Thus, the more *populous* (heavily populated) states, such as California and New York, have many more electors than do some other states. Of the total number of electors (now 538), 535 come from the 50 states and 3 from the District of Columbia.

A President must be chosen by a majority vote of the Electoral College. If no candidate gains a majority, the election is then turned over to the House of Representatives. In the House, each state can cast only one vote for any of the top three candidates. The candidate who wins a majority of this vote becomes President.

In a similar way, the election of the Vice President is turned over to the Senate if no candidate wins a majority of the Electoral College. The Senate makes its choice from the top two candidates. Each Senator casts one vote, and a majority is needed to win this election.

Reform of the Electoral College?

A presidential candidate who gains the greatest number of *popular votes* (the votes of the people) can fail to win the election. This situation, though unusual, has happened several times in the past. It can happen because the candidate

In July, 1984, the Democratic party held its National Convention in San Francisco, California. The delegates nominated former Vice President Walter Mondale for President and Representative Geraldine Ferraro for Vice President.

On November 22, 1963, President John F. Kennedy was shot dead in Dallas, Texas. Within hours, Vice President Lyndon B. Johnson was sworn in as President by federal judge Sarah T. Hughes.

who wins the most popular votes in a state gains all of that state's *electoral votes*. The loser in that state gets none. A losing candidate may win many states but lose a number of heavily populated ones (with large numbers of electoral votes) by narrow margins. Thus, votes in a state for a candidate who loses that state do not count.

Some Americans believe that the Electoral College system should be dropped. They would like to see a constitutional amendment that would replace the system with a direct popular vote. Under the new system, candidates with the most votes across the country would win.

Another proposal for an amendment would be to keep the Electoral College, but change it. The electoral votes in each state would be divided between the candidates in proportion to the popular vote of each candidate in the state. Thus, a candidate who wins three fifths of the popular vote in a state would get three fifths of the electoral votes of that state. This candidate would not get all of the votes, as he or she does in the present system.

Those who want to change or drop the electoral system have not gained enough support. People who benefit from the present system oppose such an amendment. In addition, many other Americans believe that the system works well enough despite its weaknesses. They do not want to "rock the boat" by adopting new rules for electing the President.

Terms of Office and Succession

The *inauguration* (swearing-in ceremony) of the new President and Vice President takes place at noon on the January 20 following the election. In a televised ceremony, the new President promises to "preserve, protect, and defend the Constitution of the United States."

Terms of Office Both the President and Vice President are elected to a four-year term. The Twenty-second Amendment to the Constitution (1951) limits each President to serving only two terms.

Presidential Succession If a President dies in office or cannot serve a full term, the office must be filled at once. The order in which other persons qualify is covered by law and is called the *succession*. The Vice President succeeds the President. After the Vice President, next in line for the Presidency are (in the following order):

• The Speaker of the House of Representatives.

• The President *pro tempore* of the Senate, the person who leads the Senate when the Vice President of the United States is not present.

• The Secretary of State.

• All other members of the President's Cabinet in the order in which their departments were first created.

If the Vice President must be replaced, the President makes an appointment. This appointment has to be approved by a majority of both houses of Congress.

SUMMING UP   We have seen how complicated the process of electing the President is. Long before Election Day, candidates enter state primaries. Then at conventions they seek their party's nomination. The election itself is indirect, involving the Electoral College system. Many Americans have criticized the Electoral College, but the system is likely to remain in use. Any proposed reform would need to be made by means of a constitutional amendment.

Understanding the Text

On a separate sheet of paper, write the letter of the word or phrase that best completes each of the following statements.

1. Under the Constitution, a person may be prevented from serving as President because of his or her *(a)* sex *(b)* religion *(c)* age *(d)* education.

2. A President can hold office *(a)* for only four years *(b)* for only two terms *(c)* for life *(d)* until age 75.

3. Usually, a person who wants to run for President first seeks the support of *(a)* the current President *(b)* the Electoral College *(c)* members of a political party *(d)* teachers and historians.

4. Of the following words and phrases, the one that does *not* belong with the others is *(a)* party platform *(b)* succession *(c)* key issues *(d)* planks.

5. A party's nominating convention usually takes place *(a)* several years before the election *(b)* a year before the election *(c)* in the spring of an election year *(d)* in the summer of an election year.

6. The number of electoral votes allowed to a state with three members in the House of Representatives is (*a*) nine (*b*) seven (*c*) five (*d*) three.

7. The term "popular vote" in a presidential election refers to the votes (*a*) of the Electoral College (*b*) of American citizens (*c*) of members of the House of Representatives (*d*) of a party convention.

8. One official who is not in direct line to succeed the President is the (*a*) Vice President (*b*) Speaker of the House (*c*) Chief Justice of the United States (*d*) Secretary of State.

9. According to the Constitution, if the office of Vice President becomes vacant, (*a*) the President assumes that office (*b*) the President appoints someone as Vice President (*c*) a new election is held (*d*) the Speaker of the House becomes Vice President.

10. Which of the following statements on the Electoral College system is most accurate? (*a*) It is simple and quick. (*b*) It gives equal weight to every citizen's vote. (*c*) It works fairly well to express the will of the people. (*d*) It always reflects the popular vote.

Developing Reading Comprehension Skills

Read Article II of the U.S. Constitution, on pages 607–609. Then choose the letter of the word or phrase that best completes each sentence. On a separate sheet of paper, match the sentence number with the correct letter.

1. According to Article II, Section 1, paragraph 2, the number of presidential electors per state is (*a*) two (*b*) four (*c*) equal to the number of senators and representatives that a state has in Congress (*d*) none of the above.

2. According to Article II, Section 1, paragraph 4, the day that presidential electors choose the President (*a*) varies from state to state (*b*) may be set by Congress (*c*) is always November 4 (*d*) is not discussed in this paragraph.

3. In addition to being elected, a person who wants to be the U.S. President has to meet certain requirements. These rules are listed in (*a*) Article II, Section 1, paragraph 5 (*b*) Article II, Section 2, paragraph 1 (*c*) Article II, Section 3 (*d*) Article II, Section 4.

4. A power of the President *not* mentioned in Article II, Section 2 is the power to (*a*) make treaties (*b*) be the Commander in Chief of the U.S. Army (*c*) be head of a political party (*d*) appoint Supreme Court justices.

5. As used in Article II, Section 3, the word "extraordinary" is closest in meaning to (*a*) additional (*b*) unusual (*c*) exciting (*d*) exaggerated.

Thinking About the Lesson

1. Are all the qualifications for a presidential candidate listed in the U.S. Constitution fair? Why or why not?

2. Do you think that a woman will ever become President? Explain your answer.

3. Do you believe that a presidential candidate who does not appear on television could win the election? Why or why not?

4. Why do some Americans object to the Electoral College system of electing a President? What are your views on this subject?

The Federal Court System

While Congress makes the nation's laws and the President enforces them, federal judges explain the meaning of laws. They also decide how these laws apply to everyday life. The federal court system is organized on three levels. On the lower level are the District Courts; on the next level, the Courts of Appeals. The Supreme Court sits alone at the top. All federal judges on all levels are appointed by the President, with the approval of the Senate.

Lower Federal Courts

Most court cases involving federal law are first heard in one of the over 90 *District Courts*. These courts are located all across the country and in U.S. territories.

Juries   District Courts are the only federal courts that make use of juries. A *jury* is a group of citizens chosen to hear a case in court.

One type of jury, the *grand jury*, has about 20 members. It performs a special job—deciding whether or not there is enough evidence to bring someone to trial. If the grand jury does decide that there is enough evidence, then the person accused of a crime is *indicted* (officially charged with a crime).

The other type of jury, the *petit jury*, has only 12 members. These *jurors* (members of the jury)

listen to the evidence presented in a trial. They decide whether a law has been broken and whether someone is guilty of breaking a law. They find the *defendant*, the accused person, innocent or guilty.

Criminal and Civil Cases   Federal courts hear both criminal and civil cases. In a *criminal case*, the defendant is accused of committing a crime. A crime is an act that is forbidden by law and is punishable by law. To reach a federal court, a criminal case must have involved charges of breaking a federal criminal law.

A *civil case* is one that does not directly involve any violations of criminal laws. One type of civil case brought to federal courts has to do with disputes between citizens of two states. These disputes must involve claims of more than $10,000. Other civil cases are brought to federal courts by people who believe that their rights have been violated. For instance, someone who is not allowed to vote might sue in federal courts.

Courts of Appeals

Someone who loses a case in a District Court may believe that the court's decision was wrong. This person may want to *appeal* (request a rehearing of) the case to a higher court. Such

107

an appeal can be made to a *Court of Appeals*—in the next level of the federal court system.

When a Court of Appeals receives an appeal, it does not hear the evidence again. Instead, the judges study a record of the original trial. They consider either or both of the following questions:

• Was the original trial handled properly?
• Did the District Court apply the law properly in reaching its decision?

There are 11 Courts of Appeals in the United States. They do not use juries. Instead, several judges (usually three) hear a case. The judges' decision may be unanimous, or the judges may split their votes two to one. Someone who loses a case may attempt an appeal to the U.S. Supreme Court. If no appeal is made, however, the decision of a Court of Appeals is final.

> Courts of Appeals hear cases appealed from District Courts. They also hear appeals from people affected by decisions of federal agencies, such as the Federal Trade Commission. In addition, cases heard in the U.S. Tax Court can be appealed to a Court of Appeals.

United States Supreme Court

The *United States Supreme Court* occupies the top position in the federal court system. Nine judges—the Chief Justice of the United States and eight associate justices—sit on this court.

The Supreme Court hears appeals from lower federal courts and the highest state courts. Because of its heavy workload, the Court accepts only a small number of the many appeals made to it.

Only two kinds of cases go directly to the Supreme Court:

• Cases involving ambassadors and other foreign diplomats.
• Cases involving one or more state governments.

Judicial Review In hearing a case, the Court may decide that a state or federal law is unconstitutional. If the Court makes this decision, the law is no longer in effect. Such decisions are part of the court's power of judicial review. The Supreme Court can also use its power of judicial review to check actions of the executive branch of government.

The Decision Process Nearly all cases decided by the Supreme Court are of national impor-

FEDERAL COURT SYSTEM

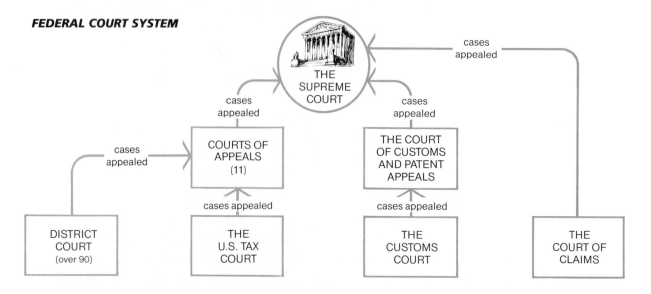

The nine justices of the U.S. Supreme Court meet and work in the building above. In 1967, Thurgood Marshall (center) became the first justice who was black. The first female justice, Sandra Day O'Connor (right), was appointed in 1981.

tance. Some involve checks on the President, Congress, or individual states. Others involve individuals or groups who may have been deprived of rights defined in the U.S. Constitution. In recent years, for example, the Supreme Court has heard cases about the rights of many Americans, including:

- Black Americans.
- Indians.
- Women.
- People accused of crimes.
- People sentenced to death by state courts.
- Public school students who are asked to take part in school prayers.

The U.S. Supreme Court has the power to overrule lower courts' decisions. The Court sometimes does this, declaring the lower courts' decisions *invalid* (not legal). The Court can also reverse its own, earlier decisions. Such reversals, however, are very rare; Supreme Court justices usually follow traditions set earlier.

Supreme Court decisions are made by majority vote of the nine justices and do not involve any juries. Such decisions are the last stages of long and difficult legal arguments. The closest

possible vote (five to four) is quite common. Rarely are decisions unanimous. The decision of the Court in a case is written down and published. It is called the *majority opinion*, reflecting the fact that often not all nine justices decide a case the same way.

Some students of government argue that the Supreme Court should not be allowed to reach decisions by a simple majority vote. They believe that Supreme Court decisions should reflect the views of more than five justices, since the decisions affect a great many Americans. Defenders of the system say that majority rule has been used by the Court since its beginning in 1789. The defenders see no compelling reason to change the system.

Dissenting Opinions Supreme Court justices who disagree with the majority sometimes write *dissenting opinions* to explain their views. A justice may also write a *separate opinion* when he or she votes with the majority but has somewhat different arguments or ideas to offer.

Special Courts in the Federal System

Several federal courts exist outside the three-level system. The names and functions of some of these special courts are the:

• U.S. Court of Claims. It can decide whether or not an individual has the right to claim money from the federal government. For example, this court would hear the claim of a person suing the government after having been injured by a National Parks Service truck.

• U.S. Customs Court. It can decide disputes about duties placed on foreign goods entering the country.

• U.S. Tax Court. It can decide disputes between taxpayers and the Internal Revenue Service.

State and Local Courts

State and local courts also play a major part in the lives of Americans. These courts, though, are separate from the federal judicial system. State and local courts handle both criminal and civil matters. The criminal cases involve violations of state and local criminal laws, but not of federal laws.

Decisions of lower state courts may be appealed to higher state courts. In rare instances, cases from state courts can go to the United States Supreme Court. (See page 108.)

The man standing in this courtroom scene is either a *defense attorney* (lawyer for the defendant) or a *prosecutor* (lawyer for the state). In jury trials, both will speak directly to the jury.

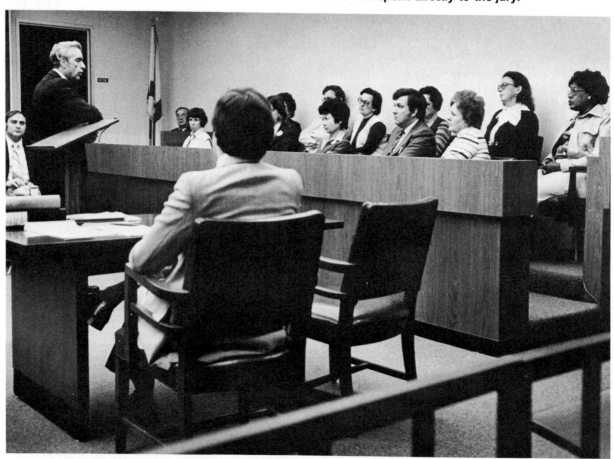

SUMMING UP   We have seen how the federal court system is organized on three levels. A court case that has been heard on all three levels would have started in a District Court. Then the case would have gone to a Court of Appeals. Finally, it would have reached the U.S. Supreme Court. This highest federal court serves as a place to appeal cases of great importance. It can also act as a check on the powers of the executive and legislative branches of the federal government. In addition to the federal courts, state and local courts are also important parts of our judicial system.

Understanding the Text

On a separate sheet of paper, write the letter of the word or phrase that best completes each of the following statements.

1. In the federal court system, the place where most cases start is the *(a)* Court of Appeals *(b)* Supreme Court *(c)* District Court *(d)* Court of Claims.

2. Juries in federal District Courts do all of the following, *except* *(a)* hear evidence *(b)* decide guilt or innocence *(c)* write dissenting opinions *(d)* decide if there is good reason for bringing a person to trial.

3. Decisions in Courts of Appeals are *(a)* made by judges *(b)* made by juries *(c)* final in all cases *(d)* usually reviewed by a higher court.

4. The President can appoint judges to the U.S. *(a)* District Courts *(b)* Courts of Appeals *(c)* Supreme Court *(d)* all of the above.

5. If the Supreme Court reaches a *unanimous decision*, the vote would probably be *(a)* five to zero *(b)* five to four *(c)* nine to zero *(d)* five to five.

6. If four Supreme Court justices disagree with the majority, *(a)* the majority decision prevails *(b)* the Court must hear the case again *(c)* the Vice President must cast the deciding vote *(d)* the case goes to the House of Representatives.

7. The Supreme Court can do all of the following, *except* *(a)* overrule a lower federal court decision *(b)* make a law *(c)* reverse its own decision *(d)* declare that a state law is unconstitutional.

8. A decision by the highest state court of Texas may reach the U.S. Supreme Court if the case *(a)* involves a claim of $1,000 *(b)* involves someone's rights protected by the U.S. Constitution *(c)* is very complicated and difficult *(d)* has led to much disagreement among Texans.

9. Of the following courts, one *not* part of the federal court system is the *(a)* California Supreme Court *(b)* U.S. Court of Claims *(c)* U.S. Tax Court *(d)* all of the above.

10. Which of the following statements about the federal court system is correct? *(a)* It is under the direct control of the President. *(b)* Its only job is to punish people who break the law. *(c)* It is one of the three branches of the federal government. *(d)* It is completely independent of acts of Congress.

Developing Skills in Reading a Floor Plan

COURTROOM FLOOR PLAN

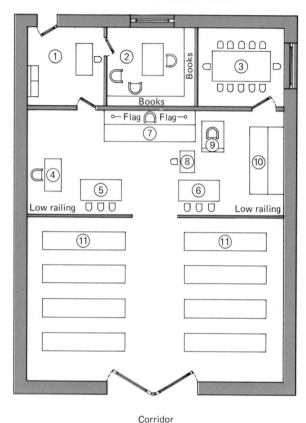

Corridor

1 Entry chamber
2 Judge's chamber
3 Jury room
4 Marshal
5 Prosecutor
6 Defendant and attorneys
7 Judge's bench
8 Court reporter
9 Witness stand
10 Jury box
11 Spectators' benches

Study the courtroom floor plan above. Then choose the letter of the word or phrase that best completes each sentence. On a separate sheet of paper, match the sentence number with the correct letter.

1. The shaded areas in this floor plan are (*a*) walls (*b*) floors (*c*) ceilings (*d*) windows.

2. If one wanted to observe a trial in the courtroom depicted, one would most likely sit on furniture represented by number (*a*) three (*b*) five (*c*) seven (*d*) eleven.

3. While a trial is in session, the judge would sit at location number (*a*) two (*b*) four (*c*) seven (*d*) ten.

4. After hearing a trial, the jury retires to a special place to decide whether or not the defendant is guilty. This place is number (*a*) two (*b*) three (*c*) ten (*d*) eleven.

5. According to the floor plan, directly in front of the defendant sits the (*a*) jury (*b*) court reporter (*c*) marshal (*d*) prosecutor.

Thinking About the Lesson

1. Is it important to have higher federal courts to which one can appeal cases lost in the lower courts? Why or why not?

2. Do you think that the U.S. Supreme Court should have the power to decide on the constitutionality of state laws? Why or why not?

3. Do you think it fair that decisions of the U.S. Supreme Court are made by majority vote? Explain your answer.

4. Why do the states have their own court systems, separate from the federal one?

The Constitution and Change

Although the U.S. Constitution is nearly 200 years old, it still works as well as ever. The Constitution has stood the test of time because of its *flexibility* (ability to bend). It has been able to *accommodate* (adapt to) change. For this reason, it is often called the "living Constitution."

Amending the Written Constitution

The Constitution was first changed while it was still being ratified. In 1791, the Bill of Rights, the first ten amendments, was added. Congress and the states were able to make these additions because the Constitution provides methods for its own amendment. (See the diagram on page 114.)

Proposal in Congress Under the most widely used method of amending the Constitution, a proposed change is introduced in Congress. Two thirds of both houses of Congress then must vote in favor of the proposed amendment. Following that step, the amendment must be ratified by the states in one of two ways:

• Approval by three fourths (now 38) of the state legislatures. Twenty-five amendments have been ratified in this manner.

• Approval by special conventions in three fourths of the states. Only one amendment—the Twenty-first—was ratified in this way.

Proposal by Constitutional Convention This method of amending the Constitution follows a different path. Two thirds (now 34) of the state legislatures may ask Congress to form a national convention to consider changes. This special convention may adopt one or more amendments. At least three fourths of the state legislatures or special state conventions must then approve any amendments so adopted.

> The Constitution itself was proposed by a national convention and ratified by state conventions. No amendment, however, has ever been approved by means of a national constitutional convention.

Debate on the Amending Process

On the one hand, some Americans think that the amending process is too slow and difficult. Many amendments have been proposed, but few of them have won the approval of three fourths of the states. In fact, after two centuries, only 26 amendments have been added to the Constitution. Critics also say that the process is unfair. They point out that 13 states are able to block the will of 37 others.

On the other hand, many other people think that slowness and difficulty are good features of the amending process. Since hasty action cannot be taken, these people say, only amendments that are really needed have a chance of being approved. Commentators point out that when a proposed amendment has widespread public support, it can be quickly approved.

Change Through Custom and Usage

The Constitution mentioned only the basic structure of government, such as Congress, the President, and a judiciary. Wisely, it did not go into great detail on how the three branches of government were to carry out their duties. The authors of the Constitution understood that, in time, various customs and familiar ways of doing things would develop. Some of those customs and habits would come to have much the same standing as written laws.

Thus, rules of government have been shaped over the years by a process sometimes called *custom and usage*. The changes made by this process have affected every branch of the government. The new customs are so important that, taken as a whole, they may properly be called the *unwritten constitution*.

The following is a list of important *innovations* (new things) that have become a part of our government. Note that they are not mentioned or described in the Constitution:

- The Cabinet system.
- The Court's power of judicial review.
- The committee system in Congress.
- The system of political parties.
- The power of the President to set broad policies to guide the nation's foreign relations.
- The *civil service system,* under which most federal civilian employees are hired and promoted through competitive tests.
- The tradition that Presidents take the lead in proposing laws to Congress.
- The power of Congress to pass laws on matters not dreamt of when the Constitution

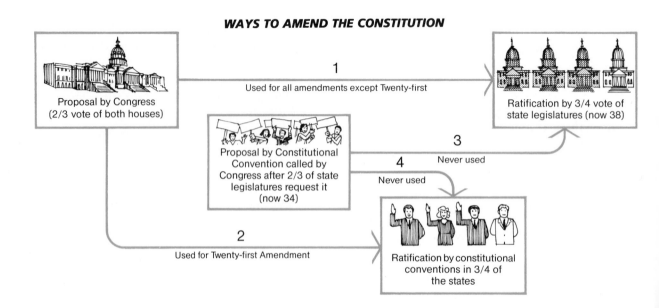

WAYS TO AMEND THE CONSTITUTION

Proposal by Congress
(2/3 vote of both houses)

1
Used for all amendments except Twenty-first

Ratification by 3/4 vote of
state legislatures (now 38)

Proposal by Constitutional
Convention called by
Congress after 2/3 of state
legislatures request it
(now 34)

3
Never used

4
Never used

2
Used for Twenty-first Amendment

Ratification by constitutional
conventions in 3/4 of
the states

Congressional committees, such as this House Rules Committee, are not mentioned in the U.S. Constitution.

was written. This power applies, for example, to laws relating to radio and television, nuclear energy, and the control of big businesses.

The list is far from complete, but it is long enough to show the great importance of the unwritten constitution.

Customs Added to the Constitution

In some cases, the unwritten constitution has eventually found its way into the written document. Starting with George Washington, for example, Presidents observed the custom of serving no more than two terms. Then, in the 1930s and 1940s, Franklin D. Roosevelt ran for President and won four times. Reacting to this break with tradition, a great many Americans thought that Washington's example should be written into the Constitution. The Twenty-second Amendment, ratified in 1951, limited future Presidents to serving two full terms.

Interpreting the Constitution

The U.S. Supreme Court can expand or otherwise change the Constitution in still another way. By interpreting sections of that document, the justices can give it new meaning. The following example shows how the Court has changed the meaning of one amendment to the Constitution.

In 1868, the Fourteenth Amendment was ratified. This amendment, guaranteeing all Americans equal protection under the law, was passed mainly to protect black Americans. Specifically, the amendment was aimed at state laws that denied blacks the same rights enjoyed by whites.

After 1868, a number of states passed laws requiring *segregated public facilities* (separate restaurants, schools, streetcars, etc., for blacks and whites). These state laws also said that such facilities should be equal for blacks and whites. For instance, parks and beaches for blacks would provide the same services as white ones. Many Americans thought that these practices were legal. In 1896, the U.S. Supreme Court agreed. In *Plessy* v. *Ferguson*, the Court stated that the Fourteenth Amendment allowed separate but equal facilities.

In 1954, the Court changed its mind on the issue of segregated schools. In *Brown* v. *Board of Education of Topeka*, it said that segregated schools did not and could not provide equal education. This court decision struck down state laws that had allowed segregation in public schools.

SUMMING UP   We have seen how the Constitution has remained useful through different periods of American history. This "living Constitution" allows for change in three major ways. First, the Constitution has provisions by which it can be amended. Second, it allows the federal government to assume new powers and new methods of dealing with problems. And third, it allows the Supreme Court to interpret provisions of the Constitution to respond to changing conditions.

Understanding the Text

On a separate sheet of paper, write the letter of the word or phrase that best completes each of the following statements.

1. The Bill of Rights is another name for (a) the written Constitution (b) the unwritten constitution (c) all of the constitutional amendments (d) the first ten constitutional amendments.

2. Most constitutional amendments have been proposed in (a) the House and Senate (b) national constitutional conventions (c) state legislatures (d) special state conventions.

3. The ratification of a constitutional amendment is solely a power of (a) the states (b) Congress (c) the courts (d) the President.

4. The Constitution is a living document because it (a) is written down (b) has worked well without change for nearly 200 years (c) can be changed and adapted from time to time to meet new conditions (d) is amended almost every year.

5. Those who support the amending process argue that it (a) checks the powers of state legislatures (b) helps to prevent hasty and unwise actions (c) makes the unwritten constitution unnecessary (d) can always be carried through quickly and easily.

6. As a result of an amendment, the Constitution now provides for (a) a two-term limit for each President (b) the offices in the President's Cabinet (c) the process of making treaties with foreign governments (d) political parties.

7. Of the following headlines, the one that best illustrates the unwritten constitution is: (a) "President Signs Tax Bill" (b) "Democratic Convention Meets to Choose Presidential Candidate" (c) "Twenty-Fifth Amendment Ratified" (d) "Impeachment Trial of Federal Judge Begins in Senate."

8. The Constitution has been expanded by all of the following, *except* (a) laws (b) court decisions (c) treaty-making (d) presidential actions.

9. The Supreme Court declared state laws allowing segregated public schools unconstitutional in (a) 1789 (b) 1868 (c) 1896 (d) 1954.

10. Which of the following statements best describes the formal process of amending the Constitution? (a) It is almost impossible to carry through. (b) It can almost always be done quickly. (c) It is the only method by which rules of government can be changed. (d) It is difficult to carry through, but it can be done if there is strong public support.

Developing Index-Reading Skills

Examine the first page of the index to the text, on page 637. Then answer the following questions. Choose the letter of the word or phrase that best completes each sentence. On a separate sheet of paper, match the sentence number with the correct letter.

1. An index to a book lists (*a*) titles of units and chapters (*b*) definitions of difficult and new words (*c*) titles of sources used in writing the book (*d*) most subjects covered in the book and on what pages they are found.

2. In any index, which of the following entries would always come before the other three? (*a*) Angola (*b*) Jackson, Andrew (*c*) Anti-Federalists (*d*) Latin America.

3. According to the index, one can find mention of Jane Addams on page (*a*) 40 (*b*) 140 (*c*) 307 (*d*) none of the above.

4. One can find a general discussion of amendments to the U.S. Constitution on page or pages (*a*) 59 (*b*) 88, 90 (*c*) 113–114 (*d*) 251.

5. An illustration of Appomattox is found on page (*a*) 96 (*b*) 246 (*c*) 248 (*d*) none of the above.

Thinking About the Lesson

1. If there had not been a means of changing the U.S. Constitution, would American society today be better off, worse off, or about the same? Explain your answer.

2. Do you think that the amending process is too long and difficult? Why or why not?

3. Why did the U.S. Supreme Court in 1954 change its mind on the question of segregated schools?

4. Some students of the Constitution have said that the "unwritten constitution" is as important as the written one. Do you agree with them? Why or why not?

5. Some Americans think that the United States has changed so much in the last 200 years that it needs a whole new constitution. What are your views on this matter?

The Constitution and Civil Rights

People in the United States are guaranteed a number of personal freedoms and property rights. Taken together, these rights are known as *civil rights*. Some civil rights were written into the Constitution. Later, amendments to the Constitution were added, increasing the protection of each American's personal freedom.

> In recent years, the term "civil rights" has developed a special meaning. It has become associated with the rights of black Americans and members of other minority groups. The struggles against segregation and for equal voting and employment opportunities are widely known as the *civil rights movement.*

Protection in the Constitution

The original, unamended Constitution ensures a number of civil rights. It:

• Guarantees the right of *habeas corpus* to people who are arrested. Because of this guarantee, a judge must look at the evidence against the accused. Then the judge has to either set a date for the trial or release the accused.

• Guarantees a trial by jury in many criminal cases (but not in impeachments). The authors

of the Constitution thought that trials decided by juries would be fairer than trials involving only a judge's decision.

• Forbids any *bill of attainder*. Such a law punishes a person for a crime without a regular trial.

• Forbids any *ex post facto law*. Such a law allows a person to be punished for an act that was not a crime when it was carried out, but was made so by a later law.

• Forbids any religious requirements for public officeholders.

The original Constitution did not satisfy all citizens of the new nation in 1789. With the memory of British rule fresh in their minds, Americans were fearful of losing their personal freedoms to another strong government. While the Constitution seemed to favor civil rights, it mentioned only a few of them.

Protection Under the Bill of Rights

Some Americans wanted other specific rights and freedoms guaranteed by the Constitution. As a result, Congress passed 12 constitutional amendments and sent the proposed changes to the states. By 1791, the states had ratified the first ten amendments—the Bill of Rights. Of

118

In 1660, Quaker Mary Dyer (center) was convicted and hanged for practicing her religion. The First Amendment was written to prevent repetition of incidents such as this one.

these ten, eight set forth personal and property rights. The other two amendments limit federal power over Americans and state governments.

First Amendment   This amendment guarantees Americans freedom of:

- Religion—the right to practice one's own religion.
- Speech—the right to speak freely, to express one's opinion.
- Press—the right to publish newspapers, books, and magazines without censorship.
- Assembly—the right to meet in public in groups.
- *Petition*—the right to ask the government to make changes.

Second Amendment   This amendment concerns Americans' *right to bear arms* (own weapons). At the time, many Americans needed guns for hunting or for personal protection. Some others belonged to a civilian militia and needed weapons to defend communities.

Third Amendment   Remember that one of the causes of the Revolution had been the British quartering laws. The Third Amendment prevents the quartering of troops in private homes.

Fourth Amendment   This amendment says that government officials can not search people or their homes without reasonable cause.

Fifth Amendment   Part of this amendment guarantees Americans the right to own and keep property. Property can not be taken away unless the government follows proper *procedures* (rules). For instance, the government has to pay people deprived of property money equal to the value of the property.

Fifth Through Eighth Amendments—Due Process   One of the most important principles in the Bill of Rights is *due process of law*. This principle, set out in several amendments, secures to people accused of crimes the right to all of the following:

- Having the help of a lawyer.
- Having a fair trial *without great delay*. (The emphasis here is on a *speedy trial*, a concept not mentioned in the body of the Constitution.)

• Having federal civil cases tried by a jury. (Previously, this right was limited to criminal cases.)

• Calling in witnesses to testify for the defendant.

• Refusing to give testimony that might be damaging to oneself. This practice is sometimes called "taking the Fifth" because it is allowed by the Fifth Amendment.

• Awaiting trial out of jail after payment of a reasonable amount of money. This money is called *bail*. Bail is returned when the defendant appears for trial. Not all defendants are released on bail, however. A judge usually has the power to keep the defendant in jail if he or she has a record of *jumping bail* (paying bail and then not appearing for trial).

• Being protected from cruel and unusual punishment.

• Avoiding *double jeopardy*. This term means being tried again for a crime after already having been found "not guilty."

Ninth Amendment This amendment asserts that Americans have other rights not mentioned in the Constitution or the Bill of Rights. These unstated rights also are protected by the federal government.

Tenth Amendment The last provision of the Bill of Rights limits the power of the federal government. It says that all powers not delegated to the federal government belong to the states or to the American people.

Protection Under Later Amendments

Civil rights have continued to be a major concern in the United States. Americans have used the amending process to give growing numbers of citizens equality under the law. Six amendments mark that progress:

• The Thirteenth Amendment (1865) prohibits slavery.

This illustration appeared in *Harper's Weekly* in November, 1867. What constitutional amendment would later guarantee blacks the right to vote?

• The Fourteenth Amendment (1868) states that all native-born Americans are citizens. It extends the safeguards of due process and "equal protection of the laws" to all Americans, including former slaves.

• The Fifteenth Amendment (1870) guarantees all adult, male American citizens (again including former slaves) the right to vote.

• The Nineteenth Amendment (1920) gives women the right to vote on the same basis as men.

• The Twenty-fourth Amendment (1964) states that no one has to pay a special tax to qualify for voting in a public election.

• The Twenty-sixth Amendment (1971) sets the legal voting age at 18 in all states.

SUMMING UP   We have seen how all Americans are guaranteed certain rights and freedoms. Some of these civil rights were mentioned in the body of the Constitution. The Bill of Rights increased the protections offered to each American's personal freedoms. Additional protection has been provided by six other amendments.

Understanding the Text

On a separate sheet of paper, write the letter of the word or phrase that best completes each of the following statements.

1. *Ex post facto* laws *(a)* protect civil rights *(b)* protect property rights *(c)* are guaranteed by the Bill of Rights *(d)* are unconstitutional.

2. Bills of attainder are often considered unfair because they *(a)* allow people to be punished without a trial *(b)* deprive women of equal rights *(c)* encourage segregation *(d)* make an act illegal "after the fact."

3. The Bill of Rights is best described as *(a)* the complete list of American civil rights *(b)* a general plan of government *(c)* a set of amendments that expands civil rights and limits the powers of government *(d)* an amendment that grants full rights to former slaves.

4. The right to freedom of speech is stated in the *(a)* First Amendment *(b)* Third Amendment *(c)* Ninth Amendment *(d)* Nineteenth Amendment.

5. The Fifth Amendment discusses *(a)* freedom of religion *(b)* the right to own property *(c)* the right of women to vote *(d)* the minimum age for voters in all states.

6. People who "take the Fifth" are refusing to *(a)* put up bail *(b)* say things in court that would make them seem guilty *(c)* accept the help of a lawyer *(d)* pay a poll tax.

7. Under the principle of due process of law, people on trial for crimes have the right to *(a)* choose the judge who will hear their case *(b)* refuse punishment set by the judge *(c)* use all legal procedures that are proper for their defense *(d)* disregard the verdict of the jury.

8. A person who insists on due process is asking for *(a)* trouble *(b)* freedom of speech *(c)* a tax refund *(d)* fair treatment in court trials.

9. The constitutional amendment that ended slavery in the United States was the *(a)* Fourth *(b)* Tenth *(c)* Twelfth *(d)* Thirteenth.

10. Which of the following statements about civil rights is *not* true? *(a)* They have been topics of discussion throughout American history. *(b)* All of these rights that we enjoy today were set down in the original Constitution. *(c)* They are the topic of many constitutional amendments. *(d)* They are of particular importance to minority groups.

Developing Glossary-Reading Skills

Look at the first page of the glossary, on page 621. Then answer the following questions about this page. Choose the letter of the word or phrase that best completes each sentence. On a separate sheet of paper, match the sentence number with the correct letter.

1. A glossary (a) summarizes each lesson (b) lists all of the subjects covered in the text (c) defines important or difficult words (d) introduces the theme of each unit.

2. In a glossary, entries are arranged in (a) the order in which they appear in the text (b) alphabetical order (c) chronological order (d) none of the above.

3. You can use this glossary to look up the meaning of (a) affiliated (b) absentee ballot (c) activist (d) Anglican.

4. "To set free of a charge by being found 'not guilty' " defines the word (a) amend (b) accommodate (c) acquit (d) abolition.

5. In the word "amphibious," the strongest stress or accent is on the (a) first syllable (b) second syllable (c) third syllable (d) fourth syllable.

Thinking About the Lesson

1. Why is it important for people who are arrested to have a trial as soon as possible?

2. Do you think that jury trials are fairer than trials decided by a judge? Why or why not?

3. Do you think that defendants should be allowed to "take the Fifth"? Why or why not?

4. Why did many Americans in 1789 want the Tenth Amendment added to the Constitution?

5. Why do you think that the authors of the Constitution did not give blacks or women the right to vote?

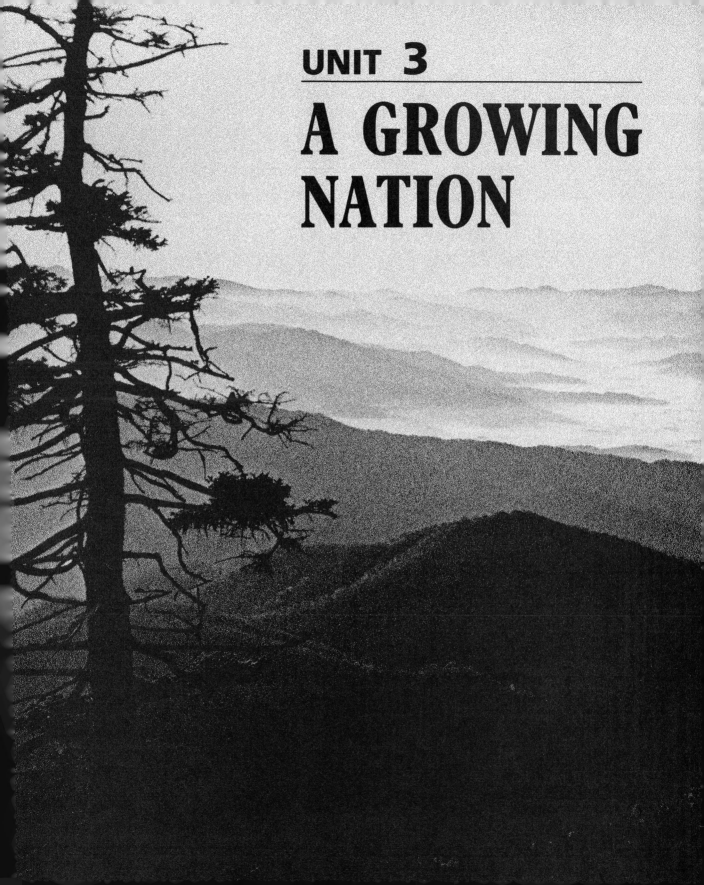

UNIT 3
A GROWING NATION

LESSON 21

The New Nation Takes Shape

Early in 1789, the government outlined by the Constitution began to work. In February, the Electoral College cast ballots for the first U.S. President. Every elector voted for George Washington. As Vice President, they selected another honored leader of the Revolution, John Adams. In March, Congress met for the first time. Then on April 30, George Washington was inaugurated, beginning his first term. All these "firsts" reinforced the belief of many Americans that 1789 was the dawn of a new age.

The New Nation

In 1789, the United States contained only about 4 million people. Most Americans lived along or near the Atlantic coast, and most farmed the land. Only a small number of people worked in factories, such as cotton mills and sugar-refining plants. These two industries, which were growing, received cotton and sugar from Southern plantations, which were also expanding in the late 18th century.

As the country's population grew, many Americans moved west in search of cheap land. At first, Indian groups living in the old Northwest Territory slowed down the westward movement. Then in 1794, General Anthony Wayne defeated an Indian force at the Battle of Fallen

Timbers, in Ohio. The resulting Treaty of Greenville (1795) favored the white settlers at the expense of the Indians. It opened up much land to the settlers and forced many Indians to move farther west.

Early Problems

Cheap land and plenty of job opportunities helped Americans feel confident about the future. Nevertheless, the new country had to face some challenging tasks:

• The lack of good roads and efficient mail service held back economic growth.
• The United States government did not have enough money to carry out all of its duties.
• At first, federal laws, federal law enforcement officers, and federal courts did not exist.
• The new nation was not treated with respect by many foreign nations. (U.S. foreign policy during the Washington administration is discussed in Lesson 22.)

Putting the Nation on Its Feet

The major goals of the new President and Congress were to make the government work and to create a sound economy.

124

Early Congressional Actions The new U.S. Senate and House of Representatives met for the first time in March, 1789. During its first months, Congress created three government departments to help the President—State, Treasury, and War. Congress also set up the offices of Postmaster General and Attorney General. The former was the head of the Post Office, and the latter served as the nation's chief legal officer. Another important step, the Judiciary Act of 1789, established the number of Supreme Court justices and created lower federal courts. Probably as important as any other accomplishment, Congress sent the Bill of Rights to the states for ratification.

Early Presidential Actions During his first year as President, Washington appointed talented

On April 30, 1789, George Washington was inaugurated as the country's first President. The ceremony took place in New York City—the nation's capital at the time.

people to head the executive departments. Fellow Virginian Thomas Jefferson became Secretary of State, while New York lawyer Alexander Hamilton got the Treasury position. Washington also named General Henry Knox as Secretary of War and Edmund Randolph as Attorney General. To head the Supreme Court, the President appointed John Jay, who had been Secretary of State under the Articles of Confederation.

New Precedents Since nearly everything done in this era was a "first," Washington was able to establish *precedents*, guides for future action. Toward the end of his first term, for example, he and the department secretaries began to meet together regularly. The group became known as "the Cabinet." Another example: Washington preferred to be addressed as "Mr. President," rather than as "Your Excellency," a European honorary title.

Financial Measures—Hamilton's Program

Alexander Hamilton, the young and skillful Secretary of the Treasury, had ambitious goals. First, he wanted to honor the *national debt* (money owed by the federal government). Next, he wanted to levy taxes to pay for government operations. Finally, he wanted to organize a sound banking system. After much congressional debate, a great part of Hamilton's program became law.

Honoring the National Debt Both individual states and Congress under the Articles of Confederation had borrowed heavily. Hamilton persuaded the new government to honor these debts. Hamilton's financial plan was expensive and called for borrowing more money. In the end, though, Hamilton was able to strengthen the new nation's *credit* (trust among lenders).

Raising Revenue One way that Hamilton raised money was to place a tax on whiskey made

The first presidential Cabinet included (from left to right after Washington): Henry Knox, Secretary of War; Alexander Hamilton, Secretary of the Treasury; Thomas Jefferson, Secretary of State; and Edmund Randolph, Attorney General.

inside the country. Taxes on domestic goods are called *excise taxes*. The whiskey excise tax was especially unpopular among the Western farmers who made whiskey.

The government also taxed goods made in other countries and brought to America. Congress had voted for a small *tariff* (tax on imported goods) in 1789. The main purpose of this tariff was to raise money. Hamilton, though, wanted a higher tariff. He was interested not only in raising money, but also in making foreign goods more expensive to buy. This *protective tariff* would encourage people to buy cheaper goods made in the United States. Hamilton, however, was not able to get Congress to pass the high tariff that he wanted.

Money and Banking Other proposals that Hamilton made helped set up a sound money and banking system. At Hamilton's urging, Congress set up a federal *mint* (a place where coins are made). Then Congress chartered the Bank of the United States. This bank was privately run, but served the government in

several ways. It issued *bank notes*, which became one of several types of money used by Americans. The bank also had the job of paying the government's bills and storing the government's extra money.

Hamilton's Critics and Supporters

Some Americans complained that Hamilton's program helped mainly the rich and raised everyone's taxes. These critics included Thomas Jefferson, the Secretary of State, and James Madison, a member of the House of Representatives. In their view, the Bank of the United States was unconstitutional. They believed that the Constitution did not clearly allow Congress to create such a bank.

Hamilton's supporters argued that his program would help the U.S. government's credit. An improved credit would give Americans confidence to invest money and to set up businesses. Americans who made such arguments leaned toward a *loose interpretation* of the Constitution.

Although the Bank of the United States was not mentioned in the Constitution, these people said that Congress had the power to create it anyway. Congress got this power, they said, from a clause in the Constitution giving Congress the right to regulate currency. At the time, currency included coins, bank notes, and paper money.

Americans who opposed Hamilton's program believed in a *strict interpretation* of the Constitution. They opposed the bank, for instance, because it was not mentioned in that document. They believed that the government should assume no powers that were not specifically stated in the Constitution.

The Success of Hamilton's Program

Hamilton's financial program was adopted during Washington's first term in office (1789–1793). The program soon began to show good results. Trust of the U.S. government improved among lenders both at home and abroad. As confidence in the new government increased,

businesses began to expand, and trade began to increase. In addition, the new national currency gained widespread acceptance.

Whiskey Rebellion During Washington's administration, the federal government became stronger and more respected. The government demonstrated its power in 1794 when a group of Pennsylvania farmers refused to pay the excise tax on whiskey. Some farmers applied tar and feathers to the tax collectors. The farmers' opposition, the so-called "Whiskey Rebellion," clearly challenged the national government.

Because Pennsylvania officials refused to send aid to the threatened tax collectors, President Washington sent a militia drawn from four states. The rebellious farmers then had to give up their resistance. Some of their leaders were arrested but were later pardoned.

The outcome of the Whiskey Rebellion showed how the government was able to enforce its laws. This new government contrasted greatly with the former, less powerful one under the Articles of Confederation.

Violence erupted in Pennsylvania in 1794. Here angry farmers tar and feather a tax collector and burn his home. (*Granger Collection*)

SUMMING UP   We have seen how economic policies of the Washington administration were shaped by Alexander Hamilton. The talented Secretary of the Treasury got Congress to pass bills that strengthened the country's finances. The new government paid off both federal and state debts. It imposed new taxes, including an excise tax on whiskey. In addition, the government created a mint and the Bank of the United States.

Understanding the Text

On a separate sheet of paper, write the letter of the word or phrase that best completes each of the following statements.

1. In 1789, most American workers were *(a)* bankers *(b)* farmers *(c)* tax collectors *(d)* skilled industrial workers.

2. Which of the following events occurred first? *(a)* the first presidential election *(b)* the Whiskey Rebellion *(c)* the inauguration of George Washington *(d)* the Battle of Fallen Timbers.

3. When Congress met for the first time in early 1789, the nation already had *(a)* good credit *(b)* a national bank *(c)* the respect of most other nations *(d)* a written Constitution.

4. Those who backed the idea of the Bank of the United States *(a)* agreed with Thomas Jefferson on the subject *(b)* favored a strict interpretation of the Constitution *(c)* wanted to give the new government broad economic powers *(d)* were against the growth of industry.

5. Of the following executive departments, the only one *not* established during Washington's administration was the Department of *(a)* Labor *(b)* War *(c)* State *(d)* Treasury.

6. The main purpose of the Tariff of 1789 was to *(a)* regulate trade between the states *(b)* discourage the drinking of whiskey *(c)* raise money for the government *(d)* discourage home manufacturers.

7. One of the main aims of Hamilton's program was to *(a)* encourage people to move west *(b)* improve travel conditions between isolated towns *(c)* win the support of Western farmers *(d)* establish good credit for the United States.

8. Hamilton's program did *not* call for *(a)* excise taxes *(b)* a government-chartered bank *(c)* new paper currency *(d)* giving the states control over all government finances.

9. The Whiskey Rebellion of 1794 was caused by *(a)* a tariff on imports *(b)* an excise tax *(c)* the need for cheap land *(d)* the creation of a mint.

10. Washington's administration is considered of great importance because it *(a)* put down a rebellion by Indians over the excise tax *(b)* used the title "Your Excellency" *(c)* wrote the Constitution of the United States *(d)* did much to get the new government started.

Developing Table-Reading Skills

OUTLAYS OF THE FEDERAL GOVERNMENT, 1792–1796
(In thousands of dollars)

Year	Department of War	Interest on the public debt	Veterans' compensation and pensions	All other	Total
1792	1,101	3,202	109	668	5,080
1793	1,130	2,772	80	500	4,482
1794	2,700	3,490	81	719	6,990
1795	2,892	3,189	69	1,390	7,540
1796	1,535	3,195	101	896	5,727

Study the table above. Then choose the word or phrase that best completes each sentence. On a separate sheet of paper, match the sentence number with the correct letter.

1. The table shows (a) federal income, 1792–1796 (b) federal taxes, 1792–1796 (c) federal expenses, 1792–1796 (d) all of the above.

2. Total federal government outlays in 1796 were (a) $896 (b) $896,000 (c) $5,727 (d) $5,727,000.

3. The only figures in the table that were less in 1794 than in 1792 were (a) Total outlays (b) Department of War outlays (c) Interest on the public debt (d) Veterans' compensation and pensions.

4. In 1795, the largest category of federal outlays shown was (a) Department of War outlays (b) Interest on the public debt (c) Veterans' compensation and pensions (d) Other outlays.

5. Outlays of the Department of War for 1796 were about what percent of the total federal outlay? (Note: To answer this question, you may need to make a mathematical calculation.) (a) 10 percent (b) 26 percent (c) 50 percent (d) 69 percent.

Thinking About the Lesson

1. Briefly explain the following statement, "George Washington was like a sculptor giving shape and form to the new government."

2. List and explain two ways in which Alexander Hamilton hoped to create a sound financial system for the new nation.

3. Imagine that you were a member of Congress who opposed Hamilton's financial program. Provide two reasons why you were critical of his ideas.

4. Do you agree with the view that the Whiskey Rebellion was a major challenge to the new nation? Why or why not?

Early U.S. Foreign Policy

In addition to domestic concerns, the Washington administration faced another set of problems—foreign policy ones. Before 1789, most countries had paid little attention to the United States. Some had taken advantage of its weaknesses. Under George Washington's leadership, however, the new nation began to win the respect of European powers.

The French Revolution

Events in France tested the U.S.-French friendship. Under King Louis XVI, France had become an ally of the United States. In 1778, the French had agreed to assist the colonies in their struggle for independence. In 1789, however, the French people rose up against the monarchy and set up a new government. By 1793, the French revolutionary government was at war with five European nations, including Great Britain. The French wanted the United States to join them in fighting the British.

Division Within the U.S. Government American leaders were divided into two *factions* (opposing groups within a larger organization) on the subject of France. Thomas Jefferson and his followers, the Democratic-Republicans, wanted to keep close ties with France. They

were sympathetic to the goals of the French revolutionaries. Hamilton and his followers, the Federalists, favored Great Britain over France. They condemned the goals and violence of the revolutionaries.

Proclamation of Neutrality In Washington's opinion, the best policy for the nation was to stay out of the European war. He wanted the United States to be neutral—not to ally itself with either side in the conflict. After a long debate, the entire Cabinet agreed to back Washington. In April, 1793, he issued the Proclamation of Neutrality, under which the U.S. stated it would favor neither side. President Washington told the American people to take no warlike actions against either France or Great Britain.

The Genêt Affair

The new French minister to the United States, Edmond Genêt, did not like the Neutrality Proclamation. In 1793, he tried to get some Americans to disobey President Washington's policy. Genêt hired private American ships and sailors, sending them out to sea to attack British warships.

Washington punished Genêt for his actions by having the French government replace the minister. A new French minister, Joseph Fauchet, arrived the next year, in 1794.

Troubles With Great Britain

In addition to its problems with France, the United States had serious difficulties with Great Britain:

• The two nations could not agree on the boundary line between the United States and Canada (then a British colony).

• The British still did not allow the United States to trade with British colonies in the West Indies. (This British policy, begun during the Critical Period, is discussed in Lesson 11.)

• The British wanted the United States to pay debts that went back to the time of the American Revolution. The claims were from British merchants and Loyalists whose properties had been seized by Patriots.

• British warships regularly captured American sailors at sea, claiming that they were deserters from the British navy. Some, but not all, of the captured sailors had served the British. Nevertheless, this British policy, called *impressment* greatly angered Americans.

• American settlers in the Northwest Territory claimed that the British were still urging Indians to attack them.

• The British refused to give up their forts in the Northwest Territory. According to the Peace Treaty of 1783, the British were supposed to have left these forts.

The Jay Treaty

In 1794, President Washington sent John Jay to London to settle the U.S.-British disputes. Jay, the Chief Justice of the United States, worked hard to get what he wanted. But the Jay Treaty met only some of the complaints made by the U.S. government:

• Great Britain gave up its forts in the Northwest Territory.

• The United States got limited trading rights in the British West Indies.

Problems With the Treaty The Jay Treaty was unpopular. It left some problems unsolved. For

Many Americans were shocked by events of the French Revolution. King Louis XVI (shown) was only one of thousands of French people who were beheaded by the *guillotine*—the device in the picture.

Americans were angered by the Jay Treaty. They considered it to be a sellout to the British. Here John Jay is *burned in effigy* (the likeness of someone displayed and burned). (*Granger Collection*)

instance, parts of the boundary between Canada and the United States were not set. (See the map on page 56.) Nor was the problem of impressment of American sailors settled. Many Americans strongly criticized Washington and Jay for negotiating the treaty.

Defenders of the treaty said that it was the best deal that the United States could get at the time. They said that the new nation was too weak to fight with Great Britain over the matters left unsettled. After a heated debate in the Senate, the treaty was finally ratified in 1795.

Agreement With Spain—The Pinckney Treaty

Spain had vast lands in North America, lying west and south of the United States. (See the map on page 56.) The Spanish government began to worry that it could not keep control of these lands from its rival—Great Britain. Because of these holdings, Spain feared the terms of the Jay Treaty. Would the treaty bring the British and the Americans closer together? Would the two countries work against Spain's interests in North America?

Because of these fears, Spain in 1795 signed an agreement with the United States called the Pinckney Treaty. Thomas Pinckney, the U.S. minister to Great Britain, had negotiated the agreement. The treaty settled three matters:

• The two nations agreed on the disputed northern boundary of Spanish Florida. (See the map on page 147.)

• Spain gave U.S. traders free use of the Mississippi River. American traders could now bring their goods down the Mississippi River to New Orleans.

• Spain also gave U.S. traders the right of deposit at New Orleans. There they could transfer their goods to ships that sailed the oceans.

Western settlers liked the treaty's last two points the best. Now, they hoped, their trade within the United States and with Europe would improve.

Washington's Farewell Advice

After two terms as President, a weary Washington decided not to run again. In 1796, he wrote a Farewell Address which contained some important advice about the future of American foreign policy. (Washington's Address appears on page 134.) Washington urged Americans to be friendly with all nations, but he warned them against making permanent *alliances* (associations of allies). He also advised that the U.S. keep out of the domestic affairs of other nations. A general term for this foreign policy is *isolationism* (remaining isolated or apart).

His advice did not surprise many people, for Washington as President had followed the same principles. Most Americans took Washington's advice seriously. His views became the basis for United States foreign policy for some time.

SUMMING UP We have seen how the Washington administration handled several important and controversial foreign policy issues. It steered clear of taking sides in the war between France and Great Britain. It got the British to settle some of the long-standing U.S. complaints against Great Britain. It successfully worked out disputes with Spain over the Florida border and trade rights on the Mississippi. By its actions in these matters, the United States earned more respect from other nations.

Understanding the Text

On a separate sheet of paper, write the letter of the word or phrase that best completes each of the following statements.

1. The word "neutrality" can best be defined as *(a)* having nothing to do with foreign nations *(b)* building a strong army and navy *(c)* failing to protect the national interests *(d)* favoring neither side in a war.

2. France and the United States entered into their treaty of alliance *(a)* during the American Revolution *(b)* during the French Revolution *(c)* early in the Colonial Period *(d)* during the Critical Period.

3. Washington issued his Proclamation of Neutrality because of *(a)* the Genêt Affair *(b)* the outbreak of war between France and Great Britain *(c)* the impressment of American sailors *(d)* the rivalry between Great Britain and Spain.

4. Most Federalists in 1793 supported *(a)* Spanish control of the Mississippi *(b)* neutrality *(c)* close ties with France *(d)* close ties with Great Britain.

5. The French minister to the United States who hired American ships and sailors to attack British ships was *(a)* Thomas Pinckney *(b)* Joseph Fauchet *(c)* Edmond Genêt *(d)* John Jay.

6. The people who overthrew their king and government in 1789 were the *(a)* British *(b)* French *(c)* Spanish *(d)* Canadians.

7. The Jay Treaty settled the problems of *(a)* British forts in the Northwest Territory *(b)* the northern boundary of Spanish Florida *(c)* the impressment of American sailors *(d)* the boundary between Canada and the United States.

8. For people in the United States in the 1790s, the issue of the right of deposit involved *(a)* Newfoundland *(b)* New Orleans *(c)* the Northwest Territory *(d)* the West Indies.

9. The terms of the Pinckney Treaty gave Americans in the West greater opportunities to *(a)* engage in trade *(b)* aid the British *(c)* join political parties *(d)* resist Indian attacks.

10. President Washington's foreign policy was designed to *(a)* favor Great Britain *(b)* help French revolutionaries *(c)* expand the size of the United States *(d)* protect the interests of the United States while avoiding a war.

Developing Reading Comprehension Skills

Read the following *paraphrased* (restated) summary of Washington's Farewell Address.

A free people should always be on guard against the false dealings of foreign governments. History and experience prove that foreign influence is one of the biggest dangers to republican government.

We should extend our commerce with foreign nations but have as little political connection with them as possible. Let us live up to agreements that we have already made with them. But as of now, let us make no more agreements. Europe has important interests that are a frequent cause of controversy. They are no concern of ours. It would be unwise for us to involve ourselves in European friendships and hatreds.

The United States is far away from Europe. This can help us follow a different course. If we remain united under an efficient government, the warring nations will come to respect our decision to remain neutral. They will not try to involve us in dangerous affairs as long as we are free to choose peace or war.

And why should we involve our future with that of Europe? Why should our peace and prosperity depend on European hopes or rivalries?

Our true policy is to steer clear of permanent alliances with any part of the foreign world, as much as we are able to do so.

I recommend friendship and trade with all nations, but we should have no favorites, even in our commercial policy.

Choose the letter of the word or phrase that best completes each sentence. On a separate sheet of paper, match the sentence number with the correct letter.

1. In Washington's opinion, the nations of Europe were (*a*) too weak to influence American foreign policy (*b*) good models for the United States to follow (*c*) not trustworthy (*d*) united by a common purpose.

2. Washington thought that new political alliances with foreign countries (*a*) should be avoided (*b*) were a necessary evil (*c*) would strengthen the United States (*d*) would guarantee a peaceful future.

3. According to the Farewell Address, one thing that would help the United States maintain its neutrality in world affairs was (*a*) its republican form of government (*b*) its distance from Europe (*c*) the hopes and rivalries of European nations (*d*) permanent alliances.

4. When Washington recommended a foreign policy free from permanent alliances, he meant that (*a*) there should be no new trade agreements (*b*) the terms of past treaties should be ignored (*c*) Americans should not debate foreign policy (*d*) there should be no new political agreements with foreign nations.

5. Of the following words, the one that does *not* belong with the other three is (*a*) alliance (*b*) treaty (*c*) isolationism (*d*) agreement.

Thinking About the Lesson

1. If you had been a member of Washington's Cabinet in 1793, which one of the following would you have supported? (*a*) close ties with France (*b*) close ties with Great Britain (*c*) neutrality. Explain your answer.

2. U.S. troubles with three European nations are mentioned in this lesson. In your opinion, which nation's actions posed the greatest problem for the United States? Explain your answer.

The Birth of Political Parties

Americans often take their political party system for granted. Actually, political parties have not always been part of the country's political process. In fact, parties were formed only partway through Washington's administration. They developed because of opposition to certain government policies. In particular, the Hamilton financial program and the Jay Treaty caused Americans to divide into two well-defined political groups.

Washington's Views on Political Parties

George Washington did not trust political parties. In his view, parties weakened the country in the following ways:

• They provoked *sectionalism*—that is, rivalries among different sections or regions of the country.

• They stirred up disagreements within communities.

• They led to disorders, and even rebellions.

• They spread false information in their attempts to win elections.

• They encouraged foreign nations to interfere in America's political life.

Many Americans agreed with Washington's views on political parties. Nevertheless, differ-

ing views among Americans on key economic and foreign issues of his administration led to the creation of these parties.

The First Political Parties

During Washington's administration, the first political parties in U.S. history emerged—the Federalists and Democratic-Republicans. They became strong rivals for national leadership.

The Federalists Federalist leaders, such as John Adams and Alexander Hamilton, believed in a strong national government. They hoped to keep it strong through a loose interpretation of the Constitution. (Discussed earlier on page 126.) Many Federalists also believed that only people of the upper classes should lead the nation. They did not want to share power with the poor or the uneducated.

Federalist policies were *conservative*. This label refers to the Federalists' great respect for tradition or doing things in old and familiar ways. Change was to come about calmly and gradually. Thus, while the Federalists admired the government of Great Britain, they feared the revolutionary one in France.

In financial matters, the Federalists supported Hamilton's program. They favored the creation of the Bank of the United States and other measures to help trade and manufacturing grow.

135

Not surprisingly, Federalists were strongest in the Northeastern part of the country, where industry and trade were concentrated.

The Federalists dominated the Cabinet and U.S. Senate from 1789 to 1801. Yet they did not have control of the Presidency until 1797—at least not in name. George Washington shared many views with the Federalists, but he did not belong to any political party. Technically, then, it was with the election of John Adams in 1796 that the nation got its first Federalist President.

Today's Republican party is sometimes viewed as a modern version of the Federalist party. Actually, the Federalists began to fade in strength early in the 1800s and ceased to exist by the late 1820s. The modern Republican party was formed many years later—in the 1850s.

The Democratic-Republicans   The Democratic-Republicans, led by Thomas Jefferson and James Madison, disagreed with the Federalists on many points. They served as the opposition party when the Federalists were in power. The program of the Democratic-Republicans, as it took shape between 1792 and 1801, included the following ideas:

• They wanted to limit the powers of the federal government through a strict interpretation of the Constitution. (Discussed earlier on page 127.)

• They favored greater power in the hands of the states, local governments, and the people.

• They opposed Hamilton's financial program, because they believed that it favored the rich.

• They claimed to speak for the interests of farmers and other working people. In fact, much of their support did come from the agricultural areas of the South and West.

• They distrusted Great Britain and favored revolutionary France.

(Top) Thomas Jefferson; (bottom) Alexander Hamilton

The strength of the Democratic-Republicans grew gradually. They gained control of the House of Representatives in 1792, only to lose that control in the elections of 1794. In 1796, a Democratic-Republican leader, Thomas Jefferson, captured the Vice Presidency, serving alongside the Federalist President John Adams. Jefferson's position in government helped the Democratic-Republicans act in their role of the vocal opposition party.

By 1801, the Democratic-Republicans were no longer the opposition. In that year, they took control of Congress, and Jefferson became the third U.S. President. He was followed into the White House by two more members of his party. For a while, members of the Democratic-Republicans wished to be known as just "Republicans." After a few decades, the party broke up into several factions. One of these, the Democrats, became the party that is still known by that name.

Two-Party System

The United States today has a *two-party system*. Each of the two major parties—the Democrats and the Republicans—represents a fairly wide range of political views. Often one party or the other gains a majority of the Electoral College. This same party may or may not gain control of one or both houses of Congress. One party may be the weaker of the two for a number of years and then become the stronger party. Differences between the parties have never been great enough to prevent them from working together in government. Even when one party takes over power from the other, the government runs smoothly.

The two-party system also includes a number of minor parties, known as *third parties*. Usually, third parties do not win major elections, but they may do well in regions of the country. Members of third parties often disagree with the views of both major parties. In time, the major parties might adopt some of the ideas of the third parties and make them into law. The federal income tax for example came about this way.

While the United States has two major parties, some democratic nations have many. In *multiparty systems*, each party represents the views of a segment of the population. Often no one party gains the support of the majority of the nation's voters. In such a situation, several political parties get together in a *coalition* (temporary alliance) to run the government.

SUMMING UP   We have seen that two political parties developed in the United States despite President Washington's misgivings. The Federalists, who dominated the government during the 1790s, favored policies that helped trade and industry. The Democratic-Republicans served as the opposition party. They favored the agricultural interests in the new nation. Although the names of the parties have changed over the years, the United States still has a two-party system.

Understanding the Text

On a separate sheet of paper, write the letter of the word or phrase that best completes each of the following statements.

1. President George Washington was against political parties because he thought that they (*a*) cost too much (*b*) tended to break up the nation's unity (*c*) might change the United States into a monarchy (*d*) would favor bankers and businesspeople.

2. American political parties first developed during the (*a*) Colonial Period (*b*) Revolution (*c*) Critical Period (*d*) administration of George Washington.

3. The Federalists supported (*a*) Hamilton's financial program (*b*) the interests of states over the interests of the federal government (*c*) the French Revolution (*d*) the right of the common people to run the government.

4. Of the following words or phrases, the one that does *not* belong with the other three is (*a*) gradual change (*b*) traditional (*c*) revolutionary (*d*) conservative.

5. The Federalist party (*a*) came to an end in the 19th century (*b*) came to an end in the 20th century (*c*) still exists as the Republican party (*d*) still exists as the Democratic party.

6. Two Americans who opposed the program of the Federalists were (*a*) Jefferson and Hamilton (*b*) Jefferson and Madison (*c*) Madison and Adams (*d*) Adams and Jay.

7. Both major political parties in the United States today (*a*) were created in the 20th century (*b*) consist of members of just one major religion (*c*) are not worried about winning elections (*d*) bring together many different groups and ideas.

8. A two-party system is (*a*) found in all democracies (*b*) common in dictatorships (*c*) well established in the United States (*d*) described in Article II of the U.S. Constitution.

9. In 1800, the agricultural interests of the nation were most clearly represented by the (*a*) Democratic-Republicans (*b*) Federalists (*c*) Whigs (*d*) none of the above.

10. A reason why political parties have become an important part of the political system is that (*a*) they are required by the U.S. Constitution (*b*) they are required by state constitutions (*c*) they have helped Americans choose their leaders and shape public policies (*d*) they were strongly supported by George Washington.

Developing Graph-Reading Skills

Examine the bar graph on page 139. Then choose the letter of the word or phrase that best completes each sentence. On a separate sheet of paper, match the sentence number with the correct letter.

1. The graph depicts political party strength, 1789–1807, in the (*a*) U.S. Senate (*b*) U.S. House of Representatives (*c*) Electoral College (*d*) state legislatures.

2. In the Second Congress, the political party that had the most seats in the Senate was the (*a*) Republican (*b*) Democrat (*c*) Democratic-Republican (*d*) Federalist.

3. The Democratic-Republicans had their largest majority during the years (*a*) 1789–1791 (*b*) 1797–1799 (*c*) 1801–1803 (*d*) 1805–1807.

4. The political makeup of the U.S. Senate was the same in the (*a*) First and Second Congresses (*b*) Fourth and Sixth Congresses (*c*) Fifth and Sixth Congresses (*d*) Third and Seventh Congresses.

5. The Federalists lost their majority in the Senate in the year (*a*) 1791 (*b*) 1801 (*c*) 1803 (*d*) none of the above.

Thinking About the Lesson

1. Conservatives today are critical of a strong federal government that might limit the rights of states and individuals. How do the views of modern conservatives compare with those of the Federalists in the late 1790s?

2. How do the views of modern conservatives compare with those of Jefferson's Democratic-Republicans?

3. Some students of government believe that a two-party system is the best political plan for running a democratic government such as the United States. Do you agree with this view? Why or why not?

POLITICAL PARTIES IN THE U.S. SENATE, 1789–1807

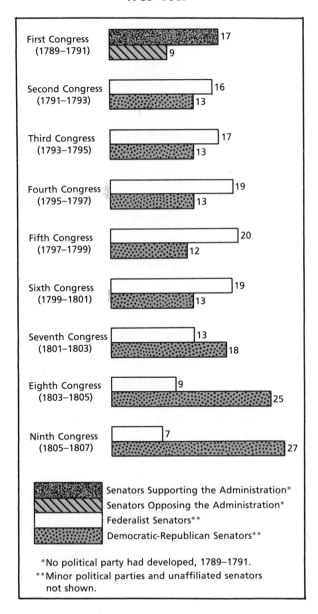

First Congress (1789–1791): 17 / 9

Second Congress (1791–1793): 16 / 13

Third Congress (1793–1795): 17 / 13

Fourth Congress (1795–1797): 19 / 13

Fifth Congress (1797–1799): 20 / 12

Sixth Congress (1799–1801): 19 / 13

Seventh Congress (1801–1803): 13 / 18

Eighth Congress (1803–1805): 9 / 25

Ninth Congress (1805–1807): 7 / 27

Senators Supporting the Administration*
Senators Opposing the Administration*
Federalist Senators**
Democratic-Republican Senators**

*No political party had developed, 1789–1791.
**Minor political parties and unaffiliated senators not shown.

John Adams and the Federalists

John Adams served as the country's second President from 1797 to 1801. His term in office was marked by a growing fight between his party, the Federalists, and the Democratic-Republicans. Adams's work was made more difficult by the fact that his Vice President was Thomas Jefferson. Jefferson was a member of the Republican party, as the Democratic-Republicans were now called.

Trouble With France

In 1797, France and England were still at war in Europe. During the war, the French had been attacking American ships that were carrying goods to England. For this reason, the United States was finding it harder and harder to remain neutral.

The XYZ Affair In 1797, President Adams sent three special ambassadors to Paris to discuss U.S. rights as a neutral. Three French agents, known as "X, Y, and Z," met them there. Soon the French agents insulted the American ambassadors. They demanded of the Americans a secret payment of money as the price of French cooperation.

The U.S. representatives refused to pay the money and told President Adams about the

matter. When news of the XYZ Affair was made public in 1798, many Americans became angry. A new national slogan arose—"Millions for defense, but not one cent for tribute." Some Americans said that they would go to war rather than pay France any money.

Unofficial Fighting For the next two years, as relations with France grew worse, Adams took steps to build up the U.S. Army. In addition, he created the Navy Department and the Marine Corps. Although war was not officially declared, fighting broke out at sea. American ships captured some 80 French vessels.

During this same time, President Adams worked for peace. In 1800, his efforts paid off. In that year, Napoleon Bonaparte, the new ruler of France, agreed to stop French attacks on American ships.

The Alien and Sedition Acts

Talk about war with France was strong during the Adams administration. Many Federalists wanted to go to war, while many Republicans opposed the idea. Some Federalists worried that French secret agents might be influencing the government's policies. In 1798, the Federalists got Congress to pass four acts directed against

140

Because France interfered with American commerce, the United States and France engaged in an unofficial naval war. Here an American vessel is defeating a French one.

both foreign agents and Adams's domestic critics. Collectively, the laws were known as the Alien and Sedition Acts.

The first act dealt with *aliens* (foreign-born persons who have not become citizens). The act required aliens to live in America for at least 14 years before applying for citizenship. Previously, aliens had to wait only five years.

Two more acts gave the President the power to deal with "dangerous" aliens. During peacetime, the President could *deport* (send back) these aliens to their country of birth. During a war, the President could either deport or jail the aliens.

A fourth act, the Sedition Act, called for the arrest or fining of citizens who violated the act. Violations included openly criticizing the government, opposing attempts to carry out the law, and attempting to rebel against the United States government.

The Federalists believed that the Alien and Sedition Acts would help their party in the following ways:

• Immigrants would have to wait much longer to become citizens and voters. Since most immigrants voted for the Republicans, this requirement would slow the growth of this party.

• Criticism of the President and Congress would be discouraged. At the time, both branches of government were controlled by the Federalists. Therefore, the Federalists believed, the acts would let them govern with less trouble.

Ten persons—mostly Republicans who worked for newspapers—went to jail or paid fines under the Sedition Act. However, many more Republicans feared being arrested under provisions of this law. The Alien and Sedition Acts became unpopular not only with Republicans, but also with the public at large. Opponents of the acts felt that they were unnecessary, despotic, and unconstitutional. After a few years, all four acts were either repealed or allowed to expire.

The Virginia and Kentucky Resolutions

In 1798 and 1799, the legislatures of Virginia and Kentucky passed resolutions critical of the Alien and Sedition Acts. Thomas Jefferson and James Madison gave prestige to the resolutions by helping to write them. They claimed that the federal government had no right to pass the Alien and Sedition Acts.

The Virginia and Kentucky Resolutions, however, did much more than criticize federal actions. The resolutions claimed the right of states to decide whether or not all acts of Congress were constitutional. But what if a state found a federal law to be unconstitutional? Then, the Kentucky Resolution said, the people of that state could rightfully refuse to obey that law. Such use of state power is called *nullification*. According to the Kentucky Resolution, a majority of the states would have to approve nullification for a law to be canceled.

Jefferson and Madison tried to persuade other states to support the Virginia and Kentucky resolutions. But they had little success. Nor did Virginia and Kentucky actually take steps to nullify the Alien and Sedition Acts. Nevertheless, the resolutions were important in at least one way. They showed how strongly some Americans disliked the Alien and Sedition Acts.

End of the Federalist Era

The Federalists, who had held power during the first 12 years of the government, served their country well:

- They started the U.S. government working.
- They created a sound financial system.
- They helped the economy develop.
- They showed that the federal government had the will and the ability to enforce its laws.
- They helped the country gain the respect of foreign nations.
- They kept the country out of wars then raging in Europe.

The Federalists did well in the congressional elections of 1798. Their success was due to Adams's handling of the XYZ Affair and his plans for building up the country's armed forces.

By 1800, however, Federalists were slipping in popularity. Many Americans objected to the Alien and Sedition Acts, which the Republicans

John Adams was the country's second President. His earlier career included negotiating the Paris Peace Treaty of 1783 and serving as U.S. minister to Great Britain, 1785–1788.

blamed on the Federalists. Increasing numbers of Americans opposed the Federalist idea of a government led by men from the upper classes only. Then, too, there was a split in the Federalist party over Adams's foreign policy. A strong faction, led by Alexander Hamilton, criticized Adams for not going to war with the French.

In the election of 1800, John Adams again ran for President against Thomas Jefferson. This time Jefferson, the Republican candidate, won the Presidency. The Republicans also won majorities in both houses of Congress. Jefferson and others thought that this election was so important that they called it the "Revolution of 1800." For the first time, the federal government went through a change in party control. Significant for the country was the fact that this changeover took place peacefully.

SUMMING UP   We have seen how the major events of the John Adams administration concerned America's relations with France. Americans rallied behind their government's handling of the XYZ Affair. Adams prepared the country for war with France but, in the end, avoided it. Without the strong feelings Americans had about going to war, the Alien and Sedition Acts would never have been enacted. The Virginia and Kentucky Resolutions were passed in reaction to these acts.

Understanding the Text

On a separate sheet of paper, write the letter of the word or phrase that best completes each of the following statements.

1. Thomas Jefferson was elected in 1796 as the (*a*) Federalist Vice President (*b*) Republican Vice President (*c*) Federalist President (*d*) Republican President.

2. The United States regarded French attacks on its ships as a violation of (*a*) states' rights (*b*) civil rights (*c*) religious freedoms (*d*) neutrality rights.

3. The XYZ Affair led to (*a*) improved relations between France and the United States (*b*) a declaration of war with France (*c*) the arrest of the French agents "X, Y, and Z" (*d*) anger toward France in the United States.

4. Leading opponents of the Alien and Sedition Acts were (*a*) Jefferson and Madison (*b*) Jefferson and Adams (*c*) Adams and Madison (*d*) Adams and Hamilton.

5. The Alien Acts did all of the following, *except* (*a*) make it more difficult for aliens to become citizens (*b*) allow the President to jail dangerous aliens during peacetime (*c*) allow the President to deport dangerous aliens during peacetime (*d*) allow the President to jail dangerous aliens during wartime.

6. The Sedition Act aimed to (*a*) give the President more power over Congress (*b*) increase immigration (*c*) protect Americans' civil rights (*d*) decrease the constant criticism of the administration.

7. If states declare a federal law unconstitutional, they are using the principle of (*a*) naturalization (*b*) neutrality (*c*) nullification (*d*) sedition.

8. Of the following events, the one that took place first was (*a*) the XYZ Affair (*b*) Adams's election as President (*c*) Jefferson's election as President (*d*) passage of the Virginia and Kentucky Resolutions.

9. The "Revolution of 1800" refers to the (*a*) Republican protests against restrictive federal laws (*b*) Federalist victory over the Republicans in elections (*c*) Republican victory over the Federalists in elections (*d*) Virginia and Kentucky Resolutions.

10. One Republican charge against the Federalists in the election of 1800 was that they (*a*) led the country into a declared war with France (*b*) failed to solve the XYZ Affair (*c*) were responsible for the Alien and Sedition Acts (*d*) were responsible for the Virginia and Kentucky Resolutions.

Developing Encyclopedia Skills

Read the following article from *The World Book Encyclopedia*, 1985 edition. Also take a look at the accompanying drawing of a set of encyclopedias. Then choose the letter of the word or phrase that best answers the following questions. On a separate sheet of paper, match the sentence number with the correct letter.

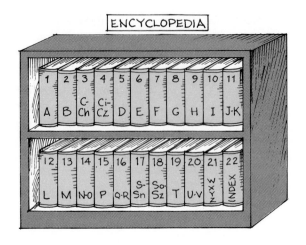

XYZ AFFAIR was the name given to an exchange of diplomatic proposals between France and the United States. In 1798, relations between the governments of the United States and France were strained. The French government grew bitter because the United States refused to help France in its war against Great Britain. French leaders became furious when the United States signed the Jay Treaty with Great Britain in 1794. This treaty brought to a peaceful settlement various American-British problems which arose from boundary and trade disputes. The angry French seized cargoes from United States ships, and forced United States seamen to serve on French vessels. The Directory then governing France refused to receive the U.S. Minister, General Charles Cotesworth Pinckney, whom President George Washington had appointed.

The next President, John Adams, had no desire to declare war on France. So he sent three special ambassadors to France to seek a peaceful settlement. The ambassadors were Pinckney, John Marshall, and Elbridge Gerry. The French Foreign Minister, Prince Talleyrand, stalled the discussions for some weeks. Then he appointed three agents to deal with the Americans. The agents insulted the Americans with various dishonorable proposals. One proposal demanded a loan for France and a large gift, or bribe, for Talleyrand. Another required payment for certain critical remarks that President Adams had made to Congress about France.

When asked for his reply, Ambassador Pinckney said, "It is No! No! Not a sixpence." The slogan "Millions for defense, but not one cent for tribute" is often credited to Pinckney. It was actually written by Robert Goodloe Harper in a magazine article.

President Adams made an official report of these proposals to the United States Congress. He did not name Talleyrand's agents, but simply referred to them as X, Y, and Z. President Adams told Congress: "I will never send another minister to France without assurance that he will be received, respected, and honored as the representative of a great, free, powerful, and independent nation."

The United States did not declare war on France, but did take steps to raise an army. American privateers received permission to attack armed French vessels. The XYZ Affair aroused indignation among citizens of both France and the United States. In 1800, a second American commission arranged for a friendly settlement with France.   EUGENE C. BARKER

See also ADAMS, JOHN (Difficulties with France); GERRY, ELBRIDGE; MARSHALL, JOHN; PINCKNEY (Charles Cotesworth); TALLEYRAND.

From *The World Book Encyclopedia*, ©1985 World Book, Inc. By permission of World Book, Inc.

1. According to the article, what were the names of the three special United States ambassadors that the President sent to France in 1797? *(a)* X, Y, and Z *(b)* Washington, Adams, and Pinckney *(c)* Pinckney, Marshall, and Gerry *(d)* Talleyrand, Adams, and Washington.

2. From which volume did the article on the XYZ Affair come? *(a)* 1st *(b)* 14th *(c)* 21st *(d)* 22nd.

3. Additional articles that give information on the XYZ Affair can be found in all of the following volumes, *except* which one? *(a)* 1st *(b)* 6th *(c)* 8th *(d)* 13th.

4. In which volume of the encyclopedia can one find a biography of John Adams? *(a)* 1st *(b)* 11th *(c)* 15th *(d)* 22nd.

5. In which volume would one look for a list of all the encyclopedia articles on almost any subject? *(a)* 11th *(b)* 15th *(c)* 22nd *(d)* none of the above.

Thinking About the Lesson

1. Do you think that John Adams was as popular a President as George Washington had been? Why or why not?

2. Do you think that President Adams handled the XYZ Affair in the correct way? Explain your answer.

3. Defend or criticize the statement, "The Alien and Sedition Acts would never be passed by Congress today!"

4. Do you think that states should have the right to nullify federal laws if they believe the laws are unconstitutional? Why or why not?

LESSON 25

Thomas Jefferson and the Growth of the Republic

Thomas Jefferson was one of the nation's truly gifted leaders. Before becoming President in 1801, he had been a lawyer, politician, author of the Declaration of Independence, and diplomat. He had also helped to organize the Democratic-Republican party. For his many contributions to the growth of the American Republic, Jefferson ranks as one of our greatest Presidents.

Jeffersonian Democracy

Unlike most Federalists, Jefferson had faith in the abilities of the common people, particularly small farmers. He believed that a central government was necessary. Nevertheless, he said that there should be as few federal controls over the states and the economy as possible.

Civil Rights Jefferson's belief in individual rights, including the right to criticize the government, guided many of his actions as President. In 1802, he signed the repeal of the first of the Alien and Sedition Acts. Once again the waiting period for immigrants who wished to become citizens was only five years. Jefferson also opposed the renewal of the rest of the Alien and Sedition Acts.

Simplicity Jefferson had simple tastes, which his election to the Presidency did not change. He put an end to fancy and expensive government ceremonies. By living without show, he made ordinary people feel closer to the federal government.

Moderate Change and Economy Much as he was a scholar and thinker, Jefferson was also a practical politician. As he had promised to do, he reversed a number of Federalist policies. Then he surprised both his supporters and opponents by keeping parts of Hamilton's financial program, including the Bank of the United States. Moreover, many Federalists were allowed to keep their government jobs after Jefferson assumed office. Other government jobs, however, were filled by Republican supporters of Jefferson.

During his first administration, Jefferson and his Secretary of the Treasury, Albert Gallatin, cut naval and other expenses. This practice was in line with the Republicans' desire to reduce the national debt. Jefferson also got Congress to put an end to a number of hated excise taxes.

During Jefferson's second administration, however, some of these policies were reversed.

146

For instance, certain excise taxes were passed into law again to pay for expanding the nation's navy. This action was thought to be necessary because of growing troubles with France and Great Britain.

A Strong Supreme Court   John Marshall became Chief Justice of the United States in 1801, just before Jefferson was sworn in as President. Under Marshall, the Supreme Court asserted its powers to rule on actions of the states. (Discussed in Lesson 27.) In addition, it declared that it had the right to decide whether or not a federal law was constitutional. This assertion of the power of judicial review was part of Marshall's decision in the famous case of 1803—*Marbury* v. *Madison*.

The Louisiana Purchase

Jefferson's greatest deed as President was to purchase the Territory of Louisiana. Buying this huge piece of land doubled the size of the United States. (See the map below.)

Background of the Purchase   Near the end of the French and Indian War in 1762, France had turned over Louisiana to Spain. Spain made it difficult for U.S. traders to use the Mississippi River. Then in 1795, representatives of Spain and the United States signed the Pinckney Treaty. For a while, Americans enjoyed free use of the Mississippi River and the port of New Orleans. Suddenly in 1800, Spain returned Louisiana to France. When Jefferson learned of

THE LOUISIANA PURCHASE

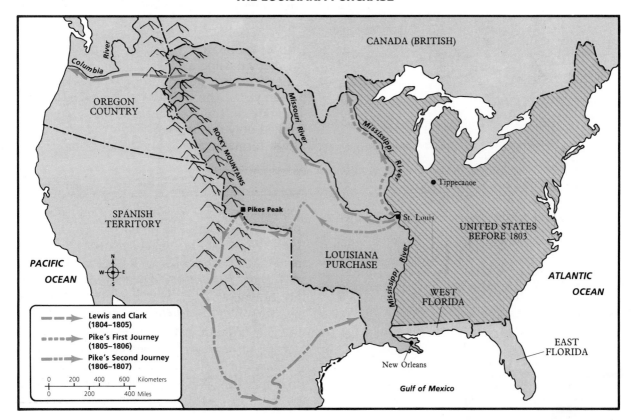

the transfer, he feared that France would again close the Mississippi to Americans.

The Purchase Is Made In 1803, Jefferson sent James Monroe to France to join Robert Livingston, the U.S. minister there. The President told the two men to make a small offer to buy the port of New Orleans and West Florida. Moreover, they were to ask France to grant rights of free *navigation* (ship traffic) on the Mississippi.

The French surprised the Americans by offering them *all* of Louisiana Territory—including New Orleans—for only $15 million. Congress and the President quickly accepted the French offer. The dollar in 1803 was worth much more than it is now. (Fifteen million dollars in 1803 currency equals about a billion dollars today.) Even so, the purchase was a bargain.

In 1791, Toussaint L'Ouverture led a slave revolt in the French colony of Haiti. L'Ouverture effectively ruled this Caribbean island from 1801 to 1802.

Why Napoleon Sold Louisiana The French ruler had several reasons for selling Louisiana Territory. Napoleon was losing control of his empire in the New World. Haiti, in the Caribbean Sea, had recently broken away from France. Moreover, France badly needed money to resume its war against Great Britain. Furthermore, if there was to be a war in Europe, France could not spare many troops or ships in the New World. Why not sell the land to the Americans rather than lose it to the British?

By buying Louisiana, Jefferson proved how practical he could be. He moved quickly to take advantage of a great opportunity, even though his act went against his political ideals:

• At this time, Jefferson was trying hard to lower the national debt. The purchase of Louisiana, however, would lead to a big increase in this debt.

• According to a strict interpretation of the Constitution, the country could gain territory only by passing an amendment. The amendment process, though, could take months or even years. The United States needed to act quickly on the French offer. Thus, Jefferson asked only the Senate to approve the treaty that formalized the Louisiana Purchase.

Importance of the Louisiana Purchase The purchase of Louisiana doubled the size of the United States and gave the country full control over the Mississippi River. Americans felt proud that their nation was expanding. Westerners were particularly grateful to the federal government for acting in their best interests. In years to come, Americans discovered incredibly rich natural resources in the region purchased from France. Its forests, water supplies, oil, coal, copper, silver, and gold all helped the new republic to grow wealthier and more powerful.

Americans in 1803 did not give much thought to the views and feelings of Indians in Louisiana Territory. Most Americans saw the West as so vast that there would always be room for everyone there. Few believed that settlers would eventually take over most Indian lands west of the Mississippi.

The struggle for land was still going on east of the Mississippi, in the old Northwest Territory. In the early 19th century, two Shawnee brothers, Tecumseh and the Prophet, toured various Indian tribes there. They urged their fellow Indians to cease giving up land to whites. As a result of their efforts, several tribes formed an Indian confederation to resist pressure from white settlers. In 1811, the governor of Indiana Territory, General William Henry Harrison, led a large military force against these Indians. At Tippecanoe Creek (Tecumseh's village), the soldiers routed the Indians and destroyed their homes. Tecumseh, though, was not there. He and many other Indians continued their fight, sometimes with British aid and encouragement.

Exploration of the Louisiana Territory

In 1804, Jefferson sent Meriwether Lewis and William Clark to explore the northwestern part of Louisiana. By 1805, they had crossed the Rocky Mountains and come within view of the Pacific Ocean. At about the same time, Zebulon Pike explored the southwestern part of Louisiana Territory. Among other sights, Pike saw a large mountain in Colorado—later named Pikes Peak. (See the map on page 147.)

The Lewis and Clark expedition strengthened U.S. claims to Oregon Country, vast lands northwest of Louisiana Territory. Lewis, Clark, and Pike paved the way for later expeditions. Encouraged by reports of these and other explorers, Americans moved westward into the newly acquired lands.

Here the Indian interpreter Sacagawea shows Lewis and Clark a way through the Rocky Mountains in their search for a route to the Pacific Ocean. As a young girl, she had been separated from her tribe—the Shoshone. On the expedition, however, Sacagawea came upon a Shoshone camp where she was reunited with her brother, now a chief.

SUMMING UP   We have seen how Thomas Jefferson, President from 1801 to 1809, continued to be concerned about civil rights. In financial matters, he introduced new ideas but also continued many of Alexander Hamilton's programs. The purchase of Louisiana was the most important accomplishment of Jefferson's administration. When he bought this large piece of land, he changed the future course of the country.

Understanding the Text

On a separate sheet of paper, write the letter of the word or phrase that best completes each of the following statements.

1. After Jefferson became President, he (a) replaced all federal workers (b) replaced some federal workers (c) replaced no federal workers (d) required all federal workers to wear fancy clothes.

2. As President, Thomas Jefferson opposed (a) the purchase of Western lands from France (b) fancy and expensive government ceremonies (c) allowing the Sedition Act to expire (d) the right of citizens to criticize their government.

3. As a member of Jefferson's Cabinet, Albert Gallatin was most concerned with (a) diplomacy (b) finance (c) defense (d) civil rights.

4. Jefferson cut the budget of the U.S. Navy because (a) he feared a revolt by officers (b) he wanted to reduce the national debt (c) he wanted to increase taxes (d) there was peace all over the world.

5. Jefferson appeared to change his political ideals when he (a) bought Louisiana Territory without waiting for a constitutional amendment (b) approved the repeal of the excise taxes (c) allowed outspoken criticisms of the government (d) defended Americans' civil rights.

6. At one time or another, Louisiana Territory was the property of all of the following nations, *except* (a) Spain (b) Great Britain (c) France (d) the United States.

7. One thing that the United States did *not* gain by buying Louisiana was (a) control of the Mississippi River (b) many natural resources (c) control of the island nation of Haiti (d) a territory that doubled the land area of the United States.

8. The northwestern part of the new territory was explored by (a) Monroe and Livingston (b) Gallatin and Pike (c) Pinckney and Hamilton (d) Lewis and Clark.

9. Jefferson was President during the (a) middle of the 18th century (b) last decade of the 18th century (c) first decade of the 19th century (d) first decade of the 20th century.

10. Tecumseh and his brother, the Prophet, organized Indians (a) in Louisiana (b) west of the Mississippi (c) east of the Mississippi (d) in Haiti.

Developing Map Skills

Study the map on page 147. Then choose the letter of the word or phrase that best completes each of the following sentences. On a separate sheet of paper, match the sentence number with the correct letter.

1. Beginning their journey west from St. Louis, Lewis and Clark in 1804 went (a) down the Mississippi (b) up the Mississippi (c) down the Missouri (d) up the Missouri.

2. According to the map, Spanish Territory was explored by (a) Zebulon Pike on his first expedition out of St. Louis (b) Pike on his second expedition out of St. Louis (c) Lewis and Clark on their 1804–1805 journey (d) Meriwether Lewis alone.

3. The eastern boundary of the Louisiana Purchase was (a) the Mississippi River (b) the Rocky Mountains (c) Oregon Country (d) the Pacific Ocean.

4. Pikes Peak is (a) west of St. Louis (b) part of the Rocky Mountains (c) south of the Missouri River (d) all of the above.

5. Lewis and Clark saw the Pacific Ocean at the mouth of the (a) Mississippi River (b) Missouri River (c) Columbia River (d) none of the above.

Thinking About the Lesson

1. Were Jefferson's policies much different from those of the Federalist Presidents who served before him? Explain your answer.

2. On entering office, some Presidents have fired large numbers of federal officeholders and replaced them with members of their own political party. Do you think that Presidents should do this? Why or why not?

3. Jefferson bought Louisiana even though the Constitution did not give him the right to enlarge the country without a constitutional amendment. Do you think that he was justified? Explain your answer.

4. Why were the explorations of Lewis and Clark and Zebulon Pike so important?

5. Was Tecumseh right in trying to persuade other Indians not to give up lands to American settlers? Why or why not?

The War of 1812

Thomas Jefferson served as President until 1809. Then James Madison, a fellow Republican, began the first of his two terms in that office. Both of these Chief Executives had sought to stay out of a series of wars between Great Britain and France. They faced the hard task of defending the country's rights as a neutral.

Trouble With Great Britain and France

Fighting between Britain and France had been causing trouble for the United States for some years. American ships trading with either country risked being attacked and seized by the other power. In 1800, Napoleon had promised to stop French attacks on U.S. ships. By 1804, however, Americans realized that the French ruler was not keeping his promise.

The British impressment of American sailors at sea, discussed in Lesson 22, continued. In addition, the British Navy in 1806 set up a *blockade* (obstacle to passage) of the French coast. Great Britain said that all American ships bound for French ports had to stop first in a British port and pay a fee. Americans became bitter over these violations of their rights as citizens of a neutral country.

Jefferson protested to both European powers. Nevertheless, the abuses continued, and many Americans began calling for war.

U.S. Trade Policies

In 1807, Jefferson got Congress to pass the Embargo Act, which applied to all trade between the United States and foreign countries. An *embargo* is a law prohibiting trade between nations. Jefferson hoped to prevent the countries that were at war from obtaining American foodstuffs and other needed goods. With the Embargo Act, Jefferson tried to force the two European powers to respect the rights of the United States as a neutral.

Results of the Embargo In fact, the Embargo Act hurt Americans more than it did the British and the French. Western and Southern farmers lost foreign markets for their crops. New England merchants and shipowners suffered from having less to trade. Despite the embargo, illegal trade continued both overseas and across the Canadian border.

Repeal of the Embargo Just before his Presidency ended in 1809, Jefferson admitted that

152

THE WAR OF 1812: NORTHERN CAMPAIGNS

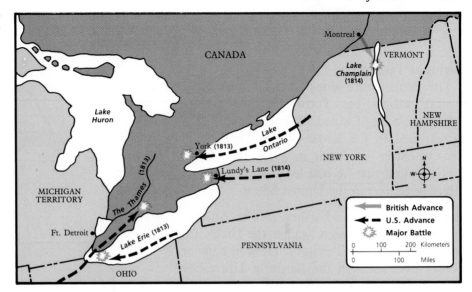

his plan had failed. He got Congress to repeal the Embargo Act only 14 months after it had become law.

Non-Intercourse Act President James Madison tried a trade policy that was a little different from Jefferson's. In 1809, Congress passed the Non-Intercourse Act, reopening trade with all nations, *except* Great Britain and France. The United States promised to renew trade with whichever of these two countries first recognized the neutral rights of Americans. This law, however, also failed to change the way the two European powers treated Americans.

Growth of Anti-British Feelings

Public anger against Great Britain became strong. This anger increased as Westerners claimed that the British in Canada were encouraging Indians to attack U.S. settlers. Some Republican members of Congress, led by Henry Clay and John Calhoun, called for an immediate war against the British. This group of men received the nickname "War Hawks."

Napoleon made good use of the anti-British feelings. Once again he promised to stop seizing

U.S. ships. Despite Napoleon's promise, French actions against Americans continued.

Americans were angry at both powers, but hostility against Great Britain was greater than hostility toward France. Why was that? Republicans were in power then, and Republicans had traditionally been anti-British and pro-French. More important, many of the War Hawks wanted to invade Canada and make that British colony part of the United States. In addition, some Westerners had designs on Florida, which was then owned by Britain's ally—Spain. A war with Great Britain might lead to an invasion of Florida. To some War Hawks, fighting for U.S. neutrality rights was just an excuse to go to war against the British.

War Is Declared

At President Madison's request, Congress declared war on Great Britain in June, 1812. During the next three years, both sides in the War of 1812 won major victories and suffered major defeats.

Fighting in the North Much of the fighting on land took place in or near Canada. While trying to seize Canada, American forces captured and then lost York (now Toronto). Similarly, the British captured and then lost Fort Detroit, in Michigan Territory.

The British were aided in their fighting by several Indian tribes. Tecumseh, the Shawnee chief, was himself killed while fighting on the British side in the Battle of the Thames, in Canada. After his death in 1813, the Indian confederation that he had led was no longer a threat to settlers in the United States.

Southern Campaign   Farther south, Andrew Jackson led a campaign against the Creek Indians of Mississippi Territory. He won a major victory over them in the Battle of Horseshoe Bend, in 1814.

Sea Battles   The most important battles of the war were fought at sea. Two American naval

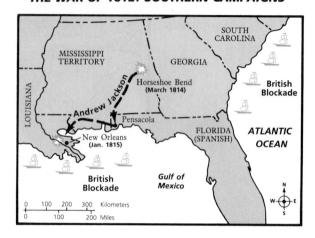

THE WAR OF 1812: SOUTHERN CAMPAIGNS

victories on inland waters halted the British advance from Canada. In 1813, Captain Oliver Perry defeated a British fleet on Lake Erie. The

This scene illustrates Tecumseh's death in 1813 in the Battle of the Thames, in Canada. The victory of American forces here under General William Henry Harrison enabled the United States to secure control of nearby Fort Detroit.

next year, Captain Thomas Macdonough won a victory over the British on Lake Champlain.

On the Atlantic Ocean, American ships, such as the *Constitution* (nicknamed *Old Ironsides*), won some brilliant victories. In general, however, the British fleet was too large for the small U.S. Navy. By the close of the war, American ships had been driven from most of the Atlantic Ocean. Furthermore, the British had blockaded most of the Atlantic coast.

British Offensive British forces conducted raids on several U.S. ports. In 1814, they captured Washington, D.C., and burned many buildings there. Both the White House and the Capitol Building went up in flames. Next the British attacked Baltimore, but they were turned back by American forces at nearby Fort McHenry.

Federalists and the War

Federalists in Congress had opposed declaring war against Great Britain in 1812. Then throughout the conflict, some Federalists refused to support the war effort. Many of them came

Francis Scott Key (above) wrote the words to "The Star-Spangled Banner" as he watched the bombardment of Fort McHenry in 1814. The song soon became popular, but more than 100 years would pass before Congress in 1931 would officially name it as the national anthem.

THE WAR OF 1812: CHESAPEAKE CAMPAIGN

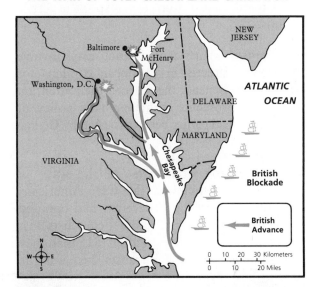

from New England, an area that suffered financially because of the fighting. The war interrupted New England's profitable trade with British merchants.

Hartford Convention Late in 1814, a group of Federalists representing all five New England states came together at the Hartford Convention. The delegates condemned the fighting, which they called "Mr. Madison's War." Some of them even threatened that their states might *secede* (leave the Union). Nevertheless, the Hartford Convention broke up without taking any specific actions.

The End of the War

The Americans won their greatest land victory at New Orleans, on January 8, 1815. Here General Andrew Jackson's forces faced a large force of British troops under Sir Edward Pakenham. The outcome of the battle may have been decided by the expert shooting of Tennesee and Kentucky volunteers. The British lost many more men than did the Americans. Neither side knew that a peace treaty had already been signed in Europe on Christmas Eve, 1814. They did not know of the treaty because news took a long time to cross the Atlantic.

Treaty of Ghent   The document ending the war was signed in Ghent, Belgium. According to the peace treaty, neither side gained or lost any land. Moreover, the treaty did not touch on the two main causes of the war—violations of neutral rights and impressment of sailors. In effect, the Treaty of Ghent simply said that the war was finally over.

> Although the treaty did not call for the United States to add any territory, the country did gain some land during the war. In 1814, U.S. forces invaded and seized Pensacola, Florida, which had been under Spanish control. (See the map on page 154.)

Lasting Results of the War

The War of 1812 did not settle the problems that existed between the United States and European countries. Nor did the United States gain British lands, as the War Hawks had hoped. Nevertheless, the war affected the country in other ways.

Economic Development   The war forced Americans to produce their own goods. During the war, Americans could not buy many imported goods from Europe. As a result, those U.S. industries that learned to make these products grew rapidly.

Patriotism   In the United States, *patriotism* (love of one's country) increased greatly. Americans began to honor new national heroes, such as Andrew Jackson and Oliver Perry. In this new spirit of patriotism, victories were remembered proudly and defeats were mainly forgotten. As patriotism grew, sectionalism became less important.

Westward Migration   The war speeded up the *migration* (movement) of Americans west. U.S. forces defeated several Indian groups that had opposed settlers taking their lands. By the end of the war, the U.S. controlled all lands east of the Mississippi except East Florida.

Foreign Respect   For the second time, the United States had proved itself in a war with the British. The Americans had not clearly won the war, but neither had the country been crushed. By standing up to the world's greatest naval power, the United States won the respect of other nations.

Isolationism   Americans did not again involve themselves directly in European conflicts for many years. Instead, they turned their attention to solving problems at home. This policy of isolationism had earlier been advocated by George Washington.

Collapse of the Federalists   In the wave of patriotism that followed the war, Americans remembered how the Federalists had opposed the conflict. As a result, the Federalists lost even more political support after 1815 than they had lost before. The Federalists' loss was the Republicans' gain.

SUMMING UP   We have seen how President Jefferson avoided getting into the war between France and Great Britain. Nevertheless, America's foreign trade suffered because of the conflict. The U.S. finally went to war in 1812. Both Great Britain and the United States won important battles on land and at sea. When the war ended in 1815, neither side could honestly claim that it had won. The war stimulated the country's economic development, patriotism, and westward migration.

Understanding the Text

On a separate sheet of paper, write the letter of the word or phrase that best completes each of the following statements.

1. The Embargo Act of 1807 was an attempt to (a) use economic power to make foreign nations respect U.S. neutral rights (b) protect new industries in New England (c) make peace between Great Britain and France (d) punish U.S. farmers for trading with Europe.

2. United States foreign policy just before the War of 1812 can best be described as (a) reckless nationalism (b) uneasy neutralism (c) dominated by close relations with Great Britain (d) dominated by an alliance with France.

3. American anger against the British was stirred up by each of the following, *except* (a) the War Hawks (b) the Federalists in New England (c) Napoleon (d) settlers in the Northwest.

4. Of the following, one *not* a cause of the War of 1812 was the (a) Treaty of Ghent (b) desire to annex Canada (c) desire to annex Florida (d) conflicts with Indians in the West.

5. One body of water that was *not* the scene of a major battle during the war was (a) Lake Erie (b) the Pacific Ocean (c) the Atlantic Ocean (d) Lake Champlain.

6. Of the following, the one that does *not* belong with the other three is (a) nationalism (b) loyalty to a region (c) patriotism (d) glorification of national heroes.

7. The country that lost land as a result of the War of 1812 was (a) Spain (b) Russia (c) France (d) Great Britain.

8. Americans took pride in their military record in the War of 1812 because they had (a) invaded and held control of Canada (b) stood up to one of the world's greatest military powers (c) burned London, England (d) controlled the Atlantic Ocean.

9. The Hartford Convention (a) led to a permanent weakening of the country (b) was strongly supported by the Republicans (c) revealed sectional opposition to the War of 1812 (d) was put down by force of arms.

10. The War of 1812 is important in the history of the United States because (a) it resulted in a crushing military defeat of Great Britain (b) the peace treaty that ended the conflict gave the United States vast new lands (c) the war strengthened the American economy and the people's patriotism (d) the peace treaty settled the question of rights of neutrals.

Developing Table-Reading Skills

VOTE IN HOUSE OF REPRESENTATIVES, JUNE 4, 1812

	For war	Against war*
New England		
New Hampshire	3	2
Vermont	3	1
Massachusetts	6	8
Rhode Island	0	2
Connecticut	0	7
Middle Atlantic		
New York	3	11
New Jersey	2	4
Delaware	0	1
Pennsylvania	16	2
Maryland	6	3
South		
Virginia	14	5
North Carolina	6	3
South Carolina	8	0
Georgia	3	0
West		
Ohio	1	0
Kentucky	5	0
Tennessee	3	0
Total	79	49

*All Federalists voted against the war.

Study the table above. Then choose the letter of the word or phrase that best completes each sentence. On a separate sheet of paper, match the sentence number with the correct letter.

1. The table shows that on June 4, 1812, (a) the United States declared war (b) the House of Representatives voted in favor of war (c) Congress voted for war (d) the Senate overturned a presidential veto.

2. A state whose representatives voted unanimously in favor of war with Great Britain was (a) Massachusetts (b) Connecticut (c) South Carolina (d) Virginia.

3. The state with the most representatives in 1812 was (a) New York (b) Pennsylvania (c) Virginia (d) California.

4. Of the following regions, the one that had the greatest number of pro-war votes in the House was (a) New England (b) the Middle Atlantic states (c) the South (d) the West.

5. The region where the number of representatives who opposed the war was greater than representatives who favored war was (a) New England (b) the Middle Atlantic states (c) the South (d) the West.

Thinking About the Lesson

1. Both British and French ships attacked and captured American trading ships before 1812. In your opinion, why were most Americans angrier with the British than with the French?

2. If you had been a member of Congress in 1812, would you have favored President Madison's request that Congress declare war? Why or why not?

3. Why did Tecumseh and other Indians fight on the side of the British in the War of 1812?

4. Why did the War of 1812 lead to further weakening of the Federalist party?

LESSON 27

Post-War Nationalism

In the years after the War of 1812, Americans showed a new sense of national pride and purpose. A high tariff, a new national bank, and new roads and canals helped the economy become strong. Supreme Court decisions strengthened the federal government at the expense of the states. In politics, the Republican party ruled without major opposition from 1817 to 1825. Because of the lack of party rivalry, these years of President James Monroe's administration were called the "Era of Good Feelings."

Economic Nationalism

National growth and prosperity have often depended on a strong economy. After the War of 1812, Congress took steps to strengthen the economy in three areas.

Industry   The British blockade during the war had helped American makers of iron and *textiles* (woven or knit cloth). Following the war, however, foreign—especially British—goods flooded the U.S. market. To prevent this flood from continuing, Congress in 1816 passed a higher protective tariff. (As we learned before, a protective tariff places high taxes on foreign goods, forcing importers to raise prices. These taxes are not added to the price of goods made by

American industries. Thus, American goods can be sold at cheaper prices.)

Banking   The charter for the First Bank of the United States had *expired* (ended) in 1811. During the war, there had been no national bank to make sure that paper money could be traded for gold or silver coins. As a result, the value of paper money had varied from place to place. To solve this problem, Congress created the Second Bank of the United States in 1816. This bank provided a new supply of currency backed by gold and silver. It helped stimulate business activity and insured confidence in the national economy.

Transportation   The country had grown greatly in size during its first three decades but still lacked a good system of *transportation* (means of getting around). Americans found traveling long distances very difficult. The country's poor transportation network had also hurt trade and weakened the spirit of national unity.

In 1811, Americans started constructing a road to the West from Cumberland, Maryland. Paid for by the federal government, this "National Road" soon reached as far west as Wheeling, West Virginia. Thus, a major highway joined the Eastern seaboard with the Ohio River, itself a major passageway between the East and the West.

159

The National Road helped, but Americans needed additional ways of getting around their growing nation. They started building canals— a cheaper form of transportation. The building of canals was paid for by the states, not the federal government. By 1825, New York State had created one of the greatest canals—the Erie Canal. This narrow strip of water extended from near Albany, New York, on the Hudson River, to near Buffalo, New York, on Lake Erie. (See the map on page 197.)

Nationalism in the Supreme Court

Chief Justice John Marshall headed the Supreme Court from 1801 to 1835. He believed in a strong national government and loose interpretation of the Constitution. His views were reflected in many Supreme Court decisions of the time. Through these and other early decisions, the Supreme Court established its power and prestige. (See Lesson 25.) In addition, it strengthened the federal government and protected certain businesses from state interference. Some of the most important Supreme Court decisions during the post-war years were:

• *McCulloch* v. *Maryland* (1819). In this case, the Court ruled that Congress has the power to establish a national bank. Then the Court said that branches of this bank may not be taxed by a state, for several reasons: (1) the power to tax is the power to destroy; (2) the bank is part of the federal government; (3) the federal government is higher in authority than the states.

• *Dartmouth College* v. *Woodward* (1819). The Supreme Court said that a state may not cancel any charter that it has granted to a college or business. The justices said that a charter is a contract, and rights of contract are guaranteed by the U.S. Constitution.

• *Gibbons* v. *Ogden* (1824). Here the Court ruled that Congress, not the states, has the right to regulate interstate commerce. The justices

By serving 34 years as Chief Justice of the United States, Marshall helped establish the prestige of the Supreme Court.

defined *interstate commerce* as any kind of business that operates in two or more states.

Unity in National Politics

In 1816, the Federalists ran a candidate for President of the United States for the last time. Their candidate, Rufus King, was soundly defeated, carrying only three states. James Monroe, the Republican candidate, won the election.

In 1820, Monroe was easily re-elected. In fact, he did not have any opposition and got all but one of the electoral votes. Through his two terms, Monroe continued nationalist programs begun under Madison, his predecessor.

In an earlier time, Republicans had favored a weak national government, while Federalists had favored a strong one. Now the Republicans had taken over most of the Federalists' ideas. The Republicans were filled with the new national spirit. They favored the idea of a strong federal government that could draw the states together.

Disunity in National Politics

Although the Republicans were the only major political party, not all Americans agreed on the issues of the day. Within the Republican party itself, factions formed that took opposing views on some issues:

• National Improvements. Although some Republicans wanted the federal government to build roads and canals, others did not. Presidents Madison and Monroe opposed federal financing of these projects. Instead, they wanted the states to finance transportation networks.

• National Bank. Many Republicans supported the Second Bank of the United States. Some, however, blamed it for an economic depression that started in 1819. They said that the bank's interest rates on loans to small businesses were too high. Opponents of the bank wanted to abolish it.

• Extension of Slavery. Republicans also differed on whether or not to admit to the Union new states that allowed slavery.

The Missouri Compromise

By 1819, nine states had been added to the original thirteen. (See the map on page 162.) Now the Union was evenly divided into two groups: 11 free states and 11 slave states. Then in 1819, Missouri, which permitted slavery, applied for admission to the Union. If Missouri were to enter as a slave state, its two new senators might give control of the Senate to the South. Northerners did not want that to happen. Thus, statehood for Missouri (and for other territories) became a political issue for the entire nation.

The House and Senate debated the Missouri question long and hard. At first, no solution proposed by either side was accepted by the other. Finally, in 1820, the Senate worked out the Missouri Compromise, which was soon agreed

The country's fifth President, James Monroe (center) was inaugurated in March, 1817. Notice the sorry state of the White House in the background. It had been burned by the British in 1814 and had not yet been rebuilt.

to by the House. The Compromise included three main points:

• Missouri was to be admitted as a slave state. The rights of free blacks in Missouri were to be protected by the U.S. Constitution. This last provision was in reaction to a proposed Missouri state constitution that would have discriminated against free blacks.

• Maine was to be admitted as a free state. Maine had been part of Massachusetts. But after the War of 1812, a movement for independence from Massachusetts grew in Maine. In 1819, the Massachusetts legislature agreed to let Maine split off into a separate state of its own.

• In Western territories, slavery was to be banned north of a line that also marked Missouri's southern border. Southerners agreed to this provision because they thought that cotton would not grow well north of 36°30′N. Missouri, a slave state, would be surrounded on three sides by areas in which slavery would not be allowed.

Many Americans thought that the Missouri Compromise had settled the slavery question once and for all. Others realized that future expansion of the country would reopen the question. They knew that the problem had merely been postponed.

THE UNITED STATES, 1821

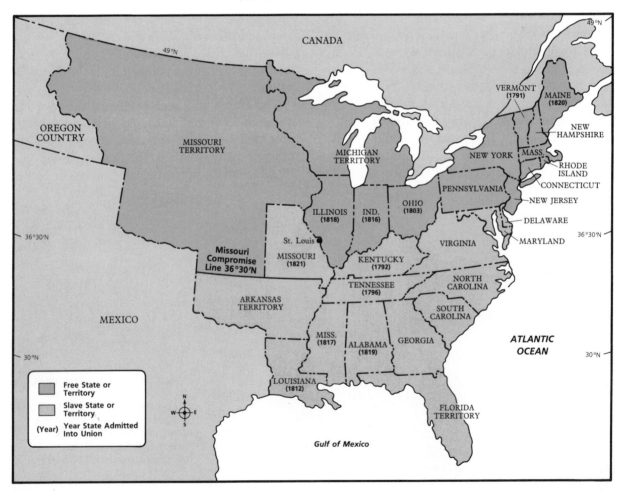

SUMMING UP   We have seen how the spirit of nationalism swept the country after the War of 1812. Internal improvements helped create a strong economy. The Supreme Court backed the federal government over the states in several key cases. Most American voters rallied to the Republican party. Unity in national politics did not last, however. Several issues, including the extension of slavery, began to divide the American people into distinct groups.

Understanding the Text

On a separate sheet of paper, write the letter of the word or phrase that best completes each of the following statements.

1. The years after 1815 were characterized by all of the following, *except* (a) low tariffs (b) a strong Republican party (c) the building of roads and canals (d) Supreme Court decisions that favored the federal government.

2. After the War of 1812, the United States set up protective tariffs as an economic weapon against (a) Federalists (b) textile manufacturers in New England (c) British manufacturers (d) cotton growers in the South.

3. The Second Bank of the United States (a) lost its charter in 1811 (b) was opposed by Congress in 1816 (c) was subject to state taxes, according to a Supreme Court decision (d) backed paper money with gold and silver.

4. The National Road (a) connected the Atlantic seaboard and the Ohio River (b) connected the Hudson River and Lake Erie (c) was paid for by the states (d) solved all of the nation's transportation problems.

5. In 1825, one way that Americans could *not* travel was by (a) roads (b) railroads (c) canals (d) rivers.

6. The Supreme Court case of *Dartmouth College* v. *Woodward* was about rights to (a) make contracts (b) regulate interstate commerce (c) tax a national bank (d) build roads.

7. The Era of Good Feelings got its name because (a) the War of 1812 had just ended (b) Madison was a popular President (c) the Republicans at this time had no major political rivals (d) the U.S. Supreme Court made popular decisions.

8. John Marshall was the (a) President of the United States, 1809–1817 (b) President of the United States, 1817–1825 (c) Chief Justice of the United States, 1801–1835 (d) Secretary of Transportation, 1807–1819.

9. Missouri was admitted to the Union in 1821 (a) as a free state (b) as a slave territory (c) at the same time as Massachusetts (d) none of the above.

10. After the War of 1812, Americans were (a) afraid to move west (b) divided on the issue of whether or not the Second Bank of the United States was good for the country (c) forced to give up the Louisiana Purchase (d) all opposed to the idea of admitting new states that allowed slavery.

Developing Map Skills

Study the map on page 162. Then choose the letter of the word or phrase that best completes each sentence. On a separate sheet of paper, match the sentence number with the correct letter.

1. St. Louis in 1821 was located in *(a)* a territory open to slavery *(b)* a state open to slavery *(c)* a territory closed to slavery *(d)* a state closed to slavery.

2. A state admitted to the Union in 1820 was *(a)* Missouri *(b)* Maine *(c)* Illinois *(d)* Mississippi.

3. Of the following, the one that was not a state in 1821 was *(a)* Maine *(b)* Missouri *(c)* Michigan *(d)* Illinois.

4. A territory that was open to slavery in 1821 was *(a)* Missouri *(b)* Michigan *(c)* Louisiana *(d)* Arkansas.

5. A slave state north of the line of latitude 36° 30′N in 1821 was *(a)* Maryland *(b)* Ohio *(c)* Louisiana *(d)* Alabama.

Thinking About the Lesson

1. What factors helped the American economy grow after the War of 1812?

2. Why did many Republicans abandon their former views and instead come to favor a strong national government?

3. In light of the debate about the extension of slavery, do you think that the label "Era of Good Feelings" fits the period 1817–1825? Why or why not?

Nationalism and the Monroe Doctrine

In the years after the War of 1812, U.S. foreign policy reflected the country's strong spirit of nationalism. During these years, the United States gained prestige by negotiating important treaties with Great Britain and Spain. These treaties enabled the country to increase in size. The strongest expression of U.S. nationalism took place in 1823 with the proclamation of the Monroe Doctrine.

Settlement With Great Britain and Spain

In the post-war years, the United States was able to settle several long-standing border disputes in its favor.

Rush-Bagot Agreement In 1817, Great Britain and the United States agreed to partial *disarmament* (giving up one's weapons). They would limit the number of armed ships they kept on the Great Lakes and Lake Champlain. By making this agreement, the two powers wanted to prevent an arms race on the major inland lakes.

Convention of 1818 The United States and Great Britain agreed to a northern border for the Louisiana Purchase. The 49th parallel (latitude 49 degrees N) was to serve as the line that

divided Canada and the United States in this area. (See the map on page 162.) On the western side of the Rocky Mountains, no border was set. Instead, the British and Americans decided that both countries' settlers could move into Oregon Country. The Convention of 1818 also dealt with the question of fishing rights. Now U.S. citizens were allowed to join Canadians in fishing the rich Atlantic waters off the coast of Newfoundland.

Parallels of latitude are imaginary lines that run east and west. They measure distances north and south of the earth's equator. The *equator* itself is a parallel, one that divides the earth's surface in half. Parallels are measured in *degrees* (°) and *minutes* (′)—a minute being a unit of measure equal to 1/60 of a degree. The equator is at 0°0′, while the North Pole is at 90°0′N. (The *N* stands for North.)

Adams-Onís Treaty Secretary of State John Quincy Adams, son of the second President, helped write this 1819 treaty with Spain. According to its terms, Spain gave Florida to the United States. In return, the United States gave up its claim to Spanish-held Texas. In addition, the U.S. agreed to pay over $5 million in damage claims made by U.S. citizens against Spain.

Behind the Adams-Onís Treaty lies an interesting story. In 1818, General Andrew Jackson had gone into Florida. He was chasing Seminole Indians who had been staging border raids on settlements in Georgia. While in Florida, Jackson and his men seized Spanish forts. Jackson had the permission of the U.S. government to enter Florida, but not to fight the Spanish.

Because Jackson broke federal orders, he was severely criticized by some Cabinet members. Nevertheless, Secretary of State Adams supported Jackson's actions. Furthermore, Adams accused Spain of encouraging hostilities against the United States. Adams told the Spanish that they had to make a choice. They either had to control the Indians in Florida or give up the land to the United States. Since Spain was too weak to control the Indians, it agreed to give up the land.

European Threats to the Americas

Events farther south than Florida were to influence U.S. foreign policy in the 1820s. In the previous two decades, people in the European colonies of Latin America had been gaining political freedom. They had been winning independence from three colonial powers—Spain, Portugal, and France. Since these Latin American revolutions were similar to the American Revolution, U.S. citizens sympathized with the independence movements.

The Quadruple Alliance In 1823, people in the United States worried that European powers might use force to overthrow the new governments in Latin America. Their fear was based on events in Europe. In 1815, four monarchies—Austria, Prussia, Russia, and France—had formed the Quadruple Alliance. Among other actions, this alliance helped put down democratic movements in Spain and Italy. U.S. leaders thought that the Quadruple Alliance might oppose democratic governments in Latin America as well.

Americans feared that European intervention in Latin America would hurt the growing U.S. trade with that area. The British, wishing to protect their Latin American trade, also were worried about the Quadruple Alliance.

A Dispute With Russia In the early 1820s, Russia threatened British and American interests in the northwest. Russia already ruled Alaska, but in 1821, Alexander I, the *Tsar*

Two of the Seminole Indians whom Andrew Jackson's forces captured in Florida in 1818 are shown being sent to be hanged at Fort St. Marks. At this time, Florida was still a Spanish colony.

Born of a well-to-do family in Venezuela, Simón Bolivar later earned the title "The Liberator." He led revolutions against Spain that resulted in the independence of Venezuela, Colombia, Ecuador, Peru, and Bolivia.

(ruler) of Russia, claimed an even larger area of North America. He not only wanted Alaska, but he also claimed the coast of western Canada and part of Oregon Country. In addition, he called for non-Russian ships to stay out of a large part of the North Pacific. The United States and Great Britain refused to give in to the Tsar's claims.

The Monroe Doctrine

In 1823, the British proposed that the United States join them in sending a warning to the other European powers. A joint declaration would tell European rulers to keep their hands off independent nations in the New World.

Adams's Views   Secretary of State John Quincy Adams had a different idea. Why, he asked, should the United States have to follow the lead of Great Britain? By acting alone, Americans could show their growing importance as a nation. In Adams's opinion, the British would support the U.S. action in any case. He believed that the British were just as interested as the United States was in keeping other powers out of the Western Hemisphere.

Monroe's Speech   President James Monroe accepted Adams's advice. In his address to Congress in December, 1823, Monroe made three main points. The substance of his speech became known as the Monroe Doctrine. He said that the United States would:

• Resist any European attempts to set up new colonies in the Western Hemisphere. In making this point, Monroe had mainly Russia in mind.

• Regard as unfriendly any act by Europeans to interfere with an independent government in the Western Hemisphere. This point was meant to protect new nations in Latin America.

• Not interfere in European affairs or in existing European colonies in the Americas.

Results of the Doctrine

The Monroe Doctrine was not immediately put to the test. The Quadruple Alliance did not invade any Latin American country. Moreover, the Russians agreed to keep out of Oregon.

We do not really know whether any European power would have invaded Latin America if the Doctrine had not been proclaimed. Even before Monroe made his famous speech, the Russians had said that they were willing to limit their claims in America. Furthermore, the other European powers were probably more impressed with British sea power than with the small United States Navy.

The Monroe Doctrine was more important for the United States in later years than it was in 1823:

• The Doctrine gave new force to the U.S. policy of isolationism. For many years, Americans stayed out of the affairs of European countries.

• In the late 1800s and early 1900s, the United States would refer to the Doctrine when pressing its own claims in Latin America. (See Lessons 55, 56, and 76.)

• In more recent times, the United States would refer to the Doctrine in countering Soviet influence in the area.

SUMMING UP   We have seen how U.S. foreign policy became nationalistic in the years following the War of 1812. During this time, the country successfully settled several outstanding matters with Great Britain. An agreement with Spain led the United States to take control of all of Florida. The spirit of nationalism was best reflected in the Monroe Doctrine. By keeping European powers as far away as possible, the United States protected its own interests.

Understanding the Text

On a separate sheet of paper, write the letter of the word or phrase that best completes each of the following statements.

1. After 1815, one way in which the United States and Great Britain improved their relations was to (a) provide for the sale of Florida to the United States (b) set up a new northern boundary of the Louisiana Purchase (c) give the entire Oregon Country to the United States (d) jointly issue the Monroe Doctrine.

2. Great Britain's reasons for opposing the Quadruple Alliance's designs in Latin America were based mainly on the British people's (a) hatred of monarchy (b) desire to maintain its trade with Latin America (c) lack of sea power (d) love of democracy.

3. Revolutions in Latin America were directed against all of the following countries, *except* (a) Russia (b) Spain (c) Portugal (d) France.

4. In advising Monroe to issue his Doctrine, Secretary of State Adams said that (a) the United States was the world's greatest sea power (b) Russia did not want the Oregon Country (c) France had been a U.S. ally in the Revolution (d) both the United States and Great Britain wanted to keep other powers out of the Western Hemisphere.

5. Monroe presented his Doctrine in the form of (a) a joint American-British statement of policy (b) a treaty with Latin American countries (c) a speech to Congress (d) a bill presented to Congress.

6. According to the Monroe Doctrine, the United States would not allow *(a)* new European colonies in the Western Hemisphere *(b)* a new type of British government in Canada *(c)* Russian economic development in Alaska *(d)* a change in the government of France.

7. In 1818, General Andrew Jackson entered Florida *(a)* in order to sign the Adams-Onís Treaty *(b)* at the request of the Spanish government *(c)* to capture Indians who had made raids into U.S. territory *(d)* all of the above.

8. Two main reasons for the success of the Monroe Doctrine were the great distance between America and Europe and *(a)* the military strength of the United States *(b)* British sea power *(c)* the decline of European monarchies *(d)* the unanimous approval of Congress.

9. With the Monroe Doctrine, the United States became the protector of the Western Hemisphere *(a)* by its own choice *(b)* at the request of new Latin American nations *(c)* with the full approval of the European monarchies *(d)* in order to honor the memory of Washington.

10. The Monroe Doctrine expressed *(a)* the spirit of nationalism in the United States *(b)* the growing strength and confidence of the country *(c)* sympathy for independence movements in Latin America *(d)* all of the above.

Developing Cartoon-Reading Skills

Study the political cartoon above. Then choose the letter of the word or phrase that best answers each question. On a separate sheet of paper, match the question number with the correct letter.

1. Whom does the man on the right represent? *(a)* the United States *(b)* Great Britain *(c)* Tsar Alexander I *(d)* a Spanish monarch.

2. Whom do the two men on the left represent? *(a)* the U.S. President and Vice President *(b)* the

Uncle Sam—"That's A Live Wire, Gentlemen!"

Federalists and Republicans *(c)* European countries *(d)* South American dictators.

3. The phrase "Monroe Doctrine" is drawn in what form? *(a)* a cane *(b)* a wire *(c)* a top hat *(d)* a wave.

4. What is the man in the center trying to do? *(a)* trade with the United States *(b)* invade Africa *(c)* put down revolutions at home *(d)* interfere in Latin American affairs.

5. What is the man on the right trying to do? *(a)* keep outsiders out of the Western Hemisphere *(b)* encourage trade with Africa and East Asia *(c)* tell Latin Americans how to run their countries *(d)* help people immigrate to the United States.

Thinking About the Lesson

1. Why did the United States and Great Britain agree to partial disarmament on the Great Lakes and Lake Champlain in 1817?

2. Why did U.S. leaders decide to proclaim the Monroe Doctrine without British sponsorship?

3. Do you think that the Monroe Doctrine is still an effective doctrine? Why or why not?

John Quincy Adams and the Breakup of the Republican Party

In the 1820s, many Americans became more critical of their government, causing the national unity of the Era of Good Feelings to break up. New political groups developed within the Republican party during the elections of 1824 and 1828. These elections also revealed that many American voters wanted a President who was different from those the country had had so far.

The Election of 1824

The Republicans were the only national party in the presidential election of 1824. Nevertheless, the party was divided by the interests of different sections of the country. Both Andrew Jackson and Henry Clay were "favorite sons" of the West. Jackson had served in politics, but he was better known as a military hero. Clay was known across the country as the Speaker of the House of Representatives. From the South came William Crawford, Secretary of the Treasury under President Monroe. Crawford might have won the election if he had not been disabled by a stroke during the campaign. The fourth candidate, John Quincy Adams, was from Massachusetts. He had been a popular Secretary of

State, but in the 1824 election his support outside the Northeast was small.

Results of the Election Jackson got the largest number of popular votes. None of the candidates, though, won the required majority of electoral votes. The Constitution states what should be done in such a situation. The House of Representatives would select the President, and each state would have just one vote. Clay, not wanting Jackson to win, threw his support to Adams, thereby ensuring Adams's victory.

> When he became President, John Quincy Adams named Henry Clay as his Secretary of State. Adams's enemies criticized this appointment, saying that a "corrupt bargain" had been made between Clay and Adams. Without having any evidence, they claimed that Adams had named Clay as a payment for Clay's support in the House vote.

The Adams Administration

Soon after Adams became President in 1825, he announced some of the programs that he wanted to see made into law. According to Adams, the federal government would:

- Build a national university.
- Finance explorations in the West, including the Pacific Coast.
- Build an *observatory* (a place to view the stars, planets, and moon through a telescope).
- Create a Department of the Interior.
- Spend much more money on transportation projects. Unlike President Monroe, Adams wanted the federal government to finance the building of roads and canals.

Adams's Accomplishments and Failures Except for obtaining funds for some transportation projects, Adams's programs did not gain the support of Congress. Critics charged that these programs would cost too much money. Furthermore, said the critics, the federal government would be taking over tasks belonging to the states.

Later in his administration, Adams took other, equally controversial stands. He opposed the way that public land in the West was being distributed. He complained about people who bought land cheap and then immediately sold it at a good profit. Westerners, however, liked the way that land sales were being handled, since cheap land was always available. In another matter, Adams attempted to help the Cherokee Indians, who were being forced off their lands in Georgia. His action was opposed by the Governor of that state and made Adams unpopular in much of the South and West.

The Tariff of 1828 The tariff issue made even more enemies for Adams in the South. The Tariff of 1828 was very high. It was hated so much that it was sometimes called the "Tariff of Abominations." Adams had reservations about the bill, but he ended up supporting it. He did so in order to protect domestic industries. Most of these industries were located in the Northeast—where Adams came from. The South, on

The country's sixth President, John Quincy Adams, was the son of President John Adams and Abigail Adams.

the other hand, hated high tariffs because they raised the price of imported manufactured goods that the South had to buy.

Part of Adams's problem was that he was a poor politician. He was not good at persuading others to support his views. He was very capable, but he lacked a warm personality. Also, he did not follow a basic rule in politics—rewarding one's followers. During his whole term in office, he named only 12 persons to positions in the executive branch of government. Furthermore, he allowed many of his opponents to keep their jobs—jobs which they had gotten during the Monroe administration.

The Rise of Democracy

Adams's opponents called him an *aristocrat*— someone from the upper classes. By the 1820s, this label had become especially damaging. When the country was first formed in 1789, state laws restricted the right to vote to men of property. Then gradually the U.S. became more democratic as new states entering the Union gave the right to vote to all white males. The older states also began to expand the number of people who could vote. From 1824 to 1828, the percentage of men who voted in presidential elections doubled.

A few states allowed free black males to vote. None gave this right to women—white or black.

By 1828, American voters were looking for a different kind of presidential candidate—one with whom they could identify. Many new voters, as well as older voters who disliked Adams's policies, supported Andrew Jackson.

The Election of 1828

The 1828 presidential election was a contest between two factions of the Republican party. Jackson led one faction and Adams the other.

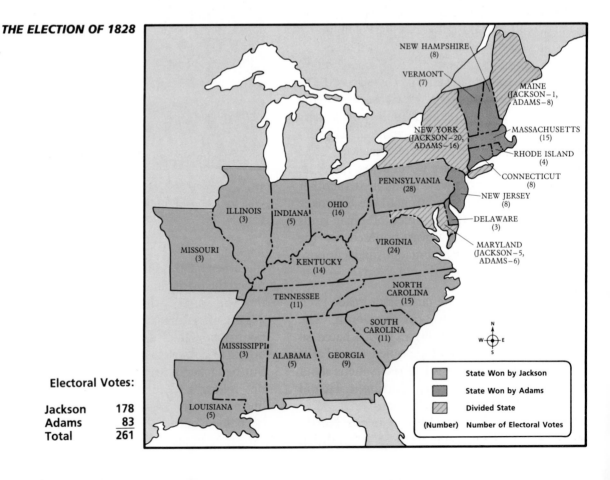

THE ELECTION OF 1828

Electoral Votes:

Jackson	178
Adams	83
Total	261

On his way to Washington for his inauguration in 1829, President-elect Andrew Jackson was enthusiastically greeted by crowds of supporters. This drawing shows Jackson on the newly built National Road somewhere between Wheeling, Virginia, and Baltimore, Maryland. (Granger Collection)

Jackson's Supporters Andrew Jackson came from a family of poor immigrants. He had been born in South Carolina and had moved to Tennessee as a young man. Tennessee remained his home state for the rest of his life. These facts partly explain Jackson's widespread popularity in the South and West. Adams's support of the Tariff of 1828 and other measures also led many Southerners and Westerners to rally around Jackson.

> Although Jackson came from a poor family, he did not remain poor. As a successful lawyer in Tennessee, he purchased much property, including a mansion—"The Hermitage"—and many slaves.

Adams's Supporters The pro-Adams group was strongest in the Northeast. They were generally conservative members of the business community. They usually favored a high protective tariff and a strong central government.

Results of the Election Jackson won by a large majority of the electoral votes. As the map on page 172 shows, he solidly won the West and the South. Adams was strongest in New England and the Middle Atlantic states (but not in Pennsylvania).

Jackson's election has been called the "Revolution of 1828" for several reasons. First, he was elected by a new kind of voter—men who were not wealthy. In recent decades, states had been eliminating property qualifications for voting. (Discussed on page 172.) Second, Jackson was the first President who did not come from an upper-class family. Third, the Western states were deciding national elections for the first time.

SUMMING UP   We have seen how John Quincy Adams served as President during a time when the Republican party was dividing into groups. Adams may have been partly responsible for this breakup. He failed to persuade enough Republicans to support his policies. Another reason for the division in the Republican party in the 1820s was the changing character of American voters. As states removed property qualifications, more and more white males voted. Perhaps these new voters wanted a candidate with a different personality and background.

Understanding the Text

On a separate sheet of paper, write the letter of the word or phrase that best completes each of the following statements.

1. The Era of Good Feelings came to an end with the election of *(a)* James Madison *(b)* Andrew Jackson *(c)* John Quincy Adams *(d)* James Monroe.

2. In the election of 1824, *(a)* Adams won by a landslide *(b)* there were factions within the Republican party *(c)* Clay threw his support to Crawford *(d)* the House finally elected Andrew Jackson.

3. Adams's support in 1824 was strongest in *(a)* New England *(b)* the Western states *(c)* the Southern states *(d)* all of the above.

4. In 1825, Adams named *(a)* Jackson as Secretary of the Interior *(b)* Clay as Secretary of State *(c)* Crawford as Secretary of the Treasury *(d)* none of the above.

5. A program that Adams did *not* advocate when he was President was *(a)* a national university *(b)* state financing of all roads and canals *(c)* high tariffs *(d)* exploration of the West and the Pacific Coast.

6. Jackson's election in 1828 *(a)* was a narrow victory *(b)* was decided in the House *(c)* ended in violence *(d)* involved many new voters.

7. Andrew Jackson *(a)* lived in Tennessee *(b)* was disabled by a stroke in 1824 *(c)* was born in Massachusetts into a wealthy family *(d)* ran for President in 1824 and 1828 as a Federalist.

8. The faction of the Republican party headed by Andrew Jackson found its strongest support in *(a)* New England *(b)* the entire Northeast *(c)* the South and West *(d)* the Middle Atlantic states.

9. The correct order in which Presidents served was *(a)* Madison, Jackson, J. Q. Adams, Monroe, and Jefferson *(b)* Jefferson, Madison, Monroe, Jackson, and J. Q. Adams *(c)* Jefferson, Monroe, J. Q. Adams, Jackson, and Madison *(d)* Jefferson, Madison, Monroe, J. Q. Adams, and Jackson.

10. Which of the following is an example of the rise of democracy in the United States? *(a)* Adams named few people to positions in the executive branch of government. *(b)* Cherokees were forced off their lands in Georgia. *(c)* Many people made profits on the sale of public lands in the West. *(d)* New states entered the Union without property qualifications for voters.

Developing Map Skills

Study the map on page 172. Then choose the letter of the word or phrase that best completes each sentence. On a separate sheet of paper, match the sentence number with the correct letter.

1. In the election of 1828, most of Adams's support came from states in the *(a)* West *(b)* Northeast *(c)* South *(d)* Southwest.

2. The states in which the vote was divided had a combined electoral vote of *(a)* 56 *(b)* 45 *(c)* 47 *(d)* 82.

3. A state that Andrew Jackson did *not* win was *(a)* Illinois *(b)* Massachusetts *(c)* Georgia *(d)* Kentucky.

4. Adams won all of the following states, *except* *(a)* Vermont *(b)* New Jersey *(c)* Delaware *(d)* Pennsylvania.

5. The map clearly shows that *(a)* Adams was elected President *(b)* the South supported Adams *(c)* Jackson won the majority of electoral votes *(d)* the House of Representatives would have to select the President.

Thinking About the Lesson

1. Do you think that it was fair that John Quincy Adams became President in 1824 even though Andrew Jackson won more popular votes? Explain your answer.

2. In light of the history of the administration of John Quincy Adams, how important do you think it is for a President to be a skillful politician?

3. Why did many of the new American voters in the 1820s favor Andrew Jackson over John Quincy Adams?

4. Why did many American business leaders favor John Quincy Adams over Andrew Jackson in the 1820s?

LESSON 30

Jacksonian Democracy

In Andrew Jackson's view, U.S. senators and representatives are expected to look after the interests of their own states and districts. Therefore, thought Jackson, the President alone has a special duty to act for the good of all of the people. This idea shaped the way in which Jackson worked as President. He approved of democratic actions and laws that he believed would benefit most Americans. He was quick to veto laws that, in his opinion, helped only a small group. Jackson's beliefs and actions in favor of ordinary Americans are often referred to as "Jacksonian Democracy."

Reforms in Federal Employment

The federal government was employing a growing number of workers, mostly in the executive branch. Jackson believed that the longer these workers held their jobs, the less likely they would be to carry out their duties in the public interest. Instead, Jackson thought, they would become more and more concerned with their own interests. The President came up with several solutions to this problem.

Rotation in Office President Jackson worried that federal workers were too *arrogant* (superior or overbearing in their dealings with others).

To counter this problem, he used the principle of *rotation in office*. According to this idea, non-elected officeholders should be replaced before they held their jobs too long. Jackson believed that by rotating people in and out of government jobs, more people would gain experience in government. In this way, he hoped, government workers might begin to see themselves as servants of the people. He also thought that, as a result of rotation, unfit and dishonest employees would be regularly weeded out.

Spoils System After Andrew Jackson became President, many new officeholders got their jobs only because they were his political friends. Jackson gave government jobs as rewards for party loyalty—loyalty to the Democratic–Republican party. This practice soon became known as the *spoils system*. President Jackson considered the use of the spoils system, in connection with rotation in office, to be democratic.

The spoils system was not really new during the Jackson administration. All Presidents beginning with Thomas Jefferson had followed it. Jackson, however, directed more attention to the practice than previous Presidents had. He was the first to use the spoils system widely.

176

BORN TO COMMAND.

OF VETO MEMORY.

HAD I BEEN CONSULTED.

KING ANDREW THE FIRST.

This cartoon shows Andrew Jackson with one foot on the Constitution and his often-used veto in hand. Was the cartoonist a supporter of the President?

The Growth of Democracy

As we learned in Lesson 29, the United States was becoming more democratic during the 1820s. More white males were gaining the right to vote. The expansion of voting rights continued during the 1830s:

• Some state constitutions were amended to permit more officials to be elected rather than appointed. In this way, voters gained more control over their government.

• In more states, property qualifications for voters were dropped. As a result, the total number of voters increased greatly.

• *Nominating conventions* (meetings of party members to name candidates for public office) began to appear for the first time. Before then, party *caucuses* (small groups of party leaders) had chosen candidates. Often these caucuses had not represented the views of most party members. Moreover, caucuses had paid little attention to the needs and desires of the people. Delegates to nominating conventions, however, were chosen by active party members. At these conventions, members could meet publicly and express their views. By 1832, all major candidates for President and Vice President were chosen at nominating conventions.

Democrats and Whigs During the Jackson years as President (1829–1837), the Republican party broke up into two separate parties. Jackson's followers began to call themselves "Democratic-Republicans," a name which was soon shortened to "Democrats." Jackson's main opponents were the "National Republicans," who by 1834 were known as the "Whigs." The Whig party, led by Daniel Webster and Henry Clay, was to remain a major political force for several decades.

Jackson and the Bank of the United States

The Second Bank of the United States still existed when Jackson became President in 1829. Ever since 1816, when it had been given a charter, the Bank had been growing richer and more powerful. It had succeeded in making the money system of the United States more stable.

Nevertheless, Jackson criticized the Bank on several counts. He said that:

• The Bank had too much power for a private business. Although the U.S. government invested in the Bank, the government did not control or own it.

• The Bank of the United States favored the interests of big businesses over the interests of small ones.

• The Bank competed unfairly with smaller state banks and tried to control their activities.

• The Bank influenced the making of laws by lending money to important politicians.

When a bill to renew the Bank's charter was passed in 1832, Jackson vetoed it. His veto became a big issue in the presidential election of that year. Jackson's victory at the polls in November convinced him that the people backed his wish to kill the Bank. Consequently, he soon took further action. First, he removed federal funds from the Bank and deposited them in state banks. Then, in 1836, he allowed the charter of the Second Bank of the United States to *lapse* (end). It no longer existed after that year. Jackson and his supporters believed that the end of the Bank was a victory for democracy.

Jackson's Indian Policy

Although Jackson claimed to believe in ordinary Americans, this attitude did not apply to American Indians. As a Westerner and military officer, he had spent years fighting Indians. President Jackson's Indian policy reflected his background.

Indian Resettlement Act   Jackson supported Congress's Indian Resettlement Act of 1830. This act called for the removal of Indians to special lands west of the Mississippi River. To provide for this removal, the United States government signed some 94 separate treaties with Indian tribes.

Indian Wars   Some Indians agreed to their removal; others resisted it. The Sac and Fox Indians of Wisconsin and Illinois fought white forces in the Black Hawk War of 1832. The Indians were soundly defeated. To the south, in Florida, the Seminoles fought a long war rather than be sent west. By 1842, they, too, were conquered.

The Cherokees also refused to move west, insisting that they be allowed to keep their lands in Georgia. When the State of Georgia passed laws to allow settlers to move onto Indian lands,

One aspect of Andrew Jackson's Indian policy is depicted in this painting "The Trail of Tears" by Robert Lindneux. The picture illustrates the mass migration of the Cherokees from Georgia, Alabama, and Tennessee to Indian Territory in the West.

the Cherokees went to court. In 1832, the U.S. Supreme Court ruled in favor of the Cherokees. This ruling, however, did not help the Indians, because President Jackson refused to enforce the Court decision. Instead, he ordered the U.S. Army to move the Cherokees and four other Indian nations to lands in the West. The Indians' long journey west has been called the "Trail of Tears." During their removal, about one fourth of the Indians died of disease, cold, and hunger. Along with other Eastern tribes, the Cherokees ended up in Indian Territory—an area that later became part of the state of Oklahoma.

How democratic was the Jackson administration? We have just seen that he did not try to protect the rights of Indians. Blacks also did not have many rights then. In fact, most black Americans were still slaves. Although some individuals and groups called for the *abolition* (ending) of slavery, neither major political party supported this view. Women of all races occupied an inferior social status during the Jackson administration. Not only did women not have the right to vote, but there was hardly any talk about giving women this right.

SUMMING UP   We have seen how the country became more democratic during Jackson's two terms as President. Political reforms continued on the local, state, and national levels. Jackson introduced rotation in office as a means of giving more people the chance to work for the federal government. In fighting against the Second Bank of the United States, Jackson thought that he was defending the interests of the average citizen. Jacksonian democracy, however, did not extend to giving blacks, women, and Indians rights enjoyed by white males. Indeed, some of Jackson's policies were undemocratic. He clearly favored removing Indians to lands west of the Mississippi, forcibly if necessary.

Understanding the Text

On a separate sheet of paper, write the letter of the word or phrase that best completes each of the following statements.

1. As President, Jackson felt that his highest duty was to (*a*) protect the jobs of federal officeholders (*b*) cooperate with Congress (*c*) end slavery (*d*) represent the people.

2. Rotation in office was a system that President Andrew Jackson (*a*) favored (*b*) opposed (*c*) ignored (*d*) had not heard of.

3. During Andrew Jackson's administration the spoils system rewarded active party members with (*a*) money (*b*) property (*c*) votes (*d*) jobs.

4. During Andrew Jackson's administration, presidential candidates began to be nominated by (a) party conventions (b) party caucuses (c) the Electoral College (d) political reformers.

5. During Jackson's Presidency, political reforms were made in all of the following areas, *except* (a) giving the vote to women (b) nominating presidential candidates (c) electing public officials (d) setting voting qualifications.

6. Jackson accused the Second Bank of the United States of all of the following practices, *except* (a) trying to control state banks (b) making loans to gain political influence (c) issuing too much paper money not backed by gold or silver (d) favoring big businesses.

7. Of the following events, one that did *not* happen in 1832 was (a) Jackson's first election to the Presidency (b) Jackson's re-election (c) Jackson's veto of the bill to recharter the Bank of the United States (d) the Black Hawk War.

8. Of the following actions, one *not* a part of Jackson's Indian policy was (a) giving Indians the right to vote (b) making treaties with Indian tribes (c) forcing Indians to move west (d) using the U.S. Army to fight Indians who resisted demands of the government.

9. Jackson showed his opposition to the Supreme Court in the Cherokee Indian case by (a) refusing to renew the bank charter (b) not enforcing the Court's decision (c) dismissing the justices of the Court (d) ending the Indian removal policy.

10. During Jackson's Presidency, steps to increase democracy were taken on (a) both the national and state levels (b) on the national, but not the state level (c) on the state, but not the national level (d) neither the national nor state level.

Developing Skills Reading a Table of Contents

Examine the Table of Contents of this book, located on pages iv–viii. Then choose the letter of the word or phrase that best completes each sentence. On a separate sheet of paper, match the sentence number with the correct letter.

1. The lesson "Jacksonian Democracy" is found in Unit (a) One (b) Three (c) Five (d) Eight.

2. Lesson 22 starts on page (a) 118 (b) 130 (c) 180 (d) 22.

3. Page 656 is the start of the (a) Preface (b) Acknowledgments (c) Glossary (d) Index.

4. In discussing the United States in the 20th century, this book treats the American people (Unit Eight) (a) after U.S. foreign policy (b) before American politics (c) after the American economy (d) none of the above.

5. If this book had a lesson titled, "The United States and India since 1947," it would most likely be found in Unit (a) One (b) Five (c) Eight (d) Nine.

Thinking About the Lesson

1. Why did Andrew Jackson consider the spoils system and the system of rotation in office to be democratic? Do you agree with him on this matter? Why or why not?

2. Which do you think were more democratic—party caucuses or nominating conventions? Explain your answer.

3. Would you have supported President Jackson's policy of resettlement of Indians to areas west of the Mississippi River? Explain your answer.

Jackson and Threats to the Union

Andrew Jackson had long believed in states' rights. At the same time, he believed that interests of the nation came before interests of states or sections of the nation. Jackson's seemingly contradictory views were put to a test in two national disputes. In these controversies, many politicians took sides according to the section of the country in which they lived.

The Sale of Public Lands

For some time, farmers had been able to buy government-owned land in the West at low prices. Land-hungry Westerners liked this practice. Some wanted the federal government to lower prices even more or to give away the land. Many people in the Northeast, however, disliked the idea of selling land at low prices. They thought that the government should make as much money as possible on land sales. Business owners feared that low prices might tempt many working people from the Northeast to move to the West.

Southern politicians supported Westerners in their fight for cheap land. In return, Southerners expected help on the tariff issue. Senate discussion of a bill to limit public land sales reached its height in the famous Webster-Hayne debates

of 1830. During these debates, the discussion soon moved beyond the issue of the sale of public lands. It took up the broader question of whether final power and authority should be vested in the individual states or the national government.

The Webster-Hayne Debates Senator Robert Y. Hayne of South Carolina spoke for both the South and the West. He defended nullification—the idea that states could nullify federal laws. In extreme cases, said Hayne, states could secede from the Union. Hayne reminded the Senate that some New Englanders, unhappy with the War of 1812, had thought of seceding. (The Hartford Convention is discussed in Lesson 26.)

In reply, Senator Daniel Webster of Massachusetts made a ringing defense of the Union. Nullification, he said, would make the Union as weak as a "rope of sand." What would happen if each of the 24 states had the right to do away with any law that it disliked? The result, answered Webster, would be disunity, chaos, and—in the end—civil war.

Jackson's Views Many Americans wondered where President Jackson would stand on this issue. He soon let them know. At a dinner party in 1830, many guests gave *toasts* (short

Daniel Webster served as U.S. senator from Massachusetts (1827–1841, 1845–1850), and U.S. Secretary of State (1841–1843, 1850–1852).

speeches before taking a drink) supporting states' rights. Jackson raised his glass and said, "Our Union—it must and shall be preserved." His remark revealed that he was on the side of a strong national government—one that could enforce its laws in all the states. In short, he believed in *national supremacy* (the idea that federal laws were superior to state laws).

Tariff Measures

In Lesson 29 we discussed the Tariff of Abominations, the high protective tariff of 1828. Congress had passed this law during the administration of John Quincy Adams. During Jackson's administration, many Southerners, including Vice President John C. Calhoun, con-

tinued to oppose the tariff. They said that the tariff increased the price of manufactured goods that all Southerners bought. This situation in turn forced Southerners to raise the price of their cotton and other exports. The higher the price of exports, the lower the volume of sales for Southerners.

In a message to Congress in 1830, Jackson spoke in favor of the 1828 tariff, saying that it was constitutional. He indicated that protective tariffs in general served a useful purpose. Even so, he suggested that a lower tariff would perhaps be fairer.

Ordinance of Nullification   In 1832, Congress passed a new tariff law—one that was lower. South Carolina, however, in its Ordinance of Nullification, declared both this law and the 1828 tariff unconstitutional. The state even threatened to secede from the Union if federal officials tried to enforce the tariff in South Carolina. Other Southern states shared this dislike of tariffs, but did not fully back South Carolina in its threat to secede.

Rejection of Nullification   In his *Proclamation to the People of South Carolina,* Jackson made some important points. He said that no state could leave the Union or refuse to obey the laws of the country. He further warned, "Disunion by armed force is treason."

The President persuaded Congress to let him use federal armed forces against the rebellious state leaders. Jackson, though, never had to resort to arms.

The Crisis Passes   In 1833, Congress passed still another tariff—a compromise that many Southerners thought was reasonable. In turn, South Carolina dropped its Ordinance of Nullification and its threat to secede. Now President Jackson could proudly proclaim that the Union was preserved.

John C. Calhoun served as U.S. Vice President under both John Quincy Adams and Andrew Jackson. Several times, he came into conflict with Jackson on the tariff and other issues. In 1828, he defended nullification in an article called the "South Carolina Exposition and Protest." Conflicts with President Jackson led Calhoun to resign as Vice President in 1832. For most of the rest of his life, Calhoun served as U.S. senator from South Carolina. This service was interrupted from 1844 to 1845 when Calhoun served as Secretary of State under President John Tyler.

Senator John C. Calhoun

End of the Age of Jackson

In spite of troubles over tariffs, land sales, and other issues, Jackson's two terms as President were times of great economic growth. The Southern cotton industry did well. Northeast industries and merchants flourished. The West was being rapidly settled.

Nevertheless, the country's rapid economic growth caused problems. In rushing to make profits, many Americans wanted to invest more money than they had. They borrowed money to make further investments. These people often got their money from state banks, which were no longer controlled by a national one. (See page 178.) To make the loans, the state banks issued more paper money—money not backed by gold or silver. A crisis developed after Jackson issued an order called the *Specie Circular*. The order required that all purchasers of public land pay in gold or silver. Soon there was a *run on the banks*. Many people rushed to the banks, demanding silver or gold for their paper money. Since the banks did not have enough gold or silver, not all the depositors could be satisfied. As a result, many banks failed.

The Panic of 1837 The failure of many banks led to a *panic*. In the Panic of 1837, news quickly spread that banks were closing their doors. Fearing that they might lose their life's savings, many Americans panicked, running to their banks to withdraw this money. This action, in turn, caused more banks to fail, because banks usually do not have enough money on hand to pay back all depositors. The nation dropped into a deep economic depression that lasted until the mid-1840s.

President Van Buren Blame for the depression fell unfairly on President Martin Van Buren, elected in 1836. Van Buren was Jackson's choice to run for President on the Democratic party ticket. As President, Van Buren was not able to deal with the economic crisis. He only made

Before becoming the country's eighth President, Martin Van Buren was a U.S. senator from New York (1821–1828), New York Governor (1829), U.S. Secretary of State (1829–1831), and Vice President (1833–1837).

matters worse. In 1840, he decided to place federal money in an Independent Treasury, a system of huge vaults located in various cities. As a result, this federal money began to disappear from circulation, and the economic depression deepened.

Elections of 1840 and 1844 After serving only one term as President, Van Buren lost a re-election bid in 1840. The victor was a military hero, William Henry Harrison. For the first time, a candidate of the Whig party won the Presidency. Nevertheless, the Jacksonian Democrats did not disappear. Harrison died after serving only one month in office, and Vice President John Tyler succeeded him. Although Tyler was also a Whig, he did not share the views of most members of his party. As a result, while he was President, the party broke into factions. By 1844, the Whigs were too weak to prevent the Democratic candidate, James K. Polk, from capturing the office of Chief Executive. Andrew Jackson died in 1845, but his influence was felt in the Democratic party for many years.

SUMMING UP We have seen how President Andrew Jackson took a strong stand against sectionalism. During two major crises, he stood for national supremacy. One crisis arose over the issue of the sale of public lands; the other, over the tariff issue. In both cases, Jackson denied the doctrine of nullification and the right of a state to secede from the Union. To some extent, Jackson's influence was felt during Van Buren's administration and later ones.

Understanding the Text

On a separate sheet of paper, write the letter of the word or phrase that best completes each of the following statements.

1. President Jackson supported (*a*) nullification (*b*) national supremacy (*c*) a national bank (*d*) the right of a state to secede.

2. Senator Robert Hayne spoke in favor of all of the following, *except* (*a*) nullification (*b*) interests of Southern states (*c*) national supremacy (*d*) secession.

3. Southern states joined the fight for cheap public lands because they (*a*) wished to sell these lands at a profit (*b*) wanted space in the Northeast for cotton plantations (*c*) thought that higher land prices were unconstitutional (*d*) wanted the West to support them in their fight against a high tariff.

4. In debating Hayne, Webster said that nullification (*a*) would undermine the Union (*b*) was a necessary action (*c*) was a New England principle (*d*) was a right guaranteed by the Constitution.

5. Jackson's actions in the nullification controversy (*a*) brought on the Panic of 1837 (*b*) won him the backing of the Cherokees (*c*) caused the rest of the South to support South Carolina in its threat to secede (*d*) upheld the authority of the federal government.

6. In 1833, the nullification crisis was resolved when (*a*) Congress passed a new tariff (*b*) South Carolina seceded (*c*) Jackson used armed force against South Carolina (*d*) Harrison died in office.

7. John C. Calhoun was (*a*) U.S. President after William Henry Harrison (*b*) U.S. Vice President under Andrew Jackson (*c*) U.S. Vice President under William Henry Harrison (*d*) Vice President of South Carolina.

8. In the Panic of 1837, many depositors in state banks became (*a*) more fearful (*b*) more confident (*c*) wealthier (*d*) happier.

9. Van Buren's creation of the Independent Treasury (*a*) helped him to be re-elected (*b*) cured the economy of its depression (*c*) began a run on the banks (*d*) deepened the depression by withdrawing federal money from circulation.

10. The first Whig candidate elected U.S. President was (*a*) Van Buren (*b*) Polk (*c*) W. H. Harrison (*d*) Tyler.

Developing Bibliography Skills

BIBLIOGRAPHY ON ANDREW JACKSON

Curtis, James C. *Andrew Jackson and the Search for Vindication*. Boston: Little, Brown and Co., 1976.

Davis, Burke. *Old Hickory: A Life of Andrew Jackson*. New York: The Dial Press, 1977.

Jackson, Andrew. *The Papers of Andrew Jackson*. Knoxville: University of Tennessee Press, 1980.

James, Marquis. *Andrew Jackson: Portrait of a President*. Indianapolis: The Bobbs-Merrill Co., 1937.

Remini, Robert Vincent. *Andrew Jackson and the Bank War*. New York: W. W. Norton, 1967.

———. *Andrew Jackson and the Course of American Empire*. New York: Harper and Row, 1977.

Schlesinger, Arthur Meier. *The Age of Jackson*. Boston: Little, Brown and Co., 1953.

Ward, John William. *Andrew Jackson: Symbol for an Age*. London: Oxford University Press, 1955.

A bibliography is a list of books, magazines, and other sources relating to a particular subject. In writing a term paper, for instance, one might include a bibliography of all the sources consulted. Look at the bibliography on Andrew Jackson, printed on page 185. Then choose the letter of the word or phrase that best completes each sentence. On a separate sheet of paper, match the sentence number with the correct letter.

1. The last name of the author of *The Age of Jackson* is (a) Arthur (b) Jackson (c) Marquis (d) Schlesinger.

2. The publisher of the book *Andrew Jackson: Symbol for an Age* is (a) Little, Brown and Co. (b) Harper and Row (c) Oxford University Press (d) London.

3. The name of a city in each entry refers to where the (a) publisher is located (b) author lives (c) author wrote the book (d) book was purchased.

4. The date at the end of each entry refers to the year in which (a) the author was born (b) the book was written (c) the author died (d) the book was published.

5. If we were to add to the bibliography the book *Andrew Jackson as a Public Man,* by William Graham Sumner (New York: Chelsea House, 1980), it would appear right after (a) *Andrew Jackson and the Bank War* (b) *The Age of Jackson* (c) *The Papers of Andrew Jackson* (d) none of the above.

Thinking About the Lesson

1. Why did many Westerners favor having the government sell its land in the West at low prices? Why did many people in the Northeast oppose this practice?

2. Explain President Andrew Jackson's opposition to the idea of nullification.

3. Some of Jackson's critics said that he could have prevented the Panic of 1837 by renewing the charter of the Second Bank of the United States. Do you agree with this view? Why or why not?

Territorial Expansion—Manifest Destiny

By 1840, the United States had already become one of the world's largest countries. It stretched from the Atlantic Ocean west to the Rocky Mountains. Many Americans, though, wanted their nation to become much larger. They looked to lands even farther west—lands through which fur trappers, missionaries, and settlers were already finding their way.

Manifest Destiny

A large number of Americans shared a common belief about the growth of their country. They believed that the United States had a God-given right to expand. They thought that their democratic government should rule from ocean to ocean. Such a westward expansion would greatly increase the size and power of the country. A larger area would create greater opportunities for industry, trade, and farming. The nation's arts and sciences also would flourish.

The belief that the United States was fated to expand to the Pacific Ocean became known as *Manifest Destiny*.

Encounters With Other Peoples

Groups of people were living in the Western part of North America before U.S. settlers arrived. These groups included Indian tribes as well as Mexican and British settlers. Manifest Destiny would affect all of them.

The Indians The explorers, trappers, traders, and missionaries who advanced to the Rocky Mountains and beyond encountered many Indian settlements. Usually these contacts were peaceful. In some instances, however, they led to violence. Many Indians were angry at the white people who were moving onto lands which they used for hunting. Moreover, some Indians did not like attempts to change their religion and way of life.

One tragic case involved the missionary couple Marcus and Narcissa Whitman. In the 1830s, they introduced Christianity to some Indian groups in Oregon Country. Later, other settlers brought measles to the same Indians, resulting in the death of some of their young. Believing they had been poisoned, the Indians in 1847 retaliated by killing the Whitmans and 12 other settlers.

The Mexicans and British Indians did not provide the main obstacle to United States expansion. The independent country of Mexico claimed ownership of the lands in the Southwest. In the Northwest, U.S. settlers came up against British claims to part of Oregon Country.

187

Mexican forces under General Santa Anna laid siege to the Alamo from February 23 to March 6, 1836, before defeating the Texan defenders. Those defenders killed in the battle included legendary frontier fighters Jim Bowie and Davy Crockett. Today, this part of the Alamo remains standing.

Texas

In 1821, Mexico had gained its independence from Spain. After that year, many U.S. settlers began moving into a part of Mexico called "Texas." They were attracted there by the low prices for land rich enough to grow cotton.

Mexican Restrictions By 1830, immigrants from the United States outnumbered Mexicans in Texas. When U.S. settlers began asking for certain rights of self-government, the Mexican government refused. Instead, it restricted existing rights of settlers who wanted to trade with the United States. The Mexican government also banned U.S. settlers from bringing additional slaves into Texas.

Revolt in Texas Because of these policies, Texans led by Sam Houston took up arms against Mexico in 1836. At first, the Mexican forces won some battles against the Texan *rebels* (revolutionaries). At the Alamo Mission, in what is now the city of San Antonio, the Mexicans wiped out almost all 185 rebel defenders. "Remember the Alamo!" became the war cry of the Texan Army in the battles that followed. A month after their loss at the Alamo, the Texans won a major battle at San Jacinto. There they even captured Antonio López de Santa Anna, the Mexican President and military leader.

In 1836, Texas became an independent country. The United States recognized the "Lone Star Republic" the following year. From the United States, Texans wanted not only recognition, but also permission to become a state. Americans in the South and the West generally favored having Texas join the Union. Opposition, however, arose among Northern antislavery groups. These Northerners did not want to add a huge slaveholding area to the country. Texas was so large that Northerners feared it might be divided into several slave states. Each of these states would then have two senators in Congress and an unknown number of representatives. In addition, many Americans believed they would have to go to war with Mexico over Texas. The issue of Texas statehood was debated in the United States for several years.

An Election Issue In 1844, the Democratic party nominated James Polk of Tennessee as its presidential candidate. Polk, a slaveholder, ran on a platform calling for the annexation of Texas. Being a shrewd politician, Polk wanted to satisfy the fears of the antislavery voters. Therefore, he also proposed that the United States take over the vast Oregon Territory at the same time. Most Americans believed that Oregon would not be settled by slave owners, since the land was too cold and mountainous for growing cotton.

Oregon

In 1818, British Canada and the United States had agreed to settle Oregon Country together. (See Lesson 28.) They had not decided, however, on a border to separate British and United States settlements. By the 1840s, more than 500 U.S. settlers had come to Oregon. Like settlers elsewhere, they were filled with "expansion fever." They wanted the United States to expand as much as possible. Some even urged that the United States claim all of Oregon Country, as far north as the southern boundary of Alaska. This Alaskan boundary line was at the parallel of latitude 54°40′N.

In the election of 1844, Polk and the Democrats took up the slogan "Fifty-four Forty or Fight!" The slogan meant that if the British did not agree to the American claims, the United States would go to war. Polk won the presidential election of 1844. As President, though, he drew back from thoughts of fighting with Great Britain. He was worried that a war with Mexico seemed likely. Therefore, he called for a compromise agreement with the British.

U.S.-British Treaty Polk believed that Great Britain would accept a proposal for a boundary at the 49th parallel of latitude. He asked the Senate to consider the idea. After the Senate

approved of the plan, a treaty was drawn up, and in 1846 the two countries signed it. The 49th parallel still serves as part of the boundary between the United States and Canada.

Outbreak of the Mexican War

In 1845, Congress agreed to admit Texas to the Union—an act which many people thought would lead to war with Mexico. Annexation, however, was only one matter of dispute between Mexico and the United States:

• Some Americans had financial claims against the Mexican government, claims that the government would not honor.

• Mexico and the United States could not agree on the southwestern border of Texas. Mexico claimed that the boundary was the Nueces River, while the United States insisted it was the Rio Grande. The latter river ran to the south and west of the Nueces. The Rio Grande as the southern boundary would add thousands of square miles to Texas. (See the map on page 190.)

OREGON COUNTRY, 1846

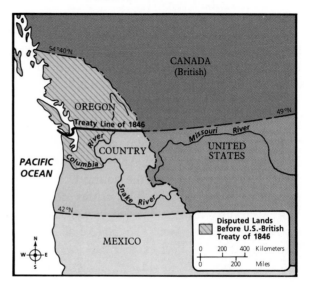

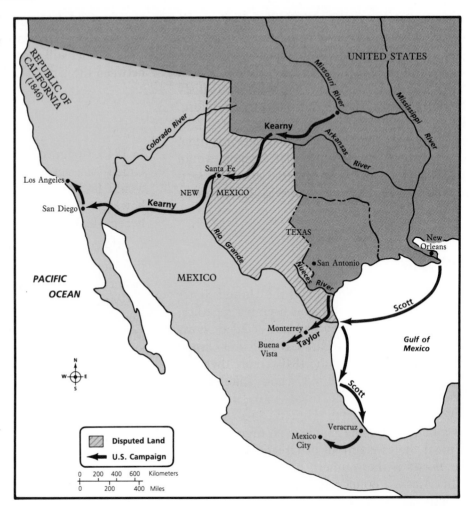

THE MEXICAN-AMERICAN WAR, 1846–1848

In 1846, President Polk sent U.S. troops into the disputed area between the two rivers. Mexico regarded this action as an invasion, and soon Mexican forces crossed the Rio Grande to attack the U.S. troops. After the Mexican attack, Polk was able to persuade Congress to declare war.

Opposition to the War Not all members of Congress favored the war. Anti-war critics included Abraham Lincoln, the young U.S. representative from Illinois. The critics accused Polk of cleverly leading Mexico into firing the first shots of the conflict. They spoke of Polk's lack of patience in dealing with the boundary issue. He was also too hasty, they said, in

sending troops into the disputed area. Many believed that Polk was chiefly motivated by the desire to take over the Mexican territories of New Mexico and California. Like Texas, these lands could be turned into slaveholding states.

The War

The war between Mexico and the United States lasted for about a year and a half. U.S. forces, led by Generals Winfield Scott and Zachary Taylor, won several easy victories. (See the map above.) General Taylor's forces made their gains in 1846 with an invasion of northern Mexico.

An 1847 campaign under General Scott went deeper into Mexico. By entering the enemy's capital—Mexico City—Scott forced the Mexicans to surrender.

During the war, U.S. troops under Colonel Stephen Kearny invaded the part of Mexico known as "New Mexico." Then they moved on to California, where U.S. settlers had declared a republic independent from Mexico. The events in New Mexico and California aided U.S. claims against Mexico when peace negotiations began.

The Peace Treaty

The Treaty of Guadalupe Hidalgo, signed in 1848, officially ended the Mexican War. With the treaty, Mexico gave up a vast area, including California and New Mexico. Today, this area makes up most of the Southwestern part of the United States. (See the map below.) The Mexican Cession, as the land was then called, had been about one fourth of Mexico. In return for all of this land, the United States agreed to pay Mexico only $15 million.

Texas Border Settlement In addition to giving up this land, Mexico finally recognized U.S. claims to Texas. The Rio Grande, not the Nueces River, came to serve as the border between Texas and Mexico.

Some Americans wanted the land just south of New Mexico Territory in order to build a railroad. As a result, in 1853 the U.S. minister to Mexico arranged to buy another piece of Mexico. For the Gadsden Purchase, as it was called, the United States paid $10 million. (See the map below.) The cost of this small strip of land was almost as much as the country paid for all of California and New Mexico. Historians have suggested that U.S. leaders paid so much for the Gadsden Purchase because they felt guilty about paying so little earlier.

GROWTH OF THE UNITED STATES, 1783–1853

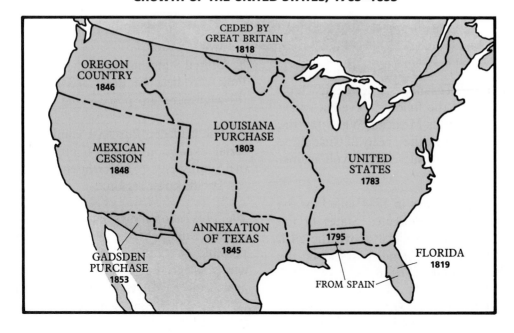

SUMMING UP   We have seen that many Americans in the 1840s wanted their country to expand westward. Regardless of other people's claims, U.S. settlers believed that they were fated to take and develop the West. Claims to Oregon were peacefully settled by a treaty with Great Britain. Taking Texas was more complicated, however. First, United States settlers in Texas declared themselves independent of Mexico. Later, Texas was admitted to the Union. Then, in 1846, the Mexican-American war broke out. As part of the peace treaty, the United States bought California and New Mexico. To round out this expansion, the United States arranged for the Gadsden Purchase.

Understanding the Text

On a separate sheet of paper, write the letter of the word or phrase that best completes each of the following statements.

1. "It is God's will that the United States stretch across the North American continent from ocean to ocean." This statement expressed the desires of U.S. settlers in the 1840s who supported (a) civil rights (b) abolition (c) Manifest Destiny (d) high tariffs.

2. Marcus and Narcissa Whitman were killed by (a) measles (b) Mexican soldiers (c) Indians (d) British settlers.

3. The revolt of Texans against Mexico took place before all of the following events, *except* (a) the United States-Mexican War (b) the Gadsden Purchase (c) the Treaty of Guadalupe Hidalgo (d) Mexico's successful revolt against Spain.

4. The Democratic party in 1844 called for the northern border of the United States in the Northwest to be set (a) just above the 54th parallel (b) at the 49th parallel (c) along the Rio Grande (d) none of the above.

5. Of the following names, the pair that best identifies an immediate cause of the Mexican-American War is (a) Nueces-Rio Grande (b) Atlantic-Pacific (c) Gadsden-Kearny (d) Guadalupe-Hidalgo.

6. The Mexican capital city was captured by (a) Zachary Taylor (b) Winfield Scott (c) Stephen Kearny (d) Sam Houston.

7. The U.S.-Canadian boundary in Oregon Country was settled by a (a) purchase (b) compromise (c) war (d) vote of the people living in Oregon

8. United States foreign policy under President Polk can best be described as (a) cautious (b) aggressive (c) peace-loving (d) isolationist.

9. The Gadsden Purchase completed the territorial expansion of the United States in the (a) Southwest (b) Northeast (c) Northwest (d) Pacific coast region.

10. This lesson shows that the territorial growth of the United States in the 1840s was made possible (a) by war only (b) by the willing agreement of the other nations involved (c) by a variety of methods, including settlement, war, purchase, and diplomacy (d) mainly by spending large sums of money to make purchases.

Developing Map Skills

Examine the map on page 189. Then choose the letter of the word or phrase that best completes each sentence. On a separate sheet of paper, match the sentence number with the correct letter.

1. In 1846, the area south of Oregon Country was owned by *(a)* Russia *(b)* Great Britain *(c)* the United States *(d)* Mexico.

2. The northern boundary of Oregon Country was *(a)* 42°N *(b)* 49°N *(c)* 54°40′N *(d)* none of the above.

3. The southern boundary of Oregon Country was *(a)* 42°N *(b)* 49°N *(c)* 54°40′N *(d)* none of the above.

4. Oregon Country was bounded on the west by *(a)* Missouri River *(b)* Canada *(c)* Mexico *(d)* the Pacific Ocean.

5. According to the 1846 Treaty, Oregon Country was divided into British and U.S. territories along the *(a)* Columbia River *(b)* Snake River *(c)* 54°40′N parallel *(d)* 49°N parallel.

Thinking About the Lesson

1. Why did the Mexican government in the mid-1830s restrict the rights of U.S. settlers in Texas to trade and own slaves? Do you think that the U.S. settlers should have protested against these restrictions? Why or why not?

2. From the point of view of a Northerner who opposed slavery, what were the advantages and disadvantages of having Texas become a state?

3. Do you think that the United States had a right to claim all of Oregon up to the border with Alaska? Explain your answer.

4. Did President James Polk make a wise decision in 1846 by compromising with the British over Oregon? Why or why not?

5. Why do many people consider the Mexican Cession to have been a bargain for the United States? Do you think that the Gadsden Purchase also was a good buy? Why or why not?

Early Economic Changes

In 1789, about 90 percent of all American workers were farmers. By 1850, this figure had declined to about 60 percent. Between these two years, the population of American towns and cities increased greatly, and the number of factories multiplied. America had begun to change from a largely agricultural nation to an industrial one.

Changes in American Agriculture

The percentage of Americans engaged in agriculture declined from 1789 to 1850. Nevertheless, farm production rose dramatically during this period. Several important inventions helped farmers to produce more:

• The *cotton gin*, invented by Eli Whitney in 1793, made the growing of cotton more profitable. Picking seeds out of raw cotton by hand had been slow, hard work. Now the cotton seeds could be removed quickly and easily by machine. Southern cotton growers began to sell more and more cotton to cloth makers in the North and in England. Slaves were in demand more than ever before. By 1850, "King Cotton" was the South's biggest crop and the nation's leading export. Alabama, Mississippi, Louisiana, Arkansas, and Texas began to replace the Old

South as cotton-growing lands. The soil in these newer states was more fertile than that in most of the Old South.

• The horse-drawn *reaper*, patented by Cyrus McCormick in 1834, increased wheat production. With this invention, a farmer could harvest many more acres of wheat than before. The reaper appeared just as the *prairies* (vast grasslands), which were ideal for growing wheat, were being settled. The reaper became a key factor in developing the huge wheat belt of the Middle West.

• The steel plow, introduced by John Deere in 1837, soon replaced the iron one. Steel, stronger and lighter than iron, was better for plowing up the hard soil of the West. With this invention (and the reaper), Americans turned the Western prairies into farmland.

The Industrial Revolution

In the 19th century, Americans experienced the same kind of rapid *industrialization* (growth of industries) that had already changed the economy of Great Britain. With this change, called the *Industrial Revolution*, the production of goods shifted from homes to factories. In factories, much work was done by power-driven machines

194

This picture shows Cyrus Hall McCormick demonstrating his reaper. In 1847, he set up a plant in Chicago, Illinois, to manufacture the machine.

The South also hoped to become a manufacturing region. It was unsuccessful in this effort for several reasons:

• The South did not have swiftly flowing rivers in good locations. Thus, the region lacked needed sources of waterpower to run factories.
• Wealthy Southerners invested most of their money in land and slaves. As a result, most had little money left to invest in factories.
• Transportation was not so well developed in the South as in the Northeast.

The First Factories

Samuel Slater helped build one of the first factories in America. After having worked in the spinning industry in England, he moved to Rhode Island in 1789. There he designed some of the country's first power-driven machines for spinning cotton thread. Previously, Americans had done this work in their homes—without the use of waterpower.

Power Loom In 1814, Francis Lowell introduced two important advances in the American textile industry. In Waltham, Massachusetts, he built the country's first power *loom* (a machine that weaves cotton thread into cloth). Then he combined under one roof both the spinning and weaving operations. For both operations, he used power-driven machines.

New Type of Worker The Waltham factory hired mostly young women and girls from New England farms. They lived in boardinghouses and had to follow strict rules while working and when off duty. Although their hours were long and the work was tiring, many textile workers enjoyed their jobs. For the first time in their lives, many of these workers could earn and save money. Furthermore, there was more to do in mill towns than in most farm communities.

instead of by hand. By 1850, over ten percent of U.S. workers made a living in manufacturing.

At first, the Industrial Revolution in America was confined largely to the Northeast. This region had many waterpower sites that were ideal for building factories. Rivers and streams could generate power by turning waterwheels. A considerable number of people in the Northeast had the money needed to build factories, buy equipment, and pay workers. Other reasons why the Northeast became an excellent place to build factories were:

• More roads, bridges, and canals had been developed there than in other parts of the country.
• Supplies of raw materials were nearby.
• Plenty of workers were available.

In the early 1830s, the fastest way to travel between Baltimore, Maryland, and Washington, D.C., was the Phoenix Line "Safety Coaches." Travel time was five hours. Passengers were "pitched about like a ship in a storm."

Interchangeable Parts   Gun-making played almost as important a part in the Industrial Revolution as did the making of textiles. In the production of muskets, Eli Whitney introduced a new idea. Previously, one skilled worker had made all the parts of a musket and then assembled it. Musket parts differed from one gun to the next; no two guns were built exactly alike. Whitney's idea, put into practice in 1800, was to make *interchangeable parts*. The same part for every gun of a certain model would be identical and usable in every product of the same model. Each worker, using machines, would probably make only one gun part. Each operation would be fairly simple, so that the factory would not need to hire skilled workers. The idea of using interchangeable parts was later picked up by other industries. The concept helped make possible *mass production* (the production of many copies of an item) in some American factories.

Before the 1840s, factories were still uncommon outside of the textile and arms industries. Then in the 1840s and afterward, industrialization increased for several reasons:

• The economic depression that began in 1837 ended in the mid-1840s, giving way to more prosperous years of factory expansion.

• Coal, used in the making of iron and steel, became available in large enough quantities for these industries to use. Coal also proved valuable in generating steam energy, which was used in some factories to power machines.

• Elias Howe invented the sewing machine in 1846. This invention brought major changes to the clothing, shoe, and leather-goods industries. In time, the cost of sewing machines became low enough so that families could buy them for use at home.

• Improvements in transportation and communications helped industries obtain raw materials more easily. Also, these improvements increased the industries' markets.

Changes in Transportation and Communications

Improved means of transportation and communications helped American industries to grow.

Transportation   By 1838, the National Road stretched from Maryland to the wheat fields of Illinois. Increasingly, Eastern cities were connected by *turnpikes*—roads built by private companies that charged tolls for their use.

Of equal importance was the growing system of canals, rivers, and lakes. By the 1830s, a person could travel inland by boat from New York City to the Mississippi River and then south to New Orleans. (See the map below.)

The steam engine brought major changes to both water and land transportation. John Fitch launched the nation's first steamboat on the Delaware River in 1787. Steamboats, however, did not become popular until after 1807. In that year, Robert Fulton demonstrated that his steamboat *Clermont* could go up the Hudson River against the current from New York City to Albany. Soon steamboats offered fast, regular service at low cost on many American waterways.

Steam also powered locomotives on the nation's growing railroads. In the 1830s and 1840s,

railroad workers laid some 9,000 miles of track—the beginning of a vast nationwide network. Trains rapidly became the fastest and most reliable form of transportation in the country. They were particularly important for inland cities that did not lie on major water routes.

Communications An advance in *communications* (systems of talking, writing, or otherwise communicating) rivaled improvements in transportation. In 1844, inventor and painter Samuel Morse opened the country's first electric telegraph line—one from Baltimore to Washington, D.C. For the first time, Americans could communicate instantly from city to city. Morse set up a company that made telegraph equipment. Within a few years, many other cities were connected by telegraph lines.

A NETWORK OF CANALS AND OTHER WATERWAYS, 1840

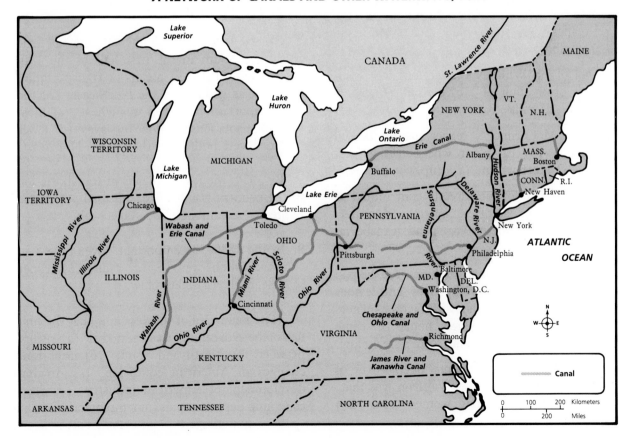

SUMMING UP   We have seen how during the first half of the 19th century the United States began to go through an Industrial Revolution. Because of key inventions, American farmers were able to produce more per acre and specialize in growing certain cash crops. Moreover, Americans changed the way that they made factory goods. Using power-driven machines, industrialists combined in one factory several operations previously done in several buildings. Some industries introduced the idea of mass production of goods, resulting in increased production and different kinds of jobs. Improvements in transportation and communications also helped industries and businesses to grow.

Understanding the Text

On a separate sheet of paper, write the letter of the word or phrase that best completes each of the following statements.

1. Preparation of prairie soil for planting crops became easier with the invention of the (a) reaper (b) steel plow (c) cotton gin (d) steamboat.

2. One of Eli Whitney's inventions led to increased production of (a) cotton (b) wheat (c) corn (d) milk.

3. Cyrus McCormick's reaper mainly helped the farmer to (a) plant wheat (b) harvest wheat (c) store wheat (d) ship wheat.

4. All of the following directly contributed to the growth of factories, *except* (a) water-power (b) investments (c) good transportation (d) slavery.

5. Elias Howe's sewing machine (a) helped the manufacture of clothing, shoes, and leather goods (b) was unpopular with factory owners (c) led to a decline in sewing at home (d) came before the invention of John Deere's steel plow.

6. Of the following statements, one *not* true of Francis Lowell's factory at Waltham was that it (a) hired many young women from New England farm families (b) used the idea of interchangeable parts for the first time (c) combined the use of a power loom and a power-driven spinning machine (d) had the country's first power loom.

7. Of the following statements, one *not* true about the South in the first half of the 19th century was that (a) means of transportation were not as good as in the Northeast (b) the most important cash crop was wheat (c) most work on plantations was done by slaves (d) fewer factories were built there than in the Northeast.

8. By 1850, the fastest means of transportation in the country was the (a) railroad (b) canal barge (c) steamboat (d) stagecoach.

9. In the 1840s, an important development in communications was the (a) radio (b) reaper (c) telegraph (d) steel plow.

10. The main idea of this lesson is that the first half of the 19th century was a period of (a) rivalry between the North and South (b) important changes in American education (c) growing development of American industry (d) deep economic depression and unemployment.

Developing Graph-Reading Skills

U.S. COTTON PRODUCTION, 1801–1850

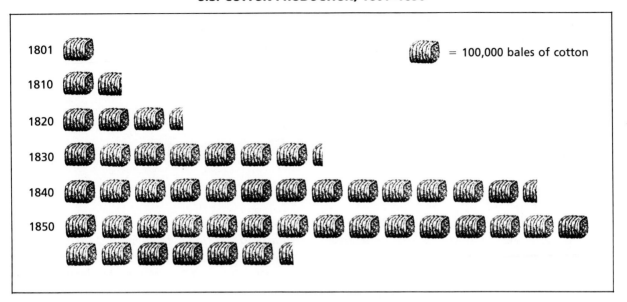

Study the picture graph above. Then choose the letter of the word or phrase that best completes each sentence. On a separate sheet of paper, match the sentence number with the correct letter.

1. Each drawn figure represents *(a)* a sugar cube *(b)* a bale of cotton *(c)* a cotton gin *(d)* 100,000 bales of cotton.

2. By 1820, cotton production had reached *(a)* about three bales *(b)* over the $3,000 level *(c)* over 300,000 bales *(d)* over 3 million bales.

3. For the years shown, cotton production was at its highest in *(a)* 1801 *(b)* 1830 *(c)* 1840 *(d)* 1850.

4. Cotton production was about 13 times over its 1801 figure in the year *(a)* 1820 *(b)* 1830 *(c)* 1840 *(d)* 1850.

5. From reading this picture graph, one can conclude that cotton production *(a)* increased greatly between 1801 and 1850 *(b)* regained the highest production level of the 18th century *(c)* reached its height during the U.S. Civil War, 1861–1865 *(d)* was highest in the South.

Thinking About the Lesson

1. Imagine that you were an American farmer in the first half of the 19th century. Would you have been interested in growing cash crops? Why or why not?

2. Explain why farm production rose dramatically between 1789 and 1850 despite the fact that a smaller percentage of Americans were farmers.

3. Would you have wanted to work in one of America's first factories if you had lived in the early 19th century? Why or why not?

4. Do you think that improvements in transportation and communications helped the West more than other regions of the country? Explain your answer.

Early Social Reforms

Americans in the first half of the 19th century were proud of their country. It had expanded greatly in size and become more democratic. Nevertheless, Americans knew that their society was far from perfect. Some, wanting *reforms* (changes that aim to improve something), joined groups or acted alone in calling for changes. American reformers lashed out against slavery and the use of alcohol. Many of them worked hard to improve education, working conditions, and the treatment of the mentally ill.

Free Public Education

In the early 19th century, most Americans generally regarded education as something reserved for the wealthy. Most parents who wanted their children educated had to hire private tutors or send the children to private schools.

Elementary Education Such thinking began to change during the 1830s and 1840s. Then towns, cities, and states gradually set up free public elementary schools. This reform was backed by working people, wanting to gain skills for better jobs, and by many employers, wanting a skilled work force. By 1850, tax-supported elementary education had become accepted in the North and the West.

Massachusetts's Example In 1837, Horace Mann, the period's most important educator, became secretary of the newly formed Massachusetts Board of Education. He worked hard to improve the *curriculum* (plan of subjects taught) and to set up *normal schools* (schools that train teachers). He also sought to lengthen the school year and to build better schoolhouses. Mann was so successful that other states copied his reforms.

Secondary Education The educational reform movement in America was less successful on the secondary level. Boston set up the nation's first tax-supported high school in 1821. By 1850, there still were few public high schools in the United States. Those that existed were mostly located in the Northeast. Not until after the Civil War did secondary public education expand the way elementary education had.

Women's Rights Movement

Most American men, even reform leaders, were unwilling to let women take more than a very minor part in public life. In the 1830s and 1840s, certain reformers openly challenged this attitude. Two white Southerners, Sarah and Angelina Grimké, came north to fight slavery.

They ended up fighting for women's rights as well. In their work, the Grimkés were joined by many other women.

Those who fought for women's rights complained that:

- Women could not vote or hold public office.
- Women could not own property.
- Women's education was usually limited to the elementary level.
- Women were not welcomed as workers in most professions or as business managers. Except for factory and teaching jobs, few opportunities for employment were open to women.

Seneca Falls Convention Lucretia Mott and Elizabeth Cady Stanton did something to help women fight for all of these rights. They organized the country's first Women's Rights Convention, held in Seneca Falls, New York, in 1848. This meeting, which claimed equal rights for both sexes, inspired women around the country to join the women's movement.

Women in Higher Education Educational advances were among the main accomplishments of the women's rights movement before 1850. In 1833, for example, Oberlin College in Ohio began admitting female, as well as male, students. In 1836, Mary Lyon, a Massachusetts teacher, opened Mount Holyoke, the nation's first permanent women's college.

> Elizabeth Blackwell defied custom by becoming a doctor in 1849. This profession had always been dominated by males in America. As a doctor, she devoted her life to the medical care of women and children.

Antislavery Movements

In Northern states, slavery had virtually ended soon after the American Revolution. In the first half of the 19th century, reformers came to call for the abolition of slavery in the South as well.

Gradual Reform At first, most reformers hoped to end slavery gradually. The Quaker journalist Benjamin Lundy represented this view, pressing first for the end of slavery in the territories. He said that after slaves were freed, they should be sent to special colonies in Africa. This idea was called *colonization.*

> Many of those who advocated colonization of blacks in Africa believed that blacks and whites could not live together in peace in North America. One group, the American Colonization Society, had limited success in sending freed slaves to Africa. Between 1817 and 1860, the organization settled some 12,000 blacks in the West African nation of Liberia.

Horace Mann (standing) pleads before the Massachusetts legislature, asking it to make important changes in the state's educational system.

Radical Abolitionists In the 1830s, some reformers began expressing more radical views on the slavery question. One of Lundy's assistants, William Lloyd Garrison, broke with his boss, demanding the immediate abolition of slavery. In 1831, Garrison set up his own newspaper, *The Liberator*, in Boston. He rejected gradual emancipation and the establishment of colonies in Africa. Believing that the U.S. Constitution protected slavery, Garrison called for the Northern states to withdraw from the Union. Garrison and others who wanted to abolish slavery were known as *abolitionists*.

Frederick Douglass was one of the most important abolitionists. As an escaped slave, he understood well the suffering of black Americans. In addition to calling for abolition, Douglass argued for black equality in both the North and the South. Although blacks were free in the Northern states, by 1850 they could vote in only a few of them.

Abolitionists used several methods to carry on their crusade. Douglass made impressive speeches on the subject and wrote editorials in his paper, *The North Star*, founded in 1847 in Rochester, New York. Other abolitionists sent petitions to Congress or campaigned for abolitionist candidates. In 1840 and 1844, the Liberty party unsuccessfully ran an abolitionist candidate for President—James G. Birney. In the 1848 election, most abolitionist voters supported the Free Soil party. (Discussed in Lesson 38.)

Labor Organizations

The first workers in America to organize labor unions were not the new factory workers. Instead, certain highly skilled *craft workers* (workers trained in a craft) formed societies in their trades. The journeymen shoemakers of Philadelphia, for instance, organized such a society in 1794. They wanted to protest low wages and other policies of the master shoemakers for whom they worked. In 1799, they *struck* (stopped working) and *picketed* (walked back and forth carrying strike signs) outside their masters' shops.

In the 1840s, Frederick Douglass carried out the nation's first "freedom rides." He took seats on railroad cars reserved for whites. He was usually removed from the cars by force.

Textile Workers At first, the new textile factories hired mostly children and women workers. The workers had to stand by their machines for 12 or 13 hours a day, six days a week. Reformers protested the use of *child labor* (work by children). The work often stunted the young people's growth and sometimes caused injuries and sicknesses.

Labor Troubles In the 1830s, workers in many industries suffered. Wages did not keep up with rising prices. As immigrants began streaming in from Europe, more people were looking for work. This situation prompted some employers to lower wages and increase hours. More labor organizations were formed and more strikes took place. Some textile workers, for example, formed the Factory Girls' Association in 1834. Between 1833 and 1837, textile workers carried out some 168 strikes in New England.

Workers' Rights Workers then did not have the same rights to organize and strike as they do today. In fact, most states either declared labor unions illegal or greatly limited their activities. A notable exception developed in Massachusetts. In 1842, the Massachusetts Supreme Court ruled that workers had the right to form labor unions.

Labor Gains In the 1830s and 1840s, unions and reformers fought hard to lower the number of hours workers spent at their jobs each day. They won a partial victory when, in 1840, the federal government put its workers on the ten-hour workday. In later years, some states would pass similar laws.

Labor unions also successfully supported other kinds of reforms. They helped to extend free public education and enact fairer tax laws. Moreover, they helped end the practice of jailing people for being in debt.

Other Reforms

In the first half of the 19th century, Americans fought for a number of other reforms.

Changing Americans' Drinking Habits Many Americans were upset by how much and how often their fellow citizens drank alcohol. They believed that drinking was both dangerous and evil. Concerned people formed local groups to combat the practice. In 1836, local societies joined together to form a national antidrinking organization—the American Temperance Union. Some members wanted to *prohibit* (ban) the sale and use of alcoholic drinks. Called *prohibitionists*, they were able to get Maine to ban drinking in

Between 1841 and 1844, reformer Dorothea Dix visited about 500 poorhouses, 300 county jails, 18 state penitentiaries, and many hospitals in Massachusetts. (*Granger Collection*)

1851. Afterward, other states followed Maine's example and began passing prohibition laws.

Reform of Prisons Dorothea Dix of Boston won fame as a social reformer in the fields of mental illness and prisons. She deplored the poor conditions of jails and poorhouses in Massachusetts. She also protested the practice of keeping mentally ill people in jails. As a result of her work, several states passed laws concerning conditions in prisons and the treatment of the mentally ill.

Ideal Communities

Throughout history, people have worked to right society's wrongs by forming special or "ideal" communities. Some of these groups were *communal*—that is, work was shared by all members of the communities. In the first half of the 19th century, Americans formed some 58 ideal communities. Most of these groups did not last long, but there were several exceptions.

Oneida Community One such community began in Putney, Vermont, in 1841 and later moved to Oneida, New York. The members farmed the land and set up factories to make steel traps and fine silverware. There were no traditional marriages, and children in the community were raised by all adults, in common. The Oneida Community prospered for more than 30 years.

Mormon Settlements In 1830 in western New York, Joseph Smith founded the Mormon religion. Soon the religious group moved to the Middle West in order to practice the religion freely. Led later by Brigham Young, Mormons ended up settling in Utah, around the Great Salt Lake, in 1847. Mainly due to the accomplishments of the Mormons, Utah became settled long before neighboring areas in the West.

SUMMING UP We have seen that in the first half of the 19th century many Americans were concerned about improving society. Some wanted to free slaves and give blacks the same rights that whites had. Others were more concerned about the rights of women or industrial workers. In the 1830s and 1840s, some states passed laws providing for free public education and improved conditions in jails and poorhouses. Not all of the demands of reformers were met during these years. Nevertheless, the discussion of society's ills set the stage for reforms later in the 19th century.

Understanding the Text

On a separate sheet of paper, write the letter of the word or phrase that best completes each of the following statements.

1. Free public schools are financed by (*a*) taxpayers (*b*) members of churches (*c*) wealthy individuals (*d*) parents of students attending schools.

2. The reform work of Garrison, Mann, and Dix was primarily carried out in (*a*) Indiana (*b*) Ohio (*c*) Connecticut (*d*) Massachusetts.

3. Horace Mann favored all of the following, *except* (*a*) shortening the school year (*b*) making students go to school (*c*) improving the curriculum (*d*) establishing teacher training schools.

4. In the first half of the 19th century, many women in America were employed as (*a*) politicians (*b*) lawyers (*c*) doctors (*d*) teachers.

5. During the same period, most women in America could (*a*) vote in elections (*b*) hold public office (*c*) own property (*d*) none of the above.

6. Factory workers in the first half of the 19th century campaigned for all of the following, *except* (*a*) labor unions (*b*) stricter punishment for debtors (*c*) shorter workdays (*d*) better pay.

7. Which of the following abolitionists was a former slave? (*a*) Sarah Grimké (*b*) William

Lloyd Garrison (c) Frederick Douglass (d) James G. Birney.

8. The settlement of black Americans in Liberia was organized by (a) the American Colonization Society (b) Lucretia Mott (c) William Lloyd Garrison (d) Frederick Douglass.

9. The Mormons were the major settlers of (a) Oneida, New York (b) Massachusetts (c) Oberlin, Ohio (d) Utah.

10. Characteristic of ideal communities in America, members (a) shared work duties (b) lived apart from each other (c) did as little work as possible (d) were supported by American taxpayers.

Developing Chronology Skills

Study the scrambled events and dates listed below. On a separate sheet of paper, draw a vertical line down the middle of the paper. Down one side, write the dates in chronological order. Down the other side, write the events that correspond to the dates.

Oberlin College admitted female students
Seneca Falls Convention held
The North Star founded
American Colonization Society founded
The Liberator founded
Mount Holyoke founded
American Temperance Union founded
Horace Mann became secretary of
    Massachusetts Board of Education

| 1833 | 1836 | 1817 | 1848 |
| 1831 | 1836 | 1847 | 1837 |

On the same piece of paper, number from one to five. Then match the number of each question with the letter of the word or phrase that best answers the question.

1. Which is the first event listed on the timeline? (a) *The North Star* founded (b) Seneca Falls Convention held (c) *The Liberator* founded (d) American Colonization Society founded.

2. Which event is at the bottom of the timeline? (a) *The North Star* founded (b) Seneca Falls Convention held (c) Oberlin College admitted female students (d) American Colonization Society founded.

3. Which two events on the timeline happened during the same year? (a) Mount Holyoke and American Temperance Union founded (b) Seneca Falls Convention held and American Colonization Society founded (c) Oberlin College admitted female students and Mount Holyoke founded (d) none of the above.

4. Which of the following dates was especially significant for those Americans who opposed drinking? (a) 1817 (b) 1833 (c) 1836 (d) 1837.

5. From reading the timeline, one can conclude which of the following? (a) Horace Mann became secretary of the Board of Education before *The Liberator* was founded. (b) Americans were able to read *The Liberator* before *The North Star*. (c) Horace Mann died before 1833. (d) Dorothea Dix attended the Seneca Falls Convention.

Thinking About the Lesson

1. Why did women have only a limited number of employment opportunities in the first half of the 19th century?

2. Was there any truth in William Lloyd Garrison's charge that the U.S. Constitution protected slavery? Explain your answer.

3. Do you think that the textile strikes of the 1830s were justified? Why or why not?

LESSON 35

Early Cultural Developments

At first, American culture was quite similar to that of Europe. As the new American nation took form, however, Americans began to create a culture of their own. By 1850, literature, painting, and music expressed truly American themes, such as the following:

- The worth of the individual.
- The great variety of human life in a large democracy.
- The glories of the rich and varied American landscape.
- American social conditions, including the institution of slavery.

Nationalism and American Writing

The pride of the new American nation was soon expressed in a growing body of literature. American writers chose to deal with American characters, regional life, and nature. Prominent among the many writers in the country's early decades were:

- Washington Irving, who wrote both history books and stories about New York City and the Hudson River Valley. His first major work, *History of New York . . .*, appeared in 1809. Readers today may be more familiar with his short stories "Rip Van Winkle" and "The Legend of Sleepy Hollow."

- William Cullen Bryant, an American poet whose first major work "*Thanatopsis*" was published in 1817. Bryant served as part owner and editor of the *New York Evening Post*, 1829–1878.

- James Fenimore Cooper, who wrote novels that described Northern frontier life in Colonial and Revolutionary times. His *The Last of the Mohicans*, first published in 1826, was one of a series of novels about a frontier scout. *The Pathfinder* (1840) was also part of that series.

- Sarah Josepha Hale, who became the first female magazine editor in the country when she began to work for *Ladies' Magazine* in 1827.

- Noah Webster, who published *The American Spelling Book* as early as 1783 and *An American Dictionary* in 1828. Webster wanted to replace the standard British texts and reference books with American ones. His books strongly influenced the way Americans used the English language.

- John James Audubon, who was not only a writer, but also a noted artist and *naturalist* (student of nature). He put together four impressive volumes of text and drawings called *The Birds of America*. The first volume appeared in 1827.

The American Renaissance

Serious American writing began to flower in the 1830s. This development, which continued for some 30 years, has been called the "American Renaissance."

Edgar Allan Poe wrote the best stories of this time. A man of strange personality and wild imagination, he originated both the detective story and horror story. Poe's highly original tales had little in common with other works by American authors. Poe was also a talented poet who effectively used words to create mysterious moods. Americans did not recognize him as a great writer until many years after his death in 1849.

Another poet, Henry Wadsworth Longfellow, won fame during his lifetime. Perhaps he was best known for his long poems *Evangeline* (1847) and *The Song of Hiawatha* (1855). Although they were heavily influenced by European models, these poems dealt with American scenes and events.

The poet John Greenleaf Whittier loved the history, daily life, and nature of his native New England. He was also a fiery reformer, dedicated to abolition and women's rights. The reformer in him spoke out in his book of poems called *Voices of Freedom* (1846).

Already in the 1820s, Nathaniel Hawthorne showed great talent in his short stories. By 1850, he was writing some of the best American novels ever written. Several of them, including *The Scarlet Letter*, were set in colonial days in New England. Others dealt with American life in the author's own day. In both settings, Hawthorne wrote of the hidden reasons that people act in certain ways.

Beginning in 1839, Herman Melville worked for several years on ships, including those that caught whales. He wrote of his seagoing adventures in his early short stories and novels, including *Typee* (1846) and *Omoo* (1847). In *Moby Dick* (1851), one of the world's greatest novels, Melville explored the role of fate in the lives of whalers.

Ralph Waldo Emerson urged American writers to turn away from European writing and create a new "literature of democracy." At first, he thought of himself primarily as a poet. His

Nathaniel Hawthorne (left) was born in Salem, Massachusetts, and lived much of his life there and in Concord, Massachusetts. Noah Webster (right) was born in West Hartford, Connecticut, and lived in various places, including Goshen, New York.

poem "The Concord Hymn," about the Revolutionary War battle, has instilled patriotism in generations of Americans. His most noted writings, however, were short essays. These pieces dealt with all kinds of serious topics, such as learning how to rely on oneself. Most of these essays were written versions of lectures that Emerson gave around the country.

Emerson's friend Henry David Thoreau was a more down-to-earth person. He loved nature, living two years (1845–1847) on the shores of Walden Pond in Massachusetts. While there, he wrote his famous book *Walden.* During the Mexican-American War, Thoreau refused to pay taxes. He did not want his tax money used to help the United States fight that war. As he later explained in his essay, "Civil Disobedience," he thought that the war furthered the interests of slaveholders.

Americans were eager to learn about the newest ideas in religion, politics, and social issues. They often went to public lectures. Many read newspapers and magazines. In the 1830s, some of the more popular newspapers reduced their price to one cent. As a result, "penny newspapers" were bought by even more readers.

Title page from Thoreau's *Walden,* published in 1854. His only other book published during his lifetime was *A Week on the Concord and the Merrimack Rivers* (1849). Visitors to eastern Massachusetts today can stop at Walden Pond to enjoy the scenery, but cannot view Thoreau's cabin, which has been torn down.

John James Audubon, portrayed here by his son John Woodhouse Audubon, was best known for his rendering of birds. He would shoot and stuff his subjects and then paint them.

Women who worked in the Lowell, Massachusetts, mills could publish their writings in this magazine. Print courtesy of Lowell Historical Society.

American Painting

After the Revolution, most American painters continued to portray important or wealthy people in their work. Both Gilbert Stuart and Charles Wilson Peale became famous for their portraits of President Washington. Peale also founded the country's first museum, in Independence Hall, Philadelphia. Another portrait artist of the period was John Trumbull. He was hired to paint four large pictures that still hang in the rotunda of the U.S. Capitol. (See the illustration on page 46.)

After 1825, an exceptional group of artists began to paint the natural beauty of American scenery. Known as the Hudson River School, these artists worked in the Hudson River Valley and neighboring New England. They specialized in landscapes. Under the leadership of Thomas Cole and others, the group dominated American oil painting for 50 years.

As the country grew, some American painters moved west. George Catlin, for instance, was attracted to studying and portraying Indian cultures. From 1829 to 1838, he painted hundreds of portraits of Indians and scenes of Indian life.

Music

A number of factors led to a growing interest among Americans in listening to music and in performing it:

- The making of inexpensive instruments in America became more widespread.
- Printing and publishing of sheet music—especially of patriotic and regional folk songs—increased.
- More schools introduced music courses, while a few devoted themselves entirely to musical training.
- In many cities, singers formed choral groups and musicians formed orchestras.
- Famous musicians began to make nationwide tours. In 1850, for example, the Swedish soprano Jenny Lind sang for audiences throughout the United States.

> Cultural tours were not limited to musicians, lecturers, and religious preachers. Americans especially welcomed traveling groups of actors and dancers. Circuses also became popular in the first half of the 19th century. Traveling performers endured many hardships to bring their cultural contributions to all regions of the land.

SUMMING UP   We have seen how Americans in the country's early decades began to create a national culture. Many well-known writers worked during the years 1789–1850. The level of writing was so high that we call the last decades of this period the "American Renaissance." Contributions of American painters, musicians, and performers also were important during this time.

Understanding the Text

On a separate sheet of paper, write the letter of the word or phrase that best completes each of the following statements.

1. The author of an important dictionary of the American language was (a) Washington Irving (b) James Fenimore Cooper (c) Noah Webster (d) Sarah Josepha Hale.

2. An American known as both a writer and an artist was (a) Henry Wadsworth Longfellow (b) John James Audubon (c) John Greenleaf Whittier (d) Henry David Thoreau.

3. The "American Renaissance" describes a period in American (a) writing (b) painting (c) music (d) all of the above.

4. The "American Renaissance" began in the (a) 1400s (b) 1790s (c) 1830s (d) 1850s.

5. All of the following are novels, *except* (a) *Last of the Mohicans* (b) *Moby Dick* (c) *The Scarlet Letter* (d) *The Song of Hiawatha*.

6. Edgar Allan Poe is remembered as (a) one of the inventors of the detective story (b) a writer of highly imaginative horror stories (c) a poet who made highly effective use of the English language (d) all of the above.

7. In his essay "Civil Disobedience," Henry David Thoreau wrote of his views on (a) the Mexican-American War (b) public drinking (c) the Civil War (d) the Hudson River School.

8. Before 1825, most American painters chose to paint mainly (a) scenery (b) Indian cultures (c) birds (d) portraits.

9. Of the following, the one who was *not* an important American painter was (a) Charles Wilson Peale (b) Jenny Lind (c) Thomas Cole (d) George Catlin.

10. As time went on, American writers and painters of the first half of the 19th century showed more and more interest in (a) imitating European artists (b) representing and interpreting American themes (c) changing the American form of government (d) gaining the approval of foreign critics.

Developing Library Skills

EXAMPLES OF LIBRARY CARDS

A

Poe, Edgar Allan
    Complete stories and poems. Garden City,
N.Y., Doubleday   c 1966

    ix, 819 p.   22cm.

B

q813
POE
            Poe the detective
    Walsh, John
        Poe the detective; the curious
    circumstances behind the Mystery
    of Marie Roget.   New Brunswick,
    N.J., Rutgers University Press
        154 p. illus.   c 1968
                    27cm.

C

813
POE
            POE, EDGAR ALLAN,   1809-1849
                                    comp.
    Howarth, William L   1940-
        Twentieth century interpretations
    of Poe's tales; a collection of
    critical essays.   Edited by William
    L. Howarth.   Englewood Cliffs, N.J.,
    Prentice-Hall   c 1971

        x, 166 p. 21cm.   (Twentieth
    century interpretations)

        A Spectrum book

        Bibliography: p. 115-116.

In a library card catalog, every book that a library has is listed on cards such as these and placed in special drawers. By knowing the author, title, or subject of a book, one can find in these drawers a card for the book. Choose the letter of the word or phrase that best completes each of the following sentences. On a separate sheet of paper, match the sentence number with the correct letter.

1. The last name of the author of the book on card "A" is (*a*) Poe (*b*) Edgar (*c*) Allan (*d*) none of the above.

2. "C" is an example of (*a*) an author card (*b*) a subject card (*c*) a title card (*d*) a bibliography.

3. The title of a book appears on the top line of a/an (*a*) author card (*b*) subject card (*c*) title card (*d*) library card.

4. An illustrated book is described in (*a*) card "A" (*b*) card "B" (*c*) card "C" (*d*) none of the above.

5. The call numbers in the left-hand margins of cards "B" and "C" tell one (*a*) where to find the books in the library (*b*) how many people have already checked out the books (*c*) how much the books cost (*d*) none of the above.

Thinking About the Lesson

1. Historians agree that the battle for U.S. cultural independence from Great Britain took longer than the struggle for political independence. What do the historians mean by the term "cultural independence"? Do you agree with the historians' view? Why or why not? Provide examples of how Americans made contributions in the fields of literature, painting, and music.

2. Select and complete one of the following library assignments: (*a*) Read a short story by Edgar Allan Poe and write a short paragraph about it. (*b*) Read a poem by Henry Wadsworth Longfellow and explain its meaning in your own words. (*c*) Look for a reproduction of a painting by George Catlin or Thomas Cole. Write a description of the painting and your reaction to seeing it.

The Development of Sectionalism

Sectionalism was not at first a major problem in the United States. The 1798 Virginia and Kentucky Resolutions, which maintained that states could nullify federal laws, had not received widespread support. As the country expanded, however, the concerns of regions or sections within it grew much stronger. Increasingly, people put the well-being of their region above national interests. In the Hartford Convention of 1814, for instance, New England states united against U.S. participation in the War of 1812. By 1850, many people of the North, South, and West had voiced clear sectional interests.

Policies Favored by Northerners

Because they lived in the manufacturing center of the nation, most Northerners strongly favored certain economic policies. These included:

• High tariffs. By increasing the prices of foreign imports, protective tariffs made domestic goods easier to sell. Now goods made abroad could not compete.

• Government-financed roads and canals. At first, many Northerners resented paying the taxes used for improvements elsewhere. Fearing a loss of business for their own Erie Canal, some New Yorkers objected to the building of canals in Pennsylvania. By the 1830s, however, more Northerners realized that roads and canals in other states helped open up new markets.

• Territorial expansion. On this issue, too, Northerners reversed their original position. At first, many Northerners opposed admission of new Western states to the Union. They believed that the new states would weaken Northern influence in Congress. Later, however, Northern business leaders saw that new states could become important markets for manufactured goods. Therefore, a large number of Northerners came to favor territorial expansion.

• High-priced public lands. Northern business leaders feared that many workers might move west if cheap land became available there. To prevent such a movement, Northern politicians favored high prices for public lands.

> Northern shippers did not always share the interests of manufacturers. High tariffs, for instance, cut down the amount of goods carried in trans-Atlantic trade. Therefore, high tariffs, meant a loss of business for shippers.

Issue of Slavery The antislavery views of many Northerners provided still another example of

By connecting the Hudson River and Lake Erie, the Erie Canal helped bring the West closer to the East. After the canal was completed in 1825, the cost of shipping a ton of grain from Buffalo to New York City fell from $100 to $5. Travel time was reduced from 20 to 6 days.

sectionalism. Antislavery groups sincerely believed that slavery was evil. Some other Northerners were merely distrustful of slavery—a system which was strange to them and from which they did not benefit.

Policies Favored by Southerners

Southerners bitterly resented Northern pressure to free the slaves or even to prevent the spread of slavery into other sections. Slavery had gone on for so long that most white Southerners—even many who owned no slaves—could scarcely imagine another way of life. The invention of the cotton gin made the Southern economy even more dependent on slave labor. Having developed a way of life based on cotton and slave labor, many Southerners supported the following policies:

• Low tariffs. Repeated attempts to develop a factory system in the South had failed. Instead, Southerners bought many factory-made goods from Europe. By favoring low tariffs, Southerners hoped to hold down the prices of the imported manufactured goods.

• Encouragement of state banks. Planters often needed credit to buy slaves, land, and equipment. Small farmers usually had to borrow money to keep going until crops could be sold. Neither group wanted to be dependent on big Northern banks, not even a National Bank. Southerners preferred to do business with local banks, over which they had some control.

• Opposition to government-financed roads and canals. In general, the South was well served by *navigable rivers* (ones that could be traveled by boats). These rivers helped Southern products get to markets in the North and also to ports in the South. After early attempts to develop a Southern canal system had failed, most Southerners opposed federal canal-building and road-building programs. These programs would have required increased federal taxes. In addition, the programs would have helped Western states, whose farmers competed directly with many Southern farmers.

• Territorial expansion and cheap public land. Since cotton growing exhausted the soil, Southern cotton growers looked to the West for new farmlands. Cheap land there would allow them to spread the plantation system. Many Southerners also hoped that the creation of new slave states would protect their sectional position within the Union.

The invention of the cotton gin by Eli Whitney in 1793 made the growing of cotton more profitable than ever before. Cotton production dominated the Southern economy and increased the demand for slave labor.

Policies Favored by Westerners

By 1850, half of the nation's population lived west of the Appalachian Mountains. Like the South, the West was primarily a farming region. As a result, Southerners and Westerners shared many concerns.

Many Westerners, however, were European immigrants or had come from the Northeast. They were used to free labor and generally opposed slavery. Thus, Westerners favored a mix of Northern and Southern positions, as the following summary shows:

• Cheap public lands. Western settlers tended to be hardworking, ambitious people who had little money. Cheap public land gave them their chance to get a good start in life by setting up farms.

• High tariffs. Westerners supported the tariffs that protected Northern manufacturing in-

terests. The manufacturing centers of the North were natural markets for Western crops. Thus, if these centers became larger and more prosperous, Western farmers would benefit.

• Government-financed roads and canals. Not many railroads had been built in the West yet. So to complement the system of navigable rivers, Western farmers needed good roads and canals.

• State banks. Most Westerners disliked the high interest rates charged by the National Bank. State banks were usually eager to grant low-interest loans, which helped Westerners prosper.

In the 1830s, President Jackson decided to raise the price of public lands in order to pay off the national debt. This action shocked many Westerners. They felt that the President—a Westerner—had betrayed them.

SUMMING UP   We have seen how by 1850 Americans' devotion to their region had become stronger. Most Westerners, Southerners, and Northerners had come to hold sectional views. The policies of Northerners and Southerners conflicted the most. Westerners tended to share concerns with Northerners on some issues and with Southerners on others.

Understanding the Text

On a separate sheet of paper, write the letter of the word or phrase that best completes each of the following statements.

1. The Hartford Convention showed that sectional feelings were developing in (a) New England (b) the old Northwest (c) the South (d) the West.

2. In time, most Northerners came to favor all of the following, *except* (a) low tariffs (b) high-priced public lands (c) territorial expansion (d) government-financed roads and canals.

3. In regard to early canal construction, relations between New York and Pennsylvania were marked by (a) cooperation (b) rivalry (c) mob violence (d) nationalism.

4. Northern manufacturers feared that cheap public lands might lead to (a) foreign competition (b) the end of the plantation system (c) westward migration of many workers (d) railroad construction.

5. Of the following developments, the one most responsible for the continuation of slavery in the South was the (a) demands of the abolitionists (b) failure to complete a Southern canal system (c) invention of the cotton gin (d) rise of state banks.

6. Most Southerners believed that government-financed internal improvements benefited (a) chiefly the South (b) chiefly the West (c) every section equally (d) no one.

7. A policy of President Jackson's that was strongly opposed by most Westerners was (a) raising the price of public lands (b) abolishing the National Bank (c) bringing the "common people" into the government (d) opposing South Carolina's threat to secede from the Union.

8. Westerners often favored high tariffs to protect Northern industries because (a) the North was a natural market for Western crops (b) most Northerners had come from the West (c) Westerners had large sums invested in Northern banks (d) the West had nothing in common with the South.

9. By 1850, half of the population of the United States lived (a) west of the Mississippi (b) west of the Appalachians (c) west of the Rocky Mountains (d) north of the 49th parallel.

10. The rise of sectionalism in the United States is explained mainly by (a) differences in religion (b) the rise of immigration (c) different economic situations and interests (d) weaknesses of the national government.

Developing Cartoon-Reading Skills

This cartoon is based on one that appeared in the *United States Weekly Telegram* in 1832.

Study the political cartoon above. Then choose the letter of the word or phrase that best completes each sentence. On a separate sheet of paper, match the sentence number with the correct letter.

1. The heavy man in the middle represents *(a)* Southerners *(b)* Northerners *(c)* Westerners *(d)* Europeans.

2. The ship in the background represents *(a)* foreign trade *(b)* improved transportation *(c)* improved communications *(d)* territorial expansion.

3. The cartoon shows sectional disagreements on the issues of *(a)* slavery and westward expansion *(b)* slavery and tariffs *(c)* tariffs and taxes *(d)* westward expansion and government-financed roads and canals.

4. The "To Let" sign probably represents the *(a)* poverty of Northerners *(b)* poverty of Southerners *(c)* plentiful housing in the West *(d)* prosperity of Northerners.

5. The cartoonist reveals sympathy with the views of *(a)* Southerners *(b)* Westerners *(c)* Northerners *(d)* farmers in all regions.

Thinking About the Lesson

1. Imagine that you had lived in the North during the 1830s and 1840s. About which one of the issues discussed in this lesson would you have been most concerned? What would have been your views on this issue?

2. Why did many Southerners favor cheap land in the West? Why did many Northern business leaders have the opposite view on this issue?

A NATION AT WAR WITH ITSELF

The Slavery Question

By the mid-19th century, slavery divided the people of the United States more than any other issue. Why were so many Americans opposed to slavery? Why did other Americans defend the institution? What actions did some people—including slaves themselves—take on the slavery question?

The Role of Slaves

As we learned in Lesson 33, the creation of "King Cotton" led to the growth of the slave system. Slavery, however, grew for other reasons as well. Slaves made life easier and more pleasant for their owners. Some slaves did the hardest jobs, such as cultivating fields, building roads, and digging canals. Some performed skilled tasks in working with wood, metal, brick, and leather. Still others took care of members of rich families and their homes.

The lowly position of slaves made even poor whites feel important by comparison. Many whites believed that they were naturally superior to blacks. Some whites used this belief in their own superiority to justify slavery. Even those blacks who had been freed found that whites continued to look down on them.

How Slaves Were Treated

The way that slave owners treated their slaves varied greatly. Some owners were kindhearted, housed and fed their slaves well, and took pride in their ownership. Most owners saw that mistreating slaves would not be smart since weakened or angry slaves would not work hard.

Other masters, however, housed their slaves in small, dirty huts and fed them poorly. Some masters whipped or branded their slaves as punishment for minor offenses.

Overseers On many plantations, *overseers* (hired managers) had complete control of the *field slaves* (those who worked in the fields). The overseers had little personal interest and no investment in the slaves. Often they worked slaves hard for long hours to produce a big crop. For their efforts, some overseers were rewarded with a bonus or a favorable new contract.

Whatever kind of master a slave had, slavery was cruel and often tragic. Masters were known to split up slave families by selling off the father, mother, or children. Some owners tried to avoid this practice. Nevertheless, breaking up slave families continued to be a widespread practice.

Slavery was an undemocratic system based

218

on false ideas of racial superiority. To be a slave was to be without dignity. Few slaves dared to hope for a better life. They had few chances for self-improvement. Laws forbade teaching slaves to read or write. Some states passed laws to prevent slaves from buying their freedom or owners from giving their slaves freedom.

Revolt and Escape of Slaves

Some slaves plotted to revolt or escape.

Denmark Vesey's Plot   In 1822, a former slave plotted the first major slave revolt of the 19th century. Denmark Vesey organized a large group of blacks from both Charleston and nearby plantations. They planned first to seize arms and then to free slaves in the area. The plot failed before any action was taken, however, because a slave informed on the conspirators. After capturing the plotters, authorities hanged Vesey and the other leaders of the plot—37

people in all. In taking such drastic action, white leaders were trying to warn all slaves against attempting any further revolts.

Nat Turner's Rebellion   In 1831, Nat Turner, a black slave who had served as a preacher, organized a rebellion of about 70 slaves. The rebels killed more than 50 white people. Whites all over the South were horrified. The Virginia state militia reacted strongly, overpowering the rebels and killing a great many blacks. Turner and some of the other leaders were captured, tried, and executed.

As a result of Turner's revolt, a number of states passed laws restricting slaves more than ever. Slaves found that they had less freedom to travel or meet together. Free blacks, too, found that their lives were becoming more difficult.

This engraving shows Nat Turner talking with fellow slaves involved in the short-lived slave rebellion of 1831. Turner, a preacher, believed that he was inspired by God to rebel. (*Granger Collection*)

Runaway slaves in the underground railroad were transported by wagons during the night. By day, they hid in cellars, attics, haylofts, or haystacks.

The Underground Railroad Many slaves tried to run away from their owners, going to Northern states and to Canada. Most of these *fugitives* (people who flee) were recaptured, but some succeeded in escaping. On the way north, free blacks and whites who hated slavery helped the fugitives. Those who helped belonged to what was called the *underground railroad*. Despite its name, it was not really a railroad. Instead, it was a system of hiding places and carefully chosen routes. "Conductors" on the railroad helped some 50,000 fugitive slaves escape to freedom between the years 1830 and 1860.

Slaves who tried to escape were sometimes pursued by professional slave-catchers. These people were paid to capture and return escaped slaves to their masters. Upon their return, slaves could expect cruel punishments.

One escaped slave became the most famous conductor the underground railroad ever had. At great personal risk, Harriet Tubman returned to the South 19 times. Each time she led blacks north to freedom, helping some 300 slaves to escape.

Southern Defense of Slavery

Most Southern whites defended slavery despite the fact that only about 25 percent of them owned slaves. Furthermore, only about one percent owned more than 20 slaves. Slavery persisted in the South because of the plantation system. Slaves were the major source of labor on plantations, and plantations dominated the Southern economy. Southern representatives in Congress spoke for and protected the interests of the plantation owners.

Southerners were quick to blame abolitionists for the discontent felt by slaves. Southern states passed laws banning abolitionist books and articles. Postal officials refused to deliver abolitionist mail. In 1836, Southern members of Congress pushed through a *gag rule*. This rule, which lasted eight years, banned the reading of abolitionist petitions in the House.

New Arguments Supporting Slavery The abolitionist movement caused a basic change in the thinking of some white Southerners. Earlier, many of them had agreed that slavery was not just, but was a necessary part of the Southern economy. Under the threat of abolition, however, many Southerners found other arguments in defense of slavery. The *Bible,* they said, allowed for slavery. Moreover, they claimed, slavery had enabled Africans to become Christians and to live in a more civilized land. Finally, they argued, most slave owners took good care of their slaves. Most slaves were always sure of food, clothing, and shelter.

These Southerners compared the welfare of slaves with that of Northern laborers. Northern "wage slaves," the Southerners claimed, lived in daily fear of losing their jobs. According to slavery's defenders, some black slaves lived better lives than did poor whites in the North.

Abolitionists counterargued that there was no comparison between free laborers and humans deprived of freedom and dignity.

Abolitionists

Beginning in the 1830s, the movement to abolish slavery gained new force, especially in the North. As we learned in Lesson 34, Americans then were becoming concerned about social reforms of all kinds. For many, the slavery system was the biggest cause for national shame. Abolitionists were inspired by Great Britain, which, in 1833, freed all slaves in the British colonies.

Abolitionists were active in many ways. Some, like the former slave Sojourner Truth, traveled widely, speaking to people throughout the North and West. Others wrote articles and sent petitions to Congress. Abolitionists held public meetings in many cities and towns.

Political Parties and Slavery In the 1840s and 1850s, abolitionists tried a new approach. They entered politics, at first by forming the Liberty party. James Birney, the candidate of the Liberty party, unsuccessfully ran for President in 1840 and 1844. The Free Soil party was the choice of many abolitionists in 1848. And after 1854, most abolitionists voted for the Republican party ticket. By 1850, more than 200,000

Americans belonged to various abolitionist societies. Nonetheless, abolitionists had not yet become a strong political force.

The North was by no means united behind the abolitionists. Some Northerners called abolitionists "troublemakers." Northern business leaders believed that abolitionist activities harmed their business dealings with Southerners. Some white factory workers in the North feared that freed slaves would compete with them for jobs.

As these fears grew, some Northerners turned to violence, breaking up antislavery meetings. A mob attacked abolitionist leader William Lloyd Garrison on the streets of Boston. In Alton, Illinois, another angry mob murdered abolitionist newspaper editor Elijah Lovejoy.

This photograph of abolitionist Sojourner Truth was taken in 1864. By then, she had spent years making speaking tours all over the North.

SUMMING UP   We have seen how slavery grew stronger in the South. We have also noted that many slaves fought the institution by fleeing the South. A few slaves resorted to violence. As slavery came under attack, many Southerners came forth to defend it.

Understanding the Text

On a separate sheet of paper, write the letter of the word or phrase that best completes each of the following statements.

1. Mistreatment of slaves took all of the following forms, *except* (a) whipping (b) branding (c) heavy taxation (d) poor diet and living conditions.

2. Most hardworking slaves could expect (a) a promotion to a better job (b) more hard work as a slave (c) freedom (d) an education.

3. Information about Denmark Vesey would most probably be found in a book about (a) plantation homes (b) the role of the plantation overseer (c) textile mills (d) slave revolts.

4. The Nat Turner rebellion led to (a) the death of more than 50 whites (b) the death of many blacks (c) state laws restricting the lives of blacks (d) all of the above.

5. A famous "conductor" on the underground railroad was (a) Abraham Lincoln (b) Elijah Lovejoy (c) Harriet Tubman (d) Denmark Vesey.

6. By founding the Liberty party, some abolitionists tried to (a) use violence to free slaves (b) help fugitive slaves escape to freedom (c) gain political power as a means of ending slavery (d) open the Western territories to slavery.

7. James Birney (a) supported slavery (b) was the Liberty party candidate for President in 1840 and 1844 (c) claimed that slaves were treated better than most Northern workers (d) all of the above.

8. Defenders of slavery used all of the following arguments to support slavery, *except* one that said that (a) the *Bible* allowed for slavery (b) slave owners usually took good care of slaves (c) abolitionists did not want to form political parties (d) slavery made it possible for slaves to become Christians.

9. Some Northern workers were against the abolitionist movement because (a) they were afraid that freed blacks might try to take over their jobs (b) they felt that slaves lived better than they did (c) they wanted to keep the plantation system going (d) they hoped to own slaves.

10. Which of the following statements about American slavery is the most accurate? (a) It depended on goodwill between slaves and masters. (b) In most cases, it was not profitable. (c) It was a cruel system that degraded blacks. (d) Most white Southerners opposed slavery.

Developing Graph-Reading Skills

U.S. COTTON PRODUCTION, 1790–1860

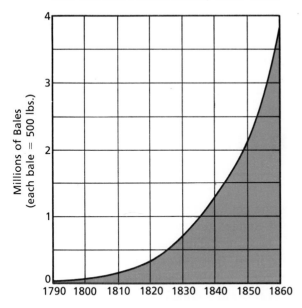

SLAVERY IN THE UNITED STATES, 1790–1860

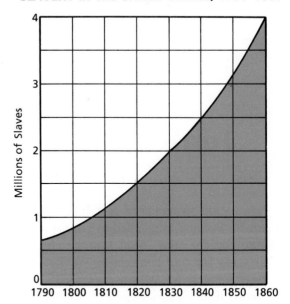

Study the two graphs above. Then choose the letter of the word or phrase that best completes each sentence. On a separate sheet of paper, match the sentence number with the correct letter.

1. The year in which cotton production went over the one-million-bale mark for the first time was *(a)* 1798 *(b)* 1810 *(c)* 1835 *(d)* 1840.

2. The ten-year period during which the growth in cotton production was the greatest was *(a)* 1820–1830 *(b)* 1830–1840 *(c)* 1840–1850 *(d)* 1850–1860.

3. In 1820, the approximate number of slaves in the United States was *(a)* 500 *(b)* 1,000,000 *(c)* 1,500,000 *(d)* 4,000,000.

4. Slavery in the United States grew the slowest during the ten-year period *(a)* 1790–1800 *(b)* 1810–1820 *(c)* 1830–1840 *(d)* 1850–1860.

5. A comparison of both graphs reveals that for the period 1790–1860 *(a)* cotton production rose while the number of slaves declined *(b)* both cotton production and the number of slaves declined *(c)* the number of slaves increased while cotton production declined *(d)* both cotton production and the number of slaves increased.

Thinking About the Lesson

1. Why was the system of hiding places and routes of escape for slaves called the "underground railroad"?

2. Why did most white Southerners support slavery even though only about 25 percent of them owned slaves?

3. Do you think that most slaves in the South lived better lives than most white laborers in the North? Explain your answer.

LESSON 38

Territorial Expansion and Slavery

Many plantation owners grew cotton in a wasteful manner. Because they failed to put nutrients back into the soil, they soon found that they were growing less and less cotton. At the same time, the demand for cotton expanded. As a result, plantation owners went west to buy new cotton lands, bringing along their slaves. As each Western territory applied for statehood, Americans debated the question, "Should slavery be allowed there?"

Territorial Expansion

As we learned in Lesson 27, the first sharp political debate over slavery occurred in 1820. At that time, both Maine and Missouri had applied for statehood. Under the Missouri Compromise of 1820, Maine came into the Union as a free state and Missouri as one that allowed slavery. The country then had an equal number of slave and free states.

This balance was redrawn in 1836 and 1837 when two more states were admitted. Michigan, a free state, offset Arkansas, a slaveholding state. Soon, however, territorial expansion again heated up the slavery debate.

Texas   Texans declared their independence from Mexico in 1836. (See Lesson 32.) They formed

224

a separate country but asked to join the *Union* (United States) as a state. If admitted, Texas would become a slave state, since many slaves already lived there. For a number of years, Northerners helped block Texas's request for admission to the Union.

Growing Support for Annexation   In 1844, Americans elected the Democratic candidate, James Polk, as President. Polk had run for office, promising to annex Texas. But a President does not have the authority to do this alone. Annexing land by the method of a treaty requires a two-thirds vote of the Senate. The pro-Texas support in the Senate, however, was not strong enough to win such a vote.

Next, supporters of annexation pressed for an alternate method—a *joint resolution of Congress*. This method of approving a treaty had never before been used to gain new territory. A joint resolution requires only a majority vote in each house of Congress and the President's signature. In February, 1845, Congress approved such a resolution, and Texas was finally annexed.

The Wilmot Proviso   The annexation of Texas was followed by a war with Mexico in 1846. Early in the war, Representative David Wilmot of Pennsylvania introduced an important bill on the slave question. The Wilmot Proviso forbade slavery in any territory that the United States might win from Mexico. Angry Southern senators were able to defeat the Wilmot Proviso, but antislavery forces in Congress would raise the issue again in later years.

The Free Soil Party

Slavery in the territories became an important issue in the presidential election of 1848. Both major parties, the Whigs and the Democrats, had strong antislavery and proslavery factions. Therefore, neither party wanted to take a stand on the issue of slavery in the new territories. The Free Soil party, however, was not afraid to come out against allowing slavery there. The Free Soilers, with former President Martin Van Buren as their candidate, captured many votes. In the process, they took much support away from Lewis Cass, the Democratic party candidate. As a result, the Whig candidate, General Zachary Taylor, became President. (Taylor was a hero of the Mexican-American War.)

The Free Soil party elected 12 U.S. representatives in the 1848 election. The rest of the House was split almost evenly between Democrats and Whigs. For two years in the lower house, the new party held the votes needed by either party to gain a majority. On many issues, the Free Soilers decided whether the Whigs or the Democrats would rule the House.

The Settlement of California

Texas and Florida came into the Union as slave states in 1845. Within a few years, two free states—Iowa and Wisconsin—were also admitted. Thus, by 1850, there was once more a balance between free states and slave states. Then in that year, California asked to join the Union as a free state.

In 1848, settlers had discovered gold at Sutter's Mill, California. In the following year, Forty-Niners, fortune seekers from all over the

During the California gold rush of 1849, Americans flocked to the region to pan for gold. They looked in streambeds for nuggets of gold that may have washed out of the surrounding hills.

United States, had flocked to California. Soon the territory had enough people to ask to become a state.

Southern Concerns

Proslavery forces were worried about California's entry into the Union. If California became a free state, then antislavery forces would control the U.S. Senate. Many proslavery Americans were also concerned about the status of slavery in other areas of the country:

• Tens of thousands of Southern slaves had run away, escaping to the North and to Canada. A federal law of 1793 had called for the return of fugitives to slave states. Some officials in the North, however, refused to help slave owners by returning escaped slaves.

• Some members of Congress were talking about banning slavery in Utah and New Mexico territories.

• Many Northerners wanted to abolish slavery in the nation's capital. They thought that the existence of slavery in the District of Columbia was a disgrace for the whole country. Supporters of slavery, however, feared abolition there, since slaveholding states surrounded the city.

The Compromise of 1850

To avoid a national crisis, Senator Henry Clay of Kentucky offered a compromise. Like all compromises, his proposal asked each side of the dispute to give up something to gain something else. The main provisions of the Compromise of 1850 were as follows:

In this 1850 scene in the U.S. Senate Chamber, Henry Clay calls for support for his compromise proposal. Senator John C. Calhoun is standing on the right. Senator Daniel Webster is seated on the left, with his hand to his ear.

• California (part of the Mexican Cession) would come into the Union as a free state.

• The rest of the Mexican Cession would be split into Utah and New Mexico territories. In each territory, settlers were to decide what would be done about slavery by voting. Deciding an issue in this manner was widely known as *popular sovereignty.*

• The slave trade, but *not* slave ownership, would be banned in the District of Columbia.

• A new, stricter *fugitive slave law* would be passed. It would require state and local officials to help capture and return runaway slaves.

Clay's proposal was hotly debated in the Senate. John C. Calhoun of South Carolina stated the proslavery position. He rejected Clay's ideas and called for an end to antislavery speeches. If such speeches continued, he said, "there will be nothing left to hold the Union together except force." Calhoun's position was weakened by the fact that he was ill during the debates. He died on March 31, 1850—before the matter had been voted on.

Senator Daniel Webster of Massachusetts supported the compromise. Although he opposed slavery, he thought preserving the Union to be more important. Many other Northerners denounced Webster. They did not want to compromise on the slavery question. William H. Seward of New York was one senator who voiced such a radical, antislavery view.

President Zachary Taylor also opposed the compromise. Some politicians thought that he might veto Clay's proposal, if passed by Congress. In the summer of 1850, however, before the opportunity arose, the President died.

The new President, Millard Fillmore, was eager to approve Clay's ideas and got the opportunity during the fall of 1850. Over a period of several months, he signed into law a number of bills that together are considered the Compromise of 1850.

The Effects of the Compromise

The Compromise of 1850 changed the map of the United States. California entered the Union as a free state in 1850. In the same year, two new territories were created—Utah and New Mexico. These territories would be open to slavery only if enough settlers there favored the institution. (See the map on page 232.)

Because senators were able to compromise, no states were to leave the Union at this time. The Compromise kept the peace between proslavery and antislavery forces for another ten years. Even so, many people on both sides of the slavery question were not satisfied.

CAUTION!!
COLORED PEOPLE
OF BOSTON, ONE & ALL,
You are hereby respectfully CAUTIONED and advised, to avoid conversing with the
Watchmen and Police Officers of Boston,
For since the recent ORDER OF THE MAYOR & ALDERMEN, they are empowered to act as
KIDNAPPERS
AND
Slave Catchers,
And they have already been actually employed in KIDNAPPING, CATCHING, AND KEEPING SLAVES. Therefore, if you value your LIBERTY, and the *Welfare of the Fugitives* among you, *Shun* them in every possible manner, as so many *HOUNDS* on the track of the most unfortunate of your race.
Keep a Sharp Look Out for KIDNAPPERS, and have TOP EYE open.
APRIL 24, 1851.

The Compromise upset many Southerners, mainly because it left the Senate controlled by antislavery forces. Southerners had little hope that any of the remaining territories would become slave states, since Utah and New Mexico were not suitable for growing cotton.

Many Northerners were also upset by the Compromise. They objected to the new Fugitive Slave Law. With this law, Northern officials now would be forced to help capture runaway slaves. And Northerners who helped slaves to escape could now be fined and even jailed.

SUMMING UP   We have seen how slavery became more and more of an issue as the country expanded. As long as each new slave state was offset by a free one, a political balance remained in the Senate. In 1850, though, there was no slave state to balance California's entry into the Union. So Henry Clay came up with a compromise to try to satisfy both sides of the question. The Compromise of 1850 defused the crisis for a number of years but did not remove the bitter feelings that had arisen in the dispute.

Understanding the Text

On a separate sheet of paper, write the letter of the word or phrase that best completes each of the following statements.

1. The Missouri Compromise of 1820 provided that *(a)* Maine was to decide by popular sovereignty whether it would be a free state or a slave state *(b)* Missouri was to come into the Union as a slave state *(c)* Wisconsin was to come into the Union as a free state *(d)* Congress would pass a new Fugitive Slave Law.

2. Admission of a territory by joint resolution requires action by *(a)* two thirds of the Senate *(b)* a majority of the Senate *(c)* the President and the Senate *(d)* a majority of both houses of Congress and the President.

3. If Congress had adopted the Wilmot Proviso, *(a)* slavery would have been banned from any territory won from Mexico *(b)* Oregon Territory would have been divided between Great Britain and the United States *(c)* the people in the territories won from Mexico would have decided the status of slavery there *(d)* the slavery issue in all territories would have been settled for good.

4. In the late 1840s, the party taking a firm position against the extension of slavery into new states was the *(a)* Whig party *(b)* Democratic party *(c)* Free Soil party *(d)* Republican party.

5. Of the following provisions, one that was *not* a part of the Compromise of 1850 said that *(a)* settlers in Utah and New Mexico were to decide themselves about slavery by voting *(b)* Texas was to join the Union as a slave state

(c) California was to join as a free state (d) the slave trade was to be banned in Washington, D.C.

6. In 1850, the phrase "popular sovereignty" was used to help settle the problem of (a) how a settler could get free land (b) whether slavery should expand into new territories (c) whether industrial or rural areas should control state governments (d) how to set voting requirements in new states.

7. The Compromise of 1850 was proposed by (a) William Seward (b) Zachary Taylor (c) Millard Fillmore (d) Henry Clay.

8. The Compromise of 1850 was opposed by all of the following, *except* (a) Daniel Webster (b) William Seward (c) John C. Calhoun (d) Zachary Taylor.

9. A result of the Compromise of 1850 was that (a) the Civil War broke out in 1850 (b) John C. Calhoun became U.S. President (c) South Carolina seceded (d) tension on the slavery issue lessened temporarily.

10. Which of the following is the most accurate statement about the issue of the extension of slavery in the 1840s? (a) Political leaders and parties paid little attention to the issue. (b) In spite of repeated efforts, no compromise could be reached on the issue. (c) It was settled by a compromise that satisfied neither side. (d) It aroused strong feelings in the South, but not in the North.

Developing Analytical Skills

Examine the poster reproduced on page 227. Then choose the letter of the word or phrase that best completes each sentence. On a separate sheet of paper, match the sentence number with the correct letter.

1. This poster was directed at (a) kidnappers (b) blacks (c) white workers (d) slave catchers.

2. According to the poster, Boston police officers were aiding (a) slave owners (b) abolitionists (c) blacks living in Boston (d) all of the above.

3. The word "fugitives" referred to (a) escaped slaves (b) freed slaves (c) army deserters (d) illegal immigrants.

4. The poster advised black people of Boston to (a) move to the South (b) surrender to the police (c) stay away from watchmen and police officers (d) help catch slaves.

5. This poster was probably written and put up by (a) the Boston city council (b) a Southern cotton growers' association (c) Northern abolitionists (d) Northern proslavery advocates.

Thinking About the Lesson

1. Why did territorial expansion lead to more conflicts over slavery?

2. Imagine that you had been a senator listening to the debates on the Compromise of 1850. Would you have voted for the Compromise? Why or why not?

3. Which group do you think received a better deal from the Compromise of 1850—the proslavery or antislavery forces? Explain your answer.

LESSON 39

Slavery Divides the Nation

The Compromise of 1850 did not really resolve the slave question in the United States. Several times in the 1850s, disagreements over slavery resulted in violence. We shall see how a number of forces and events played a part in the disputes.

Reactions to the Compromise of 1850

On the one hand, the Compromise of 1850 satisfied many Americans. On the other hand, extremists on both sides of the slavery question became angry over its provisions.

Personal Liberty Laws Northerners especially disliked the harsh, new Fugitive Slave Law, a part of the Compromise. This law made no provision for jury trials for people captured as runaway slaves. To show their opposition, nine Northern states passed *personal liberty laws*. This legislation made it harder for slave owners to capture and return runaways. Some of these laws, for instance, forbade the use of local jails to house captured slaves. Others called for jury trials before alleged runaway slaves could be returned to their owners.

Southern Discontent In reaction to the Compromise of 1850, some Southerners took extreme positions. Many state legislators in South Carolina, Georgia, and elsewhere called upon their states to secede. The efforts of these *secessionists*,

230

however, failed at this time to win a majority of any state legislature.

The Election of 1852 In the presidential election of 1852, the Whigs nominated General Winfield Scott, an antislavery candidate who did not clearly state his views on the Compromise. The Free Soilers, who nominated John Hale, came out strongly against the Compromise. The Democratic nominee, Franklin Pierce, firmly supported the Compromise of 1850. The fact that Pierce won the election probably indicates that most Americans were still in favor of the measure.

In 1852, Harriet Beecher Stowe published her controversial book on slave life, *Uncle Tom's Cabin.* This best-selling novel bitterly criticized slavery. It convinced many Northerners that slavery was an evil that had to be wiped out. Many Southerners expressed extreme anger over the publication of the book. They believed that Stowe had been unfair to the South and had spread lies about slavery.

The Kansas-Nebraska Act

In 1854, Senator Stephen Douglas of Illinois proposed a controversial bill in Congress. His

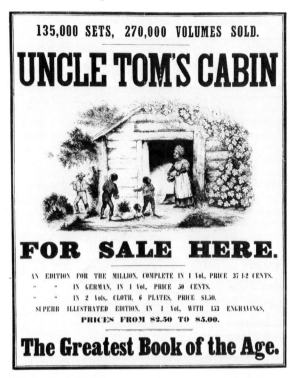

135,000 SETS, 270,000 VOLUMES SOLD.

UNCLE TOM'S CABIN

FOR SALE HERE.

AN EDITION FOR THE MILLION, COMPLETE IN 1 Vol., PRICE 37 1-2 CENTS.
" " IN GERMAN, IN 1 Vol., PRICE 50 CENTS.
" " IN 2 Vols., CLOTH, 6 PLATES, PRICE $1.50.
SUPERB ILLUSTRATED EDITION, IN 1 Vol., WITH 153 ENGRAVINGS,
PRICES FROM $2.50 TO $5.00.

The Greatest Book of the Age.

Harriet Beecher Stowe (left) was born in Litchfield, Connecticut, the daughter of a Congregational minister. Her brother, Henry Ward Beecher, became a famous clergyman. Her sister, Catharine Beecher, became a renowned educator who advocated teaching home economics and physical education to young women. The advertising poster (right) reveals how well Harriet Beecher Stowe's book *Uncle Tom's Cabin* sold.

bill provided a plan to organize for settlement the territory west of Missouri and Iowa. Settlers there would decide for themselves whether they would enter the Union as free or slave states. Douglas's plan, based on the idea of popular sovereignty, caused bitterness over the slavery issue to increase even more.

Many Northerners denounced Douglas's bill. They pointed out that it would repeal the Missouri Compromise. That law had prohibited slavery in the area where Kansas and Nebraska would be formed. The proposed Kansas-Nebraska Act would open the territory to slavery if people living there desired it.

Douglas opposed slavery, but he had several reasons for introducing his bill:

• He wanted to become President of the United States. To reach this goal, he would need the support of Southern Democrats.

• He sincerely believed in the idea of self-government. He thought that popular sovereignty was an excellent expression of that idea.

• He favored building a railroad from Illinois to the Pacific Coast. Such a railroad would go through the territory in question. The sooner the land was organized and settled, the sooner federal money might become available for the railroad.

• Some Southerners wanted Congress to fund instead a railroad from New Orleans to California. Douglas, however, wanted Southern support for his own railroad project. He hoped that if he gave in to the South on slavery, Southerners would drop their railroad project.

Douglas's bill, which became law in 1854, set up two new territories—Kansas and Nebraska. (See the map on page 232.) Many Americans quickly moved into the territories.

THE UNITED STATES, 1854

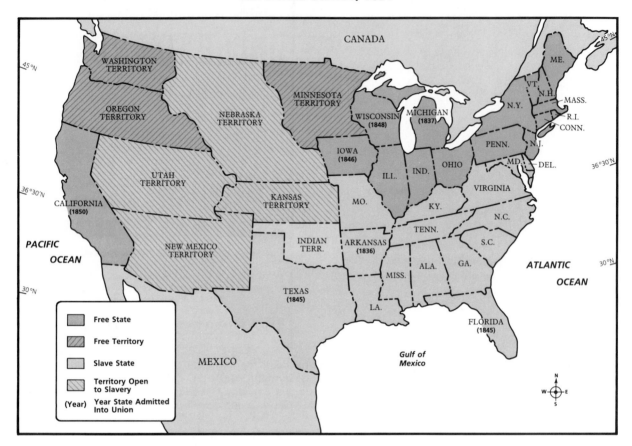

In Kansas, fighting soon broke out between proslavery and antislavery settlers. So much violence occurred that the area became known as "Bleeding Kansas." The two groups of settlers in Kansas formed separate governments. As a result, Congress could not decide whether to recognize the proslavery or the antislavery one. Congress did not settle the issue until 1861, when it allowed Kansas to enter the Union as a free state.

The Republican Party

A new political party was born out of the controversy over the Kansas-Nebraska Act. There were antislavery forces in both the Democratic and Whig parties who objected to the Kansas-Nebraska Act. Neither of the major parties, though, would come out clearly against this potential extension of slavery. Consequently, in 1854 antislavery forces from the two major parties joined with Free Soilers. They formed a new political group called the "Republican party."

The Republicans promised to prevent the spread of slavery into the territories. This pledge helped the Republicans gain supporters in the North. In time, many Whig leaders, including Abraham Lincoln, would become active Republican party leaders.

Frémont vs. Fillmore vs. Buchanan In the presidential election of 1856, the Republicans ran John C. Frémont of California. Frémont, a famous explorer of the West, opposed slavery's expansion. The Democrats and their candidate, James Buchanan, supported the Kansas-Nebraska Act. Former President Millard Fillmore ran for President as the candidate of both the Whigs and a new organization—the American party. This last group, nicknamed the Know-Nothings, opposed any more immigration.

In the 1856 election, Frémont came in second, while Fillmore ran a poor third. James Buchanan, the Democratic candidate, became President. The voting pattern showed a growing division in the country between a Democratic South and a Republican North.

The Dred Scott Decision

In 1857, the U.S. Supreme Court made an important decision on slavery. Dred Scott, a slave, had brought a case to court to gain his freedom. The key fact in the case was that his master had once taken him into free territory. Scott's lawyers claimed that once a slave goes into free territory, he or she becomes free. After deliberation, the Supreme Court denied this claim.

The Majority Opinion Chief Justice Roger Taney spoke for the majority in maintaining that slaves were a form of property. Under the Constitution, he said, Congress had no right to deprive slave owners of their property. Furthermore, said the Court, despite the Missouri Compromise, slavery was legal in every territory.

Reactions to the Decision The Dred Scott decision delighted proslavery forces, since it declared the Missouri Compromise unconstitutional. Now Southerners hoped to move more slaves into the territories. They also hoped to see more slave states enter the Union.

Antislavery forces were very upset by the Court decision. Republicans especially were bitter. Excluding slavery from the territories had been their main platform in the 1856 election.

Lincoln-Douglas Debates

In 1858, the Republican, Abraham Lincoln, speaking about slavery, attracted national attention for the first time. He held a series of debates with the Democrat, Stephen Douglas. Both men were running for the seat of U.S. senator from Illinois.

In the debates, Lincoln stated that slavery was a great evil. He opposed allowing slavery to spread beyond the states where it was already

"Bleeding Kansas," As Kansas Territory was called in 1855, was deeply divided between proslavery and antislavery populations. In this picture, opposing groups meet each other in Fort Scott, Kansas, at the time of the election of the territorial legislature. Many slaveholders from Missouri came to Kansas just to vote in that election.

legal. Lincoln conceded that there was no way of getting rid of slavery right away. He asked Douglas how, in view of the Dred Scott decision, the people of a territory could legally prevent slavery. He reminded Douglas that the Supreme Court had said that exclusion of slavery from any territories was illegal. This decision, Lincoln pointed out, contradicted Douglas's idea of popular sovereignty.

Freeport Doctrine   In Freeport, Illinois, Douglas answered Lincoln with a speech setting forth what became known as the "Freeport Doctrine." He argued that, while the people of a territory could not legally exclude slavery, they could discourage it. He said that they could make the keeping of slaves very difficult.

Douglas won the senatorial election of 1858. Because of his Freeport Doctrine, though, Douglas lost much of his Southern support. Although Lincoln lost the election, through the debates he became well-known as a strong opponent of slavery.

The Harpers Ferry Incident

Northerners were stirred up by the Kansas-Nebraska Act and the Dred Scott decision.

Southerners were equally aroused by John Brown's raid of 1859.

In that year, Brown, a white abolitionist, tried to encourage a slave uprising. He and a small band of followers seized the United States *arsenal* (weapons center) at Harpers Ferry, Virginia. From this arsenal, they hoped to get arms to supply the rebellion.

Brown and his followers took the arsenal on October 16, 1859. Soon, however, federal troops moved against them, overpowering the entire band. Brown was captured and tried by a Virginia court for treason. The court found him guilty and sentenced him to hang.

Nevertheless, white Southerners were outraged by the raid. They believed that Northerners had encouraged Brown. These Southerners accused Northerners of arousing black slaves to revolt. Many Northerners also condemned John Brown's raid. Other Northerners felt that Brown was a *martyr* (one who dies for a principle) in the cause of freedom.

John Brown's raid further divided a nation that was already upset by the Dred Scott decision, the Kansas-Nebraska Act, and other matters. Many observers thought that the proslavery and antislavery forces in the country were headed for a showdown.

Abraham Lincoln (center) and Stephen Douglas (seated at Lincoln's right) spoke to crowds of up to 12,000 listeners in their campaigns to be elected U.S. senator from Illinois.

SUMMING UP   We have seen how in 1850 most Americans hoped for compromises to heal differences between the North and the South. Then various events drove the two sections further apart. Personal liberty laws, *Uncle Tom's Cabin,* and John Brown's raid deeply angered many Southerners. Antislavery Northerners were upset by the Kansas-Nebraska Act and the Dred Scott decision. The division of the country into two main parties—Republican and Democratic—reflected the sectional split.

Understanding the Text

On a separate sheet of paper, write the letter of the word or phrase that best completes each of the following statements.

1. States passed personal liberty laws in order to (a) help slave owners recapture runaway slaves (b) give abolitionists the right to send petitions to Congress (c) make the returning of fugitive slaves to their owners more difficult (d) free all slaves in the territories.

2. Franklin Pierce was elected President in 1852 after running as the candidate of the (a) Democratic party (b) Whig party (c) Free Soil party (d) Republican party.

3. According to the Kansas-Nebraska Act of 1854, (a) slavery was barred forever from Kansas (b) Nebraska was to be organized as a slave state (c) personal liberty laws could not be passed in either territory (d) the people living in these territories were to decide whether or not to permit slavery.

4. A leader of those Americans who called for popular sovereignty was (a) Stephen Douglas (b) Harriet Beecher Stowe (c) John Brown (d) Abraham Lincoln.

5. The event that led most directly to forming the Republican party was (a) the passage of the Kansas-Nebraska Act (b) John Brown's raid (c) the Dred Scott decision (d) the passage of the Compromise of 1850.

6. The winner of the presidential election of 1856 was (a) Millard Fillmore (b) James Buchanan (c) John C. Frémont (d) Franklin Pierce.

7. One result of the Lincoln-Douglas debates of 1858 was (a) freedom for Dred Scott (b) loss of Southern support for Stephen Douglas (c) the election of Abraham Lincoln as senator from Illinois (d) the admission of Kansas as a free state.

8. The opinion of Chief Justice Roger Taney in the Dred Scott case especially pleased (a) abolitionists (b) antislavery Democrats (c) Free Soilers (d) slaveholders.

9. Because of his raid on the U.S. arsenal at Harpers Ferry, John Brown (a) was found guilty of treason (b) was judged insane and sent to an asylum (c) was found not guilty of the charge of treason (d) fled to Cuba.

10. The main idea of this lesson is that (a) the issue of slavery died out in the 1850s (b) the Kansas-Nebraska Act finally settled the question of the spread of slavery (c) John Brown led a successful slave rebellion in 1859 (d) the conflict over slavery became violent in the 1850s.

Developing Map Skills

Study the map on page 232. Then answer the following True-False questions. On a separate sheet of paper, number from one to five. After each number, write *T* if the statement is true, *F* if the statement is false, and *I* if there is insufficient information to answer the question.

1. California was admitted into the Union in 1850.

2. The map clearly shows that in 1854 slavery was not allowed in any state north of the parallel of latitude 36°30′N.

3. By 1854, Utah and New Mexico had been admitted into the Union as states.

4. In 1854, there were more free states than slave states.

5. In 1854, proslavery views were more popular than antislavery ones in Kansas, Nebraska, Utah, and New Mexico.

Thinking About the Lesson

1. Do you think that the states that passed personal liberty laws in the 1850s were right? Why or why not?

2. Do you see any contradictions between Stephen Douglas's opposition to slavery and his support of the Kansas-Nebraska Act? Explain your answer.

3. Which one of the following events do you think contributed the most to the deepening split between the North and the South—publication of *Uncle Tom's Cabin*, passage of the Kansas-Nebraska Act, the Dred Scott decision, the Lincoln-Douglas debates, or John Brown's raid? Give reasons for your answer.

LESSON 40

Southern Secession Leads to War

For years, the North and the South were in growing opposition over slavery. Events in 1860 and 1861 caused this conflict to break out into war. In November, 1860, the Republican candidate Abraham Lincoln won election as President. In the weeks and months that followed, Southern states began to secede from the Union. As a result, fighting between forces of the North and the South soon began.

The Election of 1860

The 1860 election campaign took place at a time when relations between the North and South were tense. The presidential contests were important and unusual in several ways.

Split in the Democratic Party   At a party convention, the Democrats split into two groups over the slavery issue. Southern Democrats insisted on a platform that other Democrats could not accept. Southerners wanted a platform plank calling on the federal government to protect slavery in the territories. When the Southern Democrats did not get their plank approved, they left the party, nominating their own presidential candidate, John Breckinridge of Kentucky. Meanwhile, the main Democratic party, minus its Southern wing, nominated

Senator Stephen Douglas of Illinois. Among other planks, their platform included support for Douglas's idea of popular sovereignty.

Republicans Nominate Lincoln   In 1860, the Republican party nominated Abraham Lincoln of Illinois for President. The Republican platform, which appealed mainly to Northerners and Westerners, was as follows:

- Exclusion of slavery from the territories.
- Preservation of the Union.
- Federal spending for roads and railroads.
- Protective tariffs.
- Free land for *homesteaders* (settlers on public lands).

A New Party   Former Whigs and Know-Nothings formed the Constitutional Union party and nominated John Bell of Tennessee to run for President. Their platform called for keeping the Union together through compromises on the slavery question.

With the addition of a new party, voters in 1860 had the unusual choice of four presidential candidates with four widely different platforms.

Election Results   Abraham Lincoln got about 40 percent of the popular vote, almost all from the North and West. His share of votes was not a majority, but he won more popular votes than

237

any other candidate. More important, he won a large majority of the Electoral College. As a result, Lincoln became the next President.

Secession

For many Southerners, Lincoln's victory was the last straw. During the campaign, Southern

leaders had threatened to take their states out of the Union if Lincoln won. They felt that Lincoln wanted to destroy both slavery and the Southern way of life.

In December, 1860, South Carolina left the Union. Within the next few months, six other Southern states followed South Carolina's example. These seven states joined together to form a new government—the Confederate States of America. It was also known as the "Confederacy." Representatives of its member states wrote a constitution and elected a President— Jefferson Davis of Mississippi. President Lincoln called the action of the states that seceded an *insurrection* (an action of revolt against an established government).

In April and May, 1861, four other Southern states joined the Confederacy. Virginia was part of this last group, but people in mountainous western Virginia did not want to secede. Therefore, they separated from Virginia, eventually forming the state of West Virginia. Four other slave states also decided *not* to join the Confederacy: Delaware, Maryland, Kentucky, and Missouri.

The Civil War Begins

The first shots were fired on April 12, 1861. On that date, South Carolina guns bombarded Fort Sumter in Charleston harbor. South Carolina forces wanted to take this United States fort before it received new supplies from the North. After two days of bombardment, the U.S. forces at Fort Sumter were forced to surrender.

In reaction, President Lincoln vowed to do everything needed to maintain the Union. He called for volunteers to join the United States Armed Forces. At the same time, Jefferson Davis issued a similar call for Confederate soldiers. On both sides, volunteers enlisted in large numbers. The Civil War had begun.

CHARLESTON
MERCURY
EXTRA:

Passed unanimously at 1.15 o'clock, P. M., December 20th, 1860.

AN ORDINANCE

To dissolve the Union between the State of South Carolina and other States united with her under the compact entitled " The Constitution of the United States of America."

We, the People of the State of South Carolina, in Convention assembled, do declare and ordain, and it is hereby declared and ordained,

That the Ordinance adopted by us in Convention, on the twenty-third day of May, in the year of our Lord one thousand seven hundred and eighty-eight, whereby the Constitution of the United States of America was ratified, and also, all Acts and parts of Acts of the General Assembly of this State, ratifying amendments of the said Constitution, are hereby repealed; and that the union now subsisting between South Carolina and other States, under the name of "The United States of America," is hereby dissolved.

THE
UNION
IS
DISSOLVED!

Why the War Came

The attack on Fort Sumter was the immediate cause of the Civil War. Historians agree on this point. They do not agree, however, on what was the main long-term cause of the war:

• Some historians believe that slavery was the main reason that the war started. They point to the growing Northern opposition to slavery and its extension to the territories. Many Southerners were determined to protect slavery at all costs. Neither side was willing to compromise anymore. Therefore, say these historians, war was the only solution.

• Other historians say that the war started mainly because of sectionalism. Their argument

In February, 1861, Jefferson Davis was sworn in as Confederate President on the steps of the Alabama State Capitol in Montgomery.

THE SOUTH SECEDES, 1860–1861

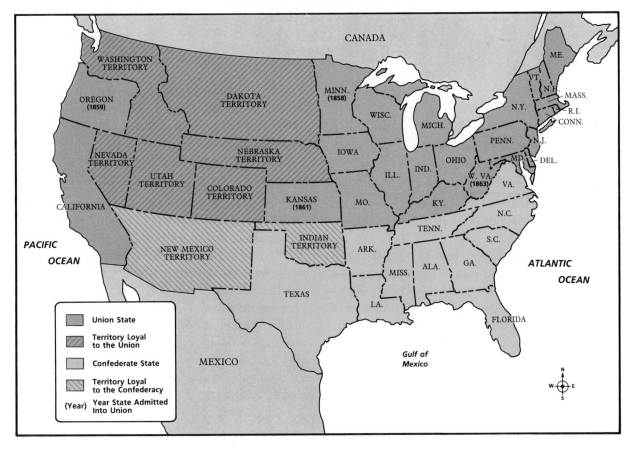

goes as follows: Different sections of the country had different economic interests. The South was mostly agricultural; the North, industrial. Each section wanted to protect its own interests against the other section. Southerners knew that they were losing political power in the federal government. To protect their economic interests, say these historians, Southerners seceded from the Union—an action that led to war.

• Still another proposed cause of the Civil War had to do with America's leaders in the 1850s. Certain historians believe that the war could have been avoided if the country had had stronger leaders. Slavery and sectionalism were important issues, these historians say, but the conflict over these issues could have been settled peacefully. Instead, Presidents, congressional leaders, and other politicians allowed matters to fall apart.

Historians will probably never settle on a single long-term cause of the Civil War. All of the above-mentioned causes, and others not discussed, played a part in starting the conflict.

Confederate Aims and Strategy

By going to war, the Southern states hoped to force the North to recognize the Confederacy as an independent nation.

Confederate military strategy had two major parts:

• To defend the South from attack by Union forces.
• To divide the North into two parts. Confederate troops would move north and, on the way, would seize Washington, D.C., Maryland, and Pennsylvania. This invasion would separate the Northeast from the rest of the Union.

Northern Aims and Strategy

The chief aim of the federal government was to maintain the Union. At first, freeing the slaves

A Job for the New Cabinet Maker

was not one of President Lincoln's goals. He stated that he would not interfere with slavery where it already existed. Later in the war, the President would change his mind about freeing the slaves.

The Northern war strategy consisted of several parts:

• To prevent European assistance to the Confederacy. The North would do this with a naval blockade of Southern ports.
• To be always on the *offensive* (attack). In this way, the North could inflict heavy losses on the South.
• To invade the heart of the South. Specifically, the North hoped to capture the Confederate capital, Richmond, Virginia, on the James River.
• To invade the Mississippi River Valley. With this invasion, the North hoped to separate Texas, Louisiana, and Arkansas from the rest of the Confederacy.

SUMMING UP   We have seen how the beginning of the Civil War closely followed several major events. In late 1860, Abraham Lincoln was elected President. Immediately, Southern states began to secede from the Union. Soon after being sworn in, President Lincoln sent supplies to Fort Sumter, in the South. To prevent this federal fort from being strengthened, South Carolina forces bombarded it. With this action, the war began.

Understanding the Text

On a separate sheet of paper, write the letter of the word or phrase that best completes each of the following statements.

1. In 1860, John Bell ran for President as the candidate of the *(a)* Free Soil party *(b)* Constitutional Union party *(c)* Republican party *(d)* Democratic party.

2. The candidate in the 1860 election who won the most popular votes was *(a)* Stephen Douglas *(b)* John Bell *(c)* John Breckinridge *(d)* Abraham Lincoln.

3. The presidential candidate who called for exclusion of slavery from the territories was *(a)* Abraham Lincoln *(b)* Stephen Douglas *(c)* John Breckinridge *(d)* John Bell.

4. Lincoln's support in the 1860 elections came *(a)* mostly from the South *(b)* mostly from the border states *(c)* mostly from the North and West *(d)* equally from all parts of the country.

5. Southern states began to secede from the Union after *(a)* Lincoln's election *(b)* the bombardment of Fort Sumter *(c)* Lincoln's call for volunteer soldiers *(d)* the formation of the Confederacy.

6. The first state to secede from the Union was *(a)* Virginia *(b)* West Virginia *(c)* South Carolina *(d)* Mississippi.

7. From Lincoln's point of view, secession of the Southern states was *(a)* a constitutional right *(b)* an insurrection *(c)* a compromise *(d)* a confederation.

8. After the election of Lincoln, most Southerners were convinced that *(a)* the North was ready for a compromise *(b)* slavery should be abolished *(c)* Southern states would have to secede from the Union and form a new nation *(d)* a new presidential election would have to be held.

9. An event or issue *not* regarded as a long-term cause of the Civil War was *(a)* the bombardment of Fort Sumter *(b)* slavery *(c)* sectional interests *(d)* poor leadership.

10. Confederates did *not* consider it part of their war strategy to *(a)* defend the South from attack *(b)* blockade the Atlantic Coast *(c)* separate the Northeast from the rest of the Union *(d)* seize Washington, D.C.

Developing Cartoon-Reading Skills

Study the political cartoon on page 240. Then choose the letter of the word or phrase that best completes each sentence. On a separate sheet of paper, match the sentence number with the correct letter.

1. The man in the cartoon is (a) Uncle Sam (b) Abraham Lincoln (c) Stephen Douglas (d) John Breckinridge.

2. The cartoonist's opinion of the man in the cartoon is largely (a) sympathetic (b) critical (c) indifferent (d) derogatory.

3. The cartoon indicates that the man (a) is a carpenter (b) is a labor union leader (c) is President of the United States (d) has just been appointed to the President's Cabinet.

4. The cartoonist probably believes that the man is acting in the interests of (a) both the North and South (b) the South (c) the North (d) labor unions.

5. The cartoonist seems to be saying that the man has to (a) widen the split between the North and South (b) repair broken furniture in the White House (c) keep the North and South together (d) investigate scandals involving labor unions.

Thinking About the Lesson

1. Explain the choices available to voters in the U.S. presidential elections of 1860. How would you have voted? Why?

2. What do you consider the major long-term cause of the Civil War? Explain your answer.

The Civil War

The Civil War was a great national tragedy. Both sides believed that they had a cause worth fighting and dying for. The Confederacy fought for recognition of its independence. The Union, on the other hand, wanted to bring back the states that had seceded. About 600,000 Americans were killed during the four-year conflict.

Northern Strengths

The Union enjoyed several advantages over the Confederacy:

• The Union had over twice as many people. Furthermore, European immigrants continued to settle in Northern states during the war. Many of these immigrants were willing to join the Union Army.

• The Union had far greater economic resources. Most banks, factories, and ships were located in the North. So were most of the railroads and many water routes. Transportation between most of the Union states was good.

• Both the North and the South grew enough food to feed their own people. Nonetheless, the South's supply routes were cut off when Union armies invaded the South.

• Both sides lost heavily in terms of men, supplies, and equipment. Even so, the North was in a better position to draft new soldiers and purchase new supplies and equipment.

• The North had a larger and more powerful navy. Thus, it was able to blockade many Southern ports and reduce the Confederate trade with Europe.

Southern Strengths

In spite of some of the North's advantages, the Union Army found the fighting difficult:

• The Union Army had to invade the South, capture its cities, and occupy its lands. On the other hand, the South, in fighting on its own soil, was defending its homeland. Thus, many Southerners were spirited fighters, convinced of the rightness of their cause.

• Most soldiers in the Confederate Army came from rural areas. They were used to living outdoors and shooting guns. Some were experienced horse riders. For these reasons, they made very good soldiers.

• The South had excellent officers. Its top general, Robert E. Lee, was one of the most able military leaders in American history. General "Stonewall" Jackson was a first-rate *strategist* (one skilled at planning battles). In the early part of the war, Confederate generals outsmarted Union military leaders again and again.

243

• The Southern coastline was some 3,500 miles long. Since the Union Navy could not close all Southern ports, a number of Confederate boats ran through the Union blockade. In this way, some much-needed foreign goods reached the South, and some Southern cotton made it to Europe.

Major Battles of the War

Both sides in the war achieved military successes and suffered defeats.

First Battle of Bull Run (1861) In this first major battle of the war, the South won and Northern forces had to retreat in disorder. Bull Run, in Virginia, was only 30 miles from Washington, D.C. The Confederate forces were so close that they could have taken the Union capital after defeating the Union Army.

Monitor vs. Virginia (1862) The iron-plated Confederate warship *Virginia* (formerly the *Merrimac*) tried to break the Union blockade. It was able to sink several Northern wooden war vessels. In March, 1862, however, the *Virginia* fought to a draw with a Union ironclad, the *Monitor*. The *Virginia* then retreated to its port for repairs and did little further damage throughout the war.

Battle of Antietam (1862) After several victories in Virginia in 1862, General Lee's forces advanced north into Maryland. At Antietam, they were stopped by Union forces under General George B. McClellan. Neither side won this battle. Yet Antietam was important in several ways:

• For a while again, battles would be fought only on Confederate soil, not in states belonging to the Union.
• France and Great Britain had been close to recognizing the Confederacy. The South's failure to win at Antietam helped change the minds of French and British officials.
• Abraham Lincoln had been waiting for a Union victory to issue the Emancipation Proclamation. (See Lesson 42.) He thought that the North's good showing at Antietam provided an opportunity to act on the slavery issue.

Battle of Vicksburg (1863) In the West, Union General Ulysses S. Grant led a major campaign

MAJOR CIVIL WAR BATTLES

Battle and location	Date	Casualties*	Who won
First Bull Run, Virginia	July, 1861	3,000	Confederate forces
Shiloh, Tennessee	Apr., 1862	24,000	Union forces
Seven Days', Virginia	June, 1862	36,000	Confederate forces
Second Bull Run, Virginia	Aug., 1862	19,000	Confederate forces
Antietam, Maryland	Sept., 1862	23,000	Neither side
Fredericksburg, Virginia	Dec., 1862	16,000	Confederate forces
Chancellorsville, Virginia	May, 1863	22,000	Confederate forces
Vicksburg, Mississippi	July, 1863	19,000	Union forces
Gettysburg, Pennsylvania	July, 1863	46,000	Union forces
Chickamauga, Georgia	Sept., 1863	34,000	Confederate forces
Chattanooga, Tennessee	Nov., 1863	12,000	Union forces
Wilderness, Virginia	May, 1864	28,000	Neither side
Spotsylvania, Virginia	May, 1864	20,000	Neither side
Atlanta, Georgia	Sept., 1864	52,000	Union forces
Petersburg, Virginia	June, 1864	30,000	Union forces

*Estimated number of dead and wounded.

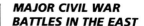

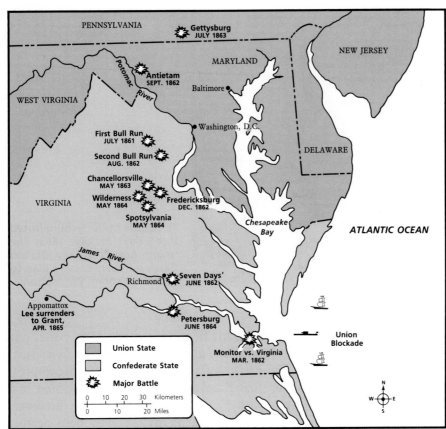

to gain control of the Mississippi River Valley. His advance south was temporarily stopped at the Battle of Shiloh, in Tennessee. Grant was able to regroup, proceed down the Mississippi, and capture Vicksburg, Mississippi. A year earlier, a Union officer, David Farragut, had captured the port of New Orleans by sailing up the river from the Gulf of Mexico. Now Union forces had full control of the Mississippi River. Texas, Louisiana, and Arkansas were cut off from the rest of the Confederacy.

Battle of Gettysburg (1863) Having achieved some more victories in Virginia in 1863, General Lee decided to invade the North again. At Gettysburg, Pennsylvania, Confederate forces met their match and suffered great losses. The battle was a turning point in the war. From then on, Lee would be on the defensive.

Sherman's March to the Sea (1864) Moving east after victories in Tennessee, Union General William T. Sherman was determined to reach the Atlantic. In 1864, the Union forces captured and burned Atlanta, Georgia. They marched on to Savannah, on the coast. Then Sherman took his forces north through South and North Carolina. On the way, the Union Army lived off the land and destroyed much Southern property.

Final Crushing of the Confederacy (1864–1865) Meanwhile, General Grant had been given command of all Union forces. As General Sherman marched north, Grant moved south. General Lee's army met Grant's army several times in 1864. Although fighting continued for months, the Southern cause was doomed. Lee's army was outnumbered. Grant's forces finally entered Richmond, the Confederate capital, in early

The Battle of Gettysburg lasted three days in July, 1863. The Union Army's victory dashed General Robert E. Lee's plan to seize Harrisburg, Pennsylvania.

April, 1865. Lee's surrender at Appomattox Court House followed a few days later (on April 9, 1865).

Foreign Affairs During the War

Both sides had trouble with foreign nations during the war.

Recognition of the Confederacy Southerners expected some European powers to recognize and aid the Confederacy. After all, Southerners believed, the French and British needed Southern cotton for their textile mills. In fact, British and French leaders tended to sympathize with the South. Nevertheless, the two European powers remained neutral because many other people in France and Great Britain favored the Union. French and British support for the Union grew even more after the Emancipation Proclamation was issued.

Relations With Russia Russia was very friendly with Northerners throughout the war. The Russian policy was partly due to Russian fears of British and French power. In the fall of 1863,

two Russians fleets visited two U.S. ports, one in New York and the other in San Francisco. The Russian visits gave Americans the impression that Russia would support the Union in a war with European powers. Russia, however, remained neutral in the Union's fight against the Confederacy.

The Trent Affair In 1861, a Union warship stopped the British steamship *Trent*. Union officers took from the *Trent* two Confederate diplomats, James Mason and John Slidell, who were on their way to Europe. The British government protested. It said that the Union had violated British rights as a neutral. To avoid a crisis, Lincoln released the Confederate agents.

The Alabama Incident Early in the war, British shipyards began building *cruisers* (large warships) for the Confederacy. The South used these ships to attack Northern commercial ships. Because many Northern ships were captured or destroyed by the British-built cruisers, the U.S. government objected. It said that Great Britain was breaking rules of neutrality. The British agreed to stop the practice, but one of the successful Confederate raiders, the *Alabama*, kept sailing. Not until 1864 was a Union cruiser able to fire on and destroy this Confederate ship.

The Maximilian Affair   The French Emperor, Louis Napoleon, took advantage of the fighting in the United States. He sent an army into Mexico—an act that U.S. officials claimed violated the Monroe Doctrine. (See Lesson 28.)

After defeating Mexican forces, the French placed their ally, the Austrian Archduke Maximilian, on the Mexican throne. During the Civil War, the United States could do little more than protest. After the war, however, the United States demanded the quick withdrawal of the French troops. The French did withdraw, but Maximilian decided to stay in Mexico. Without armed support, he was soon captured by Mexican forces and was later executed.

UNION ADVANCES IN THE WEST AND SOUTH

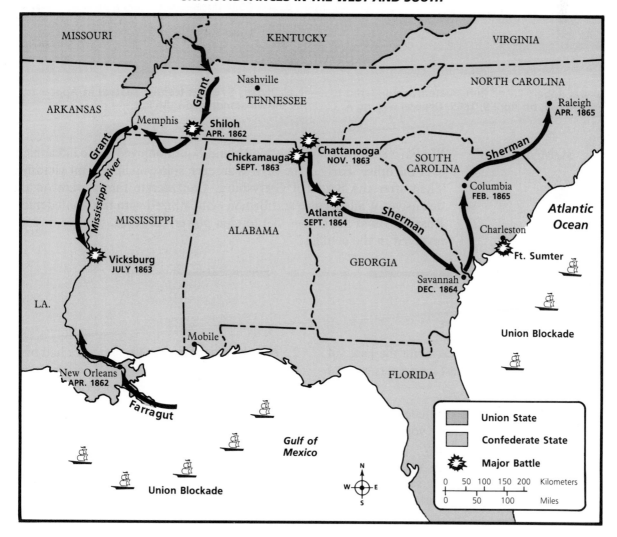

General Robert E. Lee (left, seated) surrendered to General Ulysses S. Grant (center, seated) at Appomattox Court House, on April 9, 1865. General George A. Custer is shown standing, on the left.

SUMMING UP We have seen that both the North and South enjoyed some advantages over the other. Early in the Civil War, each side won important victories. Then after the Battle of Gettysburg, Confederate forces were on the defensive. While France and Britain sympathized with the Confederacy, Russia favored the Union. No foreign power, however, became directly involved in the conflict.

Understanding the Text

On a separate sheet of paper, write the letter of the word or phrase that best completes each of the following statements.

1. The Union blockaded Confederate ports in order to prevent *(a)* British volunteers from joining the Confederate Army *(b)* trade between the South and Europe *(c)* Confederate ships from impressing Union sailors *(d)* the importation of slaves to work on Southern plantations.

2. An advantage that the Confederacy had over the Union was that it *(a)* had a larger population *(b)* had a better transportation network *(c)* fought most battles on its own soil *(d)* had more industries.

3. In 1865, the top-ranked Confederate general was *(a)* Robert E. Lee *(b)* "Stonewall" Jackson *(c)* Ulysses S. Grant *(d)* William T. Sherman.

4. The first major battle of the Civil War (a) was fought about 30 miles from Washington, D.C. (b) was won by the Confederacy (c) was called the "Battle of Bull Run" (d) all of the above.

5. The Battle of Antietam was important because it (a) was a decisive victory for the Confederacy (b) was a decisive victory for the Union (c) led the British and French to decide not to recognize the Confederacy (d) led Russia to declare war on the Confederacy.

6. The battle that helped the Union take control of the Mississippi River Valley was the (a) Battle of Gettysburg (b) Battle of Vicksburg (c) *Monitor* vs. *Virginia* (d) Battle of Atlanta.

7. The Northern general who captured Atlanta and then marched 300 miles across Georgia to the sea was (a) Robert E. Lee (b) Ulysses S. Grant (c) George B. McClellan (d) William T. Sherman.

8. The *Trent* Affair caused trouble between the Union and Great Britain because (a) the British impressed Union sailors (b) the Union was accused of violating British rights of neutrality (c) the *Trent* was a Russian cruiser (d) the *Trent* had been built for the Confederacy in Great Britain.

9. During the war, U.S. officials declared that the Monroe Doctrine had been violated by (a) Mexico (b) France (c) Cuba (d) Russia.

10. Which of the following statements best describes the Civil War? (a) It was an easy victory for the North. (b) It was a long and bloody struggle that the North won mainly because of its greater resources. (c) It was lost by the Confederacy because of unskilled military leadership and poor fighting spirit. (d) It ended in a draw because both sides were exhausted.

Developing Map Skills

Study the map on page 247. Then choose the letter of the word or phrase that best completes each sentence. On a separate sheet of paper, match the sentence number with the correct letter.

1. The ships drawn on the map represent the navy of (a) the Confederacy (b) the Union (c) Great Britain (d) France.

2. According to the map, in April of 1862, General Ulysses S. Grant was in (a) North Carolina (b) South Carolina (c) Georgia (d) Tennessee.

3. General Grant captured Vicksburg, Mississippi, in (a) April, 1862 (b) July, 1862 (c) July, 1863 (d) September, 1864.

4. New Orleans was captured in April, 1862, by (a) forces under General Grant (b) Union forces under David Farragut (c) Confederate forces under General Robert E. Lee (d) Union forces under General William T. Sherman.

5. After capturing Savannah, Georgia, in December, 1864, General Sherman and his forces went (a) north (b) south (c) west (d) east.

Thinking About the Lesson

1. What do you think was the major reason that the Union won the Civil War?

2. Explain why, despite its greater strength, the North took four years to defeat the South.

3. Why was dealing with Great Britain one of Lincoln's most difficult problems during the Civil War?

Abraham Lincoln

Today, most Americans rank Lincoln near the top of a list of the nation's great Presidents. As a young man, Abraham Lincoln was considered honest, smart, and able. Even so, few Americans thought he would become a national leader. His reputation grew in large part from his leadership of the Union during the Civil War.

Lincoln's Early Career

Abraham Lincoln was born in poverty on the Kentucky frontier in 1809. As a boy he moved west with his family, first to Indiana, and then to Illinois. In each place, his father struggled to earn a living at farming. Relying on wit and physical strength, young Abraham made many friends and tried several jobs. At different times, he worked as a clerk in a store, split logs, and served as a postmaster. During non-working hours, Lincoln read books. He studied law on his own and eventually became a lawyer.

Political Career In his first elected political office, Lincoln served in the Illinois State Legislature. In 1846, he was elected to the U.S. House of Representatives. Later, he twice failed to gain a Senate seat. At first, he belonged to the Whig party, but as the Whigs declined in strength, Lincoln joined with the Republicans.

Lincoln gained a national reputation by debating Senator Douglas in 1858. The Lincoln-Douglas debates helped him to win the presidential nomination on the Republican ticket in 1860.

Lincoln's Wartime Record

President Lincoln's main goal was to reunite the country. In pursuing this goal, he revealed patience and firmness. As Commander in Chief of the Armed Forces, Lincoln helped plan military strategy. He knew, however, that his knowledge of the military was limited. Consequently, he allowed others to take over the job of directing military operations.

At times, the North seemed to be losing the war. Many Northern Democrats and many in his own party called for an end to the war by negotiations. Nonetheless, Lincoln insisted on fighting to victory. He believed that the Union would eventually win.

The Emancipation Proclamation

Perhaps Lincoln's most important act during the war was to issue the Emancipation Proclamation on January 1, 1863. This document declared that all slaves in Confederate areas were

250

free. Remember that Lincoln had earlier said that he would not interfere with slavery where it already existed. Then, by 1863, he had changed his mind, believing that a proclamation would help weaken the Confederacy.

The Proclamation applied only to territory in rebellion against the Union. Yet it showed that the North meant to abolish slavery everywhere. After the war, slaves in the other slaveholding states were also freed.

As Union forces pushed deeper into Confederate territory, they freed the slaves whom they encountered. Not until 1865, however, did all slaves finally receive their freedom. In January of that year, Congress passed the Thirteenth Amendment, which prohibited slavery. This Amendment went into effect on December 18, when the required number of states ratified it.

President Lincoln had a talented group of men serving in his Cabinet. Here Lincoln reads a draft of the Emancipation Proclamation to (from left to right) Salmon P. Chase, Secretary of the Treasury, William H. Seward, Secretary of State, Gideon Welles, Secretary of the Navy, Edward Bates, Attorney General, Caleb Smith, Secretary of the Interior, Edwin M. Stanton, Secretary of War, and Montgomery Blair, Postmaster General.

Criticism of Lincoln

Abraham Lincoln had many enemies in both the North and the South.

Southern Critics Many Southerners hated Lincoln with a passion. They strongly disagreed with his position on slavery. In addition, they believed that he failed to understand Southern views on other matters.

Northern Critics Many Northerners also disliked President Lincoln. Abolitionists attacked him for not freeing the slaves right away. Others criticized him for the way he conducted the war. He was blamed for early defeats of the Union forces. A number of people called Lincoln a *tyrant* (ruler not restrained by laws) for taking certain actions that restricted their rights, namely:

• Freedom of the press. Lincoln had the government *censor* (shut down) newspapers that Union officials considered disloyal.
• Freedom of speech. The Union government jailed a number of *copperheads*—Northerners who sympathized with the Confederacy and criticized the U.S. government.
• Right of *habeas corpus*. (See Lesson 4.) The government jailed about 13,000 Americans without making formal charges against them.

Lincoln said that these wartime actions were necessary in a national emergency. Nevertheless, his actions made him unpopular. In 1864, many Americans believed that he could not win re-election.

The Re-Election Campaign

When Lincoln ran for re-election in 1864, he promised not to compromise with the enemy. A pro-Union Democrat from Tennessee, Andrew Johnson, ran for Vice President on the same ticket. The Republicans and pro-Union Democrats joined forces in this election as the Union party.

Lincoln's opponent was the Democratic candidate General George B. McClellan. Although McClellan had served as a Union Army commander, he criticized the way Lincoln had run the war effort. McClellan and the Democrats called for immediate steps to end the war by negotiations.

General William Sherman's capture of Atlanta in September, 1864, helped Lincoln's campaign. Nevertheless, in the months before the November elections, Lincoln did not know if he would be returned to office.

Lincoln won the election by a large majority of the electoral votes—91 percent. His margin of victory in popular votes, however, was not so large—only about 55 percent.

The Emancipation Proclamation helped to increase the number of blacks serving in the Union Army. As the Union forces conquered Confederate lands, blacks living in these areas were heavily recruited.

Lincoln's Reputation

Although Lincoln suffered much criticism, Americans have—for a number of reasons—come to regard him as one of our great Presidents.

Mastery of Language Lincoln was a master of the English language. He showed this mastery in his writings and speeches. Perhaps no one else has expressed more beautifully and clearly the ideals of democracy. His words have become a valuable heritage both for Americans and for people in other countries. Lincoln's *Gettysburg Address*, of November 19, 1863, contains several moving passages.

> Fourscore and seven years ago our fathers brought forth on this continent a new nation, conceived in liberty, and dedicated to the proposition that all men are created equal.
>
> Now we are engaged in a great civil war, testing whether that nation, or any nation so conceived and so dedicated, can long endure. We are met on a great battlefield of that war. We have come to dedicate a portion of that field as a final resting-place for those who here gave their lives that that nation might live. It is altogether fitting and proper that we should do this.
>
> But, in a larger sense, we cannot dedicate—we cannot consecrate—we cannot hallow—this ground. The brave men, living and dead, who struggled here, have consecrated it far above our poor power to add or detract. The world will little note nor long remember what we say here, but it can never forget what they did here. It is for us, the living, rather, to be dedicated here to the unfinished work which they who fought here have thus far so nobly advanced. It is rather for us to be here dedicated to the great task remaining before us—that from these honored dead we take increased devotion to that cause for which they gave the last full measure of devotion; that we here highly resolve that these dead shall not have died in vain; that this nation, under God, shall have a new birth of freedom; and that government of the people, by the people, for the people, shall not perish from the earth.

In November, 1863, Lincoln addressed Americans who had come to Gettysburg, Pennsylvania, to commemorate the battle site. Lincoln spoke only after the famous orator Edward Everett had given a two-hour long speech.

Preservation of the Union   Probably Lincoln's most important achievement was to keep the Union together. As the war dragged on, many Northerners became discouraged. Lincoln, however, had a firm faith that victory would come and the nation would hold together. He insisted on fighting to the end—until the South surrendered unconditionally. He was intolerant of those who would offer a deal to the Confederate leaders in order to end the fighting.

Strong, But Kind Personality   Lincoln's personality won over many Northerners. Even some who did not realize his greatness understood that he was honest, kind, and generous. Admirers fondly called him "Old Abe."

Self-Control   Lincoln showed unusual self-control. He often reacted to personal attacks and criticism by joking. He rarely appeared bitter, even though he suffered from depression. Nor was he puffed up with his own importance. He considered himself important only as one who served the cause of the Union.

The End of the War

President Lincoln began his second term on March 4, 1865. In his *Second Inaugural Address*, Lincoln promised not to be spiteful. He called for the government to care for all victims of the war, including orphans, widows, and soldiers on both sides of the conflict.

Assassination of Lincoln   The war ended on April 9, 1865. Shortly afterward, on April 14th, Lincoln was assassinated. The President and Mrs. Lincoln had gone to a theater to see a popular play. There an actor and Confederate sympathizer, John Wilkes Booth, shot the President from behind. Because of the assassination, Lincoln became a martyr. Northerners mourned him as a war hero and national leader who had held the Union together.

Some Southerners later wished Lincoln had lived longer. They came to believe that if he had not been killed, the South might have been treated more fairly. Lincoln might have curbed the violence and ill-feelings that characterized the post-war years.

SUMMING UP   We have seen how Abraham Lincoln went into politics after trying several other careers. He succeeded in politics, becoming one of the country's greatest Presidents. Lincoln's greatness was due to both his effective wartime leadership and his Emancipation Proclamation. Nevertheless, many criticized him for limiting certain rights during the war.

Understanding the Text

On a separate sheet of paper, write the letter of the word or phrase that best completes each of the following statements.

1. Abraham Lincoln's early years were marked by *(a)* wealth and privilege *(b)* hard work in getting an education and making a living *(c)* education in the best schools *(d)* travel throughout much of the world.

2. A public office that Lincoln did *not* hold was *(a)* Illinois state legislator *(b)* justice of the

U.S. Supreme Court *(c)* member of the U.S. House of Representatives *(d)* President of the United States.

3. As Commander in Chief of the Armed Forces, Lincoln did all of the following, *except (a)* insist on fighting the war to the bitter end *(b)* help to plan war strategy *(c)* lead men into battle *(d)* refuse to end the war by a negotiated compromise.

4. Abraham Lincoln believed that *(a)* Southern secession was good for the nation *(b)* every possible effort should be made to preserve the Union *(c)* there should be negotiations with the Confederacy to end the war through compromises *(d)* bloodshed should be avoided at all cost in saving the Union.

5. As a result of the Emancipation Proclamation, *(a)* all slaves in the United States were freed *(b)* Southern slave owners received compensation for their losses *(c)* slaves in the North were freed *(d)* slaves in areas rebelling against the Union were freed.

6. Criticisms of President Lincoln included all of the following, *except* that *(a)* he sought a third term as President *(b)* his views on slavery were too extreme *(c)* his views on slavery were too moderate *(d)* his decisions led to several defeats for the Union Army.

7. In the 1864 elections, *(a)* General McClellan was the presidential candidate of the Democratic party *(b)* Abraham Lincoln had no opposition *(c)* Lincoln had the support of most people in the Southern states *(d)* Andrew Johnson was the presidential candidate of the Union party.

8. Andrew Johnson's nomination for Vice President in 1864 showed that *(a)* Republicans refused to run on the same ticket as Democrats *(b)* Southern Democrats had political control of the federal government *(c)* Republicans and pro-Union Democrats had teamed up to win the

election *(d)* the war was being lost by the North.

9. A copperhead was someone who *(a)* had no right of *habeas corpus (b)* supported the Republican party *(c)* joined the Union Army *(d)* lived in the North but sympathized with the South.

10. Abraham Lincoln is remembered today as *(a)* a great wartime leader *(b)* a master of the English language *(c)* a kind and generous man *(d)* all of the above.

Developing Reading Comprehension Skills

Read Lincoln's *Gettysburg Address*, printed on page 253. Then choose the letter of the word or phrase that best completes each sentence. On a separate sheet of paper, match the sentence number with the correct letter.

1. In the first paragraph of the Address, Lincoln was referring to *(a)* the Declaration of Independence *(b)* the Constitution of the United States *(c)* the Bill of Rights *(d)* his *First Inaugural Address*.

2. Lincoln delivered his speech *(a)* just before the Battle of Gettysburg *(b)* during the Battle of Gettysburg *(c)* several months after the Battle of Gettysburg *(d)* after the war ended.

3. Lincoln was speaking at a ceremony that honored *(a)* Union soldiers who died at Gettysburg *(b)* Confederate soldiers who died at Gettysburg *(c)* Americans who died during the Revolutionary War *(d)* all Americans who died in all wars.

4. Lincoln said that people around the world would remember the longest *(a)* his speech *(b)* the dedication ceremony *(c)* the actions of those who fought at Gettysburg *(d)* the accomplishments of the Union generals.

5. In conclusion, Lincoln called upon his listeners to *(a)* end the war by making compromises with the enemy *(b)* stop the fighting so that all people should not perish from the earth *(c)* help form a world government *(d)* continue to defend the Union, but with greater effort.

Thinking About the Lesson

1. Many people consider Abraham Lincoln one of the greatest Presidents in United States history. Do you agree with this view? Why or why not?

2. Most historians say that Lincoln was not an abolitionist even though he issued the Emancipation Proclamation. What are your views on this question?

3. Do you think that Lincoln's mastery of the English language helped him to become a successful politician and national leader? Why or why not?

LESSON 43

The War Changes the Nation

No event in American history has been written about more than the Civil War. Americans have used various names to refer to the struggle. At first, Northerners called it the "War of the Rebellion." Southerners called it the "War Between the States" or the "War for Southern Independence." Now it is usually known simply as the "Civil War." All of these names tell us something about the conflict. The Civil War has been seen differently by different people. Despite differing points of view, everyone has agreed that the war led to major changes in American society.

A New Kind of War

The Civil War was the country's first modern war. Both sides in the conflict used weapons and methods not too different from some of those used today:

• *Repeating rifles*. They were faster and more accurate than earlier types of rifles. One soldier under cover could hold off at least three enemy attackers.

• *Trenches*. In these wide and deep ditches, soldiers sat for long periods of time. Soldiers strung wire near the trenches in order to slow down attackers. Charges against these defensive lines proved dangerous.

• Balloons. For the first time, soldiers could observe enemy lines from balloons in the air.

• Railroads and steamships. These inventions moved troops and supplies around quickly.

• Armored ships. Iron-plated ships were stronger and more powerful than wooden ones. In later wars, armored ships were commonly used in naval battles.

• The *telegraph*. With this invention, operators could send coded war messages through wires over long distances.

• Photography. For the first time, photographers made a visual record of an American war. Today, we can see photographs of groups of soldiers and the destruction caused by the war.

Total War The Civil War was the nation's first *total war*. In a total war, soldiers try to destroy enemy farms and factories, as well as enemy armies. As a result, many civilians become *casualties* (dead and wounded). Moreover, most civilians become involved in the war effort.

Contributions of Women

Women performed important duties on the home front. Many women worked in offices and factories. Others took over the running of farms and plantations. In this way, more men were able to serve as soldiers.

257

Both the North and the South had women's relief societies. These groups met to make bandages, sew uniforms, and collect medicines.

Clara Barton   Some women served as nurses. Among them, Clara Barton stood out for her efforts at gathering food and medical supplies. She brought these supplies to the front and to hospitals where soldiers lay wounded. Recognizing her abilities, the Union Army in 1864 made her a chief nurse. After the war, she helped found the American Red Cross.

Military Draft

For the first time in the nation's history, men were forced to serve in the military. This development came about because neither the North nor the South had enough volunteers.

Southern Conscription   In 1862, the Confederacy began *conscription*—the practice of compelling people to serve in armed forces. A wealthy Southerner could still avoid service in one of two ways:

• He could hire someone else to serve for him.
• He could be *exempted* (freed from obligation) if he owned or supervised at least 20 slaves.

Northern Conscription   In 1863, the Union also set up a military *draft* (system of compelling people to serve in armed forces). Here, too, the wealthy could avoid conscription. Northerners could either hire a substitute or just pay the government a fee. The draft was very unpopular in certain Northern communities. In fact, one anti-draft riot in New York City got out of hand. Angry mobs burned buildings, looted stores, and killed people. Abolitionists and blacks were often targets of the mobs.

The number of people drafted on either side was actually quite small. Most Union and Confederate soldiers were volunteers. Some Northerners volunteered because the Union paid a *bounty* (reward) for joining up.

One of the few women physicians in the Union Army, Dr. Mary Walker was captured in 1864 and held prisoner by the Confederate Army for four months.

Black Soldiers

At first, Union leaders did not want to use blacks as soldiers. Some questioned black people's ability to fight. Others worried about what slaveholders in the border states might think. Union officials were worried because they wanted the border states to remain in the Union.

As time went on, the Union's need for soldiers became great. In 1863, all-black units were formed in both the Army and the Navy. A few blacks became officers. Most of the black units, however, were led by white officers. Of 2.2 million men serving in the Union Army, almost 180,000 were blacks. The Confederacy also decided to use black soldiers, but this decision was not made until the war was almost over.

In later wars, too, blacks were to serve in the U.S. Armed Forces. Not until recent decades, though, have blacks been included with other Americans in *integrated* (mixed) units.

Financing the War

Both the Union and Confederacy needed a great deal of money to finance their war efforts. Some of the methods used to raise funds continued to be used in later years.

Northern Methods of Fund Raising   The Union obtained money in several ways:

• Excise taxes on alcohol and tobacco. These existing taxes were increased greatly.

• *Income taxes*. For the first time, the federal government levied taxes on people's incomes. In a later period, the income tax would become a major source of federal revenue.

• Tariffs. The Morrill Tariff of 1861 raised the cost of imported goods. It also provided the federal government with much-needed income. Factory owners especially liked this high tariff.

• Paper money. The Union issued paper money known as *greenbacks*. This money was not backed by gold or silver. Its value went up or down depending upon how well the Union Army was doing.

• Bonds. The Union sold war bonds to patriotic citizens and banks. To help sell the bonds, the government in 1863 set up the new National Banking System. Member banks had to put one third of their money in bonds. These banks could then issue bank notes, which became a sound currency used throughout the Union.

Southern Methods of Raising Money   The Confederacy also raised money in several ways. It, too, increased taxes, sold bonds, and issued paper money.

As the Confederacy began losing the war, Southerners doubted that their government could repay its debts. Therefore, Confederate bonds

Young men in New York City were tempted by signs such as this one at a recruiting station. Between 1861 and 1865, some 110,000 New Yorkers were recruited into the Union Army.

After the Battle of Fredericksburg, these wounded soldiers waited to be taken to a hospital.

and paper money lost much of their value. This development led to sharp price increases in the South.

Destruction in the South

The South suffered more than other sections of the country. It lost about 250,000 soldiers. Many others came home wounded. Entire farms, towns, and cities were destroyed in the fighting. Moreover, Union forces ripped up Southern railroad lines wherever they found them.

Economic Chaos During the latter part of the war, the Southern economy almost came to a stop. Although Southerners held Confederate bonds and currency, these pieces of paper had little value. Even if Southerners owned U.S. currency, they could find few items to buy. With the blockade, the Union had stopped most

of the South's foreign trade. By invading the South, the Union Army had disrupted many Southern internal trade routes. Some people who lived in Southern cities starved because supplies of food there were so scarce.

In the countryside, Southerners were generally better off because there they could grow their own food. On the other hand, their life would never be the same. Some plantations were completely destroyed when Union forces moved through the South. Many others were in a state of decline because their owners were away during the war, fighting for the Confederacy.

Post-War Life Southern society changed greatly after the war, mainly because the federal government freed all remaining slaves in 1865. Large plantations could not operate well without slave labor. In addition, owners of these plantations did not have the money to hire enough laborers to replace the slaves.

Many former slaves did not know what to do. A large number of them went to the cities to find work. There, however, they could find few jobs because the Southern economy was depressed. Some blacks ended up starving, becoming ill, or dying.

Legacy of Bitterness White Southerners were bitter. They were angry at Northerners for winning the war and occupying their lands. They resented the new status of the former slaves. They were upset by the disruption of their economy. Some former leaders of Southern society were most vocal in expressing their bitterness. New laws imposed by Congress prevented Confederate leaders from holding public office. Moreover, a good number of formerly wealthy plantation owners and owners of businesses were now poor, their plantations and businesses lost. Indeed, the "Old South" of the pre-Civil War period disappeared.

Prosperity in the North

Northerners had their share of suffering during the war. Many more Northerners died in the conflict than did Southerners. The number of Northerners wounded also was higher. In several Union states, property was destroyed by the fighting. In financing the war, federal and state governments ran up huge debts. For years Americans were repaying these debts.

On the whole, however, the war turned out to be a stimulus to the Northern economy. In order to fight, Union forces needed vast amounts of uniforms, weapons, foods, and other supplies. This need stimulated production in Northern factories and on farms. Wartime laws also helped the growth of the Northern economy. The Morrill Tariff of 1861 protected factories and farms from foreign competition. The National Bank Act of 1863 set up a new banking system.

Farmers in the North had several good years, with record crops of corn and wheat. They were able to sell some of their food in Europe.

Maintaining the Union

The Civil War had one more important result. The North's victory ensured the supremacy of the federal government over state governments. The question of whether or not states could secede from the Union was settled once and for all by 1865.

Portions of several Southern cities were destroyed during the Civil War. Here the North Western Depot in Charleston, South Carolina, lies in ruins in 1865.

SUMMING UP   We have seen how the Civil War was different from any other war that Americans had fought before. New weapons and methods of fighting were used. Women and other civilians played important roles in the war effort. Blacks served in the armed forces in large numbers.

The war changed the nation in many ways. Slaves gained their freedom. The South was devastated by the conflict. The North, however, prospered because of the war. In the end, the war proved that the Union was more important than the individual states.

Understanding the Text

On a separate sheet of paper, write the letter of the word or phrase that best completes each of the following statements.

1. The Civil War was the first American conflict in which (a) firearms were used (b) the railroad and the telegraph played important parts (c) the airplane was used (d) thousands of soldiers fought.

2. Many Southerners once preferred to call the Civil War the (a) War of the Rebellion (b) War for Slavery (c) World War I (d) War Between the States.

3. A statement about the military draft during the Civil War that is *not* true is that (a) the Confederacy drafted men before the Union did (b) the Union drafted women as well as men (c) wealthy Northerners could avoid the draft by paying the government a fee (d) people in New York City rioted against the draft.

4. Clara Barton is remembered as (a) the first female member of Congress (b) a nurse in the Union Army (c) a spy for the Confederacy (d) the first black soldier to serve in the Union Army.

5. The section of the country that suffered the most damage because of the fighting was the (a) Northeast (b) West (c) North (d) South.

6. The Civil War helped to break up the plantation system by (a) making soil less *fertile* (rich) (b) destroying forever the foreign markets for Southern crops (c) making a big change in the labor force (d) killing most plantation owners.

7. One result of the Civil War was that (a) women fought as soldiers in separate units (b) plantations grew larger (c) the pre-war Southern way of life disappeared (d) the North lost most of its factories to invading armies.

8. A group that benefited greatly from results of the Civil War were (a) slaveholders (b) plantation owners (c) Confederate leaders (d) Northern factory owners.

9. The Civil War proved that (a) the states were more powerful than the federal government (b) the federal government was more powerful than the states (c) the federal government and the states were equal in power (d) states could legally secede from the Union.

10. A statement supported by the results of the Civil War says that (a) wars are not important (b) wars often have important results apart from who wins the battles and wars (c) which side wins a war makes little difference to the people involved (d) wars are usually forgotten as soon as the fighting stops.

Developing Table-Reading Skills

THE CIVIL WAR AND OTHER U.S. WARS COMPARED

War		Number Serving	American deaths (including civilians)
American Revolution (1775–1783)		250,000	25,324
War of 1812 (1812–1814)		286,000	2,260
Mexican War (1846–1848)		78,700	13,280
Civil War (1861–1865)	Union:	2,213,000	364,000
	Confederacy:	1,500,000	258,000
Spanish-American War (1898)		307,000	2,450
World War I (1917–1918)		4,735,000	116,500
World War II (1941–1945)		16,113,000	405,400
Korean War (1950–1953)		5,720,000	54,250
Vietnam War (1964–1973)		8,744,000	56,000

Examine the table above. Then answer the following True-False questions. On a separate sheet of paper, number from one to five. After each number, write *T* if the statement is true, *F* if the statement is false, or *I* if there is insufficient information to answer the question.

1. More Americans (Confederate and Union supporters combined) died during the Civil War than during any other war listed.

2. The Korean War was the one in which the fewest number of Americans served.

3. Over 1 million Americans died during World War I and World War II combined.

4. Over 3 million Americans served during the Civil War.

5. The Spanish-American War lasted longer than any other war listed.

Thinking About the Lesson

1. Why is the Civil War considered by some historians as the nation's first modern war? Do you agree with this description? Why or why not?

2. Compare and contrast Northern and Southern methods of financing war efforts. Which side had the stronger economy? Why?

3. List and explain one *political*, one *economic*, and one *social* result of the Civil War.

Restoring the South to the Union— Reconstruction

During the 12 years after the Civil War, the country went through a process called *Reconstruction* (building again). 1865–1877 was a period during which the states of the Confederacy came back into the Union. Also during these years, the South began to rebuild its economy. American leaders disagreed on how Reconstruction should be carried out.

Why Was Reconstruction So Difficult?

Reconstruction proved to be a difficult and painful task. Rebuilding the South took many years to complete, for several reasons:

• The whole Southern economy needed to be restored. Factories and farms had been destroyed or were just not being operated. As a result, many Southerners were without work.
• The rights of 3.5 million former slaves needed to be defined and protected. These people had to learn how to earn a living on their own and live as free people.
• Southern whites needed to adjust to the freeing of the slaves. This adjustment would involve a new pattern of white-black relations.
• The seceded states needed to be brought back into the Union.

Congress and federal officials set the basic policies of Reconstruction. American leaders, however, had little experience in planning on such a large scale. Moreover, these leaders disagreed sharply as to what should be done.

Lincoln's Plan for Reconstruction

While the war was still going on, Lincoln had made plans to reunite the nation. In 1863, he had promised pardons to Southerners who took an oath of loyalty to the Union. The oath would require them to support the U.S. Constitution. They would also have to agree to obey federal laws, including ones on slavery. In a Southern state, ten percent of the voters who had voted in 1860 would need to take this oath. Then the state could form a government and come back into the Union. Only the highest Confederate leaders would be excluded from serving in public office.

Lincoln's Plan Attacked Critics of Lincoln's plan said that it was too *lenient* (soft, easy). For instance, they pointed out that Lincoln would not require the states to give blacks the vote. Furthermore, some Northerners wanted to punish Southern leaders.

Lincoln knew that firm steps would have to be taken with the South. He believed that many of these steps would be painful to Southerners. He felt, though, that there was nothing to be gained from feeling bitter and revengeful. On the whole, Lincoln's plan for Reconstruction was generous and forgiving. He believed that the Southern states had never legally left the Union. He looked on them as "erring sisters." Lincoln wanted to restore the states to full and equal status in the Union as soon as possible.

Johnson's Plan

When President Lincoln was killed in 1865, Vice President Andrew Johnson took over as President. Johnson accepted the main ideas of Lincoln's plan. He urged Southerners to organize new state governments under this plan.

Failure of Johnson's Plan President Johnson, however, was not able to gain the backing of Congress. He lacked Lincoln's ability to get along with his opponents. Johnson was criticized for being too generous to former leaders of the Confederacy, some of whom he had pardoned. To his critics, Johnson seemed not to be fully aware of the problems facing former slaves. For instance, he did not press for equal rights for black Americans.

Congressional Plan of Reconstruction

By December, 1865, all Southern states but Texas had formed new state governments. They had also elected members of Congress. Southern representatives and senators were on hand in Washington, ready to take their seats. Then Congress refused to seat these elected officials, claiming that many of them had held high positions in the Confederacy. Moreover, Congress refused to recognize the new Southern state governments. In fact, Congress rejected the whole presidential plan for Reconstruction.

Radical Republicans Northern Republicans controlled the Congress that met in December. Many of these Republicans favored a "hard peace." They wanted to place extra requirements on Southern states seeking to return to the Union. Those Republicans who held this point of view were sometimes called "Radical Republicans."

Leaders of the Radical Republicans included Thaddeus Stevens of Pennsylvania and Charles Sumner of Massachusetts. Representative Stevens argued that the nation should treat the ex-Confederate states as conquered provinces. He proposed that plantations of Confederate leaders be divided up and given to former slaves. Senator Sumner said that the Southern states had caused

These black workers in Virginia were fortunate to have jobs. Many former slaves could not find employment after the war.

their current problems by seceding. He thought that Congress could now set any conditions it wanted for readmission.

The Radical Republicans had several goals:

• To punish Confederate leaders.
• To safeguard the civil rights of former slaves.
• To keep the Republican party in firm control of the federal government.
• To make sure that the new Southern members of Congress, mostly Democrats, did not upset certain policies. The Republicans, for instance, were interested in keeping tariffs high.

In 1865, Congress set up the Freedmen's Bureau. This federal agency supplied emergency aid to freed black slaves. It gave *freedmen* (freed slaves, both male and female) food, clothing, and medical care. The Bureau also aided former slaves in adjusting to freedom. It helped them get jobs, rent lands, and set up homes. Its schools were the first for Southern blacks paid for by taxes. In 1866, Radical Republicans wanted to expand the powers of the Freedmen's Bureau. They wanted the Bureau to take to military courts cases in which freed slaves were deprived of their civil rights. President Johnson vetoed the bill to expand the powers of the Bureau. Later in 1866, this Freedmen's Bureau bill was passed over the President's veto.

The Black Codes

After the war, Southern state legislatures passed laws to limit the rights of former slaves. These laws became knows as *Black Codes*. Some of these codes allowed authorities to:

• Fine and jail blacks who did not have jobs. A black found guilty could be sentenced to serve a term as the laborer of a white person.
• Prevent blacks from attending white schools.
• Prevent a group of blacks from meeting without a white person present.

Black Codes were more severe in some states than in others. In general, the codes attempted to keep blacks under the control of whites. Many Americans realized that the new laws were not too different from former slave laws.

Citizenship for Blacks

As part of its Reconstruction program, Congress in 1866 passed a Civil Rights Act. This act was passed to weaken the Black Codes and give former slaves the right of citizenship. Under the law, blacks were now supposed to be treated the same as whites.

The Fourteenth Amendment   In 1866, Congress approved the Fourteenth Amendment to the Constitution. This Amendment, which went into effect in 1868, contained many of the

The Freedmen's Bureau set up some 4,300 schools throughout the South and taught about 250,000 blacks. This school was in Vicksburg, Mississippi.

provisions of the Civil Rights Act. It made freed slaves citizens. It guaranteed them the "equal protection of the law." The Amendment also prevented many former Confederate leaders from holding federal or state offices.

Reconstruction Acts of 1867

The elections of 1866 brought even more Radical Republicans into Congress. In 1867, it passed a series of acts that put the South under military rule. The laws divided the former Confederacy into five military districts, each one under the command of a U.S. Army general. To be let back into the Union, a state would have to ratify the Fourteenth Amendment. It would also have to prepare a new state constitution. This constitution would have to give black males the same right to vote as white males had.

Although military reconstruction was Congress's idea, President Johnson had to carry it out. To do this job, he appointed five military commanders and stationed about 20,000 U.S. troops in the South.

Readmission of States

By 1868, seven states were allowed back into the Union. The remaining states had to wait until their legislatures agreed to ratify the Fifteenth Amendment, as well as the Fourteenth.

The Fifteenth Amendment, ratified in 1870, prohibited states from denying blacks their right to vote. Many blacks in both the North and the South could now vote for the first time. Women's rights groups had urged the nation's lawmakers to give women the right to vote at the same time. Nevertheless, Congress failed to mention women in the Fifteenth Amendment.

As states were readmitted, the military governors gave up their control. Voters in the readmitted states elected new local and state officials. Federal troops, however, remained in the South until 1877.

Impeachment and Trial

President Johnson was an able man with a long record of public service. Nonetheless, he had problems because he was a Democrat dealing

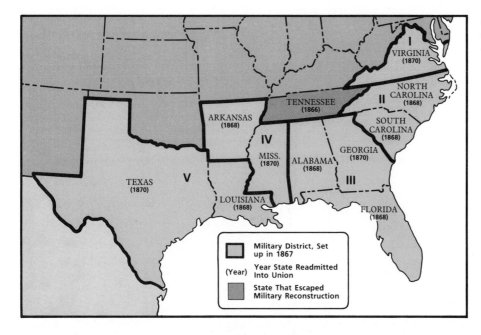

MILITARY RECONSTRUCTION IN THE SOUTH

with a Congress dominated by Radical Republicans. Furthermore, he often acted in ways that angered Congress.

• He was lenient toward the South at a time when many Americans wanted to punish the region.

• He vetoed a number of bills passed by Congress.

• He upset members of Congress by making angry remarks about them.

• He restricted the powers of the military commanders who ruled the South. Moreover, Johnson removed several commanders for being too sympathetic to the programs of the Radical Republicans.

Bad feelings between Congress and President Johnson led to a showdown. In the Tenure of Office Act of 1867, Congress barred the President from removing any important federal officials without Senate approval. In spite of this law, Johnson in 1868 dismissed his Secretary of War—Edwin Stanton. The President felt that Stanton had been working with the Radical Republicans. As a result of the President's action, the House voted to impeach Andrew Johnson.

The Impeachment Trial While the House can *impeach* (bring charges against) a President, impeachment trials are held by the Senate. Johnson's trial lasted about two months in 1868. In the end, he was declared not guilty of any crimes that could lead to his removal from office. Nevertheless, the vote was close—only one short of the two-thirds majority needed for removal. After being *acquitted* (found not guilty of the charge), Johnson continued to serve as President until his term ended in 1869. The impeachment proceedings hurt the Republicans. Public opinion began to turn against them.

In the scene below, the U.S. Senate in 1868 acts as a court to judge President Andrew Johnson after the House of Representatives had impeached him. A ticket (inset) was needed to sit in the galleries above and watch the proceedings. The Senate adjourned as a court of impeachment on May 26, 1868, having failed to convict the President.

SUMMING UP   We have seen that plans for returning the Southern states to the Union were controversial. Presidents Lincoln and Johnson had similar ideas. Under Johnson's direction, Southern states quickly formed governments. Radical Republicans in Congress, wanting to punish the South, rejected these governments and pushed their own program. The Radical Republicans kept former Confederate leaders from regaining power. They gave former slaves certain rights, including the right to vote.

Understanding the Text

On a separate sheet of paper, write the letter of the word or phrase that best completes each of the following statements.

1. The most appropriate set of dates for the period of Reconstruction is *(a)* 1861–1865 *(b)* 1865–1877 *(c)* 1870–1890 *(d)* 1860–1870.

2. A key problem of Reconstruction was *(a)* winning the war *(b)* rebuilding war-torn Southern industry and agriculture *(c)* settling a border conflict between the Union and the Confederacy *(d)* lowering tariffs to stimulate trade.

3. The main reason that it was difficult to restore the Southern states to the Union was the *(a)* high level of unemployment in the South *(b)* desire of Lincoln and Johnson to punish the South *(c)* desire of many members of Congress to punish the South *(d)* efforts of foreign nations to help the South.

4. Lincoln's feelings toward the defeated South can best be described as *(a)* harsh and stubborn *(b)* generous and forgiving *(c)* revengeful and cruel *(d)* vague and uncertain.

5. Representative Thaddeus Stevens's and Senator Charles Sumner's feelings toward the South can best be described as *(a)* very lenient *(b)* highly cooperative *(c)* severe and revengeful *(d)* willing to experiment.

6. The Reconstruction plan favored by Radical Republicans in Congress aimed to *(a)* help former slaves *(b)* punish the South *(c)* keep the Republican party in power *(d)* all of the above.

7. The main job of the Freedmen's Bureau was to *(a)* hold elections *(b)* assist former slaves *(c)* negotiate with foreign governments *(d)* provide loans to plantation owners.

8. Former slaves were especially unhappy about the *(a)* Civil Rights Act of 1866 *(b)* program of the Freedmen's Bureau *(c)* Fifteenth Amendment *(d)* Black Codes.

9. In 1868, President Andrew Johnson was *(a)* impeached by the House *(b)* tried by the Senate *(c)* found not guilty of impeachment charges *(d)* all of the above.

10. Which of the following statements best applies to the Reconstruction period? *(a)* Both the North and the South needed to rebuild their economies completely. *(b)* Americans dealt with complicated economic, social, and political problems. *(c)* The U.S. Presidents showed strong leadership abilities, while Congress appeared weak. *(d)* The Reconstruction period continues to the present time.

Developing Graph-Reading Skills

TWO AGRICULTURAL REGIONS, 1850–1880

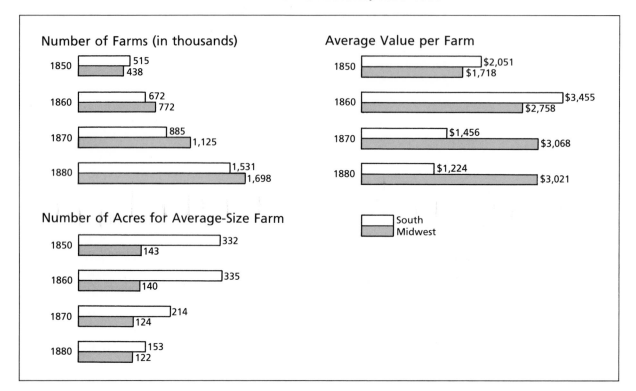

Study the graphs above. Then choose the letter of the word or phrase that best completes each sentence. On a separate sheet of paper, match the sentence number with the correct letter.

1. The three graphs are (*a*) pie graphs (*b*) line graphs (*c*) bar graphs (*d*) picture graphs.

2. From 1850 to 1880, the number of farms in the South and Midwest (*a*) increased steadily (*b*) decreased steadily (*c*) rose for 20 years and then dropped (*d*) none of the above.

3. The largest average-size farm was found in the (*a*) South in 1850 (*b*) Midwest in 1850 (*c*) Midwest in 1870 (*d*) South in 1860.

4. The average value of a farm decreased the most in the (*a*) South between 1850 and 1860 (*b*) Midwest between 1860 and 1870 (*c*) South between 1860 and 1870 (*d*) South between 1870 and 1880.

5. Information in the graphs best supports which of the following statements? (*a*) In the second half of the 19th century, the Midwestern economy changed from being agricultural to industrial. (*b*) After the Civil War, many plantations in the South were broken up into a number of smaller farms. (*c*) After 1860, the South depended less on cotton and more on other staple crops. (*d*) Usually the average value of farms decreases as the average size of farms decreases.

Thinking About the Lesson

1. Some historians believe that the social, economic, and political problems of the period after the Civil War were more difficult than those during the war. Defend or criticize this view.

2. Do you think that the Radical Republicans' Reconstruction program was too harsh on the South? Why or why not?

3. Should President Johnson have been impeached in 1868? Why or why not?

The Grant Era

Ulysses S. Grant served two terms as President, from 1869 to 1877. During these Reconstruction years, blacks in the South gained the right to vote, and many white Southerners were denied this right. Also during this time, local, state, and federal governments were rocked by scandals. The American public learned that many politicians were taking money in exchange for doing favors.

Election of 1868

The Republican party in 1868 ran the Union's most popular war hero, General Ulysses S. Grant, for President. His slogan, "Let Us Have Peace," indicated that he planned to be lenient with the South. Other leaders of the Republican party had different ideas; they called for continued military occupation of the South. Republicans used the campaign tactic of "waving the bloody shirt." They reminded voters of the Democrats' connection with the Confederacy.

In 1868, the Democrats nominated Governor Horatio Seymour of New York as their presidential candidate. They strongly criticized the Republicans' Reconstruction program. Moreover, they differed with the Republicans on the issue of how to repay *bondholders* (those who owned war bonds). The Democrats wanted

bondholders to be paid in paper money. The Republicans, on the other hand, called for repayment in gold. Republicans, often wealthier than their opponents, held more of these bonds than did Democrats.

Republican Victories Grant was elected by a solid majority of the Electoral College. In the same election, the Republicans won control of Congress and most Southern state governments. Republicans were aided by blacks, many of whom were voting for the first time. Blacks tended to see the Republican party as the party that had helped them. Democrats, however, were hurt by federal laws that prevented many Southern whites from voting.

The Grant Administration

President Grant served from 1869 to 1877—a time of great economic expansion. Western parts of the nation were quickly filling up. Railroads were connecting distant regions of the country. More and more businesses were being started, some becoming very large and powerful. Certain individuals wielded so much power that they soon owned controlling interests in a number of businesses. (Large business organizations are discussed in Lesson 47.)

President-elect Ulysses S. Grant's hometown was Galena, Illinois. In this illustration, Grant is shown with his wife and daughter as they prepare to leave Galena in 1869 for his inauguration in Washington, D.C.

Corruption During the Grant years, *corruption* (dishonesty) was widespread in governments on all levels. Important members of the House and Senate figured in scandals by taking *bribes* (money given in exchange for doing favors).

Cartoonist Thomas Nast attacked Boss Tweed (William Marcy Tweed) in this work, which appeared in *Harper's Weekly* in 1886.

Grant was not a strong leader. Misconduct was found even among members of the President's own Cabinet. In one case, the Secretary of the Treasury got a fee for giving out a contract to a private tax collector. In another case, the Secretary of War accepted bribes in return for granting someone trading rights with Indians in Oklahoma. President Grant was not directly involved in corrupt acts. Nevertheless, when some of his friends were found breaking the law, he failed to take firm action against them.

Corruption spread to state and city politics. In New York City, for example, the Tweed Ring controlled the government for nearly 20 years. This group of politicians sold jobs and handed out huge contracts to friends and supporters. The leaders of the Tweed Ring stayed in power by paying people to vote for them. Some historians say that the group cost the city more than $100 million.

The Reconstruction Governments

The state Reconstruction governments played important roles in putting the broken South

Twenty-two Southern blacks were elected to Congress in the second half of the 19th century. Although most blacks had no previous experience in government, some showed outstanding ability. Hiram Revels (on the left) served as U.S. senator from Mississippi. In the Senate, he worked for civil rights laws to aid black Americans. Others shown are (from left to right) U.S. Representatives Benjamin S. Turner of Alabama, Robert C. DeLarge of South Carolina, Josiah T. Walls of Florida, Jefferson H. Long of Georgia, Joseph H. Rainy of South Carolina, and R. Brown Elliot of South Carolina.

back together. They raised taxes to pay for the repair of roads, bridges, and buildings. They helped factories and railroads to rebuild. They aided farmers in starting to raise crops again. In addition, they reorganized and improved local governments, including local courts.

After the war, Reconstruction governments took steps to begin public school systems in the South. They set up hospitals, orphan homes, and places to aid the handicapped.

Defects of Reconstruction Governments The record of the Reconstruction governments was

not all good, however. Many state legislators were inexperienced and showed poor judgment. Some spent public money for projects that were not really needed. A number of Southern legislators turned corrupt, accepting bribes for favors. Remember, though, that corruption was widespread in many parts of the country after the Civil War.

Carpetbaggers During Reconstruction, some Northern Republicans lived in the South, helping to control Southern state governments. Because they sometimes carried their belongings

Many Southerners had this view of Northerners who lived and worked in the South during Reconstruction.

and senators. One, Pinkney B. Pinchback, served briefly as Governor of Louisiana.

Southern Resistance to Reconstruction Governments

Most Southern whites resented their loss of political power to Northern Republicans. They also resented seeing former slaves in important positions in government. If federal troops had not been present in the South, Southern whites would have prevented the Reconstruction governments from ruling.

The Klan Southern whites wanted to regain control as soon as possible. Some tried to do this by forming secret societies, such as the Ku Klux Klan. Members of the Klan strongly believed in *white supremacy* (white domination). The Klan used violence or threats of violence

in bags made of carpetlike cloth, many Southerners called them *carpetbaggers*.

Carpetbaggers became very unpopular with white Southerners. Southerners accused these Northerners of coming south just to make a quick dollar. No doubt the lure of riches motivated some carpetbaggers, but many of these Northerners sincerely wanted to help former slaves.

Scalawags A number of white Southerners worked closely with blacks and carpetbaggers. These Southerners were often planters and businesspeople with long experience in dealing with blacks. They soon found themselves criticized by other white Southerners, who called them *scalawags*.

Black Southerners Newly freed blacks played important roles in Reconstruction governments. Running on Republican tickets, blacks won many important elections. A number of blacks became state legislators and U.S. representatives

These costumes are just two of the kind that members of the Ku Klux Klan wore to disguise themselves.

against blacks and their supporters. Klan members frightened blacks from voting. In some cases, they carried arms on election day to "persuade" blacks not to vote. In other cases, Klan members "suggested" which candidate black voters should choose. Those voters who chose the "wrong" candidate might lose their jobs or be denied credit to buy food.

Return of the Democrats

After 1869, white Democrats began to regain control of Southern state governments, taking power away from Republican Reconstruction governments. This change occurred for several reasons. First, Northerners became less interested in the problems of Southern blacks. Second, Congress in 1872 restored voting rights to almost all former Confederates. Third, federal troops were withdrawn from the South in stages. Without the protection of the troops, some blacks were intimidated from voting.

The Democratic party grew stronger in other parts of the country as well. In the congressional elections of 1874, Democrats gained a majority in the U.S. House of Representatives. They had not controlled the lower house of Congress since 1859.

The Election of 1876

Democrats came close to winning the Presidency in the election of 1876. In that year, the Republican candidate for President was Rutherford B. Hayes of Ohio. He ran against the Democrat, Samuel J. Tilden of New York. Both parties favored reforms in government and an end to Reconstruction.

A Dispute   At first, Americans believed that Tilden had won by a close margin. However, a dispute arose over 20 electoral votes from 4 states, 3 of which were Southern states. Both Republicans and Democrats claimed all 20 votes— enough votes to decide the election either way.

The Settlement   To settle the dispute, Congress set up an electoral commission that included representatives of both parties. Each commission member voted for the candidate of his own party. In the end, the commission gave the disputed votes (and the election) to Hayes.

Compromise of 1877   The Democrats did not protest the decision to award the disputed electoral votes to Hayes for the following reason: In the secret "Compromise of 1877," the Democrats had agreed to let the Republican candidate win. In return, the Republicans had promised to see that federal troops were removed from the South.

The last federal troops were withdrawn from the South in 1877. With their departure, the Reconstruction era ended.

Most presidential candidates in the 19th century had campaign songs. As we see from this sheet music cover, Samuel Tilden was no exception.

SUMMING UP We have seen how Ulysses S. Grant served as President during the last eight years of Reconstruction. His Presidency was not a successful one. During his years in office, not only was his administration full of dishonest politicians, but state and local governments were as well. After 1869, white Democrats gradually regained control of the South. Along with their renewed power in that region, Democrats began to rival the Republicans in national politics as well.

Understanding the Text

On a separate sheet of paper, write the letter of the word or phrase that best completes each of the following statements.

1. Ulysses S. Grant *(a)* was a great success as President *(b)* was personally dishonest *(c)* was a weak national leader *(d)* was strongly supported by Democratic voters in the South.

2. Corruption in government after the Civil War occurred *(a)* in all sections of the country and at all levels of government *(b)* only in the big cities *(c)* mainly in the North *(d)* only in the Reconstruction governments of the South.

3. The Tweed Ring was noted for *(a)* its reform of the federal government *(b)* corruption of a city government *(c)* settlement of the disputed election of 1876 *(d)* occupation of the Southern states.

4. Hiram Revels was a *(a)* U.S. senator *(b)* Democratic candidate for President in 1876 *(c)* former Confederate leader *(d)* U.S. Army general during Reconstruction.

5. Reconstruction state governments were made up of *(a)* white members only *(b)* black members only *(c)* both white and black members, mixed together *(d)* both white and black members, organized into separate bodies.

6. One accomplishment of the Reconstruction state governments was to *(a)* do away with taxes *(b)* refuse to give blacks their rights of citizenship *(c)* discourage the building of factories *(d)* set up public school systems.

7. Most white Southerners *(a)* disliked carpetbaggers and scalawags greatly *(b)* cooperated with carpetbaggers and scalawags *(c)* paid no attention to carpetbaggers and scalawags *(d)* asked carpetbaggers and scalawags to be their leaders.

8. A major program favored by the Ku Klux Klan was *(a)* more jobs for blacks *(b)* equal rights for all *(c)* nonviolent resistance *(d)* white supremacy.

9. The politicians who regained control of Southern state governments after Reconstruction were the *(a)* white Democrats *(b)* white Republicans *(c)* black Republicans *(d)* black Democrats.

10. The disputed election of 1876 resulted in the Presidency of *(a)* Samuel J. Tilden *(b)* Ulysses S. Grant *(c)* Horatio Seymour *(d)* Rutherford B. Hayes.

Developing Chronology Skills

RECONSTRUCTION TIMELINE

Important Events:

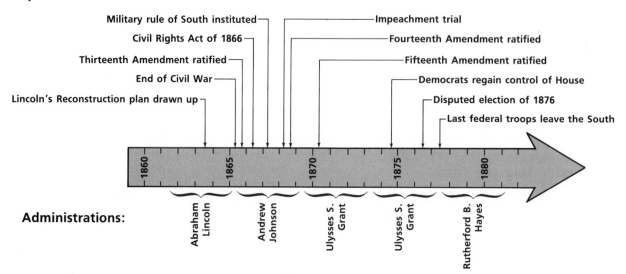

Military rule of South instituted
Civil Rights Act of 1866
Thirteenth Amendment ratified
End of Civil War
Lincoln's Reconstruction plan drawn up

Impeachment trial
Fourteenth Amendment ratified
Fifteenth Amendment ratified
Democrats regain control of House
Disputed election of 1876
Last federal troops leave the South

1860   1865   1870   1875   1880

Administrations:

Abraham Lincoln   Andrew Johnson   Ulysses S. Grant   Ulysses S. Grant   Rutherford B. Hayes

Examine the timeline above. Then choose the letter of the word or phrase that best answers each question. On a separate sheet of paper, match the sentence number with the correct letter.

1. The Civil War took place during the administration of *(a)* Abraham Lincoln *(b)* Andrew Johnson *(c)* Ulysses S. Grant *(d)* Rutherford B. Hayes.

2. A disputed election occurred during *(a)* the Johnson administration *(b)* Grant's first term *(c)* Grant's second term *(d)* the Hayes administration.

3. During Grant's first term as President, *(a)* the Fourteenth Amendment was ratified *(b)* military rule of the South was instituted *(c)* the Fifteenth Amendment was ratified *(d)* the Democrats regained control of the House of Representatives.

4. The Civil Rights Act of 1866 was passed during the administration of *(a)* Lincoln *(b)* Hayes *(c)* Grant *(d)* Johnson.

5. Of the following events, the one that happened last was the *(a)* election of Hayes *(b)* assassination of Lincoln *(c)* ratification of the Fifteenth Amendment *(d)* end of Grant's second term.

Thinking About the Lesson

1. Do you think that Presidents should be blamed if members of their administrations misbehave? Why or why not?

2. In what ways did some Southerners show their resentment toward Reconstruction programs? Do you think that their resentment and actions were justified? Why or why not?

3. Briefly explain one social and one political result of the Reconstruction period in the South.

UNIT 5

AMERICA LOOKS TO THE 20TH CENTURY

The United States Becomes an Industrial Giant

In the years after the Civil War, the United States became one of the world's great industrial powers. By 1900, it was producing more manufactured goods than any other country. The nation's history between 1865 and 1900 largely centers around the story of this astounding growth. While the growing, prosperous economy benefited many Americans, it caused problems as well.

The Growth of Industry

After 1865, the number and size of factories in the United States increased rapidly. The Industrial Revolution, discussed in Lesson 33, continued its course. As more and more workers began to operate machines, mass production became common in industries. To obtain better-paying jobs, many rural Americans moved to urban areas, where factories were generally located. Large numbers of immigrants also came to American cities to find employment.

The following examples give an idea of the extent of industrial growth after the Civil War:

• Steel production in 1865 was at a low level of 15,000 tons. By 1900, the production of raw steel had risen greatly—to over 11 million tons.

• The oil industry in 1865 was just beginning. By 1900, crude oil production was already at a healthy 64 million barrels.

• At the end of the Civil War, the country was intersected with about 35,000 miles of railway tracks. By 1900, this figure had grown to nearly 200,000. Five major railway lines crossed the Western part of the country. (See the map on page 311.)

Reasons for Industrial Growth

A number of basic factors made possible the nation's rapid industrial growth.

Natural Resources The development of industries would not have been possible without the country's rich natural resources. Then, too, scientists discovered better mining methods and better ways of separating valuable metals from ores. As a result, more and more iron, lead, copper, and other ores were mined.

Still another natural resource was the nation's vast and rich farmlands. Farmers produced not only more food, but also more raw materials, such as cotton, for industries.

Sources of Power Many American factories continued to operate with power obtained from fast-moving streams and rivers. Coal, however, became increasingly important to American industries in the second half of the 19th century. Factories burned coal to make steam; the steam powered machines used in factory production.

The development of new power sources helped industries to expand. In 1859, Edwin Drake drilled America's first oil well, in Pennsylvania. At first, oil was made into *kerosene*, a fuel burned in lamps. Later, industries used refined oil to *lubricate* (grease) machines. Not until the 20th century would oil become an important source of power in industries.

In the late 19th century, several U.S. industries began to use electrical power in their operations. This electricity was *generated* (produced) in one of two ways:

• In one way, coal was burned to make steam. A *dynamo* (electrical generator) changed the steam power into electrical power. In 1882, Thomas Edison created in New York City a large electrical power plant that used a dynamo.

• Electricity was also generated by harnessing waterpower, such as the power of a waterfall. Beginning in 1895, a large power plant in Niagara Falls, New York, produced electricity in this manner.

Inventions A number of inventions helped industries to grow larger and faster:

• Bessemer Process. For the first time, in 1864, an American factory used the *Bessemer process* to make steel rails. In this process, developed by Sir Henry Bessemer of England, workers directed blasts of air at *molten iron* (iron melted by heat). This method removed impurities in the iron and allowed steel to be made cheaply and in large quantities. So much steel was produced in America after 1865 that the era is sometimes called "The Age of Steel."

These men are watching molten iron being poured—part of the Bessemer process of making steel. Later in the 19th century, two other methods of making steel were developed—the open hearth and the electric furnace processes.

• Telegraph. The telegraph, first discussed in Lesson 33, was invented before the Civil War. After the war, telegraph companies extended lines across the United States, often alongside the new railroad tracks. In 1866, Cyrus W. Field managed to extend telegraph service across the Atlantic Ocean. His company laid an underwater cable that connected Newfoundland and Ireland. With this service, Americans could communicate quickly with people in Europe.

• Telephone. Another invention aided communication—the telephone. In 1876, Alexander Graham Bell successfully demonstrated the telephone for the first time. Not too many years afterward, businesses were using the device to reach suppliers and customers.

• Typewriter. Christopher L. Sholes of Wisconsin invented the first practical typewriter in 1868. Soon businesses that no longer wanted their letters to be written in longhand began hiring typists. The invention opened up a new field of employment for many Americans.

Thomas Alva Edison was one of the greatest inventors in history. Working hard most of his lifetime (1847–1931), he invented over a thousand useful items. Edison once said that "genius is about one percent inspiration and 99 percent perspiration." His inventions included: an electric light bulb, the phonograph, dictaphone, storage battery, microphone, motion picture equipment, and an electric generator. His favorite invention was the phonograph. Although deaf, he could hear music by pressing his ear to the machine.

Transportation   Improvements in rail transportation helped to overcome the difficulties resulting from the nation's great size. As mentioned before, railroads greatly increased the number of miles of their lines. In 1869, the first *transcontinental* (across the continent) rail line was completed. Americans could now go from one end of the country to the other by rail.

Inventor Alexander Graham Bell is shown demonstrating his telephone to interested viewers at the U.S. Centennial Exposition in Philadelphia in 1876. Bell was also an expert on speech and, in that capacity, helped train teachers of the deaf.

This print, by the successful publishers Currier and Ives, illustrates well the growth of railroads in America by the 1870s. On the right stands a Pullman Sleeping Car.

The railroad companies improved their ability to carry heavy loads safely and quickly:

• On some lines, two sets of tracks were laid so that traffic could go two ways at the same time.
• Steel rails often replaced the weaker iron ones.
• Some railroad bridges, originally made of wood, were replaced by iron or steel ones.
• In 1869, George Westinghouse introduced the air brake—an invention that made high-speed railroad travel safer. Air brakes are still used by trains today.

Passenger travel on railroads also improved after the Civil War. George Pullman's 1864 invention of the sleeping car helped make rail travel more comfortable. The introduction of dining cars was popular with many passengers.

Steam-powered boats, in use before the Civil War, became even more common after 1865. They replaced sail-powered boats on both the oceans and the country's major lakes and rivers. Now immigrants from Europe and East Asia could make a much quicker and easier journey to America. Manufacturers found that they could send their products to distant markets much faster.

Methods of Production The growth of American industries was partly due to their use of modern production methods. More and more factory owners introduced mass production techniques. They bought raw materials in large quantities and at low prices. Then they manufactured large numbers of the same item. Where possible, they had machines perform manufacturing operations.

Sources of Capital and the Free-Enterprise System The American economy was able to expand, in part because so much *capital* (money) was available. Americans could easily start new businesses or expand existing ones because banks and investors were willing to put up money for these purposes. The United States had a *free-enterprise system*, whereby almost anybody could start up a business if he or she could find the necessary capital. There were few government restrictions on business operations. (Discussed further in Lesson 47.)

Results of Industrial Growth

The growth of industries in the United States had many important results:

• Daily life for most Americans became easier. Many were able to buy new products and services, such as kerosene lamps, telephones, and phonographs.

• The country became less rural. Many people moved from farming areas to towns and cities where the new jobs were located. In 1860, about 80 percent of the American population lived in rural areas. By 1900, the figure had gone down to 60 percent.

• Millions of immigrants were attracted by new job opportunities to the shores and borders of the United States. (Discussed in Lesson 49.)

• American manufacturers had more goods to sell at competitive prices. This situation helped them in their trade with other nations.

• Some Americans gained great fortunes. Certain industrialists and other businesspeople profited from the country's industrial growth. As we shall see, however, many Americans failed to participate in the nation's growing prosperity.

Problems of Industrial Growth

The growth of industries resulted in certain problems.

Problems of Cities   Many people moved to cities after the Civil War. Some of these new urban dwellers failed to find work. Others worked at very low wages, often for long hours and in unsafe or unsanitary working conditions. The urban poor lived in *slums* (run-down buildings or neighborhoods). Their health suffered because of inadequate and unsanitary housing. (See Lessons 48 and 49 for further discussion of these problems.)

Economic Depressions   During some years, the American economy prospered. During other years, such as in 1873 and 1893, the economy went through economic depressions. To cover losses, factories reduced their production or closed their plants. Without wages, unemployed workers could buy fewer goods. Because of fewer purchases, factories cut back even more. Both depressions were followed by times of economic recovery.

One aspect of urban life in the late 19th century was a definite plus—electricity. This electric power station in New York City was one of the first in the country.

SUMMING UP   We have seen how the United States became an industrial giant after the Civil War. The growth of industries was made possible by many factors. The country had plentiful supplies of power and natural resources to set up new industries. Workers were eager to fill any job openings. New inventions and improved methods of transportation also helped the economy. The rise of industries caused basic changes in American life. Many of these changes, such as new job opportunities, were positive. In some ways, however, the growth of industries caused problems for Americans.

Understanding the Text

On a separate sheet of paper, write the letter of the word or phrase that best completes each of the following statements.

1. Between 1865 and 1900, the United States experienced a large growth in *(a)* steel manufacturing *(b)* oil production *(c)* railroads *(d)* all of the above.

2. Of the following, the one that is *not* a natural resource is *(a)* farmland *(b)* railroads *(c)* coal *(d)* iron ore.

3. Of the following, the one that was *not* a common source of power in U.S. industries of the 19th century was *(a)* waterpower *(b)* coal *(c)* steam *(d)* oil.

4. Which of the following statements about the Industrial Revolution in America is *not* true? *(a)* It began only after the Civil War. *(b)* Many new factories were built. *(c)* Mass production methods were used. *(d)* Urban areas grew in population more than rural ones.

5. Edwin Drake is known for *(a)* inventing the kerosene lamp *(b)* building a dynamo for use in New York City *(c)* drilling the first oil well in the country *(d)* laying telegraph cables along the floor of the Atlantic Ocean.

6. The Bessemer process was important in *(a)* generating electricity *(b)* sending telegrams *(c)* making steel *(d)* drilling for oil.

7. Alexander Graham Bell made an important contribution in developing the *(a)* oil well *(b)* telephone *(c)* typewriter *(d)* air brake.

8. Railroad safety was improved by *(a)* the air brake *(b)* Christopher L. Sholes *(c)* the sleeping car *(d)* all of the above.

9. As a result of industrial growth, *(a)* all Americans prospered *(b)* about 80 percent of all Americans lived in urban areas in 1900 *(c)* millions of Americans emigrated to Europe *(d)* new products and services were available for Americans to enjoy.

10. Which of the following statements about mass production is *not* true? *(a)* Machines replaced all factory workers. *(b)* Manufacturers made many copies of the same item. *(c)* Machines performed certain tasks. *(d)* Factories bought raw materials in large quantities.

Developing Graph-Reading Skills

MILES OF RAILROAD LINES BUILT IN SELECTED YEARS

Examine the picture graph above. Then choose the letter of the word or phrase that best completes each sentence. On a separate sheet of paper, match the sentence number with the correct letter.

1. The figures ▦▦▦ represent *(a)* the number of railroad companies in business each year *(b)* the number of railroad companies started each year *(c)* the number of miles of railroad lines built each year *(d)* the total number of miles of railroad lines in use each year.

2. The number of miles of railroad lines built was greatest in the year *(a)* 1855 *(b)* 1865 *(c)* 1870 *(d)* 1879.

3. If the information in the picture graph were plotted as a line graph (with the years on the horizontal axis and the mileage on the vertical axis), the low point on the line would correspond to the year *(a)* 1855 *(b)* 1865 *(c)* 1870 *(d)* 1879.

4. The combined mileage was greatest for the two years *(a)* 1850 and 1855 *(b)* 1860 and 1865 *(c)* 1865 and 1870 *(d)* 1875 and 1879.

5. From reading this graph, one can conclude that railroad construction *(a)* increased more in some years than in others *(b)* increased steadily from 1850 to 1879 *(c)* decreased steadily after the Civil War *(d)* increased steadily after the Civil War.

Thinking About the Lesson

1. The text discusses a number of reasons why industries grew rapidly in the second half of the 19th century. Which of the reasons given do you think was the most important one? Explain your answer.

2. If people had not learned how to generate electricity on a large scale, how would our lives be different today?

3. Industrial growth after the Civil War caused many changes in American society. Do you think that the benefits of this growth outweighed the problems that accompanied it? Why or why not?

The Rise of Big Businesses

The growth of industries in the United States led to the creation of many very large businesses. These companies often were organized and managed in new ways. During and after the Civil War, certain business leaders became quite wealthy and powerful. They gained so much power and influence that Congress decided to pass laws to regulate business practices.

Leaders of Big Businesses

A small group of business leaders played important roles in the growth of industry. These energetic, daring, and hard-driving "captains of industry" included:

• Cornelius Vanderbilt (1794–1877). At first, Vanderbilt was the owner of a line of steamships. Then he became an early, large-scale developer of railroads. He organized the New York Central System and soon owned railroad lines that extended as far west as Chicago.

• Jay Gould (1836–1892), part owner of the Erie Railroad. In 1868, he prevented Vanderbilt from gaining control of the Erie by issuing irregular stock. He made millions of dollars by looting the Erie Railroad treasury. He later gained control of many other railroads.

• James Fisk (1834–1872), another part owner of the Erie Railroad. In September, 1869, he and Gould tried to buy all of the gold in New York City so that the price of gold would rise. Their plan worked well until the U.S. Treasury offered its gold for sale. Then gold prices dropped drastically. Gould made millions on the scheme; Fisk avoided big losses by refusing to honor his contracts to buy gold.

• Andrew Carnegie (1835–1919). A Scottish immigrant, Carnegie became the chief owner of the Homestead Steel Works in 1888. By 1900, his company, then called the Carnegie Steel Corporation, controlled most of the steel production in the country. Andrew Carnegie sold his company in 1901, devoting the rest of his life to giving away his millions. Many libraries in America were built with Carnegie's money.

• J. Pierpont Morgan (1837–1913). Morgan was a powerful and dynamic banker. In 1901, he helped to transform Carnegie's steel company into the even larger U.S. Steel Corporation.

• James J. Hill (1838–1916). Hill was a key figure in building and managing the Great Northern, one of the country's first transcontinental railroads.

• John D. Rockefeller (1839–1937). In 1863, Rockefeller started his oil business with a refin-

ery that converted oil into kerosene. Seven years later, he set up the first great trust—Standard Oil Company. (See page 290 for a discussion of trusts.) He dominated the oil industry for many years, controlling not only production but also refining and selling.

Because of their business practices, some captains of industry were called *robber barons.* They often used their money and influence to drive out competitors. In their search for more profits, they did not hesitate to put pressure on government officials. In addition, they sometimes sold inferior goods at high prices.

Corporate Organization

Before the Civil War, most businesses were owned by individuals or families or were partnerships. In a *partnership,* two or more partners share ownership. People form partnerships usually because no one owner has enough money

Cornelius Vanderbilt (above) left about $100 million when he died in 1877. One of his heirs, his son William H. Vanderbilt, used his portion of the fortune to build an elaborate mansion on Fifth Avenue, New York City. The house had an art gallery (left) which, once a week, the owner opened to viewers.

All of the 19th century "robber barons" were men. Some women, however, ran large businesses during this period. Women who took over big companies after their husbands died included:

• Nettie McCormick, president of International Harvester Company. This corporation produced the McCormick reaper and other farm machinery.
• Anna Bissell, president of the company that made Bissell carpet sweepers.

Other women formed companies on their own in the late 19th century, including:

• Harriet Ayer, founder of a major cosmetic company.
• Mary Seymour, founder of the Union School of Stenography and Typewriting in New York City. It was the first business college in the country for women.

People who wanted to buy or sell a corporation's stock would go to a *stockbroker* (above). This drawing "The Slave of the Tape" shows a stockbroker tangled up in *ticker tape*—very long, thin paper that lists up-to-the-minute prices of stocks as received by telegraph.

to finance the company. Each partner is responsible for paying all of the debts of the business.

After the Civil War, many large and medium-sized businesses were organized as corporations. A *corporation* is a business that can sell *stock* (shares of ownership) to many different people. In this way, the business can raise the large amounts of capital needed for large-scale production.

Stockholders, the people who buy a corporation's stock, are the owners of the business. Consequently, they are entitled to share in the profits that the business earns. Usually they do not run the business. Instead, a large corporation is often run by hired managers, who do not necessarily own any shares of stock. The corporation continues in business and the managers keep their jobs when stockholders sell their stocks.

Corporations have several advantages over other types of businesses:

• The ability to raise large amounts of capital. This ability, in turn, allows the company to expand and to hire the best managers and other experts available.
• The ability to remain in business, no matter what happens to the officers and owners of the company. For example, a corporation can go on operating even when an officer or a stockholder dies.
• Limited *liability* (responsibility in the eyes of the law). For instance, if a corporation owes money, the personal property of the stockholders cannot be taken over to meet this debt.

Corporations Work Together

After the Civil War, some corporate managers started to work together with managers of other corporations in the same field. In this way, they avoided competition and kept prices high. Moreover, by such cooperation, they saved money in manufacturing, buying, and selling. Corporate managers used various means to enable their businesses to work together.

Pools This method of corporate cooperation was popular in the years just after the Civil War, especially among railroads. In a *pool*, different companies in the same field would make secret agreements. In one type of pool, managers of the companies would divide the country into sections. Each company would be assigned an exclusive section in which to do business. In another type of pool, managers set prices so that all companies charged the same for the same good or service. With both kinds of pools, prices remained high because there was no competition. These arrangements got the name "pools" because, in some instances, the companies involved would throw profits into a common pool. Then they would divide the money in the pool among themselves.

Trusts Another form of cooperation, *trusts*, became common in the 1880s. Again, as with pools, different companies in the same field of business worked together. In a trust, though, they gave over all powers of management to a single *board of trustees*. Then this board ran all of the companies much like a single business. If a board controlled enough companies, it could use its power to set prices and drive competitors out of business.

Holding Companies This form of business organization began to replace trusts in the 1890s. The *holding company* is a corporation that owns a controlling interest (by owning shares) in other corporations. In some cases, holding companies buy up firms that had formerly competed against one another. In this way, the companies avoided competition. In some industries, a super holding company controls several other holding companies.

Later the word "trust" came to be applied more loosely to any business setup that controlled supplies and prices in an industry. For instance, the word often was used this way in the expression "antitrust laws." (See page 293.)

The Government and Businesses

In the post-Civil War years, the federal government encouraged the growth of big corporations. Government leaders generally believed that large companies would help the country to prosper. To aid businesses, the government:

• Set up high tariffs to protect American firms from foreign competition.
• Enacted laws to strengthen the nation's banking system.
• Gave public lands to companies that contracted to build railroads.
• Did little to limit or control businesses. The government took no action even when it had reason to believe that some businesses were harming the nation as a whole. This policy of not interfering with the operations of private businesses is called *laissez-faire*.

Criticisms of Business Practices

In the 1880s and 1890s, Americans began to realize that some big businesses were taking unfair advantage of their growing powers. In many industries, one big company or a combination of companies was gaining control. It did this by engaging in *cutthroat competition*: it lowered prices so sharply that other companies could not compete. After the smaller rivals had been forced out of business, the giant company then raised prices without fear of competition.

A company that controls the production and sales in an industry is known as a *monopoly*.

BUSINESS ORGANIZATIONS THAT REDUCE COMPETITION

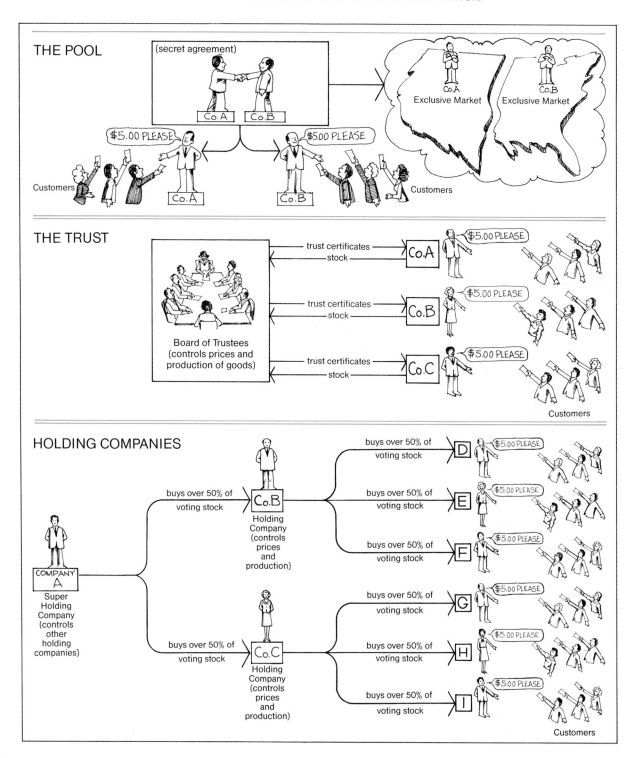

Homer Davenport's cartoon "Two Ends of the National Table" appeared in the *New York Journal.* In what ways do the two ends of the table differ?

When a company becomes a monopoly, it no longer has serious competition. Customers who want to buy a product or service must buy from the monopoly or do without.

Under monopoly conditions, giant corporations in the 19th century did the following:

• Raised prices or cut quality more or less as they wished.

• Forced railroads to grant them *rebates* (the return of part of a payment). Companies that wanted to compete with those having rebates were at a disadvantage. They did not enjoy the reduced costs of doing business that rebates provided.

Railroads, too, could be monopolies. Farmers were especially angry at railroads that charged farmers very high rates for hauling crops to market. Because of the railroad monopolies, farmers could not find cheaper rail transportation.

The End of Laissez-Faire

State governments were the first to respond to the growing complaints against the railroads. In the 1870s, several state legislatures in the Middle West passed laws that regulated railroad rates and practices. These laws stayed in effect for a number of years. Then, in 1886, the U.S. Supreme Court ruled that states could not regulate railroad traffic that crossed state borders.

Interstate Commerce Act In 1887, Congress reacted to this court decision by enacting the Interstate Commerce Act. This law outlawed pools, rebates, and other common abuses of the railroad industry. In general, the act's purpose was to make railroads behave in the public interest. A government agency, the Interstate Commerce Commission (ICC), was set up to enforce the act. At first, the ICC had few powers. Over the years, however, the powers of the ICC were expanded.

Sherman Antitrust Act The federal government ended its laissez-faire policy toward other industries as well. In 1890, Congress passed the Sherman Antitrust Act to try to prevent monopolies. The law declared illegal all combinations and agreements that *restrained* (held back or prevented) free competition. The act was specific in outlawing trusts.

The Sherman Antitrust Act, though, was weak and poorly written. Despite the act, the government lost many of its court cases against trusts. In fact, during the 1890s, the number of business combinations in the country actually increased.

SUMMING UP   We have seen that certain captains of industry led the way in creating big corporations in America after the Civil War. Some of these business leaders used questionable methods to create monopoly conditions in their industries. In the 1880s and 1890s, the federal government dropped its laissez-faire policy. It found that regulating railroads and other big companies was necessary. The government began to issue regulations to protect small businesses and American consumers.

Understanding the Text

On a separate sheet of paper, write the letter of the word or phrase that best completes each of the following statements.

1. A major contributor to the growth of big businesses after the Civil War was (a) high tariffs (b) computers (c) high corporation taxes (d) heavy regulation of businesses.

2. A phrase used by critics to describe some industrial leaders in the second half of the 19th century was (a) "Whiz Kids" (b) "War Hawks" (c) "Laissez-faire" (d) "Robber Barons."

3. A prominent railroad tycoon of the 19th century was (a) Andrew Carnegie (b) James J. Hill (c) John D. Rockefeller (d) Mary Seymour.

4. One of the nation's captains of industry in steel production was (a) Andrew Carnegie (b) Nettie McCormick (c) John D. Rockefeller (d) Cyrus W. Field.

5. Corporations can raise capital by issuing (a) money (b) travelers' checks (c) stocks (d) annual reports.

6. Before 1887, the policy of the federal government toward businesses was (a) isolationism (b) armed neutrality (c) laissez-faire (d) strict regulation.

7. The condition in which one company or group of people controls production and sales in an entire industry is called (a) a monopoly (b) laissez-faire (c) competition (d) free trade.

8. When a monopoly gains control of an industry, it is likely to result in (*a*) more competition (*b*) lower prices (*c*) higher prices (*d*) creation of many small businesses.

9. By setting up the Interstate Commerce Commission, the federal government showed its interest in (*a*) building transcontinental railroads (*b*) doing away with poverty (*c*) regulating the operations of railroads (*d*) banning interstate commerce.

10. The federal law of 1890 that outlawed trusts was the (*a*) Sherman Act (*b*) Interstate Commerce Act (*c*) ICC (*d*) Fourteenth Amendment.

Developing Diagram-Reading Skills

Study the diagrams on page 291. Then choose the letter of the word or phrase that best completes each sentence. On a separate sheet of paper, match the sentence number with the correct letter.

1. The diagrams illustrate three major ways that (*a*) people buy stock in corporations (*b*) the government controls the abuses of big businesses (*c*) businesses organize to decrease competition (*d*) businesses promote competition among themselves.

2. In a pool, managers of two or more companies (*a*) make secret agreements (*b*) divide markets among themselves (*c*) charge the same prices for the same goods and services (*d*) all of the above.

3. A board of trustees is a necessary part of (*a*) a pool (*b*) a trust (*c*) a holding company (*d*) all of the above.

4. In the diagram illustrating holding companies, company *C* (*a*) controls company *B* and is controlled by company *A* (*b*) controls companies *G*, *H*, and *I* (*c*) controls companies *D*,

E, and *F* (*d*) controls company *H* but is controlled by company *I*.

5. To be a holding company, a corporation must (*a*) own stock in more than 50 other corporations (*b*) sell all of its stock to another holding company (*c*) buy more than 50 percent of the stock of some other corporations (*d*) issue trust certificates.

Thinking About the Lesson

1. Why were all of the 19th-century robber barons in the United States men? Could women succeed in business then? Why or why not?

2. Why did corporations become such a popular way of organizing businesses in America after the Civil War?

3. For what reasons did business managers want to form pools, trusts, and holding companies?

4. Why did the federal government and state governments end their policy of laissez-faire toward businesses near the end of the 19th century?

The Growth of the Labor Movement

As industries expanded after the Civil War, so did the ranks of industrial workers. Millions of workers filled new positions in factories, warehouses, railroads, and other businesses. Many workers, though, found that they did not share in the growing wealth of the nation. As a result, they often demanded higher wages and better working conditions, joining labor unions in order to gain bargaining power. At times, they went out on strike. Because of these strikes, the decades after the Civil War were some of the most violent in American labor history.

The National Labor Union

In Lesson 34, we learned about the efforts of labor organizations that had fought for political reforms in the 1830s and 1840s. Among other issues, these groups had asked for laws establishing a ten-hour workday and the right to strike.

In the 1860s, labor groups again sought political reforms that would benefit workers. In 1866, delegates from unions across the country formed the National Labor Union. Its members wanted:

• An eight-hour workday.
• Restrictions on immigration, especially of Chinese workers. Many union members were worried that new immigrants might accept lower wages and take away their jobs.
• Producer cooperatives. In worker-owned *producer cooperatives*, members would work for themselves rather than for an employer. They would make products that the cooperative would sell.

The 600,000-member National Labor Union was successful in at least one respect. In 1868, it persuaded Congress to pass a law setting an eight-hour workday for many federal employees. The union had less success in running candidates for public office on state and federal levels. Unlike some other labor groups, it did not encourage strikes as a means of achieving workers' goals. In the 1870s, the National Labor Union lost members and then dissolved.

The 1870s—Decade of Violence

The economic depression of 1873 weakened the American labor movement. The unions were not in a strong position to make demands. In fact, some American workers had to accept pay cuts; many lost their jobs. As a result, a number of unions disbanded or lost a great part of their membership.

The declining position of labor led to a decade of violent confrontations:

• Tompkins Square Incident. In 1874, un-employed workers in New York City demon-strated on Tompkins Square. As police charged the demonstrators, the meeting turned into a riot.

• General Strike of 1877. In 1877, railway workers on many different lines around the country went on strike. In protesting wage cuts, the workers burned or otherwise destroyed rail-way equipment. They caused service to stop on some lines. In Baltimore and Pittsburgh, local authorities could not handle the violence. There-fore, federal troops had to be brought in to restore order in these cities.

The Knights of Labor

Another large labor organization, the Knights of Labor, took the place of the National Labor Union. The Knights proved to be more signif-icant than the earlier labor group had ever been. Formed on a national level in 1878, the Knights attracted both skilled and unskilled workers. By 1886, it had gained almost 700,000 members.

The Knights of Labor bargained with many employers. It sought to win various benefits for labor, including an eight-hour workday. The union educated the public on the need to outlaw child labor. Unlike the National Labor Union,

the Knights did not hesitate to call strikes. The new labor group believed in using *boycotts* when necessary and, on a number of occasions, agreed to *arbitration*.

In a boycott, a union asks its members and other people not to buy the products of an employer who, it believes, is unfair to labor. With arbitration, both sides in a labor dispute agree to call in a third party. Both sides agree in advance to abide by whatever settlement the third party makes.

Decline of the Knights of Labor Under the leadership of Terence Powderly, the Knights won a number of important strikes. It was the largest labor organization of the 1880s. After 1886, however, the union began to decline in strength, and by 1900 it had almost disappeared. Its decline was caused by several factors:

• Quarrels between skilled and unskilled workers within the organization.

• The rise of the American Federation of Labor.

• Several unsuccessful strikes organized by the Knights.

• Public reaction against the violence of the Haymarket Square Incident. On May 4, 1886,

No one knows for sure who threw the bomb in Haymarket Square, Chi-cago, in 1886. Neverthe-less, eight anarchists were convicted (four hanged) for being involved in the incident.

in Chicago, *anarchists* (people who call for the overthrow of all governments) held an outdoor demonstration. As the protest meeting was breaking up, police arrived to move the crowds away. Someone threw a bomb at the police, killing seven of them. The police opened fire, causing additional deaths and injuries. Although the Knights had nothing to do with the incident, many Americans thought that they did. The strong antilabor feelings that resulted from the Haymarket incident hurt all labor unions for many years.

The American Federation of Labor

In the 1880s, several important union leaders left the Knights of Labor. They believed that this union was not doing a good job of representing skilled workers, such as carpenters and printers. In 1886, those leaders who had left the Knights formed a new national union, the American Federation of Labor (AFL). It was made up only of *craft unions* (unions of skilled workers). Within the AFL, each union had control of its own affairs, such as who could belong to the union and when it should strike.

Samuel Gompers The American Federation of Labor grew rapidly. By 1900, it had some 500,000 members and was still growing. Much of the success of the union was due to its first president, Samuel Gompers of the Cigarmakers' Union. He kept the AFL from allying itself with any political party. He also kept the AFL from trying to reform American society. Instead, he was primarily interested in improving wages and working conditions of union members. He strongly believed that the best method of achieving these aims was to strike or threaten to strike.

The Turbulent 1890s

A number of noteworthy strikes took place in the 1890s. Of the two major labor strikes of the

Samuel Gompers, the AFL's first president, had emigrated to America from England at age 13. Within a year he had joined the Cigarmakers' Union.

decade, the first one involved a union *affiliated* (having ties) with the AFL.

Homestead Strike In 1892, the Amalgamated Association of Iron and Steel Workers battled the Carnegie Steel Corporation in Homestead, Pennsylvania. Trouble began when the company cut the wages of its union workers. Because the union refused to accept the cut, the company closed the plant to union members. This action is called a *lockout*. Workers picketed the plant and eventually occupied it.

The steel company hired 300 Pinkerton detectives as guards to regain control of the Homestead plant. As the detectives were arriving in Homestead on river barges, the strikers fired on them. After an intense battle, the detectives withdrew. Next, the steel company got the Governor of Pennsylvania to send the state militia to Homestead. The militia was able to remove the striking workers from the plant and keep them out. *Strikebreakers* (non-union workers, also called *scabs*) were hired to replace most former workers. To punish the strikers further,

The U.S. government intervened in the Pullman strike of 1894. Here troops escort a train loaded with meat from the Chicago stockyards.

the company *blacklisted* some of the union members who had lost their jobs. (They were put on a list of workers whom no steel company was likely to hire again.)

Pullman Strike The 1894 Pullman strike involved the American Railway Union, which was not affiliated with the AFL. This strike began after the company cut wages. The Pullman Palace Car Company reacted to the strike by closing its plant near Chicago. The union, led by Eugene V. Debs, retaliated by organizing a boycott. In addition, the union asked railway workers around the country not to work on any train that pulled a Pullman car. Due to this request, the strike soon spread to most railroad lines west of Chicago.

Since the Pullman strike prevented mail cars from moving, the U.S. government got involved. The U.S. Attorney General got an *injunction* (court order) that outlawed further union activities. Nevertheless, the union continued its strike. To enforce the injunction, President Grover Cleveland sent federal troops to Chicago. Eugene Debs and other union leaders

were sent to jail for refusing to obey the injunction. Because of these developments, the strike was finally broken.

> More and more, the government sided with employers by issuing injunctions and sending in troops. Injunctions were based on the idea that unions, by striking, were restraining trade. Forming a group to restrain trade had been outlawed by the Sherman Antitrust Act of 1890. Although Congress had not intended the act to be used against unions, the courts interpreted the law this way.

Non-Union Members

In 1900, some 791,000 workers belonged to unions. Nevertheless, they made up only a small part of the nation's work force of 29 million Americans. The following groups of workers were not well represented by unions:

• Unskilled workers. Most unskilled workers did not have labor unions that they could join.

The policy of the American Federation of Labor was to organize only skilled laborers.

• Female workers. Labor unions generally did not want to include the 5 million working women in their ranks. An important exception to this rule was the Knights of Labor, which at one time had about 50,000 female members. Another stronghold of female workers, the International Ladies Garment Workers Union, (ILGWU), was not organized until 1900.

• Blacks, too, faced discrimination by labor unions. Again, an exception was the Knights of Labor, which welcomed blacks as members. The United Mine Workers and several other unions also had significant black membership. Most black workers during the post-Civil War years failed to make much economic progress. By not being allowed in most craft unions, they could not enter union training programs for skilled workers.

SUMMING UP We have seen that the labor movement grew quickly after the Civil War. Groups of workers created unions in attempts to match the growing power of big businesses. Unions created three national organizations before 1900. Only one of these—the American Federation of Labor— was to last to modern times. Despite the accomplishments of unions, their future was still in doubt at the turn of the century. In 1900, only a small percentage of workers belonged to a union.

Understanding the Text

On a separate sheet of paper, write the letter of the word or phrase that best completes each of the following statements.

1. Of the following unions, the one that first formed on a national basis was the *(a)* American Federation of Labor *(b)* National Labor Union *(c)* Knights of Labor *(d)* International Ladies Garment Workers Union.

2. Of the following actions, the one that was an accomplishment of the National Labor Union was *(a)* getting Congress to pass a law for an eight-hour workday for many federal workers *(b)* having its candidate win the 1872 presidential election *(c)* striking at the Homestead Steel Plant *(d)* getting Congress to pass the Sherman Antitrust Act of 1890.

3. Federal troops were sent to Baltimore to restore order during the *(a)* Homestead Steel Strike *(b)* Pullman Strike *(c)* Haymarket Square Incident *(d)* General Railway Strike of 1877.

4. When two parties in a labor dispute agree in advance to accept a decision made by a third party, the method of settling the dispute is called *(a)* a restraint of trade *(b)* arbitration *(c)* an injunction *(d)* a lockout.

5. Union workers generally are most opposed to *(a)* strikes *(b)* scabs *(c)* benefits *(d)* boycotts.

6. The demonstration that led to the Haymarket Square Incident of 1886 was organized by *(a)* anarchists *(b)* the Knights of Labor *(c)* the United Mine Workers *(d)* the Chicago Police Department.

7. Striking workers were forcibly removed from the Homestead Steel Plant in 1892 by *(a)* Pinkerton detectives *(b)* state militia *(c)* federal troops *(d)* blacklists.

8. In the 19th century, the AFL was a federation of *(a)* craft unions *(b)* black and female workers *(c)* unskilled workers *(d)* both skilled and unskilled workers.

9. The first president of the American Federation of Labor was *(a)* Terence Powderly *(b)* Samuel Gompers *(c)* Eugene V. Debs *(d)* George Pullman.

10. Of the following weapons, one that employers did *not* use against striking workers was a/an *(a)* boycott *(b)* injunction *(c)* strikebreaker *(d)* lockout.

Developing Cartoon-Reading Skills

KING DEBS

Study the political cartoon on page 300. Then choose the letter of the word or phrase that best completes each sentence. On a separate sheet of paper, match the sentence number with the correct letter.

1. The man featured in the center of the cartoon is *(a)* George Pullman *(b)* Grover Cleveland *(c)* Andrew Carnegie *(d)* Eugene V. Debs.

2. The cartoonist put something on the man's head to indicate that the man was *(a)* powerful *(b)* a member of a royal family *(c)* a court jester *(d)* wealthy.

3. The cartoonist indicated in the drawing that the man *(a)* owned a railroad company *(b)* invented the Pullman sleeper car *(c)* headed a railway union *(d)* asked for an injunction against a railroad strike.

4. The man seems to be *(a)* thinking about how to buy a railroad *(b)* calling for the building of more railroads *(c)* preventing goods and people from being carried on the railroads *(d)* sailing up and down a river.

5. This cartoon probably first appeared in a newspaper that *(a)* was critical of the Pullman strike leaders *(b)* was owned by a labor union *(c)* favored the restoration of the monarchy in the United States *(d)* did not comment on labor-management conflicts.

Thinking About the Lesson

1. How did each of the following weaken the American labor movement? *(a)* The economic depression of 1873 *(b)* The Haymarket Square Incident of 1886.

2. What factors contributed to the growth of the American Federation of Labor in the 1880s? Why did the Knights of Labor decline in strength during this same period?

3. What groups of American workers were not well represented in labor unions by 1900? Why did these groups have so few union members?

A Nation of Immigrants and Growth of the Cities

Since the country was formed in 1789, some 50 million immigrants have come to the United States. This nation has received more immigrants than any other country in the world. From 1860 to 1900, immigration to America was quite heavy—about 14 million people. Their arrival made a great impact on the nation's political, social, and economic life. The impact was especially strong in urban areas, as immigrants contributed to the rapid growth of American cities.

Reasons for Immigration

The millions of 19th-century immigrants had a number of reasons for coming to the United States:

• Most immigrants arrived hoping to make a better living in America. Life in their homelands had been hard. For example, after repeated crop failures in Ireland and Germany in the 1840s, many Irish and Germans moved to America rather than starve. Some of these immigrants settled on the land, becoming American farmers. Others found jobs in the growing American cities and towns.

• Many immigrants came seeking freedom to practice their religion. They were fleeing religious *persecution* (cruel treatment) in their native lands. Many Russian Jews came to America because they had been subject to *pogroms* (organized mass killings of helpless people).

• Some immigrants arrived in search of political rights and social equality. In the old country, people often did not enjoy the right to vote, hold public office, or express ideas openly. In the United States, however, political freedoms were guaranteed by the Constitution. Moreover, in the United States people could rise from one social class to another much more easily than in Europe.

Periods of Heavy Immigration

During much of the 19th century, immigration to America was heavy.

1840s and 1850s During these decades, the United States experienced its first big wave of immigrants. Many of the new residents came from Ireland and Germany. England, Scotland,

302

Wales, Sweden, Norway, Denmark, France, Switzerland, and Canada also lost large numbers of their citizens to the United States.

1860s and 1870s   Americans during this period witnessed the arrival of about the same number of immigrants as in the previous two decades. (See the graph below.) Again, most of these immigrants came from Northern and Central Europe.

Immigrants often settled in groups near where other members of their nationality already lived. The Irish tended to settle in urban areas of New England and the Middle Atlantic States. Germans especially liked Pennsylvania and New York and much of the Middle West. Most Scandinavians preferred northern parts of the Middle West. There the climate was not too different from that of their homeland.

1880s and 1890s   The nature of immigration in these two decades was different from that of earlier periods. For one thing, the total number of immigrants was much larger—almost 9 million. Almost twice as many immigrants came then as had arrived between 1861 and 1880. For

another thing, a greater percentage of these new immigrants came from Eastern and Southern Europe. For instance, Russians, Poles, Greeks, and Italians now came in large numbers.

Carl Schurz was one of many 19th-century immigrants who made important contributions to American society. In his native Germany, he had tried to win freedom for his people by fighting in the German Revolution of 1848–1849. When the Revolution failed, he was forced to flee to America. Settling in Wisconsin, he soon became involved in fighting for the freedom of black slaves. During the Civil War, Schurz served as a Union Army general. After the war, he published a German-language newspaper and was elected a U.S. senator from Missouri. In Congress, Schurz fought against the corruption in the administration of his fellow Republican—President Ulysses S. Grant. Later, as Secretary of the Interior, he tried to persuade Americans to treat the Indians fairly. After retiring from government service, Schurz returned to the editing and writing of newspapers.

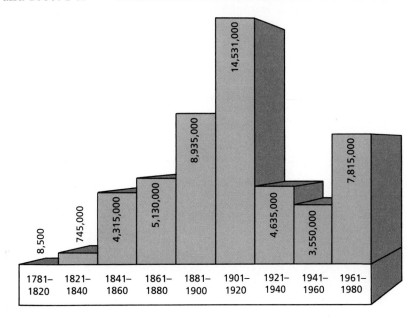

IMMIGRATION TO THE UNITED STATES, 1781–1980

1781– 1820	1821– 1840	1841– 1860	1861– 1880	1881– 1900	1901– 1920	1921– 1940	1941– 1960	1961– 1980
8,500	745,000	4,315,000	5,130,000	8,935,000	14,531,000	4,635,000	3,550,000	7,815,000

Prejudices Against Immigrants

Immigrants have often had difficulty being accepted by the people already living in the United States. Usually, the languages, religions, and ways of life of the immigrants were different enough to set them off from others. Sometimes "native" Americans felt threatened by immigrants, fearing that they might lose their jobs to newcomers.

Anti-Irish Feelings   The Irish, for instance, ran into the problem of anti-Irish feelings in the 1850s. The Irish were mainly Roman Catholic, while the majority of Americans were Protestant. Furthermore, the Irish tended to settle together in American cities, where they soon controlled local politics. Many Americans resented the Irish immigrants' new-found power. Some American workers also resented Irish immigrant workers, who often would accept jobs at wages lower than other Americans would.

Anti-Irish and anti-Catholic feelings gave rise to the Know-Nothing party, discussed in Lesson 39. This group wanted to prevent the Irish from gaining any more political power. Therefore, it proposed a law that immigrants had to live in the United States 21 years before they could vote.

The New Immigrants   Decades later, immigrants from Eastern and Southern Europe aroused the same kind of hostile feelings that the Irish had earlier. Even the children or grandchildren of immigrants criticized or made fun of the newcomers. Many Americans had *prejudices* (slanted views) against the "New Immigrants," as newcomers from Eastern and Southern Europe were called.

Beginnings of Immigration Controls

Until late in the 19th century, the U.S. government did not limit immigration. Practically anyone who chose to come to this country was free to enter and live in America. Gradually, however, many Americans began to believe that immigration should be controlled.

Selective Controls   In 1882, the United States enacted several limits on immigration. The government barred entry to:

• People who had been convicted of serious crimes.
• The insane.
• Others who were likely to become *public charges*, that is, people who would depend on society to support them.

Immigrants arriving in New York City in the late 19th century had this view of the Statue of Liberty. The large monument, installed in 1886, was a gift of the French people.

In 1880, whites in Denver, Colorado, pulled Chinese immigrants from their homes, cut off their pigtails, and in some cases *lynched* (put to death by mob action) them.

Chinese Exclusion Beginning in the mid-1850s, thousands of Chinese came to America to help build railroads in the West. Their work completed, many chose to stay in the United States.

Some Americans complained that Chinese immigrants were taking jobs away from American workers. Others complained that Chinese workers accepted low wages, causing wages to go down for all workers. The Chinese argued they were doing what they had to do to survive. They also said that Americans did not want the jobs they were performing. As a result of anti-Chinese feelings, Congress in 1882 passed a law halting further immigration of Chinese workers.

The several laws passed in 1882 to limit immigration did not significantly cut down on the total number of people coming from Europe. In fact, overall immigration in the 1880s and 1890s increased considerably from the 1860s and 1870s. (See the graph on page 303.)

The Growth of Cities

After the Civil War, the population of urban areas grew more rapidly than the population of rural ones. This urban growth matched the growth of industries and the expansion of the American economy.

Many of the immigrants who came after the Civil War settled in urban areas. The steamships that carried the immigrants landed in port cities, where many foreigners stayed to live. More jobs were available to immigrants in urban areas than in the countryside. In addition, many new immigrants lacked enough money to buy the land and equipment needed to set up a farm.

Attractions of Cities Some of the new urban dwellers were immigrants—but not all of them. People born in the United States were attracted to the cities for some of the same reasons that immigrants were. The city was a place where ambitious young people had a chance to start careers and, perhaps, get rich. Many jobs of all types opened up in urban factories, offices, stores, and other businesses. Besides, a city offered many cultural opportunities, such as museums, theaters, libraries, and schools. For many, it provided a chance for an easier and more exciting life than was possible on a farm or in a small town.

Transformation of the Cities

In the years after the Civil War, U.S. cities changed in many ways:

- They grew larger and more crowded.
- They contained more and larger factories.
- They contained more office buildings. The invention of the Otis passenger elevator in 1852 made practical the construction of taller buildings. In the 1880s, the world's first *skyscrapers* (very tall buildings) were built in the United States.

Already by 1878, steam engines were pulling elevated trains in New York City. Also shown in this picture are horsecars and other horse-drawn vehicles.

• By 1900, some 3,000 electric power plants had been constructed in America. Electric lights began to replace the old gas lamps on city streets. In homes, electric lamps were installed in place of kerosene or gas ones.

Transportation Transportation in cities improved considerably in the late 19th century. Of course, Americans also got around by walking, riding bicycles, and taking horse-drawn carriages. But successive changes in rail transportation made travel easier. The *horsecar* (a horse-drawn streetcar on rails) was an inexpensive and quick form of public transportation. Steam-powered trains, whose tracks sometimes were built above the streets, went even faster. The *cable car* (streetcar pulled by a moving cable) was first used in San Francisco in 1873. Soon other cities copied this invention. In the 1890s, electric-powered streetcars—sometimes called *trolleys*—became more common. Boston even ran part of its trolley line (1.5 miles of it) underground, making this segment of track America's first *subway*.

The Growth of Slums

The rapid growth of cities after the Civil War created many problems. Many low-income people lived in crowded housing in run-down sections of cities. The apartment buildings in which they lived were called *tenements*. Newly arrived immigrants often had to live in tenements because they could not afford better housing. In the 1890s, about half of the population of New York City lived in tenements.

Tenement life was unhealthy. Several generations of one family often lived in just one or two rooms. Some of these rooms lacked windows for light and fresh air. Residents often threw their garbage onto the street. Lack of adequate water supplies and sewage disposal systems led to *epidemics* (outbreaks of diseases) in some cities.

Photographer Jacob Riis portrayed city residents living close together in tenements. In taking pictures, Riis had to ask his subjects to stand still so that they would not blur the image.

The Battle Against the Slums

Several American reformers tried to bring the poor conditions facing slum dwellers to the public's attention.

• Jacob Riis, a Danish immigrant, wrote a book, *How the Other Half Lives* (1890), that vividly portrayed the tenements of New York City. In his book, he combined his own photographs with his journalistic writing. He was effective in convincing people that something had to be done about the slums.

• Jane Addams in 1889 established a *settlement house*, the famous Hull House, in a poor neighborhood of Chicago. It provided slum dwellers many educational, social, and health services not available to them elsewhere. Reformers set up similar settlement houses in other big cities.

SUMMING UP We have seen that, for various reasons, some 14 million immigrants came to America between 1860 and 1900. After 1880, immigration was especially heavy. The proportion of people coming from Eastern and Southern Europe increased greatly. Opposition to new immigration developed to such an extent that the federal government in 1882 imposed certain restrictions. Immigration was one of the causes of the rapid growth of cities during this period. Along with the growth and modernization of the cities came the problem of slums. Many people of low income were crowded together in areas that were dirty and unhealthy.

Understanding the Text

On a separate sheet of paper, write the letter of the word or phrase that best completes each of the following statements.

1. Immigrants came to the United States in the 19th century in order to (*a*) make a better living (*b*) seek religious freedom (*c*) gain political rights (*d*) all of the above.

2. Immigration in the 1880s and 1890s differed from that of earlier periods in that (*a*) a greater proportion of people came from Northern and Central Europe (*b*) a greater proportion came from Eastern and Southern Europe (*c*) fewer people were admitted (*d*) none of the above.

3. Carl Schurz immigrated from (*a*) Germany (*b*) the Netherlands (*c*) Italy (*d*) Russia.

4. Federal laws passed in 1882 restricted the immigration of all of the following, *except* (*a*) Chinese workers (*b*) the insane (*c*) people born in Europe (*d*) people who had been convicted of serious crimes.

5. Of the following, the best example of anti-immigrant feelings in America in the 1850s was (*a*) Hull House (*b*) the Know-Nothing party (*c*) pogroms (*d*) Jacob Riis's book, *How the Other Half Lives*.

6. America's first cable cars were used in (a) Chicago (b) San Francisco (c) New York City (d) St. Louis.

7. The Otis passenger elevator helped make possible the building of (a) cable cars (b) public baths (c) skyscrapers (d) slums.

8. The American city that had the nation's first subway was (a) New York (b) San Francisco (c) Philadelphia (d) Boston.

9. Hull House was set up by (a) Jacob Riis (b) Jane Addams (c) Carl Schurz (d) Ulysses S. Grant.

10. Which one of the following statements best reflects the relationship between immigrants and American cities in the 19th century? (a) Immigrants were the sole group responsible for the growth of cities. (b) Immigrants tended to avoid large cities. (c) Immigrants were only one of the groups that contributed to the growth of cities. (d) Only immigrants were interested in the cultural opportunities available in large cities.

Developing Reading Comprehension Skills

Read the following selection by Mary Antin, a woman who had immigrated to the United States in 1894 at age 13.

In our flat we did not think of such a thing as storing the coal in the bathtub. There was no bathtub. So in the evening of the first day my father conducted us to the public baths. As we moved along in a little procession, I was delighted with the illumination of the streets. So many lamps, and they burned until morning, my father said, and so people did not need to carry lanterns. In America, then, everything was free, as we had heard in Russia. Light was free; the streets were as bright as a synagogue on a holy day. Music was free; we had been serenaded, to our gaping delight, by a brass band of many pieces, soon after our installation on Union Place.

Education was free. That subject my father had written about repeatedly, as comprising his chief hope for us children, the essence of American opportunity, the treasure that no thief could touch, not even misfortune or poverty. It was the one thing that he was able to promise us when he sent for us; surer, safer, than bread or shelter. On our second day I was thrilled with the realization of what this freedom of education meant. A little girl from across the alley came and offered to conduct us to school. My father was out, but we five between us had a few words of English by this time. We knew the word school. We understood. This child, who had never seen us till yesterday, who could not pronounce our names, who was not much better dressed than we, was able to offer us the freedom of the schools of Boston! No application made, no questions asked, no examinations, rulings, exclusions; no machinations, no fees. The doors stood open for every one of us. The smallest child could show us the way.

This incident impressed me more than anything I had heard in advance of the freedom of education in America. It was a concrete proof—almost the thing itself. One had to experience it to understand it.

Mary Antin, *The Promised Land*. Boston: Houghton Mifflin Co., 1912, pp. 185–86.

Choose the letter of the word or phrase that best completes each sentence. On a separate sheet of paper, match the sentence number with the correct letter.

1. Before coming to the United States, Mary Antin lived in *(a)* Boston *(b)* Russia *(c)* Turkey *(d)* Union Place.

2. The first place in which Mary Antin lived when she came to the United States was a/an *(a)* big house *(b)* small house *(c)* hotel *(d)* apartment.

3. From reading this passage, one can infer that Mary Antin's religion was *(a)* Judaism *(b)* Christianity *(c)* Islam *(d)* Hinduism.

4. In her new country, Mary Antin was amazed by *(a)* streetlights *(b)* public, outdoor band concerts *(c)* free public schools *(d)* all of the above.

5. With the sentence "No application made, no questions asked, no examinations, rulings, exclusions; no machinations, no fees," Mary was commenting on *(a)* federal aid to education in the United States *(b)* the high cost of a college education *(c)* restrictions on education in the old country *(d)* calls for reforms of the American educational system.

Thinking About the Lesson

1. In the 19th century, immigrants came to the United States for many reasons. Which reason do you think was the most important? Explain your answer.

2. Why did some Americans strongly dislike immigrant groups? Were any of the anti-immigrant feelings justified? Explain.

3. Do you think that cities were better places in which to live in 1900 than they had been in 1850? Why or why not?

The Westward Movement and Indian Wars

The migration of Americans westward stepped up in the second half of the 19th century. Americans streamed west of the Mississippi in search of gold, silver, land, and new and independent lives. The West, though, was already occupied by Indian tribes, some of whom had been forced to move there from lands east of the Mississippi. Conflicts between settlers and Indians were frequent and sometimes led to what historians call the "Indian wars."

The Search for Gold and Silver

Americans moved west for various reasons. Perhaps the most dramatic movement of settlers resulted from the discovery of gold and silver deposits, such as in the:

• California Gold Rush. The discovery of gold at Sutter's Mill in 1848 led to the rapid settlement of California. So many people came to this territory that in 1850 California became a state. (California's admission is discussed in Lesson 38.)

• Pikes Peak Gold Rush. In 1858–1859, prospectors found only small amounts of gold near Pikes Peak, in Colorado Territory. Nevertheless, news of the strike brought thousands of

fortune seekers. So many of these people stayed to settle Denver and elsewhere in Colorado that the territory became a state in 1876. Soon after that date, discoveries of silver deposits encouraged many more settlers to come to Colorado.

• Comstock Lode. Beginning in 1859, rich deposits of both gold and silver were found in Western Nevada. Bustling new towns, such as Virginia City, quickly sprang up on the hillsides surrounding the mines. In 1864, Nevada, too, became a state.

• Black Hills Gold Rush. Another discovery of gold, this time in 1874, brought a rush of people to the Black Hills of Dakota Territory. The area, however, was part of the Sioux Reservation. Although the U.S. Army was supposed to keep settlers out of Indian lands, it failed to do its job. The Sioux were outraged by this and again in 1877 when the government officially opened the Black Hills to settlers.

The Search for Land

Despite the fact that many Americans believed the Great Plains to be an uninhabitable desert, the vast lands were settled gradually by ranchers and farmers. Government actions and railroad

310

expansion encouraged this settlement of the West.

Homestead Act To encourage settlement, the federal government provided free land for those who would move west. According to the Homestead Act of 1862, any adult head of household could obtain 160 acres in the West. All he or she had to do was pay a small fee and work the land for five years. By 1900, the U.S. government had granted some 600,000 homesteads.

Railroad Construction Some of the best Western lands were not open to homesteaders. Instead, the government gave this land to railroad companies as their reward for laying rail lines.

Transcontinental Railroads In the 1850s, the North and the South had differed as to where the first transcontinental railroad should be built. (Discussed in Lesson 39.) During the Civil War, though, Congress decided this issue. Soon the Union Pacific Railroad began laying tracks west starting from Omaha, Nebraska. The Central Pacific began laying tracks starting from California and moving east to meet the other line. After years of construction, the first transcontinental railroad was completed in 1869. Several others were built later.

Government Aid to Railroads To help pay the costs of constructing railroad lines, railroads sold the land alongside the tracks. The government had given the land to the railroads for this purpose. For each mile of track, the railroads got up to 40 square miles of land. After the lines were laid, these lands near the tracks became quite valuable. People wanted to settle there because these lands were easy to reach. Also, farmers and ranchers living near the lines

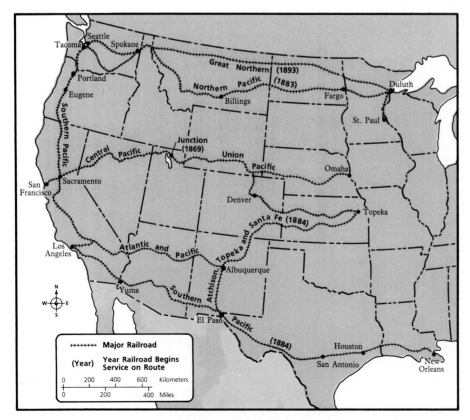

MAJOR WESTERN RAILROADS, 1869–1900

could use the railroads to ship their products to market.

The railroads helped to settle the West in another way. Previously, people crossed the plains by covered wagon or stagecoach. Now there was a faster way to go West—by train.

Ranching on the Great Plains

Farming and raising sheep and cattle were the most common occupations of the early settlers on the plains.

Cattle Raising   In the 1860s, enterprising settlers bought longhorn cattle and developed large herds of these half-wild animals. The Texas longhorns were able to survive on the dry plains. Furthermore, they could be driven long distances. The coming of railroads helped the cattle business to expand. Railroads provided ranchers with a way to get their cattle to markets in the East. Certain Western towns, such as Abilene and Dodge City, Kansas, became important *cattle centers* because they were situated on railroad lines. Even so, ranchers still had long trips to move their cattle to these towns. Their journeys, some as long as a thousand miles, became known as *cattle drives*.

Cowboys   The profession of the cowboy was an old one, having been developed by Mexicans and Texans. Cowboys were responsible for keeping track of cattle and driving them to cattle towns. Cowboys had to be skilled at riding horses and roping and branding cattle. After the Civil War, many other Americans, including Indians and blacks, became cowboys. A few women also chose this profession.

Open Range   Because the plains were not heavily settled, cattle ranchers let their animals graze on the *open range*. They did not have to fence in their cattle. They just branded them so that

In cattle drives, cowboys moved long lines of cattle along cattle trails. Several of the major trails originated in Texas and went north to Kansas.

Indians living on reservations often obtained supplies from trading posts. In this picture, Indians exchange U.S. government-issued coupons for supplies.

everyone knew which cattle belonged to which owners.

Over the years, the use of the open range by cattle ranchers began to decline for several reasons:

• Barbed Wire. In 1874, stores began selling barbed wire. American farmers began to fence in their land to keep cattle and other animals away from their crops. They also wanted to prevent their own *livestock* (horses, cows, goats, etc.) from wandering.

• Sheep Ranching. In the 1880s, a large number of sheep ranchers settled in the West. On the open range, sheep competed with cattle for the same grass. Because sheep could chew the grass closer to the ground, they usually won the competition. In view of this fact, cattle ranchers

did not like having sheep ranchers as neighbors. Sometimes conflicts between cattle ranchers and sheep ranchers turned into violent *range wars*.

• Destruction of Cattle Herds. In the mid-1880s, thousands of cattle died as a result of severe droughts in the summer and severe winter cold snaps. Those ranchers who lost many cattle had to go out of business. Others continued their operations, but on a smaller scale.

The U.S. Government and the Indians

The federal government's policies toward American Indians changed several times during the 19th century. Furthermore, the policies were often confused and contradictory. Two schools of thought predominated among government

The last "battle" between the U.S. Army and an Indian group took place at Wounded Knee, South Dakota, in 1890. There a large group of Sioux men, women, and children were arrested by the Seventh Cavalry. While the Indians were being disarmed, a shot was fired. Soon the soldiers opened fire, killing some 200 Sioux. (Granger Collection)

officials who dealt with Indians. Some officials wanted the Indians out of the way so that other Americans could settle Indian lands. Others were more concerned about protecting the rights of Indians as defined by hundreds of treaties.

Indian Removal As we learned in Lesson 30, the government under Andrew Jackson moved thousands of Indians to new lands west of the Mississippi. Government leaders thought that these Indians would never again be a problem for other Americans because they were so far away. The policy of the removal of Indians to remote parts of the country continued after Jackson left office. For the Plains Indians, this policy meant removal to areas away from railroad lines, mines, and other places where whites were settling.

Reservations As more settlers arrived in the West, Indian tribes there were placed in smaller areas called *reservations*. Often a tribe had a reservation all to itself. Other people were supposed to stay out of the reservations, and members of the tribe were not supposed to move away. The federal government assigned an Indian agent to each reservation. The reservation system, as run by the U.S. Bureau of Indian Affairs, developed many problems:

• Most reservations did not have enough land to support a tribe. Instead, the federal government had to provide tribes with food and other supplies. In part, these supplies were payments for the lands that the tribes had given up.

• Many Indians continued to hunt and fish on their traditional lands, which often were located outside the reservations. Non-Indian settlers objected to having Indians hunting and fishing near them. Bad feelings sometimes led to skirmishes and wars.

• As mentioned on page 310, some settlers moved onto reservations to look for gold and silver. The U.S. Army did not always have the power or desire to keep out these intruders.

• Some officials of the Bureau of Indian Affairs were corrupt. They pocketed funds intended for Indian tribes.

• In some tribes, there were members who did not believe that their tribal chiefs should give away, trade, or sell tribal lands. Consequently, some Indians attacked settlers who had moved onto lands given up by the tribal chiefs.

Dawes Act Many Americans disapproved of the reservation system. Instead, they wanted a policy that would encourage Indians to become more like other Americans. As a result, Congress passed the Dawes Act in 1887. This law allowed individual Indians to claim part of a reservation as their personal property. On this land they would be expected to farm. All Indians who owned property could apply to become U.S. citizens. Other provisions of the Dawes Act called for more federal funds to be spent educating Indian children.

Results of the Dawes Act In the late 1800s, a number of Indians left their reservations and found employment in towns and cities. They sold some of the best lands on the reservations to white settlers and land speculators. Most Indians, however, stayed on their reservations. Although their ways of life changed in some ways, they also kept many of their traditions.

The Dawes Act did not work well. It did not succeed in making Indians into typical American farmers. Indian traditions did not recognize the ownership of land by individuals. Tribes had traditionally held land in common, and any member could use land as he or she needed. Also, most Indians considered tilling the soil as women's work. Thus, male Indians commonly avoided farming, preferring to hunt and fish.

U.S. Army-Indian Wars

During and after the Civil War, the U.S. Army and different Indian tribes fought many battles in the West. Federal troops had the advantages of repeating rifles, railroads, and the telegraph. Indians used to their advantage the tactics of surprise and movement. In a few cases, the Indians proved to be the superior military force.

Battle of Little Big Horn The Sioux Indians had been confined to a reservation in Dakota Territory. They had retained, however, seasonal hunting rights outside the reservation along the Little Big Horn River in Montana. In the winter of 1875–1876, a group of Sioux hunters in Montana refused to return to their reservation, as required by law. These Indians were upset

because their reservation had recently been invaded by gold prospectors. Because of the Sioux's refusal to return to the reservation, the government in 1876 sent troops after them. At the Little Big Horn River, a force of 2,400 Sioux and Cheyenne under Chief Crazy Horse was waiting. The Indians easily defeated General George Custer's smaller force, killing Custer and all of his men.

Apache Wars During the 1860s, Apaches fought many battles with settlers who were moving into Arizona. Small Apache forces lived in the mountains and periodically raided the settlers. Chief Cochise led such an Apache group—one that also battled with the U.S. Army. In 1871, Cochise finally gave up, agreeing to settle his people on a reservation. Another Apache chief, Geronimo, still refused to accept reservation life. He successfully held off the U.S. Army from 1876 to 1886, often hiding in Mexico with his men. In the end, he, too, was defeated.

By 1890, all of the Indian wars in the West were over. Those Indians whom settlers had considered a threat had been defeated.

Decline of Buffalo Herds Besides defeat in battle, another development helped destroy the Indians' way of life. In the 1870s, white hunters slaughtered most of the vast buffalo herds on the plains. Many Plains Indians had been dependent on buffalo for their food, clothing, and shelter. In contrast, the white hunters killed buffalo mainly for their hides, which brought a good price back East.

Decline of Indian Population By the end of the 19th century, the number of Indians in the United States had decreased greatly. From a figure of over 1 million at the time of Columbus, the population had dropped to about a quarter of a million. Hunger and disease, not the bullets of the U.S. Army, were the main causes of the decline.

SUMMING UP   We have seen how in the second half of the 19th century the American West was settled by all kinds of people. Gold and silver prospectors, ranchers, cowboys, farmers, and townspeople poured into the West. The building of the railroads and the prospect of free land enticed many Americans. Settling the West led to conflicts with the Indians. Although various Indian groups fought with skill, the U.S. Army was victorious by 1890. In that year, the U.S. Census Bureau declared that so many settlements filled the West that a frontier line no longer existed.

Understanding the Text

On a separate sheet of paper, write the letter of the word or phrase that best completes each of the following statements.

1. The first major gold rush occurred in (a) California (b) western Nevada (c) the Black Hills (d) Colorado.

2. A federal law that allowed Americans to claim 160 acres of land in the West was the (a) Dawes Act (b) Indian Removal Act (c) Homestead Act (d) Interstate Commerce Act.

3. The building of railroads in the West (a) helped the U.S. Army to defeat Indian forces (b) brought Americans to the West in greater numbers (c) was financed, in great part, by the sale of land alongside the railroad lines (d) all of the above.

4. One of the important cattle centers in the 1880s was (a) Little Big Horn (b) Abilene (c) Virginia City (d) Sutter's Mill.

5. Range wars were conflicts between (a) cattle ranchers and sheep ranchers (b) the U.S. Army and Indian forces (c) buffalo hunters and the buffalo (d) two or more railroad lines.

6. A factor that led ranchers to stop grazing cattle on the open range was the (a) Indian wars (b) decline of the buffalo herds (c) use of barbed wire (d) all of the above.

7. The Bureau of Indian Affairs (a) was the main federal force that fought the Indians (b) managed the reservation system (c) constructed the transcontinental railroads (d) successfully defended all of the interests of American Indian tribes as defined in treaties.

8. The destruction of the buffalo herds hurt the Plains Indians because (a) they wanted to sell buffalo hides to Easterners (b) they depended on buffalo for food, clothing, and shelter (c) they rode the buffalo in cattle drives (d) the buffalo prevented the construction of the transcontinental railroads.

9. According to the Dawes Act, (a) some Indians could apply to become U.S. citizens (b) individual Indians could gain title to reservation land (c) the federal government would help educate Indian children (d) all of the above.

10. The date 1890 is important as the year in which (a) the Homestead Act was passed by Congress (b) the Pikes Peak gold rush began (c) the U.S. Census Bureau said that a frontier line no longer existed (d) General George Custer died.

Developing Map Skills

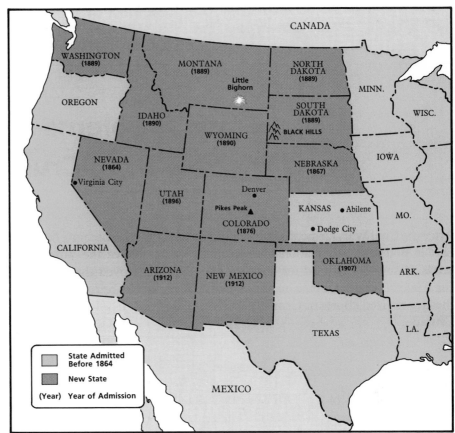

NEW STATES, 1864–1912

State Admitted Before 1864

New State

(Year) Year of Admission

Study the map above. Then choose the letter of the word or phrase that best completes each sentence. On a separate sheet of paper, match the sentence number with the correct letter.

1. The darker areas on the map indicate (*a*) states admitted into the Union between 1864 and 1912 (*b*) states admitted into the Union before 1864 (*c*) states admitted into the Union after 1912 (*d*) none of the above.

2. A state that was admitted into the Union in 1912 was (*a*) Washington (*b*) Minnesota (*c*) New Mexico (*d*) Oklahoma.

3. An example of a state that was already part of the Union before 1864 was (*a*) Utah (*b*) Idaho (*c*) Canada (*d*) Iowa.

4. The Black Hills are located in (*a*) Oregon (*b*) Nevada (*c*) South Dakota (*d*) Missouri.

5. Montana was admitted into the Union during the same year as (*a*) Wisconsin (*b*) North Dakota (*c*) Arizona (*d*) Nebraska.

Thinking About the Lesson

1. Both the lure of gold and silver and the lure of cheap and free land drew settlers to the West. Which attraction do you think was more important? Explain your answer.

2. The federal government aided the railroad companies in the West by giving them land on which to build and land to sell. Was the government right to give this kind of aid? Explain.

LESSON 51

Farm Problems
and the Agrarian Crusade

After the Civil War, farmers played an important part in politics on the national, state, and local levels. They fought hard for changes that they considered necessary. Some historians have called these organized efforts of farmers the "Agrarian Crusade."

Growth of Farm Output

In the second half of the 19th century, agricultural production expanded greatly. The growing populations of America's towns and cities needed more food and other farm products. The industrial nations of Europe also wanted America's wheat, corn, and cotton. American farmers were able to meet these demands for several reasons, as explained below.

Rise in Number of Farms Between 1860 and 1900, the number of United States farms almost tripled. Many of these new farms were established in the West.

Inventions The introduction of new farm machinery and new farming techniques helped to expand agricultural production:

• Windmill. In the dry areas of the West, water had to be brought up from wells dug deep into the earth. Windmills proved useful for this

task because the plains often had a steady wind. Once the water was brought to the surface, it moved through irrigation ditches to the fields.

• Spring-tooth Harrow. This 1877 invention broke up the soil into tiny particles.

• Twine Binder. In 1878, John F. Appleby introduced the *twine binder*, a machine which could both cut and bind wheat.

• Combine. A combination of reaper and thresher, the *combine* was introduced in the 1880s. It could cut wheat, separate the grain, and bag the final product.

Government Contributions Congress helped agriculture to expand by passing several pieces of legislation:

• In 1862, it established the Department of Agriculture. This Department gave farmers information on how better to grow crops and raise livestock.

• The Morrill Land Grant Act of 1862 set up state colleges for teaching agriculture and engineering. Eventually, 69 of these *land-grant colleges* came into existence.

• The Hatch Act of 1887 provided funds for the creation of agricultural experimentation stations in the states. These stations, run by the land-grant colleges, developed improved methods of growing crops and raising livestock.

At first, most American farmers prospered as agriculture expanded. During the Civil War, Northern farmers did well because the Union Army needed their products. These farmers benefited for several years after the war, too, because foreign farmers then were suffering crop failures. Whenever the demand for U.S. farm products increased, farm prices went up.

Serious Farm Problems

Unfortunately, American farmers became victims of their own successes. More and more often, the demand for American farm products did not keep up with the supply. Whenever this situation (called *overproduction*) occurred, farm prices dropped. For instance, the average price of wheat in 1866 was over $2.00 a bushel. By 1893, this price had dropped to just over 50 cents. (See the graph on page 324.)

In the decades after the Civil War, especially in the 1880s and 1890s, American farmers had many reasons to complain.

Economic Problems Although farmers were getting lower prices for their crops, their costs remained high:

• Their payments to banks for loans remained about the same.

• Local property taxes increased. Many farmers complained that while their taxes increased, some big businesses paid little or no taxes.

• Costs for fertilizer, barbed wire, and other farm equipment went up. Some farmers claimed that the business trusts that produced these goods kept prices high by preventing competition.

• Farmers had to pay high charges to railroads, warehouses, sales agents, and other *middlemen*. Middlemen were traders who handled farmers' goods before they reached the consumer.

• High U.S. tariffs kept the prices of foreign-made goods high. In addition, some foreign countries *retaliated* against (got even with) the United States by imposing their own tariffs. This development made it more difficult to sell U.S. agricultural products abroad.

Natural Problems In addition to economic problems, U.S. farmers suffered an unusually

Some thirty horses pulled this combine in Oregon in 1880. Compare this machine with McCormick's reaper, shown on page 195.

great number of natural calamities after the Civil War. Droughts dried up and destroyed crops in 1887 and afterward. In some years, floods caused crop damage and the *erosion* (wearing away) of soil. Crops were also damaged by insect pests and plant diseases.

Many farmers found it very difficult to make a living no matter how hard they worked. Often they were unable to meet payments on their loans. As a result, these farmers lost their farms to banks and other creditors.

Farmers found that they could not deal with their problems as individuals. They concluded that instead they would have to work in groups, using their combined economic and political powers to make changes.

The Grangers

Starting in 1867, many American farmers joined the Grange (National Grange of the Patrons of Husbandry). At first, the organization appealed to farmers' social needs, not their economic ones. Granger meetings provided an opportunity for lonely farm couples to get together and talk.

Economic Cooperation   Later, in the 1870s and 1880s, the Grangers organized farm cooperatives. In cooperatives, farmers worked together to sell their crops and to make purchases at the best possible prices. With cooperatives, they could avoid the services and costs of middlemen.

Political Influence   By the 1880s, the Grangers were helping to elect public officials who agreed with their views. In this way, Grangers influenced state legislatures to pass laws regulating railroad rates. Their pressure also led to laws regulating rates of operators of grain storage elevators.

The Grangers' fight against railroads was weakened by a U.S. Supreme Court decision in 1886. In the so-called Wabash case, the Court said that states did not have the power to regulate

The title of this cartoon is "The Iron Horse Which Eats Up the Farmers' Produce."

railroads that crossed state lines. Instead, said the Court, the power to regulate interstate commerce was reserved for Congress.

The Interstate Commerce Commission

After the Supreme Court made its 1886 decision on regulating railroads, farmers turned to Congress for help. They persuaded Congress in 1887 to pass the Interstate Commerce Act, discussed in Lesson 47. This act said that railroads did not have the right to charge farmers more than they charged others for the same service. It forbade rebates and other practices that it said were unfair. The Interstate Commerce Commission was set up to enforce this new law.

The Greenback Party

Farmers supported changes in the country's money policies as means of getting higher prices for their products. During the Civil War, the federal government had issued large amounts of greenbacks. After the war, the government began removing from circulation this paper money not backed by gold or silver. Many farmers protested the action.

They wanted more greenbacks to be issued, not fewer. If more greenbacks were in circulation, the value of the dollar would decrease. The farmers wanted money to decrease in value. They were partly motivated by the fact that they had taken out loans to finance their farms. They wanted to repay the banks with money that was less valuable than the money they had received. Moreover, farmers believed that with more money in circulation, the prices of all goods, including farm products, would rise. With more dollars in income, farmers would be better able to make payments to banks.

Political Action In 1868, Greenbackers were successful in stopping the government from removing greenbacks from circulation. In 1875, though, the federal government reversed its policy and began paying gold for greenbacks. This action was condemned by many Americans who, in the 1876 and 1878 elections, voted for candidates of the Greenback party. In 1878, some 1 million people voted for Greenback candidates. Afterward, however, the party declined in strength.

The Free Silver Movement

As the Greenback party declined, many farmers became interested in the *free silver* movement. These people believed that if more silver dollars were issued, inflation might result. With inflation, farm prices might rise. Silver miners joined farmers in calling for the government to buy more silver and make it into silver coins. Both groups also favored having the government issue more paper money, as long as this money was backed by silver.

The Free Silver movement was successful at first. In 1878, the federal government began purchasing more silver and issuing more silver dollars. In 1890, the government increased its purchase of silver even more.

Then holders of silver coins and paper money backed by silver began cashing in this currency for gold. At the time, such an exchange was legal. The result of this exchange was a sharp drop in the gold reserves held by the U.S. Treasury. To help end this drain, the government in 1893 halted its purchase and coinage of silver.

The Populist Party

In the 1890s, many American farmers became supporters of the new Populist party. Their use of the word "populist" was meant to suggest that the party stood for the interests of the common people. The party favored many reforms that its supporters believed would help workers and farmers. Changes that the Populists wanted included:

• Increased government purchase and coinage of silver.
• More government actions against monopolies.
• Government control of bank interest rates.
• Government ownership of *public utilities* (privately owned companies that provide essential services for the public), such as railroad, telephone, and telegraph companies.
• An eight-hour workday.
• A *graduated income tax*. With such a tax, the rich would pay a higher percentage of their income as taxes than would other people.
• Direct election of U.S. senators by voters. Since the Constitution required their election by state legislatures, this change would have to involve a constitutional amendment.

Most of these ideas have since become law. At the time, though, many Americans considered the proposals to be very radical.

Kansas reformer and orator Mary Lease helped form the Populist party in 1891. She was also active in the women's suffrage movement.

James Weaver, a former general in the Union Army, first ran for President in 1880 as a candidate for the Greenback party. He failed in this attempt, but did serve Iowa in the U.S. House of Representatives from 1879 to 1881 and again from 1885 to 1889. As one of the founders of the Populist party in 1891, he became its candidate for President in 1892. He was a natural choice because of his eloquent speaking voice and elegant appearance.

Election of 1892 Of all the minor political parties in American history, the Populist party was one of the strongest. In 1892, the Populist presidential candidate, James B. Weaver, received over 1 million votes. He obtained 22 electoral votes and about nine percent of the popular votes. The Democratic candidate, Grover Cleveland, however, won the Presidency.

The Populists did well in many state and local elections in the early 1890s. They elected a number of state governors and members of Congress. The party's strength declined, though, in the late 1890s.

Election of 1896

In 1896, the Democratic party adopted free silver as part of its platform. Its presidential candidate, William Jennings Bryan, argued strongly in favor of free silver. Because of his position, the Populists supported Bryan and did not run their own candidate for President.

Republican Victory Bryan ran an exciting campaign, making many fiery speeches. He lost, however, to the Republican candidate, William McKinley. Believing that McKinley opposed free silver and favored high tariffs, wealthy businesspeople had spent much money on McKinley's campaign.

William Jennings Bryan began his political career in Nebraska, where he was elected U.S. representative in 1890. In 1896, he became the Democratic candidate for President and remained the party's leader until 1912.

Return to Prosperity McKinley's election did not end the reform movement, but the farmers' campaign for free silver was over. Rich gold-fields had just been discovered in Canada. With these large supplies of gold, the U.S. government issued more money backed by gold. This new currency had much the same effect as if the government had issued more money backed by silver. The economy experienced inflation. Prices of most American goods, including farm products, rose rapidly.

At the same time, European farmers experienced crop failures. This situation increased the overseas demand for American farm products.

With the return of prosperity, most American farmers were no longer interested in having their own party. Instead, they looked after their interests through the two major political parties.

SUMMING UP We have seen that American agricultural production increased dramatically in the second half of the 19th century. After a while, this increased production hurt many farmers because farm prices fell as supply exceeded demand. The Grangers, Greenbackers, Free Silverites, and Populists fought for changes that would help the farmers. In their fight, American farmers found that their interests were often at odds with the interests of big businesses.

Understanding the Text

On a separate sheet of paper, write the letter of the word or phrase that best completes each of the following statements.

1. A factor responsible for increased agricultural production in America in the second half of the 19th century was the *(a)* settlement of the West *(b)* invention of the twine binder *(c)* passage of the Morrill Land Grant Act *(d)* all of the above.

2. After the Civil War, farmers complained because prices for farm goods were *(a)* going down *(b)* going up *(c)* remaining steady *(d)* fixed by the government.

3. From the standpoint of a farmer, an example of a middleman was the *(a)* cotton grower *(b)* consumer *(c)* sales agent *(d)* farm equipment manufacturer.

4. Farmers urged the passage of the Interstate Commerce Act in order to regulate *(a)* themselves *(b)* windmill manufacturers *(c)* railroads *(d)* electric power companies.

5. The term "greenbacks" refers to *(a)* a form of paper money not backed by gold and silver *(b)* farmers who backed increased coinage of silver *(c)* gold-backed dollars issued during the Civil War *(d)* a fighting force.

6. Farmers favored increased coinage of silver mainly because they hoped that it would (*a*) help silver miners (*b*) raise farm prices (*c*) increase their debts (*d*) help them raise better crops.

7. A presidential candidate who favored free silver in 1896 was (*a*) Benjamin Harrison (*b*) William McKinley (*c*) Grover Cleveland (*d*) William Jennings Bryan.

8. The presidential election of 1896 was a triumph for (*a*) the Agrarian Crusade (*b*) the Republican party (*c*) those who favored free silver (*d*) those who backed far-reaching reforms in American society.

9. After the election of 1896, American farmers (*a*) had no more problems (*b*) organized a new political party (*c*) worked mainly through the two major political parties (*d*) made the Populist party into one of the country's two major political parties.

10. Which of the following statements is supported by the history of farm protest in the second half of the 19th century? (*a*) Attempts to make reforms proved useless. (*b*) Reforms were easy to put into effect. (*c*) Farmers' calls for reform had their roots in the problem of falling farm prices. (*d*) Most American farmers wanted to overthrow the government.

Developing Computational and Graph-Reading Skills

WHEAT FARMING IN THE UNITED STATES, 1866–1898

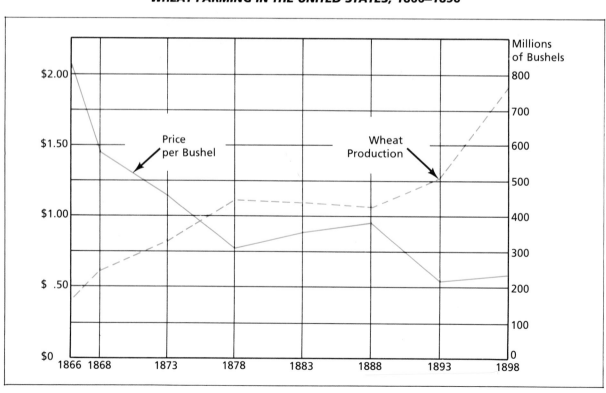

Examine the graph on page 324. Then choose the letter of the word or phrase that best completes each sentence. For some questions, you will need to make a mathematical calculation. On a separate sheet of paper, match the sentence number with the correct letter.

1. The points on the graph connected by the solid line represent (*a*) U.S. wheat production, 1866–1898 (*b*) price per bushel of wheat, 1866–1898 (*c*) acres harvested, 1866–1898 (*d*) value of all wheat harvested, 1866–1898.

2. The number of bushels of wheat produced in the United States in 1888 was (*a*) 424 (*b*) 424,000 (*c*) 424,000,000 (*d*) 385.

3. A farmer who sold 100 bushels of wheat in 1873 would have received (*a*) $117.00 (*b*) $7.71 (*c*) $1.17 (*d*) $80.00.

4. From 1866 to 1878, while (*a*) wheat production declined, the price of wheat remained steady (*b*) wheat production declined, the price of wheat decreased (*c*) wheat production rose, the price of wheat increased (*d*) wheat production rose, the price of wheat decreased.

5. In 1898, the total amount that all U.S. farmers received for wheat that they grew was about (*a*) $445,440,000 (*b*) $41,064,000 (*c*) $768,000,000 (*d*) $76,800.

Thinking About the Lesson

1. Explain how overproduction was sometimes a problem for U.S. farmers in the second half of the 19th century.

2. Why did many farmers favor greenbacks and free silver?

3. Why did the Greenback and Populist parties fail to become as large and powerful as the Democratic and Republican parties?

Toward a New South

Reconstruction strongly influenced the course of the South's economic, social, and political history for decades after it ended. Historians refer to the region after Reconstruction as the "New South." Although the South remained an agricultural region, its industries became important for the first time. During the 1880s and 1890s, Southern society underwent major changes. For instance, Southern blacks were again subjected to strict forms of segregation and restrictions on voting.

Changes in Southern Agriculture

After 1877, when Reconstruction ended, the South continued to be mainly a farming region. Nevertheless, the nature of Southern agriculture changed.

Breakup of Plantations Most big plantations were divided into smaller farms. Some of the owners of these farms worked the land themselves, often hiring blacks or whites as laborers. Many landowners, however, rented part or all of their land to others.

Tenant Farmers Farmers who rented other people's land were called *tenant farmers*. Some tenant farmers paid a fixed rent in cash. Others, called *sharecroppers*, gave the landowner a large share (usually over 50 percent) of the crops as rent. Landowners often provided sharecroppers with a house, land, tools, and seeds.

Nearby stores would supply sharecroppers with food, clothing, and other goods on credit. To make sure that they would get paid, shopkeepers insisted on a *lien* (a legal claim) on that year's crop. Some years, sharecroppers did not get enough money from their crops to pay all their bills. The shopkeepers would then put a claim on the following year's crop. Sharecroppers could remain in debt for years.

Frequently, creditors and landowners would require sharecroppers to plant only cash crops—ones that would be sold rather than eaten by the sharecroppers. This requirement affected the output of Southern agriculture, which came to emphasize cash crops.

Types of Crops Cotton remained the chief cash crop in the South. Cotton production rose from 2 million bales in 1866 to over 10 million in 1900. (Compare these figures with those of 1790–1860, on page 223.) Other cash crops, such as tobacco, rice, and sugar, also remained important. At the same time, there was a trend toward greater *diversification* (creation of a variety of something) in agriculture. Southern farmers began to grow many fruits and vegetables, including the newly popular peanut.

Wharves in New Orleans were covered with cotton bales and other products. "King Cotton" still reigned in the South.

Difficulties in Agriculture Southern farmers shared some of the problems that other American farmers of the period experienced. Prices for farm products kept falling. As a result, the Populist party and farm organizations, such as the Grange, were quite strong in the South.

Industrialization

Another major change in the South was the development of industry. During and after Reconstruction, many factories were built there. Atlanta, Richmond, and Nashville became important manufacturing centers. Since supplies of cotton were close at hand, businesspeople set up textile mills to make cotton cloth. Other major manufacturers produced tobacco and wood products.

A small iron and steel industry started in Birmingham, Alabama. This location was a good one because coal, iron, and limestone—all necessary for iron and steel production—could be mined nearby.

By 1900, railroads linked the South with other parts of the country far more effectively than before the war. Between 1865 and 1900, the number of miles of Southern railroads more than doubled.

Some Southerners hoped their industries would become as well-developed as Northern ones were. By 1900, this hope had not been realized. Although Southern industries were growing, they were not as large as those in the North.

The Solid South

Even after Reconstruction ended in 1877, many Southerners remained bitter about policies of the federal government. They blamed the Republican party for all of the following:

• Freeing the slaves.
• Keeping federal troops in the South after the war.
• Trying to give former slaves their civil rights.
• Excluding some former Confederate leaders from government for a number of years.

Once Democrats regained control of state politics in the 1870s, Republican candidates in the South faced almost certain defeat. For all practical purposes, the Democratic party was the only party, and political rivalries took place within it. The national Democratic party called the region the "Solid South" because it could depend on winning most elections there.

Race Relations in the New South

While the New South's economy was making progress, social relations between Southern blacks and whites grew worse. In the 1890s, white *racism* (belief that one race is better than others) showed more of its ugly head. Many white Southerners, as well as many white Northerners, were not willing to recognize blacks' desires for political and social equality. Instead, Southern state and local governments passed laws that aimed to *segregate* (separate) the races.

Jim Crow Laws State and local governments in the South passed laws that called for separate areas and services in public places for blacks and whites. These laws were called *Jim Crow* legislation, "Jim Crow" being a negative term applied to blacks.

One of the first Jim Crow laws was passed in Tennessee in 1881. It required whites and blacks to use separate railroad cars. By 1900, the other Southern states had adopted this requirement. Similar laws segregated blacks and whites in streetcars, riverboats, and hotels. Blacks had to use separate waiting rooms in railroad terminals and separate toilets and water fountains in parks. Perhaps most significant of all, blacks had to attend separate schools.

Supreme Court Legalizes Segregation In 1896, in the case of *Plessy* v. *Ferguson*, the U.S. Supreme Court reached an important decision about segregation. It ruled that state and local governments could require "separate but equal" railroad cars for blacks. This decision legalized segregation in other types of public facilities as well, including public schools. In practice, "separate but equal" schools for blacks were seldom equal in quality to public white schools.

Other Types of Discrimination Blacks were held back in the South in other ways. Blacks had the hardest and lowest-paying jobs. Many remained sharecroppers or farm laborers. Others worked in cities as house servants, hotel and restaurant workers, or railroad employees. A large number became unskilled or semi-skilled factory workers. Throughout the South, blacks had few chances to get better jobs.

Southern blacks also had a hard time getting equal justice. On the one hand, court trials for blacks accused of crimes were often unfair. On the other hand, those blacks accused of crimes were lucky to make it to court. Some were "brought to justice" outside the law through lynchings by white supremacy groups, such as the Ku Klux Klan.

Discrimination Outside the South

Although the problem was worse in the South, discrimination existed in other sections of the country as well. In the North and West, blacks were treated as second-class citizens. Black people were victims of discrimination in housing, employment, and education. Living in slums was a common experience among blacks. Blacks often received low wages, were kept out of good-paying jobs, and were the first to be fired when the economy declined.

Voting Restrictions

After federal troops withdrew from the South in the 1870s, blacks were left to fend for themselves. For some two decades, they continued to vote in large numbers. In the 1890s, though, Southern whites began to take away the right of blacks to vote.

Intimidation One way that whites kept blacks away from the polls was by *intimidation* (making threats against them). Blacks were threatened with violence, loss of jobs, or the loss of credit if they tried to vote. In many cases, whites carried out their warnings.

Literacy Tests In a number of Southern states, *literacy tests* became a requirement for voting. Would-be voters had to show that they could read and understand a difficult text, such as a state constitution. This task was hard for those Southern blacks who had not had a chance to learn to read. Furthermore, the tests were often given in such a way that they were harder for blacks than for whites.

Poll Taxes Southern states created another requirement for voting—the *poll tax*. People had to pay a small fee before they could vote. Most blacks (and many poor whites, too) could not afford to pay this tax.

Grandfather Clauses Literacy tests and poll taxes made it hard for many poor whites, as well as blacks, to vote. To cut down on voting restrictions for these poor whites, many Southern states added *grandfather clauses* to their constitutions. These clauses gave voting rights to all men who had voted before 1867. The clauses also applied to those whose father or grandfather had voted before that year. Since

few black people could vote before 1867, only whites were exempted from literacy tests and poll taxes. Not until 1915 did the U.S. Supreme Court declare grandfather clauses to be unconstitutional. The last poll taxes were finally eliminated in 1966. In that year, the Supreme Court ruled them illegal in state, local, and national elections.

Booker T. Washington voiced one reaction of Southern blacks to their declining status. Born into slavery, Washington worked in a coal mine after emancipation. Then he attended Hampton Institute, a black vocational school in Virginia. Upon graduation, he became a teacher, and in 1881 helped found the Tuskegee Institute, a black vocational school in Alabama.

Washington thought that blacks could best improve their lot by gaining a skill and working hard. Thus, he pushed the idea of vocational education for blacks. Many whites and blacks admired his work and his views. Some black leaders, however, disagreed with Washington's belief that blacks should avoid political protests. (Washington's views are discussed further in Lesson 72.)

Students at Tuskegee Institute had the use of up-to-date equipment in science labs. Frances Benjamin Johnston, America's first woman commercial photographer, took this picture in about the year 1900.

SUMMING UP   We have seen how the Southern economy recovered from the destruction of the Civil War. In the 1880s and 1890s, the South made noteworthy progress toward becoming industrialized. Southern blacks, however, suffered racial discrimination and segregation. They had to occupy a separate (and often inferior) place in society. Moreover, they were prevented from exercising their right to vote.

Understanding the Text

On a separate sheet of paper, write the letter of the word or phrase that best completes each of the following statements.

1. In the New South, sharecroppers *(a)* paid their rent in cash   *(b)* ran large plantations *(c)* were usually poor *(d)* owned small plots of land.

2. In the South after Reconstruction, *(a)* cotton cultivation disappeared *(b)* tobacco became the region's most important crop *(c)* farm prices generally declined *(d)* cotton production never reached its pre-war level.

3. After Reconstruction, manufacturing in the South *(a)* became less important *(b)* disappeared almost entirely *(c)* became more important than in the North *(d)* grew rapidly.

4. The term "Solid South" refers to a trend in in *(a)* politics *(b)* economics *(c)* religion *(d)* physical fitness.

5. An example of a "Jim Crow" law was one that *(a)* permitted blacks to buy property in white neighborhoods *(b)* compelled schools to mix races in classrooms *(c)* made blacks sit in separate railroad cars *(d)* prohibited hirings and firings because of race.

6. One result of the Supreme Court decision *Plessy* v. *Ferguson* was *(a)* the election of black members of Congress *(b)* federal approval of segregation of schools in the South *(c)* a decrease in the number of lynchings *(d)* the end of "Jim Crow" legislation in the South.

7. Of the following statements about poll taxes, which one expresses an opinion? *(a)* Poll taxes were voting fees. *(b)* Poll taxes were the worst form of discrimination against blacks. *(c)* An amendment to the Constitution now outlaws poll taxes. *(d)* Most blacks did not pay poll taxes.

8. The purpose of grandfather clauses in state constitutions was to *(a)* protect the voting rights of blacks *(b)* prevent the breakup of large plantations *(c)* make sure that whites would not be affected by literacy tests and poll taxes *(d)* provide funds to support elderly blacks.

9. The voting rights of blacks in the South in 1900 were *(a)* carefully protected by state governments *(b)* taken away by an amendment to the U.S. Constitution *(c)* widely violated so that few blacks could vote *(d)* unimportant because blacks did not want to vote.

10. Which of the following was *not* a prominent feature of the years 1877–1900 in the South? *(a)* the growth of industries *(b)* the growing strength of the Democratic party *(c)* a great improvement in relations between whites and blacks *(d)* the breakup of plantations.

Developing Chart-Reading Skills

SOLID SOUTH IN PRESIDENTIAL ELECTIONS, 1880–1984

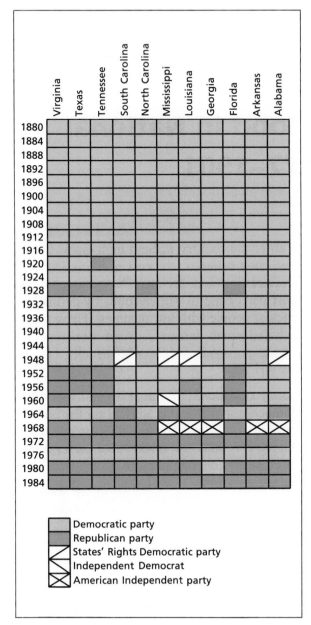

Democratic party
Republican party
States' Rights Democratic party
Independent Democrat
American Independent party

Study the chart above. Then choose the letter of the word or phrase that best completes each sentence. On a separate sheet of paper, match the sentence number with the correct letter.

1. The darkest squares on the chart represent years in which Southern states voted for (*a*) a Democratic U.S. Congress (*b*) Republican state legislatures (*c*) the American Independent party (*d*) the Republican candidate for U.S. President.

2. Beginning in 1880, North Carolina electors voted for the Democratic presidential candidate in every election until the year (*a*) 1888 (*b*) 1920 (*c*) 1928 (*d*) 1968.

3. The first election in which a Southern state voted for the Republican presidential candidate was (*a*) 1900 (*b*) 1920 (*c*) 1948 (*d*) 1984.

4. The South voted solidly Democratic during the period (*a*) 1880–1916 (*b*) 1920–1932 (*c*) 1948–1960 (*d*) 1952–1968.

5. After reading this chart, one can conclude that from 1880 to 1964 (*a*) the South usually voted Republican (*b*) Republicans were not able to win Southern states (*c*) Southern states usually voted Democratic (*d*) the South usually supported the candidate that won the election.

Thinking About the Lesson

1. In what ways was the New South different from the old one? In what ways did the region stay the same after the 1870s?

2. Why did most Southern blacks have a difficult task trying to improve their lives in the 1880s and 1890s?

3. Was Booker T. Washington's emphasis on vocational education and jobs the best course of action for Southern blacks? Why or why not?

The Conservative Mood in National Politics, 1877–1901

The two major political parties between 1877 and 1901, the Republicans and Democrats, were both conservative. In other words, members of the two parties preferred to keep things pretty much as they were. They wanted to avoid sudden and far-reaching changes. Generally, both parties supported the interests of big business. Despite their similarities, however, the Republicans and Democrats did differ on a few issues.

Political Differences

The positions of the two major political parties on tariffs and money were not the same.

Tariff Question Republicans generally favored high protective tariffs. That is, they supported high taxes on imported goods in order to protect American industries from less expensive imports. Tariffs would insure prosperity and keep workers employed at high wages, claimed the Republicans. On the tariff issue, many manufacturers supported the Republicans.

Most Democrats wanted lower tariff rates. They wanted the less expensive foreign goods to enter the country without high taxes. In that way, they believed, the cost of living for most Americans would decline. Democrats, for the most part, tried to win elections by getting the votes of people with low incomes. These voters included small farmers, urban workers, and shopkeepers—all people who usually favored low tariffs.

Money Questions In the 1870s and 1880s, the Democrats and Republicans had similar policies on money questions. In the 1890s, though, many Democrats came to favor "free silver" (the purchase and coinage of more silver) to increase the money supply. (See Lesson 51, page 321.) In contrast, Republicans supported the *gold standard*. With the gold standard, all paper money would be backed by the government with gold. The government would pay gold to those people who wanted to turn in their paper money. Reflecting the opinions of creditors and the wealthy, Republicans argued that a gold standard was the best way to prevent inflation and keep businesses prosperous.

Era of Republican Control From 1877 to 1901, the Republicans elected every President, except

332

Grover Cleveland. During these years, Republicans often tried to win votes by "waving the bloody shirt"—reminding people which party had led the fight to save the Union. This strategy was combined with ones that appealed especially to the interests of big businesses.

For a time after the Civil War, the Democrats had been very weak. Many voters had regarded the Democratic party as the "party of rebellion." In the 1870s, though, Democrats regained control of Southern political life. In addition, they elected many members of Congress from different parts of the country. Sometimes they controlled the House. Twice they controlled the Senate, too. Two times their candidate was elected President. (See the table on page 338.)

We will look at the highlights of each of the Republican and Democratic administrations, beginning with Hayes's.

Rutherford B. Hayes (1877–1881)

The Republican Rutherford B. Hayes served only a single term as President. He was able, sincere, and honest. Hayes accomplished little, though, because he did not have the support of the Democratic-controlled Congress. He was further handicapped by the way he had won the disputed election of 1876, discussed on page 276.

Among the highlights of President Hayes's term in office were:

• In 1877, he officially ended Reconstruction by removing the last federal troops from the South.

• Also in 1877, Hayes called out federal troops to put down a nationwide railroad strike. (Discussed on page 296.)

• He vetoed the 1878 Bland-Allison Act, which called for issuing more silver coins. Congress overrode his veto, however, and the bill became law.

• Hayes urged that most government employees be hired only after passing a civil service test. Tests would replace the system whereby government employees got jobs for being loyal to a political party. While Hayes was President, Secretary of the Interior Carl Schurz set up this "merit system" for his department.

Hayes's record as President showed that he was a conservative on economic matters but wanted reforms on some other issues.

To obtain many positions in the U.S. government, applicants had to pass civil service exams. Expansion of the civil service system was promoted by most Presidents of this era.

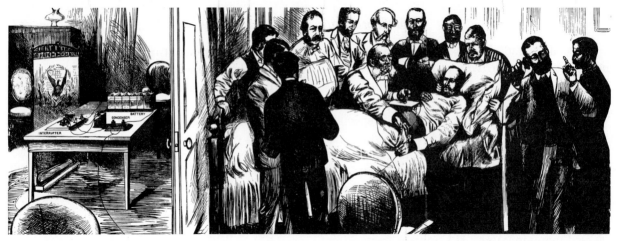

As President Garfield lies on his deathbed, inventor Alexander Graham Bell (on the right) attempts to locate the assassin's bullet with an electrical device.

James A. Garfield (1881)

In the election of 1880, the Democrats ran a Union Army general for President—Winfield S. Hancock. In their campaign, the Democrats reminded voters of how the Republicans had won the disputed election of 1876. The Democrats also called for a lower tariff. The Republicans, in contrast, favored a high tariff. Their presidential candidate, James A. Garfield, was a *dark horse*, that is, someone who unexpectedly wins a competition. Garfield had been a general in the Union Army and a member of Congress.

The Republican Garfield won the election by a large margin of electoral votes but only by some 9,000 popular ones. Moreover, the Republicans regained control of Congress in the 1880 elections. In the presidential election, James B. Weaver, the candidate of the Greenback party, ran a poor third.

Assassination A few months after Garfield had taken office, he was shot by a disappointed seeker for a federal job. The President died several months later.

Chester A. Arthur (1881–1885)

Upon Garfield's death, Vice President Chester A. Arthur became President. Before attaining this office, Arthur had been a *machine politician*—someone who works closely with political bosses and the spoils system. As President, however, Arthur fought corruption in government and backed the passage of the Civil Service Reform Act of 1883. This backing cost him the support of Republican party bosses. As a result, he was not named as the Republican candidate for President in 1884.

Tariff Question On the question of tariffs, Arthur again worked against the wishes of his party. He tried to lower tariff rates, pointing out that these taxes were providing the government with large budget surpluses. This extra money, he claimed, was being spent unwisely. The tariff passed by Congress in 1883 was only a partial victory for Arthur. It was not much lower than earlier ones.

Grover Cleveland (1885–1889)

Instead of Chester A. Arthur, the Republicans nominated James G. Blaine to be their presidential candidate in the election of 1884. Blaine had served as Speaker of the House and Secretary of State. The Democrats ran Grover Cleveland, the former Mayor of Buffalo and Governor of New York. He won the election, becoming the only Democratic President in the years 1877–1901.

As President, Cleveland was an honest leader who worked hard for various reforms:

• He took steps to improve the civil service system by adding some 12,000 federal positions to it.

• He favored low protective tariffs. He was unable, however, to get Congress to pass a bill that included tariff reductions.

• He took action to conserve the nation's natural resources. Cleveland urged the Department of the Interior to restore federal control over 81 million acres. This land had been illegally granted to ranchers, lumber companies, and railroads.

• Cleveland also helped in the passage of the Interstate Commerce Act of 1887, discussed on page 292.

Benjamin Harrison (1889–1893)

Republican Benjamin Harrison, grandson of William Henry Harrison, ran for President in 1888. He had been a lawyer and a Union Army officer and served as a U.S. senator from Indiana. Harrison was able to defeat the incumbent Grover Cleveland.

Harrison's Administration In 1888, Harrison had campaigned for a high tariff. Within two years, Congress passed such a measure—the McKinley Tariff of 1890. Other important measures passed during his administration included:

• The Sherman Antitrust Act of 1890, discussed on page 293.

• The Sherman Silver Purchase Act of 1890. This act, which increased government purchases of silver, was a compromise measure. It did not satisfy either those who favored currency inflation or those who wanted the gold standard.

Election of 1890 In the congressional elections of 1890, the Republicans lost their majority in the House of Representatives. Widespread dislike of the 1890 tariff helped bring about this Republican setback.

Grover Cleveland (1893–1897)

In 1892, the Democrat Cleveland ran again for President against Harrison—a rematch of the 1888 election. A third candidate, the Populist James B. Weaver, received fairly strong support—1 million votes. Nevertheless, Cleveland won the election, beating both the Republican and Populist candidates.

In office, Cleveland's second administration was marked by the severe economic depression of 1893. Cleveland was blamed for the depression even though he had not been in office long enough to have caused it. Cleveland himself blamed the depression on the Silver Purchase Act of 1890 and persuaded Congress to repeal that law.

In addition to being blamed for the depression, Cleveland's popularity declined because of his involvement in a labor dispute. In 1894, he ordered the use of federal troops against strikers in the Pullman railroad strike, discussed earlier on page 298.

Advocates of free silver wanted the government to mint more silver dollars, such as these coins.

TIMELINE OF PRESIDENTIAL ADMINISTRATIONS, 1877–1901

Rutherford B. Hayes
1877–1881

James A. Garfield
March 4–September 19, 1881

Chester A. Arthur
1881–1885

William McKinley (1897–1901)

The 1896 election is remembered as one of the most bitter and emotional in American history. William Jennings Bryan became the candidate of both the Democrats and Populists. The money question served as the most important issue of that campaign. Candidate Bryan called for free silver, while Republican William McKinley wanted the gold standard. In the end, McKinley was elected President.

McKinley proved to be a popular Chief Executive, perhaps because the country began to prosper once again. Business interests dominated Congress, as was shown by the passage of two laws during his administration:

• With the Dingley Tariff of 1897, protective tariffs rose to the highest levels in the nation's history.

• In 1900, the country adopted the gold standard for its money system. With this standard, the value of the dollar was set by law to equal an exact amount of gold.

Foreign Policy   A short but successful war with Spain in 1898 led the United States to *annex* (take over) overseas lands. The former Spanish colonies of Puerto Rico, Guam, and the Philippines now belonged to the United States. With this victory, it was clear that the United States had become a major world power. (This subject is discussed further in Lesson 56.)

Election of 1900   McKinley was easily re-elected in 1900, again beating the Democratic candidate Bryan. Unfortunately, McKinley was assassinated just six months after his second term began. An anarchist, Leon Czolgosz, shot the President at the Pan-American Exposition in Buffalo, New York. His death gave Vice President Theodore Roosevelt the chance to lead the country into the modern era.

Grover Cleveland
1885–1889 1893–1897

Benjamin Harrison
1889–1893

William McKinley
1897–1901

SUMMING UP   We have seen that the Democratic and Republican parties, although both conservative, differed on several issues between 1877 and 1901. During this period, the tariff was an important campaign topic, and in the 1890s, so was the money question. With the exception of Grover Cleveland, a Democrat, Republicans dominated the Presidency. Republican Presidents were Rutherford B. Hayes, James A. Garfield, Chester A. Arthur, Benjamin Harrison, and William McKinley.

Understanding the Text

On a separate sheet of paper, write the letter of the word or phrase that best completes each of the following statements.

1. Between 1877 and 1901, the Democratic and Republican parties *(a)* were formed *(b)* were in general agreement on many issues *(c)* agreed only on the tariff question *(d)* both favored free silver.

2. The political party that attempted to get votes by "waving the bloody shirt" was the *(a)* Republican party *(b)* Democratic party *(c)* Populist party *(d)* Greenback party.

3. A President of the period 1877–1901 who was *not* a Republican was *(a)* Rutherford B. Hayes *(b)* Chester A. Arthur *(c)* William McKinley *(d)* Grover Cleveland.

4. All of the following Presidents died in office, *except* (*a*) Rutherford B. Hayes (*b*) James A. Garfield (*c*) William McKinley (*d*) Abraham Lincoln.

5. President Hayes is known for all of the following, *except* (*a*) removing the last federal troops from the South (*b*) calling out federal troops because of a railroad strike (*c*) promoting free silver (*d*) urging civil service reform.

6. The Civil Service Reform Act of 1883 was passed during the administration of (*a*) Rutherford B. Hayes (*b*) James A. Garfield (*c*) Chester A. Arthur (*d*) Grover Cleveland.

7. The President who served two terms that were not *consecutive* (one right after the other) was (*a*) Benjamin Harrison (*b*) Grover Cleveland (*c*) William McKinley (*d*) James A. Garfield.

8. All of the following were passed during the administration of Benjamin Harrison, *except* the (*a*) Dingley Tariff (*b*) Sherman Antitrust Act (*c*) Sherman Silver Purchase Act (*d*) McKinley Tariff of 1890.

9. Both the Democrats and Populists ran the same candidate for President during the year (*a*) 1876 (*b*) 1880 (*c*) 1892 (*d*) 1896.

10. Which of the following statements applies best to the men who were President from 1877 to 1901? (*a*) Most of them were Democrats. (*b*) They all served two full terms. (*c*) Because of their successes in solving the nation's problems, they are considered among the greatest American Presidents. (*d*) Most of them were Republicans.

Developing Table-Reading Skills

Examine the table below. Then choose the letter of the word or phrase that best completes each sentence. On a separate sheet of paper, match the sentence number with the correct letter.

PARTY CONTROL OF THE PRESIDENCY AND CONGRESS, 1877–1901

Years	President	President's party	Major party in House	Major party in Senate
1877–1879	Hayes	Rep.	Dem.	Rep.
1879–1881			Dem.	Dem.
1881–1883	Garfield/Arthur	Rep.	Rep.	Rep.
1883–1885			Dem.	Rep.
1885–1887	Cleveland	Dem.	Dem.	Rep.
1887–1889			Dem.	Rep.
1889–1891	Harrison	Rep.	Rep.	Rep.
1891–1893			Dem.	Rep.
1893–1895	Cleveland	Dem.	Dem.	Dem.
1895–1897			Rep.	Rep.
1897–1899	McKinley	Rep.	Rep.	Rep.
1899–1901			Rep.	Rep.

1. The vertical column in the middle of the table (third from either side) provides the names of (a) U.S. Presidents (b) political parties of the Presidents (c) political parties that controlled the House of Representatives (d) political parties that controlled Congress.

2. The U.S. President who served from 1893 to 1897 was (a) Rutherford B. Hayes (b) Chester A. Arthur (c) Grover Cleveland (d) William McKinley.

3. A two-year period during which one party controlled the House and another, the Senate was (a) 1877–1879 (b) 1881–1883 (c) 1889–1891 (d) 1893–1895.

4. A four-year period during which one party controlled the Presidency and both houses of Congress was (a) 1877–1881 (b) 1881–1885 (c) 1897–1899 (d) 1897–1901.

5. An election year in which Democrats won the Presidency and a majority of both houses of Congress was (a) 1884 (b) 1887 (c) 1892 (d) 1893.

Thinking About the Lesson

1. If you had been an American voter during the 1880s, which political party would you have supported? Explain your choice.

2. Which of the following U.S. Presidents did the best job in office? (Give reasons for your choice.)

Rutherford B. Hayes
Chester A. Arthur
Grover Cleveland
Benjamin Harrison
William McKinley

3. Why did some Americans in the late 19th century favor high tariffs? Why did some others oppose high tariffs?

Cultural Developments, 1850–1900

In the second half of the 19th century, America's cultural life changed greatly. Writers, artists, architects, and musicians produced important works that reflected the nation's development. The country became one of the world's cultural centers. Americans also moved into the front ranks in education. Leaders in this field helped to make the United States into a society ready for the 20th century.

American Writers

In the 1850s, American writing was in the last decade of a rich period called the "American Renaissance." (See Lesson 35.) Ralph Waldo Emerson and Henry Wadsworth Longfellow continued to produce great works. The poet Walt Whitman began to come to public attention at this time. His collection *Leaves of Grass*, first published in 1855, celebrated American life and democracy. Many modern critics consider it a masterpiece.

After the Civil War, new writers made their mark. New York novelist Henry James became fascinated with Europe, eventually moving there. In *Daisy Miller* (1879) and other works, he compared upper-class Americans and Europeans. Stephen Crane's first novel, *Maggie: A Girl of the Street* (1893), described conditions in a New York slum. Crane was best known, however, for *The Red Badge of Courage*, published in 1895. This novel revealed in grim detail the conditions under which a soldier lived during the Civil War.

The Massachusetts poet Emily Dickinson was not widely read until after her death in 1886. Living a secluded life, she wrote mainly about thoughts and feelings. Perhaps she later became popular because many of her readers shared similar private thoughts.

Some of America's new writers came from regions of the country outside of the Northeast. Mark Twain set *The Adventures of Tom Sawyer* (1876) in Missouri, where he grew up. His *Roughing It* (1872) was based on his experiences working as a newspaper reporter in Nevada and California. The Georgian author Joel Chandler Harris, who wrote the humorous Uncle Remus stories, retold traditional black tales. His characters Brer Rabbit and Brer Fox became known to young and old alike, all across the country.

American Artists

With the building of art museums in America's larger cities, many more Americans could now see great works of art. European drawings, paintings, and works of sculpture continued to dominate American art collections. The United States, however, produced important artists of its own.

Photographer Matthew Brady took this portrait of Walt Whitman in 1866. At the time, the poet was working in Washington, D.C., as a government clerk.

Two major American painters moved to Europe, where they did most of their work. In London, James McNeill Whistler painted many fine portraits, including a famous one of his mother, done in 1872. Mary Cassatt, who had a studio in Paris, painted sensitive studies of women and children.

American painters who worked in their own country included Winslow Homer and Thomas Eakins. Homer liked to depict the people of Maine and scenes along that state's rocky coast. The Philadelphia artist Eakins often showed people engaged in strenuous sports, such as boxing and rowing. His paintings appeared quite realistic and detailed, perhaps because of his knowledge of human anatomy.

Black artist Henry O. Tanner was a student of Eakins. Tanner painted realistic scenes from the lives of black Americans.

American Architecture

The growth of big businesses after the Civil War produced many wealthy Americans. They wanted to live in comfortable but showy mansions. The houses that they built usually reflected past architectural styles of Europe rather than American ones. Nevertheless, the country's economic expansion did produce an American "first" in architecture. American cities, having become more crowded, began to sprout upward. Skyscrapers were first built in the United States, beginning in Chicago in 1884. They were made possible by the use of elevators and iron or steel frameworks.

An American designer of skyscrapers, Louis Sullivan, had a strong influence on the development of modern architecture. His most famous slogan was "form follows function." By this phrase, Sullivan meant that the shape of a

Mary Cassatt made this watercolor of herself in 1880. More information about Cassatt can be found on page 345.

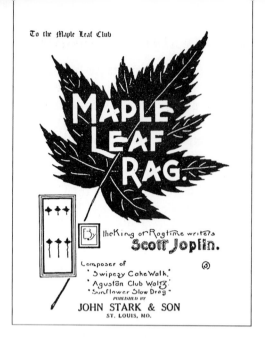

Scott Joplin named his "Maple Leaf Rag" after the Maple Leaf Club, a saloon in which he played in Sedalia, Missouri. (*Granger Collection*)

building should be determined mainly by its purpose. For this reason, he was against copying former styles of architecture, as many other architects were doing.

American Music

Americans' growing interest in music became even stronger in the second half of the 19th century. While some of the music was of European origin, Americans created their own forms of folk music.

Stephen Foster During the 1850s, Stephen Foster penned most of his famous folk songs, including "Swanee River" and "My Old Kentucky Home." Many of his works were sung in *minstrel shows*. In this type of entertainment, whites wore dark makeup on their faces to appear to be blacks. Minstrel shows continued to be popular until the early 1900s.

Civil War Songs Supporters of each side in the Civil War had their favorite songs, which they sang with enthusiasm. Confederates liked to sing "Dixie" by Daniel D. Emmett. "John Brown's Body" became the favorite tune of Union forces and their supporters.

Cowboy Songs With the settlement of the West and the growth of ranching, a new form of music was invented. Cowboys sang songs as they sat around the campfire or lay on their bunks. "Home on the Range" is one of many popular cowboy songs from the post-Civil War period.

Black Music Blacks made contributions to American music in a number of ways:

• James A. Bland wrote several popular folk songs, including "Carry Me Back to Old Virginny" and "Oh Dem Golden Slippers."
• Black *spirituals* (religious songs) were enjoyed by both blacks and whites.
• Music performed by blacks at funeral marches and other public occasions developed into jazz. Scott Joplin, a black songwriter and pianist, made popular one form of jazz called *ragtime*. His well-known work "Maple Leaf Rag" was first published in 1899.

Opera Wealthy Americans liked to support the building of opera houses and attend performances in them. One of the grandest of these, the original Metropolitan Opera House in New York City, was built in 1883. Other American cities and towns had their own opera houses. Even Central City, a mining town in Colorado, built one. Opera companies toured from one town to another, usually performing works by European composers.

Symphony Orchestras Americans also supported symphony orchestras. By 1900, several cities, including Chicago and Boston, had formed their own.

The Phonograph People living far away from urban centers had a means of listening to both serious and popular music. They could buy a phonograph. Thomas Edison invented this machine in 1877, but not until the 1890s did Americans begin to use phonographs in large numbers.

American Education

Americans have always valued education. The efforts of local and state governments to expand public education after the Civil War reflected this fact.

Kindergartens The country's first public kindergarten was set up in St. Louis in 1873. The idea caught on, and by 1900 some 3,000 kindergartens had been formed.

Elementary and Secondary Schools Public elementary school enrollment shot up from 7.5 million students in 1871 to over 14 million in 1900. High school enrollment, still far behind the lower grades, also showed a dramatic improvement—from 80,000 to half a million. High schools put less emphasis on Latin and Greek. Instead, they introduced what were considered more useful subjects, such as the sciences, business mathematics, and vocational arts.

Higher Education The number of people enrolled in programs beyond the high school level continued to grow after the Civil War. In 1870, this figure was about 52,000; in 1900, the number had increased over four times, to 238,000. This enrollment, however, represented only a small part of the country's college-age population.

Among the important trends in higher education during these years were:

• The growth of land-grant colleges in many states. These schools, set up under the Morrill Act of 1862, were financed in part by federal grants of land. At first the schools emphasized agricultural studies and engineering.

• The creation of at least one normal school in every state. Before normal schools were set up, teachers had often been hired without having had any formal preparation.

• A shift in focus in many colleges away from teaching the *classics* (Latin and Greek) toward teaching the sciences and new subjects.

• An increase in college opportunities for women. More women's private colleges, such as Vassar, Smith, and Wellesley, opened their doors. By 1901, 128 schools of higher education for women existed. Moreover, many women were able to take advantage of coeducational programs at new state universities in the West and Midwest.

• The creation of colleges for blacks. The best-known were Fisk University in Nashville (1865), Howard University in Washington, D.C. (1867), and Tuskegee Institute in Alabama (1881).

SUMMING UP We have seen how America's writers, artists, architects, and musicians all helped to enrich life in the United States. Although some Americans still looked to Europe for cultural leadership, Americans could be proud of their own contributions to the arts. Of all its cultural advances, perhaps those in education would have the greatest effect in transforming the country into a modern nation.

Understanding the Text

On a separate sheet of paper, write the letter of the word or phrase that best completes each of the following statements.

1. Of the following American writers, one *not* a part of the "American Renaissance," which ended about 1860, was (*a*) Walt Whitman (*b*) Ralph Waldo Emerson (*c*) Mark Twain (*d*) Henry Wadsworth Longfellow.

2. Of the following American writers, one known mainly as a poet was (*a*) Emily Dickinson (*b*) Henry James (*c*) Mark Twain (*d*) Joel Chandler Harris.

3. The author of the Uncle Remus stories was (*a*) Emily Dickinson (*b*) Joel Chandler Harris (*c*) Mark Twain (*d*) Henry James.

4. An American artist famous for studies of Maine's seashore was (*a*) James McNeil Whistler (*b*) Mary Cassatt (*c*) Winslow Homer (*d*) Thomas Eakins.

5. Louis Sullivan's phrase "form follows function" related to American (*a*) painting (*b*) architecture (*c*) writing (*d*) music.

6. Of the following forms of music in America, one dominated by European composers in the 19th century was (*a*) the minstrel show (*b*) the cowboy song (*c*) ragtime (*d*) opera.

7. An example of the contributions by blacks to American music was (*a*) "Maple Leaf Rag" by Scott Joplin (*b*) "Carry Me Back to Old Virginny" by James A. Bland (*c*) the spiritual "Swing Low, Sweet Chariot" sung by the Jubilee Singers of Fisk University (*d*) all of the above.

8. The public schools that had the largest enrollments in 1900 were (*a*) kindergartens (*b*) elementary schools (*c*) high schools (*d*) land-grant colleges.

9. Of the following trends in higher education, the one *not* true for the years 1850 to 1900 was (*a*) more stress put on the study of Latin and Greek (*b*) normal schools set up in every state (*c*) separate schools established for women and for blacks (*d*) land-grant colleges set up to emphasize agricultural studies and engineering.

10. An important idea discussed in this lesson is that (*a*) American cultural standards were very low in 1900 (*b*) cowboy songs were the only form of music to originate in America (*c*) America's cultural life became richer in the years 1850–1900 (*d*) most major American writers, artists, and musicians moved to Europe.

Developing Skills at Generalizing

In most forms of writing, people make *generalizations*. A generalization is a conclusion or summary drawn from facts. Most well-written paragraphs have a generalization in the form of a *topic sentence*. This topic sentence, often found at the beginning of a paragraph, expresses the main idea of a paragraph.

Facts and generalizations work well together. Generalizations need facts to back them up. Facts need generalizations to give them broader meaning.

Choose the letter of the phrase that best answers each of the following questions. On a separate sheet of paper, match the sentence number with the correct letter.

1. Which statement of fact helps support the following generalization: "Mark Twain often based his writings on his own experiences"? (*a*) Mark Twain wore a mustache. (*b*) *The Adventures of Tom Sawyer* and *The Adventures of Huckleberry Finn* were masterpieces. (*c*) Mark Twain gave lectures to supplement his income.

(d) In *Life on the Mississippi*, Twain wrote of his work as a riverboat pilot on the Mississippi.

2. Which statement of fact helps support the following generalization: "In *The Red Badge of Courage*, Stephen Crane portrayed the feelings of a common soldier in combat"? (a) Crane wrote, "Presently he began to feel the effects of the war atmosphere—a blistering sweat, a sensation that his eyeballs were about to crack like hot stones." (b) Crane effectively used strong images in describing the settings of the novel. (c) Crane had to pay to have his first novel published. (d) In 1898, Crane worked as a newspaper correspondent, reporting on the Spanish-American War.

3. Facts:
   I. The first building whose floors and walls were both supported by a metal frame was built in France in 1871. It was not called a skyscraper since it was just four stories tall.
   II. The world's first skyscraper, the Home Insurance Building in Chicago, stood from 1884 to 1931. It had ten stories.
   III. The Tacoma Building in Chicago, built in 1888, was the first to use a complete wrought-iron skeleton. It was twelve stories tall.

From the statements of fact listed above, which of the following generalizations can be made? (a) As buildings grew taller, cities did not have to spread out so far. (b) Skyscrapers made use of elevators. (c) The United States was the birthplace of the skyscraper. (d) American architects imitated earlier architectural styles.

4. Facts:
   I. Mary Cassatt was born in Pennsylvania in 1845 but lived in Paris for five years as a child.
   II. She studied at the Pennsylvania Academy of Fine Arts from 1861 to 1862. Later, from 1868 to 1874, she studied in Europe.
   III. In 1874, Mary Cassatt set up a studio in Paris and lived there until her death in 1926.
   IV. While living in France, Ms. Cassatt made periodic visits to her native land.

From the statements of fact listed above, which of the following generalizations can be made? (a) The painter Cassatt was best known for her portraits of women and children. (b) She spent much of her life away from the United States. (c) Mary Cassatt is considered by some experts to be America's most famous woman painter. (d) Her career in painting was made possible partly because of the support she received from her wealthy family.

5. In the following paragraph, identify the topic sentence.

In the last decade of the 19th century, newspaper publishing expanded, reaching more people than ever before. The number of newspapers sold each day increased from 2,800,000 in 1870 to 24,200,000 in 1900. During that same period, the number of different newspapers rose from 7,000 to 12,000. No wonder more and more young people thought of journalism as a promising career for themselves.

The topic sentence is the (a) first one (b) second one (c) third one (d) last one.

Thinking About the Lesson

1. Between 1850 and 1900, American artists made important contributions in the fields of art, architecture, literature, and music. Of which field do you think Americans had the right to feel most proud? Explain your answer.

American Foreign Policy, 1850–1900

President George Washington, nearing the end of his second term in office, made an important statement about foreign policy. He warned against having permanent alliances with foreign nations. For a good part of the 19th century, the United States followed this policy of "isolationism." Gradually, however, the country became more involved in world affairs. In the second half of the 19th century, the United States actively sought trading partners and overseas colonies.

Perry's Expedition to Japan

In 1853, Commodore Matthew Perry led a squadron of U.S. Navy ships on a trip to Japan. One of his goals was to arrange for better treatment of American sailors there. Sometimes Americans were shipwrecked in Japanese waters and had to take refuge in Japan. Another one of Perry's goals was to persuade the Japanese to open their ports to U.S. traders.

Perry came to Japan at a good time. For 200 years, the Japanese had closed their borders to foreigners. Now, though, they were ready to break out of their shell of isolation. They were impressed by Perry's ships, with their powerful cannons. They also admired the Western man- ufactured goods, such as the sewing machine, that Perry had brought with him.

U.S.-Japanese Treaty In 1854, the Japanese agreed to Perry's requests, signing a trade and friendship treaty. Within the next few years, the Japanese opened several ports to U.S. and European traders.

Secretary of State Seward

During the Civil War, the United States was too weak to get involved much in world affairs. After 1865, however, the United States actively pursued its interests in different parts of the world. William H. Seward, Secretary of State under Presidents Lincoln and Johnson, led the U.S. in this pursuit:

• Seward was strongly opposed to having a French colony on the United States' southern border. (See Lesson 41, page 247.) Accordingly, he pressed the French to withdraw from Mexico. This pressure was one of the reasons why, by 1867, Napoleon III's troops had left for France. The French puppet, Emperor Maximilian, stayed, however, and tried to retain control of Mexico. Soon Mexican forces seized the unprotected monarch and executed him.

• In 1867, Seward arranged for the United States to buy Alaska from the Russians. At the time, few Americans guessed what rich natural

In the picture on the right, Commodore Perry and the rest of the U.S. delegation are received by Japanese leaders in 1854. A Japanese artist's depiction of Perry is shown above.

resources Alaska contained. Many Americans campaigned against the purchase, but Seward was persistent. Finally, the Senate approved a U.S.-Russian treaty regarding Alaska, and the House agreed to the purchase price of $7.2 million. (See the map on page 348.)

• Seward also helped arrange for the United States to annex Midway Island in the Pacific Ocean. This island was an important stopping-off point for U.S. ships crossing the Pacific.

• In 1868, he made a deal with Denmark to buy the Danish Virgin Islands, in the West Indies. Nevertheless, the U.S. Senate failed to approve this purchase. The United States would have had to pay more for these small islands than it paid for all of Alaska. (The United States in 1917 bought the Danish Virgin Islands because it feared then that Germany might take them.)

• In 1868, Seward concluded with China an agreement that gave Americans favorable trade terms. The agreement also allowed Chinese workers to enter the United States as laborers. Most of these immigrants settled in the West, where they worked on railroad construction and other jobs.

The Grant Administration

Hamilton Fish served as Secretary of State under President Ulysses S. Grant. Fish's main accomplishment was to settle the *Alabama* claims dispute. In Lesson 41, we learned that the *Alabama*, a Confederate raiding ship, had been built in Great Britain during the Civil War. After the war, the United States asked the British for money to pay for the damage done by the *Alabama* to Union ships. Finally, in 1871, Great Britain formally expressed "regret" for the incident. It also agreed to have *arbitrators* (third parties who help settle disputes) decide on how much money should be paid to the United States. In 1872, the arbitrators decided upon the figure of $15.5 million, which the British eventually paid.

Santo Domingo President Grant had long been eager to have the United States gain overseas territories. In 1870, Grant saw an opportunity to annex Santo Domingo, a Caribbean nation that shared an island with Haiti. Grant sent a delegation there to arrange an annexation treaty with leaders of Santo Domingo. The treaty was

U.S. TERRITORIES IN THE PACIFIC, 1867–1899

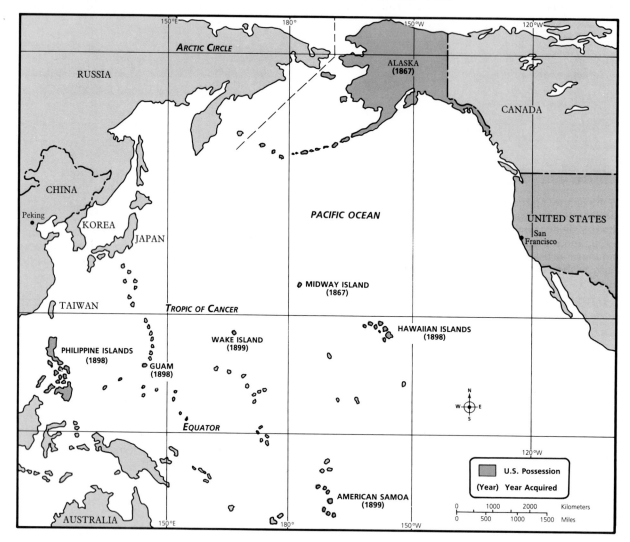

signed, but the President could not persuade the U.S. Senate to approve the pact. As a result, Santo Domingo remained independent.

Interest in the Pacific Ocean

As trade with East Asia grew, Americans became more interested in safeguarding Pacific trade routes. This interest expressed itself in several ways:

• In 1878, the United States obtained rights to have a naval base on the Samoan Islands in the South Pacific. Germany and Great Britain also had similar rights there. For a while, the three countries jointly administered the islands. Then in 1899, Great Britain withdrew, leaving Germany and the United States to divide Samoa.

• The United States was also interested in Hawaii, some 3,000 miles north of Samoa. American sugar planters had long established their presence and influence in Hawaii. In 1887, the Hawaiian government granted the United States rights to set up a naval base in Pearl Harbor. Hawaiian nationalists, however, resented this arrangement as well as the strong economic influence of Americans in Hawaii. In 1891, Queen Liliuokalani, a firm nationalist, came to the throne and tried to remove American influence. At the request of American sugar planters, U.S. Marines were used to help overthrow Queen Liliuokalani in 1893. A pro-American government was installed. Although the U.S. government had not approved the Marines' action, it decided not to reverse the course of events. In 1894, the United States recognized the new Republic of Hawaii. Many Americans now called for annexation of the islands. President Cleveland opposed this course of action, but his successor, President McKinley, favored it. Annexation of Hawaii became official in 1898.

• James G. Blaine, Secretary of State in 1881 and again from 1889 to 1892, tried to get the United States to build a canal across Central America. A waterway connecting the Atlantic and Pacific oceans would save ships the long trip around the tip of South America. The United States, though, was not able to arrange the construction of a canal at this time. The main obstacle was Great Britain, with which the United States had signed a treaty in 1850 concerning such a canal. According to the treaty, neither country had the right to build and control a waterway across Central America by itself. In the late 19th century, the British still refused to allow the U.S. to build alone.

• In 1883, the U.S. Congress approved plans for the construction of four new naval cruisers made of steel. This was the beginning of the reconstruction of the U.S. Navy. By 1900, the United States had one of the strongest navies in the world. This navy was vital to U.S. efforts to protect trade routes in the Pacific and elsewhere.

Developments in the Far East

Japan came into conflict with China over Korea, an Asian nation that had been under Chinese control for many years. Japan, wanting to gain colonies, was eager to seize Korea. Japan won an easy victory over China in a war that began in 1894 and ended the next year.

Under terms of the peace treaty, Japan got special rights in Korea. Moreover, Japan annexed Formosa (Taiwan), a large Chinese island off the Chinese coast. Japan's victory alerted the European powers to the need to prevent Japan from extending its influence in China. Soon England, France, Germany, and Russia obtained their own *spheres of influence* (areas where they dominated) in China. Reacting to these developments, some Americans expressed the fear that China might cease to exist as an independent nation. Other Americans were more worried that the United States would be left out as China was divided up by other nations.

Queen Lydia Liliuokalani succeeded her brother on the Hawaiian throne in 1891. Less than two years later, Americans living in Hawaii deposed her.

Open Door Policy   In 1899, Secretary of State John Hay sent notes to the powers involved in China. He proposed an "Open Door" policy, whereby all powers would have equal opportunities to trade with China. Most of the powers reluctantly agreed to Hay's note. Soon, however, Hay became more concerned about China's independence than about trade rights there.

The Boxer Rebellion   Many Chinese were deeply disturbed by the way their homeland was being treated by other nations. Groups of young Chinese formed secret patriotic societies to oppose the hated foreigners. One such society was called the "Boxers."

In 1900, the Boxers staged an armed rebellion in and around the capital city of Peking. About 300 Europeans were killed in the uprising and considerable damage was done to foreign property. Americans and Europeans there formed an international army to deal with the rebellion. As a result, the Boxers were soon defeated.

To penalize China, foreign nations forced it to make heavy *indemnities* (cash payments to make up for losses). Some of the powers wanted to impose other penalties, such as dividing up the country into areas to be governed by European countries. The United States opposed this idea and instead called for continued Chinese independence. The United States went a step further. It returned about half of the indemnity that it had received from China. This money went to pay for the education of Chinese students in both China and the United States.

Members of the Boxer Society (left) took up arms against foreigners in Peking in 1900. Russian sailors (below) helped defend buildings occupied by foreign diplomats and residents during the Boxer Rebellion. (*Both, Granger Collection*)

SUMMING UP   We have seen how U.S. foreign policy 1850–1900 changed from that of earlier, isolationist times. The United States opened up trade relations with Japan and expanded its trade with China. Americans became interested in gaining overseas territories. The country bought Alaska, built up its navy, and obtained island outposts in the Pacific. Some Americans were also interested in setting up colonies in the Caribbean and building a canal across Central America. As we will learn in the next lesson, U.S. actions would lead to war with a European power.

Understanding the Text

On a separate sheet of paper, write the letter of the word or phrase that best completes each of the following statements.

1. The most important result of Commodore Perry's expedition to Japan in 1853 was that *(a)* Japanese sailors in the United States were treated better than before *(b)* Japan began to trade with foreigners *(c)* American sewing machines became popular in Japan *(d)* young Japanese formed the Boxer society.

2. The country from which William H. Seward obtained the withdrawal of French troops was *(a)* Alaska *(b)* China *(c)* Mexico *(d)* Virgin Islands.

3. The *Alabama* claims dispute was settled when *(a)* Great Britain paid the United States $15.5 million *(b)* the United States paid Great Britain $7.5 million *(c)* the United States paid Russia $7.2 million *(d)* Alabama was readmitted into the Union.

4. An overseas territory that the United States did *not* acquire in the 19th century was *(a)* Hawaii *(b)* Alaska *(c)* Santo Domingo *(d)* Midway Island.

5. Before 1899, Great Britain, Germany, and the United States all had naval bases in *(a)* Hawaii *(b)* Samoa *(c)* Virgin Islands *(d)* Alaska.

6. Queen Liliuokalani *(a)* disliked American influence in Hawaii *(b)* favored more American influence in Hawaii *(c)* used the U.S. Marines to overthrow the Hawaiian government *(d)* called for the annexation of Hawaii by the United States.

7. In 1894, Japan fought a major war with *(a)* Germany *(b)* Russia *(c)* the United States *(d)* China.

8. Secretary of State Hay's "Open Door" policy related to U.S. trade with *(a)* Japan *(b)* Mexico *(c)* China *(d)* Santo Domingo.

9. The Boxers were *(a)* a group of Chinese students studying in the United States *(b)* a group of Japanese traders in Korea *(c)* a secret society of Chinese who hated foreigners *(d)* Chinese immigrants who worked on the construction of railroads in the United States.

10. United States foreign policy between the years 1850 and 1900 can best be described as concerned with *(a)* remaining isolationist *(b)* acquiring overseas colonies and expanding foreign trade *(c)* acquiring overseas colonies but not expanding foreign trade *(d)* expanding foreign trade but not acquiring colonies.

Developing Map Skills

Study the map on page 348. Then choose the letter of the word or phrase that best completes each sentence. On a separate sheet of paper, match the sentence number with the correct letter.

1. The island of Taiwan is (a) in the Eastern Hemisphere (b) off the coast of China (c) southwest of Japan (d) all of the above.

2. Of the following, the island or group of islands closest to the equator is (a) Midway Island (b) American Samoa (c) Hawaiian Islands (d) Japan.

3. Overseas lands that the United States did *not* acquire between 1867 and 1899 included (a) Japan (b) Midway Island (c) Alaska (d) Hawaiian Islands.

4. The distance between the Samoan Islands and the Hawaiian Islands is about (a) 300 miles (b) 2,600 miles (c) 5,000 miles (d) 40,000 miles.

5. Of the following distances, the longest one is between (a) Russia and Alaska (b) Hawaiian Islands and Wake Island (c) Midway Island and Taiwan (d) Midway Island and San Francisco.

Thinking About the Lesson

1. Why did the United States abandon its earlier policy of isolationism in the second half of the 19th century?

2. Why did the U.S. government want to open up or expand trade relations with Japan and China?

3. For what reasons did the United States acquire Midway Island, American Samoa, and Hawaii?

4. Why did the United States strengthen its naval power at the end of the 19th century?

5. Do you think that the United States was a true friend of China in 1899 and 1900? Why or why not?

6. Some historians have called U.S. foreign policy in the period 1850–1900 "aggressive." Do you agree? Why or why not?

The Spanish-American War

Toward the end of the 19th century, Americans were becoming even more interested in gaining overseas territories. Farmers, industrialists, and traders wanted new markets for their products and new sources of raw materials. Military leaders hoped that the country would get involved in some wars in order to build up the U.S. Armed Forces. Some nationalists believed that the country would gain prestige if its flag was raised over distant areas. It was in such an atmosphere that the United States went to war with Spain.

Causes of the War

The island of Cuba lies in the Caribbean Sea, about 90 miles off the coast of Florida. Through most of the 19th century, Cuba belonged to Spain. Then in 1895, for the second time in less than 30 years, Cubans revolted against Spanish rule. Spain, in attempting to put down the rebellion, used violent methods. United States newspapers seized on that fact, helping to build widespread sympathy for the rebels.

Yellow Journalism Many newspapers in the United States wrote of Spanish "cruelties" and Cuban "suffering." Sometimes journalists stretched the truth on purpose. Two newspapers in particular made such exaggerations—William Randolph Hearst's New York *Journal* and Joseph Pulitzer's New York *World*. Both newspapers built up their sales by printing *sensational* (thrilling) stories that were not always true. Their methods came to be known as *yellow journalism*.

The Dupuy de Lôme Letter In early February, 1898, newspapers published a letter written by the Spanish minister in Washington, Dupuy de Lôme. In the letter, Dupuy de Lôme called President McKinley "weak and a bidder for the admiration of the crowd." Its publication helped to raise anti-Spanish feeling to a fever pitch.

Sinking of the Maine Pro-war feeling reached a climax soon afterward. On February 15, 1898, the U.S. battleship *Maine* exploded in the harbor of Havana, Cuba. (See the map on page 355.) About 260 men were killed. The cause of the explosion was unknown at the time and has never been fully explained. The U.S. press, though, held Spain responsible. A new slogan appeared in newspapers, "Remember the *Maine*!" As a result, more and more Americans began calling for war. The most extreme of these nationalists were called *jingoists*.

At first, President McKinley hoped for a peaceful settlement of the crisis. The Spanish

353

EDITION FOR GREATER NEW YORK.

NEW YORK JOURNAL

AND ADVERTISER.

1168 "WANTS" GAINED LAST SUNDAY
QUICK RESULTS - - BEST RESULTS.

GAINED LAST SUNDAY "WANTS" **1168**
QUICK RESULTS - -BEST RESULTS.

NO. 5,605.   *   Copyright, 1898, by W. R. Hearst.—NEW YORK, TUESDAY, MARCH 22, 1898.—16 PAGES.   PRICE ONE CENT In Greater New York and Jersey City.   Elsewhere TWO CENTS.

JOURNAL'S COMMISSION DECLARES THAT NOTHING CAN JUSTIFY POSTPONING INTERVENTION IN CUBA!

SENATOR THURSTON.

Full Report of the Congressmen Describes Autonomy as a Failure and Cuba as Already Lost to Spain.

Spanish Campaign Marked by Slaughters as Brutal as Apache Massacres---The Insurgent Government Firmly Established Over a Great Part of the Island.

REPRESENTATIVE CUMMINGS.

BY SENATOR HERNANDO DE SOTO MONEY, SENATOR JACOB H. GALLINGER, SENATOR JOHN M. THURSTON, REPRESENTATIVE AMOS J. CUMMINGS AND REPRESENTATIVE WILLIAM ALDEN SMITH.

WASHINGTON, MARCH 21.—We went to Cuba expecting to make allowance for exaggeration due to the intense strife and bitter passion thereby engendered. We have returned convinced by personal examination and observation of the bitter inadequacy of language to tell the misery and horror of the situation. If the insurgents have waged a war of destruction against property the Spanish military authorities have in the past waged one of destruction against property and another of extermination against the Cuban people.

If the campaign of destruction is now less marked, it is because the field of military operations has been swept bare. Hardly a human habitation is visible in a rural territory co-extensive with that of the six New England States. A few plantations heavily guarded by Spanish troops, yet paying tribute to the insurgent Government, grind out less than one-tenth the normal sugar crop of the island where three years ago luxuriant fields of cane and tobacco stretched unbroken for miles. The dense vegetation of a tropical wilderness has sprung up as rank, as wild as when Columbus discovered America, to be as arduously conquered by the machete and the plough.

Half the Inhabitants in Cuba Are Dead.

From all sources, Spanish, Cuban and foreign, whether American or European, consuls or business houses, the figures practically agree that half the rural population of Cuba has disappeared from the face of the earth. In the central and western provinces, where the effect of General Weyler's order has been most severely felt, there are districts from which the whole population has been swept as if by pestilence, and of whose people less than one-fifth are to-day alive within the limits of reconcentration.

Nor have the inhabitants of the towns and cities escaped. There the poorer classes have been placed nearly on a par with the reconcentrados by the privations due to the paralysis of war. Disease and starvation have everywhere done their awful work. Spain, too, has suffered in loss of life as well as in purse and prestige. Of the 250,000 troops which she has sent to Cuba, not more than one-half will ever see their native land again. Hardly the fifth of her forces now in the island are to-day effective.

SENATOR MONEY.

The military hospitals are crowded. For the forces in the field no such thing as a medical corps is known. They are without tents or commissary. The steamships to Spain take back more invalids than offset the fresh troops brought in, and for every invalid soldier returned one is buried in a Cuban trench. The Spanish army is unpaid and discouraged; it has lost the elan and morale indispensable to military success. Members of the Commission have brought back to the United States machetes bought from the belts of Spanish soldiers on the streets of Havana and Matanzas.

Blanco Has Not Won a Single Victory.

Not a single important and successful military operation has marked the course of Spanish arms since the recall of Weyler, and the wet season will begin within six weeks, precluding further movements of critical importance until Fall. Relatively the insurgents are stronger than ever, yet lack the strength and armament to deliver a final blow.

Opportunity did not present itself to penetrate the insurgent lines, but there was no difficulty in getting in touch with men who are not only sympathizers with the cause of Cuban independence, but who themselves are in constant communication with the Insurgent Government and military leaders. From them it was learned that the Cubans were confident of being able to maintain their struggle indefinitely, and that there was a steady improvement of conditions within the territory which they controlled practically without interference from the Spanish forces.

REPRESENTATIVE W. A. SMITH.

It was pointed out that General Gomez had maintained himself within a radius of fifty miles for months In a territory from which he could easily have been driven, had he been so weak or the Spanish as strong as the latter had claimed, and that the Provisional Government at Camaguey was seemingly as firmly planted as Blanco in his palace at Havana, yet it is apparent that there is one large area of the island where the insurgents exercise permanent control.

Cubans Unconquerable by Any Spanish Force.

Each in turn raids across a region several miles in extent. The topography of the country makes it plain that only an overwhelming force and tireless pursuits could suppress forces far less numerous than the insurgents command. Any other would perish in the guerilla warfare in which the Cubans have proven such adepts.

Military termination of the war by either Spanish or Cubans is hopeless. Destruction, extermination and exhaustion seem the only immediate and unaided solution. In the meanwhile American property has

SENATOR GALLINGER.

CUBA AND THE SPANISH-AMERICAN WAR, 1898

of Manila, in the Spanish colony of the Philippines.

• A few months later, the Spaniards suffered heavy losses in a naval engagement in Santiago Harbor, Cuba.

Victory on Land   At the beginning of the war, the United States Army was poorly trained and equipped and was understaffed. Nevertheless, the United States won several quick land campaigns. It won a victory in the Battle of San Juan Hill, in Cuba. Then U.S. forces captured the nearby city of Santiago.

In the Pacific, another American land force occupied Manila. It met little resistance, since the Spanish fleet there had already been defeated. A third land force occupied Puerto Rico, a Spanish colony in the Caribbean. Completely defeated, Spain asked for peace in July, 1898.

government seemed to be willing to give in on some points. It wanted to avoid war.

Nevertheless, pro-war forces in the United States had become very strong. On April 20th, Congress passed a resolution recognizing the independence of Cuba. Congress also gave the President power to use U.S. Armed Forces to make Spain withdraw from the island. In response to the resolution, Spain declared war on the United States. The next day, April 25, 1898, McKinley signed a congressional declaration of war on Spain.

Leading Events of the War

Within ten weeks, the United States had won a complete victory over Spain.

Victory at Sea   The newly rebuilt U.S. Navy was successful on two fronts—in the western Pacific and in the Caribbean:

• The fleet in the western Pacific was commanded by Admiral George Dewey. On May 1, it destroyed a Spanish naval force near the city

The Rough Riders became America's best known volunteer regiment in the war. Led by Teddy Roosevelt (center), the cavalry unit served bravely in Cuba. Many of its members died or were wounded in a famous charge in the Battle of San Juan Hill. Roosevelt's fame as leader of the Rough Riders would help him in national politics.

Results of the War

The Treaty of Paris ended the war and provided the United States with many important rewards. Under the Treaty of Paris, Spain ceded to the United States the following colonies:

- Puerto Rico.
- Guam, an island in the western Pacific.
- The Philippine Islands. For the Philippines, the United States paid Spain $20 million.

Spain also gave up all claims to Cuba. The United States occupied the island, but promised not to annex it. (See Lesson 76 for a discussion of U.S. interests in Cuba after 1898.)

Debate Over Imperialism

In its overseas expansion, the United States made a sharp break from its former policy of isolationism. The country was clearly moving in the direction of *imperialism*, the building of an empire. This move stimulated much debate.

Anti-Imperialists   There was strong American opposition to imperialism. Many Americans

Industrialist Andrew Carnegie was one of the most outspoken opponents of U.S. imperialism.

were against the policy of taking over and governing lands far from U.S. shores. They pointed out that the United States had itself revolted against an imperial power—Great Britain.

> Anti-imperialists were greatly disturbed by the fact that thousands of U.S. troops stayed in the Philippines after 1898. There they helped put down a Filipino independence movement led by Emilio Aguinaldo. The Philippines would not gain full independence from the United States until 1946.

Supporters of Imperialism   In contrast to the anti-imperialists, many other Americans took great pride in U.S. overseas colonies. They pointed out the military advantages of having these far-flung areas under the American flag. These possessions could serve as bases and fueling stations for the U.S. Navy. With an empire, U.S. business interests were now in a better position to invest and carry on trade. Supporters of imperialism claimed that some of the people living in areas taken over by the United States would benefit. For instance, the United States would introduce better farming methods as a form of economic assistance. U.S. officials would see that schools, hospitals, roads, and other public facilities were built. Supporters of colonies said that American rule might help colonial people to enjoy more personal freedoms. Supporters pointed out that the Spanish rule in Puerto Rico and the Philippines had been oppressive.

In spite of some opposition, the McKinley administration decided to keep the lands captured in 1898. The issue of imperialism became an important one in the election of 1900, with William Jennings Bryan taking a strong anti-imperalist stand. McKinley won re-election by a wide margin. His victory seemed to settle the matter in favor of forming an American empire.

SUMMING UP We have seen that the Spanish-American War had its roots in a Cuban revolt against Spain. Many people in the United States sided with the rebels. War broke out after the *Maine* and Dupuy de Lôme letter incidents of February, 1898. Because of superior naval power, the United States quickly won the war. As a result of its victory, the United States gained an empire in two world regions—the Caribbean and the Pacific.

Understanding the Text

On a separate sheet of paper, write the letter of the word or phrase that best completes each of the following statements.

1. In the late 19th century, some Americans wanted the United States to gain overseas possessions because they believed that such areas would (a) become major sources of slaves (b) otherwise fall into the hands of Communists (c) help to build up the nation's power and glory (d) become great manufacturing centers.

2. A Spanish possession in the Caribbean in the 19th century was (a) the Philippines (b) Puerto Rico (c) Hawaii (d) Alaska.

3. Spanish forces were sent to Cuba in 1895 to (a) put down a revolt against Spanish rule (b) defend the island against United States attacks (c) help Cuba in a war against Mexico (d) enforce the Monroe Doctrine.

4. Of the following examples, the one *not* a factor in leading the United States to declare war on Spain in 1898 was (a) Spanish rule in Cuba (b) "yellow journalism" (c) the Spanish attack on U.S. Navy ships at Pearl Harbor, Hawaii (d) the desire of some Americans for expansion.

5. Joseph Pulitzer and William Randolph Hearst were (a) military leaders (b) scientists (c) newspaper publishers (d) U.S. senators who favored war with Spain.

6. Of the following events, the one that took place *last* was the (a) sinking of the *Maine* (b) formal declaration of war against Spain (c) presidential election of 1900 (d) Spanish efforts to put down a rebellion in Cuba.

7. The Battle of San Juan Hill was fought in (a) Cuba (b) the Philippines (c) Spain (d) the United States.

8. As a result of the Spanish-American War, the United States took possession of all of the following, *except* (a) Puerto Rico (b) Midway Island (c) the Philippines (d) Guam.

9. After the Spanish-American War, the United States put down an insurrection by Filipinos who wanted to (a) set up an independent Filipino republic (b) bring back Spanish rule (c) become U.S. citizens (d) become part of the Japanese Empire.

10. Which of the following best describes the Spanish-American War? (a) a long, difficult, bloody conflict (b) a war fought without bloodshed (c) a quick, one-sided victory for the United States (d) a long war fought to a draw and a compromise peace.

Developing Newspaper-Reading Skills

Examine the newspaper front page reproduced on page 354. Then choose the letter of the word or phrase that best answers each of the following questions. On a separate sheet of paper, match the question number with the correct answer.

1. What is the name of the newspaper? (*a*) The New York *Journal and Advertiser* (*b*) The New York *World* (*c*) *The New York Times* (*d*) The *Maine*.

2. The front-page article was written in Washington, D.C., on (*a*) February 15, 1898 (*b*) March 21, 1898 (*c*) March 22, 1898 (*d*) none of the above.

3. How many pages long was this issue of the newspaper? (*a*) one (*b*) 16 (*c*) 1,168 (*d*) this information not available on the front page.

4. John M. Thurston was a/an (*a*) U.S. senator (*b*) author of the front-page article (*c*) member of a group of Americans who visited Cuba (*d*) all of the above.

5. The article indicates that (*a*) Spain was in firm control of all of Cuba (*b*) the United States was intervening in Cuba (*c*) Cuban rebels were still strong (*d*) the Commission that visited Cuba sympathized with the Spanish.

Thinking About the Lesson

1. Do you think that President McKinley and Congress should have avoided war with Spain in 1898? Why or why not?

2. Why was the Spanish-American War over so quickly?

3. Was the United States right to have kept control of Puerto Rico, Guam, and the Philippines after seizing them from Spain during the war? Explain your answer.

UNIT 6

AMERICAN POLITICS IN THE 20TH CENTURY

American Presidents in the Progressive Era, 1901–1921

During the first two decades of the 20th century, Americans from many different backgrounds worked for economic and social reforms. Historians refer to these activities as "the Progressive movement" and to the years from 1901 to 1921 as "the Progressive era." Three men served as President during these years—Theodore Roosevelt, William Howard Taft, and Woodrow Wilson. Roosevelt and Wilson were key leaders of the Progressive movement. Taft also was responsible for a number of reforms.

Theodore Roosevelt (1901–1909)

In 1900, Republicans chose Theodore Roosevelt to run for Vice President on the ticket with William McKinley. This Republican team won in November, and Roosevelt became President six months later when President McKinley was assassinated.

Theodore Roosevelt turned out to be one of the nation's most active and powerful Presidents. When he took office, he was only 42 years old—the youngest person ever to serve as President.

Roosevelt brought with him a long career in public service. He had served as a New York State legislator, the New York City Police Commissioner, and Governor of New York. As Assistant Secretary of the U.S. Navy, he had helped make the country's naval forces larger and stronger. Many Americans knew about his experiences leading volunteers in the Spanish-American War. He was also well-known as a naturalist and writer.

"Teddy," as he was called, became a popular President. In 1904, when he ran against the Democratic presidential candidate, Alton B. Parker, he was easily re-elected. In all, he served more than seven years in the White House.

Historians give Theodore Roosevelt "high marks" for his performance as President for a number of reasons:

Leadership Roosevelt, as President, was a strong leader. He believed that the President should develop solutions to the nation's problems. He actively explained his ideas to the public and pushed Congress to transform his ideas into legislation.

Reform He called for giving a *square deal* (fair treatment) to the average American. Thus, his legislative reform program became known as the "Square Deal."

Theodore Roosevelt was an energetic speaker. Here he captivates a crowd in Evanston, Illinois, in 1903.

As President, Roosevelt became known as a *trustbuster* (one who seeks to break up business monopolies). Under his leadership, the federal government brought to court large corporations that had violated antitrust laws. The courts ordered several trusts to be broken up into smaller businesses. The railroads and meat-packing companies, for example, were among the main targets.

Roosevelt supported the Pure Food and Drug Act and the Meat Inspection Act, both passed by Congress in 1906. The first act made illegal the shipment or sale of impure, dangerous, or mislabeled products across state lines. The second act called for federal inspection of meat shipped across state lines. Federal inspectors were to make sure that this meat was healthy.

Theodore Roosevelt also made important contributions to the movement for *conservation* (preserving the environment). The President helped set aside valuable forest and mineral lands as national reserves. During his administration, Congress created the U.S. Forest Service to manage the national forests.

Nationalism Roosevelt wanted his country to play a major role in world affairs. With an enlarged U.S. Navy, he expanded the nation's influence in Caribbean countries and in Latin America. To further America's power and prestige, he urged that the country begin constructing the Panama Canal. (Roosevelt's foreign policy is discussed in Lesson 76.)

Election of 1908

Although he was probably popular enough to win again, Roosevelt declined to run for a third term in 1908. His personal choice, William Howard Taft, became the Republican party's candidate for President. The Democrat William Jennings Bryan ran for President for the third time. Taft won the election, getting about a million votes more than Bryan.

Eugene V. Debs, the Socialist party candidate, came in third with 400,000 votes. He had been the leader of the American Railway Union during the Pullman strike. (See Lesson 48.) In all, Debs ran for President five times—in 1900, 1904, 1908, 1912, and 1920. In 1920, he received over 900,000 votes, even though he was serving time in a federal prison.

William Howard Taft (1909–1913)

Taft had gained experience as a federal judge, civil governor of the Philippines, and Roosevelt's Secretary of War. As President, he was less willing to call for reforms and less ready to provide strong leadership than Roosevelt had been. Nevertheless, the Taft administration did take some steps in favor of reform:

• The federal government aided the cause of conservation. It took millions of acres of mineral lands and waterpower sites out of private hands.

These areas then became part of the *national domain* (land owned by the federal government).

• The civil service merit system was extended to cover more federal jobs, including the position of postmaster.

• The Justice Department continued to take to court trusts that it considered monopolies. The courts ordered Standard Oil, American Tobacco, and other companies to *dissolve* (break up) into two or more separate corporations.

Foreign Policy In 1912, Taft sent military forces to Nicaragua to protect American businesses there. Some of his critics called this policy "dollar diplomacy." They were referring to the use of American foreign policy to encourage or protect American investments abroad.

Taft had never really wanted to be President. Some years after he left the White House, Taft got the position that he had wanted all along. He became Chief Justice of the United States. Taft is the only person to have served as both U.S. President and Chief Justice.

Election of 1912

The 1912 presidential election was unusual in that it was a fairly close three-way race. In addition, all three major candidates promised more reforms and the continued regulation of businesses.

Although Taft was renominated by the Republican party, many Republicans thought he was too conservative. These Republicans joined with other reformers to form the Progressive "Bull Moose" party. They ran Theodore Roosevelt as their presidential candidate. The term "Bull Moose" arose from a statement Roosevelt made during the election campaign. He told a reporter, "I'm feeling like a bull moose."

The Democrats chose Woodrow Wilson, a former college president and, at the time, Governor of New Jersey. Wilson was also a noted student of history and government, whose books in these fields were widely read.

Because the Republicans split between Taft and Roosevelt, Wilson won the election.

President Taft is shown throwing out the first ball in a baseball game on June 9, 1910, in Washington, D.C.

As the button above illustrates, Woodrow Wilson campaigned for re-election in 1916 as a peace candidate. By 1917, however, world events forced Wilson to urge Congress to declare war. The U.S. government produced posters (right) that urged young men to enlist in the Armed Forces.

Woodrow Wilson (1913–1921)

Wilson had been born in Virginia. He was the first Southerner to be elected President since Zachary Taylor in 1848. (President Andrew Johnson had come from Tennessee but had not been elected to the nation's highest office.) Wilson's election was unusual for another reason. He was only the second Democrat to hold this office since Reconstruction.

New Freedom Wilson was a reformer who believed that the Chief Executive should be a national leader. As President, he launched a many-sided reform program which he called the "New Freedom":

• In 1913, Congress set up a new central banking system, the Federal Reserve System. The "Fed," as the system is called, consists of 12 district banks, each of which works closely with commercial banks in its district. The Fed is supervised by the Federal Reserve Board, whose members are appointed by the President. The Board works closely with the government to make the nation's currency more stable.

• Tariff duties were reduced by the Underwood Act of 1913.

• In 1914, the government's antitrust program was made stronger when Congress passed the Clayton Act. This law stated more clearly than before what was meant by "business combinations in restraint of trade." It also told what actions the government could take against these combinations. The Clayton Act helped organized workers by saying that labor unions could not be sued under the antitrust laws.

• A five-member Federal Trade Commission was created in 1914 to look into unfair business practices. The FTC was given the power to make businesses stop some of these practices. It could bring businesses to court if they failed to follow FTC orders.

• In 1916, special Land Banks were set up to make loans to farmers at low interest rates.

• A 1916 law set an eight-hour workday for employees of railroads that crossed state lines.

• Another law of that year provided civil service employees with *workers' compensation* (special pay to workers who are injured on the job and cannot work again).

Constitutional Amendments The states ratified a number of constitutional amendments during Wilson's two terms:

• The Sixteenth Amendment (1913) allowed the federal government for the first time to place taxes on the incomes of individuals and corporations. Wealthy people and businesses now had to pay a greater share of the total tax burden than before. The income tax has become the federal government's leading source of tax revenue.
• The Seventeenth Amendment (1913) called for the direct election of U.S. senators by the voters. Previously, state legislatures had elected senators.
• The Eighteenth Amendment (1919) banned the manufacture, sale, and transportation of alcoholic beverages. This *prohibition* (ban) ended in 1933 when the Twenty-first Amendment was ratified.
• The Nineteenth Amendment (1920) gave women voting rights on the same basis as men. (Discussed further in Lesson 74.)

Election of 1916 and Wilson's Second Term

Those who supported Wilson's re-election in 1916 pointed to his record of domestic reforms. They also made use of the slogan "He kept us out of war." (World War I had begun in Europe in 1914.) Wilson's Republican opponent was Charles Evans Hughes, a Supreme Court justice and former Governor of New York. Since Roosevelt decided not to run again, Wilson had no opponent from the Progressive party. Wilson easily won re-election in 1916.

Wilson's Foreign Policy Foreign policy issues often overshadowed domestic issues during Wilson's second term. Within a month of his inauguration, the country entered World War I. In 1917 and 1918, Wilson and other national leaders were busy with the war effort. They did not consider reforms to be as important as measures designed to help win the war. (World War I is discussed in Lesson 77.)

Wilson's Health Another reason that Wilson did not push for many reforms in his second term was his poor health. In 1919, he suffered a paralyzing stroke from which he never fully recovered.

Other Reforms of the Progressive Era

As a result of the work of reformers, steps were taken to improve state and city government.

Better Government Several reforms helped make it possible for the average citizen in a number of cities and states to take part in government more directly. Under the *direct primary*, members of a political party could choose the party's nominees for office through a popular election. Before, nominations had been made by party leaders. Under the *initiative*, citizens could take steps to introduce laws that they wanted a legislature to consider. Under the *referendum*, certain bills passed by lawmaking bodies had to be referred to the voters for approval before going into effect. The *recall* allowed voters to take steps to remove officials whom they no longer wanted in office.

Reformers Leaders of reform movements came from many walks of life. Included in their number were political leaders such as governors Robert LaFollette of Wisconsin, Charles Evans Hughes of New York, and Hiram Johnson of California. Writers such as Frank Norris, Ida Tarbell, and Lincoln Steffens (all discussed in Lesson 64) exposed corruption in politics and business. Perhaps the leading reform figure was Jane Addams, who established in Chicago the country's first settlement house, discussed in Lesson 49.

SUMMING UP   We have seen that many Americans from 1901 to 1921 were deeply concerned with solving some of the country's domestic problems. These people made up the Progressive movement. Because of their own views and actions, Presidents Theodore Roosevelt and Woodrow Wilson became leaders of the movement. William Howard Taft, too, was responsible for several reforms and is considered by some to have been a Progressive.

Understanding the Text

On a separate sheet of paper, write the letter of the word or phrase that best completes each of the following statements.

1. The Progressive era occurred (a) early in the 19th century (b) early in the 20th century (c) late in the 19th century (d) late in the 20th century.

2. All of the following were Presidents during the Progressive era, *except* (a) Theodore Roosevelt (b) Woodrow Wilson (c) William Howard Taft (d) Benjamin Harrison.

3. The title of "trustbuster" best refers to Theodore Roosevelt's attitude toward (a) a large navy (b) abuses by big businesses (c) the German government (d) the need for conservation of natural resources.

4. Theodore Roosevelt's reform program was known as the (a) Square Deal (b) New Freedom (c) New Deal (d) New Frontier.

5. Eugene V. Debs was (a) a reform governor of New York State (b) Chief Justice of the United States (c) a Socialist candidate for President (d) the candidate of big businesses in the election of 1912.

6. The only person to serve as both U.S. President and Chief Justice was (a) William Howard Taft (b) Woodrow Wilson (c) Theodore Roosevelt (d) Charles Evans Hughes.

7. Of the following events, the one that occurred during the Taft administration was the (a) passage of the Meat Inspection Act (b) establishment of the U.S. Forest Service (c) breakup of the Standard Oil and American Tobacco trusts (d) outbreak of the Spanish-American War.

8. In the election of 1912, Wilson was aided by the fact that the Republican vote was split between (a) Taft and McKinley (b) Theodore Roosevelt and Franklin Delano Roosevelt (c) Theodore Roosevelt and Taft (d) Debs and McKinley.

9. All of the following took place during Wilson's terms as President, *except* the (a) start of World War I (b) passage of the Pure Food and Drug Act (c) strengthening of the antitrust laws (d) founding of the Federal Reserve System.

10. Which of the following is the most accurate statement about U.S. Presidents during the Progressive era? (a) They solved the nation's major problems. (b) They prevented the United States from becoming involved in a major war. (c) They helped bring about political and economic changes that have continued to be important down to the present time. (d) They created a lot of excitement but accomplished little of lasting value.

Developing Graph-Reading Skills

POPULAR VOTE IN PRESIDENTIAL ELECTIONS, 1900–1916

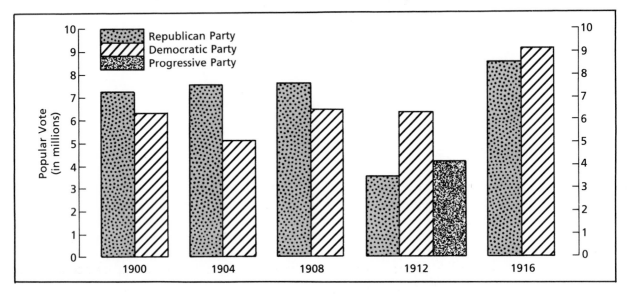

Study the bar graph above. Then answer the following True-False questions. On a separate sheet of paper, number from one to five. Write *T* if the sentence is true, *F* if it is false, and *I* if there is insufficient information to answer the question.

1. The Republican party received more popular votes than the Democrats in all five presidential elections.

2. The Democrats received the greatest number of popular votes in the election of 1912.

3. The combined Republican and Progressive vote in 1912 was greater than the Democratic vote.

4. In 1908, the Republicans received about 80 percent of the electoral vote.

5. The combined popular vote for the Democrats and Republicans in 1900 was over 10 million.

Thinking About the Lesson

1. Why are the years from 1901 to 1921 often called the "Progressive era"? Can you think of any other adjectives to describe this period in American history?

2. On a scale of one to ten (with ten being the greatest), how would you rate Presidents Theodore Roosevelt, William Howard Taft, and Woodrow Wilson? Explain your answers.

3. If you had been a registered voter in 1916, would you have voted to re-elect Wilson? Why or why not?

LESSON 58

Presidents, Parties, and Programs, 1921–1933

From 1921 to 1933, the Republicans controlled Congress, and Republican Presidents were in the White House. Presidents Warren G. Harding, Calvin Coolidge, and Herbert Hoover were all conservatives. They reflected the general conservative mood of the country and advocated policies that were favorable to business. Some reform activities continued in America in the 1920s, but these took place mostly on the state and local levels.

Warren G. Harding (1921–1923)

Woodrow Wilson wanted to run for a third term in 1920, but other Democratic leaders opposed this idea. They were convinced that he was too ill to serve again. The Democrats, however, did agree to his wish that the party campaign in favor of having the United States join the League of Nations. In the summer of 1920, the Democratic party nominated James M. Cox, a former Governor of Ohio. Cox was best known for his opposition to prohibition.

The Republicans also nominated an Ohioan—Senator Warren G. Harding. In his campaign, Harding called for a "return to normalcy." He

believed that most Americans were tired of both calls for reform and disruptions caused by World War I. The Republican platform included promises of lower taxes, higher tariffs, aid to farmers, and restriction on further immigration.

Harding won with 61 percent of the popular vote. The Republicans did very well also in Senate and House races, capturing control of both houses of Congress.

Accomplishments of the Harding Administration The Republicans carried out some of their campaign promises during Harding's years in office:

• The Emergency Quota Act of 1921 sharply cut immigration from the large numbers of the pre-war years. Under this law, each country could send to the United States only a *quota* (fixed share of a total number) of immigrants. (Discussed further in Lesson 70.)

• The government lowered some federal taxes from their high wartime levels. Moreover, it lowered the national debt. This feat was made possible by much lower government spending. The newly created Bureau of the Budget helped watch spending by taking over the work of planning federal income and expenses.

367

By posing in the White House garden, President Harding provided a "photo opportunity" for newspaper photographers.

• Higher tariffs resulted from the Fordney-McCumber Tariff Act of 1922. The tariffs had the effect of keeping out of the country imports that would have competed with American-made products. As a result, the prices of many domestic items rose greatly. Other nations followed America's lead by raising their own tariff rates.

Another important accomplishment of the Harding years was the creation of the Veterans' Bureau, now called the Veterans' Administration. This Bureau began constructing hospitals for disabled and ill former soldiers.

Scandals Harding's reputation suffered because of several major scandals involving some of his close advisers. Two of the worst of these scandals concerned the following:

• Charles Forbes, the Veterans' Bureau Director, resigned his job in 1923 after being accused of stealing federal money. The illegal actions occurred in connection with the construction of new veterans' hospitals.
• In 1923, Albert Fall, Harding's Secretary of the Interior, was accused of accepting bribes from people who leased federal oil reserves. The affair was named the "Teapot Dome Scandal" because one of the oil reserves was located at Teapot Dome, Wyoming.

Some Americans blamed the President for these scandals, saying that Harding had shown bad judgment in choosing advisers. Before all the scandals became public, President Harding fell ill and died in the summer of 1923.

Calvin Coolidge (1923–1929)

Vice President Coolidge, a former Governor of Massachusetts, became President after Harding died. Coolidge kept many of Harding's Cabinet officers, but not those involved in scandals. He also continued many of Harding's conservative policies, working for:

• Further reductions in taxes.
• Additional attempts to balance the budget by cutting spending.
• More restrictions on immigration.

Coolidge followed Harding's example when he vetoed a "bonus bill" that Congress had passed. The 1924 bill would have given each veteran of World War I a *bonus* (extra money) for serving in the Armed Forces. Both Harding and Coolidge thought that these bonuses would cost the government too much money.

Election of 1924 The popular Coolidge was the natural candidate of the Republicans in the 1924

PRESIDENTIAL ELECTIONS OF 1920 AND 1924

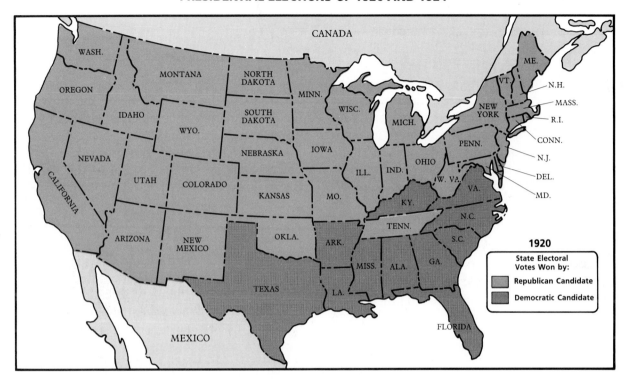

1920

State Electoral
Votes Won by:

- Republican Candidate
- Democratic Candidate

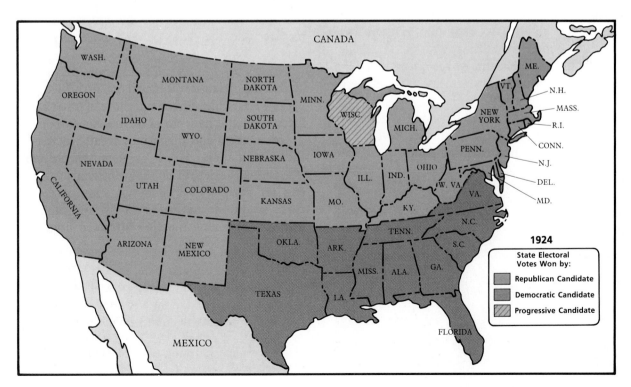

1924

State Electoral
Votes Won by:

- Republican Candidate
- Democratic Candidate
- Progressive Candidate

presidential election. The Democrats nominated John W. Davis, a wealthy lawyer from New York City. In many ways, he was as conservative as Coolidge.

A third candidate in the 1924 election, Robert M. LaFollette, stood firmly in favor of reforms. Both the Independent-Progressive party and the Socialists endorsed him. For a third-party candidate, this U.S. senator and former Governor of Wisconsin made a strong showing. LaFollette received almost 5 million votes.

Most American voters, however, were apparently satisfied with Coolidge's performance. He won the election by a landslide.

The Coolidge Presidency While serving as President, Coolidge purposely did little to make changes. Since the country was prosperous, he was content to see things stay the way they were. He vetoed several measures with which he thought the government should not be involved:

• The McNary-Haugen Farm Relief Bill. Many farmers suffered badly from declining income throughout the 1920s. In addition, farmers were producing more than they could sell. The Relief Bill would have had the government buy *farm surpluses* (products that farmers could not sell) and sell them abroad.
• A congressional bill to develop the economy of a vast region along the Tennessee River. This plan, which involved building dams to generate

electricity, was adopted in the 1930s. (Discussed in the next lesson.)

Several measures that did become law during Coolidge's administration had to do with new industries.

• In 1926, the Air Commerce Act provided for the regulation of commercial airlines by the Commerce Department.
• In 1927, the young but growing radio industry came under the control of the Federal Radio Commission.

The Golden Twenties

The years of the Harding and Coolidge administrations are sometimes called the "Golden Twenties." As we look back on these years, they seem a satisfying, even hopeful time. The "Model T" Ford and other automobiles put the nation on wheels. Americans spent more time and money on recreation than ever before. They enjoyed new forms of popular music, such as jazz, and dances based on this music. Moving pictures and the radio became extremely popular.

Charles A. Lindbergh's nonstop, solo flight across the Atlantic Ocean in 1927 thrilled the nation. His achievement and those of other early fliers opened a new era of air transportation.

Newspapers and magazines greatly increased their circulation. Some of them emphasized sensational stories, often featuring murder trials and the private lives of movie stars. A sports craze swept the nation. Football and baseball games and boxing matches attracted huge audiences.

Social Changes During the 1920s, new images and roles for women developed. The growing use of canned goods, the vacuum cleaner, and the washing machine freed many women from

These campaign buttons of 1924 helped President Calvin Coolidge stay in the White House for four more years.

routine household work. As a result, more and more women entered the job market. Daring young women, called "flappers," shocked their elders by wearing short skirts, bobbing their hair, and using cosmetics.

Prohibition The 1920s was also the era of *prohibition*. The Eighteenth Amendment, ratified in 1919, resulted in laws prohibiting the manufacture, transport, and sale of alcoholic drinks. Nevertheless, vast numbers of Americans, most of them normally law-abiding citizens, paid little attention to prohibition laws. These people bought liquor from *bootleggers* (illegal sellers) and drank in *speakeasies* (illegal bars). The illegal manufacture and sale of liquor came to be largely controlled by organized crime figures.

Economic Prosperity The U.S. economy in the 1920s was on the upswing. Owners of businesses, encouraged by the conservative policies of the Republicans, expanded their firms. Stock market prices reached new highs. Of course, not everyone shared in the prosperity. Many workers complained of low wages, and many farmers had a hard time meeting their mortgage payments. In spite of their struggles, even those who were not doing well often had strong hopes for their future.

Election of 1928

Calvin Coolidge announced in 1928 that he did not want to run for another term. Therefore, the Republican party nominated his successful Secretary of Commerce, Herbert Hoover. He had become well-known for his wartime work, organizing the sending of food to Belgium and other European countries. After the United States had entered the war, Hoover had headed the U.S. Food Administration. This agency had

PRESIDENTIAL ELECTION OF 1928

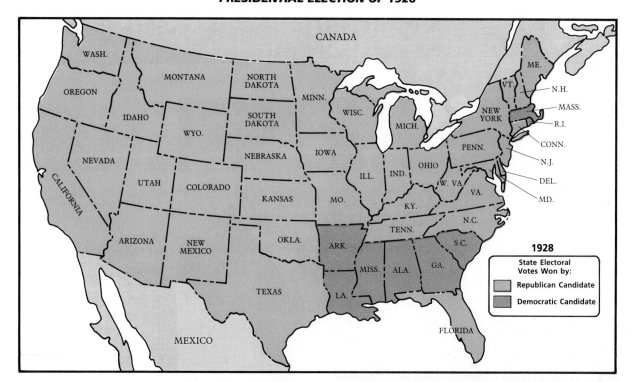

made important decisions about what food should be produced, where it should be sold, and at what price.

In 1928, the Democrats put up a strong opponent, the Governor of New York, Alfred E. Smith. He became the first Roman Catholic to be nominated for President by a major party. Some Americans may have voted against Smith because he was Catholic; some, because he was against prohibition. Hoover won the election, though, chiefly because many Americans believed that the Republicans had made the country prosperous.

Herbert Hoover (1929–1933)

Hoover, himself a millionaire, had the confidence of business leaders when he took office in 1929. Factory production was moving at record rates, and most people thought that the economy was healthy.

American farmers, however, were still suffering from low prices for farm goods and from large debts. In the presidential campaign, Hoover had promised farmers several measures, including a protective tariff for agricultural goods. As President, he tried to make good on his promises:

• In 1929, Congress passed and the President approved the Agricultural Marketing Act. This law provided for federal loans to farm cooperatives. In cooperatives, groups of farmers would buy farm surpluses at low prices and store them until prices were high again. In 1930, the government's farm program was expanded. Additional organizations were set up to buy surplus grain and cotton.

• Farmers got their protective tariff in 1930. The Hawley-Smoot Tariff turned out to be one of the highest in American history. It protected manufactured goods as well as farm products. Foreign nations reacted to the tariff by passing their own high tariffs to keep out American goods. As a result, U.S. foreign trade suffered.

Stock Market Crash The beginning of the worst economic depression in the nation's history darkened the Hoover years in the White House. The causes of the Great Depression were worldwide and could be traced back many years. Still, events in October, 1929, were instrumental in starting the decline. That month the value of stocks began a sharp decline, one that continued

Radio was introduced into many American homes in the 1920s. Herbert Hoover took advantage of that fact in his 1928 campaign for the Presidency.

for several years. The beginning of this decline was called the *Stock Market Crash*. Individual stockholders quickly lost fortunes as they scrambled to sell their stocks before prices went any lower. After the crash, many Americans went to their banks to withdraw their money. Soon the banks ran out of funds and had to close, leaving other depositors penniless.

Many businesses, lacking capital and experiencing declining sales, fired some of their employees or closed their doors. The numerous unemployed could not find new jobs. Many resorted to selling apples on street corners or standing in breadlines.

Hoover's Programs   Hoover believed in "rugged individualism," the idea that people should be able to get along on their own, with little governmental aid. At first, therefore, Hoover did little to fight the depression. Later, however, as the unemployment rate grew, the President called for some programs to help businesses, workers, and farmers. To some extent, Hoover was pushed into action by the Democrats, who by 1930 had taken control of the House of Representatives.

Some of the steps taken by Hoover and Congress to fight the Great Depression included:

• A program of public works to employ thousands of Americans. Public works projects involved the construction of highways, post offices, parks, and dams. One of the largest projects, Boulder Dam (later named "Hoover Dam"), was started in 1930.

• The creation of the Reconstruction Finance Corporation. This government agency, set up by Congress in 1932, made large loans to banks and other businesses.

• Additional help to farmers in the form of loans at low rates of interest.

These emergency measures failed to reverse the economic decline. During the presidential election of 1932, Hoover and his administration were criticized for doing "too little, too late."

SUMMING UP   We have seen that conservative views dominated politics during the period 1921–1933. Presidents Harding and Coolidge gained the goodwill of business leaders by calling for lower taxes, reduced spending, and higher tariffs. Compared to other periods in American history, the country prospered. Hoover also advocated conservative policies, but during his administration the country went into a deep economic depression. Although he tried to reverse the economic decline, he failed and was blamed for the country's problems.

Understanding the Text

On a separate sheet of paper, write the letter of the word or phrase that best completes each of the following statements.

1. The phrase "return to normalcy" best applies to the Presidency of (a) Woodrow Wilson (b) Warren G. Harding (c) Calvin Coolidge (d) Herbert Hoover.

2. The U.S. Presidents elected in the 1920s were (a) all Democrats (b) all Republicans (c) all Progressives (d) none of the above.

3. An event that did *not* occur during Harding's years as President was a (a) cut in the number of immigrants (b) lowering of federal taxes (c) lowering of tariffs (d) reduction in federal spending.

4. The newly created Veterans' Bureau (a) balanced the federal government's budget (b) ran hospitals for former soldiers (c) sold rights to U.S. oil reserves (d) bought and sold farm surpluses.

5. The Vice President who became President on the death of Warren G. Harding was (a) Franklin D. Roosevelt (b) Theodore Roosevelt (c) Herbert Hoover (d) Calvin Coolidge.

6. Charles A. Lindbergh excited the country by (a) playing jazz music (b) becoming the heavyweight boxing champion (c) flying alone in an airplane, nonstop across the Atlantic Ocean (d) performing on the radio.

7. The third-party candidate for President who in 1924 received almost 5 million votes, was (a) Robert M. LaFollette (b) James M. Cox (c) John W. Davis (d) Alfred E. Smith.

8. In 1928, Herbert Hoover (a) ran for President on the Republican ticket (b) had already become a millionaire (c) was Secretary of Commerce (d) all of the above.

9. By 1932, President Hoover was widely blamed for (a) sending too much food to Europe (b) failing to bring about economic recovery (c) causing the Teapot Dome scandal (d) all of the above.

10. The presidential administrations from 1921 to 1933 were, in general, most favorable to (a) businesses (b) labor unions (c) immigrants (d) reformers.

Developing Map Skills

Study the three maps on pages 369 and 371. Then choose the letter of the word or phrase that best completes each sentence. On a separate sheet of paper, match the sentence number with the correct letter.

1. In all three elections, the Democratic candidate was strongest in the (a) Northeast (b) Midwest (c) West (d) South.

2. The Progressive party won all of the electoral votes of one state in the election of (a) 1920 (b) 1924 (c) 1928 (d) none of the above.

3. In the 1928 presidential election, Texas gave its electoral votes to the (a) Republicans (b) Democrats (c) Progressives (d) Free Soilers.

4. In all three elections, the Republicans carried all of the states in the (a) Northeast (b) Far West (c) Midwest (d) South.

5. An example of a state that voted for the same party in all three elections is (a) Wisconsin (b) Massachusetts (c) Arkansas (d) North Carolina.

Thinking About the Lesson

1. Why did many American business leaders like the policies of the Republican Congresses and Presidents in the 1920s?

Franklin D. Roosevelt and the New Deal Era, 1933–1945

Franklin D. Roosevelt served as President during a troubled period in American history, from 1933 to 1945. During his first two terms, the government was trying to pull the nation out of the Great Depression. During Roosevelt's later years, the country was busy fighting in the Second World War.

Election of 1932

The election of 1932 took place during the worst depression in American history. Thousands of businesses and banks had failed. Twelve million workers—about 25 percent of the total—had lost their jobs. Factories and stores had shut down. Trade with other nations had almost come to a halt. Farm prices had fallen to new lows. The unemployed were selling apples on street corners, eating in "soup kitchens," and living in "shantytowns," popularly called "Hoovervilles." By 1932, desperate farmers were using pitchforks to prevent their farms and homes from being taken away for nonpayment of farm mortgages. All across the land, Americans were calling for radical action.

Despite considerable dissatisfaction with Herbert Hoover, the Republicans in 1932 kept him as their presidential candidate. For them to do otherwise would be to imply that Republican policies were not working.

The Democrats put forward Franklin D. Roosevelt, the Governor of New York and former Assistant Secretary of the Navy. This Roosevelt, a distant cousin of Theodore Roosevelt, had become known nationally when he ran for Vice President in 1920. In the next year, he contracted polio. For the rest of his life he would be unable to walk without aid. Nevertheless, he did not give up his interest in politics. In 1928, he won election to the position of Governor of New York.

"FDR," as Roosevelt was called, campaigned actively for President in 1932. Promising a "New Deal for the forgotten man," he won a decisive victory. An important reason for the Democratic victory was that voters blamed the Republicans for failing to bring about economic recovery. In contrast to Hoover, FDR would resort to massive government intervention in the economy.

The New Deal

As President, Roosevelt launched his New Deal programs, designed to bring back prosperity.

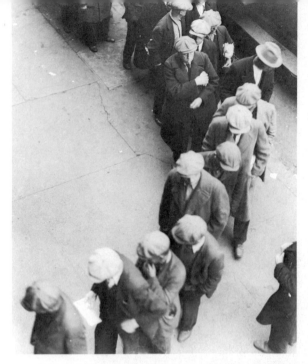

With millions of Americans unemployed, unemployment lines became a common sight in the 1930s.

His aims can be summed up in three words— relief, recovery, and reform:

• Relief to ease the suffering of millions of Americans.

• Recovery from economic collapse, so that the country's economic machinery would run again.

• Reform to prevent future breakdowns in the economy.

Roosevelt appealed to Congress and the American public to cooperate in order to reach these three goals. He called Congress into special session in March, 1933. Then in a series of radio broadcasts, called "Fireside Chats," Roosevelt explained what measures he thought needed to be taken.

Early New Deal Measures

In 1933, Congress adopted many emergency measures to provide immediate relief. Some of the early measures also helped in the economic recovery and provided long-term reforms.

New Banking Laws During the depression, rumors spread that the nation's banks were unsafe. Fearful for the safety of their deposits, depositors by the thousands withdrew their savings. Unable to meet the demands for funds, many banks closed or failed. Upon coming into office, FDR declared a four-day "bank holiday," temporarily suspending all banking operations. Meanwhile, Congress took emergency steps to have banks checked for soundness. By the time the banks did reopen, Americans had gained more confidence that their bank deposits were safe. Later in 1933, Congress set up the Federal Deposit Insurance Corporation. By insuring individual bank deposits up to $5,000, the FDIC increased public confidence in the banks even more. Several other laws were passed to regulate banking practices and to help reopen banks that had failed.

Help for the Unemployed Congress set up the Civilian Conservation Corps to hire hundreds of thousands of unemployed young men. Among other activities, the CCC built dams, planted trees, and drained swamps. The Public Works Administration also provided jobs, but less directly. The PWA gave contracts to private companies to construct many bridges, government buildings, and other public works. These companies, in turn, hired more employees to do the construction work.

Aid to Farmers Under the Agricultural Adjustment Act, farmers were given payments for agreeing to farm fewer acres. The law aimed to reduce farm surpluses. The administrators of the program hoped that without surpluses, farm prices might rise.

Regional Aid All of the states were given federal funds that were to be distributed to poor families. People in the Tennessee River Valley, in the Southeastern part of the country, got a special program. The Tennessee Valley Authority (TVA) built many dams to provide inexpensive electricity for the people and industries in the region. The dams also helped to prevent flooding and provided water for irrigation. (See the map on page 447.)

Help for Businesses The Reconstruction Finance Corporation, started under President Hoover, continued to loan money to businesses to help them expand. Businesses were also helped by the National Industrial Recovery Act (NIRA) of 1933. Under this act, businesses were asked to work together to keep prices low and to provide more jobs.

Antitrust laws were temporarily set aside as business leaders were urged to cooperate with the government in setting up industry-wide Codes of Fair Competition. These codes set wages, hours in the workweek, prices, and production in different industries. In 1935, however, the Supreme Court declared the NIRA unconstitutional. It said that Congress and the President did not have the power to approve such codes.

Reform of the Stock Exchange Many economists believed that dangerous practices on the *stock exchanges* had helped cause the crash of 1929. (Stock exchanges are places where stocks are bought and sold.) A 1933 law required that companies selling stocks disclose more information about themselves to potential investors. In 1934, a new agency, the Securities and Exchange Commission (SEC), took over the regulation of the stock exchanges.

Later New Deal Programs

After the first burst of legislation in 1933, Congress slowed down in its passage of New Deal laws. Nevertheless, a number of important measures became law in the following years:

• Social Security Act of 1935. This act was perhaps the most important single law of the New Deal. The act set up a national system of retirement pensions for the aged. It also provided an insurance program for workers to receive benefits if they became unemployed.

• The National Labor Relations Act (Wagner Act). This law of 1935 guaranteed workers the right to form unions and to *bargain collectively* (negotiate as a group) with employers. (This act is discussed further in Lesson 65.)

• The Fair Labor Standards Act of 1938. This law set minimum hourly wages and the maximum number of hours in a workweek for many

As one means to combat unemployment, the government hired work crews to improve parks.

American workers. It also barred the hiring of children under age 16 in many workplaces.

• Works Progress Administration. In 1935, the government organized the Works Progress Administration (WPA) to conduct an even larger program of building schools, sewage systems, and other public works. The WPA also hired writers to write books and plays, actors to act, and artists to paint and sculpt. The WPA provided hundreds of thousands of jobs. Its projects proved useful to many communities.

The Supreme Court and the New Deal

President Roosevelt was displeased when the Supreme Court declared several New Deal measures unconstitutional. Believing that the Court was too conservative, he decided that one way to change its rulings was to add new, more progressive members to it. He proposed to Congress a law that would add up to six more justices. Many members of Congress and the American public disliked this idea. They thought that the President was tampering with the federal government's delicate system of checks and balances. As a result, Roosevelt's so-called "Court-packing" scheme was never approved or carried out. In time, the President was able to name new Supreme Court justices to replace those who retired or died. The new justices were more sympathetic to the New Deal.

Re-Election of Roosevelt

Franklin D. Roosevelt was one of the nation's most popular Presidents. He was able to win the backing of many different political and economic groups. His supporters included blue-collar workers, members of many ethnic minorities, southern Democrats, and Democratic organizations in the big cities.

• In 1936, Roosevelt easily won re-election, beating Alfred Landon of Kansas.

After contracting polio at age 39, Franklin D. Roosevelt often used a wheelchair.

• In 1940, Roosevelt won again, this time defeating Wendell Willkie, a Republican lawyer from New York.

• In 1944, while the country was deeply involved in World War II, Roosevelt ran for a fourth term. In this election, Republicans nominated Thomas Dewey, the Governor of New York. Again Roosevelt won.

Roosevelt's election to four terms showed that he had inspired the confidence and affection of most Americans. Some historians believe that FDR's successes grew out of the needs of the time for a strong leader.

Criticism of the New Deal

Many Americans believed that the New Deal was a good thing. They felt that it was helping to solve many of the nation's ills and was bringing about economic recovery.

Critics of the New Deal, mainly Republicans, found much to criticize. They believed that the federal government was spending too much money. They claimed that it had taken too much power into its own hands, at the expense of state and local governments. They asserted that the New Deal was not really solving the country's economic problems, as shown by the fact that unemployment rose again in 1937 and 1938. Roosevelt was also strongly criticized for running for a third and fourth term. He broke a tradition set by George Washington, who had refused to run more than twice. (A number of years later, in 1951, the Twenty-second Amendment, restricting Presidents to two terms in office, was ratified.)

Popular or not, one thing was certain. The New Deal of Franklin D. Roosevelt made important changes in many areas of American life. These changes are still with us—over half a century later.

Other Developments of the Roosevelt Administration

In addition to the New Deal, several other important reforms were passed during Roosevelt's years in office.

Repeal of Prohibition The Twenty-first Amendment to the Constitution, ratified in 1933, repealed the Eighteenth. As a result, the ban on the making, sale, and transportation of alcoholic drinks was no longer the law of the land.

Tariffs Lowered By the Reciprocal Trade Agreements Act of 1934, the President gained the right to make tariff agreements with other countries. During the next several years, the United States negotiated trade treaties with 21 nations. In these treaties, the United States agreed to lower tariffs on goods coming from these countries. The 21 countries, in turn, lowered tariffs on U.S. products.

Gold Standard Dropped The United States, which had gone on the gold standard in 1900, went off it in 1933. Roosevelt believed that by lowering the value of the country's currency, prices would rise. Rising prices were supposed to stimulate businesses to expand and hire more workers.

World War II

The Second World War broke out in Europe in 1939. The United States did not officially enter the conflict until 1941, when Japanese bombers attacked Pearl Harbor, Hawaii.

From 1941 until his death in 1945, President Roosevelt attended mainly to the task of winning the war. Together with the leaders of Great Britain and the Soviet Union, he made plans that eventually led to an Allied victory. (World War II is discussed in detail in Lesson 79.) Because of U.S. involvement in the war, programs to deal with important domestic issues were put on the back burner. Many of the country's economic problems became less severe anyway. Heavy government spending involved in the war effort helped the economy to recover.

The Home Front During World War II

From 1941 to 1945, most Americans joined in the war effort with enthusiasm and unity:

• About 15 million men and women left civilian life to join the U.S. Armed Forces. (Of this number, 10 million men were drafted.)
• Industries quickly converted to war production. Factories produced vast numbers of airplanes, tanks, and other military equipment.
• Millions of women joined the work force, taking over many jobs previously thought suitable only for men.
• Farmers stepped up their production of food and other materials for both the United States and its Allies.

• The federal government introduced *wage and price controls*. Under these new rules, prices for goods and services could not go above certain levels. Moreover, workers could not be paid wages above set amounts. Labor unions cooperated with industries by pledging not to strike during the war.

• The government set up *rationing* to make sure that everyone got a fair share of scarce goods. Rationing applied to both consumers and businesses.

• Americans bought billions of dollars worth of *war bonds* to help finance the war effort. For the same purpose, they had to pay higher taxes.

SUMMING UP   We have seen how Franklin D. Roosevelt led the nation through some trying and exciting years. Serving longer than any other President, Roosevelt proposed and carried out a plan to save the American economy. Historians disagree as to what caused the economy to recover—the New Deal or World War II. All agree, however, that the New Deal left its mark on the country. Some of its laws continue to influence the way Americans live today.

Understanding the Text

On a separate sheet of paper, write the letter of the word or phrase that best completes each of the following statements.

1. The election of 1932 took place during a period of (a) economic depression (b) quick recovery (c) prosperity (d) world war.

2. The election of 1932 was considered by many a vote of "no confidence" in the administration of (a) Calvin Coolidge (b) Herbert Hoover (c) Franklin Roosevelt (d) Warren Harding.

3. The FDIC was set up in 1933 to (a) close all the banks in the country (b) build dams and other public works (c) insure bank deposits up to $5,000 (d) regulate the stock exchanges.

4. Under one New Deal agricultural program, farmers who agreed to cut production received (a) insured bank deposits of up to $5,000 (b) special payments from the federal government (c) surpluses (d) free electricity from the TVA.

5. A New Deal agency involved in constructing public works was the (a) WPA (b) SEC (c) FDIC (d) none of the above.

6. The principle of collective bargaining was guaranteed by the (a) Agricultural Adjustment Act (b) Twenty-first Amendment (c) National Labor Relations Act (d) Social Security Act.

7. The TVA helped primarily in the economic development of the (a) Southwest (b) Middle West (c) Northeast (d) Southeast.

8. Because of the U.S. Supreme Court's opposition to some New Deal laws, President Roosevelt (a) abolished the Court (b) proposed adding new members to the Court (c) resigned (d) fired six justices.

9. The United States was at war with Japan during the presidential election of (a) 1936 (b) 1940 (c) 1944 (d) all of the above.

10. Which of the following was a common criticism of the New Deal by the Republicans?

(a) It gave too much power to big businesses. (b) It was too much concerned with balancing the federal budget. (c) It led the federal government to meddle in affairs best left to state or local governments or private interests. (d) It did not pay any attention to conservation of the nation's natural resources.

Developing Graph-Reading Skills

Examine the line graph below. Then choose the letter of the word or phrase that best completes each sentence. On a separate sheet of paper, match the sentence number with the correct letter.

1. According to the graph, the number of unemployed Americans was greatest in (a) 1929 (b) 1933 (c) 1938 (d) 1940.

2. From 1929 to the beginning of 1933, unemployment in the United States (a) declined (b) increased (c) went up and down (d) remained at about the same level.

3. Between 1931 and 1937, the fewest number of unemployed was (a) around 12 million (b) between 10 and 11 million (c) between 8 and 9 million (d) between 7 and 8 million.

4. During Franklin D. Roosevelt's first term as President, the number of unemployed generally (a) increased (b) decreased (c) remained about the same (d) went up and down.

5. The United States entered World War II at a time when (a) the number of unemployed was at an all-time high (b) Franklin D. Roosevelt was serving his first term as President (c) unemployment was becoming less of a problem (d) the number of unemployed was rising.

Thinking About the Lesson

1. In what ways were several of Franklin D. Roosevelt's New Deal programs similar to certain measures advocated by Herbert Hoover? In what ways were they different?

2. Franklin D. Roosevelt was elected the U.S. President four times—more often than any other person. How would you explain this fact?

NUMBER OF UNEMPLOYED PEOPLE IN THE UNITED STATES, 1929–1942

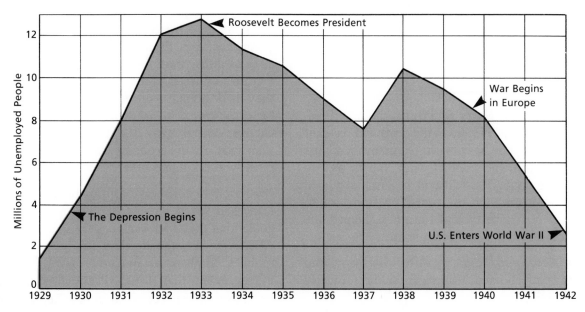

LESSON 60

Presidents and Politics After World War II, 1945–1961

Harry S. Truman and Dwight D. Eisenhower served as U.S. Presidents during the critical years after World War II. American industries then were busy adjusting to peacetime conditions. Although the country enjoyed remarkable prosperity during most of these years, many New Deal measures were continued. Moreover, both Presidents Truman and Eisenhower introduced their own legislative programs. After 1945, the nation's increasing concern about foreign threats had an effect on domestic politics. A number of prominent Americans were accused of aiding their country's enemies.

Truman's Early Policies

Vice President Harry S. Truman became President in April, 1945, upon the death of President Roosevelt. The war with Germany was just ending, but the conflict with Japan was to continue until August. President Truman guided the nation through the transition from war to peace. His honesty and bluntness helped the nation through some difficult times.

The Returning Soldiers After Germany and Japan surrendered, American soldiers eagerly

returned home. Many of them went back to the jobs that they had held before entering the service. Some took advantage of a 1944 law known as the "G.I. Bill of Rights." Under this law, they could:

• Go to college and have the government pay most expenses.
• Buy homes with U.S. government loans.
• Set up businesses or buy farms with U.S. government loans.

Retooling the Factories After the war, many of the factories that had made war materials, such as guns, were not needed. Some of these factories returned to the type of production that they had carried out before the war. Other factories closed their doors. These industrial changes caused many American workers to lose their jobs. As the economy expanded, however, most workers found other work.

The Post-War Economy During the war, Americans had saved money, because many of the goods that they had wanted were not available. After the war, the demand for homes, automobiles, appliances, and other goods became much higher than usual. President Truman,

382

fearing inflation, wanted to keep the wartime controls over prices and wages. In 1946, though, Congress dropped controls on everything except rents. As a result, the country experienced steep inflation.

As prices rose, many workers demanded higher wages. In 1946, the nation was hit by waves of labor unrest. Two of the largest strikes, one by railroad employees and one by coal workers, ended only after the government intervened.

Taft-Hartley Act   In 1947, Congress reacted against the labor unrest by passing the Taft-Hartley Act. Labor organizations hated the new law. Among other things, it allowed the government to halt strikes for a "cooling off period" of 80 days. (See Lesson 66 for more on this law.) Truman opposed the Taft-Hartley Act and vetoed it. The act's supporters in Congress, however, had enough votes to override his veto.

Partisan Politics

As often happens after a war, the party in power during World War II lost strength after the conflict ended. In 1946, the Republicans took away from the Democrats control of both houses of Congress. The Republicans felt confident that they could also win the White House in 1948.

Election of 1948   In the summer of 1948, Thomas Dewey again won the Republican nomination for President. He had been the Republican nominee in 1944 but had lost that election. Democratic leaders decided to go with Truman in 1948, even though he did not have the support of all factions of the party.

A Third and Fourth Candidate   Many Southern Democrats disliked Truman's support for the civil rights of black Americans. As a result, these "Dixiecrats" put forward their own candidate—Governor J. Strom Thurmond of South Carolina. Thurmond ran in the general election on the States' Rights party ticket. To complicate matters further, a fourth major candidate ran for President in 1948—Henry A. Wallace, Roosevelt's Vice President from 1941 to 1945. Wallace was nominated by a new Progressive party, but he had the support of some Democrats, too.

The Results   Although Dewey was expected to win, Truman campaigned vigorously. On the morning of November 3, 1948, Truman woke up to hear the news that he would be President

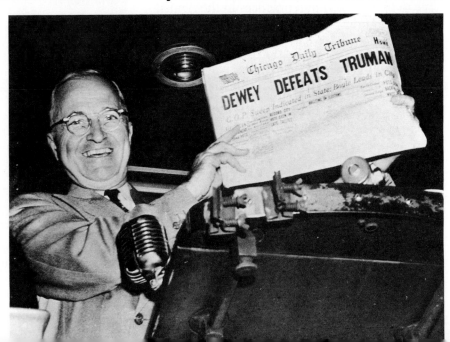

In November, 1948, the *Chicago Tribune* went to press before the results of the election were in. The real winner, Harry S. Truman, is shown enjoying the newspaper's error.

for four more years. He learned also that the Democrats had regained both houses of Congress. With a Democratic Congress, he would have an easier time of getting enacted his reform program, known as the "Fair Deal."

The Fair Deal

To some extent, Truman's Fair Deal was modeled after Roosevelt's New Deal. He wanted to offer workers, farmers, the elderly, and minorities a "fair deal" in life. Some of his proposals were:

• An extension of Social Security benefits to some 10 million more Americans. Congress passed this extension in 1950.

• Repeal of the Taft-Hartley Act. Congress failed to repeal this anti-union legislation, but it did raise the minimum wage to 75¢ an hour.

• Slum clearance and the building of low-rent housing by the federal government. The Housing Act of 1949 provided for these programs, including government *subsidies* (grants) on rents for low-income families.

• Civil rights for blacks and other minorities. Congress failed to pass a Fair Employment Practices bill. Nevertheless, the President was able to fight segregation practices in the Armed Forces and other parts of the government.

• Expansion of earlier programs in soil conservation, flood control, and *rural electrification* (bringing electricity to rural areas).

Although President Truman wanted to expand Roosevelt's domestic reforms, he met with only partial success. As we have seen, Congress was not willing to go along with all of Truman's proposals.

Questioning People's Loyalties

After the Second World War, Americans worried about the intentions and actions of their former ally—the Soviet Union. Because Soviet troops occupied Eastern Europe, Communist governments came to power there. Angered by Soviet actions, some Americans became suspicious of U.S. citizens who made favorable comments about the Soviet Union. Several Americans were accused (and a few convicted) of spying for the Soviets. Besides arresting people for spying, the government took these actions:

• In 1947, President Truman called for an investigation into the loyalty of all federal workers.

• The House Un-American Activities Committee held hearings on Communist influences in the United States.

• The U.S. Senate held similar discussions. Beginning in 1950, Senator Joseph McCarthy of Wisconsin caused considerable controversy. In a speech in Wheeling, West Virginia, he charged that some important government officials were Communists. He also claimed that

Senator Joseph McCarthy frequently gave speeches in the U.S. Senate about Communist influence in the government.

Communists had secretly made their way into many areas of American life, including the country's universities and newspaper and film industries. Although McCarthy had many supporters, public opinion began to turn against him in 1954. In that year, Americans could see Senator McCarthy on television testifying about alleged Communist influence in the U.S. Army. They saw him evading questions asked by the Army's lawyer. Soon afterward, the U.S. Senate officially *censured* (found fault with) McCarthy for insulting several Senators.

The Korean War

In June, 1950, a war broke out in Korea between Communist and non-Communist forces. Soon U.S. troops were fighting there under United Nations command. Most of Truman's efforts after 1950 were devoted to winning this war. (The Korean War is dealt with in Lesson 82.)

At home, one consequence of the war was the return of wage and price controls. Another result was a further increase in anti-Communist feelings, described above.

Election of 1952

Harry Truman decided not to run again for President in 1952. Therefore, the Democrats turned to Governor Adlai Stevenson of Illinois. Stevenson was a thoughtful person known for both his intelligence and sense of humor.

The Republicans were fortunate in having General Dwight D. Eisenhower willing to run for President on their ticket. "Ike" had become a national hero in World War II, serving as Supreme Commander of Allied forces in Western Europe. After the war, he had become president of Columbia University and then Commander of NATO forces.

Eisenhower won the 1952 presidential election by a landslide. At the same time, the Republicans gained control of both houses of Congress, but only by small margins.

Eisenhower's Programs and Problems at Home

Like many other Republican Presidents, Eisenhower usually favored the views of business leaders. He was not interested in having the federal government undertake bold, new reform programs. He thought that government regulation of the economy should be kept to a minimum. Instead, he believed the states should be given more powers. In contrast to more conservative Republicans, though, Eisenhower favored keeping and even expanding some New Deal measures. For this reason, Eisenhower became known as a moderate Republican.

Under Eisenhower's administration, the U.S. government:

• Expanded the Social Security system to cover additional groups of workers.

• Created a new executive department—the Department of Health, Education, and Welfare. (At first, HEW was headed by a woman—Oveta Culp Hobby, former commander of the Women's Army Corps.) HEW administered a modest program of *public housing* (housing owned, operated, or sponsored by governments).

• Cut government spending, taxes, and the number of federal employees. These measures were in line with the Republicans' desire to balance the budget.

• Dropped the wage and price controls that President Truman had set up during the Korean War. These controls ended even before the war was over in 1953.

• Gave to the states the rights to offshore oil deposits. Private companies found it easier to *lease* (rent) the rights to exploit oil fields from the states than from the federal government.

• Helped local school districts finance the building of schools.

During the 1952 Republican campaign for the Presidency, General Dwight D. Eisenhower addressed enthusiastic crowds. He was well known for his role in World War II.

• Set up a large federal project to construct highways. Some $25 million was spent for this purpose in 1956 alone.

Elections of 1954 and 1956   The Democrats regained control of Congress in the 1954 election. In 1956, they maintained this control.

Eisenhower's Second Term

"Ike" decided to run again in 1956 despite the fact that he had suffered a serious heart attack the year before. He easily defeated Stevenson for a second time in the election of 1956.

Civil Rights Concerns   In 1954, the U.S. Supreme Court had ruled that schools could not separate pupils in public schools on the basis of race. (Discussed on page 474.) As a result of the *Brown* v. *Board of Education* ruling, local school boards were asked to *desegregate* (end separation of races in) their schools. Some local and state officials resisted integration. Resistance by Arkansas officials led to President Eisen-

hower in 1957 sending federal troops to Little Rock. The troops maintained order while black students attended a previously all-white high school.

In 1957 and 1960, Congress passed two civil rights bills. These laws were the first important pieces of civil rights legislation since Reconstruction. They made it easier for blacks to exercise their right to vote. Local election officials who prevented blacks from voting now could face punishment.

Other Concerns   Several other significant events took place during Eisenhower's second term:

• In 1958, the United States launched into space its first satellite, *Explorer I*. The Soviet Union, though, had beaten the Americans in this early stage of the space race. They had launched their first satellite, *Sputnik I*, in 1957.

• Alaska and Hawaii were admitted to the Union as states in 1959. With this action, the country added 2 more stars to its flag, bringing the total to 50.

SUMMING UP   We have seen how President Truman dealt with the domestic problems that arose after World War II. Despite a split in the Democratic party, he was elected to a full term in 1948. The Korean War began during Truman's administration and ended during Eisenhower's. Soviet actions led to increased concerns about Communist influence at home. Congress under both administrations kept many New Deal reforms and introduced new ones. Perhaps the most important domestic events of this period were the gains that blacks made in civil rights.

Understanding the Text

On a separate sheet of paper, write the letter of the word or phrase that best completes each of the following statements.

1. The man serving as President when World War II ended was *(a)* Franklin Roosevelt *(b)* Harry Truman *(c)* Dwight Eisenhower *(d)* Adlai Stevenson.

2. Under the G.I. Bill of Rights, veterans of World War II could get *(a)* loans to buy homes *(b)* loans to set up businesses *(c)* payments from the government for most expenses of going to college *(d)* all of the above.

3. An imaginary book title that accurately reflects an event of the period 1945–1961 is *(a) Harry Truman and the Entry of the United States into the Korean War (b) Dwight Eisenhower and the End of the Social Security System (c) Dwight Eisenhower's Fair Deal (d) Franklin Roosevelt and the Fall of Senator Joseph McCarthy.*

4. In the first few years after World War II, Americans experienced *(a)* inflation *(b)* many labor strikes *(c)* rent controls *(d)* all of the above.

5. "Although he was an underdog in the presidential election of 1948, he won an unexpected victory over his Republican opponent." This statement describes the election of *(a)* Henry A. Wallace *(b)* J. Strom Thurmond *(c)* Harry S. Truman *(d)* Thomas Dewey.

6. An act or program *not* part of Truman's Fair Deal was *(a)* slum clearance *(b)* the extension of Social Security benefits *(c)* the Taft-Hartley Act *(d)* rural electrification.

7. Senator Joseph McCarthy of Wisconsin is best remembered for *(a)* working to pass civil rights acts *(b)* strengthening the Social Security system *(c)* arranging the peace that ended the Korean War *(d)* making speeches about Communist influence in America.

8. In the 1952 and 1956 presidential elections, Eisenhower's Democratic opponent was *(a)* Adlai Stevenson *(b)* Harry S. Truman *(c)* Henry A. Wallace *(d)* Thomas Dewey.

9. During the Eisenhower administration, the United States *(a)* enacted two major civil rights laws *(b)* dropped its wage and price controls *(c)* launched *Explorer I* into space *(d)* all of the above.

10. During *both* the Truman and Eisenhower administrations, *(a)* Democrats controlled Congress all the time *(b)* Republicans controlled the White House all the time *(c)* the U.S. Presidents were concerned about fighting a war in Korea *(d)* the United States launched satellites into space.

Developing Cartoon-Reading Skills

"Are You Sure You Didn't Miss Anything?"

© **1946, by Herblock in** *The Washington Post*

Study the political cartoon above. Then choose the letter of the word or phrase that best completes each sentence. On a separate sheet of paper, match the sentence number with the correct letter.

1. The figure riding in the back seat of the car represents *(a)* Franklin D. Roosevelt *(b)* Harry S. Truman *(c)* Dwight D. Eisenhower *(d)* the Taft-Hartley Act.

2. The figures in the car *(a)* have avoided the rocks *(b)* have not noticed the rocks *(c)* have gone over or hit the rocks *(d)* are about to back over the rocks.

3. The act of riding in the car represents *(a)* the experiences of labor unions with the Taft-Hart-

ley Act *(b)* a presidential election campaign *(c)* an ex-President's retirement years *(d)* a President's first year in office.

4. The cartoonist Herblock has drawn the rocks in different sizes. The one that he thinks represents the most important event or issue is labeled *(a)* "The Bomb" *(b)* "Atomic Control" *(c)* "Inflation" *(d)* "Housing."

5. The cartoonist's attitude toward the figure in the back seat of the car can best be described as *(a)* sympathetic *(b)* critical *(c)* uninterested *(d)* wildly enthusiastic.

Thinking About the Lesson

1. Was the Fair Deal a continuation of the New Deal or something quite different? Explain your answer.

2. Do you think that President Eisenhower lived up to his 1952 presidential campaign slogan, "It's Time for a Change." Why or why not?

3. During the years 1945–1961, why did more Americans than usual question the patriotism of other citizens?

Presidential Politics in the 1960s

Presidents John F. Kennedy and Lyndon B. Johnson served in the White House during the turbulent 1960s. Kennedy's youthful idealism and broad reform program were cut short by his untimely death. Johnson was able to achieve many domestic reforms, but his legislative goals were buried by an escalating war in Southeast Asia.

Election of 1960

Because of the Twenty-second Amendment, Dwight D. Eisenhower could not run for President for a third term. In 1960, therefore, the Republican party turned to Eisenhower's Vice President—Richard M. Nixon. In campaigning that fall, Nixon defended the record of the Eisenhower administration in both domestic and foreign affairs.

John F. Kennedy emerged as the most popular candidate in the Democratic primaries. This young senator from Massachusetts had the advantages of good looks and wealth. Some political experts, however, said that he could not win because of his religion. No Roman Catholic had ever been elected President of the United States.

Nevertheless, in November, 1960, Kennedy did win, defeating Nixon by an extremely narrow margin. At age 43, Kennedy became the youngest person ever elected President.

The Kennedy Program

Kennedy believed in an active Presidency. He thought that the President should be a bold leader—one who tries to find new solutions to national problems. He claimed also that the President should make every effort to convince Congress that changes were needed.

The New Frontier President Kennedy called his program of economic and social reforms the "New Frontier." For the most part, his ideas continued reforms begun during the New Deal. Examples of New Frontier laws included:

- Increases in Social Security benefits.
- A rise in the minimum wage to $1.25/hour.
- Federal Water Pollution Control Act.
- Federal housing programs. The government loaned money at low interest rates to people with moderate incomes to build homes. Also, the government built public housing projects for the elderly.
- Area Redevelopment Act of 1961. The federal government provided loans to businesses in areas of the country that were economically depressed.

389

By 1960, television had become a major new factor in politics. Presidential candidates Richard M. Nixon (left) and John F. Kennedy held four televised debates in the 1960 campaign.

• A 1962 law provided funds for retraining unemployed workers. The idea behind the program was that with new skills, these workers would have an easier time finding new jobs.

Congress did not pass all of Kennedy's New Frontier proposals. Medicare (medical aid for the elderly), federal aid to education, and other Kennedy ideas would have to wait for the next administration.

Advances in Civil Rights

President Kennedy was interested in extending the civil rights of blacks and other minorities. As President, he made sure that existing civil rights laws were enforced. For instance, the government helped many blacks to register to vote for the first time. The government also made efforts to see that all-white public schools became integrated.

Kennedy asked Congress to pass a new civil rights law—one that would be directed against discrimination in education, employment, and other areas. Such a law, however, was not passed until after Lyndon Johnson became President. During Kennedy's years in office, civil rights groups organized several large demonstrations to protest the plight of black Americans.

World Affairs

The Kennedy administration had to deal with serious challenges from Communist groups and countries. The Cuban Missile Crisis, construction of the Berlin Wall, and an expansion of U.S. military aid to South Vietnam all occurred between 1961 and 1963. (These topics are presented in more detail in Lessons 81 and 82.)

Two of Kennedy's foreign policy programs became especially popular:

• Alliance for Progress. This program, begun in 1961, provided vast amounts of U.S. financial aid to Latin America.
• Peace Corps. This government agency sends American volunteers, mostly young people, to developing countries all over the world. The volunteers work with local people on all kinds of self-improvement projects.

The Tragedy and Succession

John Kennedy was very popular. He probably would have won re-election in 1964. Instead, he was shot and killed by an assassin while riding through Dallas, Texas, on November 22, 1963.

Kennedy's death in 1963 shocked and saddened the whole nation.

Vice President Lyndon B. Johnson immediately took office as President. LBJ, of Texas, had served that state as both a U.S. representative and senator. In the U.S. Senate, where he had held the important office of Majority Leader, he had pushed for passage of many of the reforms Kennedy advocated. As President, Johnson continued many of these reforms and urged Congress to pass new ones.

The Great Society

Lyndon Johnson called his ambitious list of domestic reforms the "Great Society." Basic aims of this program included:

• Ending discrimination against minorities.
• Improving the economic conditions and opportunities of America's poor.

Civil Rights President Johnson urged Congress to pass important civil rights laws. The Civil Rights Act of 1964 barred discrimination in public places and in employment. It also upheld the right of minorities to register and vote. To some extent, this act came about because of public pressure from civil rights organizations.

Another major result of the civil rights movement was the ratification by the states of the Twenty-fourth Amendment in 1964. The Amendment barred any state or local government from requiring a citizen before voting to pay a poll tax. Before this time, poll tax laws discouraged many poor people, mostly non-whites, from voting.

In 1965, Congress passed the Voting Rights Act. With this law, the federal government could register eligible voters if the states failed to do so.

War on Poverty In 1964, LBJ launched a campaign to improve economic conditions for millions of Americans living below the poverty level. He called his campaign a "War on Poverty." During Johnson's years in office, Congress took the following steps as part of this war:

• Medicare. As an addition to the Social Security system, the Medicare program provides hospital and medical care for the elderly. Another Johnson-backed program, in which federal funds help provide medical aid for the poor, is called "Medicaid."
• Job Corps. This agency provides training in job skills for young people who have dropped out of school.
• Expanded programs of *urban renewal* (replacing slums with more modern buildings). The government built public housing projects and helped pay the rent of some poor people. To oversee these programs, Congress created a new executive branch department—the Department of Housing and Urban Development.

HUD's first head, Robert C. Weaver, was the first black to serve in a President's Cabinet.

• Special, direct aid to Appalachia, a mountainous region covering parts of several Eastern states. This area had long experienced high levels of poverty.

• Federal aid to education. For the first time, the government gave large amounts of aid to all school districts to improve educational programs. Poorer districts were usually given more money than those that were better off.

• Head Start. This new agency provided for the teaching of basic skills to poor children before they entered first grade.

Historians differ as to how effective the War on Poverty was. On the one hand, Johnson's reforms did help a large number of poor Americans. Many of these programs, such as Medicare, have been continued by later administrations. On the other hand, critics said that the War on Poverty failed to eliminate poverty in America. They claimed also that the programs were too expensive and, in some cases, poorly run. Johnson's defenders claimed that not enough funds were available to carry out all aspects of Johnson's War on Poverty. They were referring to the fact that more and more tax dollars were used to pay for the Vietnam War.

Election of 1964

Johnson became the Democratic candidate for President in the 1964 election. Although he was a Texan, many Southern Democrats did not support him. They were upset by Johnson's role in passing the new civil rights acts.

Barry Goldwater, a U.S. Senator from Arizona, ran for President on the Republican ticket in 1964. He strongly criticized the Great Society programs for bringing the federal government into new areas of people's lives.

LBJ won the 1964 election by a landslide. In addition, the Democrats strengthened their hold on Congress.

The Vietnam War

Under President Johnson, the United States became much more deeply involved in the Vietnam War. The President was determined to see South Vietnam win a military victory over its enemies. As a result, he strengthened U.S. forces in Southeast Asia until they totaled more than 500,000.

At first, Johnson's actions had the backing of most Americans. As the United States got more involved in the fighting, however, the war became less popular at home. Many Americans,

President Johnson (right) is shown conferring with black leaders (from left to right) Roy Wilkins, James Farmer, Dr. Martin Luther King, Jr., and Whitney Young.

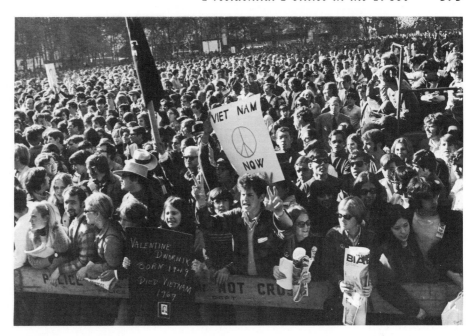

Anti-war demonstrations such as this one would eventually influence U.S. leaders to withdraw our troops from Vietnam.

especially young people, joined in anti-war rallies. A few of these demonstrations became violent. (Pro- and anti-war arguments are discussed in Lesson 82.)

In the spring of 1968, Democratic senators Robert Kennedy and Eugene McCarthy challenged Johnson for the presidential nomination. Both opposed U.S. involvement in the war. By this time, the President was tired of all the anti-war criticism directed against him. Not wanting to divide the nation and his party any longer, he announced that he would not seek re-election.

SUMMING UP   We have seen how both Presidents Kennedy and Johnson called for major domestic reforms. They both wanted laws to help America's poor and both backed major civil rights bills. Kennedy was elected President in 1960 by only a small margin. Johnson assumed that office in 1963 after Kennedy was assassinated. Then in 1964, Johnson beat his Republican opponent Barry Goldwater by a landslide. Because of U.S. involvement in the Vietnam War, however, Johnson became less popular. In 1968, Johnson decided not to seek re-election rather than risk defeat of his party at the polls.

Understanding the Text

On a separate sheet of paper, write the letter of the word or phrase that best completes each of the following statements.

1. The first Roman Catholic to become a U.S. President was *(a)* Herbert Hoover *(b)* Lyndon Johnson *(c)* John Kennedy *(d)* Alfred Smith.

2. The domestic reform program of the Kennedy administration was called the *(a)* New Frontier *(b)* Great Society *(c)* Fair Deal *(d)* New Deal.

3. An act or program *not* passed during Kennedy's administration was *(a)* an increase in Social Security benefits *(b)* the Area Redevelopment Act *(c)* public housing for the elderly *(d)* Medicare.

4. The Alliance for Progress involved U.S. foreign aid to *(a)* Africa *(b)* Latin America *(c)* Western Europe *(d)* Southeast Asia.

5. Lyndon Johnson became President in 1963 because *(a)* John Kennedy had been assassinated *(b)* Johnson had defeated Barry Goldwater *(c)* the Twenty-second Amendment had been ratified *(d)* Dwight Eisenhower had decided not to seek a third term.

6. The domestic reform program associated with the Johnson administration was called the *(a)* New Frontier *(b)* Great Society *(c)* Fair Deal *(d)* New Deal.

7. Of the following, one that became law or was ratified during Johnson's administration was the *(a)* Twenty-fourth Amendment *(b)* Voting Rights Act of 1965 *(c)* Civil Rights Act of 1964 *(d)* all of the above.

8. As President, Lyndon Johnson tried to use the power and resources of the federal government to *(a)* reduce poverty in the United States *(b)* get rid of big businesses *(c)* solve the Cuban Missile Crisis *(d)* win the war in Korea.

9. The party that named Lyndon Johnson its presidential candidate in 1964 was the same party that had four years earlier nominated *(a)* Dwight Eisenhower *(b)* Richard Nixon *(c)* John Kennedy *(d)* all of the above.

10. Which of the following statements applies to both John Kennedy and Lyndon Johnson? *(a)* He served as a U.S. senator. *(b)* He declined to run for re-election as President. *(c)* He served as Vice President of the country. *(d)* As President, he called for the creation of the Peace Corps.

Developing Reading Comprehension Skills

John Fitzgerald Kennedy

John F. Kennedy, 35th president, Democrat, was born May 29, 1917, in Brookline, Mass., the son of Joseph P. Kennedy, financier, who later became ambassador to Great Britain, and Rose Fitzgerald. He entered Harvard, attended the London School of Economics briefly in 1935, received a B.S., from Harvard, 1940. He served in the Navy, 1941–1945, commanded a PT boat in the Solomons and won the Navy and Marine Corps Medal. He wrote *Profiles in Courage,* which won a Pulitzer prize. He served as representative in Congress, 1947–1953; was elected to the Senate in 1952, reelected 1958. He nearly won the vice presidential nomination in 1956.

In 1960, Kennedy won the Democratic nomination for president and defeated Richard M. Nixon, Republican. He was the first Roman Catholic president.

Kennedy's most important act was his successful demand Oct. 22, 1962, that the Soviet Union dismantle its missile bases in Cuba. He established a quarantine of arms shipments to Cuba and continued surveillance by air. He defied Soviet attempts to force the Allies out of Berlin. He made the steel industry rescind a price rise. He backed civil rights, a mental health program, arbitration of railroad disputes, and expanded medical care for the aged. Astronaut flights and satellite orbiting were greatly developed during his administration.

On Nov. 22, 1963, Kennedy was assassinated in Dallas, Tex.

Read the short biography of John F. Kennedy reproduced from *The World Almanac and Book of Facts 1986* (New York: Newspaper Enterprise Association, 1985, p. 430). Then choose the letter of the word or phrase that best answers each question. On a separate sheet of paper, match the question number with the correct letter.

1. In which of the following sentences does the author of the biography express an opinion? (*a*) "He entered Harvard, attended the London School of Economics briefly in 1935, received a B.S., from Harvard, 1940." (*b*) "He nearly won the vice presidential nomination in 1956." (*c*) "In 1960, Kennedy won the Democratic nomination for president and defeated Richard M. Nixon, Republican." (*d*) "Kennedy's most important act was his successful demand Oct. 22, 1962, that the Soviet Union dismantle its missile bases in Cuba."

2. What was John F. Kennedy doing in 1950? (*a*) going to college at Harvard University (*b*) serving in the U.S. Navy (*c*) serving in the U.S. House of Representatives (*d*) serving in the U.S. Senate.

3. Which of the following was *not* one of Kennedy's accomplishments as President? (*a*) He commanded a PT boat in the Solomon Islands. (*b*) He forced steel companies in the United States to repeal a rise in the price of steel. (*c*) He urged Congress to spend more money on medical care for elderly Americans. (*d*) He called for railroad strikes to be settled by means of arbitration.

4. In which of the following years did John F. Kennedy *not* seek election to a federal office? (*a*) 1952 (*b*) 1958 (*c*) 1960 (*d*) 1962.

5. Who was Rose Fitzgerald Kennedy? (*a*) John F. Kennedy's wife (*b*) John F. Kennedy's mother (*c*) John F. Kennedy's sister (*d*) John F. Kennedy's daughter.

Thinking About the Lesson

1. If you had been President, would you have signed the Civil Rights Act of 1964 and the Voting Rights Act of 1965? Why or why not?

2. Some people have called Johnson's years in the White House a continuation of the Kennedy administration. Do you agree? Why or why not?

The Nixon and Ford Administrations, 1969–1977

Beginning in 1969, Republican Presidents occupied the White House for eight years. Richard Nixon scored major foreign policy triumphs, but his reputation suffered from a political scandal. After Nixon resigned, Gerald Ford took over and managed to restore Americans' confidence in their government. Both Republicans tried to check federal spending and struggled with the problem of inflation.

Election of 1968

After Lyndon Johnson had withdrawn from the race for the 1968 Democratic presidential nomination, the field was wide open. Other Democrats remained or joined in the competition:

• Robert Kennedy had the support of many anti-war Democrats and members of minority groups. In June, however, the Senator was shot and killed while campaigning in California.

• Senator Eugene McCarthy became a popular candidate among voters who called for a quick U.S. withdrawal from Vietnam.

• Most Democratic party leaders favored Vice President Hubert Humphrey. Many other Democrats, though, opposed Humphrey for his support of the Johnson administration's policy in Vietnam.

Democratic Convention Amid violent anti-war street demonstrations, the Democrats held their nominating convention in Chicago, Illinois. They ended by choosing Humphrey, thereby alienating many anti-war Democrats.

Republican Convention The Republicans nominated Richard Nixon, even though he had lost the presidential election in 1960. Nixon had also lost the race for Governor of California in 1962. In 1968, though, he campaigned hard, stressing the issues of maintaining law and order and reducing the size of the government.

The American Independent Party A third major candidate ran for President in 1968. George C. Wallace, former Governor of Alabama, led the slate of the American Independent party. He appealed especially to whites who thought that the civil rights movement was too violent and was gaining too much ground.

None of the three nominees called for immediate U.S. withdrawal from Vietnam. All seemed to want peace by means of a settlement with North Vietnam.

396

The results of the 1968 election were very close. Richard Nixon beat Hubert Humphrey by a small margin. Yet the Democrats still controlled Congress.

Developments at Home Under Nixon

President Nixon shared many of the views of his Republican predecessor in the White House—Dwight D. Eisenhower. They were both moderate Republicans, meaning that they shared most but not all of the traditional Republican beliefs. They called for less federal spending and less involvement of the federal government in the lives of Americans. At the same time, however, they kept most of the social reforms that had been in effect since the 1930s. Some of the domestic programs of the Nixon administration are described below.

Efforts to Check Inflation   In fighting the Vietnam War, the government had to spend great amounts of money on the military. High levels of defense spending contributed to the inflation problem in America. This period of rising prices had begun during the Johnson administration and continued through Nixon's years as President. At first, Nixon countered inflation by reducing *domestic spending* (federal government spending inside the country). Later, in 1972, President Nixon ordered a temporary freeze on most wages and prices. Business and labor leaders, though, immediately criticized the freeze. They thought that the measure was unfair and that it would not work well. For a while, the freeze did check inflation, but when Nixon lifted it, the rate of inflation rose again.

Revenue-Sharing   Believing that the federal government was too large and wishing to give the states more power, Nixon proposed *revenue-sharing*. Under this program, the federal government made direct grants of money to the states for them to spend as they thought best.

This idea was popular because many state and local governments could not afford certain projects. The federal government could raise money more easily than could state and local governments.

Moon Landing   A highlight of the Nixon administration was the 1969 landing on the moon by three U.S. astronauts. One astronaut, Neil Armstrong, made a memorable statement as he became the first person to step onto the moon's surface: "That's one small step for a man, one giant leap for mankind." Many Americans were proud of their space program. Others criticized it for being too costly. Critics claimed that the billions of dollars that the program cost should have been spent on worthy domestic reforms.

In 1969, Astronaut Neil Armstrong took this picture of Edwin E. Aldrin, Jr., on the surface of the moon.

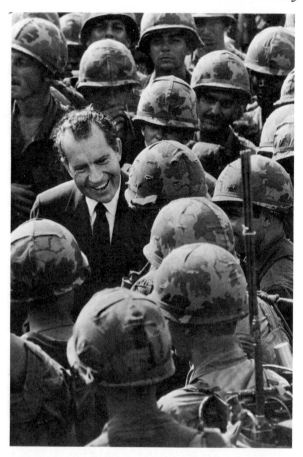

President Richard Nixon visited South Vietnam in 1969. Here he is shown mixing with U.S. combat troops stationed in Di An, northeast of Saigon.

Foreign Affairs Under Nixon

President Nixon charted several new directions in American foreign policy.

Withdrawal From Vietnam Nixon held that U.S. support of South Vietnam was fully justified as a means of checking Communism. Even so, he saw that most Americans were tired of the war and wanted an "honorable" way out. Nixon took steps to begin the withdrawal of U.S. troops. The task of defeating the North Vietnamese and their Vietcong allies was left to South Vietnam. Americans, though, promised to keep supplying the South Vietnamese gov-

ernment with money and military equipment. In early 1973, the powers involved in the war signed a peace agreement in Paris. Soon most of the remaining U.S. troops were withdrawn from Vietnam. North Vietnam then gained the upper hand over South Vietnamese forces and in 1975 won a complete victory.

A New China Policy The United States had been hostile toward the government of mainland China since the Communists took over in 1949. Richard Nixon had been one of the nation's loudest advocates of not *recognizing* (formally accepting as valid) this regime. Then in 1972, he surprised his fellow Americans by announcing that he was going to visit China. In the next year, the Nixon administration opened limited diplomatic relations with the People's Republic of China. In order to persuade China to agree to this relationship, the United States agreed to cease recognizing Nationalist China, the government located on the island of Taiwan. (See Lesson 83.)

Détente With the Soviet Union Also in 1972, Nixon became the first President of the United States to visit Moscow. The aim of his visit was to help build better relations between the two superpowers. In this way, Nixon initiated *détente* (policies aimed at reducing tensions between two nations) with the Soviet Union.

Election of 1972 Improved U.S. relations with the Soviet Union and Communist China increased Nixon's popularity. He became the natural choice of the Republicans in the 1972 presidential elections. George Wallace sought the Democratic nomination, then dropped out after being wounded in an assassination attempt. At their national convention, the Democrats were divided among several candidates. Finally, they chose Senator George McGovern of South Dakota. Although McGovern campaigned hard, Nixon won by a large margin that November.

The Democrats were able to hold on to their majorities in both houses of Congress.

> The year 1972 was the first one in which all young people age 18 through 20 could vote in a presidential election. They gained this right with the ratification of the Twenty-sixth Amendment the year before. Many young people registered and voted in 1972 and in subsequent election years. The percentage of young people voting, however, has still not reached the national average. (See the table on page 402.)

Watergate Affair

In the summer of 1972, five men employed by the Committee for the Re-election of the President, a Republican group, burglarized the Democratic party headquarters. They wanted to gather information that might damage the Democrats in the upcoming presidential election. Since the Democratic headquarters were in the Watergate complex in Washington, D.C., the affair became known as "Watergate."

For two years, the FBI, CIA, and Congress investigated members of Nixon's administration for possible involvement in Watergate. These probes exposed repeated attempts to cover up illegal and improper activities. A number of Nixon's aides, including his former Attorney General, John Mitchell, were convicted in court and sentenced to prison terms.

> Because of another scandal, a high Nixon administration official, Vice President Spiro T. Agnew, was forced to resign in September, 1973. A court found that he had been guilty of tax evasion while serving as Governor of Maryland.

President Nixon denied any involvement in Watergate, but tape recordings of conversations in the White House revealed otherwise. The tapes showed that Nixon had joined in attempts to cover up the affair.

Nixon Resigns In 1974, the House Judiciary Committee recommended that the President be impeached. The House never had to act on this recommendation. Instead, on August 9, 1974, Richard Nixon became the first U.S. President to resign.

President Gerald R. Ford

Vice President Gerald R. Ford became the country's President after Nixon resigned. Ford had served 13 straight terms as a member of Congress from Michigan, eventually becoming Minority Leader of the House. After Agnew's resignation, President Nixon had named Ford to be the new Vice President. Both houses of Congress had approved this nomination in accordance with the Twenty-fifth Amendment.

When Ford became President, there was again no Vice President. Ford filled this office by nominating Nelson A. Rockefeller, the former Governor of New York. For the first time, the country had a President and Vice President, neither of whom had been chosen by the voters.

Pardon for Nixon Shortly after taking office, Ford pardoned Nixon for any federal crimes that he might have committed as Chief Executive. Many Americans approved this action as a way of uniting the country. Other Americans criticized the pardon. Critics complained that the "man at the top" had gotten off free, while his aides had suffered tough penalties.

Amnesty Ford offered an *amnesty* (type of pardon) to some 28,000 draft evaders and deserters. These were young Americans who had hidden, fled the country, or left the Armed

President Gerald R. Ford was photographed working in the White House Oval Office with his dog "Liberty" at his side.

Services to avoid fighting in Vietnam. In return for amnesty, these men were expected to do two years of public service work. To the surprise of government officials, very few draft evaders and deserters accepted Ford's offer.

Events at Home Under Ford

In domestic matters, Gerald Ford was a moderate Republican in the tradition of Presidents Eisenhower and Nixon.

Fighting Inflation Like previous Presidents, Ford had the difficult task of fighting inflation. He did not believe in wage and price controls. Therefore, he attacked the problem by trying to reduce federal government spending. He also appealed to businesses and workers to cooperate voluntarily to keep prices and wages down. The

results of his W.I.N. (Whip Inflation Now) campaign were limited.

The Veto Power President Ford vetoed more congressional bills than any other U.S. President in a similar two-year period. He said that the government was spending too much money and was running up the national debt. This process, he claimed, was helping to cause the inflation problem. The Democratic-controlled Congress passed a number of bills to create new jobs and build public housing. Claiming that such measures would contribute to inflation, Ford refused to sign them.

Foreign Affairs Under Ford

President Ford continued several foreign policy initiatives begun by President Nixon.

Détente Ford sought to improve United States relations with the Soviet Union and China. As part of détente, the United States and the Soviet Union in 1975 agreed to the Helsinki Accords. The Soviets liked those clauses in the Accords that called for recognition of existing boundaries in Europe. Never before had the United States recognized Soviet territorial gains of World War II. Western nations liked the inclusion of clauses to protect basic human rights. For example, the Accords mentioned the right of individuals to emigrate from any country.

Southeast Asia In the spring of 1975, Communists forces had taken control of much of South Vietnam. President Ford wanted to send the South Vietnamese $700 million in emergency military aid. Congress, however, rejected the idea. It did not want the United States to become involved again in the war. By April, the Communists had conquered Saigon, the South Vietnamese capital city. The war had ended. In the same year, Cambodia and Laos also fell to Communist forces.

SUMMING UP   We have seen that two moderate Republicans served as President from 1969 to 1977. In domestic matters, Richard Nixon and Gerald Ford believed in a limited role for the federal government. In foreign affairs, both sought new directions. During Nixon's years, the United States was engaged in peace negotiations with North Vietnam. Both Nixon and Ford worked to improve United States relations with the Soviet Union and Communist China. Nixon's image was tarnished by his role in the Watergate Affair. President Ford worked to reunite the country by pardoning Nixon and giving deserters and draft evaders an amnesty.

Understanding the Text

On a separate sheet of paper, write the letter of the word or phrase that best completes each of the following statements.

1. In 1968, the Democrats nominated as their presidential candidate *(a)* George Wallace *(b)* Robert Kennedy *(c)* Hubert Humphrey *(d)* Eugene McCarthy.

2. To combat inflation, President Nixon *(a)* froze prices and wages *(b)* called for revenue-sharing *(c)* increased spending by the federal government *(d)* set up the Job Corps.

3. The Twenty-sixth Amendment, ratified in 1971, *(a)* called for equal rights for women *(b)* gave the vote to Americans 18 years old or more *(c)* changed the rules on who might succeed the President *(d)* banned poll taxes.

4. A political figure who unsuccessfully ran for President in 1972 was *(a)* Richard M. Nixon *(b)* Spiro T. Agnew *(c)* George McGovern *(d)* Gerald Ford.

5. The United States first began to withdraw its Armed Forces from Vietnam under President *(a)* Lyndon B. Johnson *(b)* John F. Kennedy *(c)* Richard Nixon *(d)* Gerald Ford.

6. By visiting Communist China and negotiating with the leaders of that country, President Nixon *(a)* ended the policy of détente *(b)* improved relations with the Soviet Union *(c)* made a historic change in U.S. foreign policy in East Asia *(d)* recognized Nationalist China.

7. Those convicted in the courts for covering up the Watergate Affair included *(a)* President Nixon *(b)* several aides to the President *(c)* Spiro Agnew *(d)* all of the above.

8. One unfortunate result of the Watergate Affair was that it *(a)* led to increased federal spending *(b)* weakened U.S. ties with its European allies *(c)* undermined the two-party system *(d)* tended to weaken the confidence of Americans in their government.

9. President Ford did all of the following, *except* *(a)* pardon former President Nixon *(b)* call for voluntary cooperation to fight inflation *(c)* offer draft dodgers an amnesty *(d)* nominate Nelson Rockefeller to be President.

10. Both Presidents Nixon and Ford *(a)* won the Presidency by large margins *(b)* advocated less government spending *(c)* named Nelson Rockefeller Vice President *(d)* resigned from office.

Developing Table-Reading Skills

PERCENTAGE OF AMERICANS WHO REPORTED THEY VOTED (BY AGE GROUP)

	1972	*1976*	*1980*	*1984*
18–20 years	48.3	38.0	35.7	40.8*
21–24 years	50.7	45.6	43.1	
25–44 years	62.7	58.7	58.7	58.4
45–64 years	70.8	68.7	69.3	69.8
65 years and over	63.5	62.2	65.1	67.7
All ages (national average)	63.0	59.2	59.2	59.9

* This 1984 figure available only for combined age group, 18–24.

Study the table above. Then choose the letter of the word or phrase that best completes each sentence. On a separate sheet of paper, match the sentence number with the correct letter.

1. The figure 58.7 represents the percentage of people reporting that they voted in 1976 and who were in the age group *(a)* 18–20 *(b)* 21–24 *(c)* 25–44 *(d)* 45–64.

2. The greatest percentage of people age 18–20 years old who reported that they voted was in *(a)* 1972 *(b)* 1976 *(c)* 1980 *(d)* 1984.

3. In 1980, the age group with the greatest percentage of people who reported that they voted was *(a)* 21–24 *(b)* 25–44 *(c)* 45–64 *(d)* 65 and over.

4. In 1972, the age group that voted in a greater percentage than the national average was *(a)* 21–24 *(b)* 25–44 *(c)* 45–64 *(d)* all of the above.

5. The national average of people reporting that they voted was highest in the year *(a)* 1972 *(b)* 1976 *(c)* 1980 *(d)* 1984.

Thinking About the Lesson

1. In 1969, U.S. astronauts landed on the moon. Do you think that the costs of this program were justified? Why or why not?

2. To fight inflation, President Nixon imposed a freeze on many wages and prices. President Ford, on the other hand, called for voluntary restraints on wage and price increases. Which method, if either, do you think should be used to fight inflation? Explain your answer.

3. President Nixon resigned in the summer of 1974 under the threat of impeachment. If he had not stepped down, should the House have impeached him? Explain your answer.

4. Do you think that Presidents Nixon and Ford made wise moves when they improved relations with the Soviet Union and Communist China? Why or why not?

LESSON 63

Presidents and Programs, 1977 to the Present

Presidents Jimmy Carter and Ronald Reagan headed the two most recent administrations. Both faced the serious domestic problems of high unemployment and inflation. Both worked to lessen government controls on businesses. In foreign affairs, the two men had to tackle different, but equally difficult problems.

James E. Carter (1977–1981)

The nation's 39th President, James E. (Jimmy) Carter, grew up in the rural community of Plains, Georgia. As a young man, he attended the U.S. Naval Academy in Annapolis, Maryland. Upon graduation, he was made an officer in the Navy, where he specialized in nuclear engineering. In 1953, after serving seven years, he left the Navy to run his family's successful peanut business. Then in 1962, he turned to politics, winning election to the Georgia State Senate and later becoming Governor of Georgia.

Presidential Election of 1976

In early 1976, Governor Carter became a candidate for the Democratic nomination for President. Though still not well-known nationally, he ran an energetic campaign and won the nomination.

Carter's opponent that fall was the incumbent President Gerald R. Ford. In the campaign, Democrats criticized Ford for failing to show strong leadership qualities. Also, they blamed him for not pulling the country out of an economic *recession* (slowdown in business activity). Jimmy Carter won a narrow victory in the November election. He had especially strong support from labor unions and minority groups.

Events at Home Under Carter

President Carter's major domestic concerns were an energy crisis and economic problems.

Energy Policies Soon after taking office, Carter proposed a bill to create a Department of Energy. He believed that this plan could be an important step in lessening the country's dependence on expensive, imported oil and gas. Like most Americans, Carter felt that the country should never again become the victim of an oil shortage, as it had become in 1973. (The energy crisis is discussed further in Lesson 84.)

President Jimmy Carter and Rosalynn Carter (holding hands with their daughter Amy) walked to the White House after the inaugural ceremony in 1977. While modern Presidents traditionally travel by limousines, Carter wanted to appear less formal.

Congress set up the Energy Department and passed other energy-related programs, including:

• Aid to private businesses that would develop new sources of energy.

• A rise in taxes on gasoline so that gas would become more expensive to consumers. If gas cost more, Americans would buy less and then less would have to be imported.

• *Decontrol* of (removing government controls on) the prices of fuels. This action had two effects. First, prices of gas and oil went up, resulting in less consumption. Next, oil and gas companies made more money. With the *incentive* (motive) of higher profits, these companies had reason to explore for more oil and gas fields.

Economic Policies   Like earlier Presidents, Carter had to deal with the dual problems of unemployment and inflation. To attack unemployment, he got Congress to pass tax cuts. With less taxes to pay, people had more money to spend and invest. Spending and investing helped the economy and led to the creation of more jobs.

Unfortunately, prices continued to rise during the Carter administration. Part of the problem was that the federal government was borrowing large sums of money to meet its expenses. In the late 1970s, the federal budget showed high and growing *deficits* (an excess of spending over income). Many economists believe that this condition leads to inflation.

Deregulation of Businesses   President Carter claimed that some prices were high because the government protected certain businesses from competition. As a result, he called for the *deregulation* of (removal of regulations from) such businesses. Congress took away from the Civil Aeronautics Board the right to set airline rates. The Interstate Commerce Commission lost its power to set rates in the trucking and railroad industries.

President Carter showed much concern for *human rights* (rights that all people should have). He named many blacks and members of other minorities to top-level federal positions. Andrew Young was appointed by Carter to the important position of U.S. Ambassador to the United Nations. Patricia Harris became Secretary of Housing and Urban Development, and later Secretary of Health, Education, and Welfare.

The administration was also involved in the fight for human rights in foreign countries. It decreased U.S. foreign aid to Bolivia and other nations that denied their citizens basic rights.

Foreign Affairs Under Carter

The most noteworthy achievements of the Carter administration were in foreign policy.

Peace Between Israel and Egypt President Carter played a major part in bringing two Middle East rivals—Israel and Egypt—to the bargaining table. In 1978, the leaders of these two countries met together with President Carter. As a result of this conference, Israel and Egypt later signed a peace treaty. (Discussed further in Lesson 84.)

Panama Canal Treaties The Carter administration negotiated important treaties with Panama. Under these pacts, the United States agreed to turn over full control of the Panama Canal to Panama by the year 2000. (See Lesson 85 for more information on these treaties.)

Relations With China Carter continued the Nixon and Ford policies of improving United States relations with China. In 1979, after a lapse of 30 years, the two nations resumed full diplomatic relations.

Decline in Carter's Popularity

President Carter became less popular in the second half of his term. He had difficulty working effectively with Congress. In addition, he was blamed by many Americans for:

• Causing the poor state of the economy.
• Being a weak President who had trouble making decisions.
• Handling the Iranian hostage crisis poorly. In 1979, Iranian *militants* (people aggressively active in a cause) had seized Americans, mostly State Department employees stationed in Teheran, Iran. Fifty-two Americans, held as hostages for 14 months, were not released until shortly after Carter left office.
• Making controversial decisions in reaction

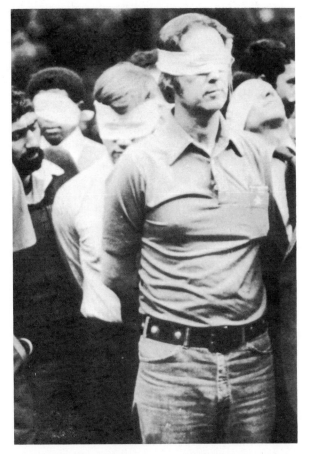

The men with blindfolds were some of the American hostages in Teheran in 1979. Iranian militants wanted to exchange the hostages for Shah Mohammad Reza Pahlavi, the former ruler of Iran who had fled the country earlier in the year.

to the Soviet invasion of Afghanistan in 1979. By banning the sale of American grain to the Soviets, Carter angered many U.S. farmers. Many Americans also disliked the President's decision to have U.S. athletes boycott the 1980 Summer Olympics, held in Moscow.

Carter's supporters strongly defended him. They claimed that he was faced by extremely difficult problems not of his making. Nonetheless, Carter was less popular when he ran for re-election in 1980 than he had been in 1976.

Ronald W. Reagan (1981–   )

The Republicans in 1980 chose Ronald W. Reagan of California to run for President. Before entering politics, Reagan had been a successful motion picture actor. He had served as head of a national labor union in the film industry. Leaving the entertainment world in 1967, he then served two terms as Governor of California.

In 1980, Reagan won the presidential election by a wide margin. At age 69, he had become the oldest person ever elected to the Presidency. In the same year, the Republicans won control of the Senate, while the Democrats kept their majority in the House.

Domestic Politics Under Reagan

Reagan held conservative ideas regarding government and the economy. He spoke of the need to "get government off the backs of the American people."

Reduction in Federal Activities The Reagan administration tried to limit the size and activities of the federal government. Reagan wanted to give many of the federal government's powers and responsibilities to the states. In line with this desire, budgets were cut for some federal social programs, such as food stamps and job-training centers. In some cases, states assumed responsibility for social programs.

Deregulation Reagan continued and broadened the deregulation policy begun by the Carter administration. Under Reagan, standards set by the Environmental Protection Administration and the Consumer Product Safety Commission were relaxed. Reagan wanted to decrease the role of government and allow businesses more freedom to make money. He believed that government regulations discouraged innovations in business practices and products.

Reaganomics Reagan's economic program became known as "Reaganomics." One of its main principles was the lowering of personal and corporate income taxes. Advocates of Reaganomics believed that if taxes were lowered, owners of businesses would have more money to invest in new factories, equipment, and other ventures. New investments would lead to increased business activity and, thus, more jobs.

Creating more jobs was an important concern of Americans in 1981 and 1982. In those years, the country was going through a recession with high levels of unemployment. Reagan's opponents in Congress wanted to attack the unemployment problem by increasing gov-

Nancy and Ronald Reagan are shown greeting supporters at the Republican National Convention in 1980.

In 1984, Democrat Geraldine Ferraro became the first female vice-presidential candidate of a major U.S. political party.

ernment spending. They believed that more federal spending should go to businesses that make goods or provide services for the government. These expanding businesses would then hire more workers. President Reagan, however, opposed this approach. He did not want to increase government spending, except for the nation's defense.

The 1984 Election   By 1984, the national economy had recovered from the recession. Production increased in many industries, and unemployment rates declined. The Reagan administration took credit for these changes and a substantial decline in the rate of inflation. The improved economy was one of the reasons that Ronald Reagan was able to win re-election in 1984. In that year, his main opponent was Walter Mondale of Minnesota—Carter's Vice President. Reagan defeated Mondale, capturing 525 out of 538 electoral votes.

Federal Deficits   President Reagan hoped to reduce deficits in the federal budget. But the tax cuts, which began in 1981, resulted in lower tax collections. The lower tax collections pre-

vented the federal government from balancing the budget. President Reagan had hoped that federal spending would be reduced enough to balance the losses caused by the tax cuts. Instead, the federal deficit continued to rise into 1986. This rise was partly due to increases in defense spending.

Citing the Soviet threat, President Reagan favored higher levels of defense spending. Crises in Central America, Grenada, and the Middle East had the effect of making Congress more willing to vote for Reagan's military budgets. Congress provided funds for costly new defense programs, such as the construction of MX missiles.

Criticisms of the Reagan Program   Many Americans disliked certain aspects of Reagan's policies. Some complained that the interests of poor people were being ignored to help big businesses and wealthy investors. Many people thought that a large defense budget was not needed—that the United States already had enough weapons to defend itself.

Critics of deregulation claimed that this policy had many weaknesses. They said that:

• By lowering certain standards, such as in the use of dangerous chemicals, and by reducing the number of federal safety inspectors, the government was taking unnecessary risks.

• With less enforcement of environmental standards, Americans could not be sure that they lived in neighborhoods free of toxic wastes.

Foreign Affairs Under Reagan

President Reagan was very active in foreign affairs, often taking strong positions on issues.

Relations With the Soviets   After Reagan took office, United States relations with the Soviet Union grew worse. In one speech, the President went so far as to label the USSR "an evil empire" for denying freedom to its own citizens. Events that contributed to the decline in relations included:

• The continued presence of the Soviet Army in Afghanistan.

• The shooting down in 1983 of a South Korean passenger jet by the Soviets.

• The U.S. installation of medium-range nuclear missiles in Western Europe in 1983 and 1984. (Discussed in Lesson 80.)

• The "Star Wars" Program (Strategic Defense Initiative). The United States decided to attempt to develop a defense system in outer space that could knock out enemy missiles and other weapons. The Soviet government, saying that such a system would allow the United States to start and win a nuclear war, strongly criticized this program.

In spite of all the troubles surrounding U.S.-USSR relations, there were some hopeful signs. In the fall of 1985, President Reagan met with the Soviet leader Mikhail Gorbachev in Geneva, Switzerland. The two men decided that this meeting would be the first in a series of summit conferences on issues about which the two countries were at odds.

Middle East Policies   President Reagan continued U.S. efforts to bring about peace in the Middle East. In 1983, fighting and civil disorder in Lebanon led the President to send U.S. Marines there. They were removed in 1984. (See Lesson 84 for a discussion of our Middle East policies.)

Central American Crises   During Reagan's years in office, the United States became involved more deeply in a civil war in El Salvador. U.S. economic and military aid to the Salvadorean government increased greatly. Moreover, the United States gave aid to forces, called "Contras," seeking the overthrow of the Nicaraguan government. (Latin American affairs are discussed in more detail in Lesson 85.)

The Caribbean   To counter growing Cuban influence in the Caribbean island of Grenada, Reagan sent U.S. forces there in October, 1983.

In Haiti, the United States had since 1967 supported the rule of the Duvalier family. First, Dr. François Duvalier and then his son Jean-Claude had ruled this poor island nation as dictators. President Reagan continued U.S. economic aid to Haiti until January, 1986, when aid was suspended. U.S. officials then said that the Duvalier regime was too corrupt and had allowed too many abuses against Haiti citizens by the secret police. The police had arrested, tortured, and killed many opponents of the Duvaliers. Fearing for his life, Jean-Claude Duvalier left riot-torn Haiti in February, 1986.

Change in the Philippines   Another leader of a country close to the United States—Ferdinand Marcos of the Philippines—fell from power in February, 1986. Marcos had been President of the Philippines since 1965. He had helped strengthen the U.S.-Filipino military alliance, allowing the United States to maintain two military bases in his country. Many Americans, though, had criticized U.S. ties with Marcos. Critics maintained that as President he had gotten wealthy through improper use of public funds. Critics charged that he had contributed to the decline of democracy in his country by rigging elections and imprisoning and killing some of his critics. One incident with which critics connected Marcos was the 1983 murder of opposition leader Benigno Aquino in 1983. Aquino was shot at the Manila airport upon arriving in the country after a 3-year exile.

In 1986, the Philippines had a presidential election. Marcos's main opponent was the widow of the slain politician, Corazon Aquino. Marcos claimed that he had won the election, but many observers believed that he had cheated. After large crowds of Filipinos demonstrated against Marcos, he was forced to leave the country. Corazon Aquino succeeded him.

The Developing Space Program

Under Presidents Carter and Reagan, the U.S. space program made great strides.

Visits to the Planets In 1977, the National Aeronautics and Space Administration (NASA) launched *Voyager 1* and *Voyager 2* into space. These twin, unmanned space probes passed close by Jupiter in 1979 and Saturn in 1980 and 1981. *Voyager 2* went on to Uranus, reaching this planet in 1986. Photographs from the space probes told us much about the moons, rings, and atmospheres of the three planets.

The Shuttle Program Meanwhile, NASA was developing a *shuttle* (reusable, manned spacecraft). The first such vehicle, called *Columbia*, was launched in 1981. Shuttles take off from launching pads with the aid of rockets. Once in orbit, they can circle the earth for many days, eventually landing on extended runways, like airplanes do. Astronauts on shuttle flights can perform scientific experiments and send satellites into orbit. Shuttle astronauts have been able to retrieve damaged satellites and repair them.

The shuttle program was temporarily halted in 1986 after *Challenger* blew up upon launching. All seven Americans aboard died, including the first civilian in space, Christa McAuliffe. She had been a social studies teacher in New Hampshire. Since that disaster, NASA has been at work finding ways to make shuttle flights safer. Some experts have suggested that NASA put more emphasis on unmanned spacecraft. They claim that these vehicles can perform many of the same functions that manned shuttles do.

In 1983, Sally K. Ride became the first female U.S. astronaut to go into space. Here she is shown working aboard the shuttle orbiter *Challenger*.

SUMMING UP   We have seen how Presidents Carter and Reagan led the United States through some difficult years. At home, the economy faltered and then regained strength. Abroad, the United States faced a stronger and more aggressive Soviet Union, bent on expanding its influence beyond its borders. While Jimmy Carter lost popularity after a few years in office, Ronald Reagan remained popular. After four years in office, he went on to win re-election in 1984 by an overwhelming majority.

Understanding the Text

On a separate sheet of paper, write the letter of the word or phrase that best completes each of the following statements.

1. Before becoming President, Jimmy Carter was a/an (a) Air Force officer (b) Governor of Georgia (c) California state senator (d) labor union officer.

2. Carter's Republican opponent in the 1976 presidential election was (a) Walter Mondale (b) Ronald W. Reagan (c) Gerald R. Ford (d) Andrew Young.

3. A step taken by Congress and the Carter administration to try to solve the energy crisis was (a) decontrol of fuel prices (b) imposition of higher taxes on gasoline (c) creation of the Department of Energy (d) all of the above.

4. A noteworthy accomplishment of the Carter administration was (a) ending the war in Vietnam (b) balancing the federal budget (c) arranging a quick release of U.S. hostages in Iran (d) helping Israel and Egypt negotiate a peace treaty.

5. Under deregulation, certain businesses (a) gained greater control over their operations (b) urged the government to fix prices (c) came under greater governmental control (d) none of the above.

6. Which of the following does *not* correctly describe Ronald Reagan as a candidate in the 1980 presidential elections? He (a) had wide experience in the entertainment industry (b) was then a Democrat (c) was a former state governor (d) was a supporter of conservative policies.

7. Among the policies favored by President Reagan was (a) raising taxes for everyone (b) drastically reducing the military budget (c) lessening the size and activities of the federal government (d) spending much more money on welfare programs.

8. The term "Reaganomics" applies to the (a) U.S. hostages in Iran (b) Reagan's economic policies (c) terms of the Panama Canal treaties (d) U.S. human rights record.

9. The Reagan administration played an active military role in (a) El Salvador (b) Grenada (c) Lebanon (d) all of the above.

10. Which of the following statements best describes the Carter and Reagan administrations? (a) They were largely free of serious problems and crises. (b) They faced serious problems in foreign affairs, but not in domestic ones. (c) They were able to reduce and balance the federal budget. (d) They had both successes and failures in dealing with domestic and foreign affairs.

Developing Reference Skills

Examine the excerpts from the *Readers' Guide to Periodical Literature*, May, 1984, Vol. 84, No. 5, printed below. This guide, which lists articles found in leading magazines, is a valuable reference tool. Each volume covers a specific time period during which articles listed were published. Within each volume, the articles are organized by author and by subject matter.

Reagan, Ronald, 1911–

16th report on Cyprus [message to Congress, November 7, 1983] *Dep State Bull* 83:29 D '83

1984 State of the Union [address, January 25, 1984] *Vital Speeches Day* 50:258-62 F 15 '84

America's commitment to peace [address, October 27, 1983] il por *Dep State Bull* 83:1-5 D '83

Anniversary of the Soviet invasion of Afghanistan [statement, December 27, 1983] *Dep State Bull* 84:37-8 F '84

Bill of Rights Day; Human Rights Day and Week, 1983 [proclamation, December 9, 1983] *Dep State Bull* 84:59-60 Ja '84

CBI recipients designated. *Dep State Bull* 84:84 Ja '84

Continuation of export control regulations [message to Congress, October 14, 1983] *Dep State Bull* 83:19 D '83

Educational excellence 1982–1983 [adaptation of address, September 28, 1983] *Am Educ* 19:2-3 D '83

In praise of American women. il pors *Ladies Home J* 101:26+ Ja '84

Age

Reagan at 73: Moses was 80. il por *U S News World Rep* 96:11 F 20 '84

Correspondence

When Americans write the president, Anne Higgins gets the mail to the chief. K. Huff. il pors *People Wkly* 21:81-2 Ja 16 '84

Relations with Congress

Amazing Grace [presidential line-item veto] *New Repub* 190:6 F 6 '84

Broader veto power wouldn't help the budget deficit [line-item authority] S. A. Wildstrom. *Bus Week* p24 F 6 '84

Congress talks back [foreign policy issues] R. Watson. il *Newsweek* 103:43-4 Ap 2 '84

Republicans close ranks on the deficit. il por *U S News World Rep* 96:11 Mr 26 '84

Rising cry: get out of Lebanon. il *U S News World Rep* 96:9 F 13 '84

Step in the right direction [budget deficits] il por *Time* 123:23 Mr 26 '84

Who cares about deficits? R. Clawson. *U S News World Rep* 96:72 F 13 '84

Religion

Presidential piety: must it be private? M. E. Marty. *Christ Century* 101:187-8 F 22 '84

Staff

Baker takes the cake. M. Kondracke. *New Repub* 190:10-12 F 20 '84

Reagan's double shuffle. J. McLaughlin. *Natl Rev* 36:23 F 24 '84

Reagan's left-hand man [R. Darman] W. R. Doerner. il por *Time* 123:28 Mr 12 '84

Ronald Reagan's Mr. Inside [R. Darman] M. Starr. por *Newsweek* 103:37-8 Mr 12 '84

State of the Union messages

1984 State of the Union [address, January 25, 1984] R. Reagan. *Vital Speeches Day* 50:258-62 F 15 '84

Democrats answer president's speech [excerpts from transcript of television program] il *U S News World Rep* 96:71 F 6 '84

Election-year gamble. S. Huntley. il por *U S News World Rep* 96:18-20 F 6 '84

State of the Union III. *Nation* 238:113 F 4 '84 The two Ronnies. il *Progressive* 48:9 Mr '84

Visit to Japan, 1983

President Reagan visits Japan and the Republic of Korea. R. Reagan. il pors *Dep State Bull* 84:1-31 Ja '84

Visit to Korea (South), 1983

President Reagan visits Japan and the Republic of Korea. R. Reagan. il pors *Dep State Bull* 84:1-31 Ja '84

Following is a list of abbreviations used in the excerpt, along with their meanings:

il	illustrated
por(s)	portrait(s)
Ja	January
F	February
Mr	March
Ap	April
N	November
D	December
Am Educ	*American Education*
Bus Week	*Business Week*
Christ Century	*The Christian Century*
Dep State Bull	*Department of State Bulletin*
Ladies Home J	*Ladies Home Journal*
Nation	*The Nation*
Natl Rev	*National Review*
New Repub	*The New Republic*
People Wkly	*People Weekly*
Progressive	*The Progressive*
US News	*U.S. News and World*
World Rep	*Report*
Vital Speeches Day	*Vital Speeches of the Day*

Choose the letter of the word or phrase that best completes each sentence. On a separate sheet of paper, match the sentence number with the correct letter.

1. The author of the first entry, "16th Report on Cyprus," was (*a*) Ronald Reagan (*b*) the Department of State (*c*) Congress (*d*) *Dep State Bull.*

2. The second entry concerned President Reagan's State of the Union message of 1984. This address appeared in *Vital Speeches of the Day* (*a*) in May, 1984 (*b*) on January 25, 1984 (*c*) on February 15, 1984 (*d*) none of the above.

3. Under the subheading "Relations with Congress," articles are arranged (*a*) chronologically (*b*) alphabetically by the first word of the articles (*c*) alphabetically by the last name of the authors (*d*) alphabetically by the name of the magazines.

4. The name of a periodical is generally followed by a volume number and then page numbers. The article listed under the subheading "Religion" can be found in *The Christian Century* in (*a*) volumes 187 and 188, page 101 (*b*) volume 22, page 84 (*c*) volume 101, pages 187 and 188 (*d*) none of the above.

5. For an article on President Reagan's 1983 visit to Japan, one would look at the periodical (*a*) *The Christian Century* (*b*) *Department of State Bulletin* (*c*) *America* (*d*) *Rolling Stone.*

Thinking About the Lesson

1. Why did President Carter want to create a Department of Energy?

2. Who benefits from deregulation of businesses? Who is harmed? Do you favor the trend toward deregulating more and more industries? Why or why not?

3. Under President Carter's direction, the United States government started a new human rights policy. It cut off aid to certain countries that were known to violate the human rights of their citizens. Do you think that the United States should try to influence the internal affairs of other nations in this way? Explain your answer.

4. Ronald Reagan has been labelled a "conservative" by many political commentators. Do you think that this label is appropriate? Why or why not?

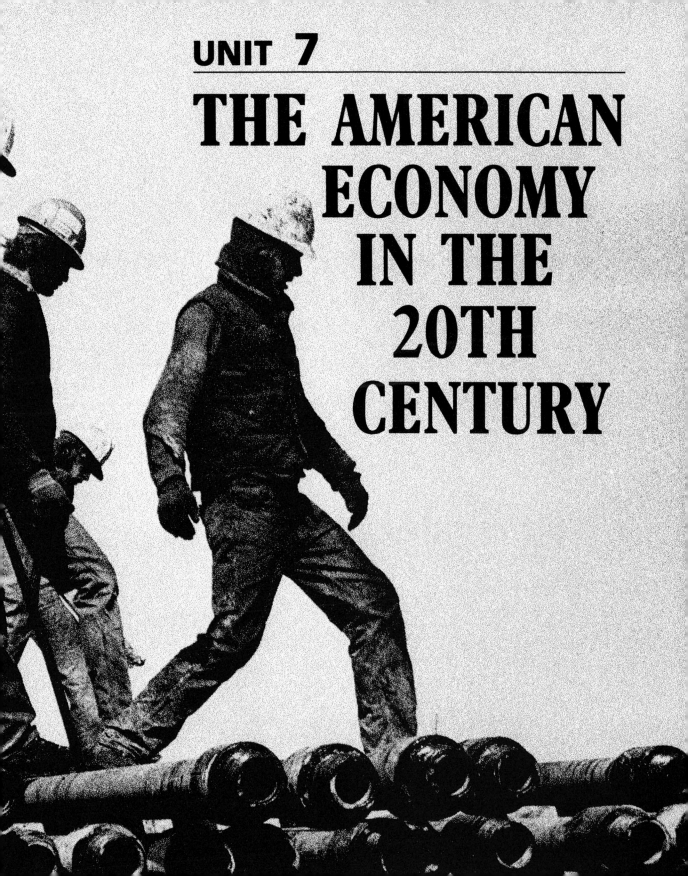

UNIT 7
THE AMERICAN ECONOMY IN THE 20TH CENTURY

Industrial Growth From 1900 to 1940

In Lesson 46, we learned that by 1900 the United States had become the world's leading producer of manufactured goods. In the 20th century, its economy grew even more powerful, despite the Great Depression of the 1930s. The American economy's ability to grow and recover was due to many factors.

Economic Expansion

From 1900 to 1940, the American economy grew tremendously. The country's annual *gross national product* (GNP), the total value of all goods and services produced in a year, rose from $19 billion to $100 billion. During this 40-year period, America's steel production leaped from 11 million tons to almost 67 million. Its crude oil production swelled from 64 million barrels to almost 1.4 billion.

This fantastic growth of American private enterprises was made possible by a number of developments.

Improved Communications The nation's telephone and mail services improved considerably in the 20th century. They both kept up with a rise in the country's population and the expanded needs of businesses. In the 1920s, radio became a new means of communicating as commercial stations began broadcasting. Later, with the appearance of commercial television in 1939, businesses had two broadcast media on which to advertise.

Improved Transportation At the beginning of the 20th century, motor vehicles provided a new and exciting way to move around. Cars, trucks, and buses were replacing the horse and buggy, creating a demand for paved roads. In a few American cities, subway systems supplied a way to get around underground. Railroad construction in the United States continued to expand until the 1920s. Although the number of miles of new railroad tracks then leveled off, railroads remained an important means of transporting both passengers and freight. Air transportation was just a dream before Orville and Wilbur Wright put a powered flying machine into the air in 1903. By 1920, airplanes were being used to carry mail across the country. Regular airline passenger and freight service also began in the 1920s.

Greater Energy Supplies After 1900, *gasoline* (a fuel made from oil) became important in running automobiles and other machines. Coal and water power, both abundant energy sources in the 19th century, continued to be relied on after 1900. These two energy sources, as well

414

as oil, were used in generating electricity. Electrical lighting of businesses and homes increased greatly in the early 20th century. In addition, more and more factories began to use electricity to run their operations.

Improved Methods of Production Mass production methods of the 19th century were refined and improved after 1900. The most remarkable improvement was the *assembly line,* used by Henry Ford in making the Model T. On assembly lines, workers performed specific, assigned tasks as the cars being assembled passed by them on large conveyer belts.

By introducing the assembly line in 1909, Henry Ford was able to produce a low-priced car that average Americans could afford. Previously, only wealthy Americans were able to buy automobiles. From 1908 to 1927, the Ford Motor Company sold over 15 million Model T's. Not only did Henry Ford help change the way Americans traveled, but he influenced worker-employer relations as well. In 1914, he greatly increased his workers' wages, setting a $5-a-day minimum wage for adult workers. This wage was very high for the time. Ford believed that raising wages was good for business. He thought that with more money, his workers would be more likely to buy his cars.

In the 1920s, automobile production replaced steel production as the country's major manufacturing industry. Automobile manufacturers and related industries employed some 4 million workers. This figure represented about nine percent of the nation's total labor force. Much of the country's economic expansion in the 1920s was due to automobile production. Then, as the economy experienced the Great Depression in the 1930s, automobile production temporarily declined.

Other Factors In addition to the above, the United States had other factors that led to the country's economic growth:

• A political environment favorable to businesses.

• Freedom from devastating wars on its soil.

These employees of the Ford Motor Company, Highland Park, Michigan, worked on an assembly line that produced the Model T.

• Good foreign markets for its goods in peacetime, and for its arms in wartime.

• A growing, relatively well-educated, and affluent population. The United States had both an excellent labor pool and a solid domestic market for its products.

Business Concentration

In the 20th century, American businesses continued the late-19th-century trend of getting together to reduce competition. Increasingly common was the *merger*, a joining together of several businesses. In a merger, a big company may "swallow up" smaller competitors. Or different companies may come together voluntarily to form a new corporation.

Two major kinds of business mergers developed—horizontal ones and vertical ones. In a *horizontal combination*, companies in the same industry, such as steel production, joined together. In a *vertical combination*, a corporation took over companies that had been supplying it. For example, a newspaper company might buy forest lands and paper mills to produce paper for its publications.

Muckrakers In the early 1900s, certain writers brought to the public's attention abuses of big businesses. These writers were called *muckrakers* because they dug up *muck* (dirt) about individuals and big corporations. Early muckrakers included:

• Ida Tarbell, who exposed the monopolistic practices of Standard Oil Company.

• Upton Sinclair, author of *The Jungle* (1906). He directed public attention to poor working conditions and unsanitary production methods in the meat-packing industry.

• Frank Norris, who exposed the power that railroads held over farmers. His best-known works were *The Octopus* (1901) and *The Pit* (1903).

Ida Tarbell (top), editor of *McClure's Magazine* (inset), wrote many articles critical of the Standard Oil Company. Lincoln Steffens, another muckraker who wrote for *McClure's*, specialized in exposing corrupt political figures.

Government Regulation of Businesses

In part because of muckrakers' disclosures, the federal government stepped up its policy of regulating harmful and unfair business practices. In addition, President Theodore Roosevelt and other government leaders realized that earlier attempts to regulate businesses had been ineffective. The Interstate Commerce Act and the Sherman Antitrust Act, discussed in Lesson 47, were now considered too weak. The Supreme Court had interpreted these laws in favor of business interests and at the expense of consumers. In addition, businesses were often able to get around antitrust laws by changing the way their corporations were organized.

Progressive Era Reforms During the Progressive era (1901–1921), Congress passed many important pieces of legislation designed to regulate businesses:

• Elkins Act (1903). This law barred companies from receiving rebates from railroads.

• Pure Food and Drug Act and the Meat Inspection Act (1906), discussed on page 361.

These two laws were among the first effective government efforts to help protect consumers.

• Hepburn Act (1906). With this legislation, Congress gave the Interstate Commerce Commission (ICC) more powers, including the right to set railroad rates.

• Mann-Elkins Act (1910). In this act, the ICC obtained the power to control the telephone, telegraph, wireless, and cable industries.

• Federal Reserve Act (1913), discussed on page 363.

• Clayton Antitrust Act (1914). The Clayton Act filled some of the holes in the Sherman Antitrust Act of 1890. The new law prohibited "cutthroat" price reductions (intended to knock out competitors by lowering prices) when these actions would help create a monopoly.

Among other provisions, the Meat Inspection Act of 1906 called for federal officials to inspect poultry that was for sale.

• Federal Trade Commission Act (1914). This act set up the FTC, which was empowered to investigate unfair business practices.

Period of Weaker Government Regulation

During most of the 1920s, a relatively prosperous time, the conservative Republican administrations favored fewer regulations of businesses. As regulations were relaxed, the number of business mergers again increased. In addition to industrial mergers, some retail businesses began to create a new kind of business organization—the *chain*. For example, several grocery store chains were formed. Some chains grew so large that they forced a number of independently owned stores to go out of business.

Businesses and the Great Depression

During the Republican administration of Herbert Hoover, the nation's economy went into a deep decline known as the Great Depression. Hoover believed in only limited government intervention to help the economy. He thought that private businesses could reverse the decline by themselves.

Democratic leaders disagreed, saying that strong reform measures and more government control of the economy were needed. In 1933, soon after Franklin D. Roosevelt took office, he laid before Congress his proposals for fighting the depression. As we learned in Lesson 59, many of these New Deal proposals became law. Important New Deal measures that provided long-term reforms of business practices included the:

• Creation of the Federal Deposit Insurance Corporation in 1933.

• Passage of the Securities Exchange Act of 1934. Firms selling *securities* (stocks and bonds) were required to file with the government information about each security offered.

• Creation of the Securities and Exchange Commission. The SEC helped protect buyers of stocks and bonds against *fraud* (dishonest acts).

• Passage of the Public Utility Holding Company Act of 1935. This act regulated holding companies that owned *public utilities* (private companies that provide essential services for the public). Because of the power of the holding companies, their public utilities had been charging high rates for electricity and gas.

Other Policies Affecting Businesses

With the New Deal, the U.S. government for the first time took on the responsibility of intervening in the economy to attain prosperity. One way that the government intervened was by spending more. It spent much money aiding farmers, the unemployed, and Social Security recipients. This spending tended to stimulate the economy. More Americans had more money to spend. Factories began to produce more goods, and businesses began to sell more goods and services.

The End of the Depression

Despite a recession in 1937–1938, the U.S. economy did recover from the depression. Many economists believe that New Deal measures were responsible. Others, however, think that increased government spending in World War II was the major reason that the economy improved.

GROSS NATIONAL PRODUCT, 1900–1940

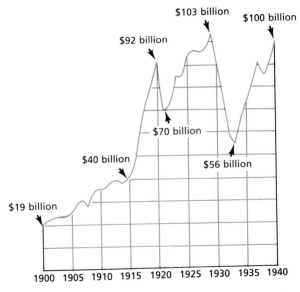

$103 billion
$100 billion
$92 billion
$70 billion
$40 billion
$56 billion
$19 billion

1900 1905 1910 1915 1920 1925 1930 1935 1940

SUMMING UP   We have seen how improvements in communication, transportation, energy supplies, and methods of production helped strengthen the U.S. economy after 1900. As the economy grew, some businesses merged and became more powerful. Responding to critics of powerful businesses, the government sought to regulate mergers. Other regulations were imposed in the 1930s as part of the efforts to fight the Great Depression.

Understanding the Text

On a separate sheet of paper, write the letter of the word or phrase that best completes each of the following statements.

1. One means of communication *not* common in the 1920s was *(a)* the telephone *(b)* mail service *(c)* radio *(d)* television.

2. A method of transportation widely used *before* the 20th century was the *(a)* railroad *(b)* truck *(c)* airplane *(d)* automobile.

3. A source of power widely used between 1900 and 1940 was *(a)* coal *(b)* waterpower *(c)* oil *(d)* all of the above.

4. From reading the lesson, we learn that Henry Ford *(a)* got rich by making conveyer belts *(b)* made Model T's on assembly lines *(c)* paid the lowest wages of any automobile manufacturer *(d)* employed about nine percent of the nation's labor force.

5. An American *not* known as a writer who exposed unfair or dangerous practices of big businesses was *(a)* Ida Tarbell *(b)* Frank Norris *(c)* Orville Wright *(d)* Upton Sinclair.

6. An example of legislation passed by Congress during the Progressive era, 1901–1921, was the *(a)* Clayton Antitrust Act *(b)* Sherman Antitrust Act *(c)* Securities Exchange Act *(d)* none of the above.

7. A federal law that provided for regulation of gas and electric companies was the *(a)* Pure Food and Drug Act *(b)* Securities Exchange Act *(c)* Public Utility Holding Company Act *(d)* Meat Inspection Act.

8. The SEC helped buyers of *(a)* automobiles *(b)* stocks and bonds *(c)* electricity *(d)* waterpower.

9. From reading this lesson, one can conclude that the regulation of businesses by the government *(a)* was greater in 1940 than in 1900 *(b)* decreased in the 1930s *(c)* was greater in 1900 than in 1940 *(d)* increased greatly in the 1920s.

10. In the 1930s, the federal government tried to improve economic conditions by *(a)* spending less *(b)* regulating the economy less *(c)* spending more *(d)* none of the above.

Developing Graph-Reading and Computational Skills

NUMBER OF TELEPHONES IN THE UNITED STATES, 1900–1940

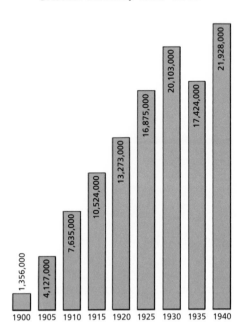

NUMBER OF TELEPHONES FOR EVERY 1,000 PEOPLE, 1900–1940

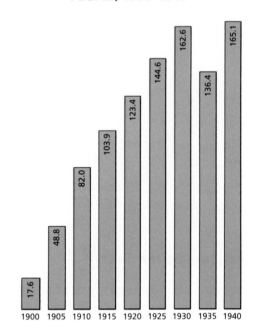

Study the bar graphs above. Then choose the letter of the word or phrase that best completes each sentence. On a separate sheet of paper, match the sentence number with the correct letter.

1. In 1900, the number of telephones in the United States was *(a)* 17.6 *(b)* 7,635,000 *(c)* 21,928,000 *(d)* none of the above.

2. In 1930, the number of telephones for every 1,000 people in the country was *(a)* 17.6 *(b)* 162.6 *(c)* 20.1 *(d)* 20,103,000.

3. Between 1900 and 1920, the number of telephones in the country *(a)* almost doubled *(b)* increased by about ten times *(c)* decreased by about five-times *(d)* remained about the same.

4. The total number of telephones in the country showed a drop from five years previously in the year *(a)* 1905 *(b)* 1915 *(c)* 1935 *(d)* none of the above.

5. Determine the population of the United States in 1910 using only the information in the graphs. The answer can be obtained through two mathematical operations. Do not look up the answer in a reference book except to check on the answer that you get by computation. In 1910, the U.S. population was approximately *(a)* 93,000,000 *(b)* 9,000,000 *(c)* 106,000,000 *(d)* 10,000,000.

Thinking About the Lesson

1. Why did the U.S. economy grow to be so strong during the first half of the 20th century?

2. What effect did the muckrakers have upon the U.S. government's attitude toward business regulation?

3. Do you think that government intervention in the economy was necessary at any time during the period 1900–1940? Why or why not?

The Changing Status of Labor

The American labor movement, which had expanded greatly in the second half of the 19th century, grew even more in the 20th. As American industry expanded, so did the ranks of skilled and unskilled workers. Some of them joined labor unions, which benefited from more favorable federal laws. Other workers did not join. Nevertheless, both union and non-union workers improved their wages, benefits, and working conditions.

The Expanding Labor Movement

As we learned in Lesson 48, the American Federation of Labor (AFL) was growing rapidly at the turn of the century. By 1900, it already had over 500,000 members. In 1920, leaders of this organization of craft unions counted 4 million members.

In 1905, some unions that had been outside the AFL formed a rival, more radical federation. The Industrial Workers of the World (IWW) differed from the AFL in several respects:

• Members of the IWW did not like *capitalism* (economic system based on private ownership of businesses and free enterprise). They wanted to replace it with *socialism* (publicly controlled economic system).

• They called for the use of violent methods, such as *sabotage*, to achieve their goals.

• They thought unions should not be organized on a craft basis. Instead, they brought both skilled and unskilled workers of an industry into the same union. Such groups were called *industrial unions* because they tried to organize the wage earners of a whole industry.

The IWW was especially strong in the West, in the lumber and mining industries. The union also gained a following in textile mills of New England and New Jersey. At one time numbering 100,000 members, the IWW began to decline in strength after World War I. By then, many Americans had become disillusioned with the union for its use of violence. In addition, the federal government had begun systematically to fight the IWW. Many IWW leaders were arrested for opposing U.S. entry into World War I.

Non-Union Workers Despite the growth of labor unions, most workers remained outside the ranks of organized labor. By 1920, only one worker in six was a union member. The AFL was partly responsible for this situation, since it did not want to organize unskilled workers. Besides, most of its member craft unions were slow to accept women workers and members of minority groups.

421

Government Actions Favorable to Workers

During the Progressive era (1901–1921), federal and state governments passed a number of laws and took many actions favorable to workers.

Anthracite Coal Strike In 1902, the United Mine Workers struck against the owners of coal mines in Pennsylvania. The miners wanted higher wages, a shorter workday, and better working conditions. Above all, they wanted their union recognized. After the strike had been going on for many months, President Theodore Roosevelt called the interested parties to the White House. Roosevelt became angry with the mine owners for refusing to consider his offer of arbitration. He threatened to send in U.S. soldiers to take over the mines. This threat changed the mine owners' attitude, and soon arbitration began. Months later, in 1903, federal arbitrators imposed a compromise settlement: a nine-hour workday and a ten-percent increase in wages. The arbitrators refused, however, to make the employers recognize the United Mine Workers or any other union.

Between 1908 and 1912, photographer Lewis W. Hine took hundreds of pictures of child laborers. Children generally did not belong to unions and were paid very low wages.

Department of Labor In 1903, Congress set up a Department of Commerce and Labor. Then in 1913, the Labor Department became separate from Commerce. The Secretary of Labor has since been a member of the President's Cabinet. The Department of Labor carries out a wide range of activities helpful to both union and non-union members.

State Labor Laws In the early 20th century, Progressive reformers enacted many state laws favorable to workers. For example, Maryland in 1902 became the first state to pass laws to compensate workers injured on the job. In 1912, Massachusetts legislated a minimum wage. Other state laws regulated working conditions, length of workday, and child labor.

Clayton Antitrust Act Organized labor got a

boost from Congress in 1914 with the passage of the Clayton Antitrust Act. Previously, some unions had been sued under provisions of the Sherman Antitrust Act. The Clayton Act declared that unions could no longer be sued under antitrust laws for restraining trade. The new law also helped organized labor because it stated that strikes and peaceful picketing were legal.

Other Federal Legislation Following the lead of several states, Congress in 1916 passed the Workmen's Compensation Act. For the first time, federal civil service employees were eligible for *disability pay* (compensation for not being able to work because of injuries). Another 1916 law—the Adamson Act—benefited railway workers on lines that crossed state borders. Among other improvements, this law gave the workers an eight-hour workday.

Labor During World War I

As the country mobilized for war in 1917, the need for workers in all kinds of industries grew. Many blacks, women, and others who had been excluded from the labor force now obtained jobs. Membership in labor unions almost doubled, partly because of favorable federal actions. (See the graph on page 427.)

National War Labor Board Government leaders thought that it was in the interest of the war effort to have fewer strikes. Therefore, in 1918 the federal government set up a board to help settle labor disputes. The National War Labor Board worked also to prevent firings of workers who were trying to organize unions.

Post-War Developments

Immediately after the war, American workers experienced especially difficult times of inflation and unemployment. Many soldiers returning home could not find jobs. A considerable number of Americans who had been employed during the war lost their jobs as industries cut back production or failed. Wages declined or did not rise as fast as prices. For these reasons, in 1919 some 4 million Americans went out on strike. Some of the best-known and most violent strikes took place in the coal and steel industries and in the Boston Police Department. Workers lost all three of these conflicts.

The 1920s During the 1920s, unions in America lost ground. From 1920 to 1923, union membership declined sharply from 5 million to 3.5 million. By 1929, it had gone down slightly more—to 3.4 million. One of the reasons for the decline was the use of government injunctions against strikes. Probably more important was the state of the American economy itself. After 1922, American workers participated in the country's rising prosperity by receiving

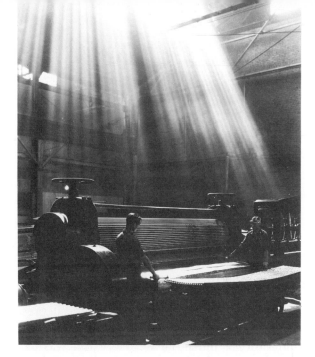

These depression-era employees of the Central Alloy Steel Corporation in Massillon, Ohio, probably felt themselves lucky to have jobs.

higher wages. As their economic position improved, workers saw less need for unions.

The Great Depression and Labor

The increased prosperity of American workers did not last long. Along with most other Americans, they suffered during the Great Depression of the 1930s. Most of those workers who did not lose their jobs had to take cuts in their salaries.

At the beginning of the depression, unions lost strength. Those workers who were employed were grateful to have jobs and usually did not wish to risk them by making demands or going out on strike. By 1933, union membership was down to 2.9 million. Gradually, however, the federal government responded to the plight of workers by aiding labor's efforts to organize.

Norris-LaGuardia Act In 1932, during the administration of Herbert Hoover, Congress passed the Norris-LaGuardia Act, which limited the use of federal court injunctions against unions. It also outlawed *yellow dog contracts* (contracts between employers and employees that prohibited employees from joining a union).

A New Deal for Labor President Franklin D. Roosevelt believed that a strong union movement was needed to help bring about economic recovery. He thought that if workers were organized, they would earn higher wages. In this way, workers would better be able to buy the products of farms and factories. If they could buy more, he reasoned, the nation would recover from the Great Depression.

In 1933, Congress passed a number of laws that Roosevelt claimed would fight the depression. Among the various early New Deal laws, the National Industrial Recovery Act was one of the most ambitious. Among other things, it set up machinery for regulating minimum wage rates and maximum working hours. The act also stated that workers had the right to join unions and bargain collectively. In 1935, the U.S. Supreme Court declared this law unconstitutional. That same year, though, Congress passed even more ambitious legislation benefiting labor.

National Labor Relations Act Also known as the Wagner Act, this 1935 law again guaranteed labor the right of collective bargaining. For this purpose, it set up the National Labor Relations Board (NLRB). The NLRB, which is still in existence, was given the power to:

• Conduct elections in a place of employment to determine whether a majority of the workers wish to be represented by a particular union. If a union wins such an election, it is *certified* (formally approved) by the NLRB.

• Take actions against an employer who tries to prevent a union from being formed or who refuses to bargain with a certified union.

• Take actions against an employer who tries to discriminate against union members or workers who want to form a union. (Sometimes employers fire or assign to less desirable jobs workers who are trying to form a union.)

Emergency Relief Appropriation Act In 1935, Congress helped many unemployed Americans by setting up the Works Progress Administration. As mentioned in Lesson 59, this organization employed millions of needy people in useful projects.

Social Security Act This important law of 1935 was designed to give greater security to American workers and their families. It provided extra income for workers after they retired. The Social Security Act also required each state to set up a system of unemployment insurance.

Fair Labor Standards Act In 1938, Congress set up minimum wages and maximum hours for workers employed by businesses in interstate commerce. An early standard was 40 cents an hour for wages and a 40-hour workweek. Those who worked over 40 hours were to be paid time-and-a-half. Over the years, the minimum wage has gone up many times. In 1986, for example, it was $3.35 an hour.

Another provision of the Fair Labor Standards Act concerned child labor. The new law forbade most instances of hiring children under the age of 16.

The reformer Frances Perkins played a pivotal role in American labor history. During the Progressive era, she investigated working conditions in factories in New York State. Later she served as head of that state's Industrial Board, where she helped push through the legislature a bill for a 48-hour workweek for women. In 1933, Perkins became the country's first female Cabinet member. President Franklin D. Roosevelt appointed her Secretary of Labor. In that position, Perkins was instrumental in drawing up the Social Security Act and other prolabor bills.

Resurgence of Union Growth

Congressional legislation, especially the National Labor Relations Act, helped American unions to grow rapidly. Total membership, which had been 2.9 million in 1933, was up to 4.1 million in 1936 and 7.3 million in 1940. (See the graph on page 427.)

Industrial Union Growth During the 1930s, mass-production industries, such as steel, rubber, and automobiles, were trying to get back on their feet. Most leaders of the AFL wanted to organize these industries on a craft basis. For example, all carpenters would join a carpenters' union; all electricians would join an electricians' union; and so on.

Other labor leaders believed that all workers—skilled, semiskilled, and unskilled—in an industry should belong to the same union. In the automobile industry, for example, welders, electricians, and every other worker would join one large industrial union. In 1935, a group of such *industrial unions*, the Committee for Industrial Organization (CIO), formed within the AFL.

Even so, some AFL leaders who believed strongly in craft unions worked against the CIO. In 1936, they suspended the CIO from membership in the AFL. As a result, the industrial unions set up their own, rival national body—the Congress of Industrial Organizations. It, too, used the initials "CIO." Under the leadership of its first president, John L. Lewis of the United Mine Workers, the CIO successfully organized millions of workers. Some of the CIO's strongest unions organized the automobile, steel, clothing, and mining industries. Within a few years, the CIO had reached a membership of about 2.5 million—half as large as that of the AFL.

Political Influence In addition to growing in size and economic importance, unions also gained political clout. The labor vote helped Franklin D. Roosevelt gain re-election in 1936, 1940, and 1944. Indeed, the endorsement of national labor unions is still sought after by many candidates for public office. Labor union endorsement, however, does not ensure victory for a candidate.

Labor violence became more common in the 1930s. Here striking dairy workers tip over a milk truck in Toledo, Ohio.

SUMMING UP   We have seen how American labor unions expanded, contracted, and again grew larger between 1900 and 1940. In addition to the AFL, two new major labor organizations—the IWW and the CIO—were formed during this period. Changing government attitudes toward unions and changing economic conditions affected the strength of labor unions. With the passage of the National Labor Relations Act during the Great Depression, labor unions became more firmly entrenched in America.

Understanding the Text

On a separate sheet of paper, write the letter of the word or phrase that best completes each of the following statements.

1. The American Federation of Labor in the early 20th century favored (*a*) organizing unions on a craft basis (*b*) using sabotage and other violent methods (*c*) bringing both skilled and unskilled workers into the same union (*d*) replacing capitalism with socialism.

2. By 1920, the Industrial Workers of the World (*a*) had begun to decline in strength (*b*) had not yet been organized (*c*) was larger than the AFL (*d*) was competing with the CIO in organizing unskilled workers.

3. President Theodore Roosevelt played a part in American labor history by (*a*) vetoing the Clayton Antitrust Act (*b*) setting up the National War Labor Board (*c*) helping to settle the Anthracite Coal Strike of 1902 (*d*) getting Congress to pass the Social Security Act of 1935.

4. During World War I, (*a*) membership in unions increased (*b*) many more women and blacks obtained jobs (*c*) the National War Labor Board was set up (*d*) all of the above.

5. The two years that immediately followed World War I were a time of (*a*) rising prices (*b*) unemployment (*c*) violent strikes (*d*) all of the above.

6. The National Labor Relations Act of 1935 (*a*) helped unions to organize workers (*b*) ended most unemployment (*c*) set up the Social Security System (*d*) all of the above.

7. The National Labor Relations Board is (*a*) an organization of business leaders (*b*) a government agency concerned with labor unions (*c*) a national labor union (*d*) a federation of labor unions.

8. Setting minimum wages and maximum hours were major provisions of the (*a*) National Labor Relations Act (*b*) Fair Labor Standards Act (*c*) Social Security Act (*d*) Clayton Antitrust Act.

9. By 1940, the Congress of Industrial Organizations was known as (*a*) the oldest labor union in the country (*b*) a federation of craft unions (*c*) a federation of industrial unions (*d*) none of the above.

10. The CIO's first president was (*a*) John L. Lewis (*b*) Samuel Gompers (*c*) Franklin D. Roosevelt (*d*) Frances Perkins.

Developing Graph-Reading Skills

RISE OF ORGANIZED LABOR, 1900–1940

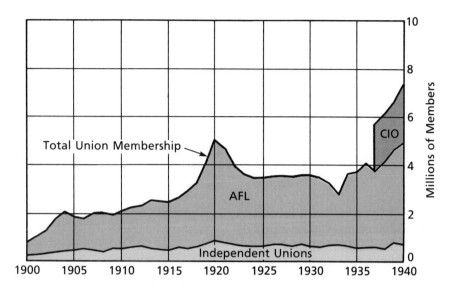

Examine the line graph above. Then choose the letter of the word or phrase that best completes each sentence. On a separate sheet of paper, match the sentence number with the correct letter.

1. In 1905, total union membership was *(a)* below 1 million *(b)* between 1 and 2 million *(c)* between 2 and 3 million *(d)* over 3 million.

2. Between 1915 and 1920, membership in the AFL *(a)* fell sharply *(b)* stayed about the same *(c)* doubled *(d)* stayed less than the membership in independent unions.

3. Between 1900 and 1930, membership in independent unions was highest in *(a)* 1910 *(b)* 1920 *(c)* 1925 *(d)* 1930.

4. Statistics for membership in the CIO first appear on the graph for the year *(a)* 1900 *(b)* 1920 *(c)* 1930 *(d)* 1937.

5. In 1940, membership in the CIO was *(a)* about 1 million *(b)* about 2 million *(c)* between 3 and 4 million *(d)* over 7 million.

Thinking About the Lesson

1. For what reasons did labor unions grow so rapidly during certain periods of the 20th century, such as from 1915 to 1920 and in the late 1930s?

2. Why did the majority of American workers *not* join any labor organizations?

3. Explain two ways in which the AFL and CIO were similar in the 1930s. Explain two ways in which they differed.

LESSON 66

Recent Trends in Industry and Labor

After four years devoted to helping fight World War II, American industry in 1946 resumed its normal, peacetime production. Although the economy has gone through several recessions since then, Americans have not had to suffer another major depression. In fact, the average standard of living for Americans has risen to new heights. Union membership continued to grow in numbers after the war, but the percentage of workers in unions, as compared to the total working population, has declined.

The Economy and the War Effort

While government controls over the economy were extensive during the depression, they soon became even stronger. In 1942, the government introduced controls to increase production of goods needed to fight the war.

Controls Over Businesses One government agency, the Office of Price Administration, worked to prevent inflation by setting many prices and rents. At the same time, the War Production Board directed companies to convert their assembly lines to produce materials for the war effort. For instance, the automobile industry was ordered to make fewer cars and more trucks and jeeps. It also began assembling tanks and airplanes.

Controls Over Labor The unemployment problem of the 1930s disappeared as more and more workers left their jobs to serve in the Armed Forces. With the growing need for workers, unions were in a strong position to strike for higher wages and better benefits. Both the AFL and the CIO, however, pledged not to strike during the war. These promises were kept for the most part. Nevertheless, the AFL and CIO could not prevent some *wildcat strikes* (ones not authorized by union leaders). The United Mine Workers, for example, went out on strike several times during the war years.

The government took steps of its own to prevent work stoppages. A new National War Labor Board worked to prevent strikes by setting wage guidelines. A 1943 law—the Smith-Connally Act—set penalties for unions that struck. It also authorized the government to seize and operate plants under threat of a strike.

Post-War Developments

Soon after the war ended, the government started to remove many of its wartime economic controls. Furthermore, the government urged factories to *reconvert* (go back to producing goods ordinarily made in peacetime). In addition, by *demobilizing* (reducing the ranks of) the Armed

These autoworkers are voting in a union election held in a factory in Flint, Michigan. The Landrum-Griffin Act of 1959 regulates how such elections are to be conducted.

Forces, the government returned many people to the work force.

Inflation Because of decontrol and the increasing demand for many goods, prices rose rapidly. Wages, however, did not keep up with the rate of inflation. Therefore, unions, no longer bound by no-strike pledges, began to strike for higher wages. In 1946 alone, about 4.6 million American workers went out on strike.

Anti-Union Feelings

During these years of frequent strikes, criticism of unions became more widespread. Critics of organized labor pointed out how long and costly some of the strikes were. Moreover, these critics claimed that some union officials had misused their powers to enrich themselves. Stories circulated about undemocratic unions whose leaders made all important decisions, regardless of what union members wanted.

Some Americans complained that unions had become too powerful. These critics said that in dealing with employers, unions often made unreasonable demands. One union practice that critics complained about was *featherbedding*. It occurred when employers were required to hire more workers than were needed.

As a result of these criticisms, the federal government and some states passed laws to limit the powers of unions and their leaders.

Taft-Hartley Act While earlier laws had outlined unfair practices by employers, this law of 1947 defined unfair union practices. The Taft-Hartley Act declared featherbedding to be illegal. The law said that there could be no *closed shops* (workplaces where only union members could be hired). Unions were prohibited from making campaign contributions to candidates for federal offices. The Taft-Hartley Act gave the U.S. President the right to postpone for 80 days strikes that "threaten national health and safety." The parties involved in a dispute were supposed to use this 80-day period to settle their disagreements.

Right-to-Work Laws The Taft-Hartley Act specifically allowed *right-to-work laws*, and, by 1955, 17 states had passed such legislation. Right-to-work laws provide that no worker can be required to join a union as a condition for getting or keeping a job. Americans who support these laws say that the laws give greater freedom to workers who do not want to join a union. Union members and their supporters strongly oppose right-to-work laws. They claim that the laws' real purpose is to weaken or get rid of unions. Many states still have right-to-work laws.

Landrum-Griffin Act In 1959, Congress passed legislation aimed against union corruption. The Landrum-Griffin Act required unions to report on their finances, hold regular meetings, and use secret ballots in their elections. It also limited the right of Communists and people convicted of serious crimes to serve as union officials.

Labor Strength Since World War II

Despite anti-union feelings and anti-union laws, labor unions grew in size in the decade after the war. They obtained many improvements in working conditions, wages, and benefits for their members.

After World War II, labor unions were able to recruit two types of workers previously not organized:

• Professional workers, such as teachers, journalists, editors, engineers, and so on.

• Local government workers, such as police, fire fighters, and sanitation workers.

Formation of the AFL-CIO   After many years of discussion, the AFL and the CIO merged in 1955. George Meany became the first president of the combined group, which at first numbered some 16 million members. The new organization was effective in lobbying for prolabor legislation and campaigning for prolabor candidates.

Less Strength in Organized Labor   Membership in labor unions has grown slightly since the mid-1950s. Unions continue to be a strong part of the economy. Nevertheless, unions' share of the work force has declined. About 81 percent of American workers today are not union members. There are several reasons for the relative decline in union strength:

• Many Americans have unfavorable opinions about unions. Some believe that unions are still corrupt despite campaigns to root out dishonest officials. Others complain that union dues cost too much and that membership in a union does not provide sufficient benefits.

• Most increases in employment in recent decades have been in the *service industries* (industries that provide services instead of products). Unions, though, find that some of these service industries workers, especially those in banking and insurance, are difficult to organize.

Some service industry workers have been organized by unions. Here Legal Aid Society employees picket for more pay and fewer hours in the work-week.

This Don Wright cartoon is part of the skills exercise on page 435. Reprinted by permission: Tribune Media Service.

• Some businesses have moved their plants to parts of the country where unions are weak or where public opinion is less favorable toward unions.

• The number of workers employed in certain mass-production industries (for example, steel, rubber, automobiles) has declined over the years. The *blue-collar workers* in these industries have traditionally been the strongest supporters of labor unions.

Changes in American Industry

After the late 1940s, the American economy prospered more than ever before. Despite several recessions, Americans enjoyed unprecedented high standards of living. Several of the developments that contributed to the country's economic growth are discussed below.

Transportation   Many of the pre-war trends in transportation continued after 1946. Fewer Americans used trains. Instead, they relied more on cars, trucks, buses, and airplanes. Air pas-

sengers and freight could move around the country much faster after airlines introduced jet engines in the 1950s. The construction of cross-country superhighways speeded up ground transportation.

Communications   In the 1960s, both the federal government and private companies developed and launched communications satellites. These sophisticated devices that circle the earth can receive, amplify, and send back radio and television signals. Using satellites, broadcasters and businesses can communicate with people over long distances.

Energy Resources   After World War II, demand for energy in the United States increased about four percent almost every year. Although the country is rich in coal, gas, and oil supplies, it still has to import much of the oil and gas that it uses.

To meet part of the energy demand, electrical utilities in the 1950s began to build nuclear power plants. By 1983, nuclear power produced about thirteen percent of the electrical energy

In the automobile assembly plant in Fenton, Missouri, robots perform vital operations. Compare this assembly line with the one shown on page 415.

used in the United States. The future of the nuclear power industry is a controversial issue. Several nuclear power plants have been shut down because of safety problems. The construction of some other plants has been delayed because of financial problems. Nuclear power plants have cost much more to build than had been expected. At most times, power companies find it less expensive to generate electricity with imported oil than with a nuclear plant. Defenders of the nuclear power industry say that their plants are safe. They also believe that new plants can be built profitably.

Power from the sun (*solar power*), wind, tides, underground heat (*geothermal power*), and falling water (*hydro power*) all provide ways to meet America's energy shortage. For various financial and technical reasons, these *clean energy sources* (ones free of pollution) still do not produce a major share of the nation's energy.

Development of Business Organizations Big businesses continued to dominate the economy after World War II. Through mergers, businesses have grown very large. In the newspaper industry, for example, certain companies have bought newspapers in many towns and cities across the country. Locally owned newspapers are becoming less common than previously.

Two other types of business combinations became widespread:

• *Conglomerate*—a large company that brings together businesses that are in different and unrelated fields. A single conglomerate, for example, might control oil wells, farmlands, a bank, a steamship line, and a chain of motion picture theaters.

• *Multinational Corporation*—a large company that owns businesses or branches in two or more countries. Many U.S. companies expanded abroad as war-torn areas of the world recovered and developing nations gained their independence.

Many giant combinations have become so complex and widespread that the government has found it difficult to regulate them under present antitrust laws.

Automation In order to lower labor costs and increase productivity, many businesses have introduced *automation*. This modern method of production involves the use of machine-controlled operations. With automation, many of the tasks used in making a product require little help from workers.

The automobile industry was one of the first to introduce automation after World War II. Since then, many other businesses, including banks and other service industries, have become automated. More than any other factor, the development of *computers* has advanced the spread of automation. Computers can help machines perform many production tasks. Furthermore, computers can *compute* (add, subtract, divide, and so on) many times faster than humans can. *Robots*, computer-controlled machines that perform manual tasks, provide the highest level of automation. So far, robots are used in a relatively small number of U.S. industries.

Officials of companies that automate say that replacing people with machines is often necessary to compete in the modern age. In some cases, the officials say, automation allows a company to expand, thereby providing new employment. Nevertheless, some unions oppose automation because workers lose jobs to machines. These workers may become permanently unemployed if they do not receive retraining for a different kind of work. As a result of automation, the number of blue-collar workers in America has declined. Jobs have been created because of automation, but they tend to be technical, white-collar positions.

Consumer Credit Another factor in the growth of the U.S. economy since World War II has been the tremendous increase in *consumer credit*. This term refers to all the different types of borrowing that individuals do in order to buy goods and services. A larger proportion of the U.S. population than ever before has borrowed money to buy homes and cars. Many Americans have credit cards or charge accounts. This form of borrowing has increased the country's money supply and has stimulated economic growth.

Foreign Competition and American Industry

Throughout most of the 20th century, until 1971, the United States had a *favorable balance of trade*, meaning that its exports exceeded its imports. Beginning in 1971, however, the country began importing more raw materials and manufactured goods than it exported. Today, for example, most videocassette recorders sold in the United States are made abroad. One out of every four automobiles and two out of every three pairs of shoes sold here are foreign-produced. This foreign competition hurts many American companies and their employees.

Reacting against the influx of foreign products into the U.S. marketplace, some American business and labor leaders have called for higher tariffs. In response, the U.S. government has sometimes raised tariff rates or persuaded foreign countries to limit sales of certain products here.

Nevertheless, not all Americans favor protective tariffs or foreign quotas. Some say that if the United States sets high tariffs or quotas, other countries will retaliate with their own barriers to trade. This foreign action will hurt the sale of U.S. products abroad. Besides, foreign competition has at least one benefit for American consumers—lower prices.

In addition to or in place of higher tariffs, Americans concerned about foreign competition offer other possible solutions:

• Getting unions and unorganized workers to agree to accept lower wages or reduced *fringe benefits*. (Fringe benefits are benefits workers seek in addition to improved wages, hours, and working conditions. They include such things as pensions, health plans, and paid vacation days.) In this way, American industries would become more competitive with foreign ones that pay less.

• Remodeling old, inefficient plants. Some U.S. factories, such as those in the steel industry, were built many years ago. Modern steel plants in Japan and elsewhere can produce steel at lower costs. To compete, therefore, U.S. industries need to remodel their outdated factories and build new ones.

• Cutting down on government regulations. Increasing numbers of Americans believe that regulations by the federal government are often unnecessary and cost businesses too much money. These critics of government regulations have called for deregulation. Beginning with the Carter administration (and continuing during the Reagan administration), the government has taken steps to end many federal regulations in the airline, trucking, banking, and other industries. (Discussed in Lesson 63.)

SUMMING UP   We have seen how the American economy rebounded after the Great Depression and World War II. Although wartime controls were relaxed after 1945, Uncle Sam has continued to influence economic developments. The government frequently intervenes in labor-management disputes. It also applies antitrust laws to newer forms of business combinations and mergers. In addition, to help weak industries and protect jobs of American workers, it has reduced foreign imports.

Understanding the Text

On a separate sheet of paper, write the letter of the word or phrase that best completes each of the following statements.

1. An action *not* part of the U.S. war effort of 1941–1945 was   (a) converting factories   (b) setting prices   (c) encouraging wildcat strikes   (d) setting wage guidelines.

2. Immediately after World War II, American workers   (a) demobilized factories   (b) suffered because of inflation   (c) went into the Armed Forces in large numbers   (d) formed conglomerates.

3. The Taft-Hartley Act   (a) outlawed unfair union practices   (b) promoted featherbedding   (c) sponsored peaceful uses of nuclear energy   (d) banned multinational corporations.

4. An example of federal legislation aimed against union corruption was the   (a) right-to-work laws   (b) Smith-Connally Act   (c) Taft-Hartley Act   (d) Landrum-Griffin Act.

5. A reason for the relative decline in union strength since the mid-1950s is that   (a) most growth in employment has been in the service industries *(b)* many companies have relocated to parts of the country where unions are weaker and less popular *(c)* the number of blue-collar workers in the United States has decreased *(d)* all of the above.

6. An example of an energy source developed since World War II is *(a)* nuclear power *(b)* coal power *(c)* communications satellites *(d)* jet airliners.

7. Results of automation in American industry include a/an *(a)* decline in the number of blue-collar workers *(b)* increase in worker productivity *(c)* need for retraining many workers *(d)* all of the above.

8. From 1971 to 1981, the U.S. foreign trade balance *(a)* was favorable *(b)* was unfavorable *(c)* involved more exports than imports *(d)* was deregulated.

9. An example of protectionism is *(a)* getting workers to agree to lower wages *(b)* erecting high tariffs *(c)* modernizing plants and equipment *(d)* deregulating industries.

10. One of the main ideas expressed in this lesson is that *(a)* most American workers belong to unions *(b)* most American businesses are inefficient *(c)* although weaker, unions remain an important force in the U.S. economy *(d)* there have been few changes in American industry in the last 40 years.

Developing Cartoon-Reading Skills

Study the political cartoon on page 431. Then choose the letter of the word or phrase that best answers each question. On a separate sheet of paper, match the question number with the correct letter.

1. Who does the man on the top represent? *(a)* businesses *(b)* labor unions *(c)* muggers *(d)* prizefighters.

2. Who does the man on the bottom represent? *(a)* businesses *(b)* labor unions *(c)* muggers *(d)* prizefighters.

3. What conclusion can one draw about the two men in the cartoon? *(a)* Both men are equally strong. *(b)* The man on the bottom is stronger. *(c)* The man on the top is stronger. *(d)* The relative strength of the two men is not indicated.

4. Which point do you think that the cartoonist is trying to make? *(a)* Labor unions are too strong. *(b)* In difficult times, workers should make sacrifices. *(c)* Businesses are taking advantage of labor unions' weaknesses to obtain concessions. *(d)* Fighting of any kind is ugly.

5. The man on the top would be most pleased with which of the following? *(a)* a ban on professional fighting *(b)* increased benefits for organized workers *(c)* lower crime rates *(d)* lower wages for organized workers.

Thinking About the Lesson

1. In 1947, the federal government by passing the Taft-Hartley Act increased its regulation of labor unions. Do you think that the act was needed? Explain your answer.

2. Do you think that your state should have a right-to-work law? Why or why not?

3. What factor do you think has been most responsible for the rapid growth of U.S. industries since 1945?

4. Has automation been good for American businesses? Why or why not?

5. In what ways have the economies of the United States and other countries become dependent upon one another? Do you see this interdependence as a problem or benefit? Explain your answer.

LESSON 67

The American Farmer in the 20th Century

As the United States developed into an industrial nation, the number and proportion of farmers in the total population declined sharply. By 1985, less than 5 percent of all Americans were engaged in farming. This figure compares with about 42 percent in 1900. Because American agriculture has become more and more productive, the country has come to need fewer farmers.

Farming Still Our Number One Industry

Farming remains very important in the U.S. economy. Today, farming and related businesses still make up the largest single industry in the country. All Americans depend on foods produced by farmers. Moreover, many other farm goods—such as cotton, wool, and plant oils—are important in U.S. manufacturing. The vast amounts of American farm products and equipment sold abroad are vital to the economy. These exports help pay for the country's imports, such as oil.

Twentieth-Century Changes

The ways in which farmers live and go about their business have changed greatly in the 20th

century. Most farmers have obtained the conveniences of modern life and are no longer isolated. The majority of farmhouses now have electricity, refrigeration, indoor plumbing, a telephone, radio, and television. Automobiles and improved roads and highways make it possible for farmers to travel quickly to nearby towns and cities. Trucks, railroads, ships, and airplanes carry their goods to local and distant markets.

Twentieth-century American agriculture is marked by technological advances. These scientific advances allow fewer farmers to produce more goods:

• Tractors have largely replaced work animals.

• Scientists have developed new varieties of wheat, corn, and rice that provide much higher *yields* (output per acre).

• From 1900 to 1975, the amount of *commercial fertilizers* (fertilizers prepared in factories) used in agriculture doubled. As much as any other factor, these fertilizers have been responsible for enormous increases in crop yields.

• The introduction of chemicals that kill insect pests also has improved the yields of many crops. These *insecticides* were widely used for a number of years. Later, some were found to be harmful to the health of humans, birds, and other animals. DDT, developed in 1939, was

436

American farmers today use many modern methods. Here a farm worker applies a chemical to crops.

banned by the federal government in 1972.

• By killing certain weeds, chemical *herbicides* (weed killers) have proved useful to many farmers. After herbicides are applied to a field, farm crops will usually grow better.

Good Times and Bad Times

Improvements in farm production have not always resulted in prosperity for U.S. farmers. At times, many have suffered to such an extent that they have had to give up their farms.

Times of Prosperity Farmers experienced prosperity during several periods in the 20th century:

• 1900–1920. For two decades after 1900, the prices farmers received for their goods generally rose. Expanding domestic industries bought more agricultural products, such as cotton and wool. Moreover, foreign countries whose economies were disrupted by World War I (1914–1918) turned to the United States for food and other farm goods.

• 1939–1955. World War II (1939–1945) was as good for the American farmer as the previous war had been. Again a vast worldwide demand for farm products raised prices of U.S. goods. Farm surpluses were no longer common. After

World War II, demand for U.S. agricultural products remained high as the United States set up the Marshall Plan. Under this plan, the government sent much food to needy Europeans and other people whose lives had been disrupted by the war. During the Korean War (1950–1953), the demand for U.S. farm goods continued. As a result, stored surpluses were used up, and farm income increased greatly. Many farmers were able to pay off their mortgages.

• The 1970s. U.S. farmers enjoyed the most prosperous period in their history during the 1970s. Between 1971 and 1979, farm income rose from $14.6 billion to $33.3 billion. The price of farmland jumped an average of 15 percent, and farm acreage increased by over 40 percent. This prosperity resulted in good measure from the sales of vast quantities of U.S. grain to the Soviet Union. Developing countries with rapidly growing populations also began to purchase our grain. (The U.S. helped these countries by lending them money to make such purchases.) As a result, the prices of U.S. grain and other farm products jumped by 75 percent.

Periods of Farm Depression Good times for American farmers were interspersed with periods of difficulty and farm depression:

• The 1920s and 1930s. When the fighting in Europe ended in 1918, after World War I, the overseas demand for U.S. products dropped drastically. American farmers' ability to produce more per acre proved to be a drawback. For many years afterward, American farmers produced more than the market required. These surpluses caused the prices of farm products to drop. At the same time, the prices of things farmers had to buy remained the same or rose.

> Many U.S. farmers who had borrowed money to buy their farms and equipment found that they could no longer make their loan payments. Many went *bankrupt*. They lost their farms to the lenders that held their mortgages. Some became farm renters instead of farm owners; others became agricultural laborers on the large farms that had survived.

• The 1980s. In the early 1980s, American farmers found themselves in serious trouble once again. While the rest of the economy was recovering from a period of recession, farm prices and exports lagged and profits declined. Many farmers struggled to pay off loans at high interest rates of 15 percent or more. Hundreds of small banks that held farm loans were in peril as bankruptcies soared. Many Americans said that this crisis was the worst since the Great Depression of the 1930s.

Farmers who had borrowed heavily at high interest rates in the 1970s found themselves in the 1980s unable to meet repayment schedules to banks. A growing number of farm bankruptcies caused farmers to ask the government for emergency financial assistance. Angry and bitter, farmers felt that they were the victims of forces increasingly beyond their control.

Government Action to Aid Farmers

Since the 1920s, the federal government has enacted a number of programs to help hard-pressed farmers:

• Tariffs. In 1921, 1922, and 1930, Congress passed tariffs that were designed to protect American agricultural goods from foreign competition.

• Farm Credit. Under various programs, the government has loaned farmers money to pay off high-interest mortgages and thus avoid bankruptcy.

Abandoned farms such as this one are becoming a more common sight in rural America as more and more farmers go bankrupt.

• Crop Reduction. Under programs established during and since the 1930s, the government has attempted to help deal with the problem of farm surplus by paying farmers to grow less. For example, farmers have received money for planting fewer acres of wheat, rice, corn, and other crops.

• Price-Support Programs. Since the late 1930s, the government has also tried to keep farm prices and farm income at reasonable levels through *price-support programs*. Farmers may take price-support loans from the government. These loans guarantee that a farmer's crop will not be worth less than the amount borrowed to grow it. If the market price of the crop is too low at repayment time, the farmer gives the crop to the government.

Under *target pricing programs*, the federal government sets what it considers to be a fair price for grain, milk, and other farm products. If the price falls below this *target price*, the government pays the farmer the difference between the target price and the real price.

When farm prices and income declined in the early 1980s, the annual cost of government farm subsidies increased sharply—from nearly $3 billion in 1980 to over $18 billion in 1983. To help balance the federal budget, the Reagan administration called for reductions in government aid to farmers. It said that the government could no longer afford to continue its farm subsidy programs.

Debate on Aid to Farmers Farm subsidies have been criticized for many years. Critics have argued that:

• These programs have not resulted in reductions in farm surpluses.

• They are very expensive, costing the government billions of dollars annually.

• Benefits to the farmer come at the expense of consumers, who must pay higher prices and higher taxes.

• The largest farms obtain the largest benefits, while the small- and medium-size farms receive much less.

Supporters of farm subsidies include farmers, farm organizations, and their representatives in Congress, who often vote as a non-partisan *farm bloc* on many farm issues. All of these people argue that agriculture is a vital industry that must receive subsidies to survive. As a result, proposals by the Reagan administration to cut farm subsidies drastically have met stiff opposition in Congress.

Decline of the Family Farm

Small *family farms*, usually of less than 360 acres, have been the traditional agricultural unit in America. Each family farm normally consists of a farm owner and family. The number of family farms has declined sharply over the last half century. Increased farm productivity in the United States has lessened the need for as many farmers as before. Family farms now make up less than 50 percent of this nation's total. Most farmers on these farms rely on income from other jobs. Some family farms are larger, medium-size farms of up to 500 acres. A medium-size farm usually employs one or more full-time workers, as well as some extra laborers at harvesttime.

In recent years, many giant farms consisting of thousands of acres have been established as large corporations. These *corporate farms* are run by managers and operated like large business organizations. They make use of the most modern equipment and methods and may employ dozens of hired hands. Because corporate farms are able to cut the cost of production, they are able to make profits more easily than can family farms. Although corporate farms comprise less than one percent of the country's farms, they take in some 60 percent of total farm income.

Migrant farm workers usually have a long workday. These workers have stopped to rest and eat a meal.

In the last 50 years, Americans have witnessed changes in the ways foods are treated to prevent spoilage. Mechanical refrigerators replaced iceboxes in most homes. Many food processors adopted the method of quick freezing developed by Clarence Birdseye in the 1920s. More and more food companies began adding chemicals to foods to slow down the spoiling of food. Thus, people are able to buy foods grown or raised far away. Moreover, they can store foods for extended periods.

Farm Labor

Growing numbers of formerly self-reliant farmers have had to give up their farms and become laborers on large farms or wage earners in cities. Some others have joined the ranks of migrant workers, who move around the country, picking crops on a number of different farms each year.

Migrant workers play an important role in American agriculture. They provide the extra "hands" needed in the fields at harvesttime. *Truck farmers* (those who grow vegetables for the market) and cotton farmers employ especially large numbers of migrant workers. Although most migrant farm workers are native-born or naturalized U.S. citizens, many others enter the country each year from Mexico and elsewhere. (Discussed further in Lesson 86.)

Problems of Migrant Workers Most migrant farm laborers live in poverty. Their pay is low, and they can be fired at any time. Employers often provide these workers with rundown housing. They sometimes charge the workers and their families high prices for needed goods and services. Because migrant workers move about so much, their children fail to get a proper education. Moreover, because of their poverty, medical care for migrant workers and their families is likely to be poor.

To improve their economic situation, some migrant workers have joined labor unions. The United Farm Workers, for example, has been especially active in organizing workers in California, Arizona, and elsewhere. Unions have been successful in negotiating contracts with growers, thereby bringing sizable benefits to their members.

SUMMING UP   We have seen that American farmers in the 20th century have gone through both good and bad times. Because of the importance of agriculture to the economy, the government has developed many farm-aid programs. Most notable have been the subsidy programs, established to keep farm income up and farm surpluses off the market. The changing nature of American agriculture in the 20th century is seen in the decline of the small-size family farm and the growth of the giant corporate farm. Another trend has been the growing number of migrant farm workers, who serve as a needed source of farm labor at harvesttime.

Understanding the Text

On a separate sheet of paper, write the letter of the word or phrase that best completes each of the following statements.

1. Twentieth-century American agriculture can be described in general terms as (*a*) backward (*b*) highly productive (*c*) free of important problems (*d*) nonproductive.

2. Of the following factors, one that helped 20th-century American farmers to grow more farm products was (*a*) tractors (*b*) new grain varieties (*c*) herbicides (*d*) all of the above.

3. Which of the following is *not* a 20th-century farm problem? (*a*) slave labor (*b*) farm surpluses (*c*) low prices for farm products (*d*) high prices for goods and services that farmers buy.

4. Of the following periods, one considered very prosperous for American farmers was (*a*) 1913–1918 (*b*) 1924–1929 (*c*) 1930–1935 (*d*) 1980–1983.

5. Since the 1930s, the federal government has tried to help farmers by (*a*) paying them to cut production (*b*) prohibiting farm sales abroad (*c*) making surpluses illegal (*d*) keeping prices of farm products low.

6. Most farmers in America today lack (*a*) electricity (*b*) knowledge of how to run a farm (*c*) enough income from sales of farm products (*d*) means of transporting crops to markets.

7. Within the last 40 years in the United States, (*a*) the number of farms has gone down, while their average size has increased (*b*) more people than ever before have gone into farming (*c*) the average size of farms has become smaller (*d*) there have been no important changes in farm size and population.

8. Corporate farms are (*a*) companies that sell products to farmers (*b*) always owned and operated by families (*c*) usually the smallest type of farm (*d*) often run by hired managers.

9. Migrant farm workers in the United States (*a*) are essential to the operation of many truck farms (*b*) usually enjoy a high standard of living (*c*) were needed in the past, but are not in demand today (*d*) usually have steady employment on one farm throughout the year.

10. Which of the following statements best applies to American farmers today? (*a*) They are prosperous and have few economic problems. (*b*) Most refuse to participate in government farm programs. (*c*) They still suffer from problems of farm surpluses and low prices for farm goods. (*d*) Most are migrant workers, employed by large corporate farms.

Developing Table-Reading Skills

LEADING PRODUCERS OF WHEAT, RICE, AND CORN, 1980
(In thousands of metric tons)

	Wheat	*Rice*	*Corn*
Australia	10,870	613	6,400
Canada	19,157	NA	100
China, Mainland	54,158	142,338	61,105
France	23,683	24	9,358
India	31,830	79,930	6,804
Indonesia	NA	29,774	4,012
Soviet Union	98,185	2,791	9,454
United States	64,619	6,629	168,787
World, total	444,603	397,597	394,056

NA = figures not available

Examine the table above. Then choose the letter of the word or phrase that best completes each sentence. On a separate sheet of paper, match the sentence number with the correct letter.

1. In 1980, the total number of metric tons of wheat produced worldwide was *(a)* 64,619,000 *(b)* 397,597,000 *(c)* 444,603,000 *(d)* none of the above.

2. The leading rice producer in 1980 was *(a)* the United States *(b)* Mainland China *(c)* India *(d)* the Soviet Union.

3. In 1980, the farm product that the Soviet Union produced more of than any other country listed was *(a)* wheat *(b)* rice *(c)* corn *(d)* all of the above.

4. The United States in 1980 produced about *(a)* twice as much wheat as India *(b)* two thirds as much wheat as the Soviet Union *(c)* over three times as much wheat as Canada *(d)* all of the above.

5. From reading this table, one can conclude that in 1980 the United States *(a)* was a leading corn and wheat producing nation *(b)* imported great amounts of rice *(c)* made more money from corn than any other farm product *(d)* had large surpluses of wheat and corn.

Thinking About the Lesson

1. What factor do you think was most important in increasing U.S. farm productivity in the 20th century? Explain your answer.

2. Do you think that U.S. farmers are better off or worse off today than they were in 1900? Explain your answer.

3. Do you agree with the statement that, in the 20th century, farming in the United States has become an increasingly subsidized industry? Explain your answer.

4. Do you think that farmers should be paid for not growing crops? Why or why not?

5. Why do some types of farms hire migrant workers? Why are so many migrant workers poor?

The Early Conservation Movement

People depend upon a number of the earth's natural resources, including clean air and water, soil, plants, and animals. All of these resources are limited. If they are *polluted* (made unclean) or destroyed, future generations will have that much less to enjoy or use. Americans first became greatly concerned about conserving natural resources in the 19th century.

> The organized movement to promote wise and efficient use of natural resources is called *conservation.* One of its purposes is to preserve the *environment* in its natural state as much as possible. The environment refers to the physical surroundings within which we all live. It includes both natural features and those made by people.
>
> The science that studies the relationship between living things and their environment is *ecology.* One of ecology's basic ideas is that there exists a *balance of nature.* In nature, the numbers of different kinds of plants and animals tend to remain the same over time. Ecologists point out that humans upset the balance of nature more often than any other living thing.

Wasteful Habits

Early European settlers in America saw the New World as a vast territory with unlimited natural resources. As a result, for centuries Americans used these resources in careless, wasteful ways. Pioneers cleared forests and early farmers plowed grasslands without knowing that their actions upset the balance of nature. When land became worn out, farmers moved on to other tracts. Miners extracted minerals without concern for future uses of the land. Americans hunted birds and other animals without thinking that they might be killing off entire species.

Occasionally, an exceptional individual would point out the dangers of waste and destruction. Thomas Jefferson stressed the need for farming methods that would help preserve the soil from water erosion. To counter erosion, he advocated *contour plowing*—plowing at a right angle to the slope of the land. The naturalist Henry David Thoreau urged people to live in harmony with nature. He recommended setting up special wilderness areas where animals could live protected from hunters.

Despite these advanced thinkers, most Americans in the nation's early years were not especially concerned about conservation.

443

In 1906, President Theodore Roosevelt (left) and naturalist John Muir together visited Yosemite National Park. They both had important roles in expanding the National Park system.

The Beginnings of the Conservation Movement

In the last decades of the 19th century, theories on conservation began to be put into practice.

System of National Parks In 1872, the federal government set up Yellowstone as the country's first National Park. Over the years, Congress created other great parks, thus forming a National Park system. The naturalist John Muir was partly responsible for getting Congress to add Yosemite and Sequoia National Parks to the system in 1891. Today, the National Park Service of the Department of the Interior administers some 79 million acres in 330 different parks and other areas. The Service preserves many resources and natural wonders and provides recreation for millions of people every year.

System of National Forests In 1891, another important conservation program was started—the nation's forest reserves. In its first ten years, the reserves grew to about 46 million acres. From 1901 to 1909, President Theodore Roosevelt added some 148 million more acres to the National Forest system. Today, the system contains over twice as much land as is in the National Park system.

The public forests are managed by the National Forest Service, created in 1905 as part of the Agriculture Department. The noted conservationist Gifford Pinchot, the Forest Service's first administrator, introduced important forestry practices, many of which are still in use. The Forest Service allows some cutting of trees on its lands. Even so, no more trees are allowed to be cut than can be replaced by one year's growth. In addition, the Forest Service insists that some trees and shrubs be left on slopes to prevent the soil from washing away. Seedlings are planted in areas where trees have been cut down or destroyed. This replanting of trees is called *reforestation*.

Parts of the National Forests are leased to private companies for cutting. This arrangement benefits both the companies and the public. The government gets money for the trees, and its employees do not have to do the cutting. Private businesses earn good profits by turning the trees into lumber or other forest products. The Forest Service leases some of its land for other commercial purposes. In certain areas, for example, it allows cattle and sheep to graze. Other lands are opened up for mining.

Theodore Roosevelt's Role in Conservation

Theodore Roosevelt became the first U.S. President to make a big push for conservation. As a young man, he became interested in natural history while living on a ranch in Dakota Territory. Later, as he traveled around the country, Roosevelt grew increasingly aware of the damage that was being done to the environment. As President, he awakened the public to the existence of environmental problems.

The National Park and National Forest systems grew rapidly during Roosevelt's administration. He also withdrew from sale millions of acres of public land that might have been mined or used to build dams.

One of Roosevelt's main accomplishments was to organize the first White House Conservation Conference, in 1908. Thirty-four state governors and many other important national figures attended this meeting. As a result of the conference, Roosevelt created a National Conservation Commission. This group made a broad survey of the country's needs in conserving its natural resources. Following the national group's example, over 40 states created their own conservation commissions.

The Dust Bowl

In large areas of the United States west of the Mississippi River, rainfall is low. As a result, the natural vegetation found there consists mainly of grasses and shrubs. In terms of agricultural use, the land is best suited for raising cattle and sheep. During wet years or with irrigation, though, people can grow wheat.

For years, ranchers successfully raised cattle and sheep in the area. Eventually, the land was *overgrazed* (too many animals were kept on a given piece of land). One result of overgrazing was the destruction of the natural cover of grass and shrubs. Clearing of land not really suited for growing crops had similar effects.

By the early 1930s, large areas of a five-state region had become barren. The loose and dry topsoil was easily blown away by the wind. From time to time, people in the region experienced *dust storms*—strong winds that carried away large amounts of soil in the form of dust. Americans called the region the "Dust Bowl"

because so many dust storms came through there. The storms caused so much damage that many people had to give up their farms. Some, such as the migrants depicted in John Steinbeck's novel *The Grapes of Wrath*, moved west to California. The Soil Conservation Service was set up, in part, to deal with the problems of the Dust Bowl.

THE DUST BOWL OF THE 1930s

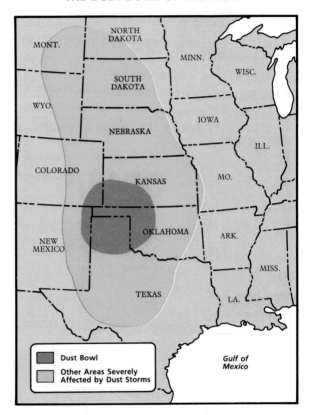

Conservation in the 1930s

Practically every U.S. President in the 20th century has given strong backing to the conservation movement. Nevertheless, historians often name Franklin D. Roosevelt as one of the most active Presidents in this field. As part of his effort to fight the Great Depression, he persuaded Congress to set up major conservation programs.

Civilian Conservation Corps (CCC) In 1933,
Congress passed a law that set up the Civilian
Conservation Corps. Until 1942, the CCC employed hundreds of thousands of young men in
conservation work. The main purpose of the
organization was to provide jobs for the youthful
unemployed. Corps members planted over 2
million acres of trees. Some members had the
additional responsibility of fighting forest fires.

Soil Conservation Service Also in the 1930s,
Congress created a government agency to deal
with the problems of erosion and low *soil fertility*
(richness of the soil). Because farmers had been
planting the same crop on a piece of land year
after year, the fertility of farmland had declined.
Poor farming methods also led to the slow
removal of topsoil by the action of water and

Artist Ben Shahn designed this poster in 1936 to
honor the work of the U.S. Resettlement Administration, one of the New Deal agencies.

wind. The Soil Conservation Service, which is
still a part of the Agriculture Department,
helped farmers to correct these problems.

Tennessee Valley Authority

One of the New Deal's most ambitious programs
was the creation of the Tennessee Valley Authority. An example of a *coordinated conservation
program,* the TVA combined different concerns
of conservationists. The project covered parts
of seven states along the Tennessee River. (See
the map on page 447.) This area had experienced
heavy flooding and erosion. In addition, its
economy had not developed as much as had
some other parts of the country. To correct
some of these problems, the TVA:

• Built huge dams on the Tennessee River,
such as the Norris and Wilson dams. It used
these dams for flood control, irrigation, and the
production of electric power.
• Distributed electric power to homes, farms,
and industries in the region.
• Improved navigation on the Tennessee River.
• Encouraged the use of modern farming
methods to increase productivity.
• Replanted forests.
• Improved public health facilities and health-
care services.
• Provided recreational facilities.

Some Americans criticized the Tennessee Valley Authority for competing unfairly with private power companies. The critics claimed that
private companies could provide many of TVA's
services—at far less cost to the American taxpayers.

Despite its critics, the TVA still serves its
many roles in the Tennessee River Valley. Its
supporters believe that the TVA is responsible
for the improved well-being of the people of
this region. In addition, say TVA's advocates,
the project has vastly reduced the area's flooding
and erosion problems.

TENNESSEE VALLEY AUTHORITY DAMS

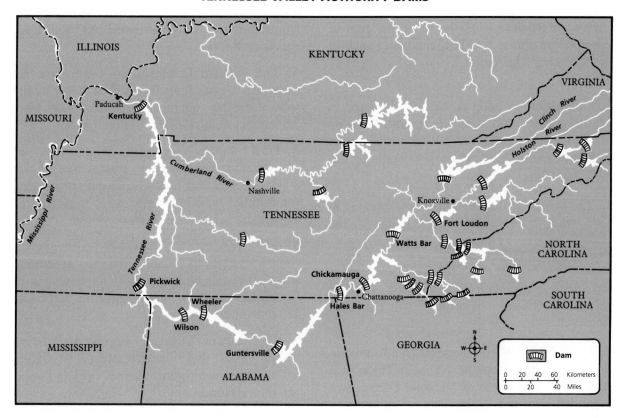

SUMMING UP   We have seen to what extent the conservation movement in the United States had grown by the 1930s. In the early days of the republic, only a few individuals had voiced concerns about conserving natural resources. By the late 19th century, these voices had become a chorus to which Congress and the U.S. President responded. As first steps, the federal government set up special agencies to manage the nation's public parks and forests. In later years, the government turned its attention to soil conservation and flood control. Some of its conservation projects grew so large that the government hired hundreds of thousands of people.

Understanding the Text

On a separate sheet of paper, write the letter of the word or phrase that best completes each of the following statements.

1. One action by early Americans designed to counter soil erosion was (*a*) contour plowing (*b*) clearing of forests (*c*) killing whole species of birds (*d*) moving on to new lands as old ones wore out.

2. The country's first National Park, created in 1872, was (*a*) Yosemite (*b*) Sequoia (*c*) the Dust Bowl (*d*) Yellowstone.

3. The first head of the National Forest Service was (*a*) John Muir (*b*) Gifford Pinchot (*c*) Henry David Thoreau (*d*) Theodore Roosevelt.

4. During Theodore Roosevelt's administration, the (*a*) system of National Parks was expanded (*b*) system of National Forests was expanded (*c*) first White House Conservation Conference was held (*d*) all of the above.

5. A conservation program begun during the administration of Franklin D. Roosevelt was the (*a*) National Park system (*b*) National Forest Service (*c*) Dust Bowl (*d*) Soil Conservation Service.

6. The Civilian Conservation Corps was *not* designed to (*a*) fight forest fires (*b*) provide jobs for the unemployed (*c*) plant trees (*d*) extract minerals from public lands.

7. Dust storms are often the result of (*a*) destroying the natural grass cover of dry land (*b*) installing faulty furnaces (*c*) limiting the number of animals grazing in a given area (*d*) setting up a National Park system.

8. The TVA activity to which private power companies objected the most was (*a*) generating and distributing electricity (*b*) improving public health care (*c*) manufacturing fertilizers (*d*) replanting forests.

9. The study of the relationship between living things and their environment is called (*a*) ecology (*b*) environment (*c*) pollution (*d*) reforestation.

10. During the years 1872–1942, the federal government was most involved with preserving which of the following natural resources? (*a*) soil (*b*) energy resources (*c*) clean air (*d*) clean water.

Developing Diagram-Reading Skills

TVA DAMS AND THE TENNESSEE RIVER IN PROFILE

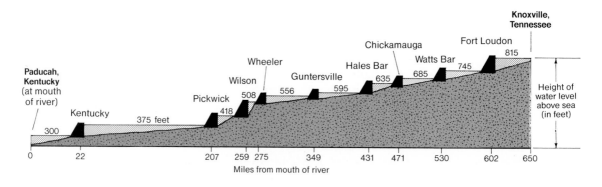

Study the profile diagram of the Tennessee River on page 448. Then choose the letter of the word or phrase that best answers each question. On a separate sheet of paper, match the question number with the correct letter.

1. Which of the following dams is downstream from the Wheeler Dam? *(a)* Wilson *(b)* Hales Bar *(c)* Chickamauga *(d)* all of the above.

2. The mouth of the Tennessee River is how many miles from the Kentucky Dam? *(a)* 0 *(b)* 22 *(c)* 300 *(d)* 375.

3. According to the diagram, the longest stretch of the Tennessee River between any two dams is how many miles? *(a)* 22 *(b)* 52 *(c)* 82 *(d)* 185.

4. The water level above the Kentucky Dam is about how many feet above sea level? *(a)* 0 *(b)* 22 *(c)* 300 *(d)* 375.

5. The drop in water level from just above Fort Loudon Dam to just below Wheeler Dam is how many feet? *(a)* 237 *(b)* 307 *(c)* 515 *(d)* 745.

Thinking About the Lesson

1. Why have Americans in the 20th century been more concerned than those of earlier generations about protecting the environment?

2. Should the National Forest Service sell companies the right to cut down trees on its lands? Why or why not?

3. Do you think that another dust bowl might develop in the United States? Explain your answer.

4. If Americans were to establish a Hall of Fame of U.S. Conservationists, why might the following individuals be nominated: Gifford Pinchot, Theodore Roosevelt, and Franklin D. Roosevelt?

Environmental Protection Today

The modern environmental protection movement has continued and expanded the conservation movement that began in the 19th century. Americans are still concerned about soil fertility, wildlife management, and protection of the nation's forests. Besides these concerns, Americans are putting more emphasis on fighting pollution of the air, water, and land.

> In modern times, with the country's increased population and industrialization, the environment is becoming more polluted than ever. Reacting to this situation, many Americans are demanding corrective measures. People who are strongly concerned about environmental problems are often called *environmentalists.*

Water Pollution

All Americans need pure water for drinking and cooking. Farmers need water to grow crops and to give to their animals. Industries make use of vast quantities of water in manufacturing processes. At the same time that water is more in demand than ever, it is being increasingly polluted. There are several major sources of water pollution in the United States today.

• Industrial pollutants, especially discharges from steel mills, paper companies, oil refineries, and chemical concerns.

• *Sewage,* in the form of waste water from homes and other buildings. Most waste water is purified in sewage treatment plants; some, however, goes untreated into lakes, rivers, and oceans.

• Agricultural runoff. Everything that washes off farmers' fields during rainstorms is called *agricultural runoff.* Often included in this runoff are portions of the fertilizers, pesticides, and herbicides that are applied to the fields. These substances can do much damage to lakes and rivers. Fertilizers that reach waterways encourage the growth of *algae* (water plants). If algae grow too much, they can cut off the supply of oxygen in the water—oxygen that fish need. With less oxygen in the water, fewer fish survive. High doses of pesticides and herbicides in lakes and rivers also can kill off many forms of life.

• Thermal pollution. Some factories and power plants use water to cool down overheated materials. When the water is dumped back into rivers and lakes, it is often warmer than it was. This *thermal pollution* can kill some aquatic plants and animals.

Federal Water Pollution Controls After World War II, the federal government began providing

450

money to local governments to build sewage treatment plants. It also began to sue major polluters. Over the years, laws concerning water quality became stricter. The Water Pollution Control Act of 1972 was a major step forward. It prohibited the discharge of any pollutant into waterways without a special permit. Moreover, it set standards of water quality.

Water Shortages Not only are many of the nation's lakes, rivers, and streams polluted, but there is also a shortage of water in some sections of the country—especially in the Rocky Mountain states and the Southwest. In some states, cities compete with one another for water to drink. The cities also compete with their area's farmers and ranchers, as well as with power plants and other industries. As a result of this competition, people in dry parts of the country make special efforts to conserve their precious water resources.

Air Pollution

We usually take air for granted. It is always around us, and we can use it without limitation and without charge.

Since the 1950s, though, Americans have become increasingly aware that the air in many places is polluted. The sources of this pollution are several:

• Power plants and home furnaces, especially those that burn coal as a fuel.

• Industries that send all kinds of wastes up their smokestacks.

• Motor vehicles. Tens of millions of cars, trucks, motorcycles, and buses send their exhaust into the air.

• Local government agencies that burn garbage and other wastes.

Air pollution can cause respiratory diseases, skin disorders, and some forms of cancer. In addition, smoke and *smog* (fog polluted by

Power plants such as this one are obvious sources of air pollution. Tall smokestacks keep emissions from falling on nearby population centers. Instead, the smoke travels long distances and lands on states downwind from the plants.

smoke) destroy the beauty of some of America's most scenic urban areas.

The U.S. Environmental Protection Agency (EPA), created in 1970, is greatly concerned about the purity of the air. For that reason, it has set air quality standards. The EPA tells individual factories and power plants how much and what kinds of *emissions* (wastes) they can send out of their smokestacks. The EPA also sets motor vehicle exhaust standards for all new cars sold in the country. Moreover, the government is phasing out the sale of leaded gas because this fuel, when burned, spreads poisonous lead along roads and highways.

Pollution of the Land

The land on which we live, grow food, and play is threatened by people who unintentionally poison it. Farmers, for instance, in trying to increase production, sometimes use pesticides and fertilizers that harm the soil and crops. In 1984, the EPA banned the use of a pesticide

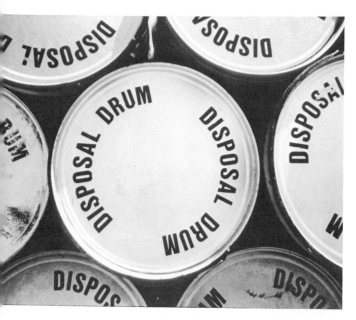

Toxic wastes are often put in metal drums, such as these, and then buried in the ground.

called EDB, saying that it might cause cancer in human beings.

In recent years, Americans have become aware of the dangers of dumping industrial wastes in the ground. They are especially worried about *toxic* (poisonous) wastes that contaminate the soil. The wastes may also spread into nearby water systems and the air. People living and working near dump sites can become ill and perhaps die from the poisons. Two cases illustrate the problem:

• Love Canal. In 1978, residents of Love Canal in Niagara Falls, New York, got some bad news. They learned that they were living above a dangerous dump site. Years before, a chemical company had deposited toxic chemicals in steel drums in this area. Some of these drums leaked toxic chemicals into the soil. Fearing for their health, residents of Love Canal moved away. They were aided in their move by the State of New York.

• In 1982, people of Times Beach, Missouri, found out that for ten years they had been living on *contaminated* (containing unwanted substances) soil. Unknown to them, one such toxic substance, dioxin, had been applied to their roads in 1971. After the discovery of this contamination, the federal government helped residents of Times Beach leave town. The government bought their homes from them. Since 1982, authorities have found dioxin contamination in 100 other Missouri communities. In fact, dioxin pollution seems to have become a nationwide problem.

In recent years, the EPA has been active in finding and investigating many toxic waste dumps—both legal and illegal ones. The federal government is giving the states money to pay for the cleanup of the most dangerous dumps. Moreover, the EPA has begun prosecuting people who have illegally dumped dangerous wastes.

The Environmental Protection Agency recommends several safe methods of disposing of toxic wastes. It says that the wastes should be burned and/or put in a *secure landfill* (underground storage area from which wastes are not supposed to leak).

Nuclear Wastes A pollution problem that especially worries environmentalists is where to dispose of nuclear wastes. These radioactive materials result from the operation of nuclear power plants and nuclear weapons factories. Nuclear wastes are dangerous and decay only after tens of thousands of years. For this reason, environmentalists want to make sure that the wastes are kept in very safe places.

Conserving Natural Resources

In addition to fighting all kinds of pollution, modern environmentalists have other pressing concerns.

Wildlife Preservation In 1940, the government set up the Fish and Wildlife Service in the

Interior Department. This agency has the job of protecting fish, birds, mammals, plants, and other types of wildlife. To do this, it has created some 350 *wildlife refuges* (places where animals and plants are protected). The Service also hatches fish eggs and stocks lakes around the country with many kinds of fish.

The nation's wildlife refuge system got a tremendous boost in 1980. In that year, Congress passed the Alaska Wilderness Act, designating 104 million acres in Alaska as wildlife refuges.

Wildlife are protected by other agencies besides the Fish and Wildlife Service. The National Park Service and many states have their own areas reserved for wildlife preservation. Furthermore, the states have fish and game laws to regulate fishing and hunting. In 1973, Congress passed a law to protect certain plants and animals found around the country. The Endangered Species Act outlawed the hunting or collecting of animals and plants that are in danger of *extinction* (dying out). Moreover, it prohibited the building of federal projects that might endanger any one of the animal or plant species put on a federal list.

Restoration of Land to Its Former Beauty In a number of ways, environmentalists have fought visual pollution:

• They have called for and obtained the expansion of the National Park system.

• They have gotten laws passed to regulate the location and appearance of junkyards.

• They have persuaded Congress and some state legislatures to pass laws concerning the number, location, and size of billboards.

• In 1977, environmentalists got Congress to pass an important *strip-mining* law. In mining for coal near the earth's surface, companies had left ugly scars. Strip mine owners now are required to restore mined land to its original form.

• In response to environmentalist pressures, many states have passed bottle laws. In order to encourage people not to litter, these states require deposits on bottles containing beverages sold to consumers. After paying a deposit, customers are less likely to throw away bottles. They are more likely to return the bottles to a store in order to get their money back.

Energy and the Environment As foreign energy sources became more expensive, business leaders and other Americans urged greater development of domestic supplies. The *extraction* (withdrawal) of coal, oil, and gas, however, can cause damage to the environment. The transportation of these resources also can cause problems, as *oil spills* along our seacoasts and rivers have shown. Environmentalists call for more controls on methods used in the extraction and transportation of energy resources. In addition, they want to see the nation rely more on nonpolluting sources of energy, such as solar and wind power.

The national symbol of the United States—the bald eagle—is an endangered species. U.S. laws prohibit killing these eagles or even disturbing their nests.

Criticism of Environmental Laws

Some business leaders say that many environmental laws are too strict and that they prevent businesses from operating profitably. The critics argue that high environmental standards discourage people from making investments. With fewer investments, the U.S. economy slows down. Environmental laws make the cost of doing business more expensive, charge the critics. They point to foreign countries with lower environmental standards, claiming that industries in those countries have an advantage. These foreign industries can produce goods more cheaply because they are not bound by laws similar to our own.

SUMMING UP   We have seen how pollution of water, the air, and the land has increased considerably since World War II. Americans have become more involved in searching for ways to stop this pollution. Many Americans are also concerned with preserving wildlife and keeping or returning the environment to its natural state. Critics of the environmental movement, however, say that it sometimes comes into conflict with the nation's goals of keeping a strong economy and developing energy resources.

Understanding the Text

On a separate sheet of paper, write the letter of the word or phrase that best completes each of the following statements.

1. A major cause of water pollution is (a) sewage treatment (b) industrial discharge (c) a wildlife refuge (d) extinction.

2. Thermal pollution from industries can be a problem because it kills some plants and animals (a) in the water (b) on land (c) in the air (d) all of the above.

3. The abundant growth of algae in water is encouraged by (a) the Environmental Protection Agency (b) the Fish and Wildlife Service (c) the use of fertilizers (d) strip-mining.

4. An activity usually *not* considered a cause of air pollution is (a) burning coal in furnaces (b) running motor vehicles (c) operating industrial plants (d) applying fertilizers.

5. The EPA has encouraged the use of non-leaded gas in (a) windmills (b) motor vehicles (c) nuclear power plants (d) solar power collectors.

6. Radioactive wastes are one of the by-products of (a) nuclear power plants (b) pesticide use (c) motor vehicles (d) coal-burning furnaces.

7. The Environmental Protection Agency has been active in (a) surveying toxic waste dumps (b) designating air quality standards (c) setting

emission standards for new cars *(d)* all of the above.

8. The Endangered Species Act was designed to *(a)* promote contour plowing *(b)* protect plants and animals in danger of extinction *(c)* regulate strip-mining *(d)* control motor vehicle emissions.

9. State bottle laws are a response to *(a)* littering *(b)* strip-mining *(c)* ugly junkyards *(d)* hot-air pollution.

10. Which of the following criticisms do business leaders often make of today's environmentalist movement? *(a)* It is concerned mainly with increasing profits of private businesses, at the expense of the public. *(b)* It tries to enforce standards so high that they often stand in the way of economic growth. *(c)* It is opposed to effective government regulation of private businesses. *(d)* It is concerned mainly with the problems of poor people, at the expense of the general population.

Developing Graph-Reading Skills

U.S. ELECTRICAL ENERGY PRODUCTION, BY SOURCES OF ENERGY

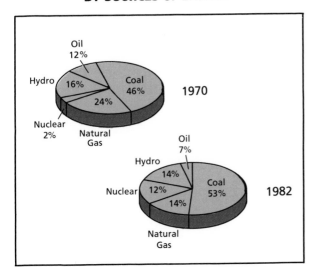

Examine the two pie graphs above. Then choose the letter of the word or phrase that best answers each question. On a separate sheet of paper, match the question number with the correct letter.

1. In 1970, natural gas accounted for what percentage of the total electrical energy produced in the country? *(a)* 2 *(b)* 14 *(c)* 24 *(d)* none of the above.

2. In 1982, over half of all electrical energy production came from one source. What was it? *(a)* coal *(b)* natural gas *(c)* nuclear power *(d)* none of the above.

3. Which of the following is an example of a source of energy whose percentage of total electrical energy production *decreased* between 1970 and 1982? *(a)* coal *(b)* nuclear power *(c)* oil *(d)* none of the above.

4. Which of the following is an example of a source of energy whose percentage of total electrical energy production *increased* between 1970 and 1982? *(a)* natural gas *(b)* nuclear power *(c)* hydro power *(d)* oil.

5. From studying the pie graphs, one can make which of the following conclusions? *(a)* The United States produced twice as much oil in 1970 as in 1982. *(b)* Of all the sources of energy shown, the relative role of nuclear power changed the most between 1970 and 1982. *(c)* Total U.S. electrical energy production was at the same level in 1982 as it was in 1970. *(d)* The United States came to rely more on imported oil and gas after 1970.

Thinking About the Lesson

1. Why did pollution become more of a problem in the United States in the 20th century than it had been in the 19th century?

2. Is air pollution a problem where you live or go to school? If so, can you explain the source or sources of the pollution?

3. Do you think that more needs to be done to clean up the country's streams, rivers, and lakes? Why or why not?

4. Do you think that federal and state governments should do more to help prevent the extinction of certain plants and animals? Why or why not?

5. Do you believe that many environmental laws are too strict and should be eased or eliminated? Explain.

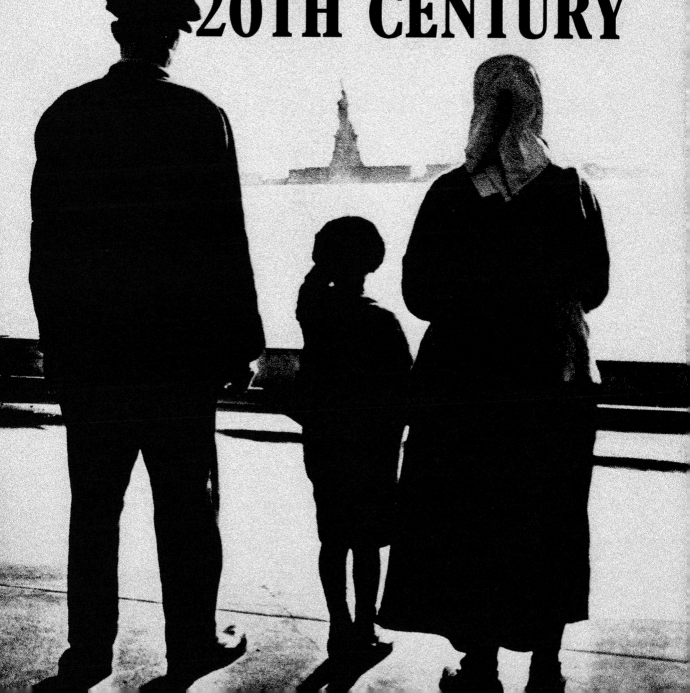

AMERICANS IN THE 20TH CENTURY

America's Changing Immigration Policies

For a long time, the United States did not limit immigration. Then in the late 19th century, the federal government began regulating who could come into the country. In the 20th century, immigration policies have changed several times. In part, these changes have reflected Americans' fear of people of different backgrounds. Another factor has been the fear among American workers that immigrants would take their jobs away.

The Great Wave

Between 1890 and 1917, a great wave of immigrants—some 18 million—came to the United States. In 1907 alone, more than 1,250,000 arrived. Western and Northern Europe continued to contribute to this *influx* (a coming in). Some seven out of every ten newcomers, however, were from countries of Southern and Eastern Europe. Especially large numbers of new immigrants came from Italy, Austria-Hungary, Poland, and Russia. Smaller numbers arrived from Greece, Finland, Armenia, and other lands. (See the graph on page 303 for general trends in immigration, 1781–1980.)

The Issue of Japanese Immigration

In the 1890s and early 1900s, tens of thousands of Japanese settled in California. Some bought farms or stores. Many more got jobs as gardeners, cooks, cannery workers, or farm laborers.

Anti-Japanese Feelings Despite the fact that most Japanese immigrants were hardworking and law-abiding, public feeling against them developed. Prejudiced Americans believed that these immigrants could not become "real Americans" because they would remain loyal to Japan. These Americans disliked seeing the Japanese immigrants holding on to Japanese customs. Some American workers did not care for Japanese-Americans for another reason—they feared competition from those Japanese workers who accepted low wages.

Anti-Japanese feelings in California led to race riots and other violent incidents. The Japanese government, though, was upset most by an action of the San Francisco Board of Education. This group ruled that Japanese children, as well as Chinese and Korean, would have to attend separate public schools.

458

Gentlemen's Agreement To head off a diplomatic crisis, President Theodore Roosevelt in 1907 arranged a "Gentlemen's Agreement" with Japan. Roosevelt promised that there would be no further moves in the United States to put Japanese children into special schools. In return, Japan agreed to stop more Japanese workers from emigrating to the United States.

The Gentlemen's Agreement solved the diplomatic crisis but did not end all Japanese immigration. During World War I, thousands more Japanese arrived in the United States to meet a new demand for farm laborers. Nor did the Gentlemen's Agreement end discrimination against the Japanese in America. In 1913, a California law restricted land ownership by Japanese. In 1920, another California law prohibited Japanese from leasing farms.

New Restrictions on Immigration

In 1917, many Americans thought that vast numbers of Europeans would soon be coming to America to escape the wartime destruction. At this time, Americans were less eager to welcome European immigrants than they had been previously. In the United States, the belief was growing that new workers and settlers were no longer needed. Because of this belief, more and more Americans were calling for further restrictions on immigration.

Many immigrants who arrived in the United States between 1891 and 1954 first landed at Ellis Island in New York Harbor. There they were inspected by health officials.

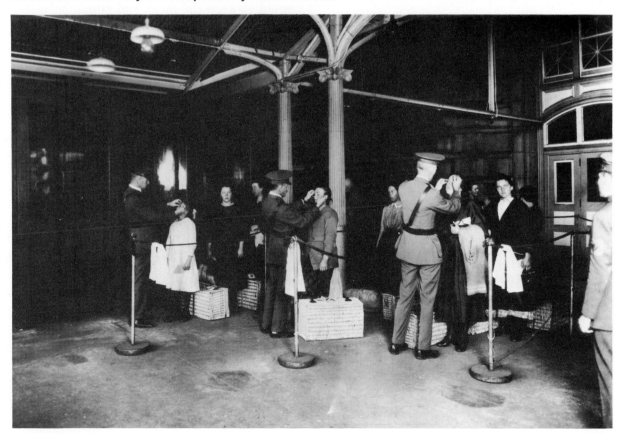

U.S. POPULATION BORN IN OTHER COUNTRIES, BY PERCENTAGE

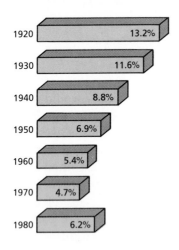

1920	13.2%
1930	11.6%
1940	8.8%
1950	6.9%
1960	5.4%
1970	4.7%
1980	6.2%

Literacy Act   As in the past, many of the immigrants during the war years were *illiterate* (could not read or write). Some Americans thought that illiterate immigrants were less desirable than literate ones. With this view in mind, Congress passed the Literacy Act of 1917. The law said that no person could immigrate to the United States unless he or she could read at least one language.

Quota System   Immigration declined during World War I but became heavy again in 1920 and 1921. During these years, America was going through an economic depression. American workers, many of whom were unemployed, did not welcome foreign competitors for scarce jobs. Newspapers blamed new immigrants for many of the labor disorders of the time. These factors contributed to the passage of laws setting quotas on immigrants from each country.

Under the Emergency Quota Act of 1921, yearly immigration from any country was limited to three percent of that nationality's population already here in 1910. Furthermore, only 357,000 immigrants were to be allowed into the country in any one year. In 1924, Congress reduced the quota to two percent of a nationality's population in the United States in 1890. This date was

chosen because at this time immigration from Southern and Eastern Europe was relatively small.

During the rest of the 1920s, the total number of immigrants was reduced several times. By 1929, only about 150,000 immigrants a year were allowed into the United States. These restrictions, though, did not apply to immigrants from Canada and Latin America. Immigrants from Japan, on the other hand, were barred completely.

One of the main purposes of the quota laws was to favor immigration from certain areas of the world. Under these laws, about four times as many immigrants could be admitted from Northern and Western Europe as from Southern and Eastern Europe. Immigration from Asian countries was severely restricted. The *national origins system*, as the plan was called, was supposed to keep the racial and ethnic balance of the country from changing.

Changes in the National Origins System

Many Americans found much to criticize about the national origins system of selecting immigrants. Critics said that the system was racist because it gave the largest quotas to Northern and Western Europeans. Some supporters of the system claimed that these immigrants would make better Americans than immigrants from Southern or Eastern Europe or from Asia.

Another criticism had to do with unused quotas. Great Britain, for example, had large quotas that often were not filled. Meanwhile, many Italians and Greeks had to wait years to come to the United States because these nationalities had been given small quotas. The law did not allow unused quotas for one nationality to be shifted to other nationalities.

Exceptions to the National Origins System
From time to time, Congress made exceptions

A majority of immigrants become U.S. citizens. Here scientist Albert Einstein (center), his secretary Helen Dukas (left), and daughter Margot Einstein take the oath of citizenship. They were all political refugees from Nazi Germany.

to the limits set by the national origins system. In the 1930s, for example, the United States admitted from Nazi Germany a small number of *refugees* (people fleeing from their homeland). As a "reward" for being an ally of the United States in World War II, China was given a quota of 105 immigrants a year in the 1940s.

After World War II, new groups of immigrants were allowed into the country in greater numbers. Foreign-born children and spouses of Americans who had served in the Armed Forces became important exceptions to the quota system. So too were hundreds of thousands of *displaced persons* (people uprooted by the war) from Europe.

McCarran-Walter Act In 1952, Congress amended the national origins system once more. The McCarran-Walter Act raised slightly the total number of immigrants from quota countries—from 150,000 to 156,000. Japan and other Asian and Pacific countries were given small quotas for the first time in many years. In addition,

the law barred would-be immigrants who were considered "politically undesirable." This phrase applied to people who belonged to the Communist party and other radical political groups.

Political Refugees Ever since 1953, the United States has accepted as extra immigrants refugees fleeing persecution in Communist countries. After the unsuccessful Hungarian uprising in 1956, tens of thousands of Hungarians were admitted into the United States. More recently, thousands of Jews from the Soviet Union have chosen to settle in the United States. Many people from Communist Cuba have also found refuge in this country.

Modern Immigration Policies

As a result of mounting criticism of existing policies, Presidents John F. Kennedy and Lyndon B. Johnson called for a totally new immigration act. Congress passed such a law in 1965.

Immigration Act of 1965   Under this law, since slightly amended, up to 170,000 people from outside the Western Hemisphere could enter the country in any year. No more than 20,000 of this total could come from any single nation. From within the Western Hemisphere, 120,000 immigrants were allowed each year. The selection of people to be admitted was based on their desirability as new Americans, not on their country of origin. People with special skills and talents were given preference. Those selected as immigrants could bring their spouse, parents, and children with them.

The Immigration Act of 1965 has changed immigration patterns in many ways:

• For the first time, a limit has been applied to immigration from countries within the Western Hemisphere.

• Many more immigrants have come from Southern European countries, such as Portugal and Greece, that previously had a backlog of applicants.

• Immigration from Great Britain, Germany, and other formerly high-quota countries of Western Europe has declined.

• More Asians have been admitted into the United States than ever before. Since 1965, for example, many immigrants have come from China, Korea, India, and the Philippines. Moreover, between 1975 and 1985, the United States permitted the entry of more than 700,000 people from Vietnam, Laos, and Cambodia. They had been uprooted by decades of wars, internal conflicts, and famines.

Illegal Immigration

In recent years, Congress has been trying to deal with some of the country's immigration problems. One of the main problems concerns *illegal immigrants*—aliens who come into the United States without official permission.

A Growing Problem   Each year, from 500,000 to 1 million foreigners come to the United States illegally. About 92 percent of these illegal immigrants cross the border from Mexico. (See Lesson 86 for a discussion of Mexican immigration.) Illegal aliens who work for low wages in the United States are resented by American workers. These Americans say that aliens keep down wages and prevent many U.S. citizens from getting jobs. Americans also complain that illegal aliens cost taxpayers a great deal of money. Some illegal aliens have obtained forged documents in order to collect food stamps, Medicaid, welfare, and unemployment benefits.

In order to solve the immigration problem, reformers have called for certain changes in the immigration laws, including:

• Penalties against employers who hire illegal aliens.

• An amnesty for a large number of illegal aliens. For instance, the law might allow those who were in the country by 1980 to become U.S. citizens.

• Stricter measures in patrolling places of entry, especially the U.S.-Mexican border.

• An increase in the number of legal immigrants allowed in each year.

Not all Americans favor such changes. Some like the way that the present system operates. They believe that all immigrants—both legal and illegal ones—provide valuable services to the American economy. For example, many immigrants work at jobs for which U.S. citizens do not wish to apply.

Leaders of Hispanic-American groups in the United States fear what might happen if such immigration "reforms" are put into law. They say that employers might discriminate against all Spanish-speaking people in trying to keep illegal aliens from their employ.

SUMMING UP   We have seen how large numbers of foreigners have come to live in the United States in the 20th century. Americans, though, have sought ways to cut down on this influx. At first, moves were made to limit Japanese immigration. Then newcomers who could not read were prevented from coming into the country. Quota laws limited immigration according to nationality. More recent laws give preference to immigrants with special skills and those who are political refugees from Communist countries.

Understanding the Text

On a separate sheet of paper, write the letter of the word or phrase that best completes each of the following statements.

1. Between 1890 and 1917, the majority of immigrants to the United States were from *(a)* Southern and Eastern Europe *(b)* Western and Northern Europe *(c)* Western Europe and Japan *(d)* Mexico and Canada.

2. The Gentlemen's Agreement of 1907 was a plan to check immigration of *(a)* people likely to become public charges *(b)* Japanese workers *(c)* Vietnamese refugees *(d)* displaced persons from Europe.

3. Of the following federal laws, the one that called for a test of an immigrant's ability to read was called the *(a)* Gentlemen's Agreement *(b)* Emergency Quota Act of 1921 *(c)* Literacy Act of 1917 *(d)* McCarran-Walter Act.

4. Of the following statements, one that supports immigration says that *(a)* immigrants take away jobs from Americans *(b)* immigrants are ignorant, dirty, and like to live in slums *(c)* immigrants are not likely to become good U.S. citizens *(d)* immigrants make important contributions to life in the United States.

5. One provision of the national origins system was to *(a)* end all limits on immigration *(b)* exclude refugees from Nazi Germany *(c)* assign quotas to immigrants from various nations *(d)* stop immigration completely.

6. The national origins system was set up to favor immigration from *(a)* Eastern and Southern Europe *(b)* Northern and Western Europe *(c)* Japan *(d)* Asia.

7. The Immigration Act of 1965 has attempted to select immigrants on the basis of *(a)* how many people of a certain nationality were already in the country *(b)* one's religion *(c)* one's ability to pay for transportation to the United States *(d)* one's desirability as a new American.

8. As a result of the 1965 Immigration Act, there has been a large increase in immigration from *(a)* Portugal *(b)* Great Britain *(c)* Canada *(d)* Germany.

9. Many Vietnamese families live in the United States. The period of heaviest Vietnamese immigration was *(a)* before 1900 *(b)* 1900–1917 *(c)* 1945–1952 *(d)* 1975–1985.

10. From reading this lesson, one can conclude that *(a)* the United States has never had an immigration policy *(b)* many Americans prefer some groups of immigrants over others *(c)* since 1917, the government has tried to keep out all immigrants *(d)* all foreigners are welcome to come to the United States to live.

Developing Table-Reading Skills

IMMIGRATION TO THE UNITED STATES BY WORLD AREAS, 1951–1980

Area	1951–1960	1961–1970	1971–1980
Europe	1,492,200	1,238,600	801,300
Asia	157,000	445,300	1,633,800
North and South America	841,300	1,579,400	1,929,400
Africa	16,600	39,300	91,500
Australia and New Zealand	5,000	13,600	19,600
Other Areas	3,300	5,500	17,700
Total	2,515,400	3,321,700	4,493,300

Study the table above. Then choose the letter of the word or phrase that best completes each sentence. On a separate sheet of paper, match the sentence number with the correct letter.

1. In the period 1951–1960, immigration to the United States was greatest from (*a*) Europe (*b*) Asia (*c*) North and South America (*d*) Africa.

2. In the periods 1961–1970 and 1971–1980, immigration to the United States was greatest from (*a*) Europe (*b*) Asia (*c*) North and South America (*d*) Africa.

3. After 1960, an area that showed a decline in the number of immigrants coming to the United States was (*a*) Asia (*b*) Africa (*c*) Europe (*d*) Australia and New Zealand.

4. From 1951 to 1980, the number of Africans who immigrated to the United States was (*a*) 16,600 (*b*) 109,800 (*c*) 147,400 (*d*) none of the above.

5. Of the total number of immigrants to the United States in the period 1971–1980, Asian immigrants made up about (*a*) 10 percent (*b*) 25 percent (*c*) 35 percent (*d*) 50 percent.

Thinking About the Lesson

1. Why was the Japanese government in the early 20th century upset by the way Japanese immigrants were being treated in the United States?

2. What was the reason behind the passage of the Literacy Act of 1917? Do you think that all immigrants should have to prove that they can read? Why or why not?

3. Do you think that the quota laws of the national origins system were fair? Explain your answer.

4. How did the Immigration Act of 1965 differ from the laws that set up the national origins system?

5. What changes, if any, would you like to see in the current immigration laws?

LESSON 71

The Immigrant Experience

Many immigrant groups have settled in the United States in the 20th century. To some extent, the experiences of all immigrants have been similar. Each group, though, has had its own set of problems in adjusting to life in America.

A Nation of Immigrants

Most Americans are either immigrants or descendants of immigrants. For this reason, the United States has been labeled "a nation of immigrants." The diverse backgrounds of Americans have combined to make American society what it is today.

In looking at American immigrant groups in the early 20th century, we can see some common patterns. At first, most immigrants had a hard time adjusting to life in America. They soon began to adopt some American customs and became familiar with life in the United States. After a longer period of time, immigrant groups became *assimilated* (formed an integral part of a society). Their former cultures were not lost, however. Some members of each immigrant group have kept traditions alive. Furthermore, certain foreign customs became American ones, adding to the total of what it means to be an American.

Adjustments to a New Way of Life

The majority of immigrants in the early 20th century arrived poor and without job skills.

Ethnic Neighborhoods New immigrants often lived in substandard housing, surrounded by Americans of the same nationality. Most large cities had separate neighborhoods for Greeks, Italians, Jews, Poles, Mexicans, and so on. Immigrants were not required to live in ethnic neighborhoods, but they felt safer and more comfortable living together. Here they could speak their native languages and preserve their cultures. Besides, at first they usually did not have enough money to live in neighborhoods with higher rents. The various nationalities in the neighborhoods would form self-help societies for each nationality. Italian-American societies, for example, would help new immigrants from Italy adjust to life in the United States.

Employment Patterns Most new immigrants lacked the skills needed to get better-paying jobs. Unskilled immigrants had to accept whatever work was offered to them. Western railroads, for example, hired many workers from Mexico to build new rail lines. Railroad companies in the East signed up many unskilled workers from Italy. Young Finnish immigrants

465

found work in the iron mines of Minnesota and the copper mines of Michigan. Unskilled Jewish immigrants—both male and female—worked long hours in urban sweatshops, making dresses and other garments. And, as we learned in Lesson 70, many Japanese-Americans were employed as farm laborers in California.

Language Difficulties Most new immigrants could not speak English, much less read or write it. This fact was another reason why they had difficulties getting better-paying work. Moreover, many new immigrants were hindered by their inability to read or write even their native language.

Some Success Stories Of course, not all new immigrants were poor, unskilled, and uneducated. A good number had gone to school and a few even had college degrees. Some had brought enough savings with them to realize their dream of buying a small farm or a business. Many immigrants, for instance, started stores and restaurants. Some others, with fewer resources, became street peddlers.

Skilled and white-collar workers were always in demand. Italian stoneworkers were quickly hired to build dams and bridges. Jewish shoemakers and tailors easily found employment in their trades. A small number of Mexican immigrants managed crews of farm laborers, while some others obtained clerical jobs.

Discrimination Against Immigrants All immigrants—whether poor or prosperous, educated or uneducated—encountered a degree of hostility from other Americans. Most immigrants, even those that were highly qualified, were excluded from the higher-paying jobs. They were often the last to be hired and the first to be fired. They were often discriminated against in housing as well. Even if the new Americans had money, they might be barred from living in certain neighborhoods.

Like other minority groups, immigrants were often unfairly criticized and ridiculed. Some individuals became the targets of anti-immigrant hate groups and were subject to verbal and physical abuse.

Jewish immigrants suffered especially sharp discrimination. Anti-Semitic groups vandalized Jewish cemeteries and synagogues. Jewish-Americans were kept out of many social clubs and other organizations. Jewish students were not allowed to enroll in some private schools, and only a limited number could attend some colleges.

Mexican immigrants, who have settled mostly in the Southwest, also found much discrimination. They were often forced to live in separate neighborhoods, called *barrios*. There, housing and health care were poor. Children of migrant workers rarely attended school. Instruction for children of Mexican immigrants who did get an education frequently took place in segregated schools.

As with other immigrant groups, Mexican-Americans had fewer job opportunities than other Americans. They usually received low wages and were often employed on a temporary, seasonal basis in agriculture.

> In some ways, the experiences of Puerto Ricans have been similar to those of Mexican immigrants. They both speak Spanish as their primary language. They have both encountered discrimination in housing and jobs. There is, however, one important difference between the two groups. Puerto Ricans have been U.S. citizens since 1917. Therefore, those who have come to the mainland are not considered immigrants.

Not all Mexican-Americans were immigrants. Mexicans had been living in the Southwest since the 17th century. By the 20th century, descendants of the older groups of Mexican-Americans had become well-established. Many owned ranches, farms, or other businesses or were employed in the professions and other well-paying jobs.

Assimilation of Immigrant Groups

Eventually, all immigrants have been faced with the question of assimilation into the larger American culture. Most have become assimilated to some degree. The speed of assimilation, however, has varied from one immigrant group to another. Italians, Puerto Ricans, and Mexicans are groups that have become assimilated more slowly than others. This situation may be due to the fact that many members of these groups came to the United States only tempo-

rarily. Considerable numbers returned to their homeland after saving substantial sums of money. Not considering themselves permanent immigrants, they had less reason to become assimilated.

Learning About America   Living in the United States, immigrants could not help but learn about the country's institutions, customs, and values. Even if they spoke only their native language at home, they probably picked up some English on the streets or at work. Besides, they could learn about the United States without knowing any English. Jewish immigrants who could read Hebrew or Yiddish newspapers learned about America in these publications. Hispanic Americans had Spanish-language newspapers, Chinese immigrants had Chinese-language newspapers, and so on.

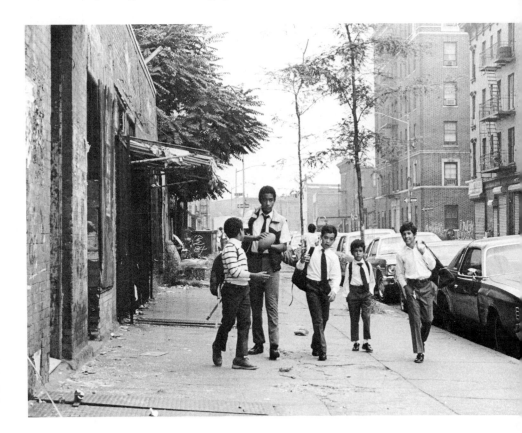

Some 1.5 million Puerto Ricans have left their island homeland to find jobs and a better life. Many of them have settled in and around New York City. Puerto Ricans frequently return to the island to visit. Moreover, as economic conditions there have improved, some have moved back to Puerto Rico permanently.

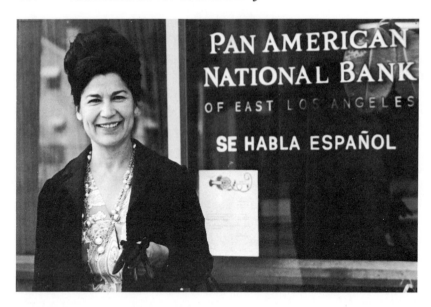

Mexican-Americans are quite influential in the Southwest. This woman chairs the board of a bank, and is president of a food company.

The Role of Education   Most immigrant groups have stressed the importance of education in order to get ahead in the United States. Some immigrant adults have gone to night school to learn English and get an understanding of American government. Mostly, though, immigrants have emphasized educating their children. In public and *parochial* (religious) schools, mixed with young people of other nationalities, immigrant children have been quick to learn about America.

First, Second, and Third Generations   Many immigrants have become *naturalized* (have gained U.S. citizenship) after passing a test proving a basic knowledge about the U.S. government. The way of life of *first-generation Americans*, though, has remained a mixture of the old and the new. They often think of themselves as primarily Greek-Americans or Mexican-Americans instead of just Americans. Full assimilation usually does not come until the *second* or *third generation* (children or grandchildren of immigrants).

Sometimes assimilation takes the form of rejecting the culture of the immigrant's homeland. Certain children or grandchildren of immigrants have refused to learn the language of their ancestors. They also have not been interested in their ethnic history, dress, foods, and other cultural traditions. Instead, they want to be like other American young people—wearing the same types of clothing, celebrating the same national holidays, and so on.

Resurgence of Ethnic Pride

For much of the 20th century, most Americans agreed that assimilation was beneficial to everyone involved. A popular theory—the *melting pot* concept—held that all national groups were melting together into one American culture.

In recent decades, however, the melting pot idea has been challenged. Many ethnic groups—both new immigrants and people whose ancestors came to America long ago—have begun to express pride again in their separate backgrounds. There has been a revival of interest in national languages, history, and customs. Americans all across the country have done *genealogical research* (studied their family's history). Ethnic food, dress, music, and dance have been celebrated at numerous ethnic fairs.

Bilingual Education Since the 1960s, leaders of Hispanic and other ethnic groups have called for *bilingual education*. They ask that teachers conduct classes partly in English and partly in the native tongue of the students. In this way, they say, some students will understand instruction better than if it was all in English. A secondary goal of bilingual education is to keep alive languages of certain ethnic groups.

Bilingual education has been instituted in a number of school systems. The U.S. government has provided schools with funds to set up programs of instruction in several languages. Bilingual education, however, has not met with the approval of all Americans. Critics say that bilingual education hinders a student's mastery of the English language. Without such mastery, they say, a person will not succeed in school and, later, in the workplace.

The Newest Immigrants

Since the 1970s, the United States has been receiving a new wave of immigrants. Hundreds of thousands of Cubans, Haitians, Mexicans, Indochinese, and Central Americans have been swelling the annual immigration rolls. Some

Americans question whether some of these newest immigrants will ever be assimilated, pointing to the increased use of languages other than English. Between 1970 and 1980, the number of Americans who speak a language other than English at home doubled. About half of these people speak Spanish as their primary language. This increase, which is continuing, reflects recent influxes of Hispanic immigrant groups.

In some parts of the country, so many people speak Spanish that Hispanic immigrants can get along without learning much English. Signs and brochures are written in both English and Spanish. Newspapers are printed in Spanish, and radio and television stations broadcast in that language. As a result, many new Hispanic immigrants have less incentive to learn English than did immigrants of earlier decades.

Some Americans worry about the growing use of Spanish in the United States. They say that its use tends to divide American society. Others say that cultural diversity can do the country no harm. Still others believe that the use of Spanish (and any other language besides English) will decline over time. They say that second- and third-generation members of ethnic groups will switch to English as most earlier immigrant groups have done.

As with earlier immigrant groups, Vietnamese-Americans have quickly learned about American culture. These young men help each other study English and other school subjects.

SUMMING UP   We have seen how different immigrant groups in the 20th century followed similar patterns of adjustment. Members of all of these groups had difficulties finding employment and being accepted by other Americans. Then after a generation or two, most immigrants became assimilated. It remains to be seen whether America's newest immigrants will also become part of the mainstream of life in the United States.

Understanding the Text

On a separate sheet of paper, write the letter of the word or phrase that best completes each of the following statements.

1. The fact that American cities developed ethnic neighborhoods such as Chinatowns and Little Italys was the result of *(a)* local laws *(b)* immigration regulations *(c)* customs and habits *(d)* international agreements.

2. The United States has been called "a nation of immigrants" because *(a)* most Americans were born in a foreign country *(b)* most Americans are either immigrants or are descendants of immigrants *(c)* immigrants run the country *(d)* none of the above.

3. New immigrants usually *(a)* were offered the better-paying jobs *(b)* took only skilled and white-collar jobs *(c)* were the last to be hired and the first to be fired *(d)* avoided jobs that were tiring.

4. In the 20th century, most new immigrants *(a)* could not speak English *(b)* could not speak any language *(c)* had gone to college *(d)* could both read and write in English.

5. An example of an immigrant group that settled mostly in the Southwest is the *(a)* Puerto Ricans *(b)* Jews *(c)* Italians *(d)* Mexicans.

6. One statement *not* true of most Puerto Ricans coming from their island to the mainland of the United States is that *(a)* their first language is Spanish *(b)* they look for opportunities to work and advance themselves *(c)* they have to apply for United States citizenship *(d)* many of them settle in and around New York City.

7. Immigrants found help in assimilating into American society by *(a)* learning the English language *(b)* studying about the American government *(c)* reading newspapers printed in their native language *(d)* all of the above.

8. An example of a resurgence of ethnic pride in America is *(a)* a Greek folk-dance festival *(b)* the popularity of the melting-pot idea *(c)* refusal to learn the language of one's immigrant parents *(d)* becoming naturalized after living in the United States ten years.

9. The major goal of bilingual education is to *(a)* teach all students in Spanish and English *(b)* help non-English-speaking students to understand their school subjects better *(c)* make Spanish an official language of the United States *(d)* have all American students learn two languages.

10. If America's newest immigrants follow the pattern of earlier immigrant groups, their use of a language other than English in the home will *(a)* decline *(b)* rise *(c)* stay the same *(d)* never develop.

Developing Cartoon-Reading Skills

'NEXT THING YOU KNOW THEY'LL BE ON WELFARE. THEN, WHEN THEY GET ON WELFARE THEY'LL WANT A BIGGER, BETTER BOAT...'

Look at the political cartoon above. Then choose the letter of the word or phrase that best completes each sentence. On a separate sheet of paper, match the sentence number with the correct letter.

1. The people on the small boat represent (*a*) vacationers (*b*) fishermen (*c*) new immigrants (*d*) new voters.

2. The two people on the big boat represent (*a*) wealthy U.S. citizens (*b*) poor U.S. citizens (*c*) new immigrants (*d*) Congress.

3. The people on the big boat believe that the people on the little boat (*a*) are rich (*b*) will soon be leaving the country (*c*) will soon be applying for welfare payments (*d*) none of the above.

4. The cartoonist is expressing the view that (*a*) having too many people on a small boat is unsafe (*b*) the United States is too crowded to allow more immigrants (*c*) the United States needs more immigrants (*d*) some Americans are prejudiced against new immigrants.

5. The cartoon best illustrates which of the following views about immigrants? (*a*) Some members of immigrant groups keep cultural traditions alive. (*b*) When immigrants come to the United States, they want a better life. (*c*) Many immigrants are hindered by their inability to read and write English. (*d*) The children or grandchildren of immigrants often reject the culture of their parents' or grandparents' homeland.

Thinking About the Lesson

1. Why have some immigrant groups had more difficulty adjusting to life in the United States than others have?

2. Why do many new immigrants want to live near Americans of the same national origin?

3. Do you think that bilingual education is a good idea? Why or why not?

4. Are the problems of recent immigrants to the United States different from those of earlier immigrants? Explain your answer.

Black Americans

America's blacks make up the country's largest minority group. In the mid-1980s, they numbered over 27 million—about 12 percent of the total population. Most blacks in America are descendants not of immigrants, but of slaves brought to this country involuntarily. Their experiences have differed considerably from the experiences of America's immigrant groups. Blacks have met more social, political, and economic discrimination than any other Americans. This lesson discusses the problems that blacks have encountered as well as the progress they have achieved in the 20th century.

> For much of the 20th century, Americans of African descent were called *Negroes.* The term came from the Spanish word for "black." They were also known as "colored people." In recent decades, however, most Negroes have preferred to be called *blacks.* Today, many black Americans also use the term *Afro-Americans,* because they are descendants of people who came from Africa.

Conditions at the Turn of the Century

In 1900, 35 years after gaining emancipation, most blacks were still poor. Most lacked skills

needed to get good jobs. More important, they suffered from discrimination in employment, housing, and other aspects of everyday living.

Southern Blacks Blacks living in the South had especially difficult times. In spite of the Fifteenth Amendment, they were rarely allowed to vote. Jim Crow laws and customs kept blacks from associating freely and equally with whites.

Northern Blacks Life for blacks in the North was somewhat better. There many had the chance to get jobs working in private homes, stores, and factories. These job opportunities accounted for the *mass migration* (large-scale population movement) of Southern blacks to the industrial cities of the North in the early 20th century. An even greater demand for workers during World War I speeded up the northward movement. In the North, though, blacks again encountered discrimination. Most labor unions there, for example, tried to keep blacks from becoming members. In most Northern cities, blacks could find housing only in separate, black neighborhoods.

Differing Approaches to Problems

Although most blacks were unhappy with their situation, they were not united on what to do

472

about it. A number of black leaders offered different solutions:

• Booker T. Washington. As we mentioned earlier, Booker T. Washington emphasized the role of vocational education. He thought that blacks could improve their lives by attending schools, such as his Tuskegee Institute. He also urged blacks to form their own businesses, creating the Negro Business League for this purpose.

• W.E.B. DuBois. DuBois actively fought against segregation and laws that deprived blacks of the right to vote. In 1909, he helped found the National Association for the Advancement of Colored People (NAACP). This organization called for greater police protection for blacks and campaigned against lynching. Moreover, the NAACP worked to get blacks employed and into labor unions.

• Marcus Garvey. A native of Jamaica, Marcus Garvey in 1916 brought his Universal Negro

W. E. B. DuBois

Booker T. Washington

Improvement Association to the United States. This group infused pride among blacks for their African heritage. Garvey did not have any hope of changing America's white-dominated society. Instead, he urged all black Americans to move to Africa. At one time, Garvey had between 500,000 and 1 million supporters.

• A. Philip Randolph. In 1925, A. Philip Randolph helped create the Brotherhood of Sleeping Car Porters and Maids. He saw unionization as the only way that blacks could make progress in the workplace. After a ten-year struggle, the Pullman Company finally recognized Randolph's union as the bargaining agent for railroad porters and maids. In 1941, Randolph was responsible for getting President Franklin D. Roosevelt to end discrimination in defense industries. Randolph did this by threatening a massive march on Washington, D.C., by black demonstrators.

By the time the United States entered World War II in 1941, the progress that blacks had made was mixed. On the one hand, a great number had found employment in industries that formerly hired almost no blacks. Many blacks had gained political influence after switching from the Republican to the Democratic party in the 1930s. On the other hand, blacks had been among the first to suffer when the American economy plunged into the Great Depression. Besides, blacks had still not gained all the civil rights that whites enjoyed.

The Civil Rights Movement

The participation of black Americans in the war marked the beginning of the modern civil rights movement. In World War II, blacks protested against having to serve in segregated fighting units. When they returned home after the war, they let it be known that they resented being treated as second-class citizens. The NAACP, the newly formed Congress of Racial Equality (CORE), and other groups pressed for full civil rights for blacks.

Presidential Actions   President Harry S. Truman took several significant steps to aid black Americans:

• In 1948, Truman ended segregation in the military. From then on, blacks and whites would serve together in the same units.
• He also prohibited racial discrimination in the hiring of federal civil service employees.

The Supreme Court on School Segregation   In 1954, the U.S. Supreme Court ruled against racial segregation in public schools. In the case *Brown* v. *Board of Education of Topeka, Kansas,* the Court said that having "separate but equal schools" was unfair to black students. In this decision, the Court overruled its 1896 decision, *Plessy* v. *Ferguson.* (See page 115.)

> We come then to the question presented: Does segregation of children in public schools solely on the basis of race, even though the physical facilities and other "tangible" factors may be equal, deprive the children of equal educational opportunities? We believe that it does. . . . To separate them from others of similar age and qualifications solely because of their race generates a feeling of inferiority as to their status in the community that may affect their hearts and minds in a way unlikely ever to be undone.
>
> Earl Warren, Chief Justice,
> for the Supreme Court of the United States,
> *Brown* v. *Board of Education of Topeka,*
> May 17, 1954.

The Court called on school districts to make plans to end segregation in the schools. When some state and local governments openly resisted the Court's decision, federal authorities began to enforce *desegregation* (the end of segregation). In 1957, the governor of Arkansas led a campaign to prevent black students from enrolling in a Little Rock, Arkansas, high school. As a result, President Dwight D. Eisenhower sent federal troops there to protect these students as they went to school. In effect, the federal government forced integration of the Little Rock schools. The United States government action served notice to other public officials that school segregation must end.

Civil Rights Acts

In 1957, Congress passed the first in a series of civil rights laws designed to insure fair treatment of minorities. The 1957 law set up a Civil Rights Division in the U.S. Department of Justice. Soon this federal agency was charging officials in several states with failing to register qualified black voters.

In August, 1963, some 200,000 people assembled in Washington, D.C., to demonstrate for the passage of civil rights laws and legislation to provide more jobs.

Civil Rights Act of 1964 In 1960, many blacks voted for John F. Kennedy because of the Democratic party's strong civil rights plank. As President, Kennedy pressured Congress to pass a new civil rights law. Passed in 1964 after Kennedy's death, the new act banned discrimination in *public facilities* (parks, buses, hotels, restaurants, and so on). It also outlawed discrimination in employment because of one's race, color, sex, religion, or national origin. Another important provision of the act said that state and local government programs that received federal money could not discriminate. Thus, many school districts were subject to loss of funds if they continued to be segregated.

Voting Rights Act of 1965 At the urging of President Lyndon Johnson, Congress passed a law to stop the use of literacy tests as a requirement for voting. The Voting Rights Act also outlawed poll taxes. Many thousands of blacks would soon vote for the first time.

Open Housing Law In 1968, Congress prohibited discrimination in the rental or sale of most houses and apartments.

Many of the nation's and states' civil rights laws were passed after long campaigns organized by civil rights activists. Dr. Martin Luther King, Jr. was one of the most effective of the country's civil rights leaders. In 1955–1956, while serving as a minister in Montgomery, Alabama, King helped blacks boycott the city's segregated buses. After founding the Southern Christian Leadership Conference in 1957, he expanded his civil rights efforts to include other communities. In Birmingham, Alabama, in 1963, he organized demonstrations by black citizens to protest citywide discrimination. King gained his largest audience later in 1963 when he spoke before 200,000 demonstrators massed in Washington, D.C. At this rally, he urged Congress to pass laws to protect blacks' civil rights. His non-violent methods were effective in organizing both black and non-black supporters. Long after his assassination in 1968, King still inspires many Americans who work for social, economic, and political equality for blacks.

Militancy Among Blacks

Despite noteworthy progress made by blacks as a result of the civil rights movement, many blacks continued to be dissatisfied with their situation. Most blacks still lagged behind whites in terms of income and educational levels. Blacks made up a greater-than-average percentage of the nation's poor. Unemployment levels among blacks remained high. Because of their poverty and because of discrimination, many blacks could find housing only in run-down areas.

In the 1960s, decades of pent-up frustration and anger among blacks exploded into riots in a number of cities. Some black militants called

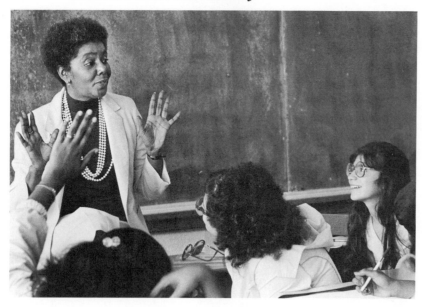

Blacks today occupy more positions of leadership in the United States than they did in the past.

for the creation of a separate black nation for black Americans.

Black Americans Today

In many ways, blacks have improved their lives in the 20th century. Their progress has been due to their own efforts and abilities as well as to favorable laws and court decisions.

Economic Progress Millions of black men and women have entered the mainstream of American economic life. They have become successful in businesses, professions, skilled trades, labor unions, and public service jobs. Earning incomes near or above the national average, these blacks have become members of the American middle class. Millions of other black Americans, however, continue to live in poverty—in both urban and rural areas of the country. Black family income on the average is only about 60 percent of the income of a white family. During the economic recession of the early 1980s, the unemployment rate for blacks was about twice that for whites.

Educational Progress The black population in America is more educated today than ever be-

fore. More and more blacks are finishing high school and going on to get a higher education. Nonetheless, there is room for improvement here, too. The percentage of young people who drop out of school continues to be much higher for blacks than for whites. (See the graph on page 478.) Moreover, racial segregation in public schools remains an unsolved problem in many communities—in both the North and the South.

Blacks in Politics In recent years, black Americans have made especially rapid progress in politics. They have been registering and voting in larger numbers than ever before. They have shown that, like other groups, they know how to use their voting strength to make practical gains. In all sections of the country, blacks have been elected to political offices. Notable have been the elections of black mayors in Los Angeles, Chicago, Philadelphia, Detroit, Atlanta, and other cities. In Congress, Barbara Jordan, Shirley Chisholm, and others worked for political causes supported by blacks and other Americans. Furthermore, Reverend Jesse Jackson sought to assert black influence on a national scale by seeking the Democratic presidential nomination in 1984.

SUMMING UP   We have seen how life for black Americans has changed considerably since 1900. In the early part of the century, black leaders offered several different solutions to the problems of blacks in America. Not until after World War II, however, did a powerful civil rights movement take shape. In the last four decades, the civil rights movement has scored many important victories. Even so, many of the movement's major goals remain unfulfilled. Overcoming the remaining obstacles is a task not just for black Americans, but for the nation as a whole.

Understanding the Text

On a separate sheet of paper, write the letter of the word or phrase that best completes each of the following statements.

1. Of the total population of the United States today, blacks make up about *(a)* 5 percent *(b)* 12 percent *(c)* 27 percent *(d)* 72 percent.

2. A black leader who emphasized the role of vocational education for improving the lives of blacks was *(a)* Booker T. Washington *(b)* W. E. B. DuBois *(c)* Marcus Garvey *(d)* A. Philip Randolph.

3. A founder of the NAACP was *(a)* Dr. Martin Luther King, Jr. *(b)* Booker T. Washington *(c)* W.E.B. DuBois *(d)* Marcus Garvey.

4. A black leader who urged black Americans to move to Africa was *(a)* A. Philip Randolph *(b)* Booker T. Washington *(c)* W. E. B. DuBois *(d)* Marcus Garvey.

5. A. Philip Randolph was responsible for getting the federal government to call for an end to discrimination in defense industries during *(a)* the Spanish-American War *(b)* World War I *(c)* World War II *(d)* the Korean War.

6. As President, Harry S. Truman *(a)* outlawed segregation in public schools *(b)* segregated the U.S. Armed Forces *(c)* banned racial dis-crimination in the federal civil service system *(d)* all of the above.

7. The U.S. President who sent federal troops to Little Rock, Arkansas, in 1957, to enforce integration of a public school was *(a)* Harry S. Truman *(b)* Dwight D. Eisenhower *(c)* John F. Kennedy *(d)* Lyndon B. Johnson.

8. The Civil Rights Act of 1964 was passed during the Presidency of *(a)* Eisenhower *(b)* Kennedy *(c)* Johnson *(d)* Nixon.

9. A civil rights leader who helped blacks in Montgomery, Alabama, boycott their bus system was *(a)* A. Philip Randolph *(b)* Marcus Garvey *(c)* Dr. Martin Luther King, Jr. *(d)* Barbara Jordan.

10. Which of the following statements reflects a major theme of this lesson? *(a)* Unlike most immigrants, few blacks have suffered from discrimination. *(b)* Since 1900, blacks in America have made considerable progress in economic, educational, and political matters. *(c)* Life for most blacks in the United States is not much different today from the way it was in 1900. *(d)* No individuals have risen within black groups and communities to take important leadership roles.

Developing Graph-Reading Skills

**WHITES AND BLACKS WHO HAVE COMPLETED HIGH SCHOOL,
BY PERCENTAGE OF THOSE 25 AND OLDER**

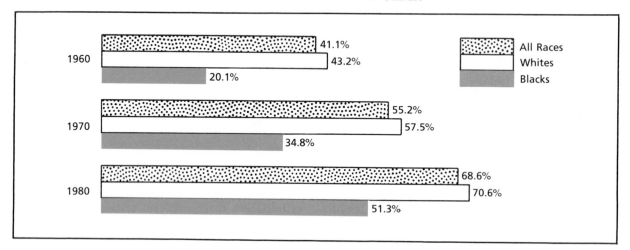

Study the bar graph above. Then choose the letter of the word or phrase that best completes each sentence. On a separate sheet of paper, match the sentence number with the correct letter.

1. One of the three bars at the bottom of the graph depicts *(a)* number of blacks who had finished high school in 1960 *(b)* number of whites who had finished high school in 1980 *(c)* percentage of blacks 25 and older who had finished high school in 1980 *(d)* percentage of all Americans 25 and older who had completed high school in 1970.

2. In 1970, the percentage of white Americans 25 and older who had completed high school was *(a)* 20.1 *(b)* 43.2 *(c)* 55.2 *(d)* 57.5.

3. Less than half of all Americans 25 and older had completed high school in *(a)* 1960 *(b)* 1970 *(c)* 1980 *(d)* none of the above.

4. A greater percentage of whites 25 and older than blacks of the same age group had completed high school in *(a)* 1960 *(b)* 1970 *(c)* 1980 *(d)* all of the above.

5. After studying this bar graph, one can conclude that *(a)* attendance at high schools in the United States was poor for every year indicated *(b)* by the year 2000, almost every American 25 and older will have graduated from high school *(c)* between 1960 and 1980, blacks narrowed the gap separating them from whites 25 and older who had completed high school *(d)* blacks in America will never achieve the same level of education as whites.

Thinking About the Lesson

1. Which of the following Americans do you think helped blacks the most in the first half of the 20th century? Give reasons for your answer.

Booker T. Washington   Marcus Garvey
W. E. B. DuBois   A. Philip Randolph

2. How did each of the following Presidents help to expand the civil rights of black Americans?

Harry S. Truman   John F. Kennedy
Dwight D. Eisenhower   Lyndon B. Johnson

3. For what reason or reasons did the U.S. Supreme Court rule that separate but equal schools were unfair?

Efforts to Combat Poverty

The most important resource any nation has is its people. In modern times, many nations, including the United States, no longer leave to chance the well-being of their citizens. One of America's main goals is to help its people make the best use of their abilities and to lead happy, healthy, and productive lives. The U.S. government, in connection with state and local governments and private agencies, is working toward that goal.

The Nature of Poverty in America

Although the United States is one of the world's richest nations, about 34 million Americans are considered poor by government standards. These people make up about 14 percent of the population. They do not have the food, shelter, clothing, and services needed to live on a "minimum level of comfort and decency."

Distribution of Poverty Poverty is particularly severe among certain groups in the U.S. population. About 34 percent of the nation's blacks and 28 percent of its Hispanics live below the poverty level. Over 34 percent of families that lack a father also are considered poor.

Pockets of poverty are scattered across the country. For example, 33 percent of the population of Newark, New Jersey, is poor. Detroit,

New Orleans, and Atlanta also have high rates of poverty. While most U.S. cities have many poor people, usually concentrated in inner city areas, some rural areas, too, are poor. In fact, the percentage of poor people is higher in the country than in *metropolitan areas* (cities and suburbs).

> The federal government determines who is poor and who is not. It sets minimum income levels, sometimes called *poverty levels,* below which individuals or families are defined as poor. For instance, in 1984, the government said that a family of four needed to earn over $10,609 a year to remain above the poverty level. Poverty levels are adjusted every year to take into account the effects of inflation.

Causes of Poverty

High rates of poverty result chiefly from economic factors, such as growing unemployment or inflation. During the recession of the early 1980s, for example, many businesses cut production or closed their doors. As a result, more and more workers joined the ranks of the unemployed. Unemployed workers and their

479

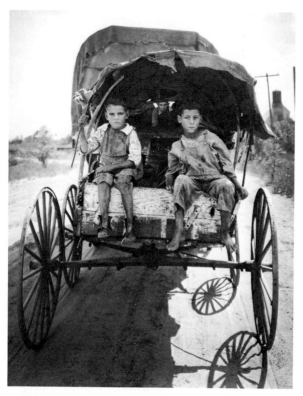

In 1931, this family rode around Texas looking for work picking cotton. Migrant workers' families are often poor.

families usually had to depend on unemployment benefits. Their standard of living declined. In some cases, their benefits ran out and they had to apply for public *welfare* (government assistance to needy individuals and families).

Personal Causes   Some Americans are poor because of personal limitations, such as being unskilled or poorly educated. Poor health and mental and physical handicaps also affect one's income level. People with the above-mentioned limitations have difficulty getting jobs. When they are employed, they usually receive low wages.

Discrimination against people because of their race, religion, sex, or age is another cause of poverty. Discrimination sometimes prevents Americans from getting good jobs and earning enough money to have a decent standard of living.

Finally, there is another major category of poor people—those living in families with a single parent. This situation causes economic problems when the parent (usually the mother) stays home to raise children instead of working at a job. Without a salary, family income is usually quite low.

Poverty as a National Problem

There have always been poor Americans. Fighting poverty, though, was not recognized as a national responsibility until the Great Depression of the 1930s. President Franklin D. Roosevelt claimed that one third of the nation was "ill-fed, ill-housed, and ill-clothed." As we learned in Lesson 59, FDR persuaded Congress to pass his New Deal proposals to fight the Great Depression and reduce poverty levels.

Since Roosevelt's time, the federal government has continued, and in some cases strengthened, its commitment to aiding the poor. President Lyndon Johnson, for instance, was especially active in this regard. His War on Poverty spent nearly $7 billion on programs to help the poor in America.

Economic Growth   A common way in which the government has attacked poverty has been to try to make the economy more prosperous. The Roosevelt administration attempted to bring about prosperity with a massive spending program. The idea behind this effort was to infuse the economy with so much money that businesses would be encouraged to expand and hire more workers. Economists then were not in total agreement that this way was the best to fight a depression or a recession. Today, economists still do not agree on what is the best way to make or keep the economy prosperous.

Government Housing Programs Millions of Americans live in run-down, crowded quarters that often lack proper sanitary facilities. Such *substandard housing* does not meet accepted standards of health and comfort. For over 50 years, the federal government has attempted to play a part in providing better housing:

• Since 1934, the Federal Housing Administration (FHA) has guaranteed loans for building and improving homes. The FHA makes it easier for would-be homeowners to get loans at affordable interest rates.

• Beginning in 1937, the federal government helped finance construction of low-cost public housing. In all parts of the country, communities, with federal and state assistance, replaced slums with new apartment buildings.

• In 1965, Congress created the Department of Housing and Urban Development to plan and coordinate housing programs.

• In recent years, the federal government has cut back on the amount of money it spends on public housing. Instead, state and local governments, as well as private developers, are expected to provide for the housing needs of Americans.

Social Security Since 1935, a growing number of Americans have been guaranteed an income under the Social Security system. Participating workers contribute money regularly to this public insurance fund. When they retire or become disabled, they receive Social Security payments. The fund also provides allowances to dependents of members who die. In 1965, Medicare, a health insurance program, was added to the Social Security system. Medicare has enabled many Americans over age 65 to pay their hospital and doctor bills.

Unemployment Insurance Authorized under the Social Security Act of 1935, the unemployment insurance system is run by the states. Employers in most industries pay into a fund. When a worker who is covered by this insurance loses his or her job, the worker can apply for unemployment compensation for a limited number of weeks.

Public Assistance Programs All the states have *public assistance programs* (programs that provide direct aid to needy individuals and families). In many of these programs, the federal government pays a large share of the costs. The states, however, often run the programs and determine who is eligible for aid. Public assistance programs administered by the states include:

• Medicaid. Under this plan, states help their poorer citizens meet rising medical costs.

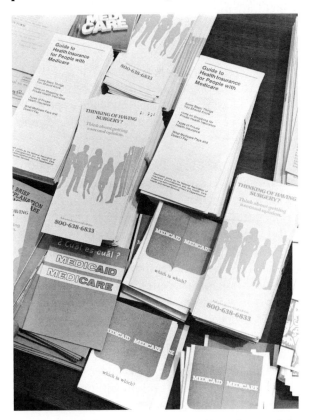

The U.S. government publishes booklets that explain who is eligible to receive Medicare and Medicaid.

• Food stamps. The U.S. Department of Agriculture administers a program that gives certain needy Americans food stamps. These stamps can be exchanged for food items at many shops.

• Distribution of surplus food. From time to time, the federal government will arrange for the distribution of surplus food. Surplus cheese and other items, obtained from American farmers under government subsidy programs, are given to needy Americans. (See Lesson 67 for a discussion of farm surpluses.)

• Aid to Families with Dependent Children (AFDC). Most of the families who receive AFDC money have no father living with them. These families need aid because the mothers stay home to care for their children and, thus, cannot work.

• Supplemental Security Income (SSI). This system provides a minimum income to poor people over 65 and those who are blind or disabled.

Aid to Education and Job Training   Lack of job skills or a basic education often leads to poverty. Several government programs attack these problems directly:

• Job Corps. Since 1964, out-of-school young adults have been receiving training in vocational skills at Job Corps centers around the country. After completing their course of training, many Job Corps graduates are able to obtain jobs.

• VISTA. The Volunteers in Service to America also has been in existence since 1964. This organization has recruited many Americans to work for a year in local projects that aid the poor. Of special concern to VISTA have been the problems of troubled youths and low-income elderly.

• Aid to education. The federal and state governments provide aid to all public school districts. To some extent, the amount of aid depends on how poor the districts are.

• Loans to needy college students. For many years, the federal government has lent money to low- and middle-income students at low interest rates.

Private Efforts

Charities, foundations, religious organizations, and other private groups are also involved in caring for poor people. Every year, Americans give billions of dollars to organizations working in this field. In some cases, these private organizations, such as the Salvation Army, can act more directly and quickly than government agencies can in providing aid to the needy.

Debate on Antipoverty Measures

Millions of Americans have benefited from federal, state, and local antipoverty measures. Despite all these programs, costing billions of dollars, poverty is still widespread in the United States.

In recent years, the number of homeless in America has soared. Charities and local governments have tried to help the homeless by providing shelter and food.

Defenders of government antipoverty programs believe that the projects have done a good job. The defenders see the programs as necessary "safety nets" for those who, for various reasons, need special help. Some concerned Americans would like to see even more tax money spent on antipoverty measures.

Critics of government antipoverty programs claim that antipoverty programs have gotten too expensive and are plagued by waste and mismanagement. Too many unqualified people, say the critics, are receiving aid—people who should be getting jobs and earning money. The system, claim the critics, discourages Americans from finding jobs. In some cases, people can get more income from public assistance than by finding a job and working. Some people receiving public assistance are penalized for taking a part-time job.

Critics and defenders of the antipoverty programs agree on at least one matter. They both believe that we cannot greatly reduce poverty unless the economy is healthy and growing. When millions of workers lose their jobs, as happened in the early 1980s, efforts to relieve poverty cannot have much success. Only a healthy economy can provide jobs for those who want to work. Only a growing economy can produce the goods and services needed to raise people's standard of living.

SUMMING UP We have seen how over the years federal, state, and local governments undertook many programs to combat poverty. The federal government took the leading role in these efforts, but it often channeled poverty funds to the states. Poverty remains a problem today. Nevertheless, Americans are divided on the question of what to do about it. Some would like to see the federal government take an even more active role in solving the problem. Other Americans believe that improving the country's economy is the best way to help people rise out of poverty.

Understanding the Text

On a separate sheet of paper, write the letter of the word or phrase that best completes each of the following statements.

1. Poverty in the United States today (a) has been practically eliminated (b) is found only in rural areas (c) is still widespread (d) is found only in big cities.

2. Of the following groups of Americans, those with a poverty level greater than the national average include (a) blacks (b) Hispanics (c) families that lack a father (d) all of the above.

3. One factor *not* considered a cause of poverty in America is (a) prosperity of the economy (b) racial discrimination (c) mental handicap (d) poor job skills.

4. Since 1934, the Federal Housing Administration has (a) administered the Social Security system (b) guaranteed loans for building and improving homes (c) distributed Medicaid funds to the states (d) printed and distributed food stamps.

5. Of the following, one *not* an aspect of the Social Security system is (a) unemployment insurance (b) the Job Corps (c) old-age insurance (d) disability insurance.

6. Vocational training is considered a way to fight poverty because (a) medical costs are rising (b) lack of job skills often causes poverty (c) farm price-support programs are often inefficient (d) vocational schools hire many VISTA volunteers.

7. An example of a private effort to help the poor is the (a) Salvation Army (b) food stamp program (c) AFDC (d) SSI.

8. A common criticism of government antipoverty programs has been that (a) poverty has already been defeated (b) the programs have sometimes been badly designed and poorly run (c) poor people do not want to be helped (d) the programs cost American taxpayers next to nothing.

9. Most defenders of government antipoverty programs believe that the programs (a) provide a valuable safety net for many Americans (b) hurt the national economy (c) will succeed despite an unhealthy economy (d) none of the above.

10. Which of the following statements best expresses the theme of this lesson? (a) The fight against poverty is usually carried out by the federal government without the participation of state and local governments. (b) The causes of poverty are unknown. (c) Private agencies are largely responsible for improving the health of the national economy. (d) The fight against poverty often involves the cooperation of local, state, and federal governments.

Developing Skills at Separating Fact From Opinion

Study the passage below on poverty in America. It includes both facts and opinions. A *fact* is something that can be proved to be true. An *opinion* is something that one believes is true or that expresses how one feels about something.

Everyone should note a recent report of the Census Bureau. This federal agency announced that the percentage of Americans who were living in poverty is the highest in 17 years. Government experts determine how much money a family of a certain size needs to earn a year to remain above the poverty level. Those families with incomes below that figure are officially called "poor."

The way that the nation treats its poor is shameful. Some 20 years ago, the Lyndon B. Johnson administration declared its "War on Poverty." That war does not seem to have been won. Despite the spending of billions of dollars of taxpayers' money, poverty remains a problem.

Perhaps we should be attacking the problem in a different manner. I call for a national conference of concerned citizens to discuss the question of poverty in America. I am sure that if intelligent and compassionate leaders from all walks of life get together, they can come up with an answer to this persistent problem.

Determine which of the following statements from the passage are facts and which are opinions. On a separate sheet of paper, number one to five. Then write *F* for statements that are facts and *O* for those that are opinions.

1. Everyone should note a recent report of the Census Bureau.

2. Those families with incomes below that figure are officially called "poor."

3. The way that the nation treats its poor is shameful.

4. Some 20 years ago, the Lyndon B. Johnson administration declared its "War on Poverty."

5. I am sure that if intelligent and compassionate leaders from all walks of life get together, they can come up with an answer to this persistent problem.

Thinking About the Lesson

1. Why do mental and physical handicaps often affect one's income level?

2. What single factor do you consider to be the most important in hindering people from rising above the poverty level? Explain your answer.

3. How important are educational and job training programs in fighting poverty? Explain your answer.

4. What roles do charities and other private organizations play in fighting poverty in the United States?

5. Do you agree with the view that the federal government spends too much on antipoverty programs? Why or why not?

Twentieth-Century Social Developments

In studying American history, we often concentrate on significant actions of government leaders. These actions make up much of what is called *political history*. Everyday activities of ordinary Americans also can have important consequences. The study of these activities, called *social history*, covers a number of topics, including education, family life, and the effects of scientific discoveries. Americans in the 20th century have witnessed many important developments in social history.

Changes in Education

In the early 1900s, a number of educators were not satisfied with the old teaching methods. For decades, elementary and secondary schools had stressed memorizing facts and behaving properly. Then new theories of teaching, called *progressive education*, stressed creativity and free expression among students. Teachers began taking students on class trips and holding group discussions. Believing that students learned at different speeds, teachers often separated them into ability groups.

Dewey's Ideas At least one reformer, John Dewey, thought that students learned by both thinking and doing. In his book *The School and Society* (1899), he wrote that certain group activities helped students become better citizens. He also believed that *manual skills* (skills using the hands) were an important part of one's education. Ella Flagg Young, Superintendent of Schools in Chicago, put many of Dewey's ideas into practice. She introduced home economics and shop classes into the Chicago schools. Many progressive education ideas such as these are still followed in Chicago and other school districts around the country.

Extension of Education In the 20th century, Americans' educational opportunities have increased greatly. While in 1900 most Americans had only an elementary school education, today most Americans graduate from high school. Moreover, many high school graduates go on to institutions of higher learning. Three of these institutions—junior colleges, community colleges, and vocational schools—are products of the 20th century. They provide important alternatives to four-year colleges and universities, both of which also have increased in number and size. The percentage of Americans who attend an institution of higher education is greater than the percentage of most other countries.

Federal Aid to Education In the 20th century, Americans have approved massive government spending on all levels of education. Some of the

486

One-room schoolhouses, such as this one, are now rare in the United States. This picture was taken in 1941 in Taos County, New Mexico.

important programs have included the following ones:

• In 1917, the federal government began funding vocational education below the college level.

• G.I. Bill of 1944. The government began offering financial aid to veterans of World War II to go to college and other schools for up to four years. Congress later extended these benefits to veterans of the Korean and Vietnam wars.

• The National Defense Education Act of 1958 provided for low-cost loans for many college students. Furthermore, the government gave many state universities funds to improve science and language teaching. Later laws extended this aid to other areas of higher education.

• In 1965, Congress set up a major program to aid elementary and secondary schools (both public and private). This program emphasized aid to school districts that had many low-income families.

Educational Problems Despite great changes in American education, many serious problems remain. Large numbers of adults and young people have difficulty reading and writing and lack basic mathematical skills. In some schools, student misbehavior hinders the ability of teachers to function. In some communities, the dropout rate among high school students is very high. Moreover, school administrators often lack the money necessary to provide basic educational programs and adequate teacher salaries.

Improved Status of Women

Since 1900, women in America have achieved some important victories. They have gained new political and social rights. They have also become more active in politics and in the competition with men for jobs.

Suffrage Movement In 1900, most American women still did not have *suffrage* (the right to vote). Only four states had granted women the same voting rights as men had. (See the map on page 493.) As a result, Carrie Chapman Catt organized a campaign to get more states to allow

U.S. SCHOOL ENROLLMENT, 1900–1980

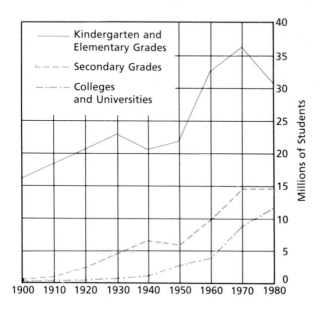

NUMBER OF YEARS OF SCHOOL COMPLETED, 1900–1980

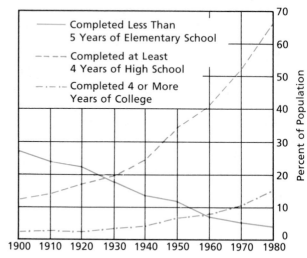

women to vote. Ever since 1878, Susan B. Anthony and other leaders of the suffrage movement had been trying to get Congress to pass a constitutional amendment to give them that right.

After 1900, these *suffragists* became more active than ever. Alice Paul took direct action against President Woodrow Wilson for failing to endorse the proposed amendment. The day before his inauguration in 1912, she organized a large protest march in Washington, D.C. In 1917, Alice Paul was again protesting in Washington, picketing in front of the White House. This time she was arrested and sentenced to seven months in prison. There she gained publicity by going on a hunger strike. Prison authorities forced her to eat rather than let her starve to death.

The Vote For Women The efforts by Alice Paul, Carrie Chapman Catt, and others finally led to victory for their cause. In 1919, Congress passed the Nineteenth Amendment, and in the following year the necessary number of states ratified it. Women now had the right to vote and run for office in all elections.

Changing Roles in the Workplace Early in the 20th century, women were still poorly paid and kept out of certain professions. Gradually, career opportunities for women improved. During World War I and World War II, women took over many jobs previously held only by men. By 1950, a third of all American women held jobs outside their homes. Today, that figure is over one half.

In the 20th century, women have moved into many important positions in government. In 1916, the people of Montana elected Jeanette Rankin to represent them in the U.S. House of Representatives. She became the first woman to serve in the House. The first female to be elected to the Senate was Hattie Wyatt Caraway, in 1932. She was elected by the people of Arkansas after completing a term of her husband, who had died in office. Frances Perkins, as Secretary of Labor under Franklin D. Roosevelt, became the first woman to hold a Cabinet office. The

U.S. Supreme Court was all-male until 1981, when President Ronald Reagan appointed Sandra Day O'Connor as a justice.

Women have made important gains in other professions as well. The anthropologist Margaret Mead gained fame after the publication of her book *Coming of Age in Samoa* in 1928. Pilot Amelia Earhart in 1932 became the first woman to fly solo across the Atlantic. In 1937, she died trying to fly around the world. Margaret Bourke-White had a successful career as a photographer, working for *Life* magazine from 1936 to 1957. Elizabeth Arden set up a cosmetics company that still flourishes. And Katherine Graham heads the large Washington Post Company, which publishes an influential newspaper in the nation's capital.

Continuing Problems In spite of the improved status of women in America, they still suffer from discrimination. On the average, women working full-time receive about 62 cents for every dollar paid to men. They are underrepresented on managerial levels in most industries. Some Americans, believing that women do not enjoy the same civil rights that men do, have called for the passage of an Equal Rights Amendment to the U.S. Constitution.

Changes in Family Life

American families have undergone major changes in the 20th century. In the past, most women thought that their main function was to raise children. Now many women combine that goal with the goal of having a career. This dual goal is one of the reasons why couples today get married at a later age than they did earlier in the century. Furthermore, once they are married, they tend to have fewer children.

The close family bonds of the 19th century

In 1912, men in Ohio were asked to vote on a measure that would give women the vote. Women in Ohio, however, did not obtain full suffrage until 1920.

seem to have grown weaker in the 20th, as witnessed by several trends:

• Many parents, wanting to be free to work, put their young children in day-care centers.

• Fewer parents are home in the afternoon when their children return from school.

• About one third of all children live with just one parent. This situation is due mainly to the rising number of divorces in the country and the growing number of children born out of wedlock.

• To some extent, the family and the home are not as important to young people as before. Instead, schools play a growing role in helping students to develop their personalities. In addition, schools provide many recreational activities, such as sports, that formerly were centered in the home or the neighborhood. Youth groups and other outside agencies also compete with the family in this regard.

All of these factors help explain why families are less stable. Many Americans are worried about the instability of the family and have called for measures to strengthen it.

An Age of Computers

The 20th century has been a time of rapid technological change. Nothing illustrates this point better than the example of how computers have changed American society.

The Invention of the Computer The first modern computers in America were built in the 1940s. Since then, engineers have been making many improvements, coming out with new models every year. The invention of the computer differs from other important inventions, such as the jet engine. Computers operate with only one raw material and one product—information. In the simplest and most general terms, this is what computers do:

• First, they accept or take in information.

• Then computers store it. Information is immediately put into the computers' memory.

• Next, they *process* (work with) the information, often arranging it in a different way. Examples of information processing include making mathematical computations and putting files in alphabetical order.

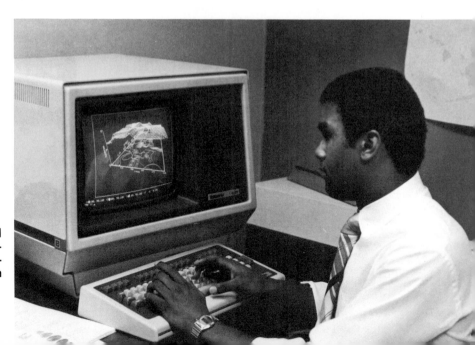

Computers are used in all kinds of work. This employee of the National Institute of Health uses one in his research.

• Finally, computers give back the processed information.

All of these operations are carried out by computers with great speed—a speed that humans cannot equal. People use computers to save time, labor, and costs. Computers are especially useful in all kinds of businesses and government organizations. American consumers also are finding uses for computers, installing them in their homes.

Benefits of Computers Computers have added greatly to the ability of our nation's economy to produce more goods and services. Through automation they have lowered costs in American factories and offices. These electronic machines have also opened up new job opportunities. Experts say that computer operators, programmers, and other computer-related workers will continue to be in demand for years to come.

Some Disadvantages The use of computers can have some harmful effects:

• Automation, which is based on computers, sometimes leads to the elimination of certain jobs. For instance, robots can now perform simple tasks, such as making a weld or fitting two or more parts together.

• Along with the growth of computer use has come the growth of computer crime. By gaining unauthorized entry into computers, dishonest computer operators have stolen *confidential* (private or secret) information. Others have transferred large sums of money to their own bank accounts.

• People who operate computers sometimes make mistakes. These computer errors, such as unintentionally transferring funds out of an account, can be costly.

• Some Americans fear that government and private agencies may use computers to invade people's privacy. Important personal financial information is available to anyone who can gain access to a computer's memory.

Computers and the Future Computers may affect the social and economic lives of Americans in ways not yet fully understood. For example, some experts believe that with the growing use of computers, populations will become less concentrated. Instead of working in vast offices, more employees could work at home or in small offices scattered around the country. Instead of going to stores, consumers could pick out purchases from lists displayed on their computers. Instead of attending schools, students could learn at home, using computers. If these trends were to develop, major cities would become less important. Populations of cities might decline, while those of rural areas might increase.

SUMMING UP We have seen how American society has undergone major changes in the 20th century. Americans were among the first people to experience mass education. American women won the right to vote in the early part of the century. They are still involved in increasing their presence and influence in the workplace. The changing roles of women in society are partly responsible for the changing nature of American families. The introduction of new technologies always affects societies. We are just learning what changes computers can have on our lives.

Understanding the Text

On a separate sheet of paper, write the letter of the word or phrase that best completes each of the following statements.

1. Today, most Americans have (*a*) obtained no more than an elementary school education (*b*) graduated from high school but not from college (*c*) graduated from a junior college or community college (*d*) graduated from a university or a four-year college.

2. One idea *not* introduced by the progressive education movement was (*a*) memorization of facts (*b*) class trips (*c*) shop classes (*d*) group discussions.

3. A well-known leader of the women's suffrage movement in America was (*a*) John Dewey (*b*) Margaret Mead (*c*) Susan B. Anthony (*d*) Sandra Day O'Connor.

4. The Nineteenth Amendment, which granted women the right to vote, was ratified by enough states to become law in (*a*) 1900 (*b*) 1920 (*c*) 1932 (*d*) 1974.

5. Jeanette Rankin was (*a*) the first woman to hold a Cabinet office (*b*) a successful photographer who worked many years for *Life* magazine (*c*) the first woman to fly across the Atlantic (*d*) the first woman to serve in the U.S. House of Representatives.

6. On the average, American women working full-time earn (*a*) about 45 percent of what men earn (*b*) about 62 percent of what men earn (*c*) about the same as what men earn (*d*) more than what men earn.

7. Concerning American family life in recent decades, it is true to say that (*a*) divorce rates have been rising (*b*) couples have been getting married when they are older (*c*) couples have been having fewer children (*d*) all of the above.

8. Of the following statements about computers, it is true to say that (*a*) both the raw material and the final product of computers is information (*b*) computers were widely used in the early 20th century (*c*) computers can process words, but not numbers (*d*) none of the above.

9. One of the disadvantages of computers mentioned in this lesson is that (*a*) computers can perform many mathematical calculations (*b*) computers can arrange files in alphabetical order (*c*) people can sometimes gain illegal entry into computers (*d*) computers work at speeds that humans cannot match.

10. Which of the following would you *least* likely consider a topic of social history? (*a*) "The Number of Presidential Vetoes by the Current Administration." (*b*) "Incidents of Juvenile Delinquency in 19th-Century Boston." (*c*) "The Role of Women in the U.S. Armed Forces During the Vietnam War." (*d*) "Have Textbooks Changed?"

Developing Map Skills

Study the map on page 493. Then choose the letter of the word or phrase that best completes each sentence. On a separate sheet of paper, match the sentence number with the correct letter.

1. In California, women got the right to vote in (*a*) 1890 (*b*) 1896 (*c*) 1911 (*d*) 1914.

2. The first state to grant women the right to vote was (*a*) Oregon (*b*) Wyoming (*c*) Utah (*d*) Colorado.

3. Before 1920, women in Indiana had the right of (*a*) full suffrage (*b*) partial suffrage (*c*) no statewide suffrage (*d*) none of the above.

GROWTH OF WOMEN'S SUFFRAGE BEFORE THE NINETEENTH AMENDMENT, 1920

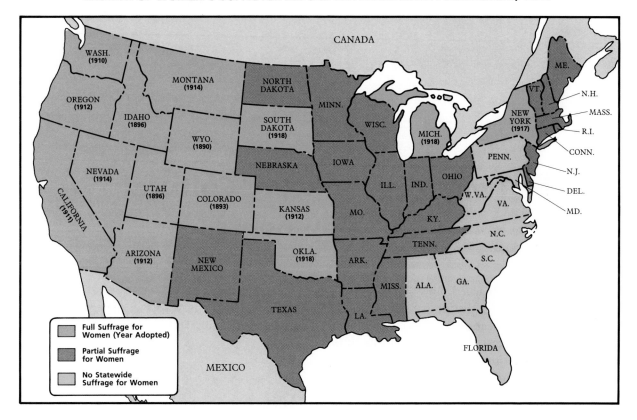

4. In Florida, women got the right to vote in (*a*) 1910 (*b*) 1912 (*c*) 1919 (*d*) 1920.

5. An example of a Northeastern state that had full suffrage for women before 1920 was (*a*) Vermont (*b*) South Dakota (*c*) Iowa (*d*) New York.

Thinking About the Lesson

1. To what extent are the ideas of the progressive education movement still followed in American schools today? Provide some examples to support your answer.

2. Do you think that the federal government should be spending more money, about the same amount, or less money on education? Explain your answer.

3. Why did women have such a difficult time getting Congress to pass and the states to ratify a constitutional amendment to give them the right to vote in all elections?

4. Do you agree with the view that American women today still suffer from some kinds of discrimination? Why or why not?

5. Do you see the increased use of computers in the United States as generally either a good or bad development? Explain your answer.

Twentieth-Century Cultural Developments

In Lesson 54, we learned how 19th-century Americans developed a distinctive national culture. In the 20th century, Americans have increased their interest in literature and the fine arts. Perhaps more important, American writers and artists have helped the United States to become a world leader in certain areas of literature, art, architecture, and music.

Literature in America

A good number of American writers have achieved distinction and recognition in the 20th century. Readers around the world have become acquainted with at least a few American authors. Moreover, several Americans have been honored with the Nobel Prize for Literature.

Early Twentieth-Century Writers The best-known American writers in the first part of the 20th century were the muckrakers. As we learned in Lesson 64, they revealed their social conscience in writing about the misery of the poor. Other authors, including the novelist Theodore Dreiser, also wrote about social problems. In *Sister Carrie* (1900), Dreiser portrayed with great realism a young working woman who made a success as an actress.

The Literature of the Twenties In the 1920s, many American novelists and poets expressed distaste for the lifestyle of these post-war years:

• Minnesota-born Sinclair Lewis believed that life in small Midwestern towns was dreary and petty. Furthermore, he thought that residents of these towns were too satisfied with their lives. He expressed these themes in two famous novels, *Main Street* (1920) and *Babbit* (1922). These works helped Sinclair Lewis win the first Nobel Prize for Literature ever awarded an American.

• In contrast to Lewis, novelist and short-story writer Edith Wharton wrote about New York City's high society. In *The Age of Innocence* (1920) and other works, she was often critical of wealthy Americans, accusing them of being mean-spirited.

• One of America's leading poets, T. S. Eliot, settled in England. In his major work, *The Waste Land* (1922), Eliot criticized Europeans for having lost their sense of values after World War I.

• The novelist F. Scott Fitzgerald often portrayed Americans as being overly concerned with seeking pleasure and wealth. In the novel *The Great Gatsby* (1925), for example, he exposed the emptiness of the life of a self-made

494

millionaire. Ironically, Fitzgerald himself followed a lifestyle of excessive drinking and partying. As a result, he suffered from alcoholism and in his later years had difficulty writing.

Other American authors followed Sinclair Lewis in winning the Nobel Prize for Literature. Those honored were:

Eugene O'Neill (1936)
Pearl Buck (1938)
William Faulkner (1949)
Ernest Hemingway (1954)
John Steinbeck (1962)
Saul Bellow (1976)
Isaac Bashevis Singer (1978)
Czeslaw Milosz (1980)

Edith Wharton is best known for her novel *Ethan Frome* (1911), which is set in rural New England.

Concerns of the 1930s and 1940s   Writers who lived through the Great Depression and the military conflicts of the Thirties and Forties often wrote about these events:

• John Steinbeck dramatized the tragic effects of the depression on rural Americans in *The Grapes of Wrath* (1939).

• Novelist Richard Wright portrayed another group of depression-era Americans—blacks living in Northern cities. One such figure, the main character in Wright's *Native Son* (1940), had a difficult time growing up in the slums of Chicago.

• Ernest Hemingway, in his *For Whom the Bell Tolls* (1940), recalled the tragedy of the civil war in Spain. The novelist, who was popular because of his strong heroes and easy-to-read style, favored the Spanish Republicans in that struggle. (See page 521.)

• Norman Mailer wrote one of the best-received novels about the American experience in World War II. *The Naked and the Dead* (1949) described the fate of 13 soldiers who battled against the Japanese.

Modern American Literature   Since the late 1940s, American writers have produced a great variety of top-quality literature. Many modern authors have dealt with the quests of individuals to discover their identities:

• Arthur Miller dramatized an aging man trying to come to terms with himself in the play *Death of a Salesman* (1949). Upon losing his job, the man found that he had little to live for.

• In 1951, J. D. Salinger published a moving novel about a schoolboy's coming of age in America. This book, *The Catcher in the Rye*, is still popular among teenage readers.

• Ralph Ellison, in his *Invisible Man* (1952), traced the story of a young, black Southerner who moved to Harlem, New York. There the main character, working to establish his identity, rejected both Communism and black racism.

• The hero of John Updike's *Rabbit, Run* (1960) was a grown man who could not accept the responsibilities of adulthood. He kept looking back to the glamour of his high school years, a time when he was a star athlete.

• Mary McCarthy's book *The Group* (1960) dealt with eight women—all graduates of Vassar College—who got together for a reunion. The novelist humorously contrasted the different paths that these women took after graduating.

• Gore Vidal presented a complex portrait of President Lincoln in *Lincoln* (1984). Earlier historical novels by Vidal included *Burr, 1876,* and *Washington, D.C.*

Science Fiction A highly imaginative type of literature gained popularity in the United States beginning in the 1930s. Science fiction stories and novels generally portray the world of the future and often have settings beyond the earth. Sometimes science fiction authors predict future technologies and social developments with remarkable accuracy. In the 1930s, 1940s, and 1950s, magazines were the source of most "sci-fi" reading. Since then, most science fiction literature has been published in paperback books. Among the most popular sci-fi writers in the last few decades have been Isaac Asimov, Ray Bradbury, Frank Herbert, and Robert A. Heinlein.

Art in America

In the 19th century, most American artists worked in a realistic manner; their finished pieces looked much like the persons or things that they were depicting. In the 20th century, some American artists have continued this tradition, while others have adopted new styles.

Realistic Artists Early in the 20th century, John Sloan painted everyday scenes of urban life. He was more interested in making comments about his subjects' lives than in creating pretty pictures. His "South Beach Bathers" (1908) expressed well the vitality and joy of ordinary people.

Edward Hopper painted realistic scenes of New England and New York City. His works, such as "Early Sunday Morning" (1930), accurately depicted qualities of light. Hopper could express deep emotions in his paintings, even when they contained no people.

The sculptor George Segal achieves a realistic look in plaster figures by making casts from live models. He often places his human figures—

Artist George Segal is shown admiring one of his sculptures. To what extent is this work realistic? To what extent is it abstract?

Frank Lloyd Wright designed the Robie House (above), built in Chicago in 1909. Wright's designs are still considered modern.

usually all one color—in realistic settings, such as a doorway or a telephone booth.

Abstract Artists Following examples set by their European counterparts, many American artists changed the way they expressed themselves. They began to work in a more abstract manner. *Abstract artists* render people and scenes in an unrealistic manner or do not even try to depict real life. Instead, they arrange lines, shapes, and colors in whatever way expresses a feeling or an idea.

After World War II, Jackson Pollack became well-known for creating large, abstract paintings that expressed much action. Pollack achieved this feeling of movement by dripping paint directly from cans onto canvases spread out on the floor.

Sculptor Louise Nevelson can evoke a variety of feelings in her works. In many cases, she glues together pieces of wood and other objects that she finds lying around. Then, in order to give the resulting large sculptures a sense of unity, she paints them all one color.

Today, some of the best artists are Americans. Artists around the world often look to the United States for the latest trends in modern art.

Architecture in America

The United States has become a center of architectural experimentation. Many new styles of architecture have developed in 20th-century America. We apply the general label *modern architecture* to all new architectural styles. Those who practice modern architecture emphasize simplicity. They use less decoration than has been common in the past.

Residential Design Frank Lloyd Wright stood out as a pioneer in the design of homes. He strongly believed in *organic architecture* (a style whose buildings seemed to grow out of the landscape). Many of Wright's houses were long and low. One could usually walk from the kitchen to the dining room to the living room without going through doors. At appropriate places, Wright had large windows built. These glass walls provided the illusion that the inside and the outside were part of the same environment. When possible, Wright used building materials, such as natural wood and stone, that blended in well with the landscape.

Large Building Design   In the 20th century, downtown urban areas have become masses of skyscrapers. One the leading architects of large buildings, Ludwig Mies van der Rohe, emigrated to the United States from Germany in the 1930s. From the outside, his sleek, uncluttered skyscrapers appeared to be all steel and glass or all concrete and glass. Like many other successful architects of tall buildings, Mies van der Rohe emphasized the buildings' *vertical* (up and down) lines.

Music in America

Americans in the 20th century have supported the development of at least two home-grown musical forms—jazz and rock. They have also made important contributions in serious music and musical comedy.

Trumpeter Louis Armstrong (center) began playing with King Oliver's Jazz Band in 1922. Later he formed his own bands, with whom he recorded many popular records.

Jazz   Although jazz came out of Southern black communities, it spread in the 20th century to all regions and groups. The 1920s became known as the "Jazz Age" because of the popularity of jazz in that decade. Jazz greats Louis Armstrong and Duke Ellington launched their careers then, while Benny Goodman, Ella Fitzgerald, and others came into prominence in the 1930s.

Today, jazz is not as popular as it once was. Jazz groups, though, still play in night clubs, and some musicians combine jazz and rock to appeal to younger audiences.

Rock   Rock grew out of two musical traditions. It was partly influenced by country and western music. The other major influence was a form of jazz called "rhythm and blues." In the 1950s, many young people danced to the beat of a new musical form known as "rock-n-roll." Thousands swarmed to concert halls or bought records of Elvis Presley and other rock stars. Presley became the most famous rock singer of all times with a string of hits, including "Heartbreak Hotel" and "Love Me Tender."

Rock soon spread to other countries. In fact, the world's most popular rock group ever, the Beatles, were British. New generations of Americans continue to be fascinated with rock music. Its popularity is helped by the availability of videotapes of rock musicians performing.

Other Musical Contributions   A number of American composers have gained worldwide reputations, working with both classical and more popular forms of music:

• George Gershwin became famous writing musical comedies for Broadway, the New York theater district. Today, though, he is best remembered for his concert music, such as *Rhapsody in Blue* and *An American in Paris*. He also composed the well-known opera *Porgy and Bess* (1935), which deals with black Americans living in Charleston, South Carolina.

• Aaron Copland has written symphonies, piano concertos, and other forms of serious music, often on American folk themes. Some of his best-known works, such as *Billy the Kid* (1938) and *Appalachian Spring* (1944), were written for ballets.

• The pianist and conductor Leonard Bernstein is also a composer of serious and popular music. Many Americans have seen his exciting musical *West Side Story*, either on stage or on film.

New Forms of Mass Culture

Americans in the 20th century took to heart three new forms of mass culture—motion pictures, radio, and television.

Motion Pictures In the late 19th century, American audiences had the opportunity to view movies for the first time. For five cents, they could sit in darkened music halls and watch black-and-white images flickering on a screen. Often the films were accompanied by a pianist. By the late 1920s, motion picture techniques had advanced enough so that movies could be shown with sound tracks. The introduction of sound led, in the 1930s, to the production of elaborate film musicals. Later developments included color photography, wide screens, sophisticated sound systems, and even outdoor theaters. For many Americans, going to the movies provided a relaxing way to spend an evening or weekend afternoon out of the home.

Radio In the 1920s, with the introduction of regular radio broadcasting, Americans in large numbers began buying radio receivers. From then until the mid-20th century, radio served as the major source of home entertainment. Extremely popular radio shows included "Amos 'n' Andy," "Fibber McGee and Molly," and "The Lone Ranger."

The electronics industry has kept pace with changing trends. Americans today can listen to music through earphones while roller-skating to work.

Television Americans began buying television sets in large numbers in the 1950s. Soon television replaced radio as the American family's major source of entertainment. To some extent, television also replaced newspapers as the public's major news outlet. Most people in the United States, for instance, kept up with the Vietnam War by watching TV news broadcasts. As television became more popular, movie theaters found that they had fewer customers. Many people preferred to stay at home and watch movies on television rather than see them in theaters. In more recent years, movie watchers have been able to purchase or rent feature films on videocassettes and watch them at home on their television screen.

SUMMING UP   We have seen how American writers, painters, sculptors, architects, and musicians have produced works of distinction in the 20th century. Some Americans working in these fields have forged new paths, thereby gaining worldwide reputations. By providing a richer national culture, these artists have helped make America a better place in which to live.

Understanding the Text

On a separate sheet of paper, write the letter of the word or phrase that best completes each of the following statements.

1. The author of the early 20th-century novel *Sister Carrie* was (a) Sinclair Lewis (b) Edith Wharton (c) Richard Wright (d) Theodore Dreiser.

2. T. S. Eliot was (a) a leading poet who wrote *The Waste Land* (b) the author of *Main Street* and *Babbit* (c) the playwright who penned *Death of a Salesman* (d) none of the above.

3. Norman Mailer's novel about American soldiers fighting in East Asia during World War II is titled (a) *The Catcher in the Rye* (b) *The Age of Innocence* (c) *The Naked and the Dead* (d) *Rabbit, Run.*

4. The first American to win the Nobel Prize for Literature was (a) Pearl Buck (b) Sinclair Lewis (c) Ernest Hemingway (d) John Steinbeck.

5. An American artist best known for painting in a realistic style was (a) John Sloan (b) George Segal (c) Frank Lloyd Wright (d) Jackson Pollack.

6. Of the following American artists, the one well-known as a sculptor is (a) Saul Bellow (b) Louise Nevelson (c) Edward Hopper (d) Ella Fitzgerald.

7. The term *organic architecture* is often associated with (a) agriculture (b) abstract art (c) "Heartbreak Hotel" (d) Frank Lloyd Wright.

8. A musical style that developed in the United States was (a) jazz (b) rock-n-roll (c) rock (d) all of the above.

9. One of George Gershwin's hits was the opera (a) *Rhapsody in Blue* (b) *Billy the Kid* (c) *Porgy and Bess* (d) *West Side Story.*

10. From reading this lesson, we can conclude that (a) more Americans write books than paint pictures (b) Americans have led the world in all cultural areas in the 20th century (c) Americans are usually included among the world's best writers, artists, architects, and musical composers (d) American music is first-class, but its art, architecture, and literature are not highly regarded.

Developing Reading Comprehension Skills

Jazz Fantasia *by Carl Sandburg*

Drum on your drums, batter on your banjoes,
sob on the long cool winding saxophones.
Go to it, O jazzmen.

Sling your knuckles on the bottoms of the happy
tin pans, let your trombones ooze, and go husha-
husha-hush with the slippery sand-paper.

Moan like an autumn wind high in the lonesome treetops, moan
soft like you wanted somebody terrible, cry like a racing car slipping away from a motorcycle cop, bang-bang! you jazzmen, bang
altogether drums, traps, banjoes, horns, tin cans—make two
people fight on the top of a stairway and scratch each other's eyes
in a clinch tumbling down the stairs.

Can the rough stuff . . . now a Mississippi steamboat pushes up the
night river with a hoo-hoo-hoo-oo . . . and the green lanterns
calling to the high soft stars . . . a red moon rides on the humps of
the low river hills . . . go to it, O jazzmen.

On a separate sheet of paper, number one through five. Then write the letter of the word or phrase that most closely expresses the meaning of the italicized word.

1. "Go to it, O *jazzmen*." (a) dancers (b) musicians (c) racing-car drivers (d) river-boat crew.

2. "in a *clinch* tumbling down the stairs." (a) easy task (b) mistake (c) weapon (d) embrace.

3. "*Can* the rough stuff . . . " (a) stop (b) preserve (c) continue (d) record.

Choose the letter of the phrase that best completes each sentence.

4. The central idea of the poem is that (a) there is much to see on a riverboat cruise (b) the sounds of jazz should be celebrated (c) danger lurks in every shadow (d) the wind makes many sounds on an autumn night.

5. The racing car and the motorcycle are mentioned in the poem because (a) they are 20th-century inventions (b) they provide settings for the poem (c) transportation is the theme of the poem (d) they make sounds similar to some jazz instruments.

Thinking About the Lesson

1. Why have many leading writers of the 20th century written about social conditions in the United States?

2. Name the 20th-century American author whom you like the best. Explain why you like this person's writings.

3. Why do some artists work in a realistic style, while others prefer a more abstract style?

AMERICA'S FOREIGN RELATIONS IN THE 20TH CENTURY

LESSON 76

Foreign Relations in the Progressive Era

In Lessons 55 and 56, we discussed U.S. foreign policy in the second half of the 19th century. In 1901, a new President, Theodore Roosevelt, took office. He was the first U.S. President to be called a "progressive," one who favors moderate, democratic reforms. Americans wondered whether the country under Roosevelt would follow a new, progressive course of foreign policy.

The Big Stick

President Roosevelt had a favorite saying: "Speak softly and carry a big stick and you will go far." This expression explains why he pushed for a rapid expansion of the U.S. Navy. He wanted the United States to be in a stronger position overseas. During his administration, the United States built many cruisers, battleships, and other naval ships.

Roosevelt used the U.S. Navy to protect and expand the country's interests in Latin America. As we shall see, he was mostly concerned about protecting U.S. citizens and their investments in Cuba, Panama, and the Dominican Republic.

Cuba Under the Platt Amendment

At the end of the Spanish-American War of 1898, the United States had freed Cuba from Spanish control. After a few years of U.S. military occupation, Cuba became independent. Nevertheless, the influence of the United States in Cuba remained strong. In exchange for withdrawing its troops, the United States demanded that Cuba put a special clause into its Constitution. This clause, which Cuba adopted in 1901, became known in the United States as the Platt Amendment. It gave the United States the right to send armed forces to Cuba to restore order whenever the United States felt they were needed.

Results of the Platt Amendment Critics of the Platt Amendment pointed out that it prevented Cuba from exercising complete political independence. In the following decades, the United States sent forces to Cuba several times. Moreover, the United States built a naval base in Cuba at Guantánamo Bay. (The United States still occupies this base, much to the irritation of the Cuban government.)

504

The Panama Canal

After the Spanish-American War, the United States again became interested in building a canal across Central America. (See Lesson 55 for a discussion of the canal idea in the 1800s.) The U.S. Navy especially wanted such a project completed. A canal would make easier the movement of naval ships from one ocean to the other. In this way, the Navy could better defend new United States territories, such as the Philippines, Hawaii, and Puerto Rico.

One likely site for the canal was the Isthmus of Panama, a narrow land area belonging to Colombia. (See the map on page 506.) U.S. officials began negotiating with the Colombians for rights to build the canal in Panama. Many disagreements, however, caused the negotiations to drag on for a long time.

A Staged Revolution President Theodore Roosevelt decided to take action. In 1903, he encouraged local leaders in Panama to stage a revolt against Colombia. The United States quickly recognized the new Republic of Panama and signed a treaty with that government. The agreement gave the United States a lease on the Canal Zone—a ten-mile-wide strip of land through which the canal was to be built. In return, the United States paid Panama $10,000,000 and agreed to a yearly rental of $250,000.

The U.S. Army Corps of Engineers, led by Colonel George W. Goethals, directed construction of the Panama Canal. Thousands of workers labored under hard and dangerous conditions. Before much work could be done, however, U.S. authorities needed to rid the area of yellow fever and other diseases. They brought in Colonel William C. Gorgas, who had had similar experiences improving health conditions in Cuba. Believing that mosquitoes carried tropical diseases, he ordered swamps drained in the Canal Zone. In that way, mosquitoes would have fewer places to lay their eggs. His efforts proved as successful in Panama as they had in Cuba. Work on the canal was completed in 1914.

The Roosevelt Corollary

Over the years, Europeans had made large loans to some of the governments in the Caribbean

During Theodore Roosevelt's administration, most U.S. warships were painted white. Thus, as a group they were known as "The Great White Fleet." The use of the U.S. Navy was an important part of Roosevelt's Big Stick diplomacy.

Sea area. Often these governments fell behind in making loan payments. When this situation developed, European powers sometimes threatened to *intervene* (interfere using force) to collect their debts.

President Roosevelt was not willing to allow European countries to use force in the Western Hemisphere. He did believe, however, that the Monroe Doctrine gave the United States the right to intervene there under certain circumstances. He was referring to times when a Latin American country had difficulty paying its debts and a European power threatened to try to collect, using force. Roosevelt's views became known as the "Roosevelt Corollary" to the Monroe Doctrine. (A *corollary* is an idea that follows naturally from existing facts.)

U.S. Intervention   Roosevelt first used the Corollary in 1905 in regard to the Dominican Republic (also called Santo Domingo). He wanted to prevent Italy and France from intervening there to collect debts. Instead, the United States intervened by sending in its troops. U.S. officials stayed in the Dominican Republic for years, helping to collect duties. The U.S. used part of this tax money to pay foreign creditors, thereby reducing chances of further intervention.

U.S. INTERESTS IN THE CARIBBEAN AND CENTRAL AMERICA, 1898–1917

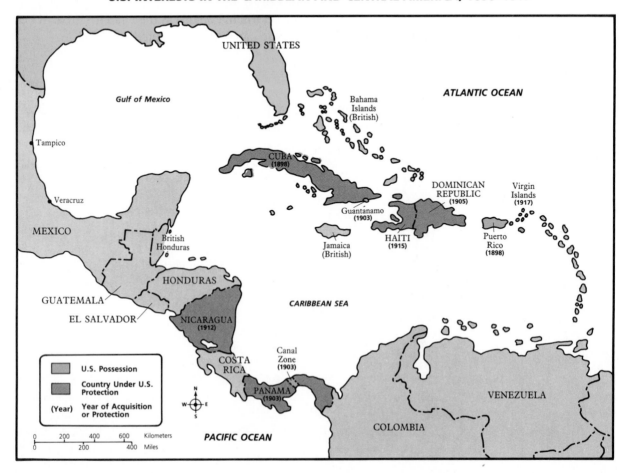

Dollar Diplomacy

President Howard Taft's policy toward Latin America was not too different from Roosevelt's. In 1912, Taft sent U.S. forces into Nicaragua to protect American lives and property there. As in the Dominican Republic, U.S. officials were stationed in Nicaragua to watch over the collection of duties. These agents also made sure that Nicaragua paid its foreign debts.

Taft's critics called his Latin American policy "Dollar Diplomacy." They felt that it was wrong to use U.S. power to protect and advance the financial interests of U.S. citizens.

Woodrow Wilson and Latin America

President Wilson continued the interventionist policy of the previous two Presidents. He kept U.S. forces in Nicaragua and sent new troops into Haiti and the Dominican Republic as well. Mexico, a large country with a large population, presented Wilson with more difficulties.

Mexican Revolution For most of the years between 1876 and 1911, Porfirio Diaz held the office of President of Mexico. He was very friendly with the thousands of Americans who invested in Mexican ranches, mines, oil fields, and railroads. Mexico, however, was not a democracy, and Diaz ruled the country with an iron fist. He was the unchallenged boss of the group of politicians, landholders, and military figures that held the most power and wealth.

In 1911, rebels overthrew the Diaz government. This event marked the beginning of the Mexican revolution, which was to last until 1917. During the revolution, one leader after another tried to control Mexico, most of them without success.

Intervention in Mexico Many U.S. business leaders asked President Wilson to intervene in Mexico to protect their interests. Wilson, at first, refused. Then events of 1914 caused him

Pancho Villa (center) played a major role in the Mexican Revolution, but he never became a ruler of the country.

to change his mind. Mexican police arrested a group of U.S. Navy sailors who had entered a forbidden zone in Tampico, Mexico. As a result of these arrests, U.S. military forces occupied the Mexican port of Veracruz. War was narrowly averted by the diplomatic efforts of Argentina, Brazil, and Chile.

In 1916, President Wilson again sent troops into Mexico. This time he wanted to capture Pancho Villa, a Mexican rebel leader. Villa had crossed the U.S.-Mexico border, raided a community in New Mexico, and fled back to Mexico. The U.S. force sent into Mexico failed to capture him. This intervention in Mexico, however, contributed to growing anti-United States feelings among Mexicans.

Constitutional Government in Mexico In 1917, Mexico under President Venustiano Carranza adopted a new constitution. This document, which provided for democratic elections, is still in use today. The new Mexican government carried out land reforms that broke up large estates and distributed land to small farmers. Moreover, it encouraged new industries and improved the railroads, highways, and ports.

U.S. Interests in East Asia

As we learned in Lesson 56, the United States became a colonial power in East Asia in 1898. As a result of the Spanish-American War, the United States obtained the Philippine Islands. Soon a group of Filipino nationalists put up a strong resistance to American control. By 1902, though, U.S. forces had put down the Filipino independence movement.

In addition to wanting to protect American interests in the Philippines, the United States had other East Asian concerns. For one thing, it wanted to maintain its trading rights in China. For this reason, the United States continued to insist on the Open Door policy there.

Russo-Japanese War In 1904, Japan upset the balance of power in East Asia by starting a war with Russia. At issue were Russian holdings in China—holdings that Japan wanted. Japan startled the world by gaining quick victories over Russia both on land and at sea.

Treaty of Portsmouth President Theodore Roosevelt played a key role in bringing the warring nations to the peace table. In 1905, he organized a peace conference in Portsmouth, New Hampshire. Under the terms of the Treaty of Portsmouth, Russia agreed to withdraw from Manchuria (in northern China). Instead of Russia, Japan became the major foreign power there, as well as in Korea. As part of the treaty, the United States recognized Japanese control over these two areas. In return, Japan accepted American control over the Philippines.

The Chinese Republic Beginning in 1905, Sun Yat-sen, a Chinese doctor, led a revolution against China's Manchu rulers. After a long

civil war, the monarchy fell in 1912. China became a *republic* (a form of government run by elected representatives) with Sun Yat-sen as its President. The United States was one of the first nations to recognize the new government.

The Chinese republic never gained control of the whole country. The civil war continued. Japan decided to take advantage of China's weakness. In 1915, Japan demanded that the Chinese government grant it many special rights. These "21 Demands," as they were called, would have gone far toward making China a colony of Japan. Strong opposition from the United States, though, prevented these demands from being put into effect.

A Progressive Foreign Policy?

In looking at the years 1901 to 1917, can we see a distinctive U.S. foreign policy? If so, was it clearly progressive? Did it differ from U.S. foreign policy in the late 19th century?

Roosevelt, Taft, and Wilson all sent U.S. troops into Latin American countries. They were all concerned with building the Panama Canal and protecting the Philippines. They all favored the Open Door policy in China. In these matters, their policies did not differ from those of the McKinley administration.

Woodrow Wilson often criticized Roosevelt's Big Stick policy and Taft's Dollar Diplomacy. Wilson said that the government should not be involved in protecting Americans' foreign investments. Nevertheless, his views on this matter did not change United States policy toward Latin America. We have to look elsewhere, such as to Wilson's plans for the League of Nations, for an example of Wilson's idealism in action.

Thus, we can say that from 1901 to 1917, United States foreign policy was not really progressive. Roosevelt, Taft, and Wilson actively intervened in other nations in much the same manner as had McKinley.

SUMMING UP We have seen how after 1900 the United States became increasingly active outside its own borders. The country built a major canal across Panama. It intervened in the political and economic affairs of Latin America. In East Asia, U.S. officials were concerned with keeping any one power from dominating China. Events in Europe would soon force the United States to become more involved in affairs there.

Understanding the Text

On a separate sheet of paper, write the letter of the word or phrase that best completes each of the following statements.

1. The Platt Amendment (a) freed Cuba from Spanish control (b) freed Cuba from U.S. control (c) allowed for U.S. intervention in Cuban affairs (d) none of the above.

2. The United States built the Panama Canal to (a) shorten the sea route from New York to Europe (b) make money for Colombian businesspeople (c) help settle the Russo-Japanese War (d) help protect U.S. possessions in the Caribbean and the Pacific.

3. The Republic of Panama was formed during the Presidency of (a) William McKinley (b) Theodore Roosevelt (c) William Taft (d) Woodrow Wilson.

4. The Roosevelt Corollary amended the (a) Monroe Doctrine (b) Bill of Rights (c) Platt Amendment (d) Mexican Constitution of 1917.

5. The term or phrase that was applied to President Taft's policy of active defense of U.S. economic interests in the Caribbean area was (a) isolationism (b) freedom of the seas (c) Dollar Diplomacy (d) the Open Door.

6. During Woodrow Wilson's administration, the United States intervened in all of the following countries, *except* (a) Mexico (b) Haiti (c) Colombia (d) the Dominican Republic.

7. Pancho Villa (a) led a raid from Mexico into the United States (b) ruled Mexico from 1876 to 1911 (c) fought tropical diseases in Cuba and Panama (d) fought for Filipino independence.

8. The United States official who helped end the war between Japan and Russia in 1905 was (a) William C. Gorgas (b) George W. Goethals (c) Woodrow Wilson (d) Theodore Roosevelt.

9. The "21 Demands" were made by (a) China (b) Japan (c) the United States (d) Mexico.

10. Which event or events were part of United States foreign affairs during all the administrations of Roosevelt, Taft, and Wilson? (a) U.S. forces were sent overseas. (b) The United States participated in a major war. (c) The United States intervened in the Mexican revolution. (d) The United States rejected the "21 Demands."

Developing Cartoon-Reading Skills

THE BIG STICK

Study the political cartoon above. Then choose the letter of the word or phrase that best completes each sentence. On a separate sheet of paper, match the sentence number with the correct letter.

1. The club that the man in the cartoon carries represents *(a)* the first baseball bat *(b)* U.S. neutrality in World War I *(c)* U.S. foreign policy under Theodore Roosevelt *(d)* William Howard Taft's Dollar Diplomacy.

2. All the nations labeled in the cartoon border the *(a)* Atlantic Ocean *(b)* Caribbean Sea *(c)* Mediterranean Sea *(d)* Pacific Ocean.

3. The ships in the cartoon represent *(a)* the United States *(b)* the Japanese Navy *(c)* Latin American governments *(d)* U.S. and European banks.

4. The cartoonist indicates that the ships are sailing by or visiting *(a)* Santo Domingo *(b)* Cuba *(c)* Venezuela *(d)* all of the above.

5. The labels "Tax Receiver," "Debt Collector," and "the Sheriff" refer to *(a)* the names of boats *(b)* typical powers of the President *(c)* U.S. officials who took over certain functions of Latin American governments *(d)* none of the above.

Thinking About the Lesson

1. Why did the United States government want to build the Panama Canal?

2. Do you think that the Monroe Doctrine gave the United States the right to intervene in the affairs of Latin American nations? Why or why not?

3. In what ways did U.S. and Japanese interests in East Asia conflict in the early 20th century?

The United States and World War I

In 1917, the United States entered the First World War. Never before had so many people suffered from such a costly and widespread conflict. The United States military efforts in Europe helped the Allies defeat the Central Powers. The country's participation in the war also influenced the course of European affairs after the fighting had stopped.

The Outbreak of War

The event that caused World War I to begin in 1914 involved Archduke Francis Ferdinand. This man was heir to the throne of Austria-Hungary—an empire that governed Europeans of many nationalities. On June 28, 1914, the Archduke was visiting Sarajevo in Bosnia, an area in the southern part of the empire. There, he and his wife were killed by a young Bosnian student who wanted Bosnia to break away from Austria-Hungary and join Serbia.

Austria-Hungary blamed Serbia for the killings and declared war in July, 1914. Because of military alliances, Germany, the Ottoman Empire, and Bulgaria joined Austria-Hungary in the war. Together, these four nations became known as the "Central Powers."

Serbia, however, was allied to Russia. As a result, Russia soon entered the war against the Central Powers. Then France and Great Britain (and later Italy and other nations) joined Russia's side in the conflict. They were called the "Allies." (See the map on page 512.)

The United States as a Neutral

At the outbreak of war, the United States declared that it was neutral. During the first years of the war, most Americans wanted their country to remain that way. A number of factors, though, drew the United States into the fighting:

• The British accused the Germans of *atrocities* (cruel acts) in carrying out the war. Newspapers in the United States often carried stories of these supposed German atrocities.

• United States citizens carried on a profitable trade with the Allies. Because Great Britain imposed a naval blockade of the Central Powers, American trade with these powers declined.

• In an effort to break the blockade, German *U-boats* (submarines) in the Atlantic began attacking Allied non-military vessels with little regard for the safety of passengers and crew. Americans were especially shocked when a U-boat sank the British liner *Lusitania* in 1915. Americans were among the many passengers killed.

• Americans became angry when the Germans invaded neutral Belgium. Americans did not

511

EUROPEAN ALLIANCES IN WORLD WAR I

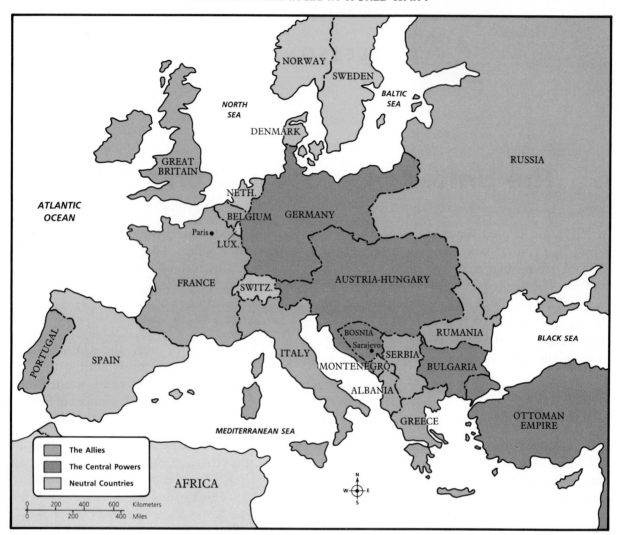

The Allies

The Central Powers

Neutral Countries

like it also when German diplomats tried to persuade Mexico and Japan to attack the United States. A German official suggested to Mexico that it could win back U.S. lands that it had lost in 1848. The U.S. government learned of this suggestion and leaked it to the press.

• Many Americans sympathized with the people and governments of the Allies. Great Britain and France had played important parts in U.S. history. Moreover, many Americans were descendants of immigrants from the British Isles.

An additional consideration was the fact that some of the Allied countries had democratic governments, which Americans admired.

All of these factors helped to convince many Americans that the United States should join the Allies. These Americans believed that their decision was both morally right and in the national interest. In April, 1917, President Woodrow Wilson delivered a war message, and Congress declared war on the Central Powers.

Not all Americans favored going to war on the side of the Allies. Many wanted the United States to remain neutral. Others wanted their country to fight on the side of the Central Powers. Pro-German and anti-British feelings were especially strong among Americans of German and Irish descent.

Participation in the War

After declaring war, the U.S. government promptly set up a system to draft an army of millions of men. Already by the spring of 1918, U.S. forces began arriving in Europe in large numbers. Under the command of General John J. Pershing, the American Expeditionary Force (AEF) eventually numbered about 2 million.

The Home Front In the United States, most Americans eagerly joined in the war effort. Because they believed that the nation was fighting for a good cause, *morale* (group spirit) was high. For this reason, most Americans accepted the military draft, willingly paid taxes, and bought war bonds. Furthermore, they accepted controls on purchases of food and fuels.

Congress put U.S. industries on a war footing. For instance, the government took over the railroads, running them until the end of the war. Of greater impact was a law that gave the President emergency powers to control the supplies and prices of many products.

The war changed the lives of many American women. Some were hired by businesses and industries to take over jobs formerly done by the men who had gone into the service. The experiences of these women helped change popular ideas of what was men's work and what was appropriate for women.

Certain Americans criticized the war effort or hindered it. Congress reacted to this problem by passing the Espionage and Sedition Acts. These laws allowed the government to impose

During the war, many American women took jobs for the first time. This woman worked as a welder.

fines and prison terms on Americans found guilty of disloyal activities.

The Armed Forces in Europe The United States brought fresh troops to Europe to join the conflict. The country also contributed vast quantities of supplies and equipment to the war effort. In the opinion of many historians, these resources turned the tide of the war in favor of the Allies.

On the sea, the U.S. Navy cooperated with the Allied fleets. It helped to protect troop and supply ships and to hunt down German submarines. The U.S. Navy also helped to enforce the Allied blockade of Germany.

The U.S. Army in Europe helped the Allies to push back German advances in France. In the fall of 1918, American forces won victories at St. Mihiel and the Argonne Forest. By early November, the Germans were ready to stop fighting. Germany and the Allies signed an armistice on November 11, 1918.

The Role of President Wilson

President Woodrow Wilson played an important role in both the U.S. war effort and the course of world history following the war.

A Wartime Leader President Wilson won re-election in 1916 by a close margin. His campaign made effective use of the slogan "He kept us out of war." When war came, however, Wilson proved to be an inspiring leader. Most Americans united behind him in mobilizing for the fight. They accepted his view that the war was being fought for idealistic and unselfish reasons. He claimed that the main goal of the war was "to make the world safe for democracy."

The Fourteen Points Above all, President Wilson wanted to frame a just peace—one fair to every country and national group. Only such a peace, he said, would be worthy of the sacrifices made in the war. He further believed that a just peace would help to prevent future wars. In a message delivered to Congress in 1918, Wilson summarized his ideas. His program, known as the "Fourteen Points," included:

• *Freedom of the seas.* Ships of all nations should have the right to sail the seas without being stopped by foreign powers.

• End of *secret diplomacy.* All countries should agree to make public any agreements with other nations.

• Free trade. All countries should gradually reduce tariffs and other barriers to trade among nations.

• Arms reductions. Each power should agree to reduce the number of its armaments.

• Peaceful settlement of rivalries over colonies.

The American soldier on the left is saying good-bye to his sweetheart. Many U.S. soldiers found themselves in France in battles such as the one below.

The victorious Allies should settle disputes over who owned certain colonies. Those who made the decisions should keep in mind the interests of the people living in the colonies.

• *Self-determination* for national minorities. National groups living under the rule of other people should decide for themselves if they wanted independence. (The map on page 516 shows new nations created from Germany, Austria-Hungary, and Russia. Russia lost territories when it made a separate peace treaty with Germany early in 1918. If Russia, ruled by the Communists since November, 1917, had stayed in the war until Germany was defeated, it might not have lost these areas. See page 520 for a discussion of Soviet Russia.)

• League of Nations. Wilson's last point was his proposal for a new international organization to protect the peace.

The Paris Peace Conference

In 1919, President Wilson went to Paris to attend the Peace Conference. There he negotiated with Prime Minister David Lloyd George of Britain, Premier Georges Clemenceau of France, and other world leaders. Lloyd George and Clemenceau disliked many of Wilson's ideas and worked against them. Wilson had to be both diplomatic and forceful to get some of his ideas included in the peace treaties.

Wilson was forced to compromise on many of his Fourteen Points, but he stood firm on his idea of forming the League of Nations. As a result, the Allied representatives wrote the League into the peace treaties. Wilson was relieved when this happened, believing that the League would be able to correct any flaws the treaties might contain.

Many historians have concluded that the peace treaties were too harsh on the Central Powers. According to the terms of one peace treaty—the Treaty of Versailles:

In 1919, Woodrow Wilson (right) met in Paris with world leaders, including British Prime Minister David Lloyd George (left) and Premier Georges Clemenceau of France.

• Germany and her allies were made responsible for starting the war.

• Germany had to give up considerable land in Europe. This land amounted to about 12 percent of Germany's former area and included about 12 percent of its population. France, Belgium, Denmark, Lithuania, and Poland gained at Germany's expense. (See the map on page 516.)

• All German colonies were to be taken away and divided among the Allies.

• Germany was to be almost completely disarmed.

• Finally, Germany was required to pay the Allies for damages caused by the war. These payments were called *reparations*.

Another treaty broke up Austria-Hungary into a number of independent countries. In still another treaty, the Ottoman Empire (after 1922 it was called Turkey) lost vast territories in the Middle East.

EUROPE AFTER WORLD WAR I

The U.S. and the Peace Treaty

President Wilson returned home from Paris in July, 1919. He was certain that the U.S. Senate would approve the Treaty of Versailles. Wilson seemed to have the support of a large part of the American public. Nevertheless, after long and bitter debates, the Senate rejected the Treaty in 1919 and again in 1920.

Historians point to a number of reasons for the Senate's actions:

• Many Americans feared becoming involved again in Europe's quarrels. Belonging to the League of Nations might lead to such an involvement.

• Republican leaders in the Senate were displeased with President Wilson. They felt that

Wilson had not consulted them enough while the Treaty was being written.

• Wilson would not accept any changes in the terms of the Treaty. If he had been willing to compromise with Senate opponents, he might have gotten the Senate to approve a revised Treaty.

• Wilson was in poor health. In October, 1919, he suffered a stroke that paralyzed him for the rest of his life. He was no longer able to campaign effectively for the League.

> In 1921, during Warren G. Harding's administration, the Senate finally ratified separate peace treaties with the former enemies. The United States, however, remained outside of the League of Nations. In the U.S.-German treaty, Germany agreed to pay for damage that had been done to U.S. properties by German submarines. The United States, in turn, agreed to pay for German property that had been seized in America during the war.

SUMMING UP   We have seen how at first the United States acted as a neutral in World War I. Then in 1917, it decided to enter the war on the side of the Allies. By the spring of 1918, American soldiers were fighting in France. U.S. participation in the war helped President Wilson to shape the peace treaties that followed. Even so, the Senate refused to approve the Treaty of Versailles and U.S. membership in the League of Nations.

Understanding the Text

On a separate sheet of paper, write the letter of the word or phrase that best completes each of the following statements.

1. Archduke Francis Ferdinand was (*a*) a Serbian revolutionary (*b*) Prime Minister of France (*c*) heir to the throne of Austria-Hungary (*d*) none of the above.

2. Two countries that fought on the same side in World War I were (*a*) Germany and Britain (*b*) France and Austria-Hungary (*c*) Germany and the Ottoman Empire (*d*) Austria-Hungary and the United States.

3. World War I took place in (*a*) the last half of the 19th century (*b*) the second decade of the 20th century (*c*) the first quarter of the 19th century (*d*) none of the above.

4. An important cause of the entry of the United States into World War I was (*a*) Germany's sinking of the British liner *Lusitania* (*b*) money owed by Germany to U.S. banks (*c*) the desire of the United States to grab Germany's colonies (*d*) the Central Powers' admiration for democratic governments.

5. Germany engaged in submarine warfare because (*a*) Germans were naturally cruel (*b*) Great Britain was also carrying on extensive submarine warfare (*c*) Germany considered the use of submarines necessary to break the British blockade (d) Germany wanted its differences with the Allies to be discussed in the League of Nations.

6. The main purpose of Woodrow Wilson's Fourteen Points was to (a) punish Germany and its allies (b) show support for Britain and France (c) express opposition to the Treaty of Versailles (d) establish a basis for a just and lasting peace.

7. At the Paris Peace Conference, David Lloyd George represented (a) Great Britain (b) the United States (c) France (d) Germany.

8. One result of World War I was that (a) Great Britain lost its colonial empire (b) the United States joined the League of Nations (c) Germany was almost completely disarmed (d) the Ottoman Empire became a major world power.

9. All of the following were reasons for the defeat in the U.S. Senate of proposals to join the League of Nations, *except* (a) a fear of getting involved in European conflicts (b) Wilson's refusal to compromise with the Senate (c) a fear that the League would not have enough power (d) Republicans' resentment over Wilson's methods.

10. Which of the following is the best statement regarding the participation of the United States in World War I? (a) U.S. participation was never supported by the majority of the American people. (b) Without U.S. participation, the Allies might very well have lost the war. (c) U.S. participation was unnecessary because in 1917 the Allies were about to win the war anyway. (d) U.S. participation made possible world disarmament after the war.

Developing Map Skills

Examine the maps on pages 512 and 516. Then choose the letter of the word or phrase that best completes each sentence. On a separate sheet of

paper, match the sentence number with the correct letter.

1. One of the Central Powers in World War I was (a) Bulgaria (b) Germany (c) Austria-Hungary (d) all of the above.

2. A European country that sided with neither the Allies nor the Central Powers in World War I was (a) Portugal (b) Russia (c) Norway (d) the Ottoman Empire.

3. A country that did *not* lose territory at the end of World War I was (a) Germany (b) France (c) Russia (d) Austria-Hungary.

4. An example of an independent nation created after World War I from land lost by Russia was (a) Alsace-Lorraine (b) Yugoslavia (c) Estonia (d) Bulgaria.

5. An example of an independent nation created after World War I from lands lost by both Russia and Germany was (a) Denmark (b) Poland (c) Albania (d) Rumania.

Thinking About the Lesson

1. Imagine that you were a member of Congress in 1917. Would you have supported President Wilson's request for a declaration of war against Germany? Why or why not?

2. How was the life of the average American back home affected by World War I?

3. Do you think that Wilson's Fourteen Points formed a sound blueprint for peace? Explain your answer.

4. Do you think that the United States should have joined the League of Nations? Why or why not?

American Foreign Policy Between the Wars

During the years following World War I, the United States tried to avoid foreign *entanglements* (ties). For instance, it refused to join the League of Nations. The country's attempt at isolationism, however, proved unsuccessful. In the 1930s, events abroad once again forced the United States to take a more active part in world affairs.

Isolationism in the 1920s

Many Americans were disappointed by the results of World War I. In joining the conflict, their country had lost thousands of lives and had spent much money. Quite a few Americans asked, "Did the results of the war justify such great sacrifices?"

Many Americans believed that the world had not become "safe for democracy" in the way President Wilson had promised. They said that selfish national interests still shaped the policies of European powers. The victors in the war continued to support huge armies and navies; most European nations kept their overseas colonies. If all of these things were unchanged, they argued, what had the United States gained in the war?

On the basis of arguments such as these, the United States followed a policy of isolationism in the post-war years. This policy was not too different from U.S. isolationism of the late 18th century, discussed in Lesson 22.

New Isolationism The new isolationism of the 1920s stressed the idea that the United States should steer clear of major foreign involvements. Instead, the country would work alone to promote its national interests. A number of events reflected this new direction in American foreign policy:

• The United States refused to ratify the Treaty of Versailles or to join the League of Nations.

• The country also refused to join the World Court. This judicial body was set up by the League of Nations in 1921 to settle disputes between nations.

• The United States reversed its pre-war policy of almost unlimited immigration. The government would now strictly control the numbers and kinds of immigrants to be admitted.

• Congress raised tariff rates in order to protect American industries. These high protective tariffs had the effect of holding down the volume of U.S. foreign trade.

519

United States Cooperation With Other Nations

In the years after World War I, the United States made some exceptions to its policy of isolationism. It signed several important international agreements.

Washington Disarmament Conference   In 1921 and 1922, the United States sponsored the Washington Disarmament Conference. Three major agreements came out of this series of meetings:

- The Five-Power Pact. Five leading world powers agreed to limit their construction of new battleships. In addition, they decided to scrap some existing ships.
- The Nine-Power Pact. Nine nations attending the conference agreed to continue the Open Door policy in China. (The Open Door policy is first discussed on page 350.)
- The Four-Power Pact. Japan, Great Britain, France, and the United States signed this agreement. They promised to work together to stop acts of aggression in the Pacific area.

In 1928, the United States and 61 other nations signed the Kellogg-Briand Pact. This agreement called for peaceful settlement of disputes and "outlawed" war as an instrument of national policy. Unfortunately, the pact had little practical effect, since the powers provided no means for enforcing it.

Better Relations With Latin America   In the 1930s, under Presidents Herbert Hoover and Franklin D. Roosevelt, United States relations with Latin America improved. Before then, the United States had been using Theodore Roosevelt's Corollary to the Monroe Doctrine to justify its intervention in Latin America.

- In 1930, the State Department said that Roosevelt's Corollary was no longer valid.

- In 1933, shortly before President Hoover left office, the United States withdrew its Marines from Nicaragua.
- Upon taking office, President Franklin D. Roosevelt said that the United States would no longer interfere in the affairs of Western Hemisphere nations. Instead, he declared, these relations would be based on the principle of voluntary cooperation. To further describe these relations, he introduced the phrase "policy of the good neighbor."
- In 1934, in accordance with the Good Neighbor Policy, U.S. Marines left Haiti. For the first time in decades, no U.S. Marines were stationed in a Latin America country.
- Also in 1934, the United States announced that it no longer had the right to intervene in Cuba. This announcement *abrogated* (canceled) the Platt Amendment of 1901.
- In 1938, Mexico *nationalized* (took over ownership of) all foreign oil companies. Many Americans wanted to punish the Mexicans by sending in troops, as the United States had done in 1914. President Roosevelt, though, opposed intervention. Instead, his administration worked out an agreement with Mexico whereby Mexico would compensate U.S. oil companies for their losses. The Mexican government began to make payments to U.S. companies in 1941.

The Rise of Dictatorships

After the First World War, *dictatorships* were set up in some of the leading nations of Europe. A dictatorship is a government controlled almost entirely by one person or by a small group of people. Usually, the people who live under this form of government lack basic rights. *Dictators* (people who rule in dictatorships) use force to crush their political opponents.

Russia   In 1917, military defeat and economic disorder led to two revolutions in Russia. In the second revolution, the Russian Communist party set up a dictatorship under V. I. Lenin. In the 1920s, another dictator, Joseph Stalin, succeeded Lenin. Until 1933, the United States refused to recognize the Soviet Union, as Russia came to be called.

Italy   Post-war economic and social conditions in Italy were very bad. These conditions helped dictator Benito Mussolini and his Italian Fascist party to come to power in 1922.

Germany   After World War I, the Germans set up a democratic government. The Weimar Republic, as it was called, could not solve the country's severe economic and political problems. As a result, in 1933 the Nazi party took over political control. The Nazi leader, Adolf Hitler, became one of the world's cruelest and most powerful dictators.

Japan   In the 1930s, Japan also came under a military dictatorship. On the surface, the Emperor appeared to rule alongside the Japanese *Diet* (parliament). Actually, however, leaders of the Japanese Army and Navy controlled the nation's government.

Spain   In 1931, the Spanish people removed their king and set up a republic. Then from 1936 to 1939, Spaniards engaged in a bloody civil war. The Nationalists, led by General Francisco Franco, defeated the Rebublicans—supporters of the Spanish Republic. Franco created a dictatorship that ruled Spain for decades.

Aggression by Dictatorships

Three of the above-mentioned dictatorships followed an aggressive foreign policy. Japan, Italy, and Germany sought to expand their borders and obtain overseas colonies.

Japanese Aggression   In 1930, Japan invaded the Chinese province of Manchuria. The Chinese, led by General Chiang Kai-shek, fought back. At the same time, however, Chiang and his

Axis leaders Benito Mussolini (center) and Adolf Hitler (right) are shown reviewing a military parade in Berlin, Germany.

Chinese Nationalist forces were fighting a civil war against Chinese Communists. The Japanese, with their more modern weapons and equipment, were able to take over a large area in China.

Both the United States and the League of Nations protested the Japanese action. Secretary of State Henry Stimson, in the Stimson Doctrine, said that the U.S. would not recognize the Japanese conquest. He claimed that the action violated several treaties, including the League of Nations Covenant, the Nine-Power Pact, and the Kellogg-Briand Pact. Despite U.S. protests, the Japanese were not discouraged from seeking even more territory. In 1937, they followed up their victory in Manchuria by invading Northern China.

Italian Aggression   In 1935, Italy sent its forces into Ethiopia, an independent country in northeast Africa. The Italian invaders, with their

AGGRESSION IN EUROPE, 1935–1939

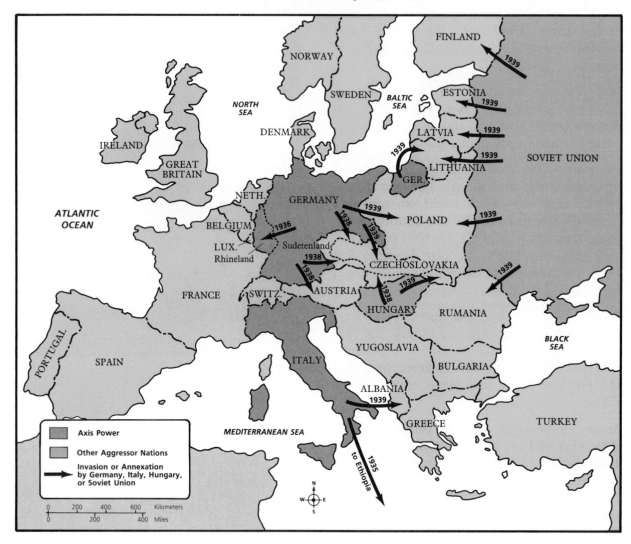

superior weapons, soon conquered Ethiopia and made it a colony. The League of Nations reacted to the invasion by applying *sanctions* (penalties) against Italy. The League asked member nations not to sell oil and other war materials to Italy. The sanctions, however, came too late. By the time they were applied, Italy already controlled Ethiopia.

German Aggression Under Hitler, Germany rearmed, thereby violating a major clause in the Treaty of Versailles. Then Germany carried out

a series of "bloodless conquests" that practically reversed the outcome of World War I:

• In 1936, the German Army occupied the Rhineland, an area along the French-German border. The territory was part of Germany but was not supposed to be armed. France and Britain failed to take action against this obvious violation of the Versailles Treaty.

• In the spring of 1938, German forces moved into Austria. Soon Austria became part of Germany.

The Nazis staged this impressive entrance of German troops into a Czechoslovak town in 1939.

• Later in 1938, Hitler threatened neighboring Czechoslovakia by demanding that it turn over its lands known as the Sudetenland. Germany claimed this area because it was inhabited by many people of German background. That September, French and British leaders met with Hitler in Munich, Germany, to discuss Hitler's demands. In return for gaining the Sudetenland, Hitler promised not to make any more territorial demands in Europe. The French and British leaders believed Hitler. In the Munich Pact, they agreed to the annexation. Nevertheless, within months of annexing the Sudetenland, Hitler broke his promise by taking over the rest of Czechoslovakia as well. The British-French policy of *appeasement* (trying to satisfy or buy off an enemy by giving in to its demands) had failed.

Formation of the Axis Alliance In the late 1930s, Germany, Italy, and Japan came together in an alliance—the Berlin-Rome-Tokyo Axis. They hoped that by forming a united front, they could prevent the democracies from acting together to stop aggression. This Axis alliance continued well into the Second World War.

The Beginning of the War

Great Britain and France had pledged to come to Poland's aid in case of an attack. When Germany invaded Poland in September, 1939, the two allies therefore promptly declared war on Germany. Nevertheless, they were powerless to prevent Poland's defeat.

The Soviet Union refused to come to Poland's rescue. In fact, just a month before, in August, Soviet leaders had made a Non-Aggression Pact with Germany. Because of this pact, the Soviets joined with the Germans in invading and dividing up Poland. Also in 1939, the Soviets invaded and occupied Estonia, Latvia, and Lithuania and parts of Finland and Rumania.

The United States Policy of Neutrality

Although the war clouds were swiftly gathering, many Americans continued to have faith in the policy of isolationism. They believed that they could remain safe behind the protection of the Atlantic and Pacific oceans. They wanted to have as little as possible to do with matters in Europe, Africa, and Asia.

In this belief, Congress passed several Neutrality Acts between 1935 and 1937. These laws forbade the selling of arms and granting of credits to warring nations. Critics of the acts claimed that the laws encouraged aggressors. They said that the laws convinced German, Italian, and Japanese leaders that the United States would not aid victims of aggression.

SUMMING UP   We have seen that isolationist sentiment was strong in the United States after World War I. Nevertheless, U.S. leaders had a difficult time in trying to follow this policy. In the 1920s, the United States took part in several international conferences. In the 1930s, the country improved its relations with its neighbors to the south. Moreover, during the 1930s, the United States kept its eyes on aggressive moves of the world's dictators.

Understanding the Text

On a separate sheet of paper, write the letter of the word or phrase that best completes each of the following statements.

1. A country that avoids foreign entanglement is following a policy of (a) imperialism (b) internationalism (c) isolationism (d) aggression.

2. In the decade after World War I, the United States (a) stayed out of the League of Nations (b) lowered tariff rates (c) opened its doors wide to all immigrants (d) joined the World Court.

3. War was "outlawed" as a means of settling international disputes by the (a) Stimson Doctrine (b) Washington Naval Conference (c) Munich Pact (d) Kellogg-Briand Pact.

4. After 1934, U.S. Marines remained in (a) Haiti (b) Nicaragua (c) Dominican Republic (d) none of the above.

5. As part of its Good Neighbor Policy, the United States (a) announced the Roosevelt Corollary to the Monroe Doctrine (b) canceled the Platt Amendment (c) sent the Marines into Mexico (d) recognized the Soviet Union.

6. A pair that does *not* correctly match a dictator with his country is (a) Mussolini-Italy (b) Franco-Spain (c) Hitler-Poland (d) Stalin-Soviet Union.

7. Of the following events, the *last* to occur was the (a) Italian conquest of Ethiopia (b) seizure of Austria by Germany (c) Japanese invasion of Manchuria (d) Washington Disarmament Conference.

8. The Munich Pact is usually associated with the policy of (a) appeasement (b) disarmament (c) opposition to aggression (d) the Good Neighbor.

9. During most of the 1930s, the United States made it a major aim of its foreign policy to (a) aid the Axis powers (b) aid victims of aggression (c) remain neutral (d) form a military alliance with the Allies.

10. Which of the following statements best expresses a theme of this lesson? (a) The United States wisely stayed out of the League of Nations. (b) U.S. foreign policy was responsible for German aggression in the 1930s. (c) Dictators in Japan, Germany, and Italy had aggressive foreign policies in the 1930s. (d) The United States was safe from foreign aggression because of the barriers of the Atlantic and Pacific oceans.

Developing Chronology Skills

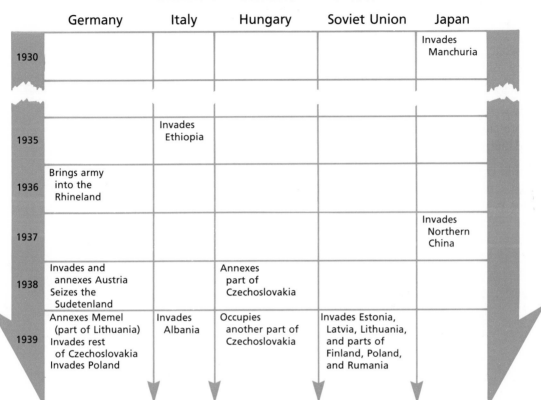

TIMELINE OF AGGRESSION—THE 1930s

	Germany	Italy	Hungary	Soviet Union	Japan
1930					Invades Manchuria
1935		Invades Ethiopia			
1936	Brings army into the Rhineland				
1937					Invades Northern China
1938	Invades and annexes Austria Seizes the Sudetenland		Annexes part of Czechoslovakia		
1939	Annexes Memel (part of Lithuania) Invades rest of Czechoslovakia Invades Poland	Invades Albania	Occupies another part of Czechoslovakia	Invades Estonia, Latvia, Lithuania, and parts of Finland, Poland, and Rumania	

Study the timeline above. Then choose the letter of the word or phrase that best completes each sentence. On a separate sheet of paper, match the sentence number with the correct letter.

1. Of the events listed on the timeline, the first one to happen was the *(a)* Italian invasion of Ethiopia *(b)* Japanese invasion of Manchuria *(c)* German invasion of Poland *(d)* German invasion of Austria.

2. In 1937, the Sudetenland was controlled by *(a)* Germany *(b)* Italy *(c)* Czechoslovakia *(d)* Japan.

3. In 1937, U.S. newspapers carried stories about *(a)* the surrender of the Polish Army to the Germans *(b)* the clash between Chinese and Japanese troops in Northern China *(c)* rumors of a possible German invasion of the Rhineland *(d)* all of the above.

4. All of the following events occurred in 1939, *except* the *(a)* Italian invasion of Ethiopia *(b)* Soviet invasion of Estonia *(c)* German invasion of Poland *(d)* Italian invasion of Albania.

5. Of the events listed on the timeline, the fourth one to happen was the *(a)* German invasion of Poland *(b)* Hungarian occupation of Czechoslovakia *(c)* German invasion and annexation of Austria *(d)* Japanese invasion of Northern China.

Thinking About the Lesson

1. To what extent did the United States follow a policy of isolationism in the 1920s? Provide some examples.

2. To what extent did the United States follow a policy of international cooperation in the 1920s? Provide some examples.

3. How was the Good Neighbor Policy different from previous United States policies toward Latin American nations?

4. Should the United States have done more in the 1930s to stop aggressive actions of other nations? Why or why not?

The United States Enters the Second World War

The United States entered World War II on the side of the Allies (Great Britain, France, and the Soviet Union) in December, 1941. By that time, the Allies had been fighting the Axis powers (Germany, Italy, and Japan) for over two years. Americans took a while to mobilize and get their forces ready. In the end, however, the United States was chiefly responsible for turning the tide of battle on the western front against Germany. Then the United States concentrated on fighting in the Pacific, where it forced Japan to surrender.

The Growing German Threat

In the spring of 1940, German forces overran Denmark and Norway. British efforts to help these two neutral countries were not effective. The Germans soon crushed Holland, Belgium, and France as well. In their *blitzkrieg* (lightning war), the Germans used thousands of tanks and planes to aid their powerful ground forces.

Many Americans believed that only Great Britain stood between them and the armed forces of Adolf Hitler, the German dictator. Under the leadership of Prime Minister Winston Churchill,

the British government pledged never to surrender.

Battle of Britain   Unable to invade Great Britain by sea, the Germans began to attack the British by air during the fall of 1940. Day and night, they pounded London and other industrial centers with bombs dropped from airplanes. The British Royal Air Force, however, shot down many bombers, thereby preventing the Germans from controlling the skies. The British efforts stopped Germany from completing its plan to conquer all of Western Europe.

U.S. Aid to the Allies

The crushing German victories of 1940 shocked most people in the United States. Increasing numbers of Americans came to realize that Hitler was bent on making Germany the ruling power in Europe. Helped by his Axis allies—Italy and Japan—Hitler's Germany might even aim for world domination.

The United States was officially neutral in the conflict. President Franklin Roosevelt, though, made no secret of the fact that he favored the Allies. Under his leadership, the country gave

527

the Allies as much aid as was possible, short of war:

• In 1939, the United States had begun to ship arms and other supplies to Great Britain and France. To do this, Congress had to amend its Neutrality Acts of 1935 and 1937.

• In September, 1940, the United States transferred 50 destroyers to Great Britain. In exchange, the British gave the United States leases on naval bases in the Western Hemisphere.

• With the Lend-Lease Act of March, 1941, the U.S. President gained the power to lend or lease war materials to nations attacked by aggressors. Great Britain and later the Soviet Union received much of this aid.

• By mid-1941, German submarines were attacking U.S. supply ships on the high seas. As a result, U.S. Navy vessels began patrolling the North Atlantic. Soon Germany and the United States were carrying on an undeclared naval war in the Atlantic.

Events of 1941

A number of important developments in 1941 influenced the course of the war.

More German Victories   In the spring, powerful German forces drove the British across North Africa into Egypt. Hitler's armies also quickly conquered Greece and Yugoslavia, in Southern Europe.

Soviets Join the Allies   In June, 1941, Hitler suddenly scrapped the German-Soviet Non-Aggression Pact of 1939. The German Army drove deep into Soviet territory, eventually as far as Leningrad, Moscow, and Stalingrad. Now, however, Hitler was fighting on two fronts at the same time. Moreover, the Soviets became an important ally of Great Britain and later the United States.

Pearl Harbor   On December 7, 1941, Japanese war planes suddenly attacked the U.S. naval base at Pearl Harbor, Hawaii. They destroyed most of the U.S. Pacific Fleet stationed there. Several thousand Americans were killed or wounded in the attack. Japan also bombed U.S. and British bases in East Asia.

U.S. Entry Into the War

On December 8th, Congress quickly reacted to the attack on Pearl Harbor by declaring war on Japan. As a result, Germany and Italy, Japan's allies, declared war on the United States.

The United States and the other Allies agreed that their first objective would be to defeat the

When the Japanese attacked Pearl Harbor on December 7, 1941, this ship, the U.S.S. *Shaw*, became one of the targets that they hit.

ALLIED ADVANCES IN EUROPE AND NORTH AFRICA, 1942–1945

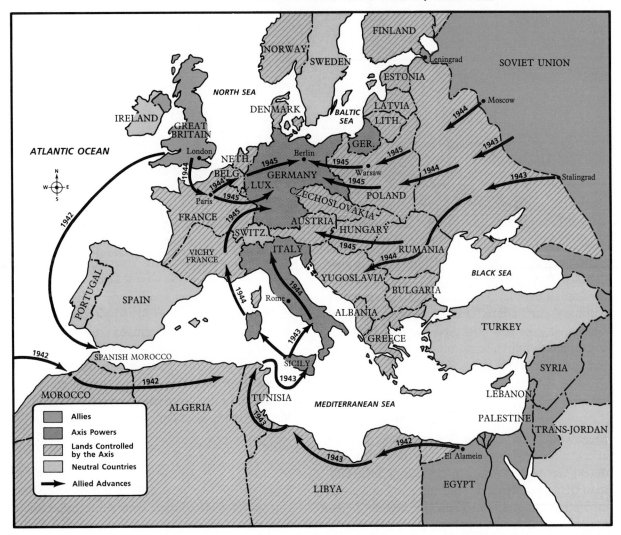

Germans in Europe. Then the Allies would turn their full attention to the Japanese in East Asia and the Pacific. Nevertheless, the Americans found that they had to conduct major operations against Japan even while fighting Germany.

North African and Italian Campaigns

In 1942, British forces won an important victory in North Africa. The British Army defeated the Germans in a major battle at El Alamein, Egypt. As the retreating Germans moved westward, American and British forces under General Dwight D. Eisenhower attacked them. Facing defeat, the German Army in North Africa surrendered to Allied forces in Tunisia in 1943. (See the map above.)

Having gained control of North Africa, the Allies next moved on to Italy. Following an invasion of the island of Sicily, they landed on the Italian mainland in September, 1943.

Many German targets were bombed by the Allies during the war. In this scene, a U.S. B-17 Flying Fortress leaves Marienburg in 1943 after dropping bombs.

Because of crushing Allied blows, the Italian dictator Benito Mussolini was overthrown by the Italian people. The new Italian government willingly surrendered to the Allies. Even so, German forces still occupied parts of Italy and continued to fight a hard, bloody war there until the spring of 1945.

The Offensive Against Germany

Meanwhile, the United States, Great Britain, and the Soviet Union combined their efforts to defeat Germany. Soviet forces stopped the German drive into Russia, winning a major victory at Stalingrad in 1943. Then the Soviets began to push the Nazi invaders back toward Germany.

Normandy Invasion In England, the United States and Great Britain prepared for an invasion of the continent. A mighty force, made up of massive land, air, and naval units, gathered along the English coast. On D-Day (June 6, 1944), this force crossed the English Channel and landed in Normandy, France. The Allied invaders, led by General Eisenhower, met heavy resistance there. Nonetheless, they were able to move eastward. Along the way, the Allies liberated parts of France, as well as Belgium, Luxembourg, and the Netherlands.

Battle of the Bulge The Allied drive was stalled for a time in late 1944 by a German counterattack. This fighting, called the "Battle of the Bulge," ended with an Allied victory. Next the Allies crossed into Germany itself. Then on April 25, 1945, British-American and Soviet forces met at the Elbe River. As the Allied forces drew closer to Berlin, they learned that Hitler had killed himself. Several days later, on May 8, 1945, Germany surrendered.

The War Against Japan

Early in the war, just after the attack on Pearl Harbor in 1941, Japan won some other major victories. Japanese forces overran the Philippines and other islands in the Pacific. They conquered the British possessions of Malaya, Singapore, and Hong Kong. They also invaded and took over the rule of the Dutch East Indies and French Indochina.

U.S. Victories in the Pacific Gradually, the tide of war turned against the Japanese. In May and June, 1942, the U.S. Navy won the important Battle of the Coral Sea and the Battle of Midway Island. With these victories, the United States stopped Japanese advances and ended Japanese threats to Australia and Hawaii.

Island Hopping   American forces in the Pacific were led by Admiral Chester Nimitz and General Douglas MacArthur. They staged a series of *amphibious* (land-and-sea) operations that conquered one Japanese-held island after another. This tactic was called *island hopping*. By late 1944, U.S. forces under General MacArthur had begun reconquering the Philippine Islands. In the first half of 1945, the United States recaptured the islands of Iwo Jima and Okinawa. Now the United States was in position to launch air attacks on Japan itself.

Despite its many defeats and losses, Japan held out. Therefore, President Harry S. Truman decided to use a new weapon—the atomic bomb—on Japanese cities. Truman said that he did this in order to avoid the loss of hundreds of thousands more American lives if the United States were to invade Japan. In August, 1945, Hiroshima and Nagasaki became the only populated targets ever to be hit by atomic bombs. Japan surrendered on September 2, 1945, in a formal ceremony aboard the battleship U.S.S. *Missouri* in Tokyo Bay.

ALLIED ADVANCES IN THE PACIFIC, 1942–1945

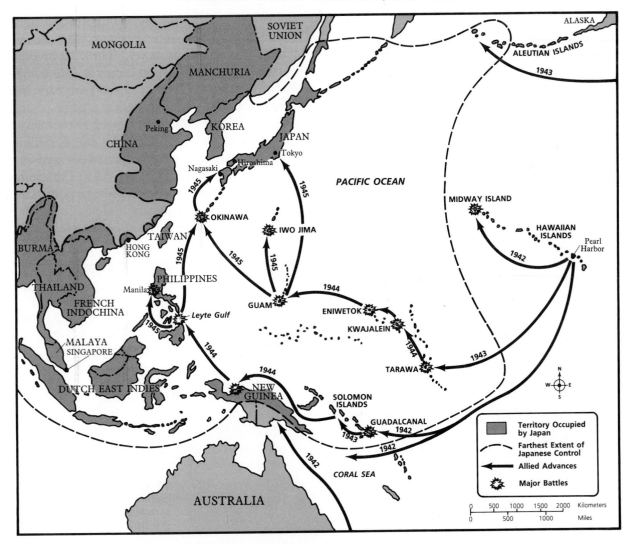

After the Japanese offered to surrender in August, 1945, crowds gathered all over the United States to celebrate.

Results of the War

World War II was probably the worst tragedy to befall the human race. Because the fighting was so widespread, more lives were disrupted and more people died than in any other conflict.

Loss of Lives Historians estimate that more than 55 million people died in the Second World War. Soviet soldiers and civilians comprised the largest group of dead—some 20 million. American losses, on the other hand, were much less—about 405,000.

The Holocaust As the victorious Allied armies drove into Poland and Germany, they found evidence of Nazi brutality. They discovered German-run concentration camps at Auschwitz, Buchenwald, and other locations. For years, the German administrators of these camps, using deadly gas, had carried out murders on a large scale. Their victims included some 6 million Jews from all parts of Europe. Many gypsies, various Slavic peoples, Catholic and Protestant leaders, labor leaders, and democratic politicians also were killed. The Nazis' systematic murder of all these people is now called the *Holocaust*.

When U.S. soldiers arrived at German concentration camps in 1945, they found some inmates who were alive, but half-starved and ill. Soldiers sprayed inmates to prevent the spread of diseases.

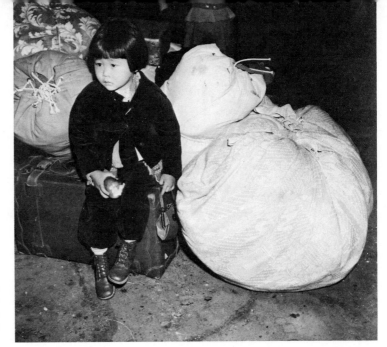

After the attack on Pearl Harbor, the U.S. government moved many Japanese-Americans away from the West Coast. They had to spend the rest of the war in camps.

Displaced Persons Millions of people in Europe and Asia lost their homes during the war. Moreover, many people lacked adequate food, clothing, fuel, money, and health services. The Allied armies that freed territories from Axis control were often responsible for dealing with these problems.

Relocated Japanese-Americans After the bombing of Pearl Harbor, people in California, Oregon, and Washington feared that they might become the next Japanese targets. Many also feared that Americans of Japanese ancestry would help Japan in an invasion. For these reasons, U.S. officials in 1942 relocated some 100,000 Japanese-Americans to camps away from the Pacific Ocean. Those relocated were virtual prisoners. Their detention was debated heatedly. Critics of relocation pointed out that relocated Japanese-Americans were loyal and many were U.S. citizens. Some came from families that had been in the United States for generations. Most important, said the critics, U.S. officials had disregarded the constitutional rights of the Japanese-Americans. They had not been charged with any crime and had never been tried for a crime in a court of law.

Occupation of Germany After the war, the Allies occupied Germany and divided it into four zones. The United States, Great Britain, France, and the Soviet Union each controlled a zone. Germany was stripped of all territories it had gained during the war. It also had to give up large areas to Poland and the USSR.

In Nuremberg, Germany, after the war, the Allies set up a special *tribunal* (court) to try Nazi leaders for "crimes against humanity." A number of those found guilty were executed; others received prison terms.

The Allies disarmed the German Army and prohibited Germany from rearming. Moreover, the defeated country had to pay reparations, mostly to the Soviet Union, for damages its invading forces had caused.

Occupation of Japan The Allies occupied Japan, too, after the war. Japan lost most of its territories outside the home islands. Like Germany, the country had to disarm. Later, a special court tried and convicted a number of Japanese leaders for crimes committed during the war. The Allies did give the Japanese one concession, however—the Emperor was allowed to stay on the throne.

SUMMING UP   We have seen how, until the United States was attacked, it resisted entering World War II. Once involved in the war, however, U.S. troops fought hard in Europe, North Africa, East Asia, and the Pacific. As in World War I, the United States helped turn the tide of war in favor of its allies.

Understanding the Text

On a separate sheet of paper, write the letter of the word or phrase that best completes each of the following statements.

1. The "blitzkrieg" was a new type of warfare used by   (a) Great Britain   (b) Germany   (c) Poland   (d) Belgium.

2. The Battle of Britain was fought mainly   (a) in the air   (b) at sea   (c) on land   (d) none of the above.

3. In exchange for giving Great Britain 50 destroyers, the United States received   (a) nothing   (b) 50 submarines   (c) title to British possessions in the Western Hemisphere   (d) leases on British naval bases in the Western Hemisphere.

4. The direct or immediate cause of the United States entry into World War II was the   (a) German invasion of Poland   (b) Japanese capture of the Philippines   (c) Japanese attack on Pearl Harbor   (d) Allied invasion of Europe.

5. German forces in North Africa were defeated by   (a) the United States alone   (b) Italy and Ethiopia   (c) Egypt and Albania   (d) combined British and U.S. forces.

6. The top commander of the Allied forces that invaded Normandy, France, in 1944 was

(a) Winston Churchill   (b) Dwight D. Eisenhower   (c) Douglas MacArthur   (d) Chester Nimitz.

7. The Battle of Midway Island, a turning point in the war, took place in   (a) North Africa   (b) the Atlantic   (c) Western Europe   (d) the Pacific.

8. Hiroshima and Nagasaki were   (a) Japanese-held islands off the coast of China   (b) German targets in the Battle of Britain   (c) Japanese cities destroyed by atomic bombs   (d) scenes of important battles in the North African campaign.

9. One result of World War II was that   (a) Japan lost most territories outside the borders of its home islands   (b) the United States took full responsibility for the occupation of Germany   (c) Nazi leaders were sentenced to death without a trial   (d) the Japanese Emperor was tried and executed.

10. From reading this lesson, one can conclude that   (a) the United States fought in World War II from the very beginning   (b) Germany and Japan were not easily defeated   (c) democratic governments always win wars   (d) Americans suffered more than did the people of any other country.

Developing Skills at Separating Fact From Opinion

In his *Memoirs*, President Harry S. Truman wrote about his decision of August, 1945, to drop two atomic bombs on Japan. He mentioned a painful alternative: he had been told that to invade Japan would cost about 500,000 U.S. lives. Truman's *Memoirs* imply that this prediction formed the basis of his decision.

Actually, there existed in 1945 an equally important reason for bombing Japanese targets. That summer, the Soviet Union was planning to enter the war against Japan. U.S. officials were of two minds about Soviet participation in the war in East Asia. On the one hand, the Soviet Union could help to force the Japanese to surrender sooner. On the other hand, the Soviet Union might take advantage of its role as an ally to seize Japanese-controlled lands and properties. It might even occupy part or all of Japan itself.

In February, 1945, at Yalta, the Soviets had promised to declare war on Japan. In exchange, the Allies had assigned the Soviets the Kuril Islands, Sakhalin Island, and an occupation zone in Korea. Moreover, the Soviets had the right to take over Japanese properties in Manchuria. U.S. officials reasoned that the sooner the Japanese were defeated, the fewer territories or properties the Soviet Union could claim. And if Japan surrendered *before* the Soviet Union declared war on that nation, maybe the Soviet Union would have no claims against Japan.

In the summer of 1945, Truman must have heard all these arguments. He also heard what might happen if the United States did not drop the atomic bombs on Japan. U.S. military advisers told him that the United States would not be ready to invade Japan until that fall. After that, it might take a year before the Japanese would surrender. During this time, the Soviet Union would be able to occupy much territory in East Asia. Thus, Soviet intentions must have been an important consideration in Truman's decision to drop the bombs on Japan.

Determine which of the following statements from the passage above are facts and which are opinions. On a separate sheet of paper, write *F* for statements that are facts and *O* for those that are opinions.

1. In his *Memoirs*, President Harry S. Truman wrote about his decision of August, 1945, to drop two atomic bombs on Japan.

2. Actually, there existed in 1945 an equally important reason for bombing Japanese targets.

3. On the one hand, the Soviet Union could help to force the Japanese to surrender sooner.

4. In February, 1945, at Yalta, the Soviets had promised to declare war on Japan.

5. After that, it might take a year before the Japanese would surrender.

Thinking About the Lesson

1. Do you think that President Roosevelt was correct in asking the United States to aid the British in 1940 and 1941? Why or why not?

2. How important a role did U.S. forces play in the Normandy invasion and the fighting against the Germans that followed?

The United States and Europe Since World War II

Since 1945, the United States has continued to play an active role in European affairs. It has cultivated military alliances with a considerable number of Western European nations. It has maintained valuable trade relations with these and other European countries. U.S. economic interests extend even to the Communist bloc nations of Eastern Europe.

U.S. Post-War Aid

As we learned in Lesson 79, much of the fighting during World War II took place in Europe. Europeans suffered millions of casualties. Moreover, their cities were ruined, industries and farms disrupted, and roads and railroads damaged.

After the war, Soviet-sponsored, Communist groups took control of many Eastern European countries. Communists were also active in France, Italy, Greece, and Turkey. In these four nations, Communists came close to either seizing power or winning national elections. U.S. leaders worried that if Communists came to power there, they would ally their nations with the USSR.

Some Americans thought that the best way to avoid further Communist expansion was to improve economic conditions in Europe. For that reason, the U.S. government gave generously to help the economies of European countries recover after the war:

• UNRRA. Beginning in 1943, the Allies spent large sums to relieve the widespread suffering in Europe. Much of the relief work was carried out by the UNRRA (the United Nations Relief and Rehabilitation Administration). Until 1947, when the organization was dissolved, the United States provided a large part of UNRRA's funds.

• Truman Doctrine. American leaders were especially worried that Communists might win control of Greece and Turkey. To counter this threat, President Truman in 1947 proposed giving these two countries economic and military aid. Under a program known as the "Truman Doctrine," the United States gave about $400 million. Partly as a result of this aid, Greece and Turkey remained non-Communist.

• Marshall Plan. Beginning in 1948, the United States spent about $12.5 billion in economic aid to Western Europe. Suggested by Secretary of State George C. Marshall, the Marshall Plan aid turned out to be highly successful. By the mid-1950s, the economies of Western European nations had recovered. Indirectly, the United States benefited from the aid as the European countries became active trading partners of the United States.

North Atlantic Treaty Organization

In 1949, the United States and certain European nations decided on another way to counter Soviet *expansionism* (increasing a country's influence or territory). They created the North Atlantic Treaty Organization. (European members of NATO are shown on the map on page 538. Canada and Iceland are also members.)

The United States has become the most powerful member of this military alliance. Americans have provided more soldiers and equipment than any other nation. The top military commander of NATO has always been an American.

Not all European nations joined NATO, however. Some, like Sweden and Switzerland, did not want to belong to any military alliance. They have remained neutral. Other nations have become part of the Soviet bloc.

Warsaw Pact As an answer to NATO, the Soviet Union in 1955 formed its own military alliance—the Warsaw Pact. In addition to the Soviet Union, Warsaw Pact members include Poland, East Germany, Rumania, Bulgaria, Czechoslovakia, and Hungary.

The Soviet Union remains by far the most powerful member of the Warsaw Pact. Member nations often set their foreign and domestic policies to correspond with those of the Soviet Union. Because Warsaw Pact nations follow the Soviet lead, they are called *satellites* of the Soviet Union. (A satellite is any country dominated or controlled by another.) The map on page 538 shows the location of Warsaw Pact nations.

At the end of World War II, Soviet troops occupied the eastern half of Germany, including this city, Leipzig. The Soviets helped Communists in East Germany set up a new government.

MILITARY ALLIANCES IN EUROPE TODAY

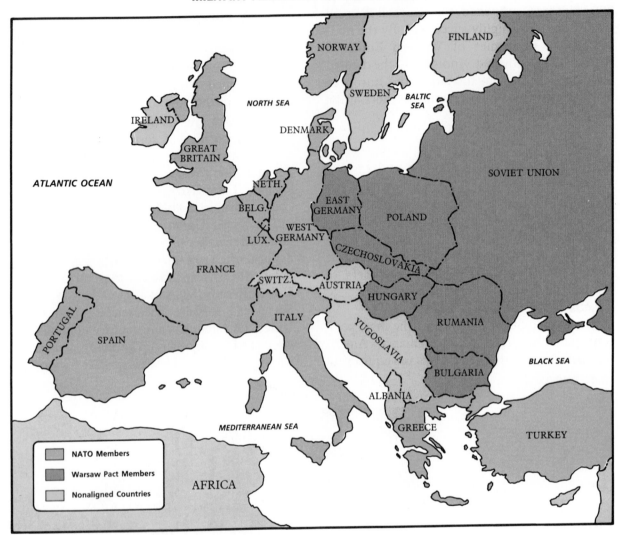

NATO Members

Warsaw Pact Members

Nonaligned Countries

Problems Within NATO Since NATO was formed, the alliance has been disrupted by disagreements among its members:

• Some Western Europeans believe that the United States has too much power in NATO. These critics want the European members to have more of a say in setting NATO's policies.

• Some NATO members do not wish to share control of their military forces with other members. Although France has retained its NATO membership, in 1966 it withdrew its armed

forces from the control of the NATO Command. Moreover, both France and Great Britain have kept their nuclear weapons out of NATO's control.

• Members of peace groups in Western Europe have called for the withdrawal of nuclear weapons from their countries. They have also opposed the U.S. policy of placing new nuclear missiles in certain European countries. These weapons are aimed at Eastern Europe and the Soviet Union. Opponents of the missiles are worried that Europe may become a battleground if a nuclear war breaks out.

• Other Europeans have a different fear. They believe that the United States might not be willing to defend them if a war with the Soviet Union begins. They say that American leaders might not be willing to risk the loss of many American lives to defend European ones.

• U.S. leaders want NATO to remain united and strong. They want nuclear missiles placed in Europe to counter Soviet ones in Eastern Europe. U.S. missiles might be withdrawn, they say, if the Soviet Union should withdraw its missiles.

• The United States also wants each NATO ally to strengthen its own non-nuclear weapon systems and increase the number of its soldiers. These efforts would help NATO defend Western Europe if the Soviet Union invaded.

In spite of some loud and angry criticisms of NATO, its policies are supported by the governments of most member nations. Moreover, most Europeans believe that a strong NATO is necessary to prevent Soviet expansion into Western Europe. Furthermore, they believe that U.S. troops and nuclear weapons are needed to help Western European nations defend themselves against the Soviets.

Economic Relations With Western Europe

U.S. leaders have long considered American economic ties with European countries to be very important. Their reasons are several:

• Western European countries such as France and West Germany are among the United States' strongest trade partners.

• U.S. investments in Western Europe are very large.

• Economic depressions and periods of prosperity in Western Europe affect the economic health of the United States.

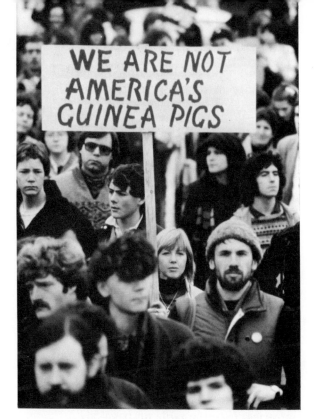

In 1982, crowds in Great Britain protested against the U.S. policy of placing more nuclear missiles in their country.

• A prosperous Western Europe is seen as a shield against Communist expansion there—whether by force or the election process.

The Common Market In 1957, many countries of Western Europe took an important action to help themselves. They formed the European Economic Community (EEC), also known as the "Common Market." The original members were France, West Germany, Italy, Belgium, the Netherlands, and Luxembourg. Since then, Great Britain, Ireland, Denmark, Greece, Portugal, and Spain have joined.

To a large extent, the EEC has helped to make much of Western Europe a single economic unit. It has practically done away with tariffs and other trade barriers among member nations. The EEC has made it possible for capital to move freely within the Common Market area. Moreover, workers of EEC nations can look for jobs in any member country.

The U.S. and the Common Market American leaders have strongly supported the Common Market. They have considered it to be good for European peace and prosperity. Strong European economies help to maintain America's prosperity and to prevent Communists from gaining more influence in Europe.

By its very nature, however, the Common Market has hindered U.S. trade with member nations. The EEC has set high tariff rates on certain products that member nations buy from outside the Common Market. U.S. farmers, manufacturers, and traders are hurt by these tariffs. In addition, surplus wheat from France and other Common Market members has been sold abroad at prices lower than what the wheat costs to grow. This practice has put American wheat farmers at a disadvantage. Nevertheless, considerable trade continues to take place between the United States and Western European countries. (See the table on page 542.)

The United States and Eastern Europe

In the years immediately after World War II, the United States had relatively few contacts with Eastern European states. These countries were well within the grip of the Soviet Union. In 1949, the Soviet Union and its European satellites formed an economic union called "COMECON." In addition to reducing trade barriers between member nations, COMECON increased Soviet control of the economies of each country.

As time went on, some Eastern European countries became more independent of Soviet control. Although Eastern European leaders wanted their nations to remain Communist, they were eager to have better economic relations with the West.

The United States has encouraged these expressions of independence. It has encouraged its own citizens to trade with Communist nations, especially Poland and Rumania. To help

Lech Walesa, leader of the independent Polish labor union Solidarity, worked as an electrician at the Gdansk Shipyard.

finance this trade, United States and other Western banks have made large loans to these countries. By 1985, Poland had the largest debt owed to the West by any Eastern European country—$31 billion worth. The Polish government has found it hard to pay back the loans or even make payments due on the interest from the loans. Because of problems such as this one, U.S. trade with Eastern Europe remains relatively limited. (See the table on page 542.)

The issue of U.S. economic relations with Eastern Europe has been controversial. Some Americans object to trading with or making loans to Communist nations. They say that these actions make the Communist regimes stronger. Other Americans defend economic relations with Communist nations as good for businesses. Moreover, they believe that the Communists' hold on these nations will naturally weaken as their people gain more contacts with the West.

Domestic unrest in Poland in the early 1980s created greater U.S. interest in that country. For the first time under Communist rule, an independent trade union movement became active there. Solidarity, led by a worker named Lech Walesa, defied Communist rulers by demanding better pay and working conditions. Members of the union also called for more personal freedom for the Polish people. Americans strongly supported the Polish workers. When the Polish government outlawed Solidarity in 1981, the U.S. government imposed trade sanctions against that country.

SUMMING UP   We have seen how the United States helped Western Europe recover from the destruction of World War II. The United States created some of its strongest trade relations and military alliances with Western European nations. In recent years, the U.S. has also gradually increased trade with and made loans to several Soviet satellite nations in Eastern Europe.

Understanding the Text

On a separate sheet of paper, write the letter of the word or phrase that best completes each of the following statements.

1. Two countries that were the object of U.S. military and economic aid under the Truman Doctrine were (a) Great Britain and France (b) the Soviet Union and Poland (c) Greece and Turkey (d) Spain and Italy.

2. The UNRRA was a (a) military alliance (b) relief organization (c) Western European trade group (d) Eastern European trade group.

3. Of the following statements about NATO, one *not* true is that (a) the United States has more soldiers in NATO than any other member (b) an American has always commanded NATO forces (c) France's armed forces are not under the control of NATO's Command (d) all European nations have joined NATO.

4. A country that belongs to the Warsaw Pact is (a) Hungary (b) Sweden (c) Great Britain (d) all of the above.

5. All of the following are members of the Common Market, *except* (a) the United States (b) Great Britain (c) France (d) Italy.

6. The Common Market (a) has banned all trade between the United States and member nations (b) has placed nuclear missiles in Europe aimed at the Soviet Union (c) has promoted free trade all over the world (d) has lowered tariffs on goods traded among member nations.

7. United States trade with Eastern Europe (a) is larger than U.S. trade with any other region of the world (b) is relatively small, but still important (c) was cut off with the formation of COMECON (d) is handled by the Common Market.

8. Poland is an example of a (a) country that benefited from the Marshall Plan (b) Soviet satellite that owes much money to Western banks (c) Soviet satellite that belongs to the Common Market (d) all of the above.

9. The dominant member of the Warsaw Pact is (a) Poland (b) Czechoslovakia (c) the United States (d) none of the above.

10. Which of the following statements best describes the policy of the United States toward the countries of Europe? (a) The United States tries to build firm ties with its friends and to improve relations with members of the Communist bloc. (b) Military matters are not important considerations in U.S. relations with European countries. (c) The United States hopes to gain complete control over the domestic affairs of Western European countries. (d) The United States depends entirely on military force to maintain its influence in Europe.

Developing Table-Reading Skills

U.S. FOREIGN TRADE, 1983
(In millions of dollars)

	Exports	Imports
Canada	$ 38,244	$ 52,130
Latin America	22,618	35,683
Western Europe	55,980	53,884
Eastern Europe	2,891	1,359
Middle East	13,796	7,135
Japan	21,894	41,183
East and South Asia	28,123	43,148
Africa	8,768	14,425
Total*	$200,538	$258,048

* The figures for world areas do not add up to the totals given because U.S. trade statistics with several Caribbean and Pacific Ocean nations are not listed.

Study the table above. Then choose the letter of the word or phrase that best answers each question. On a separate sheet of paper, match the question number with the correct letter.

1. To which country or world area listed in the table did the United States send the most exports in 1983? (*a*) Canada (*b*) Latin America (*c*) Western Europe (*d*) none of the above.

2. From which country or world area listed in the table did the United States receive the smallest amount of imports in 1983? (*a*) Canada (*b*) Eastern Europe (*c*) the Middle East (*d*) Africa.

3. What was the value of U.S. exports to East and South Asia in 1983? (*a*) $28,123,000 (*b*) $28,123,000,000 (*c*) $281,230,000 (*d*) $28,123.

4. Which was an example of a country or world area from which the United States bought more than it sold in 1983? (*a*) Japan (*b*) the Middle East (*c*) Eastern Europe (*d*) Western Europe.

5. Exports to Japan made up about what percentage of total U.S. exports shown in the table? (*a*) one (*b*) five (*c*) ten (*d*) twenty.

Thinking About the Lesson

1. Why were U.S. leaders greatly concerned about Communist influence in Europe after 1945?

2. What is the difference between economic and military aid? Which type of aid do you think was most effective in countering Communist influence in Europe?

3. Why do some Western Europeans criticize U.S. influence in NATO? Do you think that this criticism is justified? Why or why not?

4. Should Western European nations be doing more to provide for their own defense against a possible Soviet invasion? Explain your answer.

5. Do you think that United States companies should be trading with the Communist nations of Eastern Europe? Should U.S. banks loan money to these Communist countries? Explain your answers.

The United States and the Soviet Union

For decades, relations between the United States and the Soviet Union have overshadowed much of the rest of world history. Although the two powers were allies during World War II, afterward they became enemies. At times, relations between the two countries were so hostile that war seemed quite possible. At other times, tensions were reduced, and the powers were able to cooperate on a number of matters.

> The full name of the Soviet Union is the "Union of Soviet Socialist Republics," abbreviated "USSR." Sometimes the Soviet Union is called "Russia." In discussions of global rivalry, the United States and its allies are often called "the West," while the Soviet Union and its allies are called "the East."

Containment

After World War II, the United States brought most of its military forces home from Europe and East Asia. These men and women returned to civilian life.

The Soviet Union, however, kept large forces in the foreign territories that it had occupied during the war. It annexed some of these areas. Additions to the Soviet Union included Estonia, Latvia, and Lithuania and parts of Germany, Finland, Poland, Rumania, and Japan.

The presence of Soviet troops helped the Soviets to increase their influence over neighboring countries. The troops helped Communists come to power in Poland, Rumania, Bulgaria, Hungary, Czechoslovakia, and East Germany. These countries came under the control of the Soviet Union. Yugoslavia and Albania also became Communist.

United States leaders became alarmed over the Soviet actions. They decided to set definite limits upon the Soviet program of expanding its borders and influence. They would not try to remove the Soviets from any territory. Nevertheless, the United States would do everything it could to *contain* (hold) the Soviets to the lands they already controlled. This U.S. policy became known as *containment*.

Foreign Aid

At first, a major element of containment was to rebuild the economies of countries destroyed by the war. President Harry S. Truman believed that Communists were more likely to come to power in European countries where living standards were low. For this reason, the United

States spent billions of dollars on programs connected with the Truman Doctrine and the Marshall Plan. These programs are discussed in Lesson 80.

Point-Four Program   In 1949, President Truman proposed a foreign-aid program for Asia, Africa, and Latin America. His Point-Four Program emphasized giving expert advice and economic aid to *developing countries* (ones not industrialized). He wanted to improve their industries and agriculture. He also wanted to make developing countries less open to Communist influence.

In more recent decades, the United States foreign-aid program has been greatly expanded. In 1984, for example, the government spent about $15 billion in military and economic aid to countries around the world. Two of the best-known U.S. programs are the:

• Food for Peace Program. Since 1961, the United States has sent vast quantities of farm surpluses to needy foreign countries.

• Peace Corps. Introduced by President John F. Kennedy in 1961, this program has involved thousands of American volunteers. They have helped people in developing countries learn farming and building techniques. Moreover, the volunteers teach skills used in child care, sanitation, education, and the use of machinery.

Military Alliances

Another way that the United States has tried to check Soviet expansion has been to form military alliances.

NATO   In 1949, the United States joined with 11 other nations to set up the North Atlantic Treaty Organization. Most members of NATO consider the Soviet Union to be their main threat.

Organization of American States   The OAS, formed in 1948, binds the United States and Latin American nations in a military alliance.

On July 25, 1946, the United States tested an atomic bomb at Bikini Atoll (shown), in the Pacific Ocean. On September 24, 1949, the Soviet Union tested its first atomic weapons. The nuclear arms race was under way.

In 1948 and 1949, Allied transport planes such as this one flew supplies into Berlin. The Soviet Union had cut off ground transport routes between Berlin and the West.

Southeast Asia Treaty Organization (SEATO) From 1954 to 1977, eight nations were allied in the defense of Southeast Asia from Communist aggression. Besides the Soviet Union, China and North Vietnam were considered possible aggressors.

ANZUS In 1951, Australia, New Zealand, and the United States pledged themselves to the defense of the Pacific.

Mutual Defense Pacts The United States has alliances also with individual nations in various parts of the world. Signers of these *mutual defense pacts* have pledged to come to the aid of one another in case of an armed attack. U.S. allies include Japan, the Philippines, the Republic of South Korea, and Israel.

The United States has built military bases at many points around the globe. Some of these bases are located within the borders of its allies. Other bases have been set up on the soil of countries with which the United States has made special arrangements.

The Cold War

After World War II, the United States and the Soviet Union engaged in a rivalry known as the *Cold War*. For the most part, this war was not fought with guns and bullets. Instead, the two powers used mostly economic and political weapons. Each power wanted to gain the friendship and allegiance of other nations. Furthermore, the two rivals wanted to weaken each other's economic and political systems.

On several occasions, the Cold War heated up and threatened to result in a complete break in U.S.-Soviet relations.

Berlin Blockade After World War II, the four victorious powers divided Germany. France, Britain, and the United States occupied what came to be known as West Germany. The Soviets stayed in the eastern part—East Germany. The city of Berlin, which lies entirely in the Soviet zone, also was divided into a western and eastern part. Residents of Berlin were allowed access to West Germany by means of a highway and air transport.

Then in 1948, Communist authorities in East Germany suddenly cut off all land transportation between western Germany and Berlin. The aim of this blockade was to force the United States, France, and Britain out of the city. The Communists wanted to take over all of Berlin.

Led by the United States, the Western powers overcame the blockade. They organized a huge airlift, flying in thousands of tons of vital food, fuel, and other supplies to West Berlin. This effort was so effective that the Communists ended their blockade in 1949.

During the next decade, thousands of East Germans crossed into West Berlin. From there, many of these refugees moved into West Germany. The loss of so many people hurt the East German economy and embarrassed East German authorities. To stop the flight west, East Germany in 1961 built a long wall separating East and West Berlin. The Berlin Wall effectively cut down on the flow of refugees. Nevertheless, it became an embarrassing symbol of the unpopularity of the Communist regime in East Germany.

Cuban Missile Crisis Another Soviet-United States confrontation occurred in 1962. In that year, the United States announced to the world that the Soviet Union had placed nuclear missiles in Cuba. These weapons were aimed at some of the largest cities in the United States. In reaction to this threat, President John F. Kennedy took firm action. First, he put U.S. Navy ships in position around Cuba to prevent any further Soviet arms shipments there. Then he demanded that the Soviets remove the existing missiles, implying that the United States would go to war over the issue.

For several days, the world seemed to teeter on the brink of nuclear war. The crisis ended, however, when the Soviet leader, Nikita Khrushchev, agreed to withdraw the missiles.

Cooperation in the 1960s

Even at its worst, the Cold War did not end *all* forms of cooperation between the Soviet Union and the United States. In spite of bitter disagreements, the two powers recognized that they had to live in the same world. In the 1960s, they made several important agreements:

• Hot Line. In 1963, the two countries set up a special telegraph link between Moscow and Washington, D.C. Leaders of the two powers hoped that with this *Hot Line* there would be less danger of a war breaking out between them. The new means of communication could help the leaders avoid misunderstandings and delays in calling one another during an emergency.

• Nuclear Test-Ban Treaty. Also in 1963, the United States and the Soviet Union signed a limited *nuclear test-ban treaty*. They agreed to halt all further tests of nuclear devices in the air, under water, and in outer space. Subsequently, over 100 other nations joined in signing this agreement.

The Rise and Fall of Détente

In the 1970s, relations between the United States and the Soviet Union became even less strained. Although the Cold War continued, the two *superpowers* (strongest countries) found more matters on which to agree. This new spirit of cooperation, known as détente, developed during the administration of Richard M. Nixon. Nixon became the first U.S. President since Franklin Roosevelt to visit the Soviet Union.

U.S.-Soviet Trade As part of détente, trade relations between the two countries improved. The United States became a major supplier of grain to the Soviet Union.

Strategic Arms Limitation Talks (SALT) Beginning in 1969, the two powers began talks on limiting the number of nuclear weapons. By 1972, they had come up with a treaty, commonly called the "SALT I Agreement." Among other matters, this treaty called for a five-year halt to the making of certain types of *long-range nuclear weapons* (ones that can be sent from one continent to another).

Nuclear Test-Ban Treaties The two powers agreed in 1974 and 1976 to limit underground testing of nuclear weapons. These agreements expanded the terms of the 1963 Treaty on this subject.

Détente was a time of cultural exchanges and increased trade between the United States and the Soviet Union. Here Soviet people in 1976 visit an exhibit of U.S. history and technology.

SALT II In the late 1970s, the United States and the Soviet Union held another series of talks, called "SALT II." The powers signed a second treaty limiting the number of long-range nuclear weapons. Although the U.S. Senate refused to ratify the treaty, the two nations followed its terms.

Cultural Exchanges During the period of détente, the two countries sponsored cultural exchanges. Musicians, dancers, and actors of both nations visited the other nation and put on performances. Both countries also organized and sent to the other country important art shows.

Joint Scientific Activities The two powers cooperated in a number of scientific fields, including space exploration.

Strained Relations

Many Americans disliked the policy of détente. They said that the Soviets were using détente as a cover for aggressive activities. Critics of détente claimed that the Soviet Union in the 1970s was engaged in a major effort to build up its armaments. The critics also pointed out that the Soviets were expanding their influence in other countries. Vietnam, Cambodia, Angola, and Ethiopia all became Soviet allies in the 1970s. Then in 1979, the Soviet Union invaded its neighbor, Afghanistan. Soviet troops have been fighting in a civil war there ever since.

The Carter Administration For the most part, détente fell apart during the Carter administration. President Jimmy Carter denounced Soviet actions in Afghanistan. Because of Afghanistan, he cut off all U.S. grain sales to the USSR. The United States also boycotted the 1980 Summer Olympics, held in Moscow, the Soviet capital.

The Reagan Administration After Ronald Reagan took office in 1981, relations with the Soviets grew even worse:

• The United States denounced the Soviets for their part in suppressing dissent in Poland.

• President Reagan condemned the Soviet action of shooting down a South Korean airliner in 1983. Sixty Americans, including a member of Congress, were killed in this incident.

• In the early 1980s, the Soviet Union warned the United States not to install medium-range nuclear missiles in Western Europe. These missiles would be aimed at the Soviet Union. Nevertheless, in 1983 and 1984 the United States put the missiles in place. Reagan justified the action by pointing out that the Soviet Union had medium-range missiles aimed at Western Europe.

• In 1984, the Soviet Union boycotted the Summer Olympics, held in Los Angeles. Some people believe that the Soviets took this action in response to the U.S. boycott of the 1980 games.

SUMMING UP   We have seen how the Cold War developed between the United States and the Soviet Union after World War II as the Soviets extended their control over Eastern Europe. To contain further Soviet expansion, the United States helped form NATO and gave extensive economic assistance to many European nations. In the 1970s, the Cold War gave way to a new spirit of cooperation—détente. More recently, however, U.S.-Soviet relations have been marked by periods of hostility.

Understanding the Text

On a separate sheet of paper, write the letter of the word or phrase that best completes each of the following statements.

1. Of the following terms, one that does *not* belong with the others is (*a*) the West (*b*) Russia (*c*) the Soviet Union (*d*) USSR.

2. Of the following actions, the one that best describes the U.S. policy of containment is (*a*) creating Soviet satellites (*b*) sponsoring cultural exchanges (*c*) restricting the Soviet Union's influence to areas that it already controls (*d*) freeing Poland and other Eastern European countries from Soviet control.

3. Of the following, the one that was a military alliance to which the United States belonged was (*a*) Point-Four (*b*) SEATO (*c*) Food for Peace (*d*) SALT.

4. All of the following are part of the Cold War, *except* (*a*) battles between United States and Soviet troops (*b*) the creation of military alliances hostile to the other power (*c*) the Berlin airlift (*d*) the American-Soviet arms race.

5. A Cold War crisis took place in 1962 when President Kennedy (*a*) cut off wheat sales to the Soviet Union (*b*) boycotted the Olympics in Moscow (*c*) demanded the removal of Soviet missiles from Cuba (*d*) organized NATO.

6. All of the following are evidence of cooperation between the Soviet Union and the United States, *except* (*a*) the Hot Line (*b*) the Berlin blockade (*c*) the Nuclear Test-Ban Treaty (*d*) grain sales to the Soviet Union.

7. Détente began during the administration of (*a*) Harry S. Truman (*b*) John F. Kennedy (*c*) Richard M. Nixon (*d*) Jimmy Carter.

8. The policy of détente was weakened by (*a*) the Soviet invasion of Afghanistan (*b*) the shooting down of a Korean airliner (*c*) Soviet activities in Africa and Southeast Asia (*d*) all of the above.

9. The installation of U.S. medium-range missiles in Western Europe in 1983 and 1984 (*a*) was part of SALT I (*b*) was an example of a cultural exchange (*c*) was strongly opposed by the Soviet Union (*d*) had no effect on Soviet-American relations.

10. Which of the following statements best expresses a basic theme of this lesson? (*a*) The Cold War began during the Reagan administration. (*b*) The Cold War ended years ago. (*c*) The Cold War has been more intense at some times than at others. (*d*) Cold War rivalry has risen to such a frenzy that a nuclear war between the superpowers cannot be avoided.

Developing Graph-Reading Skills

SOVIET AND U.S. LONG-RANGE NUCLEAR WEAPONS, 1983

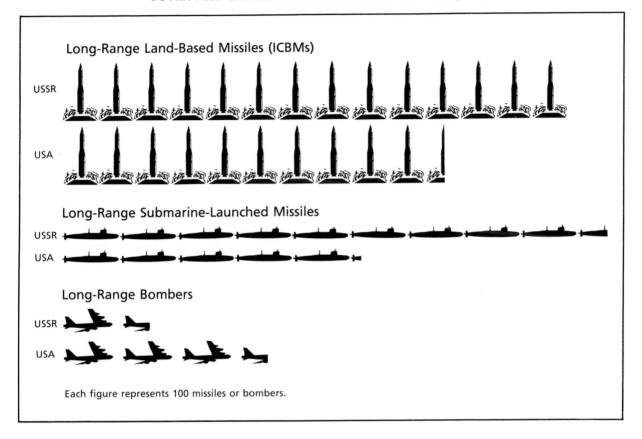

Each figure represents 100 missiles or bombers.

Study the picture graph above. Then choose the letter of the word or phrase that best answers each question. On a separate sheet of paper, match the question number with the correct letter.

1. How many ICBMs did the Soviet Union have in 1983? (*a*) 11 (*b*) 14 (*c*) 1,050 (*d*) 1,400.

2. How many ICBMs did the United States have in 1983. (*a*) 10 (*b*) 105 (*c*) 520 (*d*) 1,050.

3. About how many more long-range submarine-launched missiles did the USSR have than the United States? (*a*) 430 (*b*) 950 (*c*) 1,500 (*d*) 1,950.

4. Which of the weapons illustrated in the graph did the United States have more of than the Soviet Union? (*a*) long-range land-based missiles (*b*) long-range submarine-launched missiles (*c*) long-range bombers (*d*) none of the above.

5. A statistic *not* illustrated in the graph is the (*a*) number of submarines for each country (*b*) number of missiles carried by aircraft for each country (*c*) number of medium-range land-based missiles for each country (*d*) all of the above.

Thinking About the Lesson

1. Which military alliance of the United States do you consider the most important? Explain your answer.

2. Do you favor a return to the policy of détente with the Soviet Union? Why or why not?

3. Do you think that the Soviet Union and the United States will ever go to war against each other? Explain your answer. If you think a war is possible, describe what type of war this might be.

Wars in Korea and Vietnam

The United States has fought two major wars since 1945. Both took place in Asia—the first, in Korea, and the second, in Vietnam. The United States got involved in these two wars because it wanted to contain Communist expansion. In both cases, the wars had a strong effect on the political, economic, and social life of the United States.

Korea

Korea had been a Japanese colony from 1910 to 1945. After Japan had been defeated in World War II, the United States and the Soviet Union each sent forces into Korea. The two powers agreed to divide the country temporarily. While the U.S. Army occupied the southern half of Korea, Soviet troops controlled the northern half. The 38th parallel of latitude became the dividing line between the two zones of occupation. (See the map on page 552.)

Two Separate Countries   U.S. leaders thought that the United Nations soon would be able to hold elections in all of Korea. Most Koreans hoped that the elections would lead to the *reunification* (joining together again) of their country. The Soviet Union, however, refused to allow these elections in its zone of occupation.

Instead, it helped a Communist regime come to power in North Korea.

In the south, UN-sponsored elections held in 1948 led to the setting up of a South Korean government. By 1949, both U.S. and Soviet troops had left the divided Korean *Peninsula* (piece of land surrounded by water on three sides).

Outbreak of War in Korea

North Korea seemed intent on bringing all of Korea under Communist rule. For that reason, it invaded South Korea in 1950, overrunning most of the country.

U.S. Reaction   The United States persuaded the United Nations to declare North Korea the *aggressor* (one who starts a fight) and to authorize military action against it. Since the UN had no forces of its own, President Harry Truman sent U.S. forces to South Korea to fight under the UN flag. In time, 15 other UN member-nations supplied military aid, but on a smaller scale.

Expansion of the War   At first, the UN forces were victorious, even though the Soviets supplied the North Koreans with arms. UN troops repelled the North Korean invaders, crossed

551

the 38th parallel, and went deep into North Korea. This action caused Communist Chinese troops to enter the war on the North Korean side. The combined Communist forces were able to push the UN ones deep back into South Korea.

As neither side was able to gain a clear victory, the two sides began peace talks in 1951. The talks dragged on for almost two years while the fighting continued. Finally, in 1953, an *armistice* (a temporary end to fighting) was set. Korea was divided at about the same line as the one that had divided it before the fighting started. The Armistice Line, shown on the map, still serves as the border between North and South Korea.

Effects of the War

The Korean War affected Americans in many ways. About 54,000 U.S. soldiers were killed. The war cost U.S. taxpayers some $20 billion. As with most wars, heavy military spending resulted in inflation. The U.S. government, though, was able to slow the inflation rate by setting up wage and price controls in 1951.

Rise in Military Preparedness   The war showed the world that the United States could stop Communist aggression. The government increased the size of the U.S. Armed Forces by some 2.2 million people—to a total of 3.6 million. United States allies in NATO also undertook military expansion programs during the Korean War.

Concern About Internal Security   The war had at least one important effect on domestic politics. It fueled debates among Americans about how much Communist influence there was in the United States. (This topic is discussed on page 384.)

A Divided Korea   After the war, Korea remained divided. Communist North Korea has

been called one of the most repressive countries in the world. South Koreans have enjoyed more freedom than North Koreans, but their government, too, has been criticized for using undemocratic methods. Both Korean governments have expressed the wish for peaceful reunification of Korea. Even so, chances for success of such a plan in the near future do not look good.

THE KOREAN WAR, 1950–1953

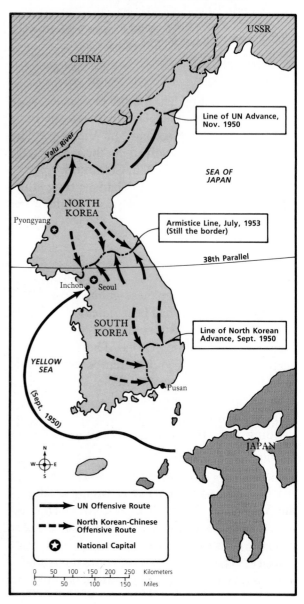

When UN forces captured Pyongyang in October, 1950, some residents of the North Korean capital celebrated. Notice the UN flag flying from the building on the right.

U.S. Defense of Korea Since the war, the United States has kept thousands of troops stationed in Korea. The United States is committed to defend South Korea in case there is another Communist invasion.

Vietnam

In the 19th century, France made a colony of a large area of Southeast Asia. Vietnam was a major part of this colonial empire known as "French Indochina." Then during World War II, Japan took control of Indochina, as well as other Asian territories. (See the map on page 531.) A Vietnamese independence movement, the Vietminh, fought the Japanese. After the war, the Vietminh turned their guns against the French, who had reclaimed their empire. For years, French forces fought the Vietminh, who were led by Ho Chi Minh, a Communist.

The United States began to get involved in the war in 1950. In that year, it gave military and economic aid to the French to help them defeat the Vietminh. U.S. leaders were worried that Communists would try to take over Vietnam as Communists had done in China in 1949.

French Defeat In 1954, the Vietminh finally defeated the French forces. By then, the French were ready to get out of all of Indochina. Leaders of interested nations met in Geneva, Switzerland, to decide on the future of the area. They divided the former French empire into the independent countries of Vietnam, Cambodia, and Laos. Vietnam itself was divided for the time being into two parts at the 17th parallel of latitude. Vietminh forces under Ho Chi Minh were allowed to keep control of North Vietnam. Non-Communist Vietnamese were to rule in South Vietnam. Elections were supposed to be held in 1956 in all of Vietnam.

SOUTHEAST ASIA, 1954–1975

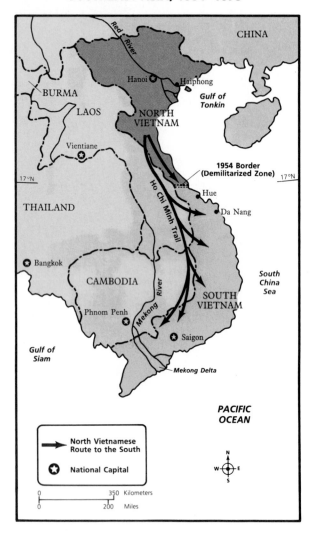

In 1960, some of Diem's opponents joined together in the National Liberation Front (NLF). The NLF came to be called the "Vietcong," which means "Vietnamese Communists." Supported by North Vietnam, the Vietcong fought the forces of the South Vietnamese government. In time, the Vietcong won many victories and controlled many areas of Vietnam.

The NLF did not comprise the only opposition to the Diem government. Buddhists complained that Diem favored the Catholics in Vietnam. South Vietnamese students protested that his methods were repressive. Even some officers in the South Vietnamese Armed Forces thought Diem was bad for their country. In 1963, a group of officers overthrew Diem and murdered him. A succession of weak, unpopular South Vietnamese governments followed.

United States Entry Into the War

In the early 1960s, U.S. aid to Vietnam was limited to money, supplies, and military advisers. As the South Vietnamese Army continued to lose ground, however, the United States became more involved.

U.S. participation in the war was based on the *domino theory*. According to this idea, if South Vietnam fell to the Communists, so would Cambodia. If Cambodia fell, Thailand would, too, and so on. Unless the United States acted, all of Southeast Asia would fall into Communist hands.

Tonkin Gulf Resolution   The United States never formally declared war on anybody in Vietnam. In 1964, though, President Lyndon Johnson did obtain congressional approval for U.S. involvement. North Vietnamese patrol boats were reported to have opened fire on two U.S. destroyers in the Gulf of Tonkin. Angered by this report, Congress passed the Tonkin Gulf Resolution. It allowed the President to "take all necessary measures" to protect American forces and prevent aggression.

The Outbreak of Civil War

Fearing that the Communists would win, South Vietnamese President Ngo Dinh Diem refused to hold elections. The United States backed Diem on this matter and supplied him with much military and economic aid. Diem diverted some of this aid to enrich himself and his relatives. For this reason, the Diem regime was widely criticized as being corrupt and undemocratic.

In 1965, U.S. planes began bombing targets in North Vietnam. Moreover, in that year the first U.S. ground forces landed in Vietnam and immediately went into combat. Soon the United States was taking on a major part of the fighting. The nature of the enemy itself changed in 1965 as North Vietnam began sending its soldiers into South Vietnam in large numbers.

Domestic Opposition to the War

The conflict dragged on for years. The United States inflicted heavy losses on the Vietcong and their North Vietnamese allies. Nevertheless, they would not surrender. Every year, the U.S. government sent more troops to Vietnam until, in 1968, over 500,000 were stationed there.

Anti-War Protests Within the United States, the war caused bitter disagreements. On a scale never before seen in the country, Americans protested U.S. involvement in Vietnam. Opposition to the war was especially strong among young people in schools and colleges. Some young men avoided the draft or deserted from the services rather than be sent to Vietnam.

Critics of the war said that the enemy did not threaten United States security. They believed that a U.S. victory in Vietnam, if possible at all, could not justify the high costs in lives and resources. Furthermore, the critics said, the United States had no right to interfere in a civil war in another country. They believed that the Vietnamese people alone should decide their own fate.

Despite the anti-war sentiment, many Americans continued to support the war effort. They believed that it was the duty of the United States to stop Communist aggression. Many supporters of the war also wanted to make sure that the United States did not lose the war.

Withdrawal of U.S. Troops

In 1969, knowing that public opinion was deeply divided, President Richard Nixon began to withdraw U.S. troops. Nixon's plan was to "Vietnamize" the war. He wanted South Vietnamese soldiers, aided by U.S. equipment and training, to take over most of the fighting.

Helicopters played an important role for U.S. forces in Vietnam. The aircraft transported soldiers and supplies in and out of the jungle.

Peace Negotiations During the Vietnamization process, National Security Adviser Henry Kissinger sought peace. He negotiated with representatives of North Vietnam and the Vietcong. In 1973, a cease-fire agreement was signed, making it possible for the United States to bring its troops home.

Results of the War in Vietnam

The Vietnam War had many consequences for the United States—most of them bad.

Communist Victory in Vietnam After the United States withdrew in 1973, the Communist forces stepped up their attack in South Vietnam. In 1975, they took Saigon, the capital city, and forced the South Vietnamese Army to surrender. South Vietnam ceased to exist as all of Vietnam became a single, Communist country in 1976.

Communists in Laos and Cambodia During the Vietnam War, local Communist groups, aided by North Vietnam, had been battling with the governments of nearby Laos and Cambodia. In 1975, these Communists—the Pathet Lao in Laos and the Khmer Rouge in Cambodia—took control of their countries. Their victories had been made easier by the withdrawal of U.S. forces from Vietnam and the defeat of the South Vietnamese government.

Although the United States lost its influence in Indochina, Communist governments in the region are far from united. In 1978, Vietnam invaded Cambodia, setting up a new Communist government there. Then in 1979, Communist China invaded Communist Vietnam, briefly occupying a small area along their common border.

Southeast Asian Refugees In 1975, the United States helped some 100,000 South Vietnamese leave their country. Many of these refugees came to the United States to live. Since then, hundreds of thousands of other South Vietnamese, Laotian, and Cambodian refugees have made their way to the United States.

Loss of Prestige U.S. prestige declined because the United States failed to win the war. Moreover, its ally, South Vietnam, suffered a crushing defeat. Some observers believe that the United States would never have been able to defeat Communist forces in Vietnam. Others believe that if the United States had stayed, it would have eventually won the war.

War Powers Act The power of the President to get the country involved in wars was another casualty of Vietnam. While only Congress can declare war, United States Presidents have on several occasions sent troops into battle without a declaration. Congress, in the War Powers Act of 1973, restricted the President's powers to take such an action. Under terms of this law, a President must notify Congress within 48 hours after sending troops abroad for combat duty. In this report, the President must explain the reasons for sending the troops. After 60 days, the President must withdraw the troops unless Congress has specifically approved the action.

Casualties The Vietnam War was the longest one in U.S. history. During the war, more than 56,000 Americans died and several times that number suffered injuries.

Economic Consequences The United States government spent some $140 billion on the war effort. It had to borrow much of this money. The resulting high national debt contributed to the country's inflation problem.

Because the government spent so much on defense, it lacked enough funds for domestic programs, such as the War on Poverty. Many projects, such as the rebuilding of inner cities, were put aside or abandoned.

SUMMING UP   We have seen how the United States fought two wars in order to stop Asian nations from falling into Communist hands. In Korea, U.S. troops entered the war soon after it had started. They have remained in Korea even though the fighting ended in 1953. In Vietnam, the United States participated only after years of fighting had occurred; its troops left Vietnam even before the war had ended.

Understanding the Text

On a separate sheet of paper, write the letter of the word or phrase that best completes each of the following statements.

1. The basic purpose of the United States entry into the Korean War in 1950 was to *(a)* defend South Korea against Communist aggression *(b)* conquer North Korea *(c)* reunify Korea *(d)* bring the Soviet Union into the war.

2. The United States fought in the Korean War *(a)* under the UN flag *(b)* against the wishes of the UN *(c)* to defend the UN *(d)* without the authorization of the UN.

3. As a result of the Korean War, *(a)* Korea was reunited *(b)* there were still two Korean states *(c)* all U.S. forces were withdrawn from Korea *(d)* all of Korea became Communist.

4. Before and after World War II, Vietnam was a colony of *(a)* Great Britain *(b)* France *(c)* the United States *(d)* Mexico.

5. In 1954, Indochina was divided into the countries of *(a)* China and India *(b)* Laos, Cambodia, and North and South Korea *(c)* North and South Vietnam *(d)* North and South Vietnam, Laos, and Cambodia.

6. Of the following people or organizations, one *not* an opponent of the government of South Vietnam in 1963 was *(a)* Ngo Dinh Diem *(b)* Ho Chi Minh *(c)* the Vietminh *(d)* the National Liberation Front.

7. The Tonkin Gulf Resolution *(a)* called for the withdrawal of all U.S. forces from Vietnam *(b)* tried to arrange a compromise peace in Vietnam *(c)* authorized the President to take military action to protect U.S. forces in Southeast Asia *(d)* called for the reunification of Vietnam.

8. The domino theory *(a)* was a plan for free trade in East Asia *(b)* described the Vietnamization of the war *(c)* demanded immediate withdrawal of U.S. forces from Vietnam *(d)* predicted the fall of other countries if South Vietnam was defeated.

9. The defeat of South Vietnam in 1975 was followed by *(a)* French rule in Indochina *(b)* unification of Cambodia and Laos *(c)* unification of North and South Vietnam *(d)* the complete triumph of Communism in Asia.

10. In both the Korean and Vietnam wars, the United States *(a)* fought under the authority of the United Nations *(b)* fought large numbers of Chinese troops *(c)* defended a non-Communist, Asian government *(d)* kept its troops in the country long after the fighting had ended.

Developing Map Skills

Study the map of Korea on page 552. Then choose the letter of the word or phrase that best completes each sentence. On a separate sheet of paper, match the sentence number with the correct letter.

1. According to the map, the North Koreans had advanced the farthest into South Korea in (a) September, 1950   (b) November, 1950 (c) January, 1951   (d) July, 1953.

2. The line of the United Nations' farthest advance into North Korea (in November, 1950) was south of the   (a) line of North Korean advance of September, 1950   (b) 38th parallel of latitude   (c) Armistice Line of July, 1953 (d) China.

3. The capital city of North Korea is (a) Pusan (b) Seoul (c) Inchon (d) Pyongyang.

4. North Korea has common borders with all of the following countries, *except*   (a) Japan (b) China (c) the Soviet Union   (d) South Korea.

5. Inchon   is   in   present-day   (a) China (b) North Korea (c) South Korea (d) none of the above.

Thinking About the Lesson

1. Do you think that the United States was right to have gone to the defense of South Korea in 1950? Why or why not?

2. Neither side won the Korean War. Should the United States have continued to fight Communist forces until they had been defeated and driven out of North Korea? Explain your answer.

3. Why was U.S. involvement in the Vietnam conflict less popular at home than its involvement in the Korean War had been?

4. Why did the governments of South Vietnam, Laos, and Cambodia all fall to Communist forces in 1975?

LESSON 83

U.S. Relations With China and Japan

Since 1945, United States concern with East Asia has centered not only on Korea and Vietnam, but also on its relations with two other countries—China and Japan. China is significant because of its great size, vast population (about 1 billion), strategic location, and growing political influence. Japan has emerged in recent years as a major economic power. Although it has a small area (about the size of California), Japan is densely populated by some 120 million people. In the production of goods and services, its economy is the second largest in the world, exceeded only by that of the United States.

China

After World War II, the Japanese troops that had been occupying much of China returned home. The Chinese Communists and Chinese Nationalists were left to resume their long-standing civil war, first discussed in Lesson 78. In this new phase of the conflict, both sides were aided by outside powers. The United States helped the Nationalists, while the Soviet Union gave military assistance to the Communists.

Communist China In 1949, the Chinese Communists, led by Mao Tse-tung, finally defeated the Nationalist forces under Chiang Kai-shek. Several million Nationalists fled the mainland and settled on Taiwan—a large island off the Chinese coast. (See the map on page 560.)

The Communists set up a new government on the mainland—the People's Republic of China (PRC). This government, which still rules, is sometimes referred to as "Communist China," "Red China," or "Mainland China."

United States' China Policy

For decades after the Communists' victory, the United States refused to recognize the PRC. Instead, the U.S. continued to accord recognition to the Nationalists on Taiwan as the only Chinese government. Moreover, U.S. officials helped the Nationalist government keep China's only seat in the United Nations. In that world organization, China held a permanent position on the Security Council.

A number of other factors contributed to the poor relations between the United States and the PRC:

• From 1950 to 1953, U.S. and Chinese troops fought each other in the Korean War. During this time, the Chinese feared that U.S. forces might cross over into their country from Korea. Meanwhile, Americans feared that the Chinese were trying to expand beyond their borders in East Asia.

• In 1950, the Soviet Union and Communist China formed a military alliance. Because of this pact, some U.S. leaders thought that China was being used in a Soviet plot to take over the world.

• Several times in the 1950s, Communist China threatened to invade Taiwan in order to reunite China. As part of this threat, Communist China bombed the Nationalist-held islands of Quemoy and Matsu. (See the map below.) In 1955, in reaction to the threats, the United States pledged itself to the defense of Nationalist-held territories.

• China and the United States were on opposite sides in the Vietnam War. As we learned in Lesson 82, U.S. troops fought against the North Vietnamese. China did not fight, but it sent to North Vietnam military and economic aid and *logistical troops* (soldiers that transport supplies).

• The United States banned U.S. citizens from trading with Communist China and restricted them from visiting that country.

• In defining their *ideology* (set of political views), the leaders of the PRC named the United States as their main enemy.

Chinese-Soviet Split

The close relations between the Soviet Union and Communist China did not last long. After the Soviet leader Joseph Stalin died in 1953, Mao Tse-tung considered himself the world's foremost Communist leader. He resented

CHINA AND JAPAN TODAY

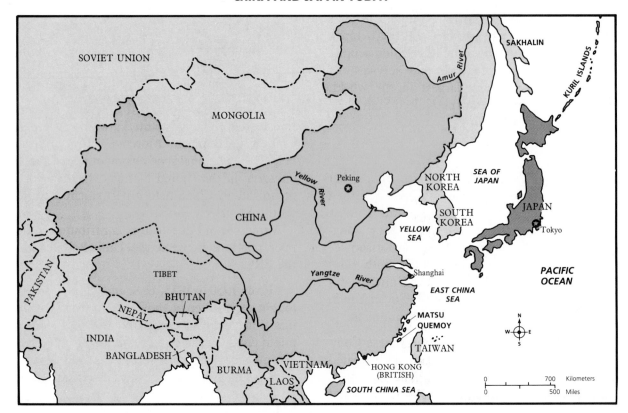

When President Nixon visited Mainland China in 1972, he and his wife Pat (center) toured a segment of the Great Wall of China. Secretary of State William Rogers (second from the right) also served on the U.S. delegation.

attempts by Nikita Khrushchev and other Soviet officials to tell China what policies to follow. Mao claimed to be the true supporter of *Marxism* (the basic ideas of Communism as set down by Karl Marx in the 19th century). Another matter of Chinese-Soviet friction involved the claims of the Soviets and Chinese to the same territories along their common border. Several times, their armed forces along the border clashed. By the late 1960s, the Chinese feared that the Soviets might invade their country.

Because of the decline in Soviet-Chinese relations, Chinese foreign policy took a new turn. China's leaders decided to improve their relations with the West, including the United States. President Richard Nixon and Security Adviser Henry Kissinger seized this opportunity.

A New China Policy

In the 1970s and 1980s, United States relations with Mainland China greatly improved. The United States stopped opposing the entry of the PRC into the United Nations. As a result, in 1971 Communist China got the UN seat formerly held by Nationalist China.

In 1972, Nixon became the first U.S. President to visit Communist China. While there, he signed agreements to open trade and cultural relations between the two countries. In following years, the United States and China exchanged groups of musicians, actors, athletes, and scholars. U.S. businesses sent representatives to China to negotiate valuable trade contracts. During the Nixon administration, limited diplomatic relations were set up. Not until 1979, though, did the United States and the PRC officially recognize each other and exchange ambassadors.

Problems With the New China Policy

Although United States-Chinese relations have improved, they are not as friendly as some observers thought they might become. A number of problems hinder further improvements, including the following:

Technology Transfers Mainland China is still a Communist country. It might again become an enemy of the United States. For that reason, many Americans oppose allowing the export of U.S. equipment that might have military uses.

Trade For a similar reason, some Americans oppose any trade with Communist China. Trade might help this potential enemy grow stronger, they say.

In recent years, another trade problem has developed. Because of a lower standard of living, China is able to produce certain goods at a much lower cost than U.S. factories can. Thus, China can flood U.S. markets with its low-cost textiles and other goods, driving U.S. competitors out of business. Fearing Chinese competition, U.S. producers have called for protective tariffs and other restrictions on Chinese imports.

Taiwan Communist China's leaders claim that Taiwan is a *province* (state) of the PRC. They say that the PRC has a right to take over Taiwan at any time. They have told the United States that restoration of normal relations is impossible until the U.S. recognizes the PRC's claim and stops selling arms to Taiwan. The United States, however, refuses the PRC's demands. Many Americans want Taiwan to remain independent. Therefore, the United States continues to sell arms to Nationalist China. Another bond that ties the United States to Taiwan is money. Many U.S. citizens carry on trade with or invest in that island nation. These Americans fear what might happen if the Communists take over there.

The U.S.-Chinese conflict over Taiwan lessened somewhat in 1982 when Mainland China announced its goal of peacefully reuniting Taiwan with the rest of China. Chinese Communist leaders promised that in such a reunification, Taiwan would be able to keep its capitalist economy. In response to this announcement, U.S. leaders agreed to reduce U.S. arms sales to Taiwan.

U.S. TRADE WITH COMMUNIST CHINA, 1972–1984

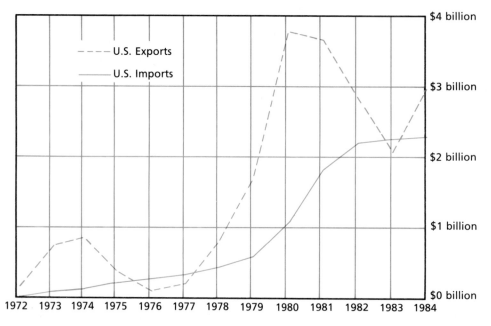

Japan

After Japan's defeat in 1945, the country was occupied by Allied forces, mostly from the United States. The Allied occupation under General Douglas MacArthur had two main aims: to create a democratic form of government and to disarm the Japanese.

Constitution of 1947

The Allies imposed on Japan a democratic form of government defined by a new Constitution that went into effect in 1947. Even though the Emperor was allowed to remain on the throne, he no longer had any political power. The strong influence of military figures in the government also ended. With the Constitution of 1947, Japan gained a new, two-house legislature. This Diet has more power to control the Prime Minister than had Japan's pre-war Diet. An independent supreme court and a bill of rights were also new features of the 1947 Constitution.

Disarmament Under its new Constitution, Japan did away with its armed forces. Furthermore, it pledged itself not to use force in its relations with other nations. The Japanese, however, believe that the Constitution allows them to set up "Self-Defense Forces." These forces now number over 200,000 people. (By contrast, the PRC has some 4 million military personnel.)

Peace Treaty

In 1951, the United States and some of its wartime Allies signed a peace treaty with Japan. By the terms of this treaty, the Allied occupation ended. Some people considered that the treaty, coming only six years after a bitter war, was very generous. For instance, the Allies did not attempt to hold back the country's economic recovery. Japan, though, was required to give up its claims to territories that it had gained before and during the war. Moreover, as we learned earlier, Japan had to remain disarmed.

The treaty was significant in that it restored Japanese *sovereignty* (freedom from foreign control). Japan could now apply for membership in the United Nations, which it joined in 1956. Japan could also enter into military alliances.

U.S.-Japanese Security Treaty

In 1951, Japan signed a treaty with the United States, whereby the larger power became Japan's protector. In return, the United States gained the right to maintain military bases and armed forces on Japanese territory. This treaty provision was especially important during the Korean War. In this conflict, the United States used Japan as a base from which to launch many of its military operations.

Over the years, the U.S.-Japanese Security Treaty has been renewed several times. Japan still allows the United States to keep bases and troops on its territory. Some Japanese, however, dislike this arrangement. They want Japan to conduct a more independent foreign policy and not act as a junior partner of the United States.

Legacy of Hiroshima and Nagasaki As we learned in Lesson 79, the Japanese are the only people who have been targets of nuclear bombs. In reaction to the Japanese experience, the Diet prohibits any nuclear weapons in Japan. For the same reason, some Japanese oppose all military ties with the United States. They are afraid that if Japan gets involved in another war, its islands may become a nuclear battleground.

The Issue of Defense A majority of Japanese people, fearing Soviet intentions in East Asia, favor military ties with the United States. This

In the last several decades, Japanese cargo ships have become an increasingly common sight in U.S. ports. This ship is visiting Seattle, Washington.

majority also wants Japan to improve its ability to defend itself. Each year the government has spent increasing amounts of money to build up its armed forces. Japanese leaders hope that Japan can soon take over from the United States the defense of the air- and the sea-lanes around their country. The United States would welcome such a development, as well as other signs of Japanese willingness to defend themselves.

Japan's Economic Growth

With the end of the Allied occupation, Japan's economy began to develop. The Japanese quickly repaired the damage done during the war. They set up many new factories that used the most modern methods and equipment. Although Japan is poor in natural resources, it has become the most prosperous country in East Asia.

Today, Japan produces a vast array of high-quality goods that compete favorably in markets all over the world. This feat makes it possible for the Japanese people to enjoy a high standard of living. Japanese exports pay for its large quantity of imports, including essential foods and oil.

Trade With the United States

Japan has become the United States' second largest trading partner. (See the table on page 542.) Japanese manufactured goods, such as automobiles and cameras, are sold in large numbers in the United States. Japan is also a leading customer for U.S. exports, especially agricultural products. This Japanese-American trade, although beneficial to both countries, has caused the United States some problems.

Trade Deficit   In recent years, Japan has been exporting much more to the United States (in dollar value) than it has been importing from this country. For Japan, this balance of trade is favorable. The United States, on the other hand, has an unfavorable balance of trade with Japan. Japanese trade policies, including trade regulations and taxes, are partly to blame for this situation. These policies make it difficult for foreigners to sell goods in Japan. In the early 1980s, U.S. trade representatives tried to get the Japanese government to remove some of its import restrictions. In 1983, the Japanese agreed, cutting tariffs on over 40 goods that were imported into Japan.

Competition Some Americans have complained that the Japanese sell their products in the United States more cheaply than U.S. competitors can. A prime example in the early 1980s was the selling of inexpensive but well-built Japanese automobiles in the United States. The low purchase prices of these cars benefited U.S. consumers. Manufacturers of U.S. cars, though, suffered from the competition and had to cut production. As a result, many American automobile workers lost their jobs. To help solve this problem, U.S. officials asked Japan voluntarily to limit its annual shipment of automobiles to the United States. From 1981 to 1984, the Japanese government imposed such quotas. American automobile manufacturers soon began to sell more cars. Nevertheless, the United States trade balance with Japan in automobiles and many other products continues to be unfavorable.

SUMMING UP We have seen how U.S. relations with Japan have been quite different from its relations with China. Japan, a defeated nation in 1945, has become a major trading partner of the United States. In addition, Japan has played an important role in U.S. security interests in East Asia. U.S. relations with Communist China, though, have not been so close. The United States established full diplomatic relations with the PRC only recently—in 1979. China, though, with its large population and rich resources, has the potential to replace Japan as the United States' major trading partner and ally in East Asia.

Understanding the Text

On a separate sheet of paper, write the letter of the word or phrase that best completes each of the following statements.

1. Of the following names, one that does *not* belong with the others is (*a*) People's Republic of China (*b*) Nationalist China (*c*) Communist China (*d*) Mainland China.

2. U.S. and PRC troops fought each other in (*a*) Korea (*b*) Taiwan (*c*) Japan (*d*) Vietnam.

3. The U.S. attitude toward the PRC in the 1950s and 1960s can best be described as (*a*) normal (*b*) indifferent (*c*) hostile (*d*) friendly.

4. The first U.S. President to visit the People's Republic of China was (*a*) Truman (*b*) Kennedy (*c*) Nixon (*d*) Reagan.

5. The United States recognized Communist China in (*a*) 1949 (*b*) 1954 (*c*) 1972 (*d*) 1979.

6. After World War II, a policy of the United States and its wartime allies was to (a) punish all of the Japanese people (b) put Japanese military leaders back in control (c) help to make the Japanese government more democratic (d) get rid of the Japanese Emperor.

7. Allied occupation of Japan ended when (a) Japan adopted the Constitution of 1947 (b) a peace treaty was signed by Japan and some of the Allies (c) the United States and Japan concluded a security treaty (d) Japan joined the United Nations.

8. One major area of disagreement between the United States and Japan in recent years concerns (a) trade policies (b) the Japanese desire to invade Taiwan (c) Japanese membership in the United Nations (d) resistance to Soviet expansion in East Asia.

9. In recent years, the United States has been encouraging Japan to (a) sell more automobiles in the United States (b) increase the size of its defense budget (c) maintain its restrictions on imports (d) disarm.

10. Japan today far exceeds China in (a) land area (b) population (c) economic development (d) size of armed forces.

Developing Graph-Reading Skills

Study the line graph on page 562. Then choose the letter of the word or phrase that best completes each sentence. On a separate sheet of paper, match the sentence number with the correct letter.

1. In 1980, U.S. exports to China were (a) under $1 billion (b) between $1 billion and $2 billion (c) between $2 billion and $3 billion (d) between $3 billion and $4 billion.

2. A year in which U.S. imports from China were closest to $1 billion was (a) 1975 (b) 1977 (c) 1980 (d) 1981.

3. A year in which U.S. exports to China were less than U.S. imports from that country was (a) 1974 (b) 1976 (c) 1979 (d) all of the above.

4. A year in which U.S. exports and imports in its trade with China were roughly equal was (a) 1973 (b) 1979 (c) 1981 (d) 1983.

5. During the period 1972–1984, the United States had a favorable balance of trade with China for (a) 3 years (b) 10 years (c) 12 years (d) 13 years.

Thinking About the Lesson

1. The People's Republic of China was established in 1949. Why did the United States wait so many years before it recognized this government?

2. Communist China has demanded that the United States end its military assistance to the Nationalist Chinese government. Do you think that the United States should give in to this demand in order to improve relations with Communist China? Why or why not?

3. Why was Japan disarmed by the Allies at the end of World War II? Should Japan now be allowed to rearm as much as it wants? Explain your answer.

4. Why are many Japanese people especially worried about nuclear weapons?

5. Why are some Americans concerned about the nature of U.S.-Japanese trade? What, if anything, should be done about this matter?

LESSON 84

The United States and the Middle East

Since World War II, the Middle East has become one of the world's leading "danger spots." Wars have broken out there again and again. Many nations outside of the region, including the United States and the Soviet Union, are concerned with the outcome of these conflicts.

Importance of the Middle East

The Middle East is one of the world's under-developed areas. Why, then, is it so important in world affairs and to the United States in particular? There are three basic reasons—the location of the region, its great oil resources, and its instability.

Strategic Location Historians have called the Middle East the "crossroads of the world." As the map on page 568 shows, the Middle East is located where Europe, Asia, and Africa meet. Since ancient times, its waterways have served as vital trade routes. These waterways include the Mediterranean Sea, the Red Sea, the Straits of the Dardanelles and the Bosporus, and the Persian Gulf. Any nation controlling one or more of these waterways could choke off shipments of essential materials. The United States wants to keep these waterways out of the hands of the Soviet Union and other unfriendly powers.

Oil Resources Middle East countries control some of the world's largest known *oil reserves* (oil still in the ground). Saudi Arabia, Iraq, Iran, Kuwait, and the United Arab Emirates are all major producers of oil. They export huge quantities to the United States and many other countries.

Middle East oil-producing nations have taken advantage of their power as suppliers of oil. In 1960, a group of them set up the Organization of Petroleum Exporting Countries (OPEC) in order to establish prices for the sale of their oil in world markets. Some non-Middle East states, such as Venezuela and Nigeria, also joined OPEC. In the 1970s, OPEC forced oil prices up sharply. Between 1973 and 1980, the cost of a barrel of *crude oil* (unrefined oil) multiplied by six. The higher prices were especially painful for developing nations in Africa, Asia, and Latin America. Oil is important to these countries not only as a fuel, but also in the production of fertilizer. As the price of oil went up in the 1970s, fewer farmers could afford to buy fertilizer. As a result, food production in many developing nations fell drastically.

To a limited extent, the United States, too, relies on Middle Eastern oil. (See the graphs on page 569.) In the 1970s when OPEC raised its prices, U.S. consumers had to endure sharp

567

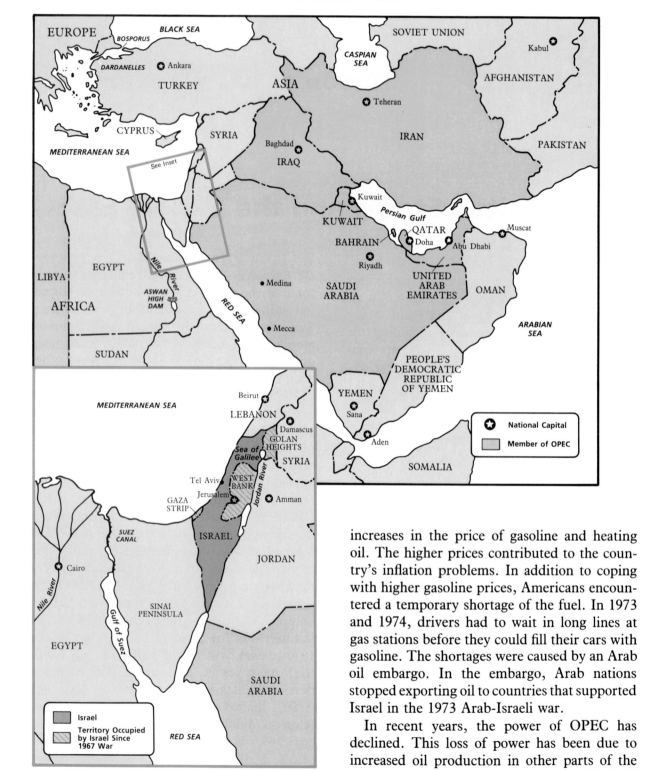

Map labels (main map):

EUROPE • BLACK SEA • BOSPORUS • DARDANELLES • Ankara • TURKEY • ASIA • SOVIET UNION • Kabul • CASPIAN SEA • AFGHANISTAN • Teheran • CYPRUS • SYRIA • IRAN • PAKISTAN • MEDITERRANEAN SEA • Baghdad • IRAQ • Kuwait • Persian Gulf • Muscat • KUWAIT • QATAR • Doha • Abu Dhabi • BAHRAIN • Riyadh • UNITED ARAB EMIRATES • OMAN • LIBYA • EGYPT • Nile River • Medina • SAUDI ARABIA • ARABIAN SEA • AFRICA • ASWAN HIGH DAM • RED SEA • Mecca • SUDAN • PEOPLE'S DEMOCRATIC REPUBLIC OF YEMEN • YEMEN • Sana • Aden • SOMALIA

See Inset

Legend:
★ National Capital
Member of OPEC

Inset map labels:

MEDITERRANEAN SEA • Beirut • LEBANON • Damascus • GOLAN HEIGHTS • Sea of Galilee • SYRIA • Tel Aviv • WEST BANK • Jordan River • Jerusalem • Amman • GAZA STRIP • ISRAEL • JORDAN • SUEZ CANAL • Cairo • Nile River • Gulf of Suez • SINAI PENINSULA • EGYPT • SAUDI ARABIA • RED SEA

Inset legend:
Israel
Territory Occupied by Israel Since 1967 War

increases in the price of gasoline and heating oil. The higher prices contributed to the country's inflation problems. In addition to coping with higher gasoline prices, Americans encountered a temporary shortage of the fuel. In 1973 and 1974, drivers had to wait in long lines at gas stations before they could fill their cars with gasoline. The shortages were caused by an Arab oil embargo. In the embargo, Arab nations stopped exporting oil to countries that supported Israel in the 1973 Arab-Israeli war.

In recent years, the power of OPEC has declined. This loss of power has been due to increased oil production in other parts of the world. Worldwide energy conservation efforts have also helped make nations less dependent on Middle East sources. As a result, OPEC has been forced to lower its oil prices. Nevertheless, the United States wants to be sure that it and its allies continue to receive enough Middle East oil to help meet energy needs.

Instability In recent decades, the Middle East has been a region of tension and turmoil. Israelis and Arabs have fought several wars. Inter-Arab political, religious, and economic differences have further complicated the tense situation.

Arab-Israeli Wars

From World War I until after World War II, the British had ruled Palestine with the approval of the League of Nations. In 1947, after Britain announced it was going to give up its control over Palestine, the UN voted to partition Palestine into an Arab state and a Jewish one. The Palestinian Arabs rejected the plan. The Jewish population accepted it and in 1948 proclaimed the state of Israel as an independent nation. The United States, the Soviet Union, and many other nations recognized the new country.

Most Arab nations and Palestinian Arabs, however, opposed Israel's existence. Within days after Israel's establishment, armies from neighboring Arab states invaded Israel in an effort to destroy it. The new Israeli Army defeated them. Jordan, meanwhile, took over most of the area that under the UN plan was supposed to become an Arab Palestinian country. This territory is called the "West Bank."

Since the creation of Israel, the Israelis and Arabs have fought five wars—in 1948, 1956, 1967, 1973, and 1982. Israeli forces have won military victories in each of these conflicts. After the 1967 war, Israel continued to occupy territories it had captured in that conflict, including:

• The West Bank of the Jordan River, from Jordan.
• The Golan Heights, from Syria.

U.S. PETROLEUM SOURCES AND CONSUMPTION, 1976–1982

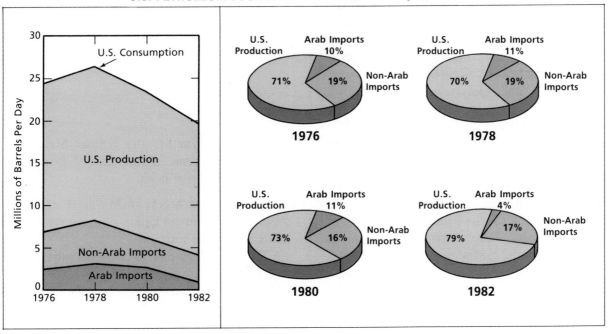

• The Sinai Peninsula and Gaza Strip, from Egypt. (See the inset map on page 568.)

Israeli leaders claimed that keeping the new territories was essential to the country's *security* (safety). Arab leaders said that peace would not be possible unless Israel returned the lands taken in 1967. Furthermore, Arab nations favored creating a Palestinian Arab nation on at least some of the territory now controlled by Israel.

Issues of Conflict

A number of factors help explain the continuing conflict between Israel and the Arabs.

Creation of Israel   Most Arabs were opposed to the creation of Israel. They say that the area formerly called Palestine—including the present territory of Israel—belongs to the Palestinians, since Palestinian Arabs have made up the large majority of the population for centuries. Palestinians say that the creation of a Jewish state dispossessed them of their land. Israelis argue that the establishment of their state is the fulfillment of their historical rights to a homeland. They say that Jews have lived in the region since ancient times, even after the Romans destroyed the Jewish commonwealth 2,000 years ago. At this time, most Jews *dispersed* (moved away) to other parts of the world, a movement called the *Diaspora.*

The PLO   The Palestine Liberation Organization (PLO), an organization of several Arab anti-Israeli groups, claims to represent the Palestinians. It has stated that it wants Israel destroyed so that the area can be settled by Palestinians. For this reason, Israel does not recognize the PLO and refuses to deal with it. Israeli leaders say that the PLO is not a legitimate government, but a gang of *terrorists.* (Terrorists are people who spread terror through violence in order to achieve political goals.) PLO attacks have cost the lives of Israeli civilians, including women and children.

Palestinian Refugees   An unresolved problem for Israel is the existence of the Arab Palestinian population, both inside and outside Israel. As Israel was being created and was fighting wars with Arab countries, many Palestinians fled from Israel to go to surrounding Arab states. They became refugees. Several hundred thousand Arab refugees continue to live in United Nations refugee camps in Jordan, Syria, Iraq, Lebanon, the West Bank, and the Gaza Strip. Others have established more settled lives, working and living in Israel and other Middle Eastern nations. Quite a number have moved to Europe and North America.

Many Palestinians look forward to the day when they can either return to their former homes or go to some other land set aside for Palestinians. However, the situation is complex. Neither Israel nor its neighboring Arab states want to take in more refugees than they already have. Nor do Israel or its neighbors want to give up territory to create a Palestinian state. Israelis fear that Palestinian Arabs are violently anti-Israel and would cause trouble if more were allowed to settle in Israel or if a Palestinian state was created next to Israel.

U.S. Policies in the Middle East

Since World War II, the United States has played a leading role in the affairs of the Middle East. Its goals have been:

• To safeguard access to Middle East oil by preventing the Soviet Union from becoming too influential in the area.

• To preserve Israel as a democratic, independent nation.

• To maintain friendly relationships with some Arab nations, particularly with those that are less hostile to the United States.

Safeguarding Access to Oil U.S. leaders fear that if the Soviet Union gains a foothold in the Middle East, it could be in a good position to cut off vital oil sources to the United States and Western Europe. In 1955, the U.S. helped organize (but did not join) the Central Treaty Organization or CENTO. This short-lived defense alliance against Soviet aggression in the Middle East consisted of Britain, Turkey, Iran, Iraq, and Pakistan. In 1958, U.S. troops were sent to Lebanon at the government's request to prevent Communist-supported rebels from seizing power. U.S. policy received a serious setback in 1979 when Soviet forces invaded and took control of Afghanistan in order to support a weak, pro-Soviet regime. U.S. leaders worried that the Soviets might next invade neighboring Iran. The Soviet Union has built up its naval fleet in the Indian Ocean and the Mediterranean Sea. The Soviets have also sought allies in the Middle East. They have given much military and economic aid to Syria and several other Arab states.

In 1980, President Jimmy Carter stated that any attempt by an outside force to take control of the Persian Gulf region would be repelled by the U.S. At about the same time, he called for the creation of a U.S. Rapid Deployment Force. It would be sent to the Middle East or other areas of the world if a military threat developed.

Support of Israel The United States was the first country to recognize Israel when it became independent. Since then, a special, close relationship has developed—one benefiting both nations. The United States and Israel have formed a military alliance. Israel receives more U.S. economic and military aid than any other country in the world.

The U.S. feels that Israel's existence as a strong, pro-West state is in America's strategic interest. Israel's military forces are considered the strongest in the Middle East. In case of a military emergency, Israel could serve the United States as a supply depot and a refueling base. Its military forces could be pooled with those of NATO or the United States.

In the United Nations, the United States has repeatedly refused to support resolutions that brand Israel as an aggressor. The U.S., like Israel, says it will not deal with the PLO until that group recognizes Israel's right to exist.

U.S. troops were first sent to Lebanon in 1958. Here Lebanese civilians watch a U.S. convoy pass by.

One of the main accomplishments of President Jimmy Carter (center) was to bring together Egyptian President Anwar Sadat (left) and Israeli Prime Minister Menachem Begin. Their 1978 meeting produced the Camp David Agreements.

Friendly Relations With Other Nations

Although the U.S. supports Israel, it has attempted to be "even-handed" with Israel's neighbors by giving them assistance as well. In order to win their support, it has given economic aid in the form of loans and grants to Jordan, Saudi Arabia, Kuwait, Egypt, and other Middle East countries. It has also sold them military weapons. In 1981, despite Israeli objections, the U.S. sold five advanced radar warning planes (called "AWACS") to Saudi Arabia. Until the Iranian monarchy was overthrown in 1979 and Iran's relations with the U.S. were severed, Iran and the United States were close. U.S. arms sales to Iran enabled that nation to play the role of "guardian" of the Persian Gulf in the 1970s. Friendly relationships have also been maintained with moderate Arab states, particularly Saudi Arabia and Jordan.

The United States has indicated that there are limits to its support of Israeli policies. In each of the wars between Israel and the Arab states, the U.S. has called for a cease-fire in order to avoid total defeat of the Arabs. The U.S. also criticized Israel for sending its troops into Lebanon in 1982 in order to wipe out PLO strongholds serving as bases for guerrilla attacks on Israel. Moreover, the U.S. has criticized Israel for increasing the number of Israeli settlements in the occupied West Bank.

U.S. Efforts at Peace and Stability

In recent years, the United States has tried to promote peace in the Middle East.

Camp David Agreements

In 1978, President Carter was able to bring together for discussions the leaders of Egypt and Israel. President Anwar Sadat and Prime Minister Menachem Begin met with President Carter at Camp David, near Washington, D.C. They drew up the Camp David Agreements which led to a peace treaty between Israel and Egypt.

Israeli-Egyptian Peace Treaty

In 1979, a peace treaty that grew out of the Agreements was finally signed. In accordance with its provisions, Israel returned to Egypt the Sinai Peninsula, taken during the 1967 war. In return, Egypt agreed to recognize Israel's right to exist. No other Arab nation had done this.

United States leaders hoped that the "Spirit of Camp David" would lead to better relations between Israel and other Arab states. There has, however, been very little progress along these lines. In 1982, both sides rejected a peace plan proposed by President Ronald Reagan. He had recommended giving the Palestinians on the West Bank and the Gaza Strip *autonomy* (self-rule) in association with the government of Jordan.

U.S. Failures in the Middle East

Two recent events in the Middle East damaged the prestige of the United States in the region: the Iranian hostage crisis and U.S. involvement in Lebanon's civil war.

Hostage Crisis In 1979, during the revolution that brought the new Islamic regime to power in Iran, militants broke into the U.S. Embassy in that country. They were angry about U.S. support for the former Iranian leader, Shah Mohammad Reza Pahlavi. The militants seized U.S. officials and employees and held 52 of them as hostages for over a year. To secure their return, the Carter administration applied diplomatic and economic pressure on the new Iranian government. U.S. forces even tried a small military operation to rescue the hostages. Nothing seemed to work. Not until early in 1981 were the hostages finally released.

Because the U.S. could not force the hostages' release for over a year, it appeared weak. The U.S. position in the Middle East was also weakened because it lost a valuable Middle East ally—the Iranian government under the Shah. The new Iranian leaders, led by the Ayatollah Khomeini were bitterly anti-American.

Fight Against Terrorism The Middle East has been the scene of many acts of terrorism. The hijacking of airlines, the blowing up of cafes, and numerous kidnappings and killings have been some of the more dramatic examples. Many terrorists support the idea of creating an independent Palestinian state. They oppose the existence of Israel and have directed much of their wrath at Israelis and supporters of Israel. Tourists, soldiers, diplomats, and businesspeople from the United States, Europe, and Israel have been typical terrorist targets.

The United States has tried to fight terrorism using several methods. It has improved security at its embassies and military bases abroad. It has urged authorities at airports in the Middle East and Europe to be more vigilant. The United States, Israel, and some European nations have exchanged information about terrorists and their plans.

People concerned about terrorism have come to believe that several Middle Eastern governments give aid and encouragement to terrorists. They believe that Libya, Syria, and Iran provide funds and weapons to terrorist groups. These governments are said to train terrorists in methods of fighting and using weapons and to provide them with places to hide.

The United States has retaliated against Libya for its support of terrorism. U.S. officials have refused to allow Americans to buy oil directly from Libya. In 1986, President Reagan went a step further by ordering the bombing of cities and military bases in Libya. The raid was a success in that the targets were hit and the U.S. lost only one plane. Critics of the bombing, though, doubted that this form of retaliation against Libya would stop terrorism.

SUMMING UP We have seen how the Middle East's strategic location and oil resources make the region very important for U.S. foreign policy. Because conflicts in the area threaten U.S. interests there, the United States would like to improve its relations with many Arab nations. This desire, however, sometimes comes into conflict with the U.S. intention of keeping its special relationship with Israel.

Understanding the Text

On a separate sheet of paper, write the letter of the word or phrase that best completes each of the following statements.

1. All of the following are vital international waterways found in the Middle East, *except* the (*a*) Red Sea (*b*) Panama Canal (*c*) Mediterranean Sea (*d*) Straits of the Dardanelles and the Bosporus.

2. An oil-producing state located in the Middle East is (*a*) Nigeria (*b*) Venezuela (*c*) Saudi Arabia (*d*) the Soviet Union.

3. All of the following statements about OPEC are true, *except* that (*a*) all members of OPEC are Arab nations (*b*) OPEC was founded in 1960 (*c*) Arab members of OPEC stopped selling oil to some countries in 1973 and 1974 (*d*) OPEC drastically raised the price of a barrel of crude oil in the 1970s.

4. From 1920 to 1948, Palestine was (*a*) controlled by the British (*b*) an independent Jewish state (*c*) an independent Muslim state (*d*) an independent Christian state.

5. The establishment of the state of Israel was supported in 1948 by (*a*) both the United States and the Soviet Union (*b*) the United States, but not the Soviet Union (*c*) all nations of the world (*d*) Israel's Arab neighbors.

6. In its 1967 war with its Arab neighbors, Israel captured (*a*) the West Bank (*b*) the Golan Heights (*c*) the Sinai Peninsula (*d*) all of the above.

7. The Camp David Agreements (*a*) led to the creation of a homeland for all Palestinian Arabs (*b*) led to a peace treaty between Egypt and Israel (*c*) were arranged by the Soviet Union (*d*) solved most political problems that Israel had with its Arab neighbors.

8. In 1979 and 1980, 52 U.S. citizens were held hostage in the U.S. Embassy in (*a*) Iraq (*b*) Lebanon (*c*) Iran (*d*) Israel.

9. In 1986, U.S. planes bombed targets in Libya in order to (*a*) force OPEC to sell more oil (*b*) help the PLO (*c*) counter Israeli influence there (*d*) retaliate against Libyan support of terrorists.

10. Of the following objectives, one *not* a part of U.S. Middle East policy is to (*a*) defend the independence of Israel (*b*) buy all the oil produced in the region (*c*) help build a firm and lasting peace (*d*) stop the Soviet Union from expanding its power and influence in this area.

Developing Graph-Reading Skills

Examine the line and pie graphs on page 569. Then choose the letter of the word or phrase that best answers each question. On a separate sheet of paper, match the question number with the correct letter.

1. In which of the years shown on the line graph was total U.S. petroleum consumption the greatest? (*a*) 1976 (*b*) 1978 (*c*) 1980 (*d*) 1982.

2. In 1976, about how many millions of barrels of petroleum did the United States import from Arab nations each day? (*a*) 1 (*b*) 2.5 (*c*) 7 (*d*) 25.

3. In which of the years shown on the line graph were petroleum imports from Arab nations the lowest? (*a*) 1976 (*b*) 1978 (*c*) 1980 (*d*) 1982.

4. In 1980, petroleum imports from Arab nations accounted for what percentage of total U.S. consumption? *(a)* 5 *(b)* 9 *(c)* 11 *(d)* 16.

5. Which of the following can one conclude from reading the graphs? Between 1978 and 1982, *(a)* the United States became less dependent upon imported petroleum *(b)* Americans used less petroleum *(c)* U.S. petroleum imports from Arab nations declined *(d)* all of the above.

Thinking About the Lesson

1. The United States has great reserves of oil and gas. It also imports much petroleum from non-Arab nations. Why then, is the U.S. government so concerned about preventing unfriendly nations from gaining control over Middle East oil fields?

2. Should the United States maintain its special political, military, and economic relations with Israel? Explain your answer.

3. Do you think that the United States should recognize the PLO? Why or why not?

4. Would it be correct to call the United States a "Middle East peacemaker"? Explain your answer.

The United States and Latin America

Since 1945, the United States has continued to seek close relations with Latin American governments. It has helped many of these nations with loans, grants, technical assistance, and military aid. On occasion, the United States has intervened in the domestic affairs of Latin American nations. Some of these acts of intervention have been designed to prevent the spread of Communism in the Western Hemisphere.

Military Cooperation

In the early 20th century, the United States had been the self-appointed defender of the Western Hemisphere. In 1948, however, the United States and Latin American nations took a step toward changing their military relationships. The United States and 22 other nations of the Western Hemisphere formed a military alliance—the Organization of American States. The OAS provides a system of collective defense against attack from both outside and within the Western Hemisphere. Members agree to cooperate to resolve disputes. Accomplishments of the OAS include:

• Peacekeeping in the Dominican Republic. In 1965, a revolt against the Dominican government led to a civil war. President Lyndon Johnson sent U.S. Marines there to protect the lives of American citizens and to prevent what he feared would become a Communist takeover. Then he asked the OAS to join the United States in the Dominican Republic. A five-nation OAS peacekeeping force remained in that country until after elections were held in 1966.

• Settlement of a border clash between El Salvador and Honduras in 1969.

The Organization of American States is not as strong a military alliance as the North Atlantic Treaty Organization. The OAS has no permanent military force. As with NATO, the United States is the most powerful member of the OAS. This alliance has often responded to U.S. requests, such as joining in the 1965 intervention in the Dominican Republic. The OAS also responded to U.S. pressure when the alliance suspended Cuba from active membership in 1964. The OAS called on members to end all diplomatic and trade relations with that Communist country.

In recent years, members of the OAS have shown less unity. Moreover, the organization has become less effective as a military alliance. The OAS, for example, did not act in 1982 when a war broke out between Argentina and Great Britain over the Falkland Islands.

LATIN AMERICA TODAY

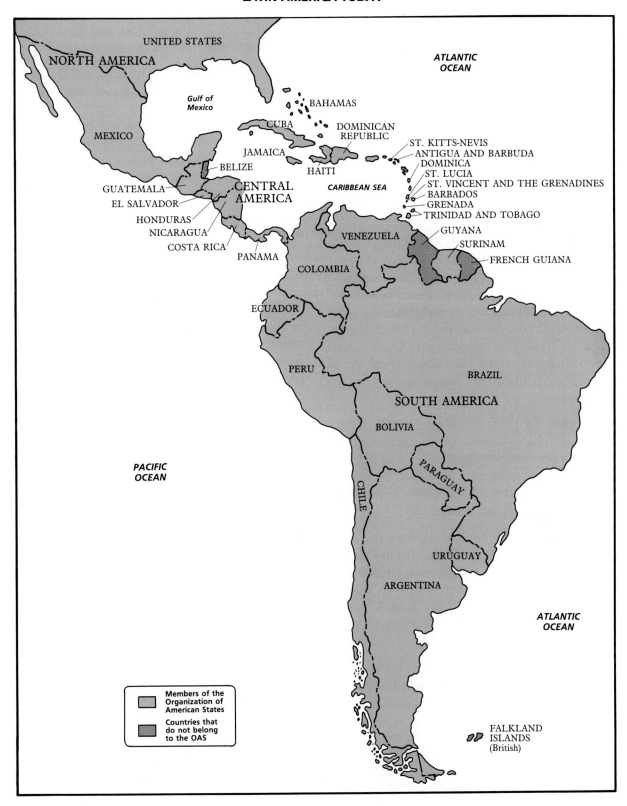

- UNITED STATES
- NORTH AMERICA
- ATLANTIC OCEAN
- Gulf of Mexico
- MEXICO
- BAHAMAS
- CUBA
- DOMINICAN REPUBLIC
- JAMAICA
- BELIZE
- HAITI
- ST. KITTS-NEVIS
- ANTIGUA AND BARBUDA
- DOMINICA
- ST. LUCIA
- ST. VINCENT AND THE GRENADINES
- GUATEMALA
- CENTRAL AMERICA
- CARIBBEAN SEA
- BARBADOS
- GRENADA
- EL SALVADOR
- TRINIDAD AND TOBAGO
- HONDURAS
- GUYANA
- NICARAGUA
- VENEZUELA
- SURINAM
- COSTA RICA
- FRENCH GUIANA
- PANAMA
- COLOMBIA
- ECUADOR
- PERU
- BRAZIL
- SOUTH AMERICA
- BOLIVIA
- PACIFIC OCEAN
- PARAGUAY
- CHILE
- URUGUAY
- ARGENTINA
- ATLANTIC OCEAN
- FALKLAND ISLANDS (British)

Members of the Organization of American States

Countries that do not belong to the OAS

Both Argentina and Britain claimed ownership of the Falkland (Maldive) Islands in the South Atlantic. The United States, being allied to both countries, was placed in a difficult situation. It ended up supporting Britain in the Falkland conflict. As a result, U.S. relations with Argentina reached an all-time low.

Relations With Cuba

In 1959, rebel forces led by Fidel Castro overthrew the Cuban dictatorship of Fulgencio Batista. The Castro regime took over foreign-owned industries (including some owned by U.S. businesses) and established close ties with the Soviet Union. In 1961, the United States broke off diplomatic relations with Cuba. Soon Castro announced that he was setting up a Communist political and economic system in that country.

Bay of Pigs   In 1961, President John F. Kennedy approved a Central Intelligence Agency plan to try to overthrow Castro. The CIA helped a group of anti-Communist Cubans living in Florida invade Cuba. This invasion at the Bay of Pigs, however, failed miserably.

Cuban Missile Crisis   Embarrassed by the Bay of Pigs incident, President Kennedy felt that he had to act forcefully in 1962 when he found out that the Soviets were putting missiles in Cuba. As we learned in Lesson 81, the United States was able to force the Soviets to back down and remove the missiles.

Recent Developments   The United States continues to refuse to open normal diplomatic relations with Cuba. United States officials argue that Castro has been trying to export revolutions in Latin America and Africa. Cuba has helped train and arm rebels in many countries, including Bolivia, Colombia, El Salvador, Guatemala, Nicaragua, Peru, and Venezuela.

From time to time, Cuba and the United States have made efforts to improve relations:

• In 1980, Castro permitted several hundred thousand Cubans to emigrate to the United States.

• The two governments permit limited trade between Cuba and the United States.

• The Cuban and U.S. governments cooperate whenever one of their nationals hijacks a plane to the other country.

Despite these and other signs of cooperation, distrust and hostility continue to keep the two countries apart.

U.S. Intervention in Latin America

In the last three decades, the United States has resumed its policy of intervention in Latin American countries. Besides the Bay of Pigs invasion of 1961 and the Dominican Republic crisis of 1965, both mentioned earlier, other U.S. actions include the following:

Premier Fidel Castro is known for making long speeches to his Cuban supporters. In this three-hour speech of September 2, 1960, Castro threatened to oust Americans from the U.S. naval base in Guantánamo, Cuba.

When the United States invaded Grenada in 1983, one of its goals was to take control of this airport from the Cubans, who had been constructing it. Members of the U.S. 82nd Airborne Division are shown guarding the airport.

• In 1954, the United States helped rebels in Guatemala overthrow a government believed to be pro-Communist.

• In 1973, CIA agents helped overthrow the government of Chile, in South America. Before the overthrow, Chile had been governed by a Socialist—President Salvador Allende Gossens.

El Salvador In 1981, the Reagan administration decided to intervene actively in a civil war in El Salvador. Salvadorean rebels were trying to overthrow the government of this small Central American country. U.S. leaders charged that the rebels were Communist-led and that they were receiving aid from Cuba and the Soviet Union. For these reasons, the United States has sent arms and financial aid to the Salvadorean government. In addition, U.S. military advisers have helped to train Salvadorean troops.

Nicaragua Also during the Reagan administration, the United States attempted to overthrow the Nicaraguan government that had come to power in 1979. This new, Sandinista regime had developed close ties with Cuba and had limited the freedom of the Nicaraguan press. It had also aided rebels in El Salvador, a neighbor of Nicaragua.

The United States backed small-scale military operations against the Sandinistas. The rebel forces, operating from Honduras and Costa Rica, were made up of Nicaraguans opposed to the government. The U.S. also tried to weaken the Sandinistas by imposing economic sanctions against Nicaragua.

Grenada In 1983, U.S. military forces invaded Grenada, a small island republic in the Caribbean Sea. U.S. leaders voiced concern about the safety of U.S. students and the growing influence of Cubans in Grenada. The United States soundly defeated Cuban and Grenadian soldiers there. The U.S. action paved the way for a new group of Grenadians to take power.

Controversy Over Intervention The issue of U.S. intervention in the domestic affairs of Latin American countries is controversial. Some people in the United States believe that intervention is sometimes necessary to prevent Communist groups from gaining control. They say that it is in the U.S. strategic interests to keep other nations non-Communist. Other Americans have problems with U.S. intervention. Critics of intervention say that the United States should not get involved in internal conflicts. They claim that often there is no real Communist threat in most places where the U.S. intervenes. In addition, critics say that in fighting supposed

U.S. ECONOMIC AID TO SELECTED COUNTRIES, 1962–1983

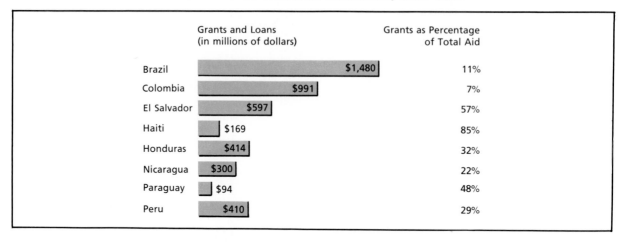

	Grants and Loans (in millions of dollars)	Grants as Percentage of Total Aid
Brazil	$1,480	11%
Colombia	$991	7%
El Salvador	$597	57%
Haiti	$169	85%
Honduras	$414	32%
Nicaragua	$300	22%
Paraguay	$94	48%
Peru	$410	29%

Communist threats, the U.S. often ends up supporting repressive, non-democratic governments. As a result, many Latin Americans look upon the United States with suspicion.

United States Economic Assistance

After World War II, Latin American economies remained underdeveloped. Poverty and illiteracy were still widespread. The economies of these countries continued to be chiefly agricultural.

Different U.S. Presidents have made efforts to provide increased economic assistance to Latin America:

• Point-Four Program. In 1949, President Harry Truman got Congress to approve the spending of hundreds of millions of dollars in economic aid. The Point-Four Program provided for technical assistance to Asia and Africa as well as Latin America.

• Alliance for Progress. In 1961, President Kennedy proposed the creation of a massive program of economic assistance—the Alliance for Progress. Made up of members of the OAS, the Alliance was to help Latin American countries develop their industries and farms. Moreover, the Alliance aimed to improve health care, build more homes and schools, and reduce illiteracy. Nations that received aid were urged to reform their tax systems so that the gap between the rich and poor would not be so great. *Land reform* (division of large farms into smaller ones) was also promoted. Over the ten years of the program's existence, the United States provided more aid than any other member. Nevertheless, even U.S. officials agreed with the program's critics that the Alliance never came close to meeting its ambitious goals.

• Peace Corps. Also because of Kennedy's urging, the United States began sending Peace Corps representatives to Latin America and elsewhere. These American volunteers have given advice to many Latin Americans on how to raise their standard of living and improve health conditions.

• Agency for International Development. Formed in 1961, AID has administered much of the U.S. government's economic and technical assistance to Latin America and elsewhere.

• Inter-American Development Bank. The IADB was founded by a group of Latin American countries to provide loans to member nations. The U.S. government has provided the IADB with much of its funds.

• International Monetary Fund and the World Bank. The United States and other wealthy nations make yearly contributions to these two United Nations banks. The banks, in turn, make loans to poor countries, including ones in Latin America.

• Private U.S. Bank Loans. Private banks in the United States have made enormous loans to Latin American nations. In the early 1980s, however, a worldwide economic slump caused problems for these lenders. Brazil, Argentina, and other nations came close to *defaulting* (not making payments) on their loans. Some U.S. bank officials worried that their banks might fail if one of these countries defaulted. As a result, the U.S. government came to the rescue, guaranteeing many of these loans.

Criticism of U.S. Aid Despite the benefits of U.S. government and private aid, many critics claim that this assistance has been inadequate. Latin American countries still have many problems. Some of their governments are unstable and often fall in military coups. Poverty and illiteracy remain widespread. Most Latin American countries suffer from runaway inflation. Critics of U.S. aid programs point out that the United States cannot solve all of the problems in Latin America. They say that the Latin American people and their governments are primarily responsible for their own future.

United States and Panama

As we learned in Lesson 76, the United States took possession of the Canal Zone in 1903. By the 1970s, many Panamanians had become dissatisfied with the situation; they wanted control of the Panama Canal to return to the Panamanian government. In the 1960s and 1970s, this dissatisfaction took the form of anti-U.S. rioting in Panama. Other Latin American nations joined Panama in calling for the United States to give up the Canal Zone and the Canal.

Treaties In 1978, after long negotiations and debate, the United States ratified treaties with Panama. With these documents, Panama in 1979 gained control of the Canal Zone. In addition, by the year 2000, Panama will take over full control of the Panama Canal itself. The treaties say that the Canal will remain neutral; all nations in the world may continue to use it. The United States, however, has reserved for itself the right to take military action if any country tries to seize the Canal.

SUMMING UP We have seen that United States relations with most of Latin America have improved since the early 20th century. The dispute over the status of the Panama Canal was settled by treaty. Some other difficult situations have been effectively handled by the OAS. Economic aid from both the United States government and private banks has been helpful to Latin American economies. Poverty, though, is still widespread in the region. Furthermore, many Latin Americans complain that the United States does not treat their governments as full equals.

Understanding the Text

On a separate sheet of paper, write the letter of the word or phrase that best completes each of the following statements.

1. A basic purpose of the Organization of American States is to *(a)* provide a place for all nations of the world to discuss their problems *(b)* bring about greater cooperation among nations of the Western Hemisphere *(c)* aid U.S. intervention in the affairs of Latin American countries *(d)* provide armed forces for NATO.

2. A nation that was suspended from active membership in the OAS was *(a)* Cuba *(b)* Bolivia *(c)* Colombia *(d)* the United States.

3. The OAS was successful in settling a border clash between *(a)* Dominican Republic and Haiti *(b)* El Salvador and Honduras *(c)* Argentina and Great Britain *(d)* Mexico and the United States.

4. In the early 1980s, the United States provided military aid in an effort to help put down a rebellion against the government of *(a)* Brazil *(b)* Nicaragua *(c)* El Salvador *(d)* Cuba.

5. The United States invaded Grenada in 1983 in order to remove the influence there of *(a)* Paraguay *(b)* Guatemala *(c)* Chile *(d)* Cuba.

6. The U.S. President who was responsible for both the Alliance for Progress and the Peace Corps was *(a)* Harry Truman *(b)* Dwight Eisenhower *(c)* John Kennedy *(d)* Ronald Reagan.

7. An example of a U.S. government organization that provides economic aid to Latin America is the *(a)* Agency for International Development *(b)* Inter-American Development Bank *(c)* International Monetary Fund *(d)* World Bank.

8. In the early 1980s, many bankers in the United States were especially worried that Latin American nations would *(a)* not want to borrow from them *(b)* go to war with the United States *(c)* not be able to pay their loans *(d)* suspend the U.S. from OAS membership.

9. In treaties made in 1978, the United States settled a long-standing dispute over the Panama Canal by agreeing to *(a)* turn over full control of the Canal to Panama by the year 2000 *(b)* limit the number of countries that could use the Canal *(c)* build another canal across Central America *(d)* leave U.S. military forces in the Canal Zone forever.

10. Which of the following statements best describes the present state of relations between the United States and Latin America? *(a)* U.S.-Latin American relations have improved, but many problems still exist. *(b)* Relations have never been so bad. *(c)* The United States no longer intervenes in the affairs of Latin American nations. *(d)* The United States is no longer interested in Latin America.

Developing Graph-Reading Skills

Study the bar graph on page 580. Then choose the letter of the word or phrase that best answers each question. On a separate sheet of paper, match the question number with the correct letter.

1. How much economic aid did the United States provide Paraguay between 1962 and 1983? *(a)* $94 *(b)* $94,000 *(c)* $94,000,000 *(d)* none of the above.

2. Which of the Latin American countries shown on the graph received the most U.S. economic aid, 1962–1983? *(a)* Brazil *(b)* Colombia *(c)* El Salvador *(d)* Peru.

3. What percentage of the economic aid that the United States provided Peru, 1962–1983, was made up of grants? *(a)* 7 *(b)* 23 *(c)* 29 *(d)* 100.

4. What percentage of the economic aid that the United States provided Honduras, 1962–1983, was made up of loans? *(a)* 25 *(b)* 32 *(c)* 48 *(d)* 68.

5. To which of the following countries did the United States provide the greatest dollar amount of economic aid, 1962–1983, in the form of grants? *(a)* Brazil *(b)* Colombia *(c)* El Salvador *(d)* Haiti.

Thinking About the Lesson

1. Why has the OAS never been a strong military alliance?

2. Do you think that the United States should ever intervene in the domestic affairs of Latin American nations? Why or why not?

3. Is the U.S. government doing enough to help the economies of Latin American countries to develop? Explain your answer.

United States Relations With Canada and Mexico

The two "next-door" neighbors of the United States in North America are Canada, to the north, and Mexico, to the south. For the most part, America's recent relations with these two countries have been friendly and cooperative. From time to time, however, the United States has had a number of disagreements with each neighbor.

The United States and Canada

For years, the United States and Canada have enjoyed close and friendly relations. They share a common, 3,000-mile-long border that is *unfortified* (not protected by military forces). The majority of the population of both countries speaks English. (Canada, though, has a large population that is French-speaking.) Since both countries were once British colonies, they share similar democratic traditions. Moreover, each country has become the other's major trading partner.

Military Cooperation Canada and the United States fought side by side in World War II. After the war, they again became allies in NATO. Both Canadian and U.S. troops have served with NATO forces in Europe.

In 1957, Canada and the United States formed a joint air defense system—the North American Air Defense Command. One of the main duties of NORAD has been to maintain a network of radar stations. This Distant Early Warning (DEW) system was set up to warn the two countries promptly if enemy bombers attack them from across the Arctic. The DEW system became outdated because of the Soviets' development of long-range missiles and other weapons. As a result, in 1985 Canada and the United States agreed to set up a new North Warning System to replace DEW.

Joint Construction Projects During World War II, Canada permitted the United States to build the Alcan Highway across Canadian territory. It was the first modern road connecting Alaska, in the north, with the state of Washington, in the south. The road, now called the "Alaska Highway," has proved very useful for travel by private and commercial vehicles, as well as military ones.

In the 1950s, Canada and the United States worked together to build the St. Lawrence Seaway. This vast system of locks and waterways allows oceangoing vessels to travel from the Atlantic Ocean to the Great Lakes. Another

THE ST. LAWRENCE SEAWAY

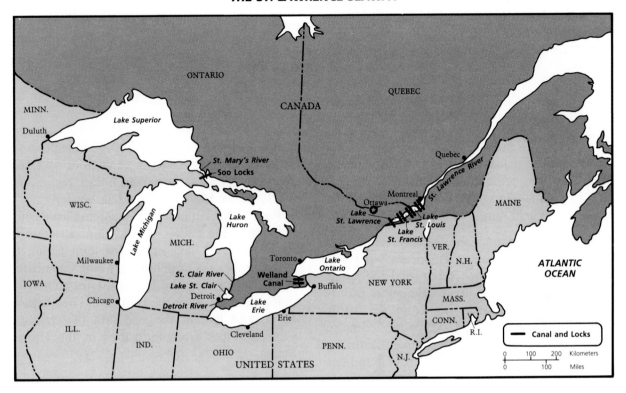

THE ST. LAWRENCE SEAWAY IN PROFILE

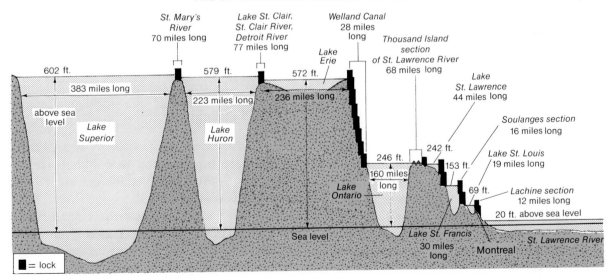

phase of the project was the building of a dam to furnish hydroelectric power. Electric power customers of both nations have benefited from this major power source.

Recent Problems in American-Canadian Relations

In recent years, relations between the United States and Canada have become somewhat strained. Two recent issues that have caused this strain include U.S. economic influence in Canada and acid rain.

U.S. Domination of Canada's Economy For many years, U.S. banks, businesses, and private individuals *invested* (committed money in order to earn more money) large sums in Canadian industries. As a result, in the 1970s foreign investors (mostly U.S.) controlled more than 50 percent of Canada's manufacturing plants. Foreign control of Canadian oil and gas industries was over 70 percent.

Many Canadians protested against this situation. Some called for restrictions or a ban on foreign investments. They wanted a *Canadianization* program whereby Canadian industries would be controlled by Canadians.

Former Canadian Premier Pierre Trudeau introduced such a program in the 1970s and again in the early 1980s. He created the Foreign Investment Review Agency to regulate foreign investments. His National Energy Program gave tax advantages and subsidies to Canadian-owned oil and gas companies. Furthermore, the government encouraged the sale of foreign-owned properties to Canadians.

U.S. officials opposed the Canadianization program. They claimed that it was unfair to U.S. businesses and investors. The United States considered taking steps to cancel certain trade agreements with Canada. As a result, in 1983 Canada eased its rules on foreign investments. Many Canadians, however, still resent U.S.

influence. The issue will probably continue to be a problem in U.S.-Canadian relations.

Acid Rain One type of environmental pollution, *acid rain*, forms when the air is full of industrial wastes (mainly sulfur dioxide). These gaseous wastes sometimes travel in the air for hundreds of miles. Eventually they combine with falling rain to form acids. The acids can pollute both land and water, and, in the process, kill plants and fish. Major sources of acid rain are industries in the Great Lakes region, on both sides of the U.S.-Canadian border.

Both Canadian and U.S. residents have complained of the effects of acid rain. Leaders of both countries have called for joint action to correct this form of pollution. Many Canadians, however, say that the United States should be doing more to solve the problem. They believe that about half of the acid rain that falls on Canada comes from industries in the United States.

The United States and Mexico

In recent decades, the United States has gotten along well with Mexico. Although the two countries disagree on some major issues, there have been no wars or border clashes, as occurred in the past. (Discussed in Lessons 32 and 76.) The economies of the two countries are closely connected by trade and investment. Moreover, each year hundreds of thousands of Mexicans come to the United States to live and work.

The Immigration Question Mexican immigrants have been coming to the United States since the 1880s. During World War II, this immigration increased because the United States had a labor shortage. Since many Americans had gone into the U.S. Armed Forces, the United States needed more laborers. Therefore, many Mexican workers crossed the border to work in U.S. factories and farms.

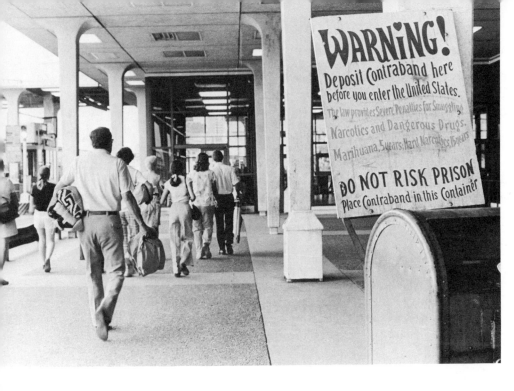

At this checkpoint on the Texas-Mexican border, U.S. customs agents will search for drugs. Because so much marijuana and other narcotics are smuggled into the United States from Mexico, drug control has become a major issue in U.S.-Mexican relations.

Since the war, many Mexicans have been coming to the United States to find temporary farm work during the harvest season. Smaller numbers have sought and found employment in plants and other industries. Their U.S. employers have come to depend upon a seasonal supply of Mexican laborers. The Mexican workers have not been welcomed by all Americans, however. Labor union leaders say that Mexican migrants, by working for lower wages, take away jobs from U.S. citizens. Furthermore, some local officials complain that these aliens put a heavy burden on school systems and welfare programs.

At various times since 1947, the U.S. government has passed laws restricting this immigration. As a result, a large percentage of the Mexicans who have come here have done so illegally. From time to time, U.S. leaders have asked the Mexican government to help stem this movement of aliens. The Mexican government, though, has usually resisted U.S. pressure on this issue. It wants the migration to continue because migration benefits Mexico. As more Mexicans move to the United States, the Mex-

ican government has fewer unemployed people to support. Moreover, Mexican workers in the United States send back to their families some $3 billion a year. These dollars help stimulate the Mexican economy.

Industrial Development in Mexico

One solution to the immigration problem is to develop more industry in Mexico. Such development would create more jobs and a higher standard of living. With an improved economy, the pressures inside Mexico that lead to immigration might weaken.

The Promise of Oil The discovery and development of new oil fields in Mexico in the 1970s provided some hope that the economy would expand. The oil industry was expected to provide many new jobs. The revenues gained from oil sales would be used to help other industries develop. Moreover, the country would have more money to improve its social services.

In 1982, a worldwide surplus of oil developed. As a result, the price of oil dropped, and

Mexico's oil exports did not bring in expected revenues. Soon Mexico had to face the problem of how to pay its huge debts to foreign lenders. Mexico had borrowed heavily to finance its industrial projects. If Mexico defaulted, many U.S. banks would be ruined. To prevent a default, the United States and the International Monetary Fund lent Mexico even more money.

Mexican leaders say that their country needs additional loans to help speed industrial development. Furthermore, they ask for trade policies that will give Mexico a better chance to sell more goods to the United States. The United States is already Mexico's major trading partner.

Independent Foreign Policy

Despite close economic ties between Mexico and the United States, Mexico sometimes has gone its own way in its foreign relations:

• In 1950, Mexico refused to agree to a proposed defense pact with the United States.

• Mexico has had friendly relations with the Communist government, headed by Fidel Castro, that has run Cuba since 1959.

• Mexican officials protested against U.S. intervention in the Dominican Republic in 1965.

• In the early 1970s, Mexico had warm relations with the Socialist government in Chile. In contrast, the United States opposed this government.

• In 1983, the Mexican Senate denounced the U.S. invasion of Grenada.

• Mexico maintains friendly relations with the Sandinista regime in Nicaragua, while the United States supports the Nicaraguan rebels.

Despite these different approaches to foreign policy questions, Mexico and the United States remain good friends. Because they are neighbors and their economies are interdependent, the two countries realize that they must work out their differences.

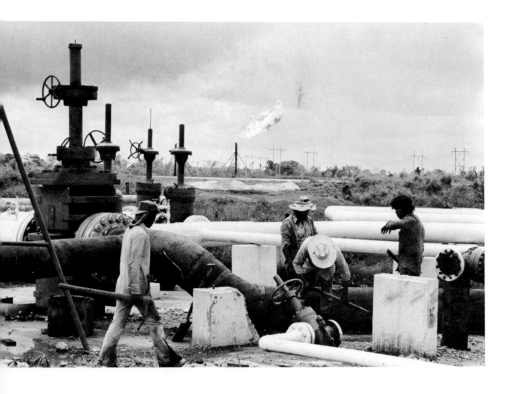

Mexicans who find employment in the oil industry are usually well paid. These men work at a gas-oil separating plant in the state of Tabasco, in Southeastern Mexico.

SUMMING UP We have seen how important Canada and Mexico have become to the United States. Both nations are major trading partners of this country. Each serves as a major area for U.S. investment. Despite some disagreements, both Canada and Mexico cooperate with the United States on many important matters.

Understanding the Text

On a separate sheet of paper, write the letter of the word or phrase that best completes each of the following statements.

1. The DEW system is a (a) group of weather stations (b) group of radar stations (c) network of highways (d) means of patrolling the U.S.-Mexican border.

2. Canada and the United States improved shipping between the Atlantic Ocean and the Great Lakes by jointly building the (a) Erie Canal (b) Suez Canal (c) Alcan Highway (d) St. Lawrence Seaway.

3. Many Canadians have urged a policy of (a) prohibiting U.S. tourists from visiting Canada (b) stationing Canadian troops in the United States (c) lessening the control of Canadian industry by U.S. investors (d) limiting the sale of Canadian products in the United States.

4. Many Canadians believe that half of the pollution that causes acid rain in Canada comes from (a) the United States (b) the Soviet Union (c) Mexico (d) the Arctic.

5. Of the following examples, one *not* a part of U.S.-Canadian military cooperation is (a) NORAD (b) DEW (c) NATO (d) Canadianization.

6. On the question of the migration of Mexicans to the United States, the Mexican government (a) has no views (b) favors closing the borders to further immigration (c) asks for the return of all Mexicans who have moved to the United States (d) wants the migration to continue.

7. Mexican immigrants in the United States (a) are sought after by United States employers (b) number in the hundreds of thousands each year (c) work mainly in agricultural jobs (d) all of the above.

8. Mexico's industrial development was helped by (a) the discovery of new oil fields in Mexico (b) a worldwide surplus of oil (c) Mexico's inability to pay interest on its debts (d) none of the above.

9. Of the following policies of the Mexican government, one that does *not* differ from a policy of the United States is (a) friendly relations with the Sandinista regime in Nicaragua (b) friendly relations with Castro's Cuba (c) membership in the Organization of American States (d) criticism of the U.S. invasion of Grenada.

10. An issue that affects United States' relations with *both* Canada and Mexico is (a) the large numbers of illegal immigrants (b) the construction of the Alcan Highway (c) a huge national debt (d) foreign investments.

Developing Diagram-Reading Skills

Examine the diagram of the St. Lawrence Seaway on page 585. Then choose the letter of the word or phrase that best answers each question. On a separate sheet of paper, match the question number with the correct letter.

1. How many feet above sea level is the surface of Lake Ontario? *(a)* 20 *(b)* 246 *(c)* 572 *(d)* 602.

2. The surface of which Great Lake is the highest above sea level? *(a)* Lake Erie *(b)* Lake Huron *(c)* Lake Superior *(d)* Lake Ontario.

3. Through how many locks would a ship travel in going from Lake Erie to Lake Ontario? *(a)* 0 *(b)* 1 *(c)* 8 *(d)* 17.

4. What is the name of the body of water that connects Lake Superior with Lake Huron? *(a)* Lake Erie *(b)* St. Mary's River *(c)* Welland Canal *(d)* Lake St. Lawrence.

5. A ship traveling through the Welland Canal from Lake Ontario to Lake Erie would do which of the following? *(a)* drop 246 feet *(b)* drop 326 feet *(c)* rise 326 feet *(d)* rise 572 feet.

Thinking About the Lesson

1. Explain why U.S.-Canadian relations have been very close in the last four decades.

2. In what ways have both Canada and the United States benefited from the Alcan Highway? From the St. Lawrence Seaway?

3. Why are some Canadians annoyed with the United States over the issue of acid rain?

4. Why are there many immigrants in the United States from Mexico? Do you think that this immigration should be restricted? Why or why not?

5. Why does the United States have close economic relations with both Canada and Mexico?

6. Why is U.S. trade with Canada much greater than U.S. trade with Mexico?

The United States and the United Nations

As we have seen in earlier lessons, the United States in the 20th century has played a leading role in world affairs. Since World War II, American foreign policy has stressed the belief that nations of the world must work together to safeguard peace. Furthermore, the United States has worked to improve economic and social conditions around the world. For these reasons, the United States helped create and has worked closely with the United Nations.

Establishing the United Nations

The United Nations was formed in San Francisco in April, 1945, at a time when the Second World War was still being fought. Hoping to prevent future wars, delegates from 50 nations met and drafted the UN Charter. Many U.S. citizens were proud that their country became one of the original members of the United Nations.

The UN was not meant to become a *superstate* (a government that would rule the world). Instead, nations that joined the UN have kept their full independence and the right to control their own affairs. Since 1945, membership in the United Nations has more than tripled. As of 1986, 159 nations belonged to the world body.

The basic organization of the UN, as set forth in its Charter, is shown in the chart on the following page.

The General Assembly

The *General Assembly* is the main body of the United Nations. Made up of delegates from all member states, the General Assembly gives every member nation a chance to express its views. For this reason, the Assembly has been called the "Town Meeting of the World."

The General Assembly has the power to admit new members to the UN. Its delegates vote on the UN budget every year. Most important, the Assembly can pass resolutions that recommend solutions to world problems. Each nation, large or small, has one vote in the General Assembly.

The Security Council

Delegates from 15 member states make up the *Security Council*. Of these 15, 5 have permanent delegations; they always have a seat on the Council. The *permanent members* are the United States, the Soviet Union, Great Britain, France, and Communist China. The ten *non-permanent members* of the Council are chosen by the General

591

UNITED NATIONS ORGANIZATION

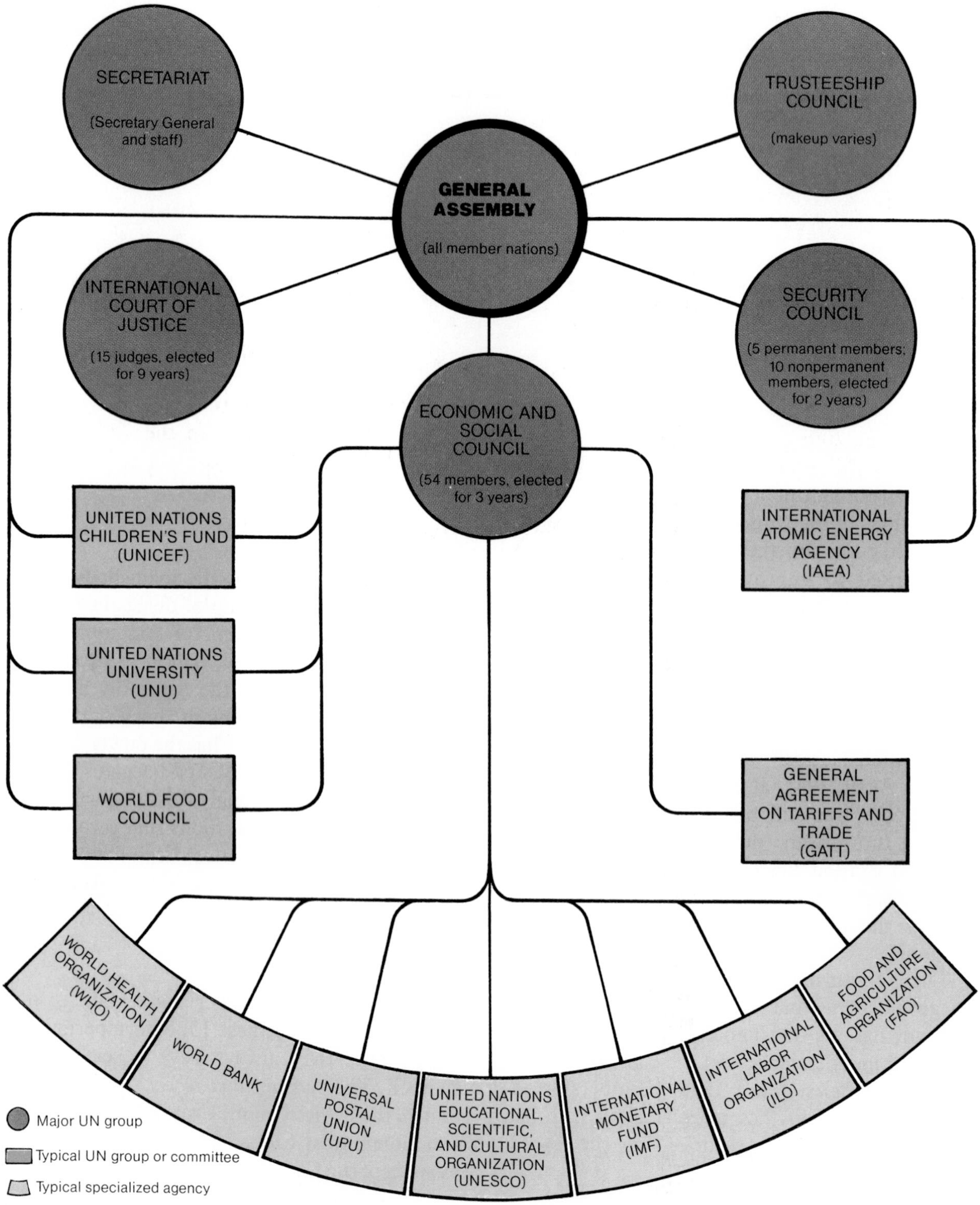

SECRETARIAT

(Secretary General and staff)

TRUSTEESHIP COUNCIL

(makeup varies)

GENERAL ASSEMBLY

(all member nations)

INTERNATIONAL COURT OF JUSTICE

(15 judges, elected for 9 years)

SECURITY COUNCIL

(5 permanent members; 10 nonpermanent members, elected for 2 years)

ECONOMIC AND SOCIAL COUNCIL

(54 members, elected for 3 years)

UNITED NATIONS CHILDREN'S FUND (UNICEF)

INTERNATIONAL ATOMIC ENERGY AGENCY (IAEA)

UNITED NATIONS UNIVERSITY (UNU)

WORLD FOOD COUNCIL

GENERAL AGREEMENT ON TARIFFS AND TRADE (GATT)

WORLD HEALTH ORGANIZATION (WHO)

WORLD BANK

UNIVERSAL POSTAL UNION (UPU)

UNITED NATIONS EDUCATIONAL, SCIENTIFIC, AND CULTURAL ORGANIZATION (UNESCO)

INTERNATIONAL MONETARY FUND (IMF)

INTERNATIONAL LABOR ORGANIZATION (ILO)

FOOD AND AGRICULTURE ORGANIZATION (FAO)

● Major UN group

▢ Typical UN group or committee

▢ Typical specialized agency

Assembly for two-year terms. The Assembly makes sure that all parts of the world are always represented on the Security Council.

The Council's Power The Security Council is one of the most powerful bodies of the United Nations. It looks into dangerous situations and recommends actions to deal with them. As a last resort, the Council may call for the use of armed force. For instance, in 1950 the Security Council voted to send UN forces to Korea after North Korea had invaded South Korea. Most of the UN forces were made up of soldiers from the United States and South Korea. This makeup came about because these two countries were the ones most interested in halting the North Korean advance.

On *substantive* (important) matters, the Council can act only when at least nine members vote "Yes." Furthermore, all five of the permanent members have to vote "Yes" or abstain. Any one of the "Big Five" can prevent action by a veto (by voting "No"). By 1983, the Soviet Union had used its veto power more than 100 times. As an ally of North Korea, the Soviet Union in 1950 wanted to veto the Council resolution on Korea. On the day the resolution was passed, though, the Soviet delegate was absent. Therefore, the USSR lost its opportunity to prevent the UN action in Korea.

Non-substantive (ordinary) matters require nine votes in favor to pass. No member country has a veto power on these issues in the Security Council.

The International Court of Justice

The International Court of Justice, often called the World Court, hears cases brought before it by governments. UN member nations are supposed to accept decisions of the Court's 15 justices. In practice, however, some decisions have been ignored, since the Court has no power to enforce its decisions. Moreover, on several occasions, the United States and some other countries have refused to recognize the Court's power to decide certain matters.

The Secretariat

Thousands of employees from all member nations work in the *Secretariat*, the "business office" of the UN. Among its duties, the Secretariat:

- Maintains records.
- Translates all official papers and speeches.
- Carries on research.

The *Secretary-General* heads the Secretariat. He or she is nominated by the Security Council and approved by the General Assembly. As the most important UN official, the Secretary-General may ask the Security Council to deal with matters that threaten world peace. The Secretary-General may also go on special peacekeeping missions to any part of the world.

The Economic and Social Council (ECOSOC)

The mission of ECOSOC is to help solve basic social and economic problems, such as poverty, illiteracy, and disease. It coordinates the work of specialized UN agencies, including the:

- *Food and Agriculture Organization.* FAO has done much to increase world food production and improve the diets of a great number of people.
- *World Health Organization.* WHO has had notable success in fighting common diseases, such as malaria and tuberculosis.
- *United Nations Economic, Scientific, and Cultural Organization.* UNESCO has carried out

In 1981, Jeane J. Kirkpatrick (center) served as the U.S. Permanent Representative to the UN. Secretary of State Alexander M. Haig, Jr., (left) was also present because he had just given a speech before the General Assembly.

major campaigns against illiteracy among adults. It has also worked to improve primary school education in countries where previously many children had never gone to school. In 1985, the United States withdrew from UNESCO because U.S. officials believed that UNESCO had become a forum for anti-U.S. and anti-Israel propaganda. The United States also claimed that UNESCO's managers were wasting funds.

• *World Bank and International Monetary Fund.* These UN bodies deal with financial problems of nations. The two organizations help poor countries develop their economies. Such development is essential if these countries are to raise the standard of living of their people.

The Trusteeship Council

UN members set up the Trusteeship Council in 1945 to deal with the former colonies of Japan, Germany, and Italy. Each *trust territory* was administered by a UN member nation. For instance, the United States took over the administration of several Japanese-controlled islands in the Pacific.

Over the years, most UN trust territories have become independent. As a result, the Trusteeship Council is no longer an important organ of the United Nations.

United States Leadership in the UN

The United States has always had close relations with the United Nations. The country played an important part in setting up the UN in 1945. In fact, its headquarters were built in New York City. Over the years, the U.S. government has contributed far more than any other nation to the finances of the UN.

Role in the Security Council and General Assembly The United States has always played a major role in the Security Council. At times, its delegates have vetoed Security Council resolutions that the United States did not favor. (The United States, however, has not used its veto power as often as the Soviet Union.)

In the General Assembly, the United States was very influential in the early decades of UN history. Many other nations followed the U.S. lead in voting on issues. Members of the *Western bloc* (a group of nations in Western Europe and the Americas) frequently voted the same way in the General Assembly. With the rapid growth of UN membership over the years, voting patterns have changed. Most members admitted in recent decades were former colonies of the Western powers. Many of these Asian and African nations now form a strong bloc of their own, often called the *Third World bloc.*

Because Third World nations now greatly

outnumber members of the Western bloc, the balance of power in the UN has shifted. The United States often finds itself at odds with the majority of General Assembly members. For example, many Assembly resolutions have condemned actions of Israel, a U.S. ally in the Middle East. Thus, the United States often finds itself in a minority in supporting Israel.

Is the UN a Failure?

Many Americans criticize the UN, saying that it has not lived up to the expectations of its founders. Critics of the world body say that:

In front of the Secretariat Building in New York City fly the flags of all nations that belong to the UN. When the United Nations celebrated its 40th anniversary in 1985, there were 159 flags.

• The UN has failed to prevent a number of wars from breaking out.

• It has failed to stop the arms race.

• It has failed to eliminate hunger and poverty.

• Many nations have ignored UN resolutions directed against them. For instance, France rejected attempts by the UN to settle France's wars in Algeria and Southeast Asia.

• Many nations have formed military alliances outside of the United Nations. Examples are NATO and the Warsaw Pact. These and other alliances are not violations of the UN Charter, but their activities tend to put the United Nations in a secondary role.

• Some nations, notably the Soviet Union, its allies, and the United States have vetoed many important Security Council resolutions.

• In the General Assembly, the smallest nation has the same power as the largest and most populous ones. Some critics would like to see this rule changed to give more power within the UN to the larger and more powerful nations.

In Defense of the UN   Although criticism of the UN has become more vocal in recent years, defenders of the organization claim that:

• The UN remains the only place in the world where ideas and opinions of all nations can be considered.

• Without cooperation among nations of the world, *chaos* (disorder) would be the rule. The UN is the only body through which such cooperation can be developed on a world scale.

• The UN has worked to relieve suffering and help people lead better lives. These activities do not get as much publicity as do the UN peacekeeping operations. Even so, they are of great importance to many millions of people throughout the world.

• The United Nations has succeeded in preventing some regional conflicts from turning into wars. Moreover, in several instances it has brought to an end full-fledged wars.

SUMMING UP   We have seen how from the start the United States has played a vital role in the United Nations. The country has been involved in UN military operations in Korea and elsewhere. It has served as a UN trustee for former Japanese colonies. The United States has contributed much money and personnel to the work of WHO, UNICEF, and the other UN agencies. Although U.S. influence in the UN has declined in recent decades, the world body still plays an important part in American foreign policy.

Understanding the Text

On a separate sheet of paper, write the letter of the word or phrase that best completes each of the following statements.

1. The United Nations was set up (a) before World War II (b) at the end of World War II (c) during the Korean War (d) none of the above.

2. A major United Nations group in which every member nation has one vote is the (a) Secretariat (b) World Court (c) General Assembly (d) Security Council.

3. Suppose that in the UN Security Council the Soviet Union voted "No" on an important resolution. This resolution would then (a) go to the General Assembly (b) be defeated, because each of the five permanent members can veto such measures (c) pass if ten "Yes" votes were also cast (d) be sent to the World Court.

4. Two permanent members of the Security Council are (a) the United States and Canada (b) the Soviet Union and Communist China (c) Great Britain and India (d) France and Austria.

5. The United Nations body that has dealt with former colonies of Germany, Italy, and Japan is the (a) General Assembly (b) UNICEF (c) Trusteeship Council (d) WHO.

6. Most of the newly independent nations of the world belong to a voting bloc in the United Nations often referred to as the (a) "Free World bloc" (b) "Communist bloc" (c) "Western bloc" (d) "Third World bloc."

7. In recent decades, U.S. influence in the General Assembly has (a) increased (b) decreased (c) remained the same (d) ceased to exist.

8. The statement that best describes the role of the UN during the Korean War is that (a) the UN started the war (b) the UN sent a military force to Korea to fight North Korea (c) the UN did not get involved (d) the UN was asked to intervene in Korea, but the Third World bloc prevented any UN action.

9. The UN has been active in promoting (a) basic education (b) higher health standards (c) welfare of children (d) all of the above.

10. Which of the following statements best summarizes the history of the United Nations since its founding? (a) It has fulfilled all of the hopes of its founders. (b) It has had many failures and disappointments, but still has been useful enough to keep the support of the United States and most other nations. (c) It has failed so badly that most nations have left it. (d) It

has given all of its attention to protecting world peace, while ignoring matters of human welfare.

Developing Chart-Reading Skills

Examine the chart on the organization of the United Nations on page 592. Then choose the letter of the word or phrase that best answers each question. On a separate sheet of paper, match the question number with the correct letter.

1. The Secretary-General is part of which UN group? (a) Trusteeship Council (b) Secretariat (c) International Monetary Fund (d) United Nations Children's Fund.

2. According to the chart, which of the following is a major UN group? (a) Secretariat (b) World Food Council (c) International Atomic Energy Agency (d) Food and Agriculture Organization.

3. Which of the following is a specialized agency? (a) Trusteeship Council (b) Security Council (c) World Food Council (d) World Bank.

4. The Economic and Social Council has how many members? (a) 5 (b) 15 (c) 54 (d) none of the above.

5. Which of the following groups does *not* come under the supervision of the Economic and Social Council? (a) International Labor Organization (b) United Nations University (c) International Court of Justice (d) Universal Postal Union.

Thinking About the Lesson

1. Why did the Allies of World War II want to create the United Nations?

2. Do you think that the "Big Five" should have the right to veto substantive matters in the Security Council? Why or why not?

3. What United Nations activity do you consider to be the most important one? Explain your answer.

4. Why has U.S. influence in the United Nations declined over the years?

5. Do you agree with the view of some Americans that the United States should withdraw from the United Nations? Why or why not?

REFERENCE AND RESOURCE UNIT

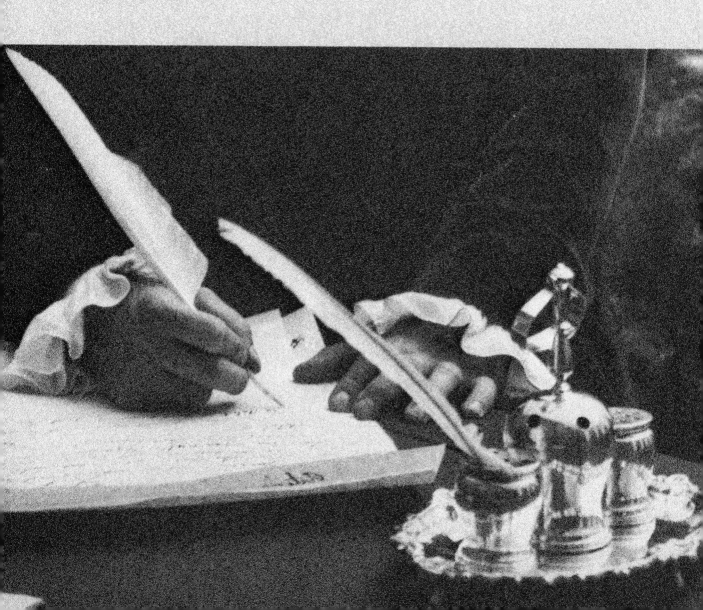

The Declaration of Independence

WHEN, in the course of human events, it becomes necessary for one people to dissolve the political bands which have connected them with another, and to assume, among the powers of the earth, the separate and equal station to which the laws of nature and of nature's God entitle them, a decent respect to the opinions of mankind requires that they should declare the causes which impel them to the separation.

Why Governments Are Created

We hold these truths to be self-evident: That all men are created equal; that they are endowed by their Creator with certain unalienable rights; that among these are life, liberty, and the pursuit of happiness.

That to secure these rights, governments are instituted among men, deriving their just powers from the consent of the governed.

That whenever any form of government becomes destructive of these ends, it is the right of the people to alter or to abolish it, and to institute new government, laying its foundation on such principles and organizing its powers in such form as to them shall seem most likely to effect their safety and happiness. Prudence, indeed, will dictate that governments long established should not be changed for light and transient causes; and, accordingly, all experience hath shown that mankind are more disposed to suffer, while evils are sufferable, than to right themselves by abolishing the forms to which they are accustomed. But when a long train of abuses and usurpations, pursuing invariably the same object, evinces a design to reduce them under absolute despotism, it is their right, it is their duty, to throw off such government, and to provide new guards for their future security.

Why We Want to Separate From Great Britain

Such has been the patient sufferance of these colonies; and such is now the necessity which constrains them to alter their former systems of government. The history of the present King of Great Britain is a history of repeated injuries and usurpations, all having in direct object the establishment of an absolute tyranny over these states. To prove this, let facts be submitted to a candid world:

He has refused his assent to laws the most wholesome and necessary for the public good.

---

* The headings are not part of the Declaration of Independence but have been provided to assist the reader. Capitalization has been modernized.

He has forbidden his governors to pass laws of immediate and pressing importance unless suspended in their operation till his assent should be obtained; and, when so suspended, he has utterly neglected to attend to them.

He has refused to pass other laws for the accommodation of large districts of people unless those people would relinquish the right of representation in the legislature, a right inestimable to them and formidable to tyrants only.

He has called together legislative bodies at places unusual, uncomfortable, and distant from the depository of their public records, for the sole purpose of fatiguing them into compliance with his measures.

He has dissolved representative houses repeatedly for opposing with manly firmness his invasions on the rights of the people.

He has refused for a long time, after such dissolutions, to cause others to be elected; whereby the legislative powers, incapable of annihilation, have returned to the people at large for their exercise; the state remaining, in the meantime, exposed to all the dangers of invasion from without and convulsions within.

He has endeavoured to prevent the population of these states; for that purpose obstructing the laws for naturalization of foreigners, refusing to pass others to encourage their migrations hither, and raising the conditions of new appropriations of lands.

He has obstructed the administration of justice by refusing his assent to laws for establishing judiciary powers.

He has made judges dependent on his will alone for the tenure of their offices and the amount and payment of their salaries.

He has erected a multitude of new offices, and sent hither swarms of officers to harass our people and eat out their substance.

He has kept among us, in times of peace, standing armies, without the consent of our legislatures.

He has affected to render the military independent of and superior to the civil power.

He has combined with others to subject us to a jurisdiction foreign to our constitution and unacknowledged by our laws; giving his assent to their acts of pretended legislation:

> For quartering large bodies of armed troops among us;
> For protecting them, by a mock trial, from punishment for any murders which they should commit on the inhabitants of these states;
> For cutting off our trade with all parts of the world;
> For imposing taxes on us without our consent;
> For depriving us in many cases of the benefits of trial by jury;
> For transporting us beyond seas to be tried for pretended offences;
> For abolishing the free system of English laws in a neighbouring province, establishing therein an arbitrary government and enlarging its boundaries so as to render it at once an example and fit instrument for introducing the same absolute rule in these colonies;
> For taking away our charters, abolishing our most valuable laws, and altering fundamentally the forms of our governments;
> For suspending our own legislatures, and declaring themselves invested with power to legislate for us in all cases whatsoever.

He has abdicated government here by declaring us out of his protection and waging war against us.

He has plundered our seas, ravaged our coasts, burnt our towns, and destroyed the lives of our people.

He is, at this time, transporting large armies of foreign mercenaries to complete the works of death, desolation, and tyranny already begun with circumstances of cruelty and perfidy scarcely paralleled in the most barbarous ages, and totally unworthy the head of a civilized nation.

He has constrained our fellow citizens, taken captive on the high seas, to bear arms against their country, to become the executioners of their friends and brethren, or to fall themselves by their hands.

He has excited domestic insurrections among us, and has endeavoured to bring on the inhabitants of our frontiers the merciless Indian savages, whose known rule of warfare is an undistinguished destruction of all ages, sexes, and conditions.

In every stage of these oppressions we have petitioned for redress in the most humble terms. Our repeated petitions have been answered only by repeated injury. A prince whose character is thus marked by every act which may define a tyrant is unfit to be the ruler of a free people.

Nor have we been wanting in attentions to our British brethren. We have warned them from time to time of attempts by their legislature to extend an unwarrantable jurisdiction over us. We have reminded them of the circumstances of our emigration and settlement here. We have appealed to their native justice and magnanimity, and we have conjured them by the ties of our common kindred to disavow these usurpations, which would inevitably interrupt our connections and correspondence. They too have been deaf to the voice of justice and of consanguinity. We must therefore acquiesce in the necessity which denounces our separation, and hold them, as we hold the rest of mankind, enemies in war, in peace friends.

Conclusion: What We Plan to Do

We, therefore, the representatives of the United States of America, in General Congress assembled, appealing to the Supreme Judge of the world for the rectitude of our intentions, do, in the name and by authority of the good people of these colonies, solemnly publish and declare; that these united colonies are, and of right ought to be, free and independent states; that they are absolved from all allegiance to the British crown, and that all political connection between them and the state of Great Britain is, and ought to be, totally dissolved; and that, as free and independent states, they have full power to levy war, conclude peace, contract alliances, establish commerce, and to do all other acts and things which independent states may of right do.

And for the support of this Declaration, with a firm reliance on the protection of divine Providence, we mutually pledge to each other our lives, our fortunes, and our sacred honor.

Signed by John Hancock of Massachusetts, as President of the Congress, and by the 55 Other Representatives of the 13 United States of America, July 4, 1776.

The Constitution of the United States

Preamble* W E, the people of the United States, in order to form a more perfect Union, establish justice, insure domestic tranquillity, provide for the common defense, promote the general welfare, and secure the blessings of liberty to ourselves and our posterity, do ordain and establish this Constitution for the United States of America.

ARTICLE I
The Legislative
Branch

SECTION 1.   A Two-House Congress

All legislative powers herein granted shall be vested in a Congress of the United States, which shall consist of a Senate and House of Representatives.

SECTION 2.   The House of Representatives

1. Election and Term of Office.   The House of Representatives shall be composed of members chosen every second year by the people of the several states, and the electors in each state shall have the qualifications requisite for electors of the most numerous branch of the state legislature.

2. Qualifications for Representatives.   No person shall be a representative who shall not have attained to the age of twenty-five years, and been seven years a citizen of the United States, and who shall not, when elected, be an inhabitant of that state in which he shall be chosen.

3. Apportionment Among the States.   Representatives [*and direct taxes*]† shall be apportioned among the several states which may be included within this Union, according to their respective numbers, [*which shall be determined by adding to the whole number of free persons, including those bound to service for a term of years, and excluding Indians not taxed, three-fifths of all other persons.*] The actual enumeration shall be made within three years after the first meeting of the Congress of the United States, and within every subsequent term of ten

---

* The headings—for the Articles, Sections, and paragraphs—are not part of the Constitution but have been added to assist the reader. Capitalization has been modernized.

† Those portions of the Constitution no longer in effect (changed by amendment or out of date) are printed in italics and enclosed in brackets.

years, in such manner as they shall by law direct. The number of representatives shall not exceed one for every 30,000, but each state shall have at least one representative; [*and until such enumeration shall be made, the state of New Hampshire shall be entitled to choose 3; Massachusetts, 8; Rhode Island and Providence Plantations, 1; Connecticut, 5; New York, 6; New Jersey, 4; Pennsylvania, 8; Delaware, 1; Maryland, 6; Virginia, 10; North Carolina, 5; South Carolina, 5; and Georgia 3.*]

4. Filling House Vacancies. When vacancies happen in the representation from any state, the executive authority thereof shall issue writs of election to fill such vacancies.

5. Election of House Officers and Impeachment. The House of Representatives shall choose their Speaker and other officers, and shall have the sole power of impeachment.

SECTION 3. The Senate

1. Number of Senators, Election, and Term of Office. The Senate of the United States shall be composed of two senators from each state, [*chosen by the legislature thereof,*] for six years, and each senator shall have one vote.

2. Expiration of Terms of Senators; Filling Vacancies. [*Immediately after they shall be assembled in consequence of the first election, they shall be divided as equally as may be into three classes. The seats of the senators of the first class shall be vacated at the expiration of the second year, of the second class at the expiration of the fourth year, and of the third class at the expiration of the sixth year,*] so that one-third may be chosen every second year; [*and if vacancies happen by resignation, or otherwise, during the recess of the legislature of any state, the executive thereof may make temporary appointments until the next meeting of the legislature, which shall then fill such vacancies.*]

3. Qualifications for Senators. No person shall be a senator who shall not have attained to the age of thirty years, and been nine years a citizen of the United States, and who shall not, when elected, be an inhabitant of that state for which he shall be chosen.

4. President of the Senate. The Vice President of the United States shall be President of the Senate, but shall have no vote, unless they be equally divided.

5. Other Senate Officers. The Senate shall choose their other officers, and also a President *pro tempore*, in the absence of the Vice President, or when he shall exercise the office of President of the United States.

6. Impeachment Cases. The Senate shall have the sole power to try all impeachments. When sitting for that purpose, they shall be on oath or affirmation. When the President of the United States is tried, the Chief Justice shall preside; and no person shall be convicted without the concurrence of two-thirds of the members present.

7. Punishment for Conviction. Judgment in cases of impeachment shall not extend further than to removal from office, and disqualification to hold and enjoy any office of honor, trust, or profit under the United States; but the party convicted shall nevertheless be liable and subject to indictment, trial, judgment, and punishment, according to law.

SECTION 4.   Congressional Elections and Sessions

1. Congressional Elections.   The times, places, and manner of holding elections for senators and representatives shall be prescribed in each state by the legislature thereof; but the Congress may at any time by law make or alter such regulations, except as to the places of choosing senators.

2. Sessions of Congress.   The Congress shall assemble at least once in every year, [*and such meeting shall be on the first Monday in December,*] unless they shall by law appoint a different day.

SECTION 5.   Organization and Rules of Congress

1. Election Returns and Attendance.   Each house shall be the judge of the elections, returns, and qualifications of its own members, and a majority of each shall constitute a quorum to do business; but a smaller number may adjourn from day to day, and may be authorized to compel the attendance of absent members, in such manner, and under such penalties, as each house may provide.

2. Rules of Procedure.   Each house may determine the rules of its proceedings, punish its members for disorderly behavior, and with the concurrence of two-thirds, expel a member.

3. Record of Proceedings.   Each house shall keep a journal of its proceedings, and from time to time publish the same, excepting such parts as may in their judgment require secrecy; and the yeas and nays of the members of either house on any question shall, at the desire of one-fifth of those present, be entered on the journal.

4. Adjournment.   Neither house, during the session of Congress, shall without the consent of the other, adjourn for more than three days, nor to any other place than that in which the two houses shall be sitting.

SECTION 6.   Congressional Privileges and Restrictions

1. Salaries and Special Privileges.   The senators and representatives shall receive a compensation for their services, to be ascertained by law and paid out of the Treasury of the United States. They shall in all cases, except treason, felony, and breach of the peace, be privileged from arrest during their attendance at the session of their respective houses, and in going to and returning from the same and for any speech or debate in either house, they shall not be questioned in any other place.

2. Restrictions.   No senator or representative shall, during the time for which he was elected, be appointed to any civil office under the authority of the United States, which shall have been created, or the emoluments whereof shall have been increased, during such time; and no person holding any office under the United States shall be a member of either house during his continuance in office.

SECTION 7. Ways to Pass Bills

1. Revenue Bills. All bills for raising revenue shall originate in the House of Representatives; but the Senate may propose or concur with amendments as on other bills.

2. Presidential Approval or Veto of Bills. Every bill which shall have passed the House of Representatives and the Senate, shall, before it becomes a law, be presented to the President of the United States; if he approves, he shall sign it, but if not, he shall return it, with his objections to that house in which it shall have originated, who shall enter the objections at large on their journal, and proceed to reconsider it. If after such reconsideration two-thirds of that house shall agree to pass the bill, it shall be sent, together with the objections, to the other house, by which it shall likewise be reconsidered, and, if approved by two-thirds of that house, it shall become a law. But in all such cases the votes of both houses shall be determined by yeas and nays, and the names of the persons voting for and against the bill shall be entered on the journal of each house respectively. If any bill shall not be returned by the President within ten days (Sundays excepted) after it shall have been presented to him, the same shall be a law, in like manner as if he had signed it, unless the Congress by their adjournment prevent its return, in which case it shall not be a law.

3. Congressional Actions Subject to Presidential Approval or Veto. Every order, resolution, or vote to which the concurrence of the Senate and House of Representatives may be necessary (except on a question of adjournment) shall be presented to the President of the United States; and before the same shall take effect, shall be approved by him, or being disapproved by him, shall be repassed by two-thirds of the Senate and House of Representatives, according to the rules and limitations prescribed in the case of a bill.

SECTION 8. Powers Granted To Congress

1–17 Delegated or Enumerated Powers. The Congress shall have power:

1. To lay and collect taxes, duties, imposts, and excises, to pay the debts and provide for the common defense and general welfare of the United States; but all duties, imposts, and excises shall be uniform throughout the United States;
2. To borrow money on the credit of the United States;
3. To regulate commerce with foreign nations, and among the several states, and with the Indian tribes;
4. To establish a uniform rule of naturalization, and uniform laws on the subject of bankruptcies throughout the United States;
5. To coin money, regulate the value thereof, and of foreign coin, and fix the standard of weights and measures;
6. To provide for the punishment of counterfeiting the securities and current coin of the United States;
7. To establish post offices and post roads;
8. To promote the progress of science and useful arts by securing for limited times to authors and inventors the exclusive right to their respective writings and discoveries;

9. To constitute tribunals inferior to the Supreme Court;
10. To define and punish piracies and felonies committed on the high seas and offenses against the law of nations;
11. To declare war, [*grant letters of marque and reprisal,*] and make rules concerning captures on land and water;
12. To raise and support armies, but no appropriation of money to that use shall be for a longer term than two years;
13. To provide and maintain a navy;
14. To make rules for the government and regulation of the land and naval forces;
15. To provide for calling forth the militia to execute the laws of the Union, suppress insurrections, and repel invasions;
16. To provide for organizing, arming, and disciplining the militia, and for governing such part of them as may be employed in the service of the United States, reserving to the states, respectively, the appointment of the officers, and the authority of training the militia according to the discipline prescribed by Congress;
17. To exercise exclusive legislation in all cases whatsoever, over such district (not exceeding ten miles square) as may, by cession of particular states, and the acceptance of Congress, become the seat of government of the United States, and to exercise like authority over all places purchased by the consent of the legislature of the state in which the same shall be, for the erection of forts, magazines, arsenals, dock-yards, and other needful buildings;—and

18. Implied Powers; The Elastic Clause. To make all laws which shall be necessary and proper for carrying into execution the foregoing powers, and all other powers vested by this Constitution in the government of the United States, or in any department or officer thereof.

SECTION 9. Powers Denied to the Federal Government

1. May Not Interfere With the Slave Trade Prior to 1808. [*The migration or importation of such persons as any of the states now existing shall think proper to admit shall not be prohibited by the Congress prior to the year 1808; but a tax or duty may be imposed on such importation, not exceeding ten dollars for each person.*]

2. May Not Suspend the Writ of *Habeas Corpus* Except in Emergency. The privilege of the writ of *habeas corpus* shall not be suspended, unless when in cases of rebellion or invasion the public safety may require it.

3. May Not Enact a Bill of Attainder or an *Ex Post Facto* Law. No bill of attainder or *ex post facto* law shall be passed.

4. May Not Levy a Direct Tax Except in Proportion to Population. [*No capitation or other direct tax shall be laid, unless in proportion to the census or enumeration herein before directed to be taken.*]

5. May Not Levy an Export Tax. No tax or duty shall be laid on articles exported from any state.

6. May Not Favor the Ports of One State Over Those of Another. No preference shall be given by any regulation of commerce or revenue to the ports of one state over those of another; nor shall vessels bound to, or from, one state, be obliged to enter, clear, or pay duties in another.

7. May Not Spend Federal Funds Without Congressional Approval and Public Accounting. No money shall be drawn from the Treasury, but in consequence of appropriations made by law; and a regular statement and account of the receipts and expenditures of all public money shall be published from time to time.

8. May Not Grant Titles of Nobility. No title of nobility shall be granted by the United States; and no person holding any office of profit or trust under them, shall, without the consent of the Congress, accept of any present, emolument, office, or title, of any kind whatever, from any king, prince, or foreign state.

SECTION 10. Powers Denied to the States

1. Unconditional Denial of Various Powers. No state shall enter into any treaty, alliance, or confederation; grant letters of marque and reprisal; coin money; emit bills of credit; make anything but gold and silver coin a tender in payment of debts; pass any bill of attainder, *ex post facto* law, or law impairing the obligation of contracts, or grant any title of nobility.

2. May Not Levy Import and Export Taxes Without the Consent of Congress. No state shall, without the consent of the Congress, lay any imposts or duties on imports or exports, except what may be absolutely necessary for executing its inspection laws; and the net produce of all duties and imposts, laid by any state on imports or exports, shall be for the use of the Treasury of the United States; and all such laws shall be subject to the revision and control of the Congress.

3. May Not Prepare For and Wage War Without the Consent of Congress. No state shall, without the consent of Congress, lay any duty of tonnage, keep troops, or ships of war in time of peace, enter into any agreement or compact with another state, or with a foreign power, or engage in war, unless actually invaded, or in such imminent danger as will not admit of delay.

ARTICLE II. **The** **Executive** **Branch**

SECTION 1. The President and the Presidential Office

1. Term of Office. The executive power shall be vested in a President of the United States of America. He shall hold his office during the term of four years, and together with the Vice President, chosen for the same term, be elected as follows:

2. Number of Presidential Electors per State. Each state shall appoint, in such manner as the legislature thereof may direct, a number of electors, equal to the whole number of senators and representatives to which the state may be entitled in the Congress; but no senator or representative, or person holding an office of trust or profit under the United States, shall be appointed an elector.

3. Election Procedures of the Electoral College and Congress. [*The electors shall meet in their respective states, and vote by ballot for two persons, of* *whom one at least shall not be an inhabitant of the same state with themselves. And they shall make a list of all the persons voted for, and of the number of votes for each; which list they shall sign and certify, and transmit sealed to the seat of the government of the United States, directed to the president of the Senate. The president of the Senate shall, in the presence of the Senate and House of Representatives, open all the certificates, and the votes shall then be counted. The person having the greatest number of votes shall be the President, if such number be a majority of the whole number of electors appointed; and if there be more than one who have such majority, and have an equal number of votes, then the House of Representatives shall immediately choose by ballot one of them for President; and if no person have a majority, then from the five highest on the list the said House shall in like manner choose the President. But in choosing the President the votes shall be taken by states, the representation from each state having one vote. A quorum for this purpose shall consist of a member or members from two-thirds of the states, and a majority of all the states shall be necessary to a choice. In every case, after the choice of the President, the person having the greatest number of votes of the electors shall be the Vice President. But if there should remain two or more who have equal votes, the Senate shall choose from them by ballot the Vice President.]*

4. Election Day.   The Congress may determine the time of choosing the electors, and the day on which they shall give their votes; which day shall be the same throughout the United States.

5. Qualifications for the President.   No person except a natural-born citizen, [*or a citizen of the United States, at the time of the adoption of this Constitution,*] shall be eligible to the office of President; neither shall any person be eligible to that office who shall not have attained to the age of thirty-five years, and been fourteen years a resident within the United States.

6. Filling a Vacancy.   [*In case of the removal of the President from office, or of his death, resignation, or inability to discharge the powers and duties of the said office, the same shall devolve on the Vice President, and the Congress may by law provide for the case of removal, death, resignation, or inability, both of the President and Vice President, declaring what officer shall then act as President, and such officer shall act accordingly, until the disability be removed, or a President shall be elected.*]

7. Salary.   The President shall, at stated times, receive for his services, a compensation, which shall neither be increased nor diminished during the period for which he shall have been elected, and he shall not receive within that period any other emolument from the United States, or any of them.

8. Oath of Office.   Before he enter on the execution of his office he shall take the following oath or affirmation:—"I do solemnly swear (or affirm) that I will faithfully execute the office of President of the United States, and will to the best of my ability, preserve, protect, and defend the Constitution of the United States."

SECTION 2.   Powers of the President

1. Military, Executive, and Judicial Powers.   The President shall be Commander in Chief of the Army and Navy of the United States, and of the militia of the several states, when called into the actual service of the United

States; he may require the opinion, in writing, of the principal officer in each of the executive departments, upon any subject relating to the duties of their respective offices, and he shall have power to grant reprieves and pardons for offenses against the United States, except in cases of impeachment.

2. Treaty Making and Appointive Powers.   He shall have power, by and with the advice and consent of the Senate, to make treaties, provided two-thirds of the senators present concur; and he shall nominate, and by and with the advice and consent of the Senate, shall appoint ambassadors, other public ministers and consuls, judges of the Supreme Court, and all other officers of the United States, whose appointments are not herein otherwise provided for, and which shall be established by law; but the Congress may by law vest the appointment of such inferior officers, as they think proper, in the President alone, in the courts of law, or in the heads of departments.

3. Appointments During Recess of the Senate.   The President shall have power to fill up all vacancies that may happen during the recess of the Senate, by granting commissions which shall expire at the end of their next session.

SECTION 3.   Further Powers of the President

He shall from time to time give to the Congress information of the state of the Union, and recommend to their consideration such measures as he shall judge necessary and expedient; he may, on extraordinary occasions, convene both houses, or either of them, and in case of disagreement between them, with respect to the time of adjournment, he may adjourn them to such time as he shall think proper; he shall receive ambassadors and other public ministers; he shall take care that the laws be faithfully executed, and shall commission all the officers of the United States.

SECTION 4.   Impeachment

The President, Vice President, and all civil officers of the United States, shall be removed from office on impeachment for, and conviction of, treason, bribery, or other high crimes and misdemeanors.

ARTICLE III.
The
Judicial
Branch

SECTION 1.   The Federal Courts: Supreme and Lower Courts

The judicial power of the United States shall be vested in one Supreme Court, and in such inferior courts as the Congress may from time to time ordain and establish. The judges, both of the Supreme and inferior courts, shall hold their offices during good behavior, and shall, at stated times, receive for their services a compensation, which shall not be diminished during their continuance in office.

SECTION 2.   Jurisdiction of the Federal Courts

1. Cases Tried in Federal Courts.   The judicial power shall extend to all cases, in law and equity, arising under this Constitution, the laws of the United States, and treaties made or which shall be made, under their authority; to all cases affecting ambassadors, other public ministers and consuls; to all cases of admiralty and maritime jurisdiction; to controversies to which the

United States shall be a party; to controversies between two or more states; [*between a state and citizens of another state;*] between citizens of different states; between citizens of the same state claiming lands under grants of different states, and between a state, or the citizens thereof, and foreign states, citizens, or subjects.

2. Original and Appellate Jurisdiction of the Supreme Court.   In all cases affecting ambassadors, other public ministers and consuls, and those in which a state shall be a party, the Supreme Court shall have original jurisdiction. In all the other cases before mentioned, the Supreme Court shall have appellate jurisdiction, both as to law and fact, with such exceptions, and under such regulations as the Congress shall make.

3. Rules Regarding Trials.   The trial of all crimes, except in cases of impeachment, shall be by jury; and such trial shall be held in the state where the said crimes shall have been committed; but when not committed within any state, the trial shall be at such place or places as the Congress may by law have directed.

SECTION 3.   Treason

1. Definition of Treason; Requirements for Conviction.   Treason against the United States shall consist only in levying war against them, or in adhering to their enemies, giving them aid and comfort. No person shall be convicted of treason unless on the testimony of two witnesses to the same overt act, or on confession in open court.

2. Punishment of Treason Limited to the Guilty Person.   The Congress shall have power to declare the punishment of treason, but no attainder of treason shall work corruption of blood or forfeiture except during the life of the person attainted.

ARTICLE IV.
Relations
Among
the States
and Between
States and
the Federal
Government

SECTION 1.   Regarding Official Acts

Full faith and credit shall be given in each state to the public acts, records, and judicial proceedings of every other state. And the Congress may by general laws prescribe the manner in which such acts, records, and proceedings shall be proved, and the effect thereof.

SECTION 2.   Regarding Citizens and Fugitives

1. Exchange of Privileges of Citizenship.   The citizens of each state shall be entitled to all privileges and immunities of citizens in the several states.

2. Extradition: Return of Fugitives From Justice.   A person charged in any state with treason, felony, or other crime, who shall flee from justice, and be found in another state, shall on demand of the executive authority of the state from which he fled, be delivered up, to be removed to the state having jurisdiction of the crime.

3. Return of Fugitive Slaves and Indentured Servants.   [*No person held in service or labor in one state, under the laws thereof, escaping into another, shall in consequence of any law or regulation therein, be discharged from such service or* *labor, but shall be delivered up on claim of the party to whom such service or labor may be due.*]

SECTION 3. New States and Territories

1. Admission of New States. New states may be admitted by the Congress into this Union; but no new state shall be formed or erected within the jurisdiction of any other state; nor any state be formed by the junction of two or more states, or parts of states, without the consent of the legislature of the states concerned as well as of the Congress.

2. Regulations for Federal Territories and Properties. The Congress shall have power to dispose of and make all needful rules and regulations respecting the territory or other property belonging to the United States; and nothing in this Constitution shall be so construed as to prejudice any claims of the United States, or of any particular state.

SECTION 4. Federal Guarantees to the States

The United States shall guarantee to every state in this Union a republican form of government, and shall protect each of them against invasion; and on application of the legislature, or of the executive (when the legislature cannot be convened) against domestic violence.

**ARTICLE V.
Amendments
to the
Constitution**

The Congress, whenever two-thirds of both houses shall deem it necessary, shall propose amendments to this Constitution, or, on the application of the legislatures of two-thirds of the several states, shall call a convention for proposing amendments, which, in either case shall be valid to all intents and purposes, as part of this Constitution, when ratified by the legislatures of three-fourths of the several states, or by conventions in three-fourths thereof, as the one or the other mode of ratification may be proposed by the Congress; provided that [*no amendments which may be made prior to the year 1808 shall in any manner affect the first and fourth clauses in the Ninth Section of the First Article; and that*] no state, without its consent, shall be deprived of its equal suffrage in the Senate.

**ARTICLE VI.
Other
Provisions**

1. Acceptance of Previously Contracted Public Debts. All debts contracted and engagements entered into, before the adoption of this Constitution, shall be as valid against the United States under this Constitution, as under the Confederation.

2. The Constitution: Supreme Law of the Land. This Constitution, and the laws of the United States which shall be made in pursuance thereof, and all treaties made, or which shall be made, under the authority of the United States, shall be the supreme law of the land; and the judges in every state shall be bound thereby, anything in the constitution or laws of any state to the contrary notwithstanding.

3. Official Oath of Office; No Religious Test. The senators and representatives before mentioned, and the members of the several state legislatures, and all executive and judicial officers, both of the United States and of the several states, shall be bound by oath or affirmation, to support this Constitution;

but no religious test shall ever be required as a qualification to any office or public trust under the United States.

**ARTICLE VII.
Ratification**

The ratification of the conventions of nine states shall be sufficient for the establishment of this Constitution between the states so ratifying the same.

**Amendments
to the
Constitution**

AMENDMENT I (1791).   Freedom of Religion, Speech, Press, Assembly, and Petition

Congress shall make no law respecting an establishment of religion, or prohibiting the free exercise thereof; or abridging the freedom of speech, or of the press; or the right of the people peaceably to assemble, and to petition the government for a redress of grievances.

AMENDMENT II (1791).   Right to Keep and Bear Arms

A well-regulated militia, being necessary to the security of a free state, the right of the people to keep and bear arms shall not be infringed.

AMENDMENT III (1791).   Regulations for Quartering of Troops

No soldier shall, in time of peace, be quartered in any house, without the consent of the owner; nor in time of war, but in a manner to be prescribed by law.

AMENDMENT IV (1791).   No Unreasonable Searches

The right of the people to be secure in their persons, houses, papers, and effects, against unreasonable searches and seizures, shall not be violated; and no warrants shall issue but upon probable cause, supported by oath or affirmation and particularly describing the place to be searched, and the persons or things to be seized.

AMENDMENT V (1791).   Rights of Accused Persons and Protection of Private Property

No person shall be held to answer for a capital, or otherwise infamous, crime, unless on a presentment or indictment of a grand jury, except in cases arising in the land or naval forces, or in the militia, when in actual service in time of war or public danger; nor shall any person be subject for the same offense to be twice put in jeopardy of life or limb; nor shall be compelled, in any criminal case, to be a witness against himself; nor be deprived of life, liberty, or property, without due process of law; nor shall private property be taken for public use, without just compensation.

AMENDMENT VI (1791).   Other Rights of Accused Persons

In all criminal prosecutions, the accused shall enjoy the right to a speedy and public trial, by an impartial jury of the state and district wherein the crime shall have been committed, which district shall have been previously ascertained by law, and to be informed of the nature and cause of the accusation; to be confronted with the witnesses against him; to have compulsory process for obtaining witnesses in his favor, and to have the assistance of counsel for his defense.

AMENDMENT VII (1791).   Trial by Jury in Most Civil Cases

In suits at common law, where the value in controversy shall exceed twenty dollars, the right of trial by jury shall be preserved, and no fact tried by a jury shall be otherwise reexamined in any court of the United States than according to the rules of the common law.

AMENDMENT VIII (1791).   No Excessive Bail or Cruel Punishments

Excessive bail shall not be required, nor excessive fines imposed, nor cruel and unusual punishments inflicted.

AMENDMENT IX (1791).   Rights Reserved to the People

The enumeration in the Constitution, of certain rights, shall not be construed to deny or disparage others retained by the people.

AMENDMENT X (1791).   Powers Reserved to the States

The powers not delegated to the United States by the Constitution, nor prohibited by it to the states, are reserved to the states respectively, or to the people.

AMENDMENT XI (1798).   No Suits in Federal Courts by Individuals Against a State

The judicial power of the United States shall not be construed to extend to any suit in law or equity, commenced or prosecuted against one of the United States, by citizens of another state, or by citizens or subjects of any foreign state.

AMENDMENT XII (1804).   New Rules for Electing the President and Vice President

The Electors shall meet in their respective states, and vote by ballot for President and Vice President, one of whom, at least, shall not be an inhabitant of the same state with themselves; they shall name in their ballots the person voted for as President, and in distinct ballots the person voted for as Vice President, and they shall make distinct lists of all persons voted for as President, and of all persons voted for as Vice President, and of the number of votes for each, which lists they shall sign and certify, and transmit, sealed, to the seat of government of the United States, directed to the president of the Senate; the president of the Senate shall, in the presence of the Senate and House of Representatives, open all the certificates and the votes shall then be counted; the person having the greatest number of votes for President shall be the President, if such number be a majority of the whole number of electors appointed; and if no person have such majority, then from the persons having the highest numbers not exceeding three on the list of those voted for as President, the House of Representatives shall choose immediately, by ballot, the President. But in choosing the President, the votes shall be taken by states, the representation from each state having one vote; a quorum for this purpose shall consist of a member or members from two-thirds of the states, and a majority of all the states shall be necessary to a choice. [*And if the House of Representatives shall not choose a President whenever the right of choice shall devolve upon them, before the fourth day of March next following, then the Vice President shall act as President, as in the case of the death or other constitutional disability of the President.*] The person having the greatest number of votes as Vice President shall be the Vice President, if such number be a majority of the whole number of electors appointed, and if no person have a majority, then, from the two highest numbers on the list, the Senate shall choose the Vice President; a quorum for the purpose shall consist of two-thirds of the whole number of senators, and a majority of the whole number shall be necessary to a choice. But no person constitutionally ineligible to the office of President shall be eligible to that of Vice President of the United States.

AMENDMENT XIII (1865).   Abolition of Slavery in the United States

SECTION 1.

Neither slavery nor involuntary servitude, except as a punishment for crime whereof the party shall have been duly convicted, shall exist within the United States, or any place subject to their jurisdiction.

SECTION 2.

Congress shall have power to enforce this article by appropriate legislation.

AMENDMENT XIV (1868).   Protection of Civil Liberties

SECTION 1.   **Definition of Citizenship; Due Process of Law and Equal Protection of the Laws.**

All persons born or naturalized in the United States and subject to the jurisdiction thereof, are citizens of the United States and of the state wherein they reside. No state shall make or enforce any law which shall abridge the privileges or immunities of citizens of the United States; nor shall any state deprive any person of life, liberty, or property, without due process of law; nor deny to any person within its jurisdiction the equal protection of the laws.

SECTION 2.   **Reduction of Representation of States Denying Vote to Citizens.**

Representatives shall be apportioned among the several states according to their respective numbers, counting the whole number of persons in each state, excluding Indians not taxed. But when the right to vote at any election for the choice of electors for President and Vice President of the United States, representatives in Congress, the executive and judicial officers of a state, or the members of the legislature thereof, is denied to any of the [*male*] inhabitants of such state, being [*twenty-one*] years of age and citizens of the United States, or in any way abridged, except for participation in rebellion, or other crime, the basis of representation therein shall be reduced in the proportion which the number of such male citizens shall bear to the whole number of [*male*] citizens [*twenty-one*] years of age in such state.

SECTION 3.   **Exclusion of Former Confederate Leaders From Public Office.**

No person shall be a senator or representative in Congress, or elector of President and Vice President, or hold any office, civil or military, under the United States, or under any state, who, having previously taken an oath, as a member of Congress, or as an officer of the United States, or as a member of any state legislature, or as an executive or judicial officer of any state, to support the Constitution of the United States, shall have engaged in insurrection or rebellion against the same, or given aid or comfort to the enemies thereof. But Congress may, by vote of two-thirds of each house, remove such disability.

SECTION 4.   **No Repayment of the Confederate Debt.**

The validity of the public debt of the United States, authorized by law, including debts incurred for payment of pensions and bounties for services in suppressing insurrection or rebellion, shall not be questioned. But neither the United States nor any state shall assume or pay any debt or obligation incurred in aid of insurrection or rebellion against the United States, [*or any claim for the loss or emancipation of any slave;*] but all such debts, obligations, and claims shall be held illegal and void.

SECTION 5.

The Congress shall have power to enforce, by appropriate legislation, the provisions of this article.

AMENDMENT XV (1870).   Right to Vote

SECTION 1.

The right of citizens of the United States to vote shall not be denied or abridged by the United States or any state on account of race, color, or previous condition of servitude.

SECTION 2.

The Congress shall have power to enforce this article by appropriate legislation.

AMENDMENT XVI (1913).   Income Taxes

The Congress shall have power to lay and collect taxes on incomes, from whatever source derived, without apportionment among the several states, and without regard to any census or enumeration.

AMENDMENT XVII (1913).   Direct Election of Senators

SECTION 1.   **Election by the People.**

The Senate of the United States shall be composed of two senators from each state, elected by the people thereof, for six years; and each senator shall have one vote. The electors in each state shall have the qualifications requisite for electors of the most numerous branch of the state legislatures.

SECTION 2.   **Regulations Regarding Vacancies and Temporary Appointments.**

When vacancies happen in the representation of any state in the Senate, the executive authority of such state shall issue writs of election to fill such vacancies: Provided that the legislature of any state may empower the executive thereof to make temporary appointments until the people fill the vacancies by election as the legislature may direct.

SECTION 3.

[*This amendment shall not be so construed as to affect the election or term of any senator chosen before it becomes valid as part of the Constitution.*]

AMENDMENT XVIII (1919).   Prohibition

SECTION 1.   **No Manufacture, Sale, or Transportation of Intoxicating Liquors.**

[*After one year from the ratification of this article the manufacture, sale, or transportation of intoxicating liquors within, the importation thereof into, or the exportation thereof from, the United States and all territory subject to the jurisdiction thereof for beverage purposes is hereby prohibited.*]

SECTION 2.   **Enforcement.**

[*The Congress and the several states shall have concurrent power to enforce this article by appropriate legislation.*]

SECTION 3.   **Ratification Required Within Seven Years.**

[*This article shall be inoperative unless it shall have been ratified as an amendment to the Constitution by the legislatures of the several states, as provided in the Constitution, within seven years from the date of the submission hereof to the states by the Congress.*]

AMENDMENT XIX (1920).   Right of Women to Vote

SECTION 1.

The right of citizens of the United States to vote shall not be denied or abridged by the United States or by any state on account of sex.

SECTION 2.

Congress shall have power to enforce this article by appropriate legislation.

AMENDMENT XX (1933). No "Lame Duck" Members of Congress; Presidential Successions

SECTION 1.   **Revised Dates for Terms of President, Vice President, and Members of Congress.**

The terms of the President and Vice President shall end at noon on the 20th day of January, and the terms of senators and representatives at noon on the 3rd day of January, of the years in which such terms would have ended if this article had not been ratified; and the terms of their successors shall then begin.

SECTION 2.   **Revised Date for Sessions of Congress.**

The Congress shall assemble at least once in every year, and such meeting shall begin at noon on the 3rd day of January, unless they shall by law appoint a different day.

SECTION 3.   **Presidential Succession in Unusual Circumstances.**

If at the time fixed for the beginning of the term of the President, the President-elect shall have died, the Vice President-elect shall become President. If a President shall not have been chosen before the time fixed for the beginning of his term, or if the President-elect shall have failed to qualify, then the Vice President-elect shall act as President until a President shall have qualified; and the Congress may by law provide for the case wherein neither a President-elect nor a Vice President-elect shall have qualified, declaring who shall then act as President, or the manner in which one who is to act shall be selected, and such person shall act accordingly until a President or Vice President shall have qualified.

SECTION 4.   **Congress and Presidential Election in Unusual Circumstances.**

The Congress may by law provide for the case of the death of any of the persons from whom the House of Representatives may choose a President whenever the right of choice shall have devolved upon them, and for the case of the death of any of the persons from whom the Senate may choose a Vice President whenever the right of choice shall have devolved upon them.

SECTION 5.   **Effective Date of This Amendment.**

[*Sections 1 and 2 shall take effect on the 15th day of October following the ratification of this article.*]

SECTION 6.   **Ratification Required Within Seven Years.**

[*This article shall be inoperative unless it shall have been ratified as an amendment to the Constitution by the legislatures of three-fourths of the several states within seven years from the date of its submission.*]

AMENDMENT XXI (1933).   Repeal of Prohibition

SECTION 1.   **Repeal of Eighteenth Amendment.**

The eighteenth article of amendment to the Constitution of the United States is hereby repealed.

SECTION 2.   **Control of Liquor Left to the States.**

The transportation or importation into any state, territory, or possession of the United States for delivery or use therein of intoxicating liquors, in violation of the laws thereof, is hereby prohibited.

SECTION 3.   **Ratification Required Within Seven Years by State Conventions.**

[*This article shall be inoperative unless it shall have been ratified as an amendment to the Constitution by conventions in the several states, as provided in the Constitution, within seven years from the date of the submission hereof to the states by the Congress.*]

AMENDMENT XXII (1951).   Limitation on Presidential Terms

SECTION 1.   **No More Than Two Elected Terms as President.**

No person shall be elected to the office of the President more than twice, and no person who has held the office of President, or acted as President, for more than two years of a term to which some other person was elected President shall be elected to the office of the President more than once. [*But this Article shall not apply to any person holding the office of President when this Article was proposed by the Congress, and shall not prevent any person who may be holding the office of President, or acting as President, during the term within which this Article becomes operative from holding the office of President or acting as President during the remainder of such term.*]

SECTION 2.   **Ratification Required Within Seven Years.**

[*This article shall be inoperative unless it shall have been ratified as an amendment to the Constitution by the legislatures of three-fourths of the several states within seven years from the date of its submission to the states by the Congress.*]

AMENDMENT XXIII (1961).   Presidential Electors for the District of Columbia

SECTION 1.   **Number of Electors.**

The District constituting the seat of Government of the United States shall appoint in such manner as the Congress may direct:

A number of electors of President and Vice President equal to the whole number of senators and representatives in Congress to which the District would be entitled if it were a State, but in no event more than the least populous State; they shall be in addition to those appointed by the States, but they shall be considered, for the purposes of the election of President and Vice President, to be electors appointed by a State; and they shall meet in the District and perform such duties as provided by the twelfth article of amendment.

SECTION 2.

The Congress shall have power to enforce this article by appropriate legislation.

AMENDMENT XXIV (1964). No Poll Tax in Federal Elections

SECTION 1. Citizens to Vote Without Payment of a Poll Tax.

The right of citizens of the United States to vote in any primary or other election for President or Vice President, for electors for President or Vice President, or for senator or representative in Congress, shall not be denied or abridged by the United States or any state by reason of failure to pay any poll tax or other tax.

SECTION 2.

The Congress shall have the power to enforce this article by appropriate legislation.

AMENDMENT XXV (1967). Presidential Disability and Succession

SECTION 1. Filling a Presidential Vacancy.

In case of the removal of the President from office or of his death or resignation, the Vice President shall become President.

SECTION 2. Filling a Vice Presidential Vacancy.

Whenever there is a vacancy in the office of the Vice President, the President shall nominate a Vice President who shall take office upon confirmation by a majority vote of both houses of Congress

SECTION 3. Vice President as Acting President.

Whenever the President transmits to the President *pro tempore* of the Senate and the Speaker of the House of Representatives his written declaration that he is unable to discharge the powers and duties of his office, and until he transmits to them a written declaration to the contrary, such powers and duties shall be discharged by the Vice President as Acting President.

SECTION 4. Resumption of Power by the President.

Whenever the Vice President and a majority of either the principal officers of the executive departments or of such other body as Congress may by law provide transmit to the President *pro tempore* of the Senate and the Speaker of the House of Representatives their written declaration that the President is unable to discharge the powers and duties of his office, the Vice President shall immediately assume the powers and duties of the office as Acting President.

Thereafter, when the President transmits to the President *pro tempore* of the Senate and the Speaker of the House of Representatives his written declaration that no inability exists, he shall resume the powers and duties of his office unless the Vice President and a majority of either the principal officers of the executive department or of such other body as Congress may by law provide transmit within four days to the President *pro tempore* of the Senate and the Speaker of the House of Representatives their written declaration that the President is unable to discharge the powers and duties of his office. Thereupon Congress shall decide the issue, assembling within forty-eight hours for that purpose if not in session. If the Congress, within twenty-one days after receipt of the latter written declaration, or, if Congress is not in session, within twenty-one days after Congress is required to assemble, determines by two-thirds vote of both houses that the President is unable to discharge the powers and duties of his office, the Vice President shall continue to discharge the same as Acting President; otherwise, the President shall resume the powers and duties of his office.

AMENDMENT XXVI (1971).   Lower Voting Age

SECTION 1.   Voting Age Set at Eighteen.

The right of citizens of the United States, who are eighteen years of age or older, to vote shall not be denied or abridged by the United States or any state on account of age.

SECTION 2.

The Congress shall have the power to enforce this article by appropriate legislation.

Glossary

abolition doing away with something, such as slavery.

abolitionist person who calls for an end to slavery.

abrogate to do away with or cancel.

abstract artist one who intentionally creates art that does not closely reflect how things or people really look.

academy private school, usually above the elementary level.

accommodate to make room for or adapt to something new.

acid rain rain polluted with acidic substances, such as sulfur dioxide, thought to enter the air from coal power plants and other sources.

acquit (ə′-kwit) to set free of a charge by finding "not guilty."

adjourn (ə-′jərn) to end a session or meeting of a group such as Congress.

adobe (ə-′dō-bē) brick made of sun-dried clay.

affiliated having ties with a group.

Afro-American an American of African descent.

aggressor one who starts a fight or war.

agricultural runoff everything that washes off farmers' fields during a rainstorm, including fertilizers, pesticides, and herbicides.

algae (′al-jē) plants that grow in water.

alien foreign-born person who has not become a citizen of the country in which he or she resides.

alliance association of several nations who are allies.

allies nations united by treaty calling on each to help the others in time of war.

ambassador person who lives in a foreign nation and represents his or her country there.

amend to change.

amendment change or alteration, such as in a law or document.

amnesty type of pardon granted by a government to a large group of individuals.

amphibious (am-′fib-ē-əs) relating to or adapted for both land and water.

anarchist person who wishes to live in a society that has no government.

annex (ə-′neks) to take over something, such as a territory.

Anti-Federalist   member of the political group that opposed ratification of the U.S. Constitution.

appeal   to take a case to a higher court for rehearing.

appeasement (ə-'pēz-mənt)   to satisfy or buy off an enemy by giving in to its demands.

appoint   to name someone officially to a position.

arbitration   action whereby both sides in a dispute call in a third party and agree in advance to abide by this person's decision.

arbitrator   person chosen to settle differences by arbitration.

aristocrat   person of the upper class.

armistice ('är-mə-stəs)   temporary end to fighting.

arrogant   acting superior in dealing with others.

arsenal   place where weapons are stored.

assembly   group of people, such as a legislature.

assembly line   arrangement of machines and workers in which work passes from operation to operation until the product is finished.

assimilate   to bring someone into the cultural traditions of a population.

astrolabe   small instrument once used in navigation; it measures the angle between the horizon and a star.

atrocity (ə-'träs-ət-ē)   cruel or brutal act.

automation   machine-controlled operations.

autonomy   situation where people have self-government.

aye   affirmative vote; yes.

bail   money paid to obtain release of a prisoner from jail while awaiting a trial.

balance of nature   situation in which the number of plants and animals in nature remains roughly the same over a number of years.

balance of trade   relationship between a country's exports and imports; it is favorable when exports are greater than imports.

bank note   type of money issued by banks.

bankrupt   financially ruined.

barrio   neighborhood of a U.S. city in which many Mexican-Americans live.

Bessemer process   method of making steel that uses blasts of air to remove impurities from molten iron.

bilingual education   teaching of subjects in two languages: the native tongue of students and the major language of society.

bill   written draft of a law.

bill of attainder   law that punishes a person for a crime without giving that person a trial.

bill of rights   list of rights guaranteed by a government.

black   someone of African origin.

Black Codes   Southern state laws passed to limit the rights of blacks in the late 19th century.

blacklist   to put someone on a list of people who are to be punished, for instance by not being hired in an industry.

blitzkrieg ('blits-krēg)   military campaign conducted with great speed and force.

blockade   attempt to obstruct traffic to and from an area, often by means of armed force.

blue-collar worker   wage earners whose work duties call for the wearing of work clothes or protective clothing.

board of trustees   group of people who run a business trust.

bond   document that one buys from a government or corporation that promises purchasers their money back, with interest, after a stated amount of time.

bondholder   one who owns a government or corporate bond.

bonus   something in addition to what is expected.

bootlegger   one who makes, sells, or transports liquor illegally.

bounty   reward or premium given by a government.

boycott   agreement not to buy something from someone as a means of expressing disapproval.

bread colonies   the Middle Colonies, which had a surplus of grains.

bribe   money given in exchange for doing favors.

budget   written estimate of expenses and income for a set time period.

burgess   delegate to the legislature of colonial Maryland or Virginia.

burn in effigy   to display and burn the likeness of someone as a protest.

Cabinet   group of advisers to the U.S. President.

cable car   streetcar that moves by means of a cable moving overhead or below street level.

calendar   chart of dates and events.

Canadianization   program whereby Canadian industries are to be controlled by Canadians.

capital   money or property that is used to produce more money.

capitalism   economic system in which natural resources and means of production are privately owned and prices, production, and distribution of goods are determined mainly by competition in a free market.

caravel   type of small sailing ship used during the 15th and 16th centuries.

carpetbagger   Northerner living in the South shortly after the Civil War.

cash crops   products that farmers grow to be sold rather than used or consumed by themselves.

casualty   person who dies or is injured in a war or other calamity.

cattle center   area where cattle were driven to be sold.

cattle drive   movement by cowboys of a vast herd of cattle to a cattle center.

caucus ('ko-kəs)   small group of people belonging to the same political party.

cede ('sēd)   to give up or yield, often by treaty.

censor   to suppress or delete communications thought to be harmful or dangerous.

censure   to blame or find fault with someone.

century   period of time of 100 years.

certify   to approve or declare formally.

chain   group of similar retail businesses under a single management, ownership, or control.

chairperson   leader of a meeting or committee; term was traditionally called "chairman."

chaos ('kā-äs)   state of disorder.

charter   legal document or contract.

charter colony   type of colony in which English rulers gave a trading company land and certain rights to govern in the New World.

checks and balances   system that gives each of the three main branches of the federal government certain powers to limit the other two.

child labor   work done by children, often for long hours with little pay.

civil case   court case that does not directly involve a violation of criminal laws.

civil rights   personal freedoms and property rights.

civil rights movement   struggle of minorities for equal rights in such areas as employment opportunities and housing.

civil service system   practice by which federal civilian employees are hired and promoted using competitive tests.

civil war   armed conflict among groups within one country.

civilian   person not on active duty in a military, police, or fire-fighting force.

classics   study of Greek and Latin literature.

clean energy source   source of energy that is non-polluting.

closed shop   workplace where only union members may be hired.

cloture   vote to limit the time of a debate in a legislative body.

coalition   temporary alliance of certain parties, persons, or states.

Cold War   hostile relations between the U.S. and the USSR following World War II.

collective bargaining   negotiations between employers and employees concerning wages and working conditions.

colonization   to set up a colony in a foreign land.

colony   group of people living in a new land who have political ties to a parent country.

combine   harvesting machine that is both reaper and thresher; it can cut wheat, separate the grain, and bag the final product.

commerce   trade of goods on a large scale.

commercial fertilizer   factory-made product used to enrich the soil.

committee   group of people who meet and discuss possible courses of action; groups of senators or representatives who discuss and debate bills and recommend them for consideration by the House or Senate.

communal   having to do with sharing work or property among members of a community.

communications systems of talking, writing, or otherwise communicating.

communism set of beliefs concerning the overthrow of capitalism and its replacement with state-owned and state-run economic institutions.

compromise to settle a dispute by the method in which each party gives up something that it wants.

compute to perform mathematical calculations.

computer electronic device that can store, recall, and analyze information.

concurrent powers powers shared by the federal and state governments.

conference committee group of U.S. senators and representatives who work together to arrive at a bill acceptable to both the House and the Senate.

confidential private; secret.

confiscate to seize something (by an authority).

conglomerate large company that combines businesses from different and unrelated fields.

Congress U.S. Senate and the House of Representatives acting together.

conscription government practice of compelling its people to serve in armed forces; draft.

consent of the governed as stated in the Declaration of Independence, people willingly give their government the powers it needs to do its job.

conservation preservation and protection of natural resources.

conservative having great respect for tradition; not wanting major or abrupt changes.

constitution set of basic principles and rules of government.

consumer credit borrowing by private individuals.

containment policy of limiting another country to the land it already controls; also, limiting the influence of another country.

contaminated containing unwanted substances.

continent one of seven large divisions of land on the earth.

contour plowing plowing at a right angle to the slope of the land.

convention meeting of delegates called for a specific purpose.

coordinated conservation program major conservation program that combines many different concerns of conservationists.

copperhead Northerner who sympathized with the Confederacy.

corollary idea that follows naturally from existing facts.

corporate farm farm run as a business corporation.

corporation business that sells stock to raise capital; owners of the stock become owners of the business.

corruption dishonesty.

cotton gin machine used to separate seeds from raw cotton.

Court of Appeals one of 11 courts that make up the middle level of the federal court system.

craft unions labor unions of skilled workers.

craft worker workers skilled in a specific craft.

credit reputation as a borrower who does or does not repay loans promptly.

creditor one who lends money.

criminal case court case in which the defendant is accused of an act that is forbidden and punishable by law.

crude oil unrefined oil; oil in its natural state.

cruiser large warship.

Crusades religious wars that took place in the Middle East from the 11th to the 13th centuries.

culture distinct way in which a group of people live; also, the appreciation of art, music, and literature.

cure to prepare something in order to preserve or use it.

currency coins and paper money; in some cases, bank notes.

curriculum (kə-'rik-yə-ləm) plan of subjects to be taught in schools.

custom way of doing things in everyday life.

custom and usage a process by which rules of government have been shaped and reshaped over the years.

cutthroat competition engaging in business practices so that other companies cannot compete.

dark horse one who unexpectedly wins a competition, such as a party nomination to run for an office.

deadlock inaction or standstill because neither of two opposing groups will give in.

debtor ('det-ər) one who owes money and cannot pay back the debt.

decontrol act of removing a specific government regulation or law.

default to fail to make payments on a loan.

defendant person accused of committing a crime.

defense attorney lawyer for the defendant.

deficit ('def-(ə)-sət) excess of spending over income.

degree measure of distances on the earth between two lines of latitude or two lines of longitude.

delegate (v.) to assign to another.

delegate (n.) person who represents others, such as at a convention.

delegated powers powers set aside to the federal government by the Constitution.

demobilize to discharge large numbers of people from the armed forces.

democracy government in which people rule themselves, usually by means of elected representatives. Also, a way of life that provides personal freedoms and equal rights and opportunities.

deport to send someone back to another country.

depression period of extremely low economic activity and high unemployment.

deregulation policy of removing government restrictions and regulations.

desegregation reversal of the policy of keeping races separate.

détente (dā-tä(n)t) policies aimed at reducing tensions between nations.

developing country one that is not industrialized.

Diaspora (dī-'as-p(ə)rə) settling of Jews outside Palestine after their exile from Babylonia.

dictator person who rules in a dictatorship.

dictatorship government controlled almost entirely by one person or a small group of people.

Diet Japanese Parliament.

direct primary system that allows members of a political party to nominate candidates by a secret ballot, instead of having this done by party leaders.

disability pay compensation to a worker who can no longer work because of an injury or other impairment.

disarmament giving up or reducing the number of one's weapons.

disperse to scatter; to spread out; to move away to many places.

displaced person someone uprooted from his or her home; refugee.

dissenter one who publicly disagrees with authorities, such as an established church.

dissenting opinion written views of a Supreme Court justice who disagrees with the majority opinion.

dissolve to break up something, such as a corporation.

district area of a country or state.

District Court one of over 90 federal courts located throughout the country where most cases involving federal law are first heard.

diversification creation of variety.

domestic spending federal government spending inside the country.

domino theory belief that if one nation becomes Communist-controlled, neighboring nations will also fall to Communists.

double jeopardy being tried again for a crime after having already been found "not guilty."

draft system of compelling people to serve in the armed forces; conscription.

due process of law procedures that police and courts observe to protect the rights of criminal defendants.

dust storm strong winds that carry away large amounts of dry soil.

duty tax on imports; tariffs.

dynamo small generator that makes electricity.

ecology study of the relationships between living things and their environment.

economic   related to the earning and spending of money, and the making and using of goods and services.

elastic clause   section of the Constitution that gives Congress its implied powers.

election campaign   candidate's large-scale effort to win support from voters.

electors   members of the Electoral College.

Electoral College   group of individuals elected by voters to vote on their behalf for President and Vice President; votes are cast in each state and sent to Congress, where they are counted.

electoral vote   vote cast by a member of the Electoral College.

embargo   law prohibiting trade between nations.

emissions   substances (often wastes) discharged into the air.

empire   several territories ruled by one person.

entanglement   involvement with someone or something.

environment   physical surroundings within which one lives.

environmentalist   person strongly concerned about environmental problems; modern term for conservationist.

epidemic   sudden, rapid outbreak of a disease.

equal representation   situation in which each state or district, regardless of size, has the same number of representatives in a legislative body.

equality   as stated in the Declaration of Independence, all people are born with equal rights.

equator   imaginary east-west line that divides the earth in half; is equal distance from both poles.

erosion   wearing away of something by action of wind, water, or glacial ice.

established church   country's official religion.

ex post facto **law**   legislation that allows a person to be punished for an act that was not a crime when it was carried out, but was made so by a later law.

excise tax   tax on production, sale, or consumption of goods within a country.

executive branch   one of the three parts of the national government, headed by the President.

executive privilege   one of the President's expanded powers that allows the President to refuse demands by Congress for information.

exempt   free from obligation.

expansionism   trend toward increasing a country's influence or territory.

expire   to come to an end.

exploration   voyage or journey of discovery.

export   to send goods out of a country.

extinction   dying out of a plant or animal species.

extraction   withdrawal or removal of something.

fact   something that can be proved to be true. Compare with *opinion*.

faction   group that is at odds with other members of an organization.

family farm   farm owned and run by one family.

farm bloc   congressional supporters of farmers; they vote the same on many farm issues.

farm production   growing of crops and raising of livestock.

farm surplus   farm products for which there are no customers.

featherbedding   union practice of requiring employers to employ more workers than are needed.

federal   of or relating to the national government.

federalism   system under which power is distributed between the national government and the states.

Federalist   one who favored ratification of the Constitution.

fertile soil   ground capable of providing abundant plant growth.

field slave   slave who works in the fields.

filibuster   extended debate used by senators to prevent passage of a bill.

finance   to raise money for some project.

first-generation Americans   immigrants who come to the country as adults.

flexibility   ability to bend or adapt to change.

foreign diplomat   representative of a foreign government.

fraud   dishonest act or acts.

free enterprise system economic system under which private businesses operate with little or no government control.

free silver movement group that wanted to raise farm prices by getting the government to issue more silver coins and silver-backed currency, thus causing inflation.

free trade trade without government restrictions.

freedmen freed slaves, both male and female.

freedom of assembly right to meet in public.

freedom of petition right to petition or ask the government to make changes in its laws and rules.

freedom of religion right to practice the religion of one's choice.

freedom of speech right to speak in public.

freedom of the press right of newspapers and other publishers to print what they want.

freedom of the seas condition that allows ships of all nations to use the world's seas without hindrance.

fringe benefit benefit a worker receives that has a money value but is not part of basic wages.

frontier unsettled lands beyond a settled area.

fugitive one who flees or escapes prison or slavery.

fugitive slave law legislation that required state and local officials to help capture and return runaway slaves.

gag rule rule that banned the reading of abolitionist petitions in the House of Representatives.

gasoline fuel made from oil.

genealogical research the study of the histories of families.

General Assembly main body of the United Nations, made up of delegates from all member states.

generalization conclusion or summary drawn from facts.

generate to produce something, such as electricity.

geothermal power energy from underground heat.

ghetto separate neighborhood in which an ethnic group tends to live because of discrimination.

glacier large mass of ice that slowly moves across a land area.

gold standard government policy of promising to pay gold to people who want to turn in paper money.

gospel set of religious beliefs.

graduated income tax a tax on income in which the rich pay a higher percentage than other taxpayers.

grammar school public grade school.

grandfather clause state law that eliminated literacy tests and poll taxes for people who had voted before 1867 and for their descendants.

grand jury special jury that decides if there is enough evidence to bring someone to trial.

greenbacks paper money, issued by the Union, that was not backed by gold or silver.

gross national product total value of goods and services produced by a country during a period (such as a year).

guillotine machine used to execute people by cutting off their heads.

habeas corpus right to know about criminal charges made against one, so that one can defend oneself; also, the right not to be held in jail except as the law provides.

hearing public meeting to inform people (such as committee members) about a particular subject.

herbicide chemical used to kill weeds.

hogan Navajo structure built with logs covered by mud.

holding company corporation that owns controlling interest in competing corporations and sets policies for these corporations.

Holocaust Nazis' systematic murder of millions of Jews and other groups in Europe.

homesteader one who settles on public lands.

horizontal combination type of business merger in which companies in the same industry join together.

horsecar horse-drawn streetcar on rails.

Hot Line telegraph/teleprinter link between the heads of the U.S. and Soviet governments.

House the U.S. House of Representatives; the lower house of Congress.

human rights basic rights that all people should enjoy.

hydropower energy from falling water, often in connection with a dam.

ideology (īd-ē-'äl-ə-jē) set of political and economic views.

igloo Eskimo house; applies not only to structure made of blocks of snow and ice, but also to more permanent houses made of sod, stone, or wood.

illegal immigrant one who enters a country without official permission.

illiterate unable to read and write; opposite of *literate.*

illumination lighting.

immigrant person who comes from another country to settle.

impeach to charge a public official with misconduct in office.

impeachment charge against a public official of misconduct in office.

imperialism doctrine urging the building of an empire.

implied powers ability of Congress to pass laws on subjects that are not directly mentioned in the Constitution.

imply to indicate something indirectly.

import to bring goods into a country.

impoundment the refusal of the President to spend funds approved by Congress.

impressment act of seizing something for public use or service.

inaugurate to officially install someone in office.

inauguration (in-ȯ-g(y)ə-'rā-shən) ceremony in which an official is installed in office.

income tax government tax on people's income.

indemnity sum of money paid or received to make up for losses.

indentured servant person who earned passage to America by promising to work for seven years.

independence complete self-government.

indict (in-'dīt) to charge officially with a crime.

industrial union union of both skilled and unskilled workers of one industry.

Industrial Revolution rapid growth of industry that began in Britain in the 18th century and in the United States in the 19th century.

industrialization growth of industries; transformation to an economy based on factory production.

inflation major increases in prices.

influx flow of people or things into a place.

initiative (in-'ish-ət-iv) system that allows citizens to introduce laws that they want a legislature to consider.

injunction court order stating that something must be done or not done.

insecticide chemical used to kill insects.

insurrection act of revolt against an established government.

integrate to mix things or people.

integrated state of being mixed together, such as mixed races.

interchangeable parts pieces of an item that are the same in every model and can be used in the production of multiple copies of that model.

interpret to explain the meaning of something.

interstate commerce business activity that takes place in two or more states.

intervene to interfere, often by using force or threats of force.

intimidation making of threats against someone to cause fear.

invalid not legal; having no force or effect.

invest to use money to buy something that will earn interest or make a profit.

irrigation ditch long hole dug to move water to farming areas.

island hopping going from island to island; tactic used by U.S. forces in World War II in the Pacific.

isolationism policy of refraining from making alliances.

Jim Crow a negative term for black Americans; also discrimination against blacks.

jingoist ('jin-gō-əst) one who displays extreme nationalism, often aggressively.

joint resolution of Congress official views on a subject by a majority of both houses of Congress;

signed by the President, it has the force of law.

judicial branch one of the three parts of the national government, headed by the Supreme Court.

judicial review power of the judicial branch of government to review actions of the executive branch and acts of Congress.

judiciary (ju-'dish-ē-erē) the judicial branch of government; also, a system of courts.

jump bail to fail to appear for one's trial after having posted bail.

juror member of a jury.

jury group of citizens chosen to hear a case in court.

kerosene fuel made from oil; commonly used in lamps before electricity was available.

laissez-faire policy of non-interference, such as a government not interfering with businesses.

land reform division of large farms into smaller ones.

land speculator person who buys and sells land for profit.

land-grant college state college that originally was financed by a federal grant of land.

lapse to come to an end; to go out of existence.

lease to rent.

legislative branch one of the three parts of the national government, headed by Congress.

legislative process way in which legislators consider bills and either reject or pass them.

legislature group of people who have the power to make laws.

lenient ('lē-nē-ənt) soft; easy; not firm or harsh.

liability responsibility in the eyes of the law.

lien (lēn) legal charge upon property to pay a debt or duty.

literacy test exam to determine whether one can read or write or both; was used in the South to reduce number of eligible black voters.

livestock farm animals kept for use or profit.

living quarter place to eat and sleep.

lobbying attempt to influence the vote on a bill in Congress.

lobbyist person hired by groups to persuade members of Congress on how they should vote.

lockout closing of a plant to union members in order to resist employees' demands or to gain concessions.

logistical troops soldiers that transport supplies but do not fight.

logrolling action of legislators who do favors for each other in order to help pass each others' favorite bills.

long-range nuclear weapon nuclear weapon that can be sent from one continent to another.

loom machine that weaves cotton thread into cloth.

loose interpretation (of Constitution) belief that government can assume certain powers that are not specifically stated in the Constitution.

Loyalist American colonist who supported British rule over the colonies.

lubricate to apply oil or grease to something to make it move more easily.

luxury something that provides pleasure and comfort, but is not necessary.

lynch ('linch) to put to death without legal authority, by mob action.

machine politician one who belongs to a highly organized political organization that uses the spoils system.

magnetic compass device used to determine direction by means of a magnetic needle, which always points north.

maize (māz) Indian corn.

majority any number over one half of a total.

majority opinion views of over one half of a body, such as the U.S. Supreme Court.

majority party political party that controls a majority of seats in a legislative body, such as the House or Senate.

malaria deadly disease spread by mosquitoes.

Manifest Destiny belief that the United States was fated to expand west to the Pacific Ocean.

manual skill skill involving use of the hands.

manufacture to make products (by hand or machine) suitable for use.

manufactured goods   products that have been made by hand or by machine.

martyr ('märt-ər)   one who dies for a principle or strong beliefs.

Marxism   basic ideas of communism as set down by Karl Marx in the 19th century.

mass migration   large-scale population movement.

mass production   manufacture of many copies of an item, usually by machine.

media   systems of mass communication, such as television, radio, newspapers, and magazines.

melting pot   idea that the United States is a gigantic melting pot in which different nationalities mix together and form one culture.

mercantilism   theory in which it was stated that the best way for a country to become powerful was to store up large amounts of gold and silver.

mercenary   soldier who serves only for pay (as opposed to being drafted or joining service for patriotic reasons).

merchant   a trader.

merger   joining together of several groups, such as two corporations.

metropolitan area   one city and its surrounding suburbs.

middleman   agent (male or female) who buys goods from producers and sells them to retail merchants or consumers.

migrant worker   one who moves around, taking on temporary work assignments.

migrate   to move from one place or country to another.

migration   movement of people or animals from one place or country to another.

militant   someone aggressively active in a cause.

militia (mə-'lish-ə)   group of armed and trained civilians.

minstrel show   type of stage show in which whites wore dark makeup to appear to be blacks.

mint   place where coins are made.

minute   a 60th part of a degree of longitude or latitude.

minuteman   militia member during the American Revolution, so named because he was supposed to be ready at a minute's notice.

moderate   one whose political views are not extreme.

modern architecture   architectural styles developed during the 20th century.

molten iron   iron melted by heat.

monopoly (mə-'näp-ə-lē)   company that dominates the production and sales in an industry; also, the condition in an industry that has such a company.

morale (mə-'ral)   a group's spirits.

mortgage ('mȯr-gij)   document showing that if a loan is not repaid, certain property will be transferred to the lender.

Moslem   follower of the Islamic religion.

muck   dirt, filth.

muckraker   one who searches out and exposes apparent misconduct of prominent individuals or companies.

multinational corporation   large company that owns businesses in two or more countries.

multiparty system   political system consisting of many political parties, none of which holds a monopoly of power.

musket   type of heavy gun once carried by a soldier.

mutual defense pact   alliance between two nations, calling on each to come to the aid of the other in case of an attack.

national bank   bank established by Congress.

national debt   money owed by the federal government.

national domain   land owned by the federal government.

national origins system   immigration laws involving quotas of immigrants from various countries.

national supremacy   idea that federal laws are superior to state laws.

nationalism   love of one's country; loyalty and devotion to that country.

nationalize   to take over ownership of property by the national government.

natural-born citizen   U.S. citizen who was born in the United States.

naturalized   having become a citizen of a country.

navigable ('nav-i-gə-bəl)   capable of being traveled on by ships.

navigation ship traffic.

Negro someone of African descent; the term is no longer widely used in the United States.

neutral not taking either side in a dispute, such as a war.

nominate to choose or name a candidate for election.

nominating convention meeting of party members to name candidates for public office.

non-permanent member country that is chosen by the UN General Assembly to have a seat on the Security Council for a two-year period.

non-substantive ordinary; nonessential.

non-violent resistance opposition to authorities without behaving violently.

normal school school that trains teachers, often requiring a two-year course.

nuclear test-ban treaty agreement to halt further testing of nuclear devices.

nullification action of a state declaring a U.S. law invalid within that state.

observatory place to view the stars, moons, and planets through a telescope.

offensive relating to, or designed for, attack.

oil reserves quantities of oil still in the ground.

oil spill leakage of oil into the environment from a pipeline or an oil tanker.

open range vast, unfenced prairie where sheep and cattle can graze.

opinion belief that something is true; one's feelings about something. Compare with *fact*.

organic architecture design style in which buildings seem to grow out of the landscape.

overgraze to keep grazing animals on a given piece of land for too long a time.

overproduction the production of more goods than there is a demand for.

override to annul or cancel the decision of one body by an opposing decision of another body.

overseer hired manager of something such as a plantation.

panic sudden, widespread fright concerning financial affairs, such as fear that banks might go broke.

parallels of latitude imaginary lines that run east-west around the earth and are used to measure distances north and south of the equator.

paraphrase to rewrite something in another way but with the same meaning.

pardon the freeing of a suspected or convicted criminal from any further trial or punishment.

parish school school financed and run by a church.

Parliament ('pär-lə-mənt) Britain's lawmaking body.

parochial having to do with a parish or religion.

partnership business owned privately by two or more people.

Patriot American colonist who favored independence from Great Britain.

patriotism love of one's country.

patronage distribution of government jobs on the basis of favorable service to a political party.

peninsula body of land surrounded by water on three sides.

permanent member country that always has a seat on the UN Security Council.

persecute to make someone suffer because of his or her beliefs.

persecution the condition of being persecuted.

personal liberty laws legislation passed in Northern states that made it more difficult for slave owners to capture and return runaway slaves.

petit ('pet-ē) **jury** jury of 12 people who decide if someone is guilty of breaking a law.

picket to walk back and forth carrying signs in a labor strike.

pigeonhole to set aside; to shelve.

pirate seagoing robber.

plank each of the main items of a party's platform.

plantation large farm that usually grows great amounts of one crop and is cultivated by resident workers.

platform political party's official views on key issues.

pocket veto type of veto that the President can make by doing nothing with a bill that Congress has passed. Can only be made when Congress passes a bill within the last ten days of a session.

pogrom (pō-'gräm) organized mass killing of helpless people.

political   relating to governments and the exercise of power.

political history   study of elections and actions of government officials.

political union   formal association of groups by means of a common government.

poll tax   fee that had to be paid before one could vote; was introduced in Southern states to prevent most blacks from voting.

pollute   to make something unclean, such as the air or a river.

pool   method of corporate cooperation that eliminated competition through secret agreements on sales territories or prices.

popular sovereignty   ('säv-(ə)-rən-tē) pre-Civil War doctrine that gave people living in some newly organized territories the right to vote as to whether or not slavery would be permitted there.

popular vote   votes of the people (as opposed to votes of the Electoral College).

population   number of people in a group or geographical area.

populous   heavily populated.

pork-barrel legislation   law or laws that benefit only one state or district.

postal system   organization that collects, sorts, and delivers mail.

poverty level   federally determined minimum yearly income, below which people are defined as poor.

prairie   large area of grasslands.

precedent   ('pres-əd-ənt) action that serves as a guide or rule for future actions.

prejudice   ('prej-əd-əs) slanted view, often hostile.

presiding officer   one who runs a meeting; a president of a group.

price-support program   federal loan program aimed at keeping farm prices and income at steady levels.

primary election   election held to test candidates' popularity with the voters of their political party.

principle   basic truth.

printing press   machine that makes multiple copies of books, pamphlets, and other materials.

procedure   rule or method of doing something that involves a series of steps.

process   to conduct a series of actions or operations.

producer cooperative   association of workers in which the association sells products made by the workers.

progressive education   new theories about teaching that were popular in the early 1900s; among other things, the theories stressed student creativity and free expression.

prohibit   to ban; to forbid by authority.

Prohibition   ban on the manufacture, transport, and sale of alcoholic beverages.

prohibitionist   one in favor of banning the sale and use of alcoholic drinks.

property qualification   requirement of owning a certain amount of property before being allowed to vote.

proprietary colony   colony established when English rulers gave gifts of land to close friends and people of high birth.

proprietor   one who received a land grant from English rulers.

prosecutor   lawyer who represents a government.

protective tariff   high tax on imported goods designed to encourage people to buy cheaper domestic goods.

province   administrative district or division of a country (similar to a state in the United States).

public assistance program   government program that provides direct aid to needy individuals and families; welfare.

public charge   one who depends on welfare for support.

public facilities   places open to the general public, such as buses, hotels, and restaurants.

public housing   apartment buildings and other housing owned, operated, or sponsored by a government.

public utility   privately owned company that provides essential services, such as electricity and water, to the public.

quota   fixed number; a proportional part or share.

racism   belief that one race is superior to others; the practice of this belief.

radical someone whose political views are considered extreme.

ragtime an early form of American jazz.

range war violent conflict between cattle ranchers and sheep ranchers over use of the open range.

ratification official approval of something, such as the Constitution by the states.

rationing government system of dividing up scarce goods among the population.

raw materials crude or processed material (such as lumber, furs, and iron ore) that can be converted into new and more useful products.

reaper ('rē-pər) machine used to harvest wheat and other grains.

rebate return of part of a payment.

rebel someone who violently opposes something; a revolutionary.

rebellion open resistance to authority.

recall system that allows voters to remove officials whom they no longer want in office.

recession slowdown in business activity.

recognize a country to formally accept it as legitimate.

Reconstruction period of rebuilding the South that took place just after the Civil War; also, the process of readmitting states that had seceded.

reconvert to return industries to their previous, pre-war state.

redcoat British soldier during the time of the American Revolution; (term refers to the color of soldier's uniform).

referendum system that allows bills to be referred to voters for their approval.

reforestation replanting of trees after a forest has been cut or burned.

reform change that aims to improve something.

refugee (ref-yù-'jē) one who flees a country or area to escape danger or persecution.

regulatory agency organization formed by an act of Congress to regulate transportation companies or other industries.

Renaissance (ren-ə-'sän(t)s)) from the French word meaning "rebirth," a period of renewed interest in learning, sciences, and the arts in Europe.

reparations payment for damages caused by a war, demanded by the victor from a defeated enemy.

repeal to declare a law no longer legal.

repeating rifle rifle with which one can make shot after shot without reloading.

representative government type of government in which people elect officials to represent them.

reprieve (ri-'prēv) delay of court-ordered punishment of someone.

republic form of government run by elected representatives or by an elected president.

reservation area of land set aside for Indians by the federal government.

reserved powers as stated in the Tenth Amendment to the Constitution, all powers not given to the federal government belong to the states.

restrain to hold back; to prevent.

retaliate to get even with; to get revenge.

reunification to join together again.

revenue-sharing system whereby the federal government shares its tax income with the states.

revolution attempt to overthrow a government.

right of deposit right to transport goods to a foreign port from where they may be shipped elsewhere.

right to bear arms one's right to own weapons.

right-to-work law legislation providing that no worker can be required to join a union as a condition for getting or keeping a job.

robber baron businessperson who becomes wealthy and powerful using unsavory methods.

robot computer-controlled machine that performs manual tasks.

rotation in office system designed to replace non-elected officeholders so that they do not hold their positions too long.

royal colony English colony directly controlled by the king.

run on a bank occurrence when many depositors withdraw money from a bank or make other demands on it.

running mate person chosen to run for a subordinate office (such as Vice President) who is paired with the candidate of a higher office on the same ticket.

rural   relating to the countryside.

sabotage (′sab-ə-täzh)   destruction of property to hinder an operation.

sanctions   penalties imposed by an international organization or country on a country that violates international laws or principles.

satellite   country politically and economically dominated or controlled by another, more powerful country.

scab   derogatory term for a non-union worker hired to replace a striking worker; strikebreaker.

scalawag   Southern white who associated closely with blacks and carpetbaggers during Reconstruction.

search warrant   document issued by a judge that allows police to search a suspect's home or business.

secede   to leave or withdraw from an organization, such as a state leaving the Union.

secessionist   one who calls upon a state to secede from the Union.

secret diplomacy   making of secret agreements between nations.

Secretariat   business office of the United Nations, responsible for maintaining records, doing research, and translating official documents.

Secretary   title given to the heads of all executive departments of the U.S. government.

sect   religious group or denomination.

section   an area of one square mile. According to Land Ordinance of 1785, 36 sections equals one township.

sectionalism   rivalry among different parts of a country.

secure landfill   underground storage area from which toxic wastes are not expected to leak.

securities   stocks and bonds.

security   safety.

Security Council   the permanent council of the United Nations, having primary responsibility for the maintenance of peace and security.

segregate   to separate things or people by categories; to separate people by race.

segregated public facility   public place (such as a restaurant, school, or bus) reserved for only one race.

self-determination   right of national groups living under the rule of others to declare independence.

Senate   upper house of Congress.

seniority   having to do with a person who has worked or been someplace the longest time; in congressional committees, one also has to belong to the majority party to have seniority.

sensational   producing excitement or thrills.

separate opinion   written views of a Supreme Court justice who votes with the majority but has different arguments or ideas to offer.

separation of church and state   no government control of religions or control by religions of the government.

separation of powers   system whereby the three branches of the federal government check and balance each other.

service industry   industry that provides a service rather than a product.

session   meeting or series of meetings of a body, such as a legislature.

settlement house   private establishment providing education, health, and social services for poor people in cities.

sewage   waste matter carried off by sewers.

sharecropper   farmer who does not own the land on which he or she works and who gives the landowner a large share of the crops as rent.

siege (sēj)   military blockade of an armed city, fort, or other place.

slum   rundown neighborhood or building.

smog   mixture of fog and smoke.

smuggle   to import or export goods illegally and, thereby, avoid duties or bans.

social history   study of the everyday activities of people in the past.

socialism   economic system in which workers or the state would own and control means of production and distribution and would set prices and wages.

solar power   energy from the sun.

sovereignty   independence; freedom to rule one's country.

speakeasy illegal drinking establishment during prohibition.

Specie Circular order issued by Andrew Jackson that required that all purchasers of public land pay in gold or silver.

speedy trial trial called without great delay.

sphere of influence land where a foreign power claims exclusive rights of trade and other activities.

spirituals emotional, religious songs developed by American blacks.

spoils system procedure of giving government jobs as a reward for party loyalty or service.

stock piece of paper representing a share of ownership in a corporation.

stock exchange place where many stocks are bought and sold.

Stock Market Crash period of sharp decline of stock values that began in October of 1929.

stockbroker person who buys and sells stocks for others.

stockholder one who owns stock in a corporation.

strategist one skilled at planning military campaigns and battles.

strategy overall plan.

strict interpretation (of Constitution) belief that the government should assume no powers that are not specifically stated in the U.S. Constitution.

strikebreaker non-union worker hired to replace a striking union worker. *Scab* is a derogatory term for a strikebreaker.

strip-mining process of extracting ore from giant pits instead of from underground tunnels.

subsidy ('səb-səd-ē) government grant to help pay for something regarded as advantageous to the public.

subsistence farming type of agriculture in which farm families consume almost all of what they produce.

substandard housing houses and apartments that do not meet accepted standards of health and comfort.

substantive important, essential.

succession replacement of an elected official who does not serve a full term.

suffrage right to vote.

suffragist one who advocates voting rights, especially for women.

superpower one of the strongest countries in the world.

superstate government that would rule the world.

Supreme Court highest court in the federal court system, it hears appeals from lower federal courts and the highest state courts.

surplus amount of something remaining when all that is needed has been used.

target price fair price set by the federal government for farm products involved in subsidy programs.

tariff tax on imported goods.

telegraph device used to send coded messages electrically by wires.

tenant farmer one who rents and farms another's land.

tenement run-down, crowded apartment building.

tepee cone-shaped tent made of hides, used by Plains Indians.

terrorist one who causes terror in order to achieve political goals.

textiles woven or knit cloth.

thermal pollution heated water discharged into rivers, lakes, and oceans.

third parties minor political parties in a political system dominated by two major parties.

Third World bloc group of developing nations that are not aligned with either the Soviet or Western blocs.

ticker tape long strip of paper used in machines that receive and print reports on stock prices.

topic sentence sentence that expresses the main idea of a paragraph, often the first one.

total war war in which the total population and resources of a country are involved.

Tory American colonist who remained loyal to the British and opposed the Revolution.

township area of 36 square miles.

toxic poisonous.

traitor one who commits a disloyal act against his or her country.

transcontinental from one end of a continent to the other.

transportation means of travel from one place to another.

treaty formal agreement between nations.

trial by jury court trial in which a group of citizens decide the guilt or innocence of the accused.

trolley electric-powered streetcar.

truck farmer one whose business is to grow vegetables for the market.

trust type of business arrangement in which different companies in the same field of business have a common board of trustees; also, any type of business arrangement that reduces competition.

trust territory former colony that is administered by another country through the UN Trusteeship Council.

trustbuster one who seeks to break up business monopolies.

tsar ('zär) Russian ruler.

turnpike road built by a private company that charges tolls for use of the road.

twine binder machine that both cuts and binds wheat.

two-party system political system dominated by two major political parties.

tyrant ('tī-rənt) brutal ruler not restrained by laws.

U-boat German submarine.

unalienable (ən-'āl-yə-nə-bəl) **rights** rights that governments have no authority to take away.

unanimous (yù-'nan-ə-məs) consent or agreement by all.

unconstitutional illegal according to the Constitution.

underground railroad system of hiding places and travel routes set up to aid fugitive slaves.

unfortified not protected by military forces and forts.

Union another term for the United States.

unwritten constitution customs not specifically mentioned in the Constitution that have become part of the rules of government.

urban renewal replacing slums with more modern buildings.

vertical in the direction of top to bottom, up and down.

vertical combination type of business merger in which a corporation takes over its suppliers.

veto to refuse to approve something, such as the President vetoing a bill passed by Congress.

wage and price controls federal laws that set wages and prices for goods and services.

welfare government financial assistance to needy individuals and families.

Western bloc group of non-Communist nations in Western Europe and the Americas.

White House home and workplace of the U.S. President.

white supremacy (sü-'pre-mə-sē) doctrine that calls for white domination over other races.

wigwam Indian hut covered with bark, hides, or reed mats.

wildcat strike labor strike not authorized by union leaders.

wildlife refuge place where animals and plants are protected by law.

workers' compensation payments made to people who were injured on the job and cannot work.

World Court United Nations International Court of Justice.

writ of assistance document that allowed officials to search buildings and ships for smuggled goods; type of search warrant.

yellow journalism publication of sensational newspaper stories.

yellow-dog contract employer-employee contract that prohibits employees from joining a labor union.

yield amount or quantity of something produced (in agriculture, yield often measured per acre).

Index

ACKNOWLEDGMENTS

Archive Pictures, Inc.—78 (Michael O'Brien), 102 (Charles Harbutt), 413 (Alen MacWeeney), 437 (Gregory J. Lawler), 440 (Rebecca Collette), 452 (Jeff Jacobson), 476 (Sylvia Plachy).

H. Armstrong Roberts—1, 123.

The Bettmann Archive—4, 10, 13, 17, 23, 29, 30 (bottom), 40, 51, 53 (bottom), 58, 64, 104, 119, 120, 125, 131, 141, 149, 155, 161, 166, 188, 195, 208 (both), 214, 220, 233, 234, 238, 239, 246, 251, 253, 260, 266, 273 (top), 275 (left), 276, 281, 282 (both), 284, 289, 297, 304, 306 (bottom), 312, 313, 319, 320, 322 (both), 327, 333, 335, 347 (both), 359, 362, 363 (left), 368, 370, 372, 376, 377, 383, 384, 391, 404, 415, 416 (top), 425, 489, 495, 498, 507, 510, 515, 521, 523, 532 (bottom), 545.

Bettmann Newsphotos (United Press International)—386, 398, 400, 405, 406, 532 (top), 555, 561, 572.

Black Star—110 (John J. Lopinot), 407 (Anthony Suau).

Brown Brothers—305.

Culver Pictures, Inc.—169, 296, 416 (inset).

Dover Publications, Inc.—41, 53 (top), 72, 136 (top), 259, 288 (bottom), 306 (top).

FDR Library (Suckley)—378.

The Granger Collection—24, 30 (top), 45, 127, 132, 173, 203, 219, 314, 342, 350 (both).

John Hancock Mutual Life Insurance Co.—201.

Library of Congress—36, 46, 54, 77 (right), 83, 88, 95, 109 (center), 160, 177, 196, 248, 268 (both), 273 (bottom), 274, 275 (right), 283, 292, 298, 300, 329, 334, 355, 361, 423, 444, 446, 457, 530.

Lowell Historical Society—209.

Maryland Historical Society, Baltimore—77 (left).

NASA—397, 409.

National Archives—6, 96, 207 (left), 217, 258, 261, 265, 279, 341 (top), 392, 417, 422, 459, 461, 475, 480, 487, 503, 505, 513, 514 (both), 528, 533, 537, 544, 571.

National Gallery of Canada, Ottawa, gift of the Duke of Westminster, 1918–34.

National Institute of Health—490.

National Portrait Gallery, Smithsonian Institution—136 (bottom), 182, 183, 184, 202, 221, 231 (left), 288 (top), 336–337 (all), 341 (bottom), 349, 356, 473 (both).

The New-York Historical Society—65, 126, 213, 226, 231 (right), 240, 252, 354.

The New York Public Library—28, 142, 148, 154, 167, 171, 207 (right), 227 (Schomburg Center for Research in Black Culture), 363 (right).

Photo Researchers—103 (Renee Lynn), 393 (Christa Armstrong), 429 (Michael Hayman), 430 (Bettye Lane), 432 (Tom McHugh), 438 (David Plowden), 451 (Bruce Roberts), 453 (Karl H. Maslowski), 467 (Barbara Rios), 468 (Hella Hammid), 469 (David M. Grossman), 481 (Arthur Tress), 482 (Chester Higgins, Jr.), 496 (Hans Namuth), 497 (Tom McHugh), 499 (F. B. Grunzweig), 547 (Robert Houser), 564 (Ned Haines), 587 (Bettye Lane), 588 (Georg Gerster).

Princeton University Library, Graphic Arts Collection—225.

Supreme Court Historical Society—109 (left and right).

Sygma (Stuart Franklin)—539.

Texas Department of Highways—188.

Ron Tunison—598.

United Nations—594, 595.

Virginia Museum of Fine Arts—71.

The White House—69, 84, 97.

Wide World Photos—390, 540, 553, 578, 579.

Woolaroc Museum, Bartlesville, Oklahoma—178.